W9-ADP-858

Gramley Library
Salem Academy and College
Winston-Salem, N.C. 27108

THE GRAIL

ARTHURIAN CHARACTERS AND THEMES
VOLUME 5
GARLAND REFERENCE LIBRARY OF THE HUMANITIES
VOLUME 1510

ARTHURIAN CHARACTERS AND THEMES

NORRIS J. LACY, *Series Editor*

THE GRAIL
A CASEBOOK

EDITED WITH AN INTRODUCTION BY
DHIRA B. MAHONEY

GARLAND PUBLISHING, INC.
A MEMBER OF THE TAYLOR & FRANCIS GROUP
NEW YORK AND LONDON
2000

Gramley Library
Salem Academy and College
Winston-Salem, N.C. 27108

Published in 2000 by
Garland Publishing, Inc.
A Member of the Taylor & Francis Group
19 Union Square West
New York, NY 10003

Copyright © 2000 by Dhira B. Mahoney

All rights reserved. No part of this book may be reprinted or reproduced or utilized
in any form or by any electronic, mechanical, or other means, now known or hereafter invented, including photocopying and recording, or in any information stor-
age or retrieval system, without permission in writing from the publisher.

10 9 8 7 6 5 4 3 2 1

Library of Congress Cataloging-in-Publication Data

The Grail: a casebook / [edited by] Dhira B. Mahoney.
    p.   cm.—(Arthurian characters and themes ; vol. 5)
  (Garland reference library of the humanities ; vol. 1510)
      Collection of twenty essays, seven of which were written for this work.
      Includes bibliographical references and index.
      ISBN 0-8153-0648-2 (alk. paper)
      1. Grail—Romances—History and criticism. 2. Arthurian romances—
    History and criticism. 3. Literature, Medieval—History and criticism.
    4. Arthurian romances—Adaptations—History and criticism. 5. Knights and
    knighthood in literature. 6. Quests (Expeditions) in literature. I. Mahoney,
    Dhira B. II. Series. III. Series: Garland reference library of the humanities ;
    vol. 1510.
PN686.G7G73   1999
809'.93351—dc21   99-34171
                                                          CIP

Printed on acid-free, 250-year-life paper.
Manufactured in the United States of America

Gramley Library
Salem Academy and College
Winston-Salem, N.C. 27108

CONTENTS

Series Editor's Preface

This is Volume V of "Arthurian Characters and Themes," a series of casebooks from Garland Publishing. The series includes volumes devoted to the best-known characters from Arthurian legend: Tristan and Isolde, Arthur, Lancelot and Guenevere, Merlin, Gawain, and Perceval. One volume is also devoted to Arthurian women in general. A single volume, the present one, treats an Arthurian theme rather than characters.

Each volume offers an extended introductory survey and a bibliography and presents some twenty major essays on its subject. Several of the essays in each volume are newly commissioned for the series; the others are reprinted from their original sources. The previously-published contributions date from the past two decades for the most part, although a few older, "classic," essays are included in several of the volumes, the criterion being the continuing importance of the study. All contributions are presented in English, and most volumes include essays that are translated into English for the first time.

Heaviest emphasis remains on the development of the legend and its characters and themes during the Middle Ages, but each volume also gives appropriate attention to modern, even very recent, treatments. Similarly, the central focus is on literature, but without excluding important discussions of visual, musical, and filmic arts. Thus, a number of the volumes are intentionally interdisciplinary in focus.

The proliferation of scholarly studies of Arthurian material continues at a daunting rate. When the *Bibliographical Bulletin of the International Arthurian Society* began publishing annual bibliographies, the first volume (1949) included 226 items (books, articles, and reviews). That number has increased regularly, to the point that some 700 items are now listed per year, and the 1996 bibliography offered over 800. Furthermore, the major contributions to Arthurian scholarship are often dispersed widely through North America, Europe, and elsewhere, and in books and articles that are, in some instances, available in few libraries.

As a result, it is extraordinarily difficult even for the professional medievalist to keep abreast of Arthurian scholarship, and it would be very nearly impossible for the non-scholar with serious Arthurian interests to identify and locate a score of the major scholarly contributions devoted to a particular character or theme. These difficulties clearly dramatize the value of this series, but they also remain an insistent reminder that even the most informed selection of major essays requires us to omit many dozens, perhaps hundreds, of studies that merit attention. Editors have attempted to remedy this situation insofar as possible by providing introductions that discuss other authors and texts and by compiling bibliographies that document a good many important studies that could find no room in these volumes. In addition, many of the contributions that are included here will themselves provide discussions of, or references to, other treatments that will be of interest to readers.

This volume, edited by Dhira B. Mahoney, includes a detailed introduction examining the literary and artistic history of the Grail, from its earliest development to very recent explorations in text and in visual media. The volume thereafter offers twenty essays, twelve covering the medieval period and eight the postmedieval. The essays examine Grail origins, literary interpretations of the Grail in medieval French, German, and English texts as well as in modern English fiction and poetry, and representations of the Grail in visual and filmic arts. Seven essays are new, written for this volume; those are the contributions of Glenys Witchard Goetinck, Janina P. Traxler, Alison Stones, Felicity Riddy, Linda K. Hughes, Debra N. Mancoff, and Raymond H. Thompson. In addition, the article by Friedrich Ranke, originally written in German, appears in English here for the first time.

Because permissions from copyright holders sometimes prohibited us from modifying the texts in any way, the decision was made to present all of them in their original form, with changes generally limited to the correction of obvious typographical errors. However, in some cases authors have, with permission, chosen to update, expand, or rework their contributions.

The necessity to reproduce many essays in the exact form of their original publication inevitably produces some inconsistencies, especially in documentary form. In addition, style, usage, and even spelling (British vs. American) may vary as well. Offsetting these inconsistencies is the advantage of having in one's hand a substantial selection of the finest available studies, new as well as previously published, of one of the central symbols associated with the Arthurian legend.

Such a volume could not be produced without the generosity of museum officials and editors of presses and journals, who kindly gave permission for us to reproduce illustrations and articles. We are pleased to express our gratitude to all of them. Appropriate credits accompany essays and plates.

Norris J. Lacy

THE GRAIL

Introduction

DHIRA B. MAHONEY

The Holy Grail is a standard symbol in the English language for an object of search far-off, mysterious, out of reach. In popular usage it represents the ultimate achievement in the particular context in which it is invoked: "System designers have yet to find the Holy Grail of one-hundred-percent accuracy in matching fingerprints or avoiding false matches," or "The Holy Grail of Artificial Intelligence is to create a machine as intelligent as a human." Implied in the usage is the idea of difficulty, exclusivity in the search, even the impossibility of ever attaining it. On some occasions, it connotes not the goal of the search, but the search itself, the quest that drives men (for it is traditionally men who search) unstintingly.

In its various manifestations through the ages, the Grail is embodied in many different objects, a bowl, a cup, a goblet, a platter, a reliquary that holds the Eucharist, a dish with a severed head, a precious stone. It may be associated, in different versions, with a Lance or a Spear, with a sword, with a carving dish, with silver knives; it may appear floating in the air, sliding down a beam of light, carried by a maiden, a youth, or angels; it is guarded variously by maidens, wounded kings, and Knights Templar. It has the power to provide inexhaustible nourishment and to serve the food and drink one most desires. Though it is frequently veiled or covered, or hidden in light, it irradiates and beautifies its beholders. It can heal wounds and even confer immortality; yet it is also associated with blight, destruction, and the Waste Land.

Shrouded in mystery itself, it may also be associated with mysteriousness, with the need to ask questions: the failure to ask questions about it results in devastation and grief. The search for it is exclusive, limited to a few, the elect. Only the pure can find it, and they must suffer hardships and undergo terrible tests of courage and faith to do so. It is frequently surrounded by taboos, by codes that must be broken to find the way, by fearful punishments for presumption or improper action in the search: looking into the Grail is perilous. Because the search is exclusive, it may be antisocial; it may break up a society, destroy the homosocial bonds that held it together, present new values that undermine or challenge those on which the society depends. Alternatively, it may establish a new community, of those who are bonded together by the search.

Not only is the Grail elusive, it is sometimes illusory, resulting in disappointment; those who search for a precious object find a simple wooden or pewter bowl, or something that is not a vessel at all. All their preconceptions of it were erroneous. The search is associated with failure, inaccessibility, disaster, yet the Grail is still the symbol of hope, of healing, of something beyond the mundane, the earthly, transcending normal life. For those who truly search for it, life will be forever changed, never the same again; for some it may cease altogether. It has religious and mythic dimensions, beyond specific, organized religion: though the best-known versions of the legend link it firmly with Christ and the Passion, it has never been officially endorsed by the orthodox Church.[1]

THE THREE STRAINS

As A.T. Hatto has observed, "There never was a story of *the* Grail, and never could be. On the other hand there were stories of as many different Grails as there were writers or syndicates exploiting the potent name."[2] The best that can be done in this introduction is to identify the most influential and best-known versions of the legend and to disentangle some of the traditions that connect them. It is possible to speak of three separate but overlapping traditions or strains in the medieval period: the Perceval strain, the Joseph of Arimathea strain, and the *Queste* strain. A brief account of these three follows here, organized chronologically; fuller discussions of the individual texts will follow later, arranged by language.

1. Perceval

The Perceval strain begins with the earliest Grail romance, written in Old French verse by Chrétien de Troyes between 1180 and 1190, *Perceval*, or *Le Conte du Graal* ("The Story of the Grail"), the last of his works. In this romance Perceval is the chief quester. The Grail is a mysterious and unexplained serving dish, which is carried with other talismans (including the Lance) in procession before Perceval at the castle of the Fisher King. Perceval fails to ask the crucial questions about the Grail and the Lance and is bitterly reproached for it by the Ugly Maiden. If he had asked the questions, the Fisher King's wound would have been cured, and imminent devastation and social upheaval in the land prevented. Chrétien's romance was never finished; but within fifty years, at least four different writers picked up his narrative and wrote Continuations, developing Perceval's adventures as well as those of his fellow Arthurian knight Gauvain (Gawain).[3] In two of the *Perceval* Continuations, the question is asked, and the Fisher King is healed; in the Third Continuation, Perceval becomes the Grail King after the Fisher King's natural death.

Chrétien's romance was the source for a translation and adaptation into Middle High German verse, *Parzival*, composed between 1200 and 1210 by Wolfram von Eschenbach. In this version, most of Chrétien's central narrative elements are retained, though the Grail is a stone, guarded by an elect company. The narrative ends with Parzival returning to the Grail Castle, asking the question, healing the Fisher King, and finally reigning as the Grail King himself with his wife and children. Another version of the Perceval story was also written in the early thirteenth century, in Old French prose, by an anonymous writer who clearly knew Chrétien's romance, though he does not actually refer to it. This is *Perlesvaus*, known in English as *The High History of the Grail*. Here Gawain, Lancelot, and, finally, Arthur are questers as well as Perlesvaus (Perceval); the narrative begins with the consequences of Perlesvaus's failure to ask the question. Finally, the Middle Welsh *Peredur* is seen by some scholars as also deriving from Chrétien's work (the manuscripts date to the late thirteenth century), though other scholars maintain that it represents an earlier version predating Chrétien's.[4] The central quester here is Peredur (corresponding to Perceval), who is rebuked by the Ugly Maiden for failing to ask a question about the bleeding Lance; if he had, his uncle the Lame King would have been healed and the kingdom restored to peace and tranquillity instead of strife. The Grail procession in *Peredur* is, however, very different from Chrétien's: the dish that is carried past Peredur holds a severed head swimming in blood.

2. Joseph of Arimathea

This strain provides a pre-Arthurian history of the Grail. Some ten years after Chrétien's *Perceval*, between 1191 and 1202, Robert de Boron composed the Old French verse romance *Joseph d'Arimathie* ("Joseph of Arimathea"), the only full surviving text of a conjectured trilogy. Joseph of Arimathea was the knight whose tomb was to be used for Christ; the Grail is the vessel from which Christ drank at the Last Supper, and which Joseph uses to catch Christ's blood when washing the body after the Deposition. It is taken into the desert by Joseph and his relatives. Though Joseph dies in the Holy Land, his descendants will bring it to Britain, to the vale of Avalon; the connection between the Grail and Arthurian Britain is thus made only at the end of the romance. In the early thirteenth century, Robert's verse romance was translated into prose, providing a version also known as *Joseph d'Arimathie*, or *Le Petit Saint Graal* ("The Little Holy Grail").[5] This was also credited, probably erroneously, to Robert. From the prose romance was developed *L'Estoire del Saint Graal* ("The History of the Holy Grail"), the first branch of the vast anonymous compilation in Old French prose known as the *Lancelot-Graal* or the Vulgate Cycle (1215–35). *L'Estoire* describes the adventures of Joseph and particularly his son Josephes in great detail, tracing their roles in the evangelization of the East and the West and recounting the bringing of the Grail to Britain, where it is ultimately lodged in the Castle of Corbenic. Two Middle English translations were based on the *Estoire*, the alliterative verse *Joseph of Arimathie* in the mid-fourteenth century and Henry Lovelich's *History of the Holy Grail* in the early fifteenth century.[6]

3. The *Queste*

The impetus for the third Grail strain is provided by *La Queste del Saint Graal* ("The Quest for the Holy Grail"), the fourth branch of the *Lancelot-Graal* or the Vulgate Cycle.[7] Here, the focus shifts to Galaad, Lancelot's son. Although many knights of the Round Table embark on the Quest, only three questers come close to achieving it, Bohort (Lancelot's cousin), Perceval, and Galaad; Galaad achieves the supreme Vision of the Grail, which is the dish of the Last Supper. Also on the Quest are Lancelot himself, who achieves only a partial vision because of his sinful love for Guinevere, and Perceval's sister, who dies on the journey. The three chief questers sail on the Ship of Solomon and arrive at the holy city, Sarras, in the last leg of their journey. Translations and adaptations of the Vulgate *Queste* survive in many languages,[8] one of the best known being Sir Thomas Malory's Middle English "Tale of the Sankgreal," Book 6 of the *Morte Darthur*.[9] (Malory's version is the starting point for almost all the postmedieval variations in English, such as Tennyson's "The Holy Grail.") Still recognizably belonging to the

Queste strain, though some important details are added or changed, is the Post-Vulgate *Roman du Graal* ("Romance of the Grail"), which continues the second branch of the Vulgate Cycle, *Merlin,* by adding to it the *Suite du Merlin* ("Continuation of Merlin").[10] It is in the *Suite* that we find the motif of the Dolorous Stroke, executed by Balain on King Pellehan, causing devastation to the land and a wound that can be healed only by Galahad in the Quest. This narrative provides a completely alternative account of the Waste Land and the Maimed King from the *Perceval* strain.[11] The motif also appears in Malory, since his Book 1, "The Tale of Arthur," is based on the *Suite du Merlin*.

TALISMANS AND MOTIFS

Talismans

Certain objects and motifs are common denominators of the Grail story, but they do not appear in every version, nor in the same combinations. First, of course, is the Grail object itself. The French word *graal* is derived from the medieval Latin *gradale* ("in stages"), designating a dish or platter that was brought to the table at various stages during the meal. *Graal* is used as a common noun in this sense in Old French literary texts without any of the associations it later acquires in the development of the legend. In its first appearance in Chrétien de Troyes's *Perceval* or *Le Conte du Graal*, it is described simply as *un graal* (a common noun accompanied by the indefinite article); it is a serving dish of costly workmanship, made of gold and decorated with the finest precious stones in the land, borne in a procession with other items and giving off an unearthly radiance. It is distinguished by its beauty, appropriate for a rich man's castle, but it has at this point no spiritual connotations. Only later, in the hermit's explanation of the procession, is the reader told that it contained a single Mass wafer and was therefore holy–"Tant sainte chose est li graals" ("such a holy thing is the grail," 6425).

The Continuators of *Perceval* added food-producing and other magical attributes to the Grail and progressively christianized the vessel, but it was Robert de Boron, writing some ten to fifteen years after Chrétien, who made the leap to explicit identification with Christian sacramental tradition, identifying it as the vessel of the Last Supper, which Joseph of Arimathea used to catch Christ's blood when he was washing the body after the Deposition. Thus Chrétien's *un graal* ("a grail") becomes *Le Graal* ("the Grail"), explicitly Christian, and twice hallowed. Joseph's

Grail has the power to feed (it sustains him for years in prison), to punish sinners, and to provide an ineffable sense of well-being for the elect; it is also Joseph's guide through the wilderness on his journey westward: he consults the Grail by praying to it when he has a question and is answered by the Holy Spirit or an angel. The Grail's associations with the Last Supper (where Christ invited the disciples to eat his body and drink his blood in the form of bread and wine) and its centrality in the spiritual life of Joseph's band make it "a prototype of the chalice of the Mass."[12] In the *Queste del Saint Graal* and Malory's "Tale of the Sankgreal," its appearance is accompanied by radiance, silence, and beauty: all the knights are struck dumb, they appear beautiful to one another, and the Grail provides the food and drink they like best. Other, distinctive forms for the Grail have already been mentioned: in Wolfram's *Parzival*, it is a precious stone, which provides the faithful with all the food they desire, renews the Phoenix, and wards off death. Its power is renewed every Good Friday by a visit of a dove bringing a wafer. In *Perlesvaus*, the Grail is the vessel in which Christ's blood was saved, but during the procession it may appear in many forms, showing a child within it or a crucified king above it. The most important form it takes is the chalice, which, according to the narrative, has been to this point unknown in Arthur's kingdom. In *Peredur*, it could be argued, there is no Grail at all, since the object is a platter holding a severed head and Peredur's failure is to ask the Question as to the identity of the murdered man.

Another talisman most frequently associated with the medieval Grail is the bleeding Lance, carried by a youth in the Grail procession, sometimes held so that the drops of blood will fall into the vessel; in Chrétien's *Perceval*, the Lance is unexplained, but in the First and Third Continuations it is identified with the spear that the Roman centurion Longinus thrust into Christ's side on the Cross. In some versions, such as the Post-Vulgate Cycle and Malory, the Lance is the instrument that has wounded the Maimed King, but blood dripping from the Lance also heals the wound when administered by the destined quester, Galahad. In *Parzival*, the Lance (or spear) has wounded Anfortas and must be thrust into his wound periodically to reduce his pain, but it is Parzival's asking of the Question that finally heals the Maimed King.

In some versions, there is a third talisman: the silver *tailleor* (trencher, or carving dish), carried by a second maiden. Little is made of the history or symbolism of this object, though the Third *Perceval* Continuation associates it with the Crucifixion, claiming it was used to cover the Grail and protect Christ's blood.

A final talisman is the marvelous sword, which is given to Perceval before the procession in *Perceval* and which prediction claims will be broken. In the Second Continuation, Perceval joins the two pieces, but there is still a hairline crack; not until the Third Continuation is the repair complete. Its significance is never made fully clear, though it seems to have some connection with the vengeance theme that is latent in the *Perceval* strain.[13] In the Third Continuation, that theme comes to the fore, when the sword is identified as the instrument that killed the Fisher King's brother and wounded the King when he handled it. (The wound is healed miraculously when the brother's murder is avenged.) In the Vulgate *Queste*, the broken sword, which wounded Joseph of Arimathea, is mended by Galaad.

Motifs

A major motif is the role of the Fisher King. Sometimes, this figure is identical with the Grail King; sometimes, the two are separate figures related by blood. In the *Perceval* strain, the Fisher King is also the Maimed King, afflicted by a mysterious and apparently incurable wound, frequently through the thighs, sometimes explicitly in the sexual organs. (He is called the Fisher King, we are told in *Perceval*, because he fishes for recreation instead of hunting, which his wound has prevented him from doing.) The cause of the wound varies; it may be a sexual transgression punished by wounding in battle, as in *Parzival*, or may have been inflicted in battle before the story begins, as in *Perceval*. In *Perceval* and *Parzival*, Perceval's failure to ask the question prevents the healing of the wound and prolongs the Fisher King's pain, whereas in *Perlesvaus*, the failure to ask the question is itself the cause of the Fisher King's illness (not wound). In the Joseph of Arimathea strain, however, there is no sense of a wound or transgression associated with the Grail guardian: Bron or Hebron, Joseph's brother-in-law in Robert de Boron's *Joseph*, is called the Rich Fisherman because he provided the fish for the Table of the Grail at the first ritual that weeded out the sinners from the company of the elect. The name is a mark of distinction: Charles Williams tells us that the "fish caught by Bron is the image of our Lord in the imagination of the young Church," since the initial letters in Greek of the formula "Jesus Christ, Son of God, Saviour" form the word *icthus* or fish.[14] In the *Estoire*, the Rich Fisherman is Alain, Bron's youngest son, who catches a fish that is miraculously multiplied to feed the sinners who have been denied food by the Grail. Subsequent Grail guardians each take the name after Alain.

When the Grail King is a separate figure from the Fisher King, he is also frequently ill or very old. In *Perceval* he is the Fisher King's father, unseen and fed only by the Mass wafer; in *Parzival* he is the Fisher King's great-grandfather, Titurel, unable to die because he continually gazes on the Grail. In the *Queste* strain, it is the Grail King, Pelles, who is younger, while his father is the wounded Fisher King, Pellehan, who will be healed only at the coming of Gaahad. Pelles is the King of Corbenic Castle, where Lancelot will be tricked into sleeping with the Grail princess and fathering Galaad.

The second major motif is the Waste Land, closely connected with the wound of the Maimed King. The land is devastated, infertile, or at war. In the Perceval strain, the Waste Land is linked to the Question Failure, which either causes the devastation or prevents its recovery. (In the *Perceval* Continuations, Gauvain and Perceval do, respectively, restore the Waste Land by asking the Question.) In the *Queste* strain, on the other hand, the Waste Land is caused by the Dolorous Stroke, which varies according to the version. In the Vulgate *Queste* (as predicted in the *Estoire*), the Stroke is committed with the sword from Solomon's ship, wielded by King Varlan when he pursues King Lambor; in the Post-Vulgate Cycle, on the other hand, the Stroke is committed with the Lance, seized by Balain in a moment of rash ignorance at Corbenic and used to strike King Pellehan through the thighs. In both cases, only the coming of Galaad will restore the land. Whereas in the Vulgate *Queste* the restoration of the land is separated from the healing of the Maimed King, in the Post-Vulgate Cycle Galaad's action of applying blood from the Lance to the wound heals both King and land simultaneously. It is this link between the healing of the Fisher King and the restoration of fertility to the land that gives support to the Ritualist theories of origin proposed by Jessie Weston and discussed below.[15]

THEORIES OF ORIGIN

Scholars have always been fascinated with the question of the origin of the Grail legend. Among the many theories of origin, three have been most popular: the Christian, the Ritualist, and the Celtic. The Christian theory has many variations; some proponents argue that the objects of the Grail procession evoke the Catholic liturgy, forming a precursor to the Mass. The Grail would be understood as a ciborium or container of the Eucharist, the *tailleor* (carving dish) as the paten of the Mass, and the Lance as the weapon that pierced Christ's side on the Cross. An alternative Christian theory traces analogies between the Grail procession and Byzantine liturgy, as in the St. John Chrysostom Mass. (Neither interpretation explains the fact that it is women who carry the *graal* and the *tailleor*, which would generally be forbidden by the early Church.) Other Christian readings provide allegorical interpretations of the procession.[16]

The Ritualist theory, propounded chiefly by Jessie Weston, argues that the origins of the now Christianized legend lie in Middle Eastern vegetation ritual and are linked with the cults of Attis, Orisis, and Adonis, in which the chief features are the death and rebirth of the god-king. The death or mutilation of the king is required to make the waters flow and restore fertility to the land. Perceval's visit to the Grail Castle thus represents an aborted initiation into a fertility rite; similarly, the Lance and the Grail are sexual symbols, representing the male and female organs, respectively. Though few scholars now subscribe to this theory of origin, Weston's writings are particularly influential on twentieth-century literature, ever since they inspired the central symbols of T.S. Eliot's "The Waste Land," published in 1922.

The Celtic theory, of which R.S. Loomis was the most famous proponent, suggests that the ultimate source of the Grail legend lies in Irish sagas, in which mortal heroes visited the palaces of pagan gods, "where they were feasted on vessels of plenty."[17] (In Welsh tradition, the Horn of Bran and the Platter of Rhylgenydd are both providers of unlimited food and drink.) The material was transmitted through Breton *conteurs* (storytellers) to the French and the Anglo-Normans. Loomis argued that the horn of plenty, "cors beneïz," was mistranslated and confused with "cor benoit," the sacred body of Christ, thus leading to Corbenic as the name of the Grail Castle and the increasing christianization of the story.[18] The Bleeding Lance and the Fisher King also have analogues in Irish literature, while Welsh literature provides a mythological hero named Bran, who is wounded in the foot. The Ugly Maiden also recalls the Sovereignty of Ireland, a goddess who has the power to appear both as a beautiful young and a loathly old woman; in some versions of the *Perceval* strain, the Grail-Bearer and the Ugly Maiden are clearly metamorphoses of the same person. For a detailed discussion of these issues, see Glenys Goetinck, "The Quest for Origins," Chapter 1 of this volume.

The sections that follow discuss in greater detail the various medieval versions of the Grail legend mentioned above, tracing them chronologically and by language. (By far the greatest number of versions are in Old French.) In some cases, it has been necessary to summarize the plot of the work in order to differentiate it clearly from the rest of the tradition.

THE MEDIEVAL LEGEND IN FRENCH

Chrétien de Troyes's *Perceval* or *Le Conte du Graal* ("The Story of the Grail")

Little is known about Chrétien other than that he lived and was probably born in Troyes, in Champagne, and received a classical education as well as clerical training. *Perceval*, written probably between 1180 and 1190,[19] is the last of his Arthurian verse romances, and it is unfinished. In his prologue Chrétien explains that the romance was commissioned by Count Philip of Flanders, who gave him the book called "li contes del graal" and asked him to put it into verse.

Perceval is a young Welshman who has been kept hidden away in the forest by his mother, endowed with great natural strength and skill but knowing nothing of knightly behavior or the courtly world. He is the quintessential Fool, an untutored naïf, and much comedy is created in the early sections by his self-centeredness and ignorance of courtly or even civilized etiquette, especially when he takes people's advice too literally. Perceval's gradual socialization and education is a major theme of the first part of the romance, as he not only learns society's customs, but also learns to care about the feelings of others.

The romance opens with Perceval meeting five armed knights in the forest. Having never seen knights before, he is fired with the desire to seek the court and become one, despite his mother's reluctance. Though she swoons with grief as he rides off, he does not turn back. Various encounters with civilization follow, including the incident of the Tent Maiden, whom he kisses by force, and the battle with the Red Knight, who has insulted the court and humiliated the queen. Perceval demands the Red Knight's armor from Arthur and is told contemptuously by Kay, the seneschal, to go and fetch it. He kills the Red Knight with a javelin but does not know how to remove the armor and has to be helped by a squire from the court. His next encounter is with a nobleman, Gornemant of Gohort, who teaches him how to use his newly acquired arms and weapons and also advises Perceval that he should avoid excessive speech. Perceval proves his knightly training by rescuing the beautiful Blancheflor from a besieging suitor. Though she and Perceval promise each other love, and spend some nights in embraces, Chrétien suggests that Perceval does not consummate his love. Increasingly remorseful over his treatment of his mother, he leaves Blancheflor, determined to find out if his mother is still alive.

Perceval's "education" has led him to the most important adventure, at the Grail Castle. He comes upon two men fishing, one of whom invites him to come to his castle, which he will find by riding to the top of the rock. At first Perceval sees nothing, but the castle suddenly appears, and he enters, being welcomed, and drawn to a large hall where an enormous fire is burning between four columns. The fisherman is his host, seated on a bed, from which, he says, he is unable to rise. As Perceval and his host converse, a squire enters with a sword, forged by a wonderful smith, which is given to Perceval. Next, a squire passes in front of them holding a lance, from the tip of which single drops of blood well up and flow down. Mindful of Gornemant's advice, Perceval asks no question about this occurrence, nor does he when two more squires pass holding blazing candelabra. After them comes a maiden who bears "un graal" (a wide, deep dish), which casts such a brilliant light that it dims the candles. It is made of gold and set with the finest gems. After this maiden comes another, holding a silver platter. Still the youth fails to ask a question. Tables are brought in and rich food is served, including sumptuous meats carved from the silver platter; at each course, the Grail passes before them, but still the youth does not ask, thinking it will be more polite to wait till morning. But when he wakes the next morning, the castle is empty; his horse and arms are waiting for him, but as he rides across the drawbridge, it rises underneath him and he must make a mighty leap to avoid being hurt. Outside, he calls, but no one responds. It is too late to ask questions now.

The next incident explains Perceval's error. A maiden mourning over a dead knight turns out to be his cousin. She tells him that the Fisher King was wounded between his thighs in battle, and fishing is the only sport he can resort to now. By not asking the question about the Grail, Perceval has failed to cure the king's wound. Furthermore, by abandoning his mother, he caused her to die of grief. She tells him, also, that the sword he was given will fail him in his moment of need, but it can be repaired by Trebuchet, the smith who made it. During this conversation, Perceval for the first time articulates his own name, which he has not known before. In pursuing the Proud Knight who killed his cousin's lover, Perceval brings to an end the adventure of the Tent Maiden. Meanwhile, the various defeated knights he has been sending to Arthur's court have whetted Arthur's interest, and the court sets out to find him. Outside the camp, Perceval falls into a love reverie at the sight of three drops of blood on the snow from a wounded bird (they remind him of his lady's complexion), and when knights come out to challenge him, he knocks them down (including Kay). Only Gawain's courtesy persuades Perceval to accept a welcome into the court. He has avenged his humiliation by Kay and fulfilled his earlier promises.

Gramley Library
Salem Academy and College
Winston-Salem, N.C. 27108

It takes the visit of the Ugly Maiden to the court to give Perceval and the court a new direction. Hideous, her features described by comparison to animals, she reproaches Perceval explicitly for his failure to ask questions about the Lance and the Grail, which has condemned the Fisher King to continued suffering and his kingdom to misfortune. While other knights vow to pursue the quests she has described, Perceval in shame vows to seek the Grail Castle again and ask the questions he should have asked. This is clearly a turning point for Perceval, as he rejects the chivalric quests in order to pursue the Grail, to rectify the consequences of his failure. After this the narrative follows the more conventionally chivalric adventures of Gawain, which include his championship of the Maid with Little Sleeves and an accusation of treason, with the combat postponed for a year.

At this point the narrative returns to Perceval, who has spent five years in successful pursuit of knightly fame and has totally forgotten God. It is Good Friday, and he sees a procession of penitents, who rebuke him for bearing arms on this holy day. When Perceval reveals his ignorance about the day, the leader tells him about Christ's Passion and directs Perceval to the hermit who has just received their confession. In remorse, Perceval seeks the hermit and acknowledges his sin: he failed to ask the questions at the Fisher King's. The hermit reveals to him that his true, original sin, which caused his silence, was that he caused his mother to die of grief when he left her. The man served by the Grail is the hermit's brother, and both of them are Perceval's maternal uncles; the Fisher King is the Grail King's son and therefore Perceval's cousin. The Grail King's life is sustained by the Mass wafer brought in the Grail, and he eats no other food. The hermit-uncle enjoins Perceval to attend Mass every morning as a penitent and administers communion. Perceval shares the hermit's frugal fare and vows to change his ways. This is the last we hear of him. The narrative returns to Gawain, following a series of adventures that end with Gawain's pledge to fight a challenger before Arthur and the messenger arriving at Arthur's court to announce it. At this point the narrative breaks off.

The unfinished nature of Chrétien's romance provides much mystery and ambiguity, and has led to speculation as to how he would have ended it. It is clear, however, that the interweaving of Perceval's and Gawain's adventures is intended to contrast the two knights.[20] Perceval's meeting with the hermit-uncle turns his adventures in an explicitly Christian direction. His spiritual blindness for five years, not knowing or observing Christian rituals, shows another plane of ignorance from the innocence of knightly

Cramley Library
Salem Academy and College
Winston-Salem, N.C. 27108

society and custom that characterized him in the first part of the romance. First from his cousin and then from the Ugly Maiden, he learned that his failure to ask the fateful questions perpetuated the Maimed King's suffering; from his uncle, he learns that the original, worst sin was his abandonment of his mother, which trapped his tongue in silence. Perceval's journey is into increasing involvement with humanity, first on the social level, then on the spiritual level. (It is significant that he learns about the second king and the inner room only when he is ready for the information, in other words, fully penitent.) Furthermore, his meeting with the hermit restores him to the Grail nobility, the family of which he is a vital part (see Pickens, 247, 278). The implication at the end of the hermit episode is that he will enact his penances, find the Fisher King's castle, and ask the questions he failed to ask before. But we can only guess that, since Chrétien returns to the more secular adventures of Gawain and leaves the narrative unfinished. Not surprisingly, Chrétien's Continuators provide endings, elaborating and intensifying the Christian and sacramental elements hinted at in the hermit episode, as well as extending and concluding Gawain's adventures.

As for the Grail itself, Chrétien has provided only a glimpse. It is initially "un graal," a dish or platter, only later "li graals" ("the grail"). Its mysterious destination during the procession indicates the nature of the multiple questions Perceval should have asked; not what is it, or what does it contain, but where is it going and whom does it serve? How can the lance bleed? Why does it bleed? As Emmanuèle Baumgartner suggests, a great number of enigmas are presented in the scene.[21] Rupert Pickens observes that one essential theme of the *Conte du Graal* is perception of meaning and the failure to communicate. "The point of the Grail and Lance questions in their various versions is that questions lead to questions and, ultimately, to fruitful, revelatory discourse with another human being–communication with the Fisher King" (285). In the hands of the *Perceval* Continuators, however, the emphasis shifts from whom the Grail serves to what it contains, and thereby to its significance, allowing an account of its Christian origins; here we come closer to the Grail we are familiar with, in the narratives of Robert de Boron or in the Vulgate *Queste*. Chrétien's version is purposefully ambiguous, inconclusive, and suggestive. Its power lies in that very inconclusiveness, in Perceval's failure to ask questions about it, in the narrator's failure (or refusal) to describe or explain it to his readers. The Grail procession is mysterious precisely because the narrative refuses to interpret it, focusing only on Perceval's reaction (Pickens, 280).

Perceval **Continuations**

The First Continuation, written ca. 1200 and known in the early part of the twentieth century as the Pseudo-Wachier Continuation, develops the adventures of Gauvain, allowing him to witness the Grail procession in the Fisher King's Castle and ask the question about the Bleeding Lance, though he fails to repair the broken sword. This version adds food-producing attributes to the Grail and explains the Lance as the spear used by the Roman centurion Longinus to pierce Christ's side on the Cross. Gauvain's asking the question about the Lance partially restores the Waste Land; however, he falls asleep before asking about the Grail. The Second Continuation, written shortly after the First, returns to focus on Perceval's adventures, including the pursuit of a white stag. Perceval returns to the Grail Castle and attempts to repair the broken sword. He rejoins the pieces, but there is still a hairline crack, indicating that he is not yet worthy to understand the mysteries of the Grail. The Third Continuation, written ca. 1230 by Manessier, was composed independently of but contemporaneously with the Continuation by Gerbert de Montreuil; in fact, they probably provided competing conclusions. In the two manuscripts that contain Gerbert's massive Continuation, Paris B.N. fr. 12576 and B.N. n.a. fr. 6614, the scribes have suppressed his conclusion and inserted his narrative between the Second Continuation and Manessier's, leading to some inconsistencies and repetition. The majority of the manuscripts omit Gerbert's Continuation and have the Third Continuation following directly after the Second.

Gerbert's narrative shows Perceval taking his broken sword to the smith who originally forged it, Trebuchet. The smith repairs it and dies shortly after. By asking the questions about the Lance and the Grail (in the Second Continuation), Perceval succeeds in making the waters flow and restoring the Waste Land; however, he does not learn the answers to the questions, nor does he heal the Fisher King. Gerbert introduces more tests of Perceval's courage and faith, including the Perilous Seat at Arthur's court (that swallows up unworthy knights who try to sit on it), and the white shield with the red cross, which similarly cannot be wielded by anyone but the destined Grail quester. Among the many episodes is Perceval's marriage to Blancheflor, which is not, however, consummated, as both bride and groom decide to preserve their virginity to save their souls. Gerbert's Continuation intensifies the Christianizing tendencies of the previous two Continuations, adding much allegorical (and typological) interpretation[22] of episodes as well as overt sermonizing on the theme of confession. One episode, in which King Mordrain (previously the heathen Evalac of Sarras) is wounded in the battle to rescue Joseph of Barismachie (Arimathea) and lies in a chapel for three hundred years, clearly resurfaces in the Vulgate *Estoire du Graal*. At the end of Gerbert's Continuation, Perceval returns to the Grail Castle and successfully mends the broken sword.

In the Third Continuation, by Manessier, Perceval's questions to the Fisher King are answered. The Lance is the spear of Longinus, and the Grail is the vessel in which Joseph caught the blood that ran down Christ's side on the Cross (but it is *not* identified as the cup of the Last Supper, as in Robert de Boron's poem). The silver trencher carried in the Grail procession was used during the Crucifixion to cover the Grail and protect the blood. Joseph was sustained in prison by the Grail (as in Robert de Boron) and on his release brought the Grail and the Lance to Logres. The Fisher King is descended from him, and the Grail maiden is the King's daughter.

Perceval also learns the secret of the broken sword. It was the instrument that treacherously cut down the Fisher King's brother, wielded by the Knight of the Red Tower. The Fisher King wounded himself by handling the sword and will not be healed until the death is avenged. Perceval promises to carry out the revenge and sets out after the killer. Other adventures intervene, including the adventure of the chapel with the Black Hand, and two episodes when Perceval is tempted by the Devil, first in the form of a black stallion and second in the guise of the beautiful Blancheflor. Also narrated is Boors's dilemma, when he is forced to choose between saving his brother Lyonel from death or a beautiful virgin from rape, and Perceval and Ector's battle, after which the Grail appears to heal their wounds.[23] Finally, Perceval defeats and kills the Knight of the Red Tower and returns to the Grail Castle, to find a miraculously healed Fisher King. Subsequently, when the Fisher King dies of joy, Perceval reigns as Grail King for seven years, until he decides to retire to a hermitage, taking with him the Grail and the Lance. The Grail sustains Perceval entirely for ten years, and when he dies, the Grail and the Lance are taken to heaven and not seen on earth again.

It is possible that the last two Continuators were familiar with Robert de Boron's *Joseph*; alternatively, they may have been independently driven toward progressively greater christianization of the Grail symbolism. Whatever the reason, they increasingly shift the emphasis from questions about the destination of the Grail to focus on the Grail itself, as a mysterious covered object that the quester desires to see more openly.[24] The result is a narrative whose closing sections would not be out of place in the *Queste*.

Robert de Boron's *Joseph d'Arimathie*

Robert is the author of a trilogy in Old French verse, comprising *Joseph d'Arimathie* (originally edited as *Le Roman de l'Estoire dou Graal* ["The Romance of the History of the Grail"]), the *Merlin*, and a conjectured *Perceval*. Only *Joseph* (3,154 lines) and 502 lines of *Merlin* survive, in a single manuscript, but evidence of the content of the trilogy and Robert's intentions is provided by the close prose redactions of all three romances made by an unknown writer in the early thirteenth century: the prose *Joseph*, the Huth *Merlin*, and, possibly, the Didot-*Perceval*. At the end of the *Joseph* poem, Robert tells us that he told his story to his patron, identified as Gautier de Montbéliard, Lord of Montfaucon, who embarked on the Fourth Crusade in 1202. The *Joseph* is therefore dated between 1191 and 1202, since it clearly postdates Chrétien's *Perceval*. Though Robert is generally considered a mediocre poet, he is credited with bold and innovative vision in seeing the potential of Chrétien's *graal*: by linking Chrétien's mysterious and unexplained vessel explicitly with the events of the Last Supper, the Crucifixion, the symbolism of the Eucharist, and Apocryphal tradition, Robert brought the Arthurian material into the context of universal sacred history.[25]

In Robert's poem, Joseph is a paid soldier of Pilate, who admires Jesus but dares not reveal his devotion for fear of the Jews, who are intensely jealous of Jesus. After the Crucifixion Joseph asks Pilate for Jesus' body, to inter it in the rock tomb made for himself. The vessel used for the Sacrament at the Last Supper has been saved, and Pilate gives it to Joseph because he loved Christ so much. (This extremely anti-Semitic text takes care almost to exonerate Pilate, who is represented as virtually powerless against rich and influential Jews.)[26] When Joseph takes down the body and begins to wash it for burial, the wounds continue to bleed, so he brings the vessel to catch the blood. After the Resurrection and disappearance of Christ's body from the tomb, the Jews seek vengeance on Joseph and throw him into a tower with a deep dungeon. God appears to Joseph, bringing the vessel, which casts such radiance that it lights up the dungeon. He explains the "secrets of the Grail": the link between the vessel, the Last Supper, and the Eucharist. The Table of the Last Supper is echoed by the altar of the Mass, and the various elements of the Eucharist are "signs" that will recall Christ's Passion. Joseph must keep the vessel and entrust it only to three people after him; those who see the vessel will be members of Christ's company, and whenever they perform the service their hearts will overflow with joy.

The miraculous vessel sustains Joseph for many years, until the fall of Jerusalem, when Vespasian releases him from prison and enacts a brutal revenge against the Jews, killing many and selling the rest into slavery. Obtaining exemptions for his sister and brother-in-law, Hebron or Bron, Joseph leads them with a small band of believers into the desert. During their sojourn there, the vessel becomes a test for the virtuous. God tells Joseph to build a table in imitation of the Last Supper table and place the vessel on it. Bron is to catch a fish and lay it beside the vessel. Only those who have maintained faith will be able to sit at the table and experience indescribable sweetness and delight, since the vessel will not tolerate the presence of sinners. One of the seats is left empty, waiting for the chosen one; when Moysés, a member of the excluded company, tries to take the empty seat, he is swallowed up by the earth.

Bron and his wife have twelve handsome sons, who take wives, all except the youngest, Alain. Joseph is told by God that the virtuous Alain is to lead his brothers and sisters westward, preaching the word of Christ. The next day, divine directions send a certain Petrus also to the wild westward lands, to the vale of Avaron (Avalon). Joseph is then told that his brother-in-law Bron will be called the Rich Fisherman, in honor of the fish he caught for the altar, and will be the new guardian of the Grail. Joseph will die here, but Bron will also go westwards, and await his grandson (the issue of Alain),[27] who will ultimately take over the guardianship of the Grail, thus symbolizing the Trinity.

Robert ends with an enigmatic epilogue indicating that he will recount later what happened to Alain, to Petrus, to Moysés, and to the Rich Fisherman, but that he must put these four stories aside to narrate a fifth one, presumably the *Merlin*. (This narrative recounts the story of the birth of Merlin and the birth and coronation of Arthur.) The third part of Robert's trilogy is possibly represented by the Didot-*Perceval*, called after a former owner of the manuscript to distinguish it from Chrétien's romance.[28] This prose romance focuses on Perceval, here the son of Alain le Gros, who comes to Arthur's court without his mother's knowledge and attempts to sit in the Perilous Seat. Darkness sweeps over the court, the stone splits, and a voice announces that the Grail is in the land and that the Fisher King (Bron, Perceval's grandfather) will not be cured of his illness until a knight who has surpassed all others visits him and asks the Grail Question. Perceval vows to seek the Fisher King, and a number of adventures follow, many of them derived from the Second Continuation. Perceval makes two visits to the Castle, failing to ask the Question on the first occasion but succeeding on the second. The Fisher King is healed, the enchantments of Britain cease, and the history of the Grail is told to Perceval. Many of the details correspond closely to *Joseph*, but others differ markedly; for instance, the Lance, which is not mentioned in *Joseph*, is identified as the spear of Longinus. Bron dies and Perceval becomes the Fisher King. Merlin dictates these events to Blaise, who writes them down. Some manuscripts of the Didot-*Perceval* contain a further section, a kind of *Mort Artu* ("Death of Arthur"), describing Arthur's conquest of France, the Roman wars, Mordred's treachery, and Arthur's removal to Avalon. The trilogy thus formed provides the point of departure for the massive Vulgate Cycle (see below).

Since Robert sends Petrus to the "vale of Avaron" (Avalon), the end of his *Joseph* hints at an assocation between Joseph of Arimathea and Glastonbury, in Somerset. Avalon was first identified with Glastonbury by Gerald of Wales, an identification perhaps prompted by the purported "discovery" at Glastonbury Abbey in 1191 of the skeletons of Arthur and Guinevere, a well-publicized event with which Robert may have been familiar.[29] Though the Abbey had not initially claimed Joseph as its founder, the legend of his apostolic mission to England was soon developed and fostered by the monks. Just before 1250, interpolations in a manuscript of William of Malmesbury's *De Antiquitate Glastoniensis Ecclesiae* ("Concerning the Antiquities of the Abbey of Glastonbury," ca. 1129) mention Joseph as the leader of a band of twelve missionaries sent to Britain by the apostle Philip, and refer to the Arthurian story as authority for the incident. By 1382 the tradition of Joseph as founder of the Abbey had been fully established, and at the end of the century John of Glastonbury's *Chronicle* gives a definitive account of the occasion, dating it to A.D. 63. Also repeated in John's account is the enigmatic prophecy of Melkin (*not* to be identified with Merlin) that Joseph's body would be found near the old church, buried with two silver cruets holding Christ's blood and sweat.[30] By the fifteenth century, Joseph's reputation as the first evangelist of Britain was so firmly established that it could be invoked at four great Church councils to give precedence to Britain as the first European country to be converted to Christianity (Lagorio, "The Evolving Legend," 220–24).

Perlesvaus

The anonymous author of *Perlesvaus*, known in English as *The High Book of the Grail*, also knew the tradition of Glastonbury, since he claims that the source of his romance is a Latin account recorded by a Flavius Josephus from the narrative of an angel and kept at a religious house on the Isle of Avalon (clearly identifiable as Glastonbury by the reference to the tombs of Arthur and Guinevere). *Perlesvaus* was written in Old French prose in the early thirteenth century. Despite the author's claim of a fictional source, it is clear that he expects his audience to be fully familiar with Chrétien's *Perceval* or *Le Conte du Graal* although he nowhere makes a direct reference to it. Indeed, this romance may be seen as a palimpsest of Chrétien's, which hovers as a ghostly offset behind its elaborate narrative.[31] Perlesvaus, the hero, both is and is not Perceval; his name is glossed early on as "Per-les-vaux," meaning "he who has lost the Vales," in a reference to his inheritance, the Vales of Kamaalot, the recovery of which becomes a major thread in the narrative. The author must also have known Robert de Boron's work, or at least the Didot-*Perceval*, since Perlesvaus's father was Alain le Gros, and his ancestry is traced to Joseph of Arimathea, whose shield he frequently carries. The Grail is the vessel that received Christ's blood from the Cross; the Fisher King is one of his maternal uncles, and Pelles, the Hermit-King, another. A third maternal uncle is the evil King of the Castle Mortal, whom Perlesvaus must fight in order to regain the Grail Castle and the holy talismans.

Perlesvaus's first visit to the Grail Castle has taken place before the narrative begins: there are constant references to his failure to ask the Question, and to the many consequences of that failure—the Fisher King's languor, war and anarchy in Britain, the baldness of the Maiden of the Cart, the degeneration of Arthur's court. Indeed, the first quester, who has the chance to redeem Perlesvaus's failure, is Gawain; as he approaches the Fisher King's castle via many distractions and lesser quests, he is continually reminded of that failure and warned not to repeat it. The cumulative effect of anticipation is quite powerful, so that when Gawain finally sits at the meal and the Grail procession passes in front of him, the reader cannot believe he will fail. The Grail appears to him as a chalice, then with a child in its center, and finally with the crucified Christ above it; also, three drops of blood fall from the Lance on the table. However, although the procession passes three times and the knights cry out to Gawain, he is too rapt in his visions to hear them and fails to ask the question.

The second quester is Lancelot, who arrives at the Grail Castle but confesses to the hermit that he cannot give up his love for the queen. Because of his refusal to repent of his sin, the Grail does not even appear to him. Interwoven with his and Gawain's adventures are the attempts by both knights and Perlesvaus's sister, Dandrane, to find Perlesvaus (Dandrane is looking for the Good Knight who may deliver her mother from the Lord of the Fens). Unlike Chrétien's knight, Perlesvaus's fault lies in the past, and he is now a transformed knight. His story moves from successful personal revenge (he exacts a grisly punishment on the Lord of the Fens when he regains his lands) to a more messianic role: he defeats the Knight of the Dragon and saves all the souls oppressed by him, he recaptures the Grail Castle from the King of the Castle Mortal, which allows the Grail to return, and, finally, he defeats the Black Hermit, who is sent alive into a deep foul pit by his followers. He never does ask the Grail Question, however, because the Fisher King dies before he gets there.

The final quester is Arthur himself: after the reconquest of the Grail Castle, Arthur sees two suns in the sky, signifying the union of temporal with spiritual power, [32] and a voice announces that he too should seek the Grail. In Arthur's vision the Grail takes on five transformations, but only the last form, that of the chalice, is actually described; both chalice and bell have been unknown in Logres and are shown to Arthur as models of the symbolic objects he should now duplicate and distribute to churches in his realm for the continued celebration of the Christian faith.

As may already be apparent, the Crusading flavor of the narrative is extremely strong. The main theme is the supplanting of the Old Law (meaning not only the Jewish religion but all heathen faiths) by the New Law, and the promulgation of the New Law through other lands, often by forcible conversion, as well as the constant need to defend it when established. The picture is of a militant Christianity, often brutal and violent. Arthur's kingdom is threatened, however, not only from without, but also by treachery within, representing not only the battle against the external enemies of Christianity but also the moral struggle within every Christian. The complicated interlaced narrative cannot be reduced successfully to a rigid allegorical system with one-to-one correspondences, but it is clear that an intermittent typology is operating.[33] Events and characters recall New Testament events, without representing them. Perlesvaus's failure to ask the question recalls Adam's sin, but his victory over the King of the Castle Mortal reflects Christ's victory over death.[34] Perlesvaus wins the Circle of Gold (the crown of thorns set in gold and jewels), and Gawain, who wins the sword that beheaded St. John the Baptist, may be seen as the Precursor. Both defend the New Law, as does Arthur. Even Lancelot, who is barred from seeing the Grail because of his love for the queen, is able to free Albanie and other lands from the false faith. In the final episode Perlesvaus retires to the Grail Castle, where his mother and sister have also come; after their death, he distributes the relics among the hermits and disappears on a magical boat. The Grail itself is seen no more, and the castle crumbles into ruins, though the chapel survives intact. No one who visits the castle returns, except for a couple of enthusiastic Welsh knights, who reappear many years later, radically changed. It has become a place of mystery and indescribable mystical experience. As Angus J. Kennedy, in "Punishment in the Perlesvaus," Chapter 5 of this volume, and Thomas E. Kelly have suggested, the inconclusive nature of the end of the romance underscores the idea that redemption for humankind is an ongoing struggle.

The Vulgate Cycle

Some ten years after *Perlesvaus*, the vast compilation known as the Vulgate Cycle, or the *Lancelot-Graal* (1215–35), began to be written. With its five roughly sequential branches, the Cycle is an extensive rewriting of the many versions of the Arthurian story that precede it. Traces of the prose *Joseph* and *Merlin*, Chrétien's *Perceval* and its Continuations, and the Didot-*Perceval* can all be identified as layers in the composition of the Vulgate Cycle. As E. Jane Burns observes, "In the medieval system of rewriting, a reformulated text becomes to a degree the author's own invention without ever really losing its former character. The literary work resides in a continuum of transformations, each different from but as valid as its predecessor."[35] The narrative method of the Vulgate Cycle employs *entrelacement*, or the interlace technique, whereby themes and stories are developed by interweaving the narrative threads. One character's adventures may be pursued for some folios, then be picked up again much later, while other characters' adventures intervene. The narrative thread disappears for a while and reappears later in the weave; yet, as in a tapestry, it has continued behind the fabric, away from the reader's view. This technique allows the writer to keep the adventures of a number of characters going simultaneously.

For our purposes, the most important branches of the Vulgate Cycle are the *Estoire del Saint Graal* ("The History of the Holy Grail"); the last part of the *Lancelot* proper, which prepares for the *Queste*; and the *Queste del Saint Graal* ("Quest of the Holy Grail"). The *Estoire* is a highly Christianized elaboration of the prose *Joseph d'Arimathie*, focusing on Joseph and his descendants, in particular his son Josephes, a character invented to provide the purity and holiness that makes him worthy to become the first Christian Bishop, and to parallel Galaad in the *Queste*. Though this branch comes first in the chronology of the Vulgate Cycle, it was probably written last, to provide the prophecies and antecedents of the events in the *Queste*.[36]

An unidentified first-person author who is ordered in the Prologue to transcribe the book previously written by Christ, the "estoire" itself, and Robert de Boron, translating from Latin to French, all claim to be authors or narrators of this text at different points.[37] The ascription to Robert de Boron indicates the authoritative tradition with which the narrative aligns itself and the Joseph of Arimathea strain to which it belongs. As in Robert's original verse romance, Joseph is the noble knight, a secret Christian, who catches Christ's blood after the Crucifixion in a bowl ("escuele") that he rescued from the utensils of the Last Supper and who is sustained for forty-two years in prison by this miraculous vessel. On his release, God tells him he must give up all his wealth and the comforts of home, taking only the vessel, and, with his wife and relatives, spread the Christian message throughout the world. Joseph's issue from his son Galaad I, born after their departure, will fill foreign lands and provide the "new people of the Crucified One," the congregation for the new faith.

Joseph and his companions make their way to Sarras, capital city of the Saracens, where their first task is the conversion of King Evalach and his relatives. Joseph's son Josephes, having taken a vow of chastity, is granted a vision of the symbolic instruments of the Passion within the ark or tabernacle of the Lord, among which are the "escuele" (the vessel), the bleeding Lance, and a covered chalice with a paten for administering the Eucharist. He is then instructed in the mysteries of the Eucharist (the Sacrament of Christ's body and blood)[38] and consecrated as the first bishop of this New Law, Christianity.

The conversions of Evalach, baptized Mordrain, and his brother-in-law Seraphe, baptized Nascien, require Joseph to present Mordrain with the red-cross shield, symbol of Christ's conquest over death. Nascien is shown the ark and names the vessel "the Grail," arguing the spurious etymology of its derivation from the verb "agréer," to be pleasing.[39] His presumption in looking too closely into the Grail is punished by blindness, later cured by an angel who anoints his eyes with blood from the Lance. The angel predicts the *Queste*, when marvels will happen through the land because good men will desire knowledge of the Grail and the Lance. Only one mortal will see the full marvels of the Grail, and he will be the last of Nascien's line.

The narrative is indeed full of prophecies, as events in the *Estoire* anticipate and are fulfilled by events in the *Queste*, creating a complex system of cross-references. Both this narrative and the whole Arthurian world await the "bon chevalier," the Good Knight who will bring to an end the adventures of the Grail, in other words Galaad. One such linking event is the description of Solomon's ship, seen by Nascien, which will be encountered by the "bon chevalier" during the *Queste*. Following the advice of his wife, Solomon has provided the ship itself, the marvelous bed with its three spindles carved from cuttings of the Tree of Life, one white, one green, and one red, as well as the sword with strange straps, so that his descendant the "bon chevalier" will know that he (Solomon) knew the truth about his birth. The sword belt and straps, made of unworthy material, are to be left untouched until the coming of a princess who will replace them with what she most values in the world. The description of Solomon's ship is repeated closely in the *Queste*,[40] when Galaad, Bohort, and Perceval find the ship, and Perceval's sister replaces the sword belt with one woven from silk and gold thread and her own hair.

The *Estoire* narrative is also full of journeys, as Joseph and his son separately wander through the Middle East, guided by God and sustained by the Grail, eventually making their way to Great Britain, where they are joined by Nascien and finally Mordrain. The most spectacular journey is made by 150 of the faithful who cross the sea on the hem of Joseph's garment, while those more sinful have to wait for Nascien and more conventional transport. The narrative also features a number of miracles, and punishments for presumption: just as Nascien was blinded when he looked too closely into the Grail, Mordrain is blinded and paralyzed for the same offense. He prays that he may be allowed to live until the coming of Galaad, and his request is granted as he waits two hundred years.[41] Similarly, Moysés asks to sit in the empty seat at the Grail Table, between Josephes and Bron, and is carried off in flames for his hypocrisy. In Brocéliande, Joseph brings a Saracen back to life by means of the Grail, to prove the power of the Christian god over Mahomet, Apollo, and other heathen gods.

Ultimately, the wanderings and testings begin to come to a close, when Bron's youngest son, Alain, who has vowed to remain a virgin, catches a fish that is miraculously multiplied to feed the sinners who were denied food from the Grail. Alain is named the Rich Fisherman and appointed the next Grail guardian by Josephes before he dies. The King of the Land Beyond, cured of leprosy by the Grail, builds a splendid stronghold for it, named Corbenic (Chaldean for "The Holy Vessel"). Here the Grail resides, guarded by a succession of Rich Fishermen descended from Joshua, Alain's brother. One of these guardians, Lambor, is killed by Varlan when the latter seizes the sword destined for Galaad from Solomon's ship, causing two lands to become waste, a condition that will be relieved only by the coming of the "bon chevalier." Lambor's son is Pellehan, wounded between the thighs in battle (a wound that will also be healed with the coming of Galaad), and Pellehan's son is Pelles, on whose daughter Lancelot will father Galaad.

In this way, the history is brought up to date with the Arthurian present. The third section of the *Lancelot* branch prepares the way for the Grail, as a new note creeps into the chivalric setting with the prophecies of the Good Knight who will sit in the Perilous Seat and bring to an end the adventures of the Grail. The Grail itself makes its first appearance, to Gauvain at Corbenic. Since the description of its appearance here is repeated on subsequent occasions virtually unchanged, it is worth giving in detail. First, a white dove flies into the hall carrying a golden censer in its beak, and the sweetest possible odors fill the hall. Everyone is struck silent, but cloths are laid on the dinner tables and all pray while waiting. A most beautiful maiden then appears, carrying a splendid vessel; as she passes in front of each knight, he bows, and the tables are filled with the most delightful nourishment, while it seems as if all the spices of the world are present.

The Grail has appeared to Gauvain, however, only to mark how unworthy he is.[42] It feeds everyone but him, and on the following night he fails the adventures of the Palace of Adventures, leaving in disgrace. It is Lancelot for whom the people of Corbenic have been waiting: he achieves the feats Gauvain could not achieve, such as delivering a naked lady from a tub of boiling water and fighting a lion that issues from a tomb, and witnesses the Grail procession. But, with the connivance of King Pelles, Lancelot is deceived into sleeping with Pelles's daughter under the impression that she is Guinevere. This act engenders Galaad, who will restore the Waste Land and by his own virginal perfection will offset the princess's loss of virginity.[43]

Lancelot's cousin Bohort is also twice granted a vision of the Grail at Corbenic, though he is temporarily blinded when its cover is removed. Perceval is similarly privileged. On his arrival at court a miracle marks him as one of the Grail knights, and when he and Lancelot's brother Hector are wounded nearly to the death, the Grail appears to heal them both. Lancelot, too, is healed by the Grail of his madness, after being banished by Guinevere. The groundwork has been laid for the *Queste*: the Grail's marvelous qualities have been established and the questers marked off from the rest, contrasted with the unworthiness of Gawain. At the end of the *Lancelot* branch, Galaad is sent to be brought up by his aunt, Pelles's sister, at her abbey of white nuns, till the age of fifteen.

In the *Estoire*, we were following the Joseph of Arimathea strain. The *Queste del Saint Graal* brings us to the third Grail strain, with its focus on Galaad. It also heralds a new juncture in the Cycle, introducing a new value system. Where, previously, the appearances of the Grail have been interspersed between secular, chivalric adventures, now chivalric events, visions, and dreams are equally and consistently reinterpreted by a series of resident hermits, recluses, and priests, according to a new register of signification. This constant allegorical and typological interpretation[44] has prompted some scholars to read this text as essentially a religious treatise for which the Arthurian setting is an entertaining background. Albert Pauphilet, for instance, having identified the services and practices described in the *Queste* as Cistercian, argues that conveying religious doctrine was the primary purpose of its writers: "Sous l'apparence chevaleresque, c'est la grand aventure de l'homme qui est ici exposée: c'est un tableau de la vie chrétienne telle que pouvait l'observer ou la rêver une conscience du treizième siècle" ("Under the chivalric surface, it is the grand adventure of man that is revealed: it is a picture of the Christian life as a conscience of the thirteenth century could imagine or dream it").[45] Other scholars, such as Emmanuèle Baumgartner, argue that the *Queste* should not be read independently of its links with the rest of the Cycle and that the religious aspect has been introduced to enhance and dignify chivalry. Its evangelization is strictly reserved for the characters of its own fictional world, the Arthurian knights.[46] Laurence de Looze, in Chapter 6 of this volume, reminds us that although events are constantly interpreted and reinterpreted by the hermits, those interpretive scenes are *within* the text and are themselves narrative events. The *Queste* is a metafiction, a story of interpretations of the events of its own narrative, and the reader is required to become a hermeneutician along with the knights of the quest.

The plot of the *Queste* is elegant and tightly knit. Galaad's arrival at Camelot heralds the Quest, as he sits unharmed in the Perilous Seat and draws the sword from the stone. The inscriptions on the seat and on the stone, the announcements of the old man who leads Galaad in and, later, of a strange maiden, as well as Galaad's performance at the tournament, all confirm in various ways that Lancelot's primacy as the best knight is ended and that this new knight will bring the adventures of the Grail to an end. His arrival is climaxed by the appearance of the Grail itself, for the first time at Camelot: with cracking of thunder and unearthly radiance, it enters, covered with white silk and moving without visible means of support. All are struck silent. The Grail fills the hall with the odors of all the spices of the world and feeds every man with the food he most desires. Gauvain makes the first vow, that he will not rest till he sees openly what is now obscured, and many other knights follow him, causing Artus to lament that this will break up the Round Table, as many knights will not return. Next day, a formal oath is taken on the relics, led by Galaad, who vows to learn the truth about the Grail. No women are to accompany the knights, they are told, and only those who are fully confessed of their sins should set out on the Quest.[47]

The Quest itself progresses both spatially and temporally, as the interlaced narrative follows the adventures of individual knights through the pathless forest, on uncharted sea voyages, and, finally, to Corbenic and the Holy City. As the narrative progresses, the spiritual hierarchy of the knights is delineated. Gauvain and Hector belong to the majority group of knights, who will never understand the significance of these new adventures and will therefore never encounter any; they go home in disgust. Lancelot is the intermediate figure, the repentant sinner, who begins to understand the Quest's significance and is granted a partial vision of the Grail. The three elect, Bohort, Perceval, and Galaad, are allowed to embark on the magic ship, and from there onto Solomon's ship, where Perceval's sister joins them. The climactic experience for Bohort and Perceval is at Corbenic, where they participate in the Eucharist administered by Christ himself; though they accompany Galaad and the Grail to the holy city of Sarras, it is only Galaad who sees the final vision and experiences complete union with the Divine.

For Galaad, there are no temptations; his progression represents simply "the unveiling of a destiny."[48] He acquires the red-cross shield originally given by Joseph of Arimathea to Evalach, and makes the right choice of path through the trackless forest. For the other questers, the narrative traces a spiritual progression. Lancelot begins to understand his sinfulness when the Grail appears to heal a sick knight and he can only lie there motionless. Through a series of conversations with hermits and recluses, he confesses his sin with Guinevere and begins penance for it, wearing a hairshirt and vowing to sin no more with any woman. Perceval, in his turn, embarks on a series of tests and temptations, culminating in a narrow escape from seduction by a diabolical maiden. Subsequently, Bohort, too, undergoes a series of tests that climax when he is forced to choose between saving a virgin from rape or his brother Lionel from death. As their respective trials conclude, Bohort and Perceval join Galaad on the magic ship, from where, guided by Perceval's sister, they embark on a second ship, the Ship of Solomon. The description, history, and significance of this ship has already been given us in the *Estoire*: this is the fulfillment of the earlier predictions. Galaad draws the sword from the scabbard, and Perceval's sister produces the new belt for the sword, woven from gold threads and her hair. At the culmination of this sequence, Perceval's sister sacrifices herself by giving her blood to save a princess with leprosy. When she dies, the companions build a boat for her embalmed body and set it afloat.

At this point the companions separate. Lancelot sails for a time on Perceval's sister's ship, sustained by the Holy Ghost and accompanied for a time by Galaad. Eventually, Lancelot arrives alone at Corbenic, in bright moonlight; passing two guardian lions, he moves through the apparently empty palace, till he hears beautiful singing. Here is an open door, with intense light pouring out. He kneels and sees the Grail resting on a table, covered with a red silk cloth, attended by angels. An old man is conducting Mass. Lancelot has been warned by a voice not to enter the room, but when he sees the old priest elevating the Host and apparently supporting three men in his hands, he runs to help him and is struck down by a fierce hot wind. He has mistaken transubstantiation for true corporeal reality. He lies motionless for twenty-four days (corresponding to the twenty-four years he was in the Devil's service), tended by the people of the castle. When he recovers, he understands that his Grail Quest is over, and returns to Camelot.

Meanwhile, Galaad has been continuing to fulfill the prophecies. Mordrain, having waited for four hundred years, dies in his arms, with his wounds miraculously healed. Perceval and Bohort join Galaad again, and the three companions arrive at Corbenic, where Galaad joins the pieces of Joseph's broken sword. At vespers, the skies darken, and a voice banishes all those who are not companions of the Quest from the room. Nine other knights enter to share the service.[49] The Maimed King is carried in, and Josephes, the first bishop, descends from the sky. Four angels place candles, a red silk cloth, and the Lance beside the Grail, on the silver Table. Josephes takes the host (in the form of bread) from the Grail; when he elevates it, the form of a child enters the bread, and he returns it to the vessel. He invites the twelve knights to sit at the Table and be nourished by this exquisite and celestial food, and vanishes. As the knights do so, weeping and in fear, a naked man issues from the Grail and speaks to them, saying, "I can no longer conceal Myself from you." They are served from the Grail, which is the platter from which Christ and his disciples ate the Paschal Lamb. Though others in the palace have been fed by the grace of the Holy Vessel, that was material food: this is heavenly.

At the end of the service, Christ tells Galaad that he, Bohort, and Perceval must take the Grail to Sarras, to the spiritual palace. The Grail is

leaving Logres, because the people have not respected it or served it correctly. But first Galaad is to heal the Maimed King with blood from the
Lance. He does so, and Christ ascends.

At the shore the companions find Solomon's ship waiting for them,
with the Grail on its Table, covered with the red silk cloth. Galaad had
felt such intense joy when he witnessed the mysteries at Corbenic that he
wished he could die at that moment, and he prays daily to repeat the experience. The companions arrive at Sarras, to find Perceval's sister's
ship, with her body, waiting for them. They bury her richly, but are
thrown in prison by the king of the city, who is an unbeliever. The Grail
sustains them, and on the king's death a year later the people choose
Galaad as king. He suffers this earthly existence for another year, but finally comes the day when the three companions, making their daily
prayer to the Grail, see Bishop Josephes kneeling before it, surrounded
by angels. He conducts Mass and invites Galaad to look into the Grail.
Galaad, trembling violently, sees the mysteries, and prays to pass, in this
state of bliss, into eternal life. Kissing Bohort and Perceval, and sending
greetings to his father, Lancelot, Galaad kneels and dies. A hand appears,
seizes the Grail and the Lance, and carries them up to heaven, never to be
seen on earth again.

In grief, Perceval and Bohort retire to a hermitage, though Bohort
retains his secular clothing. When Perceval dies a year later, Bohort returns to Camelot, to narrate the adventures of the Grail to scribes who
record it and store it in the library at Salisbury, after which Walter Map
translates the account from Latin into French, at the request of King
Henry II.[50]

The process of the narrative has been a gradual unveiling of the
meaning of the Grail, but what, ultimately, it symbolizes is open to dispute. Scholars have provided many interpretations: that it is the presence
of Christ, that it is a symbol of God's grace, that it is a representation of
the Eucharist.[51] The Grail is first of all an object: as Christ informs the
celebrants at Corbenic, it is the platter of the Last Supper, in which the
Paschal Lamb was served. On the literal level, it is therefore a relic with
Eucharistic associations; yet at the same time, it has undeniable Pentecostal associations, with the imagery of its first appearance at court, and
the spring that withdraws from Lancelot, described by the hermit as "la
douce parole de l'Evangile" ("the sweet words of the Evangelist") and
"la grace del Saint Graal" ("the grace of the Holy Grail"). Given these
double associations, Matarasso argues that the Grail is a "double manifestation of the Son and the Spirit" (*Redemption*, 194). At the same time,

what the questers seek is not the Grail itself, but the Truth that it contains: Galaad's vow, repeated by the whole court after him, is to seek "la verité del Saint Graal." By the time Galaad truly "sees" the Grail, questers and readers alike have learned its history, the history of the Lance, the adventures of Logres, and the theological truths the Grail stands for. Galaad not only "sees" but "knows" the Grail.[52] Baumgartner suggests that the Grail provides an image of each quester's personal vision of God and the divine mysteries. For Gauvain and Hector it is essentially a material object, providing inexhaustible nourishment. For Lancelot, the repentant sinner, it is the source of healing Grace. For the three elect it is the concrete manifestation of the divine mystery. For Galaad alone it is the naked vision, the moment when the Bread becomes Life, the origin of all things ("Les Aventures du Graal," 27).

Ultimately, as Sandra Ness Ihle reminds us, the meaning of the Grail can never be complete:

> . . . the essence of the Grail in the *Queste* is its mystery; to identify it specifically is to ignore the diversity of its manifestations and the interpenetration of images attached to it. Since even those who achieve it–and especially Galahad, who sees it openly and directly revealed–cannot express what they see, it is obvious that its truths are ineffable and ultimately inexpressable. Galahad, at the moment he sees the Grail secrets revealed, is transported to heaven; one cannot be illumined with that bright light and continue in mortal life. . . . The truth of the Grail is adumbrated. We know all we can of it through the partial views provided by each device. The hand comes from heaven to remove the Grail; beyond what the author has told us, we can say and see no more. (40)

The Post-Vulgate Cycle, or *Le Roman du Graal* ("The Romance of the Grail")

Between 1230 and 1240, an anonymous writer whose aim was to create a more homogeneous work out of the Vulgate Cycle composed what is known as the *Roman du Graal,* or the Post-Vulgate Cycle.[53] This romance, a comparatively recent postulation by Fanni Bogdanow, has not survived in a complete form but must be reconstructed from widely scattered fragments in Old French and extant translations in Spanish and Portuguese.[54] The major change made by the Post-Vulgate writer was to leave out most of the *Lancelot,* thus de-emphasizing the adultery between Lancelot and Guinevere as the cause of the downfall of the Round

Table and emphasizing in turn the consequences of Arthur's incest with King Lot's wife. By including in the *Suite du Merlin* the story of Balain, the knight with two swords, who commits the Dolorous Stroke with the holy Lance at Corbenic, an episode that looks forward to the arrival of Galaad in the *Queste*, the Post-Vulgate writer has created a new and different set of links and prophecies from those in the Vulgate. Merlin puts Balain's sword in a block of marble and sends it floating down the river, to arrive at Camelot on the same day as Galaad. It is therefore Balain's sword that Galaad removes from the stone, whereas in the Vulgate *Queste* the sword in the stone had no provenance. Balain's sacrilegious blow wounds Pellehan through the thighs, making him the Maimed King and causing the Waste Land, wounds that will be healed only at the advent of Galaad; Pellehan recalls Balain's blow when he is healed. At the same time as links between the *Suite* and the *Queste* are created, many of the Vulgate links between the *Estoire* and the *Queste* are severed. Though the Post-Vulgate *Estoire* is not much changed from the Vulgate (judging from the *Livro de Josep Abarimatia*), Bishop Josephes's role in the Post-Vulgate *Queste* is considerably diminished: he appears at only one of the Grail liturgy scenes. Therefore, the Dolorous Stroke in the *Suite* becomes the dominant antecedent to Galaad's redemption, rather than the actions of Josephes.

The story of Balain le Sauvage (Balin the Wild) is affecting and tragic. Known as the Knight of Two Swords because he keeps a sword after releasing it from the enchanted scabbard of a damsel, Balain embarks on a series of adventures, each of which ends disastrously, and with a repeated prediction of his death. He is noble and a splendid fighter, but despite his best intentions, he continually causes death or suffering to those he attempts to help. The climax of his adventures comes when he arrives at Pellehan's castle, seeking Garlon, an invisible knight who has caused him great injury. Garlon is Pellehan's brother, and when Balain kills Garlon at a feast in the castle, Pellehan attacks Balain, breaking his sword. Balain flees through the castle searching for another weapon, and enters a room where, on a silver table, rests a vessel of silver and gold in which stands a lance. Despite a warning voice, Balain seizes the Lance and strikes Pellehan through the thighs. The castle begins to shake, inhabitants fall unconscious, and a terrible voice announces, "Now begin the adventures of the Kingdom of Adventures." Because impious hands have touched the Lance, sacrilege has taken place, and devastation and misery will result for twenty-two years. Balain rides away sorrowing, through a land that lies waste as if struck by lightning, with many people lying dead.

His own fate is not much better. Despite warnings, he accepts an un-
marked shield in replacement for his own and ends up fighting an unknown knight to defend an island. Too late, Balain discovers that he is
fighting his own brother and that they have wounded each other to the
death. Merlin buries the brothers, and places Balain's sword in the stone,
with an inscription that it can be removed only by "the best knight in the
world."

This section of the *Suite du Merlin*, therefore, anticipates the Post-
Vulgate *Queste*,[55] which is very different from the Vulgate. Though most
of the central episodes of the Vulgate *Queste*, and the primacy of the
three questers, are retained, they are interwoven with the adventures of a
great number of other knights familiar from the Prose *Tristan*, such as
Erec, Meraugis, Sagremor, Arthur the Less, Palamedes and the Bête
Glatissant (Questing Beast), as well as Tristan himself. Indeed, the Grail
does not appear at Camelot until Tristan returns to court to make the
Round Table complete. The elegant interlace of the Vulgate *Queste*, with
its tightly knit progression in virtue and its spiritual hierarchy of
questers, is quite dissipated. The doctrinal interpretation of dreams and
allegorical incidents is considerably lessened. In the Ship of Solomon
episode, for instance, the narrative alludes to the explanation of the three
spindles from the Tree of Life given to Nascien (in the *Estoire*) but does
not repeat it; thus a whole level of typological significance is excised.

The most striking alterations are in the scenes of the Grail liturgy.
Lancelot's visit to Corbenic follows the Vulgate closely until he comes to
the entrance of the Grail chamber. Though he sees a great light and the
Holy Vessel, covered, on a silver table, there is no Mass and no transubstantiation. Whereas in the Vulgate he was driven to enter the forbidden
chamber because he thought the old priest needed help to support the
transubstantiated Host, in the Post-Vulgate version he desires only to un-
veil the Grail, to see the Vessel. Instead of a burning wind, unseen hands
pull him back and render him unconscious. Similarly, the experience of
the questers at Corbenic is significantly altered. First of all, one of the
questers is Palamedes the Saracen, who has just achieved the adventure
of the Questing Beast and been baptized; he is even present among the
twelve who receive the Host. Galaad heals the Maimed King first, with
blood from a silver basin into which the Lance has been bleeding. There
is no Josephes, and the crucial Mass does not take place until vespers,
when the knights are called back into the Grail chamber, to feed on the
heavenly food. Christ serves them, but he is not naked and does not appear from the Grail;[56] nor does he identify the Grail as the dish of the

Last Supper. It is true that when each knight takes the Host, he thinks he is "putting a living man into his mouth" (*Lancelot-Grail*, V, 280), so the Eucharistic significance of the service has not been quite lost; however, the Post-Vulgate description loses the charming and touching concrete representations of transubstantiation that characterized the Vulgate Grail scenes. The Post-Vulgate *Queste*, therefore, retains the mystery but not the mysticism, and certainly not the doctrine, of its source.

THE MEDIEVAL LEGEND IN GERMAN

Wolfram von Eschenbach, *Parzival*

The German contribution to the Grail legend is extremely important. Between 1200 and 1210, Wolfram von Eschenbach reworked, expanded, and completed Chrétien de Troyes's *Perceval* or *Le Conte du Graal*, in 25,000 lines of rhymed couplets in Middle High German, titled *Parzival*.[57] Though Wolfram acknowledges his debt to Chrétien in his epilogue, he claims that his primary source is a Provençal poet named Kyot, who found in Toledo a manuscript written in a "heathenish tongue" (presumably Arabic) by one Flegetanis, a scholar whose background was Jewish on his mother's side and heathen on his father's; the manuscript contained rudimentary information about a sacred object left on the earth by the neutral angels. Kyot studied Latin books to find out more about the subject and eventually discovered in "Anjou" the whole tale that Wolfram is now telling (Hatto, 213–14, 232–33). Scholars are generally agreed that this chain of transmission (worthy of Umberto Eco) is a fiction to provide Wolfram with authority.

The main narrative details of Wolfram's epic are recognizable from Chrétien: the untutored boy Parzival, the arrival at court, the rescue of and marriage to a beautiful woman, the castle with the maimed Fisher King and the failure to ask the question, the arrival at Arthur's camp, the blood on the snow, the reproach of the Ugly Maiden, Parzival's despair and rejection of God, his second setting out, his meeting with the hermit and confession. As in Chrétien's romance, after he leaves the court for the second time Parzival's adventures are interlaced with those of Gawan, and Gawan's adventures are also similar to the French source, including the Damsel with Little Sleeves, the Proud Maiden, and the magical castle that contains the queens who are his relatives. But Wolfram adds new narrative elements, in providing both a conclusion and a "prequel" to Chrétien's unfinished narrative. The conclusion brings

Parzival and Gawan together in combat, closing Gawan's adventures with a marriage to the Proud Maiden, and Parzival's with his return to the Grail Castle, his asking of the question that heals the wounded King, and his installation as the Grail King, with his wife and son. In the "prequel" to Parzival's story, two books detail the adventures of his father and mother, Gahmuret and Herzeloyde; the latter withdraws with her child to the wilderness after Gahmuret's death, thus explaining the boy's lack of knowledge of the court and knightly ways. Wolfram also adds an Eastern/Oriental element that remains as a background through the story, for Gahmuret's first liaison is with a Moorish princess, Belacane, which results in a particolored child, with a skin patterned in black and white. Parzival thus has a half-brother, Fierefiz, a rich and noble "Infidel," with whom he fights and is reconciled at the end of the work, bringing him to the Grail Castle where he is baptized. Baptism allows Fierefiz to see the Grail and to marry the Grail Maiden, Repanse de Schoye, subsequently founding a Christianizing dynasty in India.[58]

Wolfram's main differences from Chrétien, however, lie in more than narrative additions. As Hatto notes, Chrétien's romance sets a foreground of "clarity and intensity . . . against an elusive and often mysterious background," whereas Wolfram provides "a very highly organized background" (430), a background that fills in details and supplies explanations. Wolfram provides names for every character, including many whom Chrétien prefers to designate with a periphrasis, and detailed genealogies, frequently linking characters by turning them into blood relations. The Red Knight whom Parzival kills for his armor becomes Ither, a cousin, and killing him is a sin added to Parzival's load. The Ugly Maiden is named Cundrie the sorceress and given a marvelous genealogy. Wolfram's descriptions of the "splendid material culture"[59] of the courts, of courtly etiquette, of spectacle and ceremony, of feudal hierarchies, are rich and detailed; he reveals an intimate knowledge of falconry, heraldry, organized warfare, astronomy, gemology, and medicinal lore.

The greatest difference between Wolfram and Chrétien, however, is in Wolfram's concept of the Grail and its guardians, detailed in two crucial chapters, 5 and 9. Wolfram's "Gral" is not a dish but a stone, left on earth by banished angels neutral in the divine war; it can be carried only by a virgin, Repanse de Schoye, who is the sister of the Maimed King, Anfortas. The Grail procession, described in Chapter 5, is an elaborate ceremonial, preceded by a page carrying a bleeding Lance, at which the whole company weeps and mourns. A hundred couches draped in quilts are provided for the spectators, and the procession requires eighteen maidens to precede the Grail Princess. The Grail provides all kinds of food and drink to the company, whatever one stretches one's hand out for; but it does not provide happiness: these are sorrowful people, "wholly given up to mourning" (128). The Grail Castle, named Munsalvaesche (Mount Savage), appears only to those who are meant to see it and is guarded by a company of knights, an order of "templeis"[60] dedicated to this service and required to remain chaste.

All these matters are explained in Chapter 9, the doctrinal center of the work, when Parzival encounters his uncle, the hermit Trevrizent, on Good Friday. The Grail company is nourished by the stone, which wards off death. The power of the stone is renewed every Good Friday, when the Holy Spirit in the form of a dove lays a wafer on it. The Grail company is a select group drawn from many countries, including both men and women, called to its service as children when their names appeared on the stone; while at Munsalvaesche they cannot marry, but are sometimes sent out to other countries that ask for them, as indeed happened to Parzival's mother, Herzeloyde. (Thus Parzival is destined for the Grail.) The Grail King may marry; however, Anfortas pursued a secular love service and was in punishment wounded in the scrotum, a wound from which he cannot recover, living in agony. Thus Anfortas's transgression is a sexual one, requiring an explicitly sexual punishment. An inscription on the stone informed the company that the chosen knight would come and ask the Question that would heal Anfortas but that no one should forewarn him. Parzival did arrive, but though he saw the marks of suffering, he failed to ask, "Sire, what ails you?"

Thus the Question in Wolfram's work is subtly altered from that in Chrétien's, and Parzival's sin is lack of compassion. Nor is this sin causally linked, as it is in Chrétien, with Parzival's mother's death, though that sin is also to be laid at his door, along with the killing of Ither. Parzival has been prevented by his immature blindness from recognizing the need to ask the Question. In his first encounter with the Grail, he perceived only the material aspects, the rich trappings of the ceremony and the attendant maidens.[61] After his sojourn with the hermit, however, Parzival is characterized by remorse and humility. Two potentially mortal battles (with Gawan and Fierefiz) are interrupted by recognition before bloodshed can take place, and it is a chastened Parzival who returns to the castle to heal his uncle. As Cundrie, now the messenger of good news, tells him, "You have won through to peace of soul" (p. 388).

Parzival's ultimate achievement is to exercise his magnificent courage and ability in the service of the Grail. Whereas love service is a constant theme through the work, and women are criticized for not rewarding the knights who have served them, it is clear that secular love service is antagonistic to the Grail; when Anfortas is healed, he vows to fight only in the service of the Grail, never more for the love of woman (407). Yet, whereas the realms of the spiritual and the secular were essentially antithetical in Chrétien, Wolfram appears to be reaching for a synthesis. The Grail King is allowed to marry, to create a dynasty; Parzival and his beloved Condwiramurs have a delighted and passionate reunion in the meadows outside Munsalvaesche at the end. It appears that when Parzival has mastered his passions and achieved true humility, he may lead the Grail community.[62] As James Poag suggests, "It is apparently a journey toward healing, restoration, consolation, and fullness of life, not only for the quester-hero and his uncle Anfortas, but for all mankind, for the Grail Company is a sort of missionary society. The men and women of Munsalvaesche, called by God, go out to guide various principalities of the known medieval world in the West and East" (66). For Wolfram, the Grail family is the "divinely ordained instrument in the affairs of the world."[63]

THE MEDIEVAL LEGEND IN WELSH

Peredur (Historia Peredur vab Efrawc, "History of Peredur, son of Efrog")

Peredur is one of three Middle Welsh tales which are close analogs to romances by Chrétien de Troyes, the other two being *Owein* and *Gereint*. All three tales were included in a collection translated by Lady Charlotte Guest, titled the *Mabinogion*. John K. Bollard observes that "the basic materials of *Peredur* . . . are Welsh in origin, and there are clear parallels with earlier Irish literature and with common Celtic themes."[64] Scholars disagree on the exact relationship of the Middle Welsh romance to Chrétien's *Perceval*; the manuscripts of the Welsh text belong to the late thirteenth century, but the text is clearly copied from earlier manuscripts and also shows evidence of oral tradition. Some scholars have argued that it is derived from Chrétien's romance, whereas others, notably Glenys Goetinck and Jean-Claude Lozachmeur, claim that the original form of the legend predated Chrétien.[65] The first part of *Peredur*'s narrative is very similar to *Perceval*, with the addition of the theme of the Witches of Caer Loyw, warrior women who, despite their hostility to Peredur, instruct the young knight in the use of arms and horsemanship. This part concludes with the reception of Peredur into Arthur's court. After this, however, the narrative diverges in another direction, introducing a new love theme (Peredur's love for Angharad Golden Hand, during which he is known as the Mute Squire) and an extensive sequence of interlocked adventures involving castles, hosts, monsters, tournaments, and a miller's family (during which Peredur is known as Peredur Long-Spear and later The Knight of the Mill) that culminates in Peredur's union with the Empress of Constantinople, with whom he rules for fourteen years. The oldest manuscript of *Peredur* concludes with this episode.[66] Others pick up Chrétien's story again by bringing in the visit of the Ugly (or Black) Maiden to Arthur's court, and the new quests by Gwalchmai (Gawain) and Peredur; these are broadly similar to Chrétien's narrative but severely truncated. The conclusion of the Welsh romance brings Peredur back to his uncle's castle, the Fortress of Wonders, but provides a totally different explanation for the marvelous incidents that have intervened.

Bollard characterizes the narrative structure of *Peredur* as a "series of episodes interrelated and interlaced by textual cross-reference, by structural parallelism, and by verbal echoes" (30). Verbal and structural repetition is, indeed, the most noticeable feature of the romance; it becomes, on occasion, incremental repetition. There is a pleasing folktale element to the narrative. Events take place most frequently in threes: Peredur strikes the marvelous sword against an iron column three times, being unable to mend the pieces on the last try; the King of the Round Valley yields to Peredur only at the third plea by his womenfolk; the tournament for the hand of the empress lasts for three days, the first two of which Peredur misses because he is in a love trance; three challengers offer goblets in the final test before he wins the empress; and so on.

The most significant sequence, from our point of view, is that which corresponds to Chrétien's Grail procession. To this point, the narratives have been fairly similar, though the Welsh author makes both Peredur's first tutor and the Fisher King his maternal uncles, and both lame. At this second fortress, known later as the Fortress of Wonders, the procession is preceded by the incident with the sword that breaks. The procession itself begins with two youths carrying a great spear bleeding in three streams of blood. This is followed by two maidens carrying a large dish holding a man's severed head, surrounded by quantities of blood. Both movements are met with loud lamentation. Peredur fails to ask questions about either. In the later sequence corresponding to Chrétien's Good Friday meeting of Perceval and the hermit, Peredur does indeed meet a priest, on Good Friday, and remains with him for three days, but there is no mention of confession or penitence, no explanation of the secrets of the Grail, and the priest is not his uncle. It is not till the final episode, when Peredur has found the fortress again and rejoined his uncle and Gwalchmai, that a youth kneels before him and reveals that he was the Black Maiden who set him a number of tasks and was also the bearer of the head and the bleeding spear. The head, he tells Peredur, was that of his cousin, killed by the Witches of Caer Loyw, who also lamed his uncle. Peredur has been fated to avenge them, which he accomplishes at the end of the narrative with the help of Arthur's court.

The absence of food-bearing attributes of the dish, the severed head swimming in blood, the bleeding lance, the lamentation at their passing, and the final identification of the head as Peredur's relative combine to indicate that, unlike Chrétien's mysterious and quasi-religious symbol, the procession in the Welsh romance emphasizes the vengeance theme latent in the original form of the legend.[67] *Peredur* is undoubtedly closely related to other Grail romances and belongs to the *Perceval* strain; yet, in one sense, it could be argued that it is not a Grail romance at all.[68]

THE MEDIEVAL LEGEND IN ENGLISH

Sir Thomas Malory's *Le Morte Darthur*

In the process of recycling, reinvention, and reinterpretation that characterizes the transmission of the Grail legend through medieval literature,[69] one of the most influential versions was Sir Thomas Malory's *Morte Darthur*, written in Middle English prose in 1469 or 1470 and printed by William Caxton in 1485.[70] There is no space here to discuss the controversy that still rages about the identification of the historical Malory;[71] regardless of who he was, we can be sure only that he was a knight and that he was in prison while he was writing sections of his book. Caxton stated that Malory had taken his book from certain books of French and "reduced" them into English. "As the Frenssh boke seyth" is Malory's frequent formula to provide authority for his narrative, but his sources were in Middle English as well as Old French: the alliterative *Morte Arthure* and the stanzaic *Le Morte Arthur* in English as well as the Vulgate Cycle, Post-Vulgate Cycle, and the prose *Tristan* in Old French. Caxton's comment that Malory "reduced" the French books into English[72] is an apt description of the process by which Malory adapted and translated his sources: he worked by abridging, simplifying the interlace structure, cutting down or excising episodes, reducing the vast cast of characters typical of the French, naming characters left unidentified in the source, and turning narrative into dialogue. In the early stages his translation is close and sometimes pedestrian, but by the last two books of the *Morte Darthur* he moves backward and forward between French and English sources with considerable freedom and originality. Above all, he creates a prose style of great power and emotional force.[73] It is Malory's version, whether original, expurgated, modernized, or adapted for children, that has been *the* version of the Arthurian legend for English speakers from sixteenth-century England to twentieth-century America, influencing countless poets, artists, and adult and child readers.[74]

In the sections of the *Morte Darthur* dealing with the Grail legend, Malory sticks close to his sources. The relevant sections are the Balin episode of Book 1 ("The Tale of Arthur"), the Lancelot-Elaine section of Book 5 ("The Tale of Sir Tristram") and the whole of Book 6 ("The Tale of the Sankgreall"). Book 1 is based on the Post-Vulgate *Suite du Merlin*, Book 5 on the prose *Tristan* (though the Lancelot-Elaine section was borrowed by the writers of the prose *Tristan* from the Vulgate *Lancelot*), and Book 6 on the Vulgate *Queste del Saint Graal*. Malory's shift from the Post-Vulgate *Suite* (in Book 1) to the Vulgate *Lancelot* and *Queste* (in Books 5 and 6) causes some confusion, since the forward links in the Post-Vulgate *Suite* anticipate a Post-Vulgate form of the *Queste*, whereas the Vulgate *Queste* fulfills somewhat different prophecies, made mostly in the *Estoire*. However, we see Malory attempting to forge new links between the Balin episode and the Vulgate *Queste*. After the Dolorous Stroke, Malory adds a forward link announcing that Pellam will never be healed till the advent of Galahad and identifying the occupant of the mysterious bed in the Grail chamber as Joseph of Arimathea. As in the *Suite du Merlin*, Merlin places Balin's sword in the stone, sending it down the river to arrive at Camelot simultaneously with Galahad; but Malory adds a passage to Galahad's speech when he pulls out the sword, recalling Balin's tragic fate and the Dolorous Stroke (863.3–9).[75] Galahad's adventures are thus established as a redemptive counterpart to Balin's destructive ones. Yet certain competing patterns of cross-reference survive from the shift between Post-Vulgate and Vulgate that, paradoxically, add to the pervading sense of mystery of the work.

Malory's Balin, The Knight with Two Swords, is an almost self-contained narrative embedded in the larger story of Arthur consolidating his kingdom. It is close to its Old French source, though much abridged (compare the discussion above of the Post-Vulgate Cycle); the result is a swifter-moving, more direct narrative that intensifies the fated nature of Balin's actions and leads with a sense of inevitability to Balin's commission of the Dolorous Stroke on King Pellam. Balin is still the unlucky knight, acting on impulse, spreading destruction around him despite his best intentions; but Malory's greater emphasis on his knightly potential, his "worship," makes his death more poignant, a source of great sorrow and loss to Arthur's fellowship. In the *Suite*, Balin's tragic death is seen as a direct retribution for the violation of the sanctuary involved in the Dolorous Stroke; Malory makes the Stroke a result of Balin's failure to save Columbe from killing herself (72.25–32), and Balin's death more a result of fate, never fully explained but hauntingly powerful.[76] The cadences of Balin's cry of discovery are particularly moving: "O, Balan, my broder! Thow hast slayne me and I the, wherefore alle the wyde world shalle speke of us bothe" (90.9–10). Within this universe, each action sets in motion a chain of consequences that can be neither predicted nor avoided. All the knight can do is to "take the adventure" that will come to him (e.g., 70.19–20, 89.1–4).[77]

Small changes also mark Malory's redaction of the Lancelot-Elaine section of the prose *Tristan*. Whereas in the Vulgate (the ultimate source) the first appearance of the Grail at Corbenic is to Gauvain, Malory only alludes to Gawain's visit without describing it, focusing instead on Lancelot's visit, during which he frees the boiling lady[78] and kills the dragon in the tomb, witnesses the Grail, and is subsequently enchanted into sleeping with Pelles's daughter, Elaine, in the belief that she is Guinevere (the incident that Charles Williams described as a "mystical substitution").[79] As in the Vulgate, Bors also witnesses the appearance of the Grail (though Malory conflates two visits into one), meets the child Galahad, and achieves the adventures of the Palace of Adventures. Similarly, Percival is healed by the Grail after fighting Ector: it appears to the two knights after Percival's prayer to Christ, and Percival, because he is a virgin, has a "glemerynge of the vessell and of the mayden that bare hit," whereas Ector cannot see either. Finally, Lancelot is also healed from his madness by being laid in the Grail chamber. Throughout this section, Lancelot and other knights have been reminded that his supremacy among the Arthurian knights is about to be superseded; though he will remain the best of "all erthly synfull" knights, in religious matters he will be surpassed by others, especially Galahad. The way has been prepared for "The Tale of the Sankgreal" and for the dichotomy between terrestrial and celestial values that characterizes its progression.

Malory's "Sankgreal" also stays close to its (Vulgate) source, though it is about one-third shorter. The spiritual hierarchy of knights, with Gawain and Ector at the bottom, the three elect at the top, and

Lancelot in the middle, is faithfully retained, as are the tests that define them. The episodes of the Ship of Solomon and the sacrifice of Percival's sister are all reproduced, though the narrative of Solomon's ship, conveyed in the *Queste* through the authorial voice, is put by Malory in Percival's sister's voice. Though in his other Books Malory tends to disentangle the interlace structure of the French, he faithfully reproduces the modified interlace of the Vulgate *Queste*. His chief changes come in omitting the passages retelling events of the *Estoire*, especially the narrative history of Joseph of Arimathea. Whereas such digressions serve in the *Queste* to link past and present, collapsing time and preparing for Galaad's achievement, Malory shows that he is not interested in such "communication between the centuries" (Ihle, p. 117). Similarly, he prunes much of the doctrinal explanation of dreams and symbols, excising a whole level of typological explanation.[80]

One subtle but significant change takes place in Malory's conception of the Grail vessel itself. As in the *Queste*, Christ announces to the communicants at Corbenic that it is "the holy dysshe wherein I ete the lambe on Estir Day" (1030.19–20), but Malory appears to consider that it also holds Christ's blood, for he adds a reference to that effect during Balin's invasion of the Grail chamber (85.23–26), as well as in the *incipit* to his "Tale of the Sankgreal": "But here folowyth the noble tale of the Sankegreall, whyche called ys the holy vessel and the sygnyfycacion of blyssed bloode off our Lorde Jesu Cryste, whyche was brought into thys londe by Joseph off Aramathye" (845–46). As Ihle establishes in her Chapter 2, Malory "consistently narrows and concretizes references" to the Grail (32). What in his source is ineffable, impossible to know fully or to limit to one symbolic interpretation, becomes for Malory essentially the Eucharistic vessel, the vessel that contains Christ (44). It is still, however, an object of great mystery and reverence, as its first appearance at Camelot demonstrates. As in the *Queste*, it is announced with thunder and unearthly radiance, and all the knights are struck dumb with awe; the hall is filled with good odors, and "every knyght had such metis and drynkes as he beste loved in thys worlde" (865.30–31). Also as in the *Queste*, the presence of this ineffable object is, paradoxically, apprehended through the physical senses; however, Malory adds one detail not in the French. The grace of the Holy Ghost that illuminates the company allows every knight to see the others "by their seemynge, fayrer than ever they were before" (865.22–23). The experience of shared ecstasy is manifested in unearthly beauty. Finally, Malory adds an original scene to the end of his Quest, in which Lancelot and Bors, meeting at Camelot, swear a special bond of brotherhood with each other for the rest of their lives. Being so close to the Grail has changed them forever.

Vinaver claims that Malory's "one desire seems to be to secularize the Grail theme as much as the story will allow" (1535), and Ihle similarly argues that Malory's narrative judges success and failure by standards of moral rather than spiritual excellence (127 ff.); yet the Quest still signifies, for Malory, a completely different order of adventure from the rest of the *Morte Darthur.*[81] Vinaver himself concedes that, despite all Malory's alterations, "it is through his version and not through the French *Queste* that the symbol of the Grail has reached in our imagination that degree of reality without which no symbol can live" (1541–42).

POSTMEDIEVAL LITERATURE: NINETEENTH AND EARLY TWENTIETH CENTURY: BRITISH AND AMERICAN

The period from the sixteenth century through the eighteenth has been called the Dark Ages of Arthurian literature: Spenser, Dryden, and Fielding utilized the figure of King Arthur in essentially non-Arthurian contexts, Milton and others planned and abandoned Arthurian projects, but there was a comparative dearth of new treatments of the legend in general. Of the Grail there was nothing, perhaps because it had become so strongly identified with Roman Catholic tradition. It took the revival of medievalism that began toward the end of the eighteenth century and flowered at the beginning of the nineteenth to give a new impetus to the Arthurian legend and, thereby, the Grail story. The revival was fueled to a large extent by the antiquarian interest and industry of writers and scholars like Sir Walter Scott, Bishop Percy, and Joseph Ritson, who were responsible for recovering and editing ballads and medieval romances, and the renewed interest of scholars in philological studies. The strongest impulse came from the reediting of Malory, unpublished since 1634. Three new editions of Malory appeared in 1816 and 1817 (the last a fine, if expensive, edition by Robert Southey) and a further one in 1858, making the text available to poets and painters like Alfred, Lord Tennyson, William Morris, Edward Burne-Jones, and Dante Gabriel Rossetti.

The chief architect of the Arthurian Revival was Tennyson, whose attraction to the medieval period was in part inspired by his rejection of Victorian commercialism and industrialism, though he used the past as a mirror to reflect the moral condition of the present. His poem "Sir Galahad" was circulated among university friends after 1834 and published with three other Arthurian poems in 1842. It became immensely popular, inspiring such paintings as George Frederic Watts's "Sir Galahad" and embodying an ideal of muscular male piety that captured the Victorian sensibility.[82] Galahad's militant chastity enables him to surpass all others in martial vigor, at the same time that it drives him onward to pursue the vision of the Grail. His zeal separates him from ordinary mortals who remain in the "dreaming towns" he leaves behind, and sustains him through storm and driving sleet as he braves "waste fens" and climbs the heights to his goal. Though the Grail is a far-off ideal, there is no hint that it is unattainable: on the contrary, angelic voices assure him, " 'O just and faithful knight of God! / Ride on! the prize is near.' " It is easy to understand why the poem (and the paintings associated with it) should have inspired generations of schoolboys and young men. When Edward Burne-Jones dreamed of a charitable brotherhood that would work in the slums of East London and be named The Order of Galahad, he urged a potential member to learn the poem by heart.[83]

The success of Tennyson's early Arthurian poems led him eventually to publish, in stages, the poems that make up the *Idylls of the King*, given their final arrangement only in 1892. Based essentially on Malory (though the story of Geraint and Enid derives from the *Mabinogion*), these narratives and dramatic monologues add psychological development to Malory's spare text, as well as presenting Tennyson's vision of a potentially ideal civilization destroyed by sensuality, materialism, and spiritual blindness. The first four Idylls were published together in 1859 and contained no Grail episode. Nearly a decade intervened before the poet took up the legend again, chiefly because of his uncertainty as to how to treat the Grail. In a letter of 1859, he wrote: "I doubt whether such a subject could be handled in these days, without incurring a charge of irreverence. It would be too much like playing with sacred things. The old writers *believed* in the Sangreal."[84] The answer he found was to approach the episode from a completely new perspective, that of a failed quester, and the result was "The Holy Grail," published with other Idylls in 1870.

The poem is a dramatic dialogue between Percivale and Ambrosius, a monk in the monastery to which Percivale has retired after the Quest. As David Staines observes, what Tennyson focuses on is not so much the Grail as the responses of various figures to it. By choosing Percivale's point of view, Tennyson makes the "failed quest the poem's centre."[85] Unlike the Holy Grail of "Sir Galahad," this Grail is almost unattainable, a will of the wisp, a delusion and a distraction from the proper social duties of Arthurian knights. Only those who experience true religious ecstasy can achieve it.

The Grail is the cup from which the Lord drank at the Last Supper, brought by Joseph of Arimathea to Glastonbury, where it healed those who could approach it, but when times grew evil, it disappeared; now it has come again. The first to see the Grail is Percivale's sister (unnamed), who has retired to a convent after a disappointment in love. It appears to her in her cell, sliding down a beam of light, "rose-red, with beatings in it, as if alive" (117–18). From her, the news spreads to other Arthurian knights, affecting Galahad most of all: he "believed in her belief" (165). Galahad comes to court to brave the Siege Perilous, and the Grail appears to all the knights, with a cracking and riving noise, down a long beam of light. But it is covered with a "luminous cloud," so no one can actually see it, as Percivale's sister and Galahad have seen it. They all swear oaths to go on the Quest, to see it openly. Arthur has not been present at the scene; when he is told, he is angry, claiming that only Galahad is truly suited for this mission. Noble deeds will go undone while these knights "follow wandering fires / Lost in the quagmire!" (319–20). This ominous prophecy of failure, of misguided direction, underlies the poem.

On the Quest, Percivale is racked by self-doubt, loneliness, and thirst. He suffers a series of hallucinatory visions, which crumble into dust, and fears the Grail itself may do the same. Eventually he finds a hermit in the valley who tells him he does not yet have the true humility to see the vision: "Thou hast not lost thyself to save thyself / As Galahad" (456–57). Galahad appears, and they celebrate Mass together; whereas Percivale sees only the "elements" of the Mass, Galahad sees the actual transubstantiation. Galahad tells Percivale that he has continued to see the Grail as a "blood-red" vision, leading him on as he has journeyed through the world, conquering and converting the pagans. Now, however, the time has come to go to the holy city itself. Percivale accompanies him as they climb a terrible hill, through swamps and lightning storms. Galahad forges ahead, dodging the lightning bolts, crossing bridges that fail after him, appearing ultimately in a boat, perhaps, or in the sky, far from Percivale. The vision is hallucinatory, phantasmagoric, doubtful. The holy city appears far off, "like one pearl" (527), with a "rose-red sparkle" to it that Percivale knows comes from the Grail. Without knowing how, Percivale finds himself back with the hermit.

Riding over shattered remnants of sculpture in the city, the destruction caused by a terrible storm, the few remaining knights return to court to report on their experiences. When Percivale tells Arthur of his desire to retire from the world, the king turns away. Gawain, the frivolous, saw nothing to report. (He was unaware even that there was anything to seek.)

Bors glimpsed the Grail through a gap in the wall of his prison but will not speak of what he saw. Lancelot was granted a vision of the Grail from the door of the chamber at Carbonek, but his sin and lack of faith prevented him coming any closer. Arthur sums up the significance of the search: Bors, Lancelot, and Percivale have each seen according to their capacity for seeing. But the Quest has been a terrible thing; it has decimated the Round Table. Arthur himself would not have taken the vow, because of his sense of duty toward the land. For ordinary man, secular duty is paramount, but the vision may still come, unbidden, and recall to him his true spiritual nature.

The "Holy Grail" parallels versions of duty and kingship: Galahad is king of the spiritual city, Arthur attempts "to create the spiritual city in his earthly sphere" (Staines, 750). Percivale is offered the chance to rule in a secular kingdom with his former love, to be "as Arthur," which would be more suitable for him, but he rejects it. Though he learns humility, he is unable to translate his knowledge into fruitful action in the secular world; he can only withdraw into the contemplative life. Whereas the medieval Quest operated on the certainty that the next life was perfection, and this one only a shadow, Victorian times have no such consolation. The contemplative life, it is implied in this poem, is misguided and wasteful–indeed, Percivale has died and the poem's voice is heard only as flashback. The final line of the poem indicates that he has not understood the king's message and has misdirected his life: "So spake the King: I knew not all he meant."

Tennyson's poem is, ultimately, a "study of human responses to the spiritual world" (Staines, 753). The Quest has been a distraction and a failure for almost all, yet the power of the vision is still admitted. The descriptions of the Grail are always beautiful, sensuous, even sensual (in contrast to the descriptions of secular, heterosexual love), but at the same time they have a miragelike quality. Galahad's apotheosis was seen by Percivale, immensely beautiful, but far off, mysterious, and hallucinatory. We wonder if it took place at all.

The poet's innovations have been to make Percivale's sister the initiator of the Quest and to sever the connection between Galahad and Lancelot, making Galahad even purer and more removed from the world than in Malory. Lancelot is only reputed to be Galahad's father, and there is no mention of the "mystical substitution" (as Charles Williams calls it) with the body of Elaine, no sense of prophetic fulfillment. Indeed, in the Idyll "Balin and Balan" (written in 1872–74 but not published till 1885), King Pellam is old and deluded; a former pagan, he has now converted with excess zeal, almost to the point of Papism, living in celibacy and surrounded by relics.[86] In Malory, the Dolorous Stroke that Balin commits on Pellam is linked prophetically with Galahad; Tennyson's narrative omits the Dolorous Stroke altogether. Balin finds the Lance in Pellam's chapel but uses it only to vault out of the window. There is no hint that Pellam's castle is Corbenic, or that the Grail might be within.

Five years before the publication of Tennyson's Grail poem, the eccentric Cornish vicar Robert Stephens Hawker published at his own expense *The Quest of the Sangraal*, including it later in his *Cornish Ballads and Other Poems*, with a title page announcing that this was "a second edition." He thus underlined that his poem had preceded Tennyson's.[87] Hawker's blank-verse narrative shows a stern and militant Arthur announcing the Quest to his knights by telling them the story of Joseph of Arimathea bringing the Cup to Avalon, from where it disappeared, driven away by the evil of men. Merlin has announced that "the land is lonely now," but he has also prophesied that a king arisen "from Keltic loins" would call a quest for "the vanished vase of God." Arthur calls for questers, evoking an enthusiastic response from his knights; Gawain urges the company to "search the regions! one by one, / And pluck this Sangraal from its cloudy cave." The four questers, Lancelot, Perceval, Tristan, and Galahad, disperse to the four quadrants of the earth, but Arthur remains behind because of his kingly responsibilities. (One wonders whether Tennyson's similar idea was suggested to him by Hawker in their conversations about Arthurian matters.)[88] Arthur hopes, however, that success in the Quest will bring fame to him and to the land of Cornwall. Yet he is afraid that God may be angry with this land "too fond of blood."

The poem ends somewhat obscurely, with Merlin and Arthur standing on the walls of Dundagel (Tintagel) after a storm, seeing three visions: the first is a retrospective view of Arthur's wars, the second shows Galahad, successful in the Quest, holding up the Grail from which light "gushe[s] . . . in flakes" to transform the land. The third looks into a grim future, with the chalice "void," and more wars, not noble hand-to-hand combat but death hurled from "the metal of the mine."[89] Merlin utters a fierce warning to England, which should reawaken the ancient cry, "Ho! for the Sangraal! vanished vase of heaven."

Hawker's poem has a quaint charm. The exuberant militancy of the knights and the symbolism of the Grail strike quite a different note from Tennyson's poem; the Quest is not a diversion from the duties of the Arthurian knights but a means of restoring glory to the lonely land, specifically Cornwall. Arthur exhorts his knights that achievement will mean a fierce battle, on behalf of God: "If bevies of foul fiends withstand your path, / . . . . / Plunge in their midst, and shout 'a Sangraal!'" The poem may indeed "allegorize Tractarian themes," such as the restoration of Church power over encroaching political power,[90] but if so, the message is obscure. Hawker's Celtic researches and identification with Cornish history would seem to be a stronger inspiration.

Tennyson and Harker were not the only Victorians to write about the Grail. William Morris includes two short poems in his *Defence of Guenevere and Other Poems*, "Sir Galahad, A Christmas Mystery" and "The Chapel in Lyoness." Both are light, elegant lyric-dramatic vignettes, focusing on the conflicting claims of secular and religious love. In "A Christmas Mystery," Galahad contrasts lover-knights like his father, Lancelot, and Palomydes, driven and sustained by their love for women, with his own loneliness and barrenness. Then Christ speaks to him in a chapel, reminding Galahad that His love will always accompany him. Angels and virgin saints console and strengthen Galahad until Bors, Percivale, and Percivale's sister arrive at the chapel with news of failure and death among the knights on the Quest: "In vain they struggle for the vision fair." Morris's second poem is even more fragmentary. Ozanna of the hardy heart (Ozanne Le Cure Hardy in Malory) lies dying in a chapel, to which come Galahad and Bors. The episode is conveyed dramatically, by the three speakers. Ozanna dies holding a tress of golden hair to his heart but realizes, "My life went wrong." Bors and Galahad are left musing, ambivalent about the force of this secular love that has sustained their fellow knight.

Like Tennyson, Morris believed that industrialized Victorian society, with its emphasis on capitalism and progress, had lost the integrity and simplicity of medieval times. He tried consciously to recover that spirit, both in art and in the many crafts he developed and practiced privately and commercially.[91] In this, he was aided by his friends Edward Burne-Jones and Dante Gabriel Rossetti. Morris's fascination with Arthurian themes began in childhood, when he used to ride his pony through Epping Forest wearing a child-sized suit of armor; it flowered in Oxford, when he used to read Malory aloud to Burne-Jones; and it was intensified by his friendship with the painter Rossetti. Rossetti included Morris and Burne-Jones in the group he gathered to paint frescoes for the Debating Hall of the Oxford Union, using scenes from Malory. Though the project was ultimately a failure, owing to the painters' inexperience with the medium, the restored panels and surviving sketches for certain scenes are witness to the abiding attraction of Arthurian subject matter.[92]

Rossetti and Burne-Jones were particularly absorbed by the Grail theme, the latter returning to it throughout his life. Both were inspired by Galahad's achievement and intrigued by Lancelot's failure. Rossetti's sketch for the Oxford Union Hall shows Lancelot asleep outside the Grail Chapel, with the figure of Guinevere, her arms extended in the branches of an apple tree, standing between him and the Grail; in Burne-Jones's tapestry of the same scene, it is an angel that bars the way into the Grail Chapel.[93] Rossetti depicted Galahad many times, including a scene of the knight at a shrine in the illustrations for the Moxon edition of Tennyson's poems in 1857; Burne-Jones also painted Galahad as a pure, serene youth, riding untroubled past scenes of worldly pleasure. However, the most splendid example of Burne-Jones's dedication to the Grail theme is his set of designs for six tapestry panels showing the Quest, commissioned by W. K. D'Arcy and woven at Morris's Merton Abbey Tapestry Works from 1890 to 1894 (three partial sets were later woven from the designs, for other clients). The panels demonstrate Burne-Jones's love of beauty and the Pre-Raphaelite debt to medieval tapestry and Quattrocento painting. In the final panel, "The Attainment," Bors and Percival stand on the left, separated by a group of angels from the Grail Chapel, at the door of which kneels Galahad, gazing in at the radiant Grail, which rests on an altar before three more adoring angels. The rich reds of the standing angels' wings stand out strongly against the dark, mysterious forest background; the foreground is filled with stylized clumps of flowers reminiscent of the "milles-fleurs" tradition of medieval tapestry, but still dark, while lilies bloom outside the Chapel. The eye is led by the composition and the colors to the radiant, glowing interior of the Chapel on the right, where Galahad will surely enter. This is not the austere, world-rejecting atmosphere of the medieval *Queste;* though Galahad's union with divine beauty is clearly predicted, there is no hint of impending death.[94]

In nineteenth-century America, the influence of Tennyson's poetry and Pre-Raphaelite painting is less than might be expected. The Grail story appears not to have captured literary imaginations, perhaps because it did not lend itself conveniently to an American nationalist agenda. The American attitude to the Grail might almost be summed up in Mark Twain's contemptuous reference to it in *A Connecticut Yankee at King Arthur's Court* (1889). Admittedly, the aim of Twain's novel is satirical, debunking not only medieval chivalric ideals but also contemporary American culture,[95] but it is noteworthy that Twain's narrator, Hank, devotes only one paragraph to the Grail Quest, in which he describes the annual forays of knights to search for an object they would not recognize nor know what to do with if they found it. "Every year expeditions went out holy grailing, and next year relief expeditions went out to hunt for *them*. There was worlds of reputation in it, but no money."[96]

Indeed, nineteenth-century American writers, those who treat it at all, tend to demystify the Grail story, emphasizing rather its moral or ethical aspects. Ralph Waldo Emerson wrote an unpublished prose sketch in which Arthur himself went on the Grail Quest, and Richard Hovey planned but did not finish a series of verse dramas on the Arthurian cycle: of the dramas completed, *The Birth of Galahad* (1898) is notable for making Guenevere the mother of Galahad, who is entrusted to Guenevere's dear friend Ylen (Elaine) to bring up as her own to protect the lovers (Taylor and Brewer, p. 177). James Russell Lowell utilizes the Quest for his charming poetic fable *Sir Launfal* (1848), which is in fact only tangentially Arthurian. The character of Sir Launfal is probably derived from Marie de France's Old French lai of the twelfth century, *Lanval*; it is nowhere else associated with the Grail story, but for Lowell he provides a useful figure without former associations to carry the moral of his story, set in an indeterminate medieval time. Sir Launfal vows to find the Grail, and the poem narrates his dream before he sets off; as he leaves his castle on a springtime morning he throws a gold coin contemptuously to a leper at the gates. In the next scene of his vision, he has returned, in the bitter weather of Christmastime, old, gray, and unsuccessful, barred from entering his former castle because of his now beggarly appearance. He shares his last crust of bread and water from the brook in a simple wooden bowl with the leper, who is then transformed into Christ. Sir Launfal wakes from his dream, recognizing that the Grail was here all along: it represented charity given with love and compassion for humanity: "The gift without the giver is bare."

Lowell's choice of a nontraditional Grail knight universalizes and democratizes the Grail theme, showing that the search is open to all, not just the chosen few. Similarly, the nature imagery that frames and threads itself through the text evokes an Edenic vision that can sustain "a new world order based on charity."[97] Though the narrative adds little of significance to the development of the legend, it reveals the versatility of the Grail symbol, to tell a Christian parable. In contrast, Edwin Arlington Robinson's long narrative poem *Lancelot* (1920), the second of his Arthurian poems, places the Grail Quest entirely in the background, a haunting memory for Lancelot, who has returned to Camelot after his unsuccessful pursuit. The focus of Robinson's poem is the love affair between Lancelot and Guinevere, and, although he follows the outlines of

Malory's story, he invents some dramatic and emotional new scenes between the lovers, notably the last confrontation between Guinevere and Lancelot at Joyous Garde before he returns her to Camelot and Arthur. While the rain pours down outside, Guinevere's passionate appeal beats fruitlessly against Lancelot's grieved stoicism. Guinevere's "white and gold" beauty has stood, and still stands, between Lancelot and "the Light" that drew him, and he is torn between the two "gleams." At the end, when Arthur and Modred are dead, Lancelot returns to Britain, to this "played-out world," and confronts Guinevere at the convent in Amesbury. He finds a wan, pathetic penitent, who recognizes now as she did not before that there is no world for them. As Lancelot rides away in grief, he is gradually comforted by the "living Voice," urging him in a new direction; Galahad's face rather than Guinevere's hovers in vision before him. The poem ends: "But always in the darkness he rode on, / Alone; and in the darkness came the Light."[98]

Robinson is vague about what "the Light" actually symbolizes in his poem, other than to distinguish it clearly from "the Light of Rome." It is still a stirring symbol, but this seems to be the closest that American writers wish to come in spiritualizing the Grail. Even painters prefer to emphasize the moral virtues inculcated and fostered by the Quest, as in Edwin Austin Abbey's Frieze painted for the Book Delivery Room in the Boston Public Library (1895–1901). This consists of fifteen panels depicting the Quest, focusing on Galahad, whose "figure, in scarlet, is the brilliant recurring note, all the way round the room."[99] Abbey's interpretation of the legend, though it draws elements from different traditions, is dependent chiefly on the *Queste* and Perceval strains, which he folds together, giving Perceval's role to Galahad. The first panel shows Galahad as an infant held in the arms of a nun, stretching his own arms out to the Grail held by an angel above him, while the last panel shows Galahad at his apotheosis, with Joseph of Arimathea holding before him the uncovered Grail, and behind him the Golden Tree of Life that he has built. In between come panels showing Galahad as a youth taking the oath of knighthood, coming to court to begin the Quest, and failing at the Grail Castle to ask the question that will heal Amfortas. After being reviled by a Loathly Lady and her two companions, Galahad undergoes adventures with allegorical significance, defeating the Seven Deadly Sins (in the form of knights) and releasing the Captive Virtues (in the form of maidens), marrying Blancheflor but leaving her on the morning after their wedding. These trials have prepared him to return to the Grail Castle and heal Amfortas. (The questions, the healing of Amfortas, and the marriage with Blancheflor belong to the *Perceval* strain, but the battles and the Castle of Maidens are from the *Queste*.) After this, we remain with the *Queste* strain: Galahad rides through a restored land to come to Solomon's ship, on which, accompanied by Bors and Percival, he sails to Sarras, guided by the Grail held by an angel in the prow of the ship. It is at Sarras that he gains his apotheosis.

Though Abbey's interpretation does not ignore the religious dimension of the legend (nuns, angels, and Galahad's red-cross shield are featured in many scenes), Galahad is not the aggressively virginal hero of the Vulgate *Queste* or Malory; his marriage to Blancheflor and the allegorical battles show that his progression to make himself fit for the Grail is a moral rather than a spiritual one. Abbey's contemporary Sylvester Baxter claims that the Grail of the Frieze symbolizes "illumination of the soul through the wisdom that comes with the right use of knowledge."[100] The legend carved upon the Frieze reads, "The Commonwealth Requires the Education of the People as the Safeguard of Order and Liberty" (Baxter, 18). Abbey's Grail Quest was, therefore, an entirely appropriate subject for the library, endorsing the virtues that lead to good citizenship. It was apparently known through photographs to all school children and college students of the time (O'Shaughnessy, 311).

This view of the legend as a paradigm of gentlemanly moral behavior no doubt also fueled the number of late nineteenth-century abridgments and modernizations of Malory made in America for children, such as those by Sidney Lanier (*The Boy's King Arthur*, 1880)[101] and Howard Pyle (*The Story of the Grail and the Passing of Arthur*, 1910). In these versions, the adultery of the lovers and the Catholic significance of the Grail Quest were thoroughly suppressed, while the virtues of courage, humility, and manliness were endorsed. Pyle's tetralogy is a complete retelling, rather than an abridged version with modernized spelling; his combination of text and illustration democratizes the Arthurian legend, suggesting that "the moral equivalent of knighthood" is available to anyone and that it does not require only the best and purest of knights to achieve the Grail.[102] The most overt milking of the Arthurian ideal for its value to boys' education can be found in the movement of the Boy Scouts of America. The English founder, Sir Robert (later Lord) Baden-Powell, had claimed that every boy could be a knight in search of the Holy Grail and would gain his reward from God if he did his duty cheerfully, bravely, and unselfishly. A charming imaginative reconstruction of the ideal can be seen in the 1917 film made by the Edison Company titled *The Knights of the Square Table*, which combines a Boy Scout troop, a gang of delinquent boys, and the Grail legend from Lowell's "Vision of Sir Launfal" to provide a moral fable in which Boy Scout values are both triumphant and redemptive.[103]

NINETEENTH AND EARLY TWENTIETH CENTURY: THE CONTINENT

As in English-language literature, a hiatus occurs on the Continent after the end of the medieval period in developments of the Grail legend. In sixteenth-century France, literary energies were spent in compilations and adaptations of Arthurian material rather than new versions, and subsequently both Renaissance and neoclassical writers scorned medieval subjects in favor of classical and biblical ones. German writers of the seventeenth and eighteenth centuries were competing with the French neoclassicists, whom they saw as their models. With the German Romantic movement at the turn of the nineteenth century, however, began a new interest in medieval subjects, coupled with antiquarian and scholarly activities, including the publication of critical editions of Middle High German poets such as Wolfram von Eschenbach. In terms of new versions of the Arthurian legend, the most important new works, influencing countless others in both France and Germany, were Richard Wagner's operas, of which *Parsifal*, presented in 1882, offers a unique version of the Grail legend.

Parsifal was the last opera Wagner wrote, and the culmination of a lifetime's thought. He had first read Wolfram's *Parzival* in 1845.[104] Later he read and reread it and other versions of the legend, trying to develop his first concept of the healing and redemption of an old man laden with knowledge and grief by the initially careless, ignorant young man who is destined to be his heir. The shape of the work was also strongly influenced by his reading of Arthur Schopenhauer and the latter's interest in the Buddhist doctrine of renunciation. The opera was presented in Wagner's own theater, the Bayreuth Festspielhaus, and performed there almost exclusively for thirty years.

Wagner called his opera *Ein Bühnenweihfestspiel* ("a Consecration Festival Play"), and the term sums up its stately, quasi-religious atmosphere. (It has been the tradition at Bayreuth that audiences do not applaud after Acts 1 and 3, the Grail-temple scenes).[105] The work reflects Wagner's lifelong aim to integrate the words of opera with the music and the stage picture into an indissoluble whole. With *Parsifal*, he goes even farther: whole passages proceed without dialogue, their significance conveyed by gesture, movement, and music. The stage picture becomes "ersichtlich gewordene Taten der Musik," or "acts of music become visible."[106] Though the text is comparatively short, the opera lasts more than four hours in performance, as music, ritual, and pageantry fill the stage.

Wagner's chief innovation was to cut the number of characters and tighten the action, focusing on the Grail Castle sequences. From Wolfram's poem he retains five main characters: Amfortas (the Grail King), Parsifal,[107] Kundry (who combines the roles of Parzival's cousin and Cundrie, the Ugly Maiden), Klingsor the enchanter (from a minor episode concerning Gawan), and Gurnemanz (who combines the roles of tutor and Trevrizent, the hermit-uncle). Titurel, Anfortas's grandfather in Wolfram, is here Amfortas's father and has a minor role.

From his reading of Chrétien de Troyes, Wagner had decided that the name "Le Roi Pescheoir" (the Fisher King) resulted from a confusion with "Le Roi Pécheur" (the sinner king) (Beckett, p. 20); certainly he emphasizes the massive guilt of Amfortas, giving the narrative a new direction and tension by focusing on this character at the beginning of the opera, when the nature and circumstances of his incurable wound are described, as well as the prophecy that it would be healed only by an Innocent Fool. Amfortas is wounded in the side, not the genitals like his counterpart in Wolfram, but the suggestion of sexual transgression is no less strong; it is because he succumbed to the seductive wiles of Kundry that Klingsor was able to wound him and steal the Spear. Having Amfortas wounded in the side, with the Spear that once wounded Christ, does, however, set up a deliberate Christological parallel and contrast.

Wagner's other major change from his source is the "Gral." It is no longer Wolfram's precious stone, though it does retain the stone's capacity to confer immortality; here, it is the Cup of the Last Supper, and the Grail-feast that Parsifal witnesses is not a banquet but, explicitly, a form of the Eucharistic service. Amfortas's duty is to conduct the service (though he is not a priest), to uncover the Grail, lift it out of its shrine, and pass it over the bread and wine that the knights of the brotherhood will then partake of. The service is a "Liebesmahle," a "Love-Feast," and the Grail glows with a red radiance as it fills again with blood; the holy food restores the faith and strength of the Grail knights, just as witnessing the Grail uncovered keeps Titurel and Amfortas alive. It is supremely ironic that the service that reminds the participants of the blood shed by Christ in his loving sacrifice to save humanity also continually renews Amfortas's pain and guilt—the wound bleeds anew each time. Wagner also fuses Wolfram's different spears into one, identifying it with the Spear of Longinus and making it the actual instrument of Amfortas's agony. As a result of Amfortas's sin, the Spear has been separated from the Grail. Parsifal's achievement will be to return it to the vessel and heal Amfortas's wound.

The most important change Wagner made from his source is his creation of Kundry. By excising all the other women of Wolfram's poem, including the Grail maiden, he can focus on this one enigmatic and ambiguous figure. Kundry is both the direct instrument of Amfortas's sin and the source of his redemption through Parsifal. She is the reincarnation of other treacherous women in history, Gundryggia and Herodias, and is doomed to suffer because she witnessed the Crucifixion and laughed at the suffering of Christ. Her double nature may have been suggested to Wagner by the transformation of the Ugly Maiden to the Sovereignty of Ireland figure in *Peredur* (Beckett, 21); wherever he got the idea, it became the pivoting motivation for his opera and for Parsifal's redemption, when he is able to resist her seduction while his predecessor was not.

The plot of the opera is tightly controlled. As we have said, it begins in the Grail kingdom, outside Monsalvat, where the old knight Gurnemanz tells the history of Amfortas to some young squires. He tells, also, how Titurel received the Grail from the angels and was commissioned to protect and serve it and the Spear. Only the chaste can join the brotherhood of the Grail, and Klingsor, a knight who aspired to the brotherhood, castrated himself to control his raging lust but was still rejected by Titurel. Only "der reine Tor" ("the innocent Fool"[108]), "durch Mitleid wissend" ("made wise through pity"), can heal Amfortas, and for him they all wait. Kundry is present, an enigmatic and wild-eyed figure, who has apparently helped the brotherhood; Gurnemanz does not associate her with the "furchtbar schönes Weib" ("the woman of terrible beauty") who seduced Amfortas. Parsifal blunders in, apparently knowing little about himself and his background. Gurnemanz takes him to the Castle to witness Amfortas conducting the Grail-service. Parsifal watches Amfortas's agony but does not understand what he sees; Gurnemanz calls him a fool and pushes him out. The music, however, has told us, with the phrases associated with the Innocent Fool, that Parsifal is the one they are waiting for, and an unseen voice repeats the motif.

Act 2 shifts to the magic garden of Klingsor, who reminds the audience of his desire for revenge against the brotherhood of the Grail and orders Kundry to seduce Parsifal. Parsifal easily resists Klingsor's knights and the bevy of flower-maidens that surround him, but he is more vulnerable to Kundry, now in the form of a beautiful, seductive woman lying on a couch of flowers. She tells him of his birth and his mother's death;

when he collapses in grief she offers her own consolation, ending by kissing him on the mouth. Parsifal tears himself from her arms, calling out "Die Wunde! die Wunde! Sie brennt im meinem Herzen!" ("The wound! The wound! It burns in my heart!"), while the music recalls Amfortas's last cry for mercy. Carolyn Abbate observes, "It is an extraordinary moment. Parsifal literally becomes Amfortas, taking on the wounded king's musical identity as he does the terrible burden of Amfortas's suffering. This exact quotation from the aria is like the turning of a musical key that sets Parsifal's memory free."[109] He begins now to understand what he saw at the Grail Castle. He can resist Kundry when she pleads with Parsifal to give her one hour of embraces to save them both and leave Klingsor's garden with the Spear that the enchanter has unsuccessfully hurled at him.

Act 3 begins on Good Friday, in a hermit's glade beside a holy spring. Gurnemanz is the hermit, and Kundry is now in penitent's garb. Parsifal arrives, in black armor and carrying the Spear, and reveals that he has been wandering on pathless ways throughout the world. Gurnemanz tells him that Amfortas has neglected his office, refusing to uncover the Grail; the Grail knights are bewildered and without guidance, and Titurel is dead. Parsifal collapses in grief and self-reproach and is revived by water from the holy spring, while Kundry unarms hims and washes his feet, drying them with her hair in an obvious reminiscence of the repentant sinner Mary Magdalene. Gurnemanz anoints Parsifal as the new Grail King. Parsifal's first task in this new office is to take the holy water and baptize Kundry to restore her faith. The Good Friday magic is abroad in nature, the meadows are smiling, and all creatures rejoice at the reminder of "Gottes Liebesopfer" ("God's loving sacrifice") and the redemption of humanity. Parsifal kisses Kundry's forehead in benediction, canceling out her lustful kiss in Act 2. The three move toward Monsalvat, where Amfortas, conducting the Eucharistic service for Titurel's funeral, is still reluctant to reveal the Grail. He begs for death, but Parsifal steps forward with the Spear and touches it to the wound: only the instrument that inflicted the wound can heal it. As Parsifal raises the Spear in ecstasy, blood flows again from its tip. The Spear can be returned to the Grail, and the shrine opened again. Parsifal is the new Grail King. The music enters its "long, shimmering conclusion" (Beckett, 58), and a dove descends and hovers over Parsifal's head, while Kundry sinks lifeless to the ground. The curtain falls on the final "tableau of reconciliation" (Beckett, 58).

Wagner's former disciple Friedrich Nietzsche deplored what he claimed was Wagner's prostration to the Christian cross (Beckett, 113–14);

Wagner himself saw his opera as a means of restoring a weakened pride in Germany's glorious Aryan past.[110] This is not the place to discuss Wagner's anti-Semitism, but it is undeniable that his opera has been intricately involved in his country's history. Hitler's adoption of Bayreuth as the Nazi "cultural shrine" (Beckett, 121) is only one indication. On the other hand, the opera's Christian (and Buddhist) message of renunciation and responsibility is clearly and strongly transmitted in performance. It is necessary that Parsifal wander through the world, feeling his predecessor's guilt and pain. Only by Parsifal's knowledge and suffering can Amfortas's wound be healed, Kundry be released from her torment, and the Grail be rescued from neglect or disappearance. The Grail represents Christ's continuing presence among men, and by revealing it again to the world Parsifal confirms that presence. Wagner insisted that Parsifal was not a Christ-figure; he is, rather, redeemed man who shows Christ's continued redemptive power.

As an artistic work *Parsifal* proved enormously influential in the Continental tradition, giving rise to many imitations and adaptations in different media throughout the twentieth century. Richard von Kralik's opera *Der heilige Gral* ("The Holy Grail," 1912) provides a prelude to Wagner's story in explaining Amfortas's loss of the Spear, and uses a choir of angels in imitation of Wagner's chorus. (Von Kralik's fascination with the Grail legend had previously resulted in an ambitious poetic chronicle, *Die Gralsage* ["The Legend of the Grail," 1907]). Similarly, Eduard Stucken's Grail Cycle, a sequence of eight plays written between 1901 and 1924, combines religious mysticism with "fin-de-siècle aesthetic" in weaving together a number of Arthurian themes around the connecting thread of the Grail legend. Although performed successfully in Europe, the plays are now largely forgotten.[111] The opera has also inspired film, both in Europe and the United States. In 1904 Edwin Porter produced a version of Wagner's opera for Thomas Edison, an ambitious affair of eight episodes, with elaborate sets and exaggerated acting. Edison hoped to synchonize phonographic recordings with the film, but the technology did not yet exist. The film had to be withdrawn from circulation when the owner of the copyright successfully sued Edison.[112] More recently in Europe appeared the innovative and controversial *Parsifal* by Hans Jürgen Syberberg (1981–82). In this four-hour-long film of Wagner's opera, the action is staged partly in the cracks and crevices of a gigantic death mask of the composer, fifteen meters long. Other deliberately nonrealistic devices include the use of puppets and the playing of Parsifal by both a male and a female figure (the two separate when Kundry kisses Parsifal and do not rejoin till the film's end).[113]

Thus in fiction, poetry, drama, and film, German artists drew from both Wagner and Wolfram, a trend that was intensified in the resurgence of interest in national cultural history exhibited after 1970 in both states of divided Germany. In France both the Symbolist poets and modern novelists were similarly inspired by Wagner or by Tennyson.[114] The most important direction, however, to be seen in treatments of the Grail legend occurred as a result of two seminal works published in English in the second decade of the twentieth century.

TWENTIETH CENTURY: BRITISH AND AMERICAN

In 1920 appeared what would prove to be one of the most influential books on the modern treatment of the Grail legend, Jessie Weston's *From Ritual to Romance*. Drawing on material from Sir James Frazer's *Golden Bough* (1911–15) as well as other anthropologists, Weston argued the presence of an archetypal initiation myth in the legend of the Grail. The story of the Fisher King whose impotence can be cured only by the proper asking of ritual questions about the Cup and the Lance by a quester shows the vestiges of ancient vegetational cults focusing on the death and resurrection of a god/king, regarded as the Life Principle. The resurrection of the god is linked to the restoration of the land, the freeing of the waters and the cycle of the seasons. The Lance and the Cup were originally male and female fertility symbols, which Christianity later identified with the Cup of the Last Supper and the spear of the Crucifixion, creating a late and misleading layer of interpretation. (The Christianizing of the legend was made possible because the Fisher King can be related to the use of the fish symbol in early Christianity.) At the root of the Grail myth, claims Weston, "lies the record, more or less distorted, of an ancient Ritual, having for its ultimate object the initiation into the secret of the sources of Life, physical and spiritual."[115]

Weston's book strongly influenced one of the seminal poems of the modern period, T.S. Eliot's *The Waste Land*, which appeared in 1922. In a general note to his poem, Eliot indicated that "not only the title, but the plan and a good deal of the symbolism of the poem were suggested" by Weston's book. As Taylor and Brewer observe, "Hitherto the story of the Grail, mediated by Malory or Wolfram, had been seen simply as medieval romance or as religious propaganda; now it took on fresh resonance as emanating from the dark abyss of time" (236). What Weston enabled Eliot (and writers after him) to do was to free himself from the Grail narrative and to utilize the pure myth, placing it in new contexts.

The symbols of the Waste Land and the Fisher King become for Eliot the most powerful "objective correlatives" (to use Eliot's own term) of the cultural and spiritual sterility of a modern world devastated by the Great War.[116] The despair and horror of that war, the facelessness of modern urbanized society, the devaluation of the sacred, the celebration of lust without love, the loss of sublimity and true emotion in human relationships, are all evoked in this portrayal of a land that is only "A heap of broken images, where the sun beats / And the dead tree gives no shelter, the cricket no relief, / And the dry stone no sound of water" (22–24). Though much of the poem focuses on London, the "Unreal City," images of contemporary Europe also weave in and out. Eliot's technique of juxtaposing seemingly disconnected scenes and conversations, of making classical myth rub shoulders with the contemporary scene, of evoking whole literary complexes with brief quotations or allusions, makes the poem extremely rich, but obscure and difficult to interpret. Dante, Arnaut Daniel, Shakespeare, Spenser, Webster, Kyd, Marvell, Goldsmith, Swinburne, Wagner, Verlaine, Nerval, and the Hindu Upanishads are only some of the writers and writings layered through the poem in fragments alongside conversations in the pub or snatches of music-hall song. The crowd that flows over London Bridge (62) represents at one and the same time the faceless workers swarming toward London's financial district, the souls of the dead from World War I, and the souls that Dante saw in hell ("I had not thought death had undone so many" [63]). The Waste Land is not simply a place, but a state of mind.

The polyvocalic nature of the poem, its dazzlingly multiple effects, [117] contribute to its obscurity, and the final message is ambiguous. The few symbols Eliot draws from the Grail myth seem to emphasize sterility and despair. In "The Fire Sermon" section, while "fishing in the dull canal," the Fisher King sees a rat "dragging its slimy belly on the bank" (187–89), creating an image that evokes only disgust and hopelessness. Similarly, in the last section, "What the Thunder Said," while towers fall in the decayed cities of Europe, there is only "rock and no water and the sandy road" (332), and "voices [sing] out of empty cisterns and exhausted wells" (385). The Chapel Perilous is empty, a "decayed hole among the mountains" (386), with the door swinging in the wind. In the same passage, a "damp gust / Bringing rain" ushers in a faint hint of relief, but we cannot be too sure of this, since water is an ambiguous symbol in the poem. The rain that the thunder presages and that the Ganges is awaiting has not arrived. The possibility of renewal comes from an unlikely source, as Western civilization is jostled by Eastern philosophy.

The Hindu gods provide a possible answer, couched in the stern Sanskrit injunctions of "Datta," "Dayadhvam," and "Damyata" ("Give, Sympathize, Control," or, more fully, "Give alms; be compassionate; control yourselves.") The passage suggests that the way out of the Waste Land requires the individual to break out of the prison of isolation, of the ego, to have both self-discipline and compassion for humanity. (We may be reminded that the Question in Wolfram's *Parzival* was not "Whom does the Grail serve?" but "What ails you?") The last eleven lines of the poem provide the most dense and puzzling juxtapositions, drawing together nursery rhyme, classical myth, French and English poetry into an enigmatic nonconclusion. The Fisher King sits on the shore, "Fishing, with the arid plain behind me," but wonders if he should "at least set my lands in order?" The fragments of different cultures and civilizations are pulled together like Ezra Pound's iron filings drawn together by a magnet, and crystallized into the famous line, "These fragments I have shored against my ruins" (431). The final lines of the poem repeat the thunder's commands and deliver the Sanskrit blessing from the Upanishads—"Shantih shantih shantih," meaning "Peace." The hope of renewal may be fleeting and illusory, but it is not completely denied.

Eliot's use of selected Grail symbols is heavily weighted toward their despairing and negative aspects, and *The Waste Land* may easily be read as a secular poem.[118] In contrast, a small group of Anglo-Catholic writers of the early part of the century responded positively to the sacramental quality of the Grail symbol. Among them is the highly underrated British writer Charles Williams, who was fascinated with the Arthurian legend throughout his unfortunately brief life. His prose studies on the legend were unfinished when he died, but his drafts were collected by his close friend C.S. Lewis into an essay titled "The Figure of Arthur," published together with Lewis's commentary on Williams's poems in *Arthurian Torso* (1948). "The Figure of Arthur" reveals that Williams considered the Grail theme central to the Arthurian legend, and another of his essays, published in a collection by his friend Anne Ridler, clarifies what Williams saw as the most important innovation in the development of the Grail, the invention of Galahad.[119] Williams's comments on the birth of Galahad (taken from Malory's version) are worth quoting in full. He has been discussing Lancelot's welcome to the Grail Castle by King Pelles:

> There is about this a known predestination: "the king knew well that Lancelot should [get a child upon his daughter.]" Lancelot is here the predetermined father of the great Achievement; he is the noblest lord in

the world, the kindest, the bravest, the truest. But he will not have to do with any woman but the Queen. . . . And Galahad must certainly be the child of the Grail-princess and certainly not of Guinevere. How is it to be done? It is brought about by holy enchantment and an act of substitution. Lancelot is deluded (as it were, by a courtesy of terrible condescension) into riding "against the night" to another castle, where he is received "worshipfully with such people to his seeming as were about Queen Guinevere secret." He is given a cup of enchanted wine and taken to the room where the supposed Queen is: "and all the windows and holes of that chamber were stopped that no manner of day might be seen."

I am not unaware that the substitution of one woman for another is common enough in the romances; it is the kind of substitution that makes this so thrilling. The vision is of "the best knight," labouring in that three-fold consciousness of God, the King, and Guinevere, received into the outlying castle of the Mysteries, and then by the deliberate action of spiritual powers drawn on into a deeper operation. He dismounts: around him are those who seem to be the Queen's servants, but it is not so; the assumed forms, the awful masks, of this sacred mystery attend him; he is taken to a chamber as dark as the night of the soul; and there the child who is to achieve the Grail is begotten.

This concept of the "mystical substitution" (194) that enables the conception of Galahad is central to Williams's poetic treatment of the Arthurian story, as seen in his unfinished poetic cycle, comprising two sequences, *Taliessin Through Logres* (1938) and *The Region of the Summer Stars* (1944). Though the two sequences were published together in one volume by Oxford University Press in 1955, and are frequently discussed as a single series, I prefer here to discuss the volumes separately.[120] As we have noted, the Grail was for Williams the thematic core of the Arthurian story: it "is not, as in Tennyson, only for the elect; it is for all" ("The Figure of Arthur," 84). Nathan Comfort Starr observes, "Williams conceives of the Grail as an idea or presence, an emanation of the Divine Order"(172). We do not see the actual quest, rather scenes and dramatic monologues that illuminate different aspects of it. *Taliessin Through Logres* is a mosaic of different voices and stanza forms, with first-person speakers such as Lamorack, Palomides the Saracen knight, Bors, Percivale, and Taliessin, "the king's poet," who is a participant and observer of much of the action, as well as an impersonal third-person narrator. The story is not told in a clear narrative sequence but has to be pieced together from allusive and elliptical passages. Williams makes some substantial changes to the central Arthurian narrative inherited from Malory, not only in the addition of the "Druid-born" bard and seer Taliessin,[121] but also in having Bors marry and have children, and in developing the character of Percivale's sister, named Blanchfleur[122] in the first series and Dindrane in the second. She is the princess whom Taliessin loves but who retires to a convent at Almesbury, becoming instrumental in bringing up Galahad, Lancelot's son. In "The Son of Lancelot," Merlin and his sister Brisen (both here children of Nimue) collaborate to rescue the infant Galahad at his birth: Brisen assists at the birth; Merlin, in the shape of a white wolf, saves the baby from the hungry gray wolf into which Lancelot has been transformed in his madness and carries the baby on his back though the snow to Blanchfleur at Almesbury. Galahad is a Messianic figure (though Williams insists that Galahad does not represent Christ, rather "man's capacity for Christ"):[123] he is known equally as "the High Prince," and "the Child," and "the Infant." In "The Coming of Galahad," the central event is seen from the point of view of Taliessin, who explains the significance of Galahad's arrival: he has brought all the dissonant images together, fitted the stone to the shell,[124] enabled "the redaction/ of categories into identity." Yet, although Galahad is "Sanctity / common and crescent," he is also human. In "Percivale at Carbonek," the speaker watches Galahad weep for his father, Lancelot, asking pardon for his very existence, which required Lancelot to be unfaithful to Guinevere. Not until he receives forgiveness (from Bors on behalf of Lancelot) can Galahad enter Carbonek to heal the wounded king.

In Williams's poems, Arthurian geography has mystic and Christian significance. As he explains in the Preface to *The Region of the Summer Stars*, as well as in his essay "Notes on the Arthurian Myth" (178–89), the Empire represents creation, with its center in Byzantium. Logres is Britain, regarded as a province of the Empire, and west of Logres is the region of Broceliande, in which is Carbonek; further west of Broceliande is the holy state of Sarras. In the antipodean seas lies Williams's equivalent of hell, the state of P'o-l'u governed by its headless Emperor, with its blind and octopoid tentacles. The symbolic geography is important because the concept of organic order is central to William's vision. The major threat to that order is the impulse toward autonomy, schism, making categories: the Byzantine Emperor's Acts of Identity create and maintain unity. In "The Last Voyage" (from *Taliessin*) when the three questers, Bors, Percivale, and Galahad, drive through the waves on the Grail ship, with the body of Blanchfleur at the prow, they are journeying toward "the safe tension / in each alloted joint of the knotted web of empire, / multiple without dimension, indivisible without uniformity." Also central to Williams's vision is the concept of Largesse–the generous love of others "not for themselves but for the divine qualities they exhibit" (Moorman, 70.)[125] Largesse leads to the doctrine of Exchange, or "substitution," the willing assumption of another's burden, the ultimate form of which is the sacrifice of self (Taylor and Brewer, 253). Blanchfleur/Dindrane becomes the supreme symbol of such sacrifice, because she allowed herself to be bled to save a lady from leprosy ("The Last Voyage").

Six years after *Taliessin*, Williams published *The Region of the Summer Stars*, six poems that fill out and intensify the themes raised in the earlier sequence, though with less variety in voice and stanza-form. Williams makes it clear in the Preface that "the argument of the [whole] series is the expectation of the return of Our Lord by means of the Grail and of the establishment of the kingdom of Logres (or Britain) to this end by the powers of the Empire and Broceliande." In this second sequence, Taliessin is more an actor than an observer; his coming to Broceliande and later Logres is described, the Company that forms from his household is instrumental in countering the division and dissolution caused by Mordred, and the slave-girl freed by him in "The Departure of Dindrane" acquires spiritual significance in her choice of continued service rather than freedom or marriage. In the last poem, "The Prayers of the Pope," Arthur's wars with Lancelot and Mordred's cynical ambition for power are cosmic, threatening the destruction of the Empire, the triumph of the antipodean realm of P'o-l'u, and the delay if not the prevention of the Second Coming. It is the combination of the Pope's prayer, the innate strength of Broceliande (the roots of the trees resist the slimy tentacles of the giant octopods), the loyalty and Largesse of Taliessin's Company, and the coming of the three "lords of the quest" that defeats the evil forces in a movement equivalent to the Harrowing of Hell. Schism and division are forestalled, unity is preserved: "The roses of the world bloomed from Burma to Logres; / pure and secure from the lost tentacles of P'o-l'u, / the women of Burma walked with the women of Caerleon." Despite the potential for destruction, despite the visions of Taliessin that pictured both the establishment of Logres and its Fall, there is still hope of renewal of the Empire, as the consuls and lords feel it "revive in a live hope of the Sacred City" ("The Prayers of the Pope").

Williams's achievement is to create in his poetic cycle a much more universal myth than the narratives that he drew from: his poems evoke the cosmic battle between good and evil, which is not confined to any

particular period of the past. His style makes his poetry extremely difficult, in a way quite different from Eliot's fragments and quotations; his
technique of allusion and anticipation is highly elliptic, his metrical
schemes are unusual (he was strongly influenced by Gerard Manley
Hopkins,)[126] with a heavy use of internal rhyme, alliteration, and asso-
nance. His imagery is also extremely concentrated, linking abstract and
concrete terms in the same phrase in jarring and confusing ways. Yet he
thoroughly repays the effort it requires to read his poetry.

Williams could be called a "mystical" writer, and he was probably
strongly influenced, during the period that he was a member of it, by the
ideas of an occult society founded by A.E. Waite, called the Hermetic
Order of the Golden Dawn, of which W.B. Yeats was also a member. At
the turn of the century, the decline in orthodox religion gave space for exploration of occultism, spiritualism, psychic research, and a renewal of
interest in mysticism (Taylor and Brewer, 239–40). Waite himself wrote
a long book on Grail symbolism in 1909, *The Hidden Church of the Holy
Graal: Its Legends and Symbolism*,[127] tracing the essence of the Grail
mystery to the secret words of Christ to Joseph of Arimathea in Robert
de Boron's work (Starr, 151–53), and emphasizing the Grail's sublime
spiritual power.

Perhaps as a result of Waite's influence, a handful of British novelists were motivated to take the Grail story "straight," not retelling it as a
remote medieval narrative, but exploring the idea of the Grail's actual
reappearance in a modern setting. Arthur Machen was the first to treat
this theme in his long short story *The Great Return* (1915), in which the
narrator comments on the strange and unexplained phenomena occurring
in a remote Welsh village by the sea. Lights appear on the sea, bells
sound on land, a mysterious radiance and the perfume of incense fills a
formerly Nonconformist church. The strange manifestations range from
the healing of a young girl in the last stages of tuberculosis to the restoration of love and friendship to a warring community. The effectiveness of
the story lies in its method of reporting–newspaper accounts, glimpses,
villagers' reminiscences are all filtered through the half-skeptic, half-be-
lieving voice of the narrator, as he comes to believe it is the Grail. Less
successful is Machen's second Grail fiction, *The Secret Glory* (1922),
which describes a sensitive Welsh boy, Ambrose Meyrick, bullied and
beaten at a second-class British public school, who is strengthened by
the memory of seeing the Grail kept by its hereditary keeper in a remote
Welsh farmhouse, when he was ten years old. His revolt from the brutality and hypocrisy of public-school morality and its deadening effects on

the imagination and the spirit leads him eventually to throw away a brilliant career at University and take the Grail to the Middle Eastern deserts. He is captured by Turks and crucified, dying in the religious ecstasy of martyrdom and fulfilling what had been predicted for him, "the glorious Quest and Adventure of the Sangraal." Unfortunately, the primary motivation of the novel seems to be a savage excoriation of the British public-school system (there is no doubt a strongly autobiographical element in the novel), and the theme of the Grail visions is secondary. The motivation for Meyrick's martyrdom is inadequate, and the event itself is described from a distance, reported in a brief Epilogue.

Machen was a Celticist, a strong believer in the vigor of the older Celtic Christianity before it was stamped out by Rome. Charles Williams, whose poetry we have just examined, was a High Anglican, but he too explores the effect of the reappearance of the Grail in a novel that develops Machen's suggestions more fully and universally, *War in Heaven* (1930). This novel has been described as satire, romance, thriller, morality play, and glimpses of eternity all rolled into one. The Graal,[128] a plain, somewhat battered silver chalice, turns up among the church vessels in an obscure English village, Fardles. The Graal is "a gate," not powerful in itself but a repository of power. Its identification sets loose a murder mystery and adventure story as the forces of evil and unmotivated malevolence are unleashed against the forces of good in an attempt first to simply possess and then to subvert the power of the chalice. The defenders of the Graal are an unlikely trio, a Roman-Catholic duke, a young idealistic publisher's assistant, and the archdeacon who first identified it. They represent three ways of seeing the Grail: the duke seizes onto its ancient tradition in his denomination (he wants to take it to the Vatican for safety); the publisher's assistant, Mornington, is drawn to it because of its romantic literary history; and Archdeacon Davenant worships it out of simple faith in the manifestation of God. The forces of evil are led by the owner of the publishing firm, Gregory Persimmons, who murders those in his way and gratuitously drives a young wife insane because he has designs on her child. Persimmons's black magic and his alliance with an anti-Christian Greek and an old Jewish man are almost too powerful to resist, and one of the questers, Mornington, loses his life. In a stunning culmination, the evil forces attempt the ultimate sacrilege, the spiritual contamination of the archdeacon by fusing his soul with that of a criminal. Finally, it is only the appearance of the Graalkeeper, Prester John, both messenger of Christ and Christ himself, that defeats them and delivers both archdeacon and child from the peril of losing their souls.[129]

The title of Williams's novel comes from the Book of Revelation: "There was war in heaven: Michael and his angels fought against the dragon; and the dragon fought and his angels, and prevailed not . . . ." Williams has universalized and updated the Grail myth by placing it in the twentieth century. What the defenders of the Grail must fight is not so much evil as "pulverizing nihilism" (Starr, 162). As Starr points out, Machen had restored the Eucharistic significance to the Grail, but Williams provides a different emphasis: "the Sacred Vessel is not simply to be sought and found, but to be *preserved* against an onslaught undreamed by the Fisher-King" (Starr, 166).

Strongly similar in theme, and undoubtedly influenced by it, is C.S. Lewis's novel *That Hideous Strength* (1945). However, the rise of Fascism and the horrors of World War II have intervened since Williams's novel, and Lewis's novel is darker and more sweeping, with a more contemporary political and science-fiction edge. It is the third of Lewis's Space Trilogy (the other novels being *Out of the Silent Planet* and *Perelandra*), but the only one of the three to utlilize the Arthurian myth. Perhaps again influenced by Williams, Lewis sees English history as a continual struggle between Logres and Britain, Logres representing the spiritual ideal, the idea of excellence, that is in constant conflict with the materialistic, self-seeking and secular Britain. In the sixth century, the idea of the perfect society was almost achieved; since then, in every age, the Pendragon of the time has gathered around himself the "little Logres" that gives "the tiny shove or almost imperceptible pull, to prod England out of the drunken sleep or to draw her back from the final outrage into which Britain tempted her" (Chap. 17. iv).

The "final outrage" attempted here is a design on the fate of the human race. It takes the form of the scheming by N.I.C.E (the National Institute of Co-ordinated Experiments), a monstrous and totalitarian organization, to take over Edgestow, a small university town in the Midlands, employing terror tactics, control of the press, and the establishment of its own police force. Ultimately, it will govern England, and all the world. All natural processes will be extinguished, and mechanical or disembodied Mind will dominate. Behind N.I.C.E. is in fact a more terrible and powerful force, the supernatural beings Lewis introduced in his earlier novels, the bad eldils. Against them is only a small and diverse Company of humans (and animals) that has assembled around Elwin Ransom, also known as Mr. Fisher-King, at the Manor in the village of St. Anne's. Ransom is also the Pendragon, inheriting the office from a direct line back to the sixth century; he has an incurable wound in his heel, which will be healed only when he returns to the planet Venus, which he visited in a previous novel. Both sides are trying to harness the power of Merlinus Ambrosianus, the sixth century Druid sage lying in suspended animation for fifteen centuries under Bracton Wood in Edgestow; it is Ransom's Company that Merlinus voluntarily joins when he revives. Harnessing the power of the planetary gods, Merlinus subverts a ceremonial banquet at N.I.C.E. and releases all the animals that were incarcerated for experimentation. The final cataclysm obliterates Edgestow by earthquake and flood; but Venus (Perelandra) is hovering over St. Anne's, and animal and human couples together are restored in a joyous upswell of reunion and sexual celebration. The central couple thus saved are Jane and Mark Studdock, whose marriage was disintegrating at the beginning of the novel through negligence and lack of understanding. The presence of Venus brings them together in a kind of epithalamium, with a hint that the next Pendragon will be born on this night.

That Hideous Strength is not strictly a Grail novel: there is no mention of the Grail. However, what the Pendragon guards is a spiritual power equivalent to the Grail, the force that inspires those moments in history when Logres appears to break through to revitalize and heal materialistic Britain. The picture of totalitarianism at work in a small country town is credible and horrifying, as is the seduction of Mark by a Kafkaesque institution. A similar attempt to bring the Grail into the twentieth century, but very different in style and feeling, is John Cowper Powys's mystical-realistic novel *A Glastonbury Romance* (1933), which has as its cast the inhabitants of Glastonbury and its surrounding regions in the early twentieth century. The lives of nearly fifty characters are intertwined in this novel, covering a range of occupations and classes from the local landowning Marquis to the lowest starving poor. Powys taps all the legendary associations of Glastonbury and the Arthurian story, English, Welsh, and continental: Joseph of Arimathea, the earliest Christian church built out of wattle, and Glastonbury Abbey rub shoulders with the cauldron of Ceridwen, apple orchards and Avalon, Fisher Kings and fish, while the action swirls against the background of historic and prehistoric sites–the Tor, Wirral Hill, Chalice Hill, St. Michael's Tower, the ruins of the Abbey, Stonehenge, and the dwellings of the aboriginal Lake Village people. Though Arthurian allusions are woven intricately through the novel, there are no exact correspondences: Sam Dekker, for instance, the vicar's son, having an affair with a married woman, is clearly a Lancelot figure, but when he takes a vow of celibacy to serve Christ and abjures the woman, he is Galahad, or perhaps Perceval leaving Blancheflor;[130]

and when he sees a vision of the Grail, he is pierced by a Lance in the vitals like the Fisher King. The charismatic prophet Johnny Geard, mayor of Glastonbury and founder of a new religion, is a Merlin-figure, intending to revive the Cymric (Celtic) Grail; yet when he channels the Grail's power through himself to heal a diseased woman in the Grail Fountain, he imagines that he is plunging the Bleeding Lance into her cancer in a reminiscence of Galahad. At the same time, allusions may be employed in reverse: a monstrous inversion of the Dolorous Stroke takes place when the local madwoman, Mad Bet, who is a kind of Grail Messenger, incites a tramp to crush with an iron bar the skull of the man she loves.[131] Such repetitions and inversions convey the impression that the myth is continually playing out in different forms in human lives (Taylor and Brewer, 280).

The central conflict of the novel is between Geard, who wishes to revive the holy past of Glastonbury and make it a religious center drawing pilgrims from all over the world, and the local industrialist Philip Crow, who wishes to exploit the local resources and develop the town economically. Also in conflict with the capitalist Crow are a group of Communists who succeed in establishing an experimental commune in the town. Geard's plans for Glastonbury begin with a massive Midsummer Pageant, which combines Arthurian tableaux with a Passion play: Part 3 of the Pageant, based on Cymric mythology, has to be abandoned when the Welsh antiquary playing Christ so identifies with his part that he collapses on the Cross. (The description of the pageant is a seriocomic delight: the local poet's text is staged by members of Dublin's Abbey Theatre, who have been invited for their professional expertise; the actors are mostly townspeople, but they also include a famous French mime, imported for satirical effect; the pageant is staged so far from the audience that no lines can be heard, and the audience has to follow the action from a printed program; the event itself is threatened by a band of strikers fomented by Communist agitators who almost mob the Marquis.) Later, Geard has a massive Saxon arch built over the Grail Fountain on Chalice Hill, and stages a grand opening of the religious center during which he performs a miracle by bringing a dead child back to life (though newspaper accounts afterward disagree over whether a true miracle occurred).

It is impossible to do justice here to the complex plot of the novel: love affairs, marriages, adulteries, births of legitimate and illegitimate children, attractions both heterosexual and homosexual (though the latter is only hinted at) take place among the different classes, and a strong erotic strain runs through the action. The Grail itself is a force that inspires the erotic element of human nature, a force of both destruction and fertility. No one religion is privileged in this novel: orthodox Anglican Christianity is represented side by side with Cymric Druidism, prehistoric paganism, and the new charismatic cult founded by Geard. The range may be seen most clearly in the visions of the Grail given to the two Holy Men in the book, Sam Dekker, the "new Anglo-Saxon saint," and Johnny Geard. Sam's vision takes place in a coal barge, heralded by a cracking of the darkness: he is racked with pain and experiences the sensation of being pierced from below by a Lance, after which he sees before him a crystal chalice holding water streaked with blood, in which swims a shining fish. The description of the vision draws clearly on orthodox Christian symbolism and shows Sam's identification with the crucified Christ. Geard's vision of the Grail, however, takes place during the climactic event of the novel, a terrible Arctic-born flood that overwhelms the region; Geard drowns while saving Philip Crow, but he dies willingly. In his death throes he sees a vision–the Grail in its "fifth shape," hovering above the tower on Glastonbury Tor. That fifth shape is not revealed, but it is terrifying; and the spot where Geard drowns is exactly above "where the ancient Lake Villagers had their temple to the neolithic goddess of fertility."[132]

For Powys, the Grail is more than a Christian object; it is pre-Christian, even pre-Cymric. It is "a morsel of the Absolute, and a broken-off fragment of the First Cause" (748). The First Cause, however, is essentially dualist in nature, inspiring both great good and great evil, violence, cruelty, and hatred as well as selfless love (Taylor and Brewer, 280–82). The forces of the Grail may be harnessed against the dark aspects of the First Cause, as Geard harnesses them when he heals the woman in the Grail Fountain, calling on its creative rather than its destructive energy (708). Ultimately, however, it is unknowable: as Powys observes in his 1953 introduction, "Whether we shall find the beyond-life of which [the Grail] is a symbol when we perish, or whether we shall vanish with it into oblivion, we . . . will never know" (xvi).

LATE TWENTIETH CENTURY: FICTION AND FILM

Unlike the novels of the first half of the twentieth century, late twentieth-century fiction has difficulty in treating the Grail legend seriously. Writers omit it or marginalize it, or dance around its edges by parodying it. Sometimes they simply exploit it for comic effect,[133] as in David Lodge's wickedly funny satire on contemporary academic institutions, *Small World: An Academic Romance* (1984). The hero of this novel is Persse McGarrigle, a junior university lecturer from Ireland on a quest for a beautiful girl he first sees at an academic conference in the British Midlands. (Lodge's prologue compares the yearly round of academic conferences to medieval pilgrimages.) Persse follows his lady from conference to conference around the world, ending up at the Modern Language Association Convention in New York, in December. A number of romance conventions are parodied in the narrative, but the Grail legend provides the material for the climax, which takes place during the Convention, at the Forum for the Function of Criticism. The outgoing chair, UNESCO Professor Arthur Kingfisher, sexually and intellectually exhausted, is electrified when Persse asks the unanswerable question, "What do you *do* if everyone agrees with you?" As a wave of warm moist air courses through frozen Manhattan, Kingfisher is restored to sexual vigor, marriages are revived, new romantic liaisons made, and long-lost children are united with their parents in the best romance manner.

For Lodge the Grail legend is simply a vehicle to expose the sterility and exhaustion of contemporary academic literary studies; it is only one of the weapons in his comic arsenal. In contrast, most postwar writers have difficulty in retelling the myth without disillusion and despair. Even T.H. White treats the Quest obliquely in *The Ill-Made Knight*, the third part of *The Once and Future King*.[134] Though he can display his characteristic irreverent humor by having King Pelles tell Lancelot, "I have some sort of holy dish in my castle at Carbonek, together with a dove which flies about in various directions holding a censer of gold in its beak" (Chap. 9), when it comes to describing the arrival of the Grail at court White directs the reader to Malory, saying:"That way of telling the story can only be done once" (Chap. 28). The Quest itself is narrated indirectly: as the lesser and unsuccessful knights come trailing in to court, first Gawain, then Lionel, and finally Agglovale recount the achievements, respectively, of Galahad, Bors, and Percivale's sister. Only when Lancelot returns, beaten and exhausted, does the court get a firsthand account of the Grail Quest, limited to his own, incomplete, experience.[135] The cumulative effect is of a court bewildered and lost, unable to comprehend this mystery that excludes all but the chosen few.

In general, late-twentieth-century fiction writers display the modernist nostalgia for lost certainties and systems that has been described in the discussion of T.S. Eliot, above. Familiar themes are parodied and inverted: anti-quests and anti-Grails predominate. One such absurdist treatment is Thomas Berger's *Arthur Rex: A Legendary Novel* (1978), where the Grail is demystified and desacralized completely. We never see the Grail, except in dream or false vision. Galahad never achieves it; on the contrary, pale from an unidentified terminal illness, he kills his father, Lancelot, on the final battlefield without recognizing him. Percivale is allowed to heal the Maimed King by asking the innocent question, "Why do you suffer?" but he too dies in the apocalyptic final battle along with the rest. The ultimate modernist Grail novel is, however, Walker Percy's *Lancelot* (1977), set in the contemporary American South.[136] From his asylum cell, the narrator, Lancelot Andrewes Lamar, tells his story to a priest/psychiatrist friend called Harry, also identified as "Percival and Parsifal, who found the Grail and brought life to a dead land" (Chap. 2). Jealousy has poisoned Lancelot's view of the world since he discovered his wife Margot's infidelity with a movie director. Determined to prove it, he pursues, as he calls it, a Quest for "an unholy Grail" (Chap. 6). Illusion and invention are at the heart of the novel: the movie company is engaged in making a movie at Lancelot's New Orleans mansion, Belle Isle; Margot has restored the mansion and reinvented Lancelot as the ideal Southern gentleman, while Lancelot, after his discovery that his second daughter was not fathered by him, remakes himself as a quester to root out Margot's sin. At the climax of the narrative, he blows up the mansion, killing his wife and her new lover. Life has been too fragmented, too full of deceptions, too ambiguous for Lancelot; he announces that he "will not tolerate this age." His vision of the new world order is a clean, austere one where there will be no confusion between the honest man and the thief, the lady and the whore, but also one where women submit willingly to male violence and rape.

Lancelot has cast himself in the role of quester: he claims that his medieval namesake was "one of only two knights to see the Grail" (Chap. 5). Not only is he defining his life by myth, he is remaking the myth to suit himself. Worse still, he identifies himself with the wrong part of the myth; he is not Lancelot, but the Fisher King,[137] wounded to the heart by jealousy and distorted vision, with the world become waste through the poisoning of love. His compulsion to confront his wife with her lover is partly fueled by "the desire to feel the lance strike home to the heart of the abscess and let the puss out" (Chap. 8). Yet when he kills the lover he feels only coldness and emptiness. "I have nothing to ask you after all because there is no answer. There is no question. There is no unholy grail just as there was no Holy Grail" (Chap. 9). But his "confession" to Percival has been a form of healing; he is to be released, apparently sane. Both he and Percival will make new beginnings, but the novel's enigmatic ending leaves us guessing as to whether the new beginning will be according to Lancelot's way of total nihilism or Percival's renewal of faith.

If Percy's *Lancelot* is the ultimate modernist novel, expressing sorrow and pain for the loss of coherence in the universe, the ultimate postmodern Arthurian novel is Donald Barthelme's *The King* (1990). The postmodernist sensibility may be distinguished from the modernist by its celebration of the loss of coherence; fragmentation, instead of being a symptom of despair, is an exhilarating, liberating phenomenon.[138] In postmodernism, the distinction between what is real and what is simulated collapses: everything is a model or image, all is surface without depth.[139] Barthelme's tour-de-force of black comedy collapses periods of the past and proceeds in fragments of narration (frequently the dialogue of unidentified observers), so that it is impossible to separate reality from illusion. Arthur's kingdom has survived (without explanation) into the Britain of World War II: Arthur listens daily to radio broadcasts by the traitor Lord Haw Haw and complains about the policies of Winston Churchill. The Grail Quest has become an arms race for the cobalt bomb, the formula for which is found in sets of equations mysteriously appearing in a box of Girl-Guide cookies, an inscription on the heel of a Hanged Man, and the paper wrapping around the mace that Lancelot left in the men's room at a pub. Building the superweapon would be the answer to Mordred, who holds all London hostage, but Arthur refuses to do so: "It's not the way *we* wage war." When it is pointed out that the enemy is likely to build it if Arthur does not, the king responds: "The essence of our calling is right behavior, and this false Grail is not a knightly weapon."[140] The identification of the Grail with an instrument of mass destruction has not been made merely for its shock value: in this universe there is no true Grail. The romantic past is not simply deflated by the commercialist present, as in many comic Arthurian novels: here, the two cannot be separated. By refusing to use the bomb, Arthur has given up an advantage and is doomed to lose the war; yet the prophesied apocalypse does not quite take place. Though Arthur and Mordred fight "the greatest battle that ever was" (134), neither is killed. Mordred escapes and joins the Nazis, while Arthur and Guinevere retreat to the mountains. Though "legend requires a tragic end" for them (156), they are in no hurry for it; meanwhile, Lancelot lies under an apple tree and dreams of Guinevere.

French postwar authors also reflected the modernist loss of certainty and avoidance of closure. Whereas writers like Anouilh and Sartre tended to adapt classical myth to modern settings, the surrealist Julien Gracq was influenced by the Grail myth throughout his work.[141] His 1938 novel *Au*

Château d'Argol ("The Castle of Argol") is described by the author as a "demoniac version" of Wagner's *Parsifal*, but owes a greater debt, as the author also acknowledges, to Gothic horror novels and Edgar Allan Poe.[142] The narrative sets a triangle of two male intellectuals, Albert and Herminien, and the woman they both love in a remote castle overlooking an enormous forest, which almost appears to come alive. Indeed, nature is the primary character in this novel, which abounds in rich, sensuous, but phantasmagoric descriptions, both ominous and joyful, of the forest, the night sky, the sea, and the river. The link with the Grail seems to rest solely on the revelation (found in a small engraving of Parsifal healing Amphortas) that far from being a redeemer, Parsifal is intextricably implicated in the Grail King's guilt: the blood that spreads from the wound is the same substance that irradiates the Grail. Similarly, Albert and Herminien cannot break the sinister bond that holds them together even after the woman's death, and the relationship ends in murder. This oblique vision of the legend and the preoccupation with blood manifest themselves also in Gracq's 1948 play *Le Roi pêcheur* ("The Fisher King"), which inverts and parodies Wagner's opera. Though Gracq retains Wagner's characters, he alters their relationships. Amfortas now has the central role, tormented by his monstrous incurable wound; Kundry caused it by seducing him, but now, converted, she lives in the castle, tending him devotedly.

The opening scene shows desolation at Montsalvage: the forest is encroaching on the castle, all the knights are cold, aging, full of lassitude. Amfortas's wound is poisoning the whole community. All await the coming of "Le Simple" (The Fool) who will save them. But Clingsor reminds Amfortas that his healing will also mean his death: "La page sera tournée, le livre clos, la tourment effacé" ("The page will be turned, the book closed, the torment wiped out").[143] When Perceval arrives, he is overwhelmed by Kundry's beauty but repelled by the idea that she tends Amfortas's wound, just as he is terrified and repelled by the castle, which reeks of blood, not the red blood of battle, but the tainted blood of sick women. The castle is empty, like a stopped clock. It is Perceval's role to give it significance, to bring new life.

However, Amfortas, reluctant to give up his power even though it means relief of his torment, offends the pure Perceval by hinting that Perceval is only a reflection of himself, secretly desiring to commit the same sin. Perceval pushes him away, opening the wound, and is disgusted as it gushes blood, which only Kundry can stanch. He tries to leave, but Kundry persuades him to stay and witness the Grail ceremony that evening. Amfortas offers Perceval the kingship of the Grail, which will appear before him any moment, accompanied by light, music, fragrance, and nourishment; however, at the same time he reveals that to be the Grail King, to breathe the air of divinity, is a terrible burden. The Grail signifies closure and the death of adventure. "Là où tu entres finit l'espoir et commence la possession" ("Where you enter, hope is finished and possession begins," 141).

We do not witness the Grail ceremony directly but have it reported to us. When Perceval sees the Grail, he kneels but remains silent, refusing to ask the question that can be asked only once. He leaves, and Amfortas remains the Grail King. When Kundry reproaches him, Amfortas defends himself: he treated Perceval better than a messiah. He treated him like a man, gave him the right to choose. But the surrealist hero rejects both quiet and certitude. As Robert L. Sims observes, "Acceptance would signify a fatal cessation of the marvelous interrogation of the world" (46). Thus the expectations of the myth have been frustrated. The Grail hero has refused the Grail, and Amfortas and Kundry must await the coming of another "Simple."

Similarly avoiding closure is a later French work, the absurdist novel *Graal Flibuste* by Robert Pinget (definitive edition, 1966). Pinget's writing has prompted critics to compare him with proponents of the "nouveau roman" ("the new novel"), such as Alain Robbe-Grillet and Samuel Beckett.[144] His deliberate rejection of chronological narrative (with its illusion of cause and effect) and refusal to locate the narrative in landmarks of the "real" world are designed to call "reality" into question. *Graal Flibuste* is a tour-de-force of comic invention and exuberant wordplay, true Nonsense in the vein of Lewis Carroll or Edward Lear.[145] The novel takes its title (an untranslatable phrase that combines *Grail* with *piracy* or *buccaneering*) from a deserted baroque temple described in the first chapter and never mentioned again, though a later chapter attempts to explore the genealogy of the temple's apparent deity or monarch. The narrative is a reverse Grail Quest, a parody of a travelogue whose linear progression is constantly subverted by nonsequiturs, flashbacks, and digressions. The fantastic realm in which the unnamed narrator wanders with his horse, Clotho, and his coachman, Brindon, contains such strange hybrid species as tiger-birds, butterfly-monkeys, vines whose strings of fruit are tiny humans talking to one another, cherry trees whose fruit becomes human eyeballs. If the novel is a quest, it is never clear what is being sought, and closure is never achieved–in fact, it is feared. As the novel ends, the travelers are approaching the open sea; but as they follow a valley they come out not to the sea but a massive portal, a triumphal arch, with a city vista stretching out around it. The portal, its ornamental sculpture described in great detail, symbolizes new directions and adventures, the impossibility of conclusion.

Though written later than *Graal Flibuste*, René Barjavel's novel *L'Enchanteur* ("The Enchanter," 1984) returns to a more straightfoward fictional method, though his Arthurian characters converse in modern dialogue and the narrative introduces witty anachronisms (e.g., Merlin succors an old widow by filling her cupboard with canned goods, all with modern pull-top lids). Barjavel combines Merlin's story with the Grail theme, making Merlin the real architect and mastermind of the Quest. His goal is to find and educate the knight who will achieve the Grail; he chooses first Arthur, then Perceval, then Lancelot, each time disappointed when his chosen knight fails to remain chaste. Finally, he lights on Galahad. The origin of the Grail is traced to a clay cup made by Eve to catch the blood from Adam's wound after the removal of the rib; as she held it to the wound, the blood ceased to flow and the wound healed. The cup was broken by the angel guarding the gate when Adam and Eve were expelled from Eden. It turns up again, repaired, as the cup used in the miracle at Cana and again as the vessel of the Last Supper; finally, it is brought by Joseph of Arimathea to Britain, where it remains in the Castle of Adventures, guarded by the Wounded King. Therefore, all through its history it has been associated with blood and the wound, "qui sont la douleur du monde dont elle est le remède" ("which are the world's sorrow, for which it is the cure").[146] Similarly, it is associated with humanity (the clay it is made of is the same clay from which Adam was formed). In announcing the Quest to the Round Table knights, Merlin explains that the Grail is linked to "l'equilibre du monde" ("the world's balance"); every now and then that balance is threatened, and a chaste, courageous, devout hero is required to seek the Grail, restoring to humankind the strength to continue its difficult path (90).

FILM

The newest medium for the exploration of Arthurian themes in the late twentieth century is film. Again, however, the Grail is marginal or conspicuously absent from many filmmakers' visions, as, for example, the MGM *Knights of the Round Table* (1953) or the more-up-to-date *First Knight* (1995), both of which write out the Grail completely. Even the celebrated *Monty Python and the Holy Grail* (1975), directed by Terry Gilliam and Terry Jones, has as its chief joke that the film never shows the Grail, except as a vision in the sky when an irritable God orders the knights out on the Quest. The closest this example of inspired lunacy comes to showing a Grail is the Grail-shaped beacon used to lure unsuspecting knights to Castle Anthrax, the Castle of (voracious) Maidens. No completion of the Quest is possible, because the twentieth century breaks into the illusion: policemen with paddy wagons round up and arrest the few remaining Arthurian knights for the murder of the modern historian who has been commenting on the action, and a hand covers the camera.[147]

In Steven Spielberg's *Indiana Jones and the Last Crusade* (1989), the Grail myth is utilized for entertainment and adventure but given a serious subtext. The archaeologist Indiana Jones (Indy) sets out to rescue his father, a medievalist who has spent his life researching the whereabouts of the Grail, which is both the cup used at the Last Supper and the vessel that caught Christ's blood at the Crucifixion. It was entrusted to Joseph of Arimathea and then lost for one thousand years till it was found by three knights of the First Crusade. Since it can confer eternal life, it is a talisman of great power, eagerly sought by villains, chief among whom are Nazis, since the film is set in 1938. The Grail becomes, in fact, a weapon against National Socialism, whose philosophy is antagonistic to all religions and to humanist culture.[148] As Professor Jones insists, "The quest for the Grail . . . is a race against evil: if it is captured by the Nazis the armies of darkness will march all over the face of the earth." In a dizzying sequence of adventures and narrow escapes, Indy and his father salvage the vital clues to the location of the Grail, dodge the Nazis, and end up in a climactic confrontation at the temple of the Grail, somewhere in the Arabian desert.[149] Like the medieval Grail, it is protected by the secrets of the ages, by booby traps and taboos. Indy must pass three tests, tests of humility, courage, and faith, to penetrate the inner chamber where the Grail is guarded by an ancient knight, the remaining Crusader. The final test is to choose the right goblet from a bewildering array of items on the altar: the Nazi villain chooses the richest-looking one, drinks from it, and dies horribly. The correct choice is the humble wooden cup suitable for a carpenter.

As in medieval legend, the Grail separates the worthy from the unworthy. The Austrian art historian Elsa refuses to heed the warning not to take the Cup beyond the boundary; when the temple is riven apart and the earth opens up, she dies, still reaching for the Cup in her greed. Indy almost follows her, until his father convinces him to let it go. Success in this Quest lies not in the recovery of a precious object, for that is withdrawn forever from the human race, but in the self-discovery the Quest has necessitated. As one of the characters observes, "The search for the

Cup of Christ is the search for the divine in all of us." Indy has had to learn to *believe* in the Grail, in order to heal his dying father; his renunciation of the Cup gains him something more precious than power and immortality–love. Father and son rediscover their bond; though they return to bickering at the end, for one moment, while Indy hangs over the chasm held only by his father's hand, his father recognizes him as an equal and calls him by his chosen name, "Indiana."

One of the few modern films to take the Grail seriously is Eric Rohmer's *Perceval le Gallois* (1978), a stylized and deliberately nonrealistic setting of Chrétien de Troyes' *Perceval* or *Le Conte du Graal*. Rohmer consciously "distances" his material by using medieval music, having his characters and singers comment on the action like a chorus, and using a set modelled on illuminations in medieval manuscripts. The actors use stylized and artificial gestures, and the effect is a conscious recreation of a medieval text.[150] Rohmer follows faithfully the major scenes of the Perceval section of his source, as well as two episodes from the Gauvain section, but departs radically from his original by concluding the film with a Latin Passion play of the Crucifixion, thus giving an explicit Christian coloring to Chrétien's text. Since the actor playing Perceval also plays Christ in this Passion play, the identification between the two is complete. Perceval not only comes "to understand the historical fact of Christ's sacrifice; he actually becomes Christ" (Williams, Chapter 20 in this volume). As critics have suggested, Rohmer's is a "profoundly Catholic, highly moralized interpretation of Chrétien's romance."[151]

Whereas French Arthurian cinema reflects primarily the French cultural reception of a brilliant literary tradition,[152] John Boorman's *Excalibur* (1981) draws directly on the Anglo-American associations of Arthurian legend. Ostensibly adapted from Malory by Rospo Pallenberg, Boorman's film divorces the Grail from its Christian context and treats it as a rather confused fertility symbol. Arthur's sickness is reflected in the land, which is also diseased: Arthur begs his knights to find the Grail, for "only the Grail can restore leaf and flower." The Quest itself is developed in haunting images of bleak, wintry landscapes, with knights fighting through hail and snow. Percival, questing for ten years, comes upon skeletons in armor and corpses whose eyes are pecked out by crows. The horror, however, is being engineered by the demon child Mordred and his evil mother, Morgana; when Percival refuses their blandishments, he is hung on a tree and receives a vision of the Grail, a chalice floating in the air. A voice asks him "What is the secret of the Grail? Whom does it serve?" Percival is unable to answer on this occasion, but after suffering and travail he receives a second chance to do so. The secret of the Grail is that Arthur and the land are one.

The Grail in Boorman's film has taken on ritualist and anthropological associations. Arthur is himself the Maimed King, and his healing simultaneously restores the land.[153] Whereas in Chrétien's paradigm Perceval was supposed to have asked the question, here he is supposed to provide the answer. Since Boorman has, from the start of his film, emphasized the Celtic dimensions of the myth by building up Merlin as a Druidic figure muttering Welsh spells and "loosing the dragon's breath," it is not surprising that his Grail should be divested of its Christian, and especially Catholic, significance. On the other hand, by employing the Grail as a fertility symbol, Boorman has difficulty reconciling it with the symbolism of the sword Excalibur, which has already been identified with the health of the kingdom and the potency of the king. According to Boorman, the film shows humanity's loss of touch with the world of magic and nature, and the Quest is a form of transcendence, an attempt to regain that lost world. But without a clearer link with Merlin (who has up to now represented the lost world of the old gods), the Grail can only, as in Perceval's vision, hover in the air without any support.

A far more successful attempt to incorporate Jessie Weston's motifs of the Maimed King and the Waste Land into film narrative is Terry Gilliam's *The Fisher King* (1991), with script by Richard LaGravenese. Here, the Grail Quest is set in contemporary New York, a veritable Waste Land. Despite the film's contemporary images of homeless people and street violence, it is really a modern fantasy, capturing the vision of an alienated society and fragmented, incoherent human life common to modernist fiction. The central figures are Jack Lucas, a former radio talk-show host, now racked with guilt for having encouraged a deranged fan to commit mass murder in a restaurant, and Parry, the former professor of medieval studies whose wife was one of the murder victims. Parry, half insane, living in a basement and consorting with the homeless, is clearly Percival, the Fool, and Jack is the Fisher King, emotionally crippled, unable to love or feel loved. In truth both are psychically wounded, and are needed to heal each other. Parry, the innocent, childlike figure, must teach Jack to let go of the world, to feel sympathy for the "bungled and the botched," to lie naked at night in Central Park and watch the clouds. Jack has to take over Parry's Quest in order to restore him from a catatonic state after being attacked by teenage thugs. Parry's Quest is to recover (actually, steal) the Grail from the "castle" of its owner, Langdon Carmichael, a dying real-estate billionaire.

The film is full of comic and parodic moments. Parry's Blancheflor is an awkward maiden who knocks over everything she touches; Jack's girl-friend, Ann, when asked if she knows of the Holy Grail, says, "Yeah, I know that one; that was like Jesus's juice glass." The Grail itself is Parry's delusion: it turns out to be a cup awarded to "Little Lannie Carmichael" for his help with the school Christmas pageant. But, as in *Indiana Jones*, it is not the object itself that matters, but the quest for it. By taking the risk of stealing it (climbing into Carmichael's mansion), Jack has made a human connection; when he brings the cup to Parry, it heals him. Feeling flows again for them both. They are able to grieve, to express and receive love. Parry's demons (terrifying visions of a Red Knight, accompanied by violence and disintegration) are presumably put to rest.

The version of the myth central to the film, told by Parry to Jack in the park, is not medieval, but is strongly influenced by Jungian thought, specifically the writings of Robert A. Johnson.[154] The Fisher King caused his own wound by his hubris, burning his hand by reaching into the fire for the Grail; he is cured ultimately by the Fool, who asks "What ails you, friend?" and hands him drink simply because he is thirsty. The Grail becomes a symbol of compassion, of human connection, of risking one-self for another; as Johnson would argue, Jack's quest mirrors the process of Jungian individuation (Osberg, 210). Gilliam's version of the myth is from Chrétien out of Jung via Weston, and the end is somewhat facile (the last scene shows Jack and Parry lying naked in Central Park, while the city explodes in a firework display); yet he creates a funny and sometimes touching film. It seems that modern (and postmodern) ver-sions of the Grail myth work best when transplanted into the modern day. As Gilliam notes, "Luckily the myth is strong enough to be pushed around in many directions" (Osberg, 200).

CONCLUSION

The very indeterminacy of the Grail symbol allows for multiple interpre-tations, for appropriation by orthodox Christianity or heterodox religious groups, even by New Age psycho-religion: "The way to the Grail lies within," writes John Matthews (introduction to "Temples of the Grail," *Table*, 69); "The quest for the Grail . . . suggests a quest for self-discov-ery. You are finding yourself at the same time that you are searching for the Grail."[155] It lends itself to exploitation by groups with differing agen-das. In the Middle Ages it supported and endorsed nationalist aspira-tions: the legend that Joseph of Arimathea, by bringing the Grail from the

Middle East to England, converted England to Christianity even before the establishment of the Church in Rome was invoked at the Council of Pisa in 1409 to support England's primacy as a Christian nation.[156] The monks of Glastonbury even meddled with documents to establish that Joseph had brought the Grail to their site. In the fifteenth century John Hardyng similarly exploited the associations of Glastonbury to endorse English nationalism in his secularized version of the Grail Quest, bringing Galahad's heart and his red-cross shield back to England to be buried at the Abbey.[157] At the same time, some scholars speculate that the development of the Grail romances reflects the desire of Western Christendom to compensate for the loss of Jerusalem in 1187 and the subsequent failure of the Crusades.[158] Through its Christianization by Robert de Boron, the Grail represents a literary alternative to the lost holy places; Joseph of Arimathea brings the Grail to the West, and Galahad returns it to the Holy Land, from where it is taken back to heaven, "where no one can dispute ownership" (Knight, 231).

In the Victorian period the Grail could be associated with the renunciation of dangerous sexuality–only the pure in heart and body can achieve it–or with the ideals of duty and self-sacrifice by which colonial civil servants justified their roles in the imperialist project. In the public arena, pictorial representations could support the sanctioned royal allegory of stability and power.[159] Moreover, in the nineteenth century it has always been able to stand for a nostalgic return to medieval values in reaction to the materialism and dehumanization of the Industrial Revolution. In the twentieth century, between and after two world wars, it has been used to symbolize the barrenness, the spiritual emptiness of society, or the psychic woundedness of individual humans. Early twentieth-century British mystical writers imported the myth into contemporary times in order to repudiate Fascism; yet at the same time, the theater that Wagner built at Bayreuth to stage his *Parsifal* was adopted by Adolf Hitler as a cultural shrine to National Socialism. Whereas the thirteenth-century *Queste del Saint Graal* presents a distinctly mysogynistic view of women, who are categorically barred from embarking on the Quest,[160] post-Freudian interpretations focus on the vessel as a symbol of the female, particularly in its associations with blood, which evokes menstruation,[161] or as a representation of the mother, providing "nourishment, protection, and perfect union" to the Grail knights.[162] As Martin B. Shichtman suggests, the Grail is an empty vessel which can be filled with any kind of ideology.[163] Yet throughout its transformations, it remains an enduring symbol of aspiration, of the hope of something Other in this materialistic world.

CONTENTS OF THIS VOLUME

Of the twenty essays that follow, seven have been written specially for this volume; the other thirteen are previously published essays, some being classics on the topic. The selection is designed to convey the great range of treatments of the Grail legend, though it can by no means represent all the primary texts. Scholarly articles rarely focus on the Grail object exclusively: most of the essays in this volume consider the Grail in the context of the thematic development of the respective texts, or they examine specific motifs, such as the Quest and the Waste Land. Modernist and postmodernist texts are particularly fascinated with the latter motif, which expresses so effectively the loss of faith and meaning in the modern age.

In the first essay, "The Quest for Origins," written for this volume, Glenys Witchard Goetinck surveys theories of the origin of the Grail legend: those of pagan origin (ancient vegetation cults, initiation rituals, the cult of the Mother Goddess) as well as those from Celtic legend, or from Christian, Hebrew, or Byzantine allegory and ritual. In the second half of her essay, she explores the relationship between the Welsh romance of *Peredur* (in which the platter in the procession carries a severed head) and Chrétien's *Perceval* (in which the dish contains a Mass wafer). Arguing that *Peredur* represents the earlier version, she traces the steps by which the head becomes a Mass wafer, suggesting that both versions ultimately derive from Indo-European initiation myth, assimilated into Celtic mythology. The severed head is a "dieu sans corps" (god without body), a symbol of divinity. The ultimate source of the Grail Quest, she speculates, is "a myth as old as humanity," the search for the secret of creation.

The next essay arrives at a somewhat similar conclusion from a different direction. In *The Grail Legend*, Emma Jung and Marie-Louise von Franz apply Carl Gustav Jung's theory of archetypes to the Grail material. Chapter 7, reprinted in this volume, explores the symbolism of the Grail as vessel. Jung and von Franz examine examples of life-giving vessels in Celtic mythology and consider the etymology of the word *graal* as well as its forms and attributes in the various Grail romances. In many cultures, the vessel is a maternal symbol, linked with the grave, associated both with death and rebirth. (The grave may also house hidden treasure, both material and nonmaterial.) The form of the vessel that contains Christ's blood holds his soul-substance; but Christ's grave is found empty. The most essential attribute of the Grail is, therefore, its emptiness, an emptiness which is necessary for the separation of human consciousness from the unconscious, and the emergence of Anima. The quest for the vessel is, therefore, a means to discover Anima, the soul.

The next seven essays treat individual Old French texts. Jean Frappier's classic essay on Chrétien's *Perceval* or *Le Conte du Graal*, translated by Raymond Cormier, emphasizes the work's strangeness and ambiguity, maintaining that its incomplete state is essential to its charm. Exploring the motifs of the *graal*, the bleeding Lance, the Fisher King, and the Waste Land, Frappier also discusses some of the theories of their origin, concluding that in the *Conte du Graal* we have a delicate adaptation by Chrétien of disparate pagan, probably Celtic, elements, into a setting that has Christian significance. The crucial modulation is the hermit's declaration that the *graal* contains the Mass wafer rather than the large fish it might be expected to contain. Here is the new *sen* (meaning) given by Chrétien to his received and already adapted *matière* (subject matter). The mysterious, ambiguous effect of the narrative is therefore created by the two different levels of meaning, sacred and profane, the one superimposed upon the other.

Sara Sturm-Maddox's essay, "*Tout est par senefiance*: Gerbert's *Perceval*," demonstrates the progressive christianization of the Grail theme in the *Perceval* Continuations. She argues that the Continuation by Gerbert de Montreuil provides a loop in Perceval's adventures, not just a deferral of the conclusion. These adventures are framed by the Fisher King's pronouncement that Perceval must expiate his "sin" before he can learn the secrets of the Grail. The emphasis on breaking and repairing of the Sword and Perceval's mistaken assault on the gate of Paradise with another sword indicate that he must learn a new conception of secular chivalry, set in the context of theological discourse. Perceval returns to the Grail Castle not with answers to the old questions, but with a new set of questions, aimed at elucidating a larger *senefiance*. Sturm-Maddox has provided her own translations of quotations from Old French.

Angus J. Kennedy examines the narrative and symbolic functions of the Waste Land theme in *Perlesvaus*. The results of Perlesvaus's failure to ask the questions about the Grail and the Lance are manifest throughout Arthur's kingdom, in the physical blighting of the land, the decline of chivalry, internal dissension and war, and in individual characters such as the bald Maiden of the Cart. Yet these effects are not completely reversed after Perlesvaus's reconquest of the Grail Castle, as might be expected. Symbolically, then (though the symbolism is not consistently imposed through the work), the Waste Land signifies unredeemed humanity, as well as the imperfections of the Old Law (the Jewish faith) in contrast to the New Law. The author has skillfully reworked the myth to support his militant view of Christianity. The Waste Land is not a geographical location but a spiritual state, and the inconclusive ending of the romance signifies that the process of redemption is ongoing.

In "Failure in Arthurian Romance," Elspeth Kennedy shows that the theme of failure serves to emphasize the unattainable nature of the Grail Quest. Chrétien's unfinished *Conte du Graal* prompts us to speculate how he would have completed it. If he followed the pattern of his other romances, he would have had Perceval follow his initial failure not simply by a return to the Grail Castle but by a new kind of journey. In *Perlesvaus*, the memory of Perceval's failure in a previous text directs the narrative, but Perlesvaus redeems and transcends the earlier failure by his military achievement. Yet the setting of the Grail theme in the wider context of Arthurian wars and the establishment of the New Law gives a different emphasis, so that neither total failure nor definitive success can be contained within the narrative. In the *Lancelot-Graal* cycle, Lancelot is the triumphant hero until the preparation for the *Queste* predicts his displacement at the pinnacle of chivalry by his chaste and perfect son, Galahad. Thus in the *Lancelot-Graal* cycle we have a "hero who fails and never redeems his failure." The various approaches demonstrate that the Grail "cannot be won on human terms."

Where Elspeth Kennedy would interpret the *Queste del Saint Graal* as an allegory, Laurence de Looze prefers to apply the language of semiotics to the text. The *Queste* disinherits the old code of *fin amor*, replacing it with the new code of promised salvation. Knights must become hermeneuticians, except for Galahad, who is fluent in the language already–his search for the Grail is a search for the pure signified, without intermediary. For Lancelot, biblical parables partake in the semiological system he must learn, but his chance to redeem himself is sacrificed by the exegetical demands of the narrative. The *Queste* is "primarily a story of interpretations of the events of its own narrative," and the reader must also become a hermeneutician.

Janina P. Traxler approaches the *Queste* from another perspective in her original essay, "Dying to Get to Sarras: Perceval's Sister and the Grail Quest." She asks (1) why is a female required for the role, and (2) once granted entrance to the narrative, why must she die before getting her reward? Perceval's sister is vital to the completion of the *Queste*, providing the history and the straps for Galaad's sword. She becomes the virginal Mary-figure to pair with the Christlike Galaad, showing why a female is necessary to the narrative. However, medieval theological assumptions about woman prohibit the possibility of her participation in the Grail liturgy. The *Queste* author solves the problem by drawing on another genre, hagiography, to turn Perceval's sister into a virgin martyr, sacrificing her blood to save a leprous lady. "In the world of the *Queste*, the best woman is . . . dead virgin."

In the last of this group of essays Alison Stones's original study examines medieval visual representations of the Grail. "Seeing the Grail: Prolegomena to a Study of Grail Imagery in Arthurian Manuscripts" focuses on illuminations in *Lancelot-Graal* manuscripts, particularly the *Estoire* and the *Queste*. Stones finds that the depiction of the Grail is not consistent, either within a text or in the work of one illustrator. The similarity between the Grail liturgy and the sacrament of the Mass makes it not surprising that illustrators would adapt Eucharistic models from Christian art, and, indeed, some illustrations take care to represent the miracle of transubstantiation. However, in the *Queste* the Grail may be shown as a chalice or paten and even a covered ciborium (vessel that holds the host), [164] whereas in the *Estoire* it may also be a shallow bowl (the "escuele" of the text). The rules are clearly flexible and the depiction of the Grail decided on an *ad hoc* basis. Stones argues that the emphasis on blood rather than bread seen in the illustrations of the *Tavola Ritonda* may be connected to the popular cult of the Holy Blood in areas where the manuscripts were produced. Also unusual are the depictions of the Grail in its healing function, where the power comes from the vessel itself rather than its contents.

The three essays that follow treat texts in Middle High German and Middle English. Friedrich Ranke's classic essay "The Symbolism of the Grail in Wolfram von Eschenbach" has been reprinted frequently but is here translated into English for the first time, by Adelheid Thieme. Ranke provides a philological study of the properties and nature of the Grail in *Parzival*, observing that the description is a mixture of fabulous and Christian elements. The miraculous stone, which is so heavy that it can be carried only by a completely chaste person, dispenses unlimited food and prolongs life for those who view it. Its strength is renewed every Good Friday when a dove descends from heaven to lay the host on it. Wolfram has departed most particularly from Chrétien in having the Grail shed no radiance from itself and in having it guarded by the neutral angels. The crucial and obscure phrase describing the Grail, "lapsit exillus," is interpreted by Ranke in the light of the similar phrase, "lapis exilis," given to the miraculous stone from the earthly paradise that teaches humility to the eponymous hero in the Alexander legend. Ranke concludes that Wolfram's Grail is the stone of humility, fittingly guarded by the neutral angels, who refused to join a battle motivated by pride. In desiring to synthesize Christian and chivalric ideas, Wolfram has his hero Parzival struggle to overcome the sin of pride, taking the first steps toward that goal under the tutelage of the hermit.

In "The Truest and Holiest Tale: Malory's Transformation of *La Queste del Saint Graal*," I compare Malory's "Sankgreal" with its Old French source, arguing that while Malory faithfully reproduces the dichotomy between worldly and spiritual chivalry of the *Queste*, he cuts down its typological significance and subtly transforms its message. Choosing to follow the Vulgate rather than the Post-Vulgate *Queste* of the Prose *Tristan*, Malory successfully transmits its substitution of new meanings for established chivalric values, given most vivid form in the temptations of Bors and Perceval. The pivotal figure is Lancelot. The "instability" that characterizes him in Malory should be interpreted as a failure of perseverance rather than weakness of will. He cannot withdraw from the world as long as Guinevere is still a part of it; only when she has withdrawn is he able to do so. Whereas in the French romance celestial chivalry replaces and negates terrestrial chivalry, for Malory they are complementary rather than competitive aspects of life, one available only after the other has lost its meaning.

Felicity Riddy focuses on another Middle English version of the Grail Quest in her original essay "Chivalric Nationalism and the Holy Grail in John Hardyng's *Chronicle*," showing the fifteenth-century chronicler adapting the Grail legend to suit his nationalistic agenda. Hardyng is less interested in the Grail than in the symbol of the red-cross shield of Joseph of Arimathea (which, as the arms of St. George, had recently become an important national symbol). He recounts Joseph bringing relics of Christ to Glastonbury and adds the new item that Joseph presented the red-cross shield to the first king of England, thus giving the shield a secular genealogy going back to Arthur and, beyond him, Brutus. Though Hardyng's is the only chronicle version of the Arthurian legend to include the Quest, his Quest is severely truncated and shorn of its mystical aspects. Galahad, the legitimate son of Lancelot and Pelles's daughter, collects the red-cross shield from Glastonbury and achieves the Grail in Wales, subsequently taking both objects to the Holy Land to found a chivalric Order of the Holy Grail (reminiscent of the many secular orders founded in Europe in the fourteenth and fifteenth centuries). After Galahad's death, Percival and Bors bring his heart, encased in gold, back to Glastonbury, where it is buried, along with the red-cross shield.

Thus the Grail itself has almost disappeared from this version of the Quest, and the focus is on the nationalist symbolism that can be milked from the red-cross shield, evoking a lost dream of England's greatness in the light of its present weakness against France.

The Grail legend in the Victorian period is the subject of the next two essays. Linda K. Hughes exposes underlying issues of sexuality and religion in Victorian society in her original essay "Scandals of Faith and Gender in Tennyson's Grail Poems," examining these poems in the light of the dominant ideologies of the day, especially the backlash against the Oxford Movement. What was considered by the critics of the Oxford Movement a dangerous tendency toward excess in ritualized Catholicism, with its focus on male celibacy, forms the subtext of "The Holy Grail," the second of Tennyson's Grail poems. Unlike the popular celebration of virginity in "Sir Galahad," "The Holy Grail" offers a more ironic and complicated treatment. Not only is the vision of the Grail itself ambiguous, possibly destructive to human society, but the impulse toward male celibacy and the denial of heterosexual desire required in the Quest are also dangerous and suspect. Finally, in Tennyson's third Grail poem, "Balin and Balan," the primitive and superstitious tendencies of Roman Catholicism are revealed even more clearly.

Debra N. Mancoff's essay " 'Pure Hearts and Clean Hands': The Victorian and the Grail" is revised, with permission, from her catalog essay for the Dumont/Bayerisches National Museum (1995). Mancoff looks at the engagement of Victorian painters with the Grail legend. Tennyson's enormously popular lyric "Sir Galahad" captured the imagination of the Victorian public by presenting a youth who epitomized Victorian boyhood. The public focused on his character rather than the reason for his Quest. It was difficult for some artists (and for Tennyson himself) to explore the more spiritual aspect of the legend: William Dyce's fresco *Religion: The Vision of Sir Galahad* presents the character as active rather than mystical. Dante Gabriel Rossetti was able to show Galahad as a solitary mystic, led on by a sumptuously dressed Grail Maiden, but he was more interested in the failed quest of Lancelot, showing him barred from the Grail by the figure of Guinevere. Only Edward Burne-Jones truly identified with the mystical elements of the theme, returning to it throughout his life. His Galahad is serene and beautiful; in *The Attainment*, the final scene of the Merton tapestries, Galahad kneels at the door of the Grail Chapel as the petitioner who will be rewarded by a vision of beauty.

The remaining essays treat manifestations of the Grail theme in the twentieth century. Charles Moorman's chapter on T.S. Eliot from his book examines the way that myth shapes and informs Eliot's vision in *The Waste Land*, arguing that a "sacramental" point of view underlies all of Eliot's work. The central image of the Waste Land, derived from Jessie Weston's work, provides a perfect "objective correlative" for the modern world, devastated by moral and spiritual wounds; it also acts as a matrix for the extraordinary collection of disparate experiences and allusions that Eliot draws together in his poem. The sacramental view is opposed to the "dissociated sensibility" characteristic of the modern temper. The Grail myth can hold out a faint possibility of revitalization to the maimed ruler and the sterile land.

Karl Heinz Göller tackles the obscure but richly rewarding universe of Charles Williams's poetry in "From Logres to Carbonek: The Arthuriad of Charles Williams." (Part 7 has been omitted, with permission.) Göller provides a detailed and sensitive analysis of the narrative and thematic development of Williams's poetic sequence. For Williams, the second coming of Christ was to be achieved by means of the Grail, and by the establishment of a society of harmony and wholeness, based on selfless love. His major innovation was to denationalize the Arthurian myth, by making Arthur's kingdom part of the Byzantine Empire. The poems' focus is on Taliessin, a Welsh bard, who is granted a vision of the Empire when he meets Merlin and his sister, Brisen; the poems concerning Taliessin and his servant establish the themes of exchange, sacrifice, and substitution, the contrast between egotistic isolation and coinherence. The coming of Galahad suggests the possibility of coinherence, while Mordred's "meditation" presents a cynical view of the Grail as a "cooking pot," a trivial magic device. The final catastrophe is experienced in "The Prayers of the Pope," with its echoes of World War II and past barbarian invasions. The Pope prays against disintegration and schism; the Round Table is dead, but Taliessin's household may survive and hold out a dream of the advent of Sarras.

From Williams's poetry to Walker Percy's novels is a great leap, yet J. Donald Crowley and Sue Mitchell Crowley see in Percy's fictional output a similar attempt to restore the sacramental to a desacralized (post)modern culture. In *Lancelot*, Percy presents us with an antihero in search of an unholy Grail. Lancelot Andrewes Lamar's "confession" to his friend Father John, whom he used to call Percival, structures the novel, and the two friends are deeply interdependent upon one another. Lance suffers from a Kierkegaardian despair as he confronts the secrets of his father's embezzlement and his mother's probable adultery. Central to Lance's disillusion is his discovery of his second wife's infidelity, which drives him to his unholy quest, to document and prove her sin, a quest that culminates in murder and the discovery of nothingness at the heart of evil. Yet in Lance's final conversations with Percival, the latter's affirmations suggest an alternative path from his nihilistic one, a path that–just faintly–admits the possibility of grace.

In "The Grail in Modern Fiction: Sacred Symbol in a Secular Age," Raymond H. Thompson makes a rapid survey of the enormous range of modern fiction that transposes characters and motifs from the Grail legend or retells the Quest in a contemporary setting. Such novels and short stories belong to the genres of fantasy, historical fiction, and ironic fiction. In the second half of his essay, Thompson examines four novels that either rationalize the Grail or exploit it for its comic and ironic possibilities: Parke Godwin's *Firelord*, Jim Hunter's *Percival and the Presence of God*, Thomas Berger's *Arthur Rex*, and Naomi Mitchison's *To the Chapel Perilous*. As Thompson observes, organized religion suffers heavy criticism in all four works; ultimately, the spiritual journey is a solitary one.

The last two essays discuss modern versions of the myth translated onto film. Martin B. Shichtman demonstrates the continued fascination of modern writers and filmmakers with Jessie Weston's vision of the Grail Quest as a "romanticized version of ancient fertility rituals." Both *Apocalypse Now* (1979) by Francis Ford Coppola and *Excalibur* (1981) by John Boorman draw on Weston's master narrative. For Coppola Vietnam is the Waste Land, filled with images of death, insane destruction, and sexual frustration. Kurtz is the Maimed King, and Willard the film's Grail Knight, but his task is more ambiguous than his prototype's. He can heal the land only by annihilation. Boorman's film, though putatively dependent on Malory, is also heavily indebted to Weston. The Grail Quest represents an atttempt to regain the time of magic and harmony with nature. Arthur is identified with the land; he becomes emasculated, first by the adulterous affair, next by his sister Morgana's evil. He himself is the Maimed King and Perceval is the Grail Knight who must suffer the ordeals of the Quest to save him. Perceval's encounters with the Grail are greatly altered from the sources (the Grail asks the questions!); though his eventual success results in a temporary restoration of health and virility to Arthur, the episode is symbolically confused and unexplained.

Linda Williams analyzes Eric Rohmer's technique in *Perceval le Gallois* (1978), a fascinating and strangely moving film adaptation of Chrétien's *Perceval*. Beginning with his own faithful modernization of Chrétien's verse text, Rohmer rejects the common tendency to use visual and narrative realism in filming a medieval subject. Chrétien's self-conscious narrator is recreated in the combination of sung narration by a chorus (sometimes a single voice) and spoken third-person narration by the characters, who alternate narration with direct dialogue. Highly original is Rohmer's addition of a "coda" in which the characters enact a pantomime of Christ's Crucifixion in the Hermit's chapel, with the actor who played Perceval playing Christ. Perceval not only understands Christ's passion but internalizes its meaning. The most innovative techniques, however, are spatial: the patently artificial set, with stylized, metallic trees and interchangeable castles, flat lighting, and the liberal use of gold, recall medieval illumination. The mannered movement and gestures of the actors and the restriction of movement by the semicircular set also add to the impression of continuous narrative characteristic of medieval illumination. Rohmer's "subversion of rationalist and realist space," argues Williams, effectively reveals the kinship between medieval and postmodern literature.

The last essay has brought us back full circle, to the first enigmatic literary text that introduced the Grail and started the exploration of the legend. The inexhaustible vessel, with its extraordinarily varied manifestations, has provided food for countless works in art and popular culture, in many genres and media. Mysterious, secret, and elusive, it continues to entice artists, writers, and readers alike.

ACKNOWLEDGMENTS

It is impossible to name all the colleagues who have assisted this project with informal advice and recommendations, but Lori Walters, Alan Lupack, Debora Schwartz, and Sandra Ihle deserve special mention, as does Gary Kuris for his advice throughout the planning stages. In particular, however, I would like to thank the following: Glenys Goetinck, Janina Traxler, Alison Stones, Felicity Riddy, Linda Hughes, Debra Mancoff, and Raymond Thompson, for writing original essays for this volume and revising them with patience and good-humor; Sara Sturm-Maddox, for providing translations of the Old French quotations in her article; my reading group at Arizona State University, Corinne Schleif, Juliann Vitullo, and Diane Wolfthal, for their pertinent comments on the Introduction; Adelheid Thieme, for translating Friedrich Ranke's article and for early assistance with the bibliography; my research assistant Judith Mara Kish, for the massive job of scanning, proofing, and editing the previously published articles and for other invaluable help; Norris Lacy, for his unfailingly tactful, patient, and courteous guidance and editing throughout the project; and, finally but most important, my husband, James Mahoney, for reading countless versions of the Introduction, for providing active assistance with modern French fiction, and for his sustained emotional support through a quest that seemed as long as any in medieval romance.

NOTES

Works that are cited in full in the Select Bibliography appear in these Notes in abbreviated form. Studies designated by an asterisk are included in this volume.

1. One can only speculate on the reasons for this. One possibility is that once the Grail became identified with the Eucharist, the narrative tradition came into conflict with the Church's desire in the twelfth century to regulate and control the performance of the Mass and to limit the administration of the sacraments exclusively to the clergy, who were males. See Miri Rubin, *Corpus Christi*, pp. 49–50, and "The Eucharist and the Construction of Medieval Identities," in *Culture and History, 1350–1600: Essays on English Communities, Identities and Writing*, ed. David Aers (Detroit: Wayne State University Press, 1992), pp. 46–50. The Grail procession in Chrétien de Troyes's *Perceval* would be highly threatening to such constructions of hierarchy and authority. In the Vulgate *Queste*, it is true, Bishop Josephes (the first bishop of Christendom) administers the Eucharist to the select three; but this literary tradition conflicts with the historical tradition of apostolic succession. Furthermore, endorsing Joseph of Arimathea's line might strengthen the British Church to a degree that would make Rome uncomfortable.

2. Foreword, *Parzival*, trans. Hatto, p. 7.

3. They are known as the First or Gawain Continuation (ca. 1200), the Second or Perceval Continuation (written shortly after the First), the Third Continuation, by Manessier (ca. 1230), and the Continuation by Gerbert de Montreuil (also ca. 1230). Only one manuscript, B.N. fr. 12576, includes Chrétien's *Perceval* as well as all four Continuations, thus providing a "complete" *Perceval* romance of some 63,550 lines.

4. See *Glenys Witchard Goetinck, "The Quest for Origins," and *Peredur*, pp. 302–03.

5. A Dutch version of the prose *Joseph* also exists, Jacob van Maerlant's *Historie van den Grale* ("History of the Grail"), written in verse, ca. 1261.

6. Also should be mentioned the French poem *Sone de Nansai* ("Dream of Nansai"), composed in the second half of the thirteenth century. Set in the period of the Crusades, it has no connection with Arthur's court, bringing its eponymous

hero to Norway. However, it does tell the story of Joseph of Arimathea, who gets wounded in the thighs in Norway and acquires the title of the Fisher King. Thus the Maimed King and the Waste Land motifs appear, as well as the Grail, in a non-Arthurian context. See Loomis, *The Grail*, pp. 135 ff.

7. It has also been called the Pseudo-Map Cycle, since Walter Map is claimed as author of two of the branches, despite the fact that he died in 1209. The five branches of the Vulgate Cycle are *L'Estoire del Saint Graal*, mentioned above, *L'Estoire de Merlin* ("The Story of Merlin"), the *Lancelot en prose* ("The prose Lancelot"), *La Queste del Saint Graal* ("The Quest of the Holy Grail"), and *La Mort Artu* ("The Death of Arthur"). The first two branches were composed after the others, though they stand first in the chronological sequence of the narrative.

8. E.g, the German prose *Die Gral-Queste* ("The Grail Quest," early thirteenth century), included in the *Prosa-Lancelot* compilation, a condensed version of the same, Ulrich Füetrer's *Buch von dem Heiligen Gral* ("Book of the Holy Grail"); the Dutch verse *Die Queeste vanden Heiligen Grale* ("The Quest of the Holy Grail," ca. 1300), included in the *Lancelot-Compilatie* ("Lancelot Compilation:); the Italian prose *Inchiesta del Sangradale* ("Quest of the Holy Grail," early fourteenth century); the Catalan prose *Storia del Sant Grasal* ("Story of the Holy Grail," fourteenth century); the Irish prose *Lorgaireacht an tSoidhigh Naomhtha* ("Quest of the Holy Grail," fifteenth century); the Welsh *Y Seint Greal* ("The Holy Grail," fifteenth century), which contains a translation of the Vulgate *Queste* and the *Perlesvaus*. See Reiss, Reiss, and Taylor, eds. *Arthurian Legend and Literature: An Annotated Bibliography*, for details of the many versions. The Italian prose *Tavola Ritonda* ("The Round Table," ca. 1325) includes an abbreviated and perfunctory version of the Quest, but it is an independent version chiefly based on the French Prose *Tristan*, so should not be included in this list.

9. Two "witnesses" to Malory's text exist, the Winchester Manuscript, discovered in 1934, and Caxton's printing of 1485. The two versions are significantly different in numbering: the Winchester Manuscript is divided into eight Books or Tales, whereas Caxton's is divided into twenty-one Books, usually indicated by Roman numerals. I follow the Winchester numbering and titles of the Books, as edited by Eugène Vinaver, *The Works of Sir Thomas Malory*, 3 vols., 3rd ed., rev. P.J.C. Field (Oxford: Oxford University Press, 1990).

10. Bogdanow, "The *Suite du Merlin*," pp. 325-35.

11. As the Comparative Table that follows this Introduction demonstrates, the Question Failure and the Dolorous Stroke never exist together in the same text.

12. See O'Gorman, "The *Gospel of Nicodemus*," p. 120.

13. See Lozachmeur, "Recherches sur les origines," 45–63, and *Goetinck, "The Quest for Origins."

14. "The Coming of the Grail," in C.S. Lewis, *Arthurian Torso*, p. 73 and n. 2.

15. *Alison Stones, in "Seeing the Grail," suggests that an illumination in the *Queste* in which the Grail vessel is touched to the king's genitals might well have given Weston the idea.

16. See Jean-Claude Lozachmeur and Shigemi Sasaki, "Researches on the Mystery of the Grail, Part II: Modern Critical Hypotheses," *Avalon to Camelot*, 1, no. 4 (1984), 20–23. Geoffrey Ashe argues that it is Celtic Christianity, dominated and superseded by Roman Catholicism, that is evoked in the Grail story, which accounts for the sense of nostalgia, the loss of a golden age: see "The Grail of the Golden Age," in Matthews, ed. *At the Table of the Grail*, pp. 11–28.

17. Loomis, "The Origin of the Grail Legends," pp. 274–94.

18. Loomis, "The Origin of the Grail Legends," p. 294, and *The Grail*, pp. 60–61.

19. Pickens, p. 232.

20. See Busby, pp. 46–54.

21. Baumgartner, "*Del Graal Cui L'An Servoit*," pp. 137–44. See also Pickens, pp. 275, 283–85.

22. In allegorical interpretation, events are given a spiritual meaning: when Bohort dreams of a pelican piercing its own breast in order to feed its offspring with blood, the pelican represents Christ. In typological interpretation, events are projected onto the plane of universal sacred history, as when Galaad prefigures the Messiah. For the classic explanation of typology, or "figura," see Erich Auerbach, "Typological Symbolism in Medieval Literature," *Yale French Studies*, 9 (1952), 3–10, also "Figura," *Scenes from the Drama of European Literature* (1959; Minneapolis: University of Minnesota Press, 1984), pp. 11–76.

23. Perceval's temptations are reworked in the Perceval section of the Vulgate *Queste*, as is Boors's dilemma in the Bohort section. The battle between Perceval and Ector reappears at the end of the Vulgate *Lancelot*, also in the Post-Vulgate prose *Tristan*, which is why it also appears at the end of the Tristram section of Malory's *Morte Darthur*.

24. See Baumgartner, "From Lancelot to Galahad," pp. 20–21. Manuscript illuminators also shared in the process of christianizing the Grail. Unable to think retroactively of the Grail as an ordinary object, the illuminators of the Continuations progressively identified it as a liturgical vessel: see Baumgartner, "Les scènes du Graal et leur illustration," in *Les Manuscrits de Chrétien de Troyes*, I, 489–503. Only one manuscript of the *Conte du Graal* proper depicts the Grail (see *Alison Stones, "Seeing the Grail.")

25. Though Joseph of Arimathea appears in the canonical Gospels, the episode of his imprisonment by the Jews and miraculous release comes from the apocryphal *Gospel of Nicodemus*. See Zbigniew Izydorczyk, Introduction, *The*

Medieval *"Gospel of Nicodemus,"* pp. 4–5, and O'Gorman, "The *Gospel of Nicodemus,"* pp. 120–22.

26. See the sophisticated discussion by Joan Tasker Grimbert.

27. The contradiction between this prophecy and the statement that Alain remained a virgin is not explained in this text.

28. It has never been ascribed to Robert, but it fits his description of the third part of the trilogy.

29. See Antonia Gransden, "The Growth of the Glastonbury Traditions and Legends in the Twelfth Century," in Gransden, *Legends, Traditions and History in Medieval England* (London: Hambledon Press, 1992), pp. 153–74, esp. p. 170. Gransden suggests that the Glastonbury monks invited Gerald to attend the exhumation and to write it up afterwards. For fuller discussions of the tradition, see Carley, *Chronicle,* Introduction, pp. xlviii–lvii, Loomis, *Grail,* pp. 249–70, and Lagorio, "The Evolving Legend," 209–31.

30. Note that Hardyng's *Chronicle* also endorses the tradition that Joseph was buried at Glastonbury (see *Felicity Riddy, "Chivalric Nationalism and the Holy Grail").

31. See Lacy, *"Perlesvaus* and the *Perceval* Palimpsest," 263–71.

32. See Nitze, *"Perlesvaus,"* p. 265.

33. See Thomas E. Kelly, pp. 91–102.

34. Nigel Bryant, introd. and trans., *The High Book of the Grail: A Translation of the Thirteenth-Century Romance "Perlesvaus"* (Cambridge, Eng.: D.S. Brewer, 1978, 1996), pp. 5–7.

35. See E. Jane Burns, Introduction, Lacy, ed. *Lancelot-Grail,* I, xix–xxv.

36. Michelle Szkilnik argues that the *Estoire* was written not just to provide origins for events in the *Queste,* but also to show readers how the *Queste* should be read. See *"L'Estoire del Saint Graal:* réécrire la *Queste,"* pp. 294–305.

37. See Burns, *Lancelot-Grail,* I, xxii–xxv and *Arthurian Fictions,* pp. 35–54, for a discussion of the fictitious multiple authors of the Vulgate.

38. By eating the body and blood, the Christian becomes one body with Christ, incorporated into the Christian community. For a full discussion of the practice and symbolism of the Eucharistic sacrament in medieval times, see Rubin, *Corpus Christi,* Chap. 1, esp. pp. 35–63.

39. This explanation is very popular in Grail accounts, appearing in Helinandus, Robert de Boron's *Joseph* (where it is Petrus who supplies the spurious etymology), the Didot-*Perceval,* and elsewhere (see *Emma Jung and Marie Louise von Franz, "The Central Symbol of the Legend: The Grail as Vessel").

40. To be precise, the *Estoire* repeats the description composed earlier for the *Queste.*

41. This becomes four hundred years in the *Queste.*

42. Gauvain is "too caught up in a literal vision of the world, . . . more dazzled by the beauty of the lady carrying the Grail than by the Grail itself," observes Baumgartner, "From Lancelot to Galahad," p. 21.

43. See Baumgartner, "From Lancelot to Galahad," for an interesting discussion of the rearrangement of lineages in the process of the legend's transformation from Chrétien's poem and its Continuations to the Vulgate Cycle.

44. See above, note 22, for a definition of these terms.

45. Pauphilet, p. 26. See also Matarasso, *Redemption*, esp. pp. 205–41. In her Introduction to her translation, *The Quest of the Holy Grail*, Matarasso describes the *Queste* as "a spiritual fable," and "an anti-romance" (pp. 9, 15).

46. Baumgartner, *L'Arbre et le pain*, pp. 21, 142–54, and "Les Aventures du Graal," pp. 23–28.

47. Virginity is at a premium in this text. As Jill Mann suggests, "It is because the intact, inviolate, virgin body is an image of spiritual wholeness that sexual temptations loom so large in the adventures of the Grail knights" ("Malory and the Grail Legend," p. 214). Mann is discussing the narrative common to both the *Queste* and Malory's "Sankgreal." For a fully theorized discussion of the issue of gender in the *Queste*, see E. Jane Burns, "Devilish Ways: Sexing the Subject in the *Queste del Saint Graal*," *Arthuriana* 8.2 (1998), 11–32.

48. Mann, "Malory and the Grail Legend," p. 210. See also Robert S. Sturges: Galahad's adventures "simply serve as rituals to be performed by the chosen one," p. 73.

49. There has been no preparation for these knights, who presumably appear so that the celebrants of the Mass will number twelve, in imitation of the disciples at the Last Supper.

50. This is another fictitious author ascription, since Map, a man of letters at the court of King Henry II of England, died in 1209, some sixteen to twenty years before the *Queste* was composed.

51. These interpretations are offered by Pauphilet (*Études*, p. 25), Gilson, Lot-Borodine, and Hamilton, respectively. For a thorough discussion, see Matarasso, "The Holy Grail: Its Meaning and Symbolism," in *Redemption*, pp. 180–204.

52. Ihle, p. 34.

53. Since, like many other texts, it was attributed to Robert de Boron, it is also known as "the Pseudo-Robert de Boron Cycle."

54. See Bogdanow, "The Post-Vulgate Cycle," in Lacy et al., *New Arthurian Encyclopedia*, for identification of the Old French fragments and Spanish and Portuguese texts on which the reconstruction is based. The romance presumably comprised an early history of the Grail (a version similar to the Vulgate *Estoire*), followed by a prose *Merlin*, to which was added the *Suite du Merlin* ("Continua-

tion of Merlin"), some sequences from the first version of the Prose *Tristan*, some sequences from the Agravain section of the Vulgate *Lancelot*, and a *Queste* and a *Mort Artu*, both significantly different from the Vulgate versions. Bogdanow is engaged on an edition of the romance. The text used for this discussion is the translation by Martha Asher of the Post-Vulgate Cycle, Parts I-III, in Lacy, ed., *Lancelot-Grail*, Vols. IV and V.

55. The *Suite* survives in two Old French manuscripts, as well as in the following redactions: Malory's "Tale of King Arthur," the Galician-Portuguese *Livro de Josep Abarimatia* ("The Book of Joseph of Arimathea"), and the Spanish *El Baladro del Sabio Merlin* ("The Cry of Merlin the Wise"). The post-Vulgate *Queste* is found in some newly discovered Old French fragments and the translations into Galician-Portuguese and Spanish, *A Demanda do Sancto Graal* (In Quest of the Holy Grail) and *La Demanda del Sancto Grial* (The Quest of the Holy Grail), respectively. See Bogdanow, "The Post-Vulgate Cycle," in Lacy et al., *New Arthurian Encyclopedia*, for fuller details.

56. The Vulgate Christ was clearly the crucified Christ, naked and wounded in the hands, feet, and body; the Post-Vulgate presents the risen Christ, in white robes, with a face so bright they cannot look at it.

57. Hatto, Foreword, *Parzival*, trans. Hatto. Quotations are taken from this translation.

58. Their son is named Prester John, and all subsequent kings of the land have the same name. The Grail, however, remains in the West. In a long stanzaic romance known as *Der Jüngere Titurel* ("The Later Titurel"), written ca. 1270 and based on *Titurel* fragments by Wolfram von Eschenbach, a certain Albrecht describes the early history of the Grail family and the erection of the Grail Temple by Titurel, and finishes, quite unlike *Parzival*, with the removal of the Grail to India, the realm of Prester John. See *Titurel: Wolfram of Eschenbach*, transl. and studies, Charles E. Passage (New York: Frederick Ungar, 1984), Chaps. 1 and 2.

59. Groos, p. 121.

60. Hatto translates this term as "Templars"; see p. 438.

61. Northcott, pp. 409–28.

62. See Poag, pp. 86–88.

63. Sidney Johnson, "Wolfram von Eschenbach," in Lacy et al., *New Arthurian Encyclopedia*, p. 522.

64. Introduction, "The Story of Peredur, Son of Efrog," in *The Romance of Arthur II*, p. 29.

65. See Lozachmeur, "Recherches sur les origines," 45–48, 54; Goetinck, *Peredur*, pp. 302–03, and the detailed discussion in *Goetinck, "The Quest for Origins."

66. See Idris Llewelyn Foster, "*Gereint, Owein*, and *Peredur*," in Loomis, ed. *ALMA*, pp.199–201.

67. See Lozachmeur, "Recherches sur les origines," 45–63, and *Goetinck, "The Quest for Origins."

68. Though it was presumably seen as a Grail romance by the scribes who included it with a Welsh translation of the Vulgate *Queste* in a manuscript known as *Y Seint Greal*. See Lloyd-Morgan, pp. 78–81.

69. And, indeed, medieval literary texts in general. See Douglas Kelly, "*Translatio Studii*: Translation, Adaptation, and Allegory in Medieval French Literature," *Philological Quarterly*, 57 (1978), 287–310.

70. Malory's colophon states that the work was finished in the ninth year of the reign of King Edward IV. See above, note 9, for a discussion of the two "witnesses" to the text: the Winchester Manuscript, discovered in 1934 and edited by Eugène Vinaver (third edition by P.J.C. Field); and Caxton's printing of 1485, titled *Le Morte D'Arthur*. As previously noted, Vinaver's numbering of books rather than Caxton's is followed here, and page references are to the three-volume third edition.

71. R.M. Lumiansky, "Sir Thomas Malory's *Le Morte Darthur* 1947–1987: Author, Title, Text," *Speculum* 62 (1987), 878–97, and P.J.C. Field, *The Life and Times of Sir Thomas Malory* (Woodbridge, Eng.: D.S. Brewer, 1993), represent the two main schools of thought on this issue.

72. Malory's own description of the "Tale of the Sankgreal" is that it was "breffly drawyn oute of Freynshe" (1037.9).

73. For good discussions of Malory's style, see P.J.C. Field, *Romance and Chronicle: A Study of Malory's Prose Style* (London: Barrie and Jenkins, 1971), and Mark Lambert, *Malory: Style and Vision in "Le Morte Darthur"* (New Haven: Yale University Press, 1975), esp. Chap. 2.

74. See Marylyn Jackson Parins, ed. *Malory: The Critical Heritage* (London: Routledge, 1988), Introduction, pp. 1–39, for the reception of Malory's work through the last five centuries; also Barry Gaines, *Sir Thomas Malory: An Anecdotal Bibliography of Editions, 1485–1985* (New York: AMS Press, 1990).

75. See Murray J. Evans, "*Ordinatio* and Narrative Links: The Impact of Malory's Tales as a 'hoole book,'" in Spisak, ed. *Studies in Malory*, pp. 29–52, esp. pp. 32–36.

76. Among other small changes, Malory omits the warning voices that tell Balain in the *Suite* not to enter the Grail chamber or to touch the Lance; the terrible consequences of the Stroke are therefore more inexplicable.

77. See Mann, "'Taking the Adventure,'" pp. 71–91.

78. A common error made by critics of Malory and such redactors as T.H.White is to identify this lady with Elaine, the Grail Princess, but comparison with the source shows that the two are separate figures.

79. See the discussion of Charles Williams's poetry in the Introduction. Pelles is presumably the son of Pellam of Lystenoyse (corresponding to Pellehan in the Old French), who was rashly wounded by Balin (but not, in Malory, through the thighs). Pellam is usually identified as the Maimed King, but occasionally Pelles is also given that designation (863.8, 989–90), possibly because of the lingering confusion between the Vulgate and Post-Vulgate references.

80. See Ihle's careful comparative analysis throughout Chapter 4, and *Dhira B. Mahoney, "The Truest and Holiest Tale."

81. See *Mahoney, "The Truest and Holiest Tale."

82. For the relationship between George Frederic Watts's painting and the poem, see Marilyn Lincoln Board, "Art's Moral Mission: Reading G.F. Watts's *Sir Galahad*," in Mancoff, ed. *Arthurian Revival: Essays*, pp. 132–54, and *Debra N. Mancoff, " 'Pure Hearts and Clean Hands.' "

83. See Taylor and Brewer, p. 69. The ideal of self-disciplined dedication to a noble cause in a hostile environment also lent itself easily to young colonial administrators in the far reaches of the British Empire: see, e.g., Mark Girouard, *The Return to Camelot: Chivalry and the English Gentleman* (New Haven: Yale University Press, 1981), Chap.14, Knights of the Empire.

84. See Hallam Tennyson, *Alfred Lord Tennyson: A Memoir by His Son*, 2 vols. (New York: Macmillan, 1987), I, 456–57.

85. Staines, 747.

86. See the discussion by *Linda K. Hughes, "Scandals of Faith and Gender."

87. Kay J. Walter and Terence Allan Hoagwood, Introduction, *Cornish Ballads and Other Poems, by Robert Stephen Hawker, A Facsimile Reproduction of the 1869 Edition* (Delmar, NY: Scholars Facsimiles and Reprints, 1994), pp. 8–9.

88. See Taylor and Brewer, p. 87.

89. Hawker later explained that these were references to the Battle of Waterloo and the Armstrong Gun (Taylor and Brewer, p. 87).

90. See Walter and Hoagwood, Introduction, *Cornish Ballads*, pp. 8–10.

91. Such crafts included stained glass, embroidery, painted furniture, hand-knotted rugs, tapestries, wallpaper, tiles, and woven and printed textiles, executed by "The Firm" (Morris, Marshall, Faulkner, & Company). Morris also practiced medieval calligraphy, producing his own illuminated manuscripts, and his life-long interest in decorated books culminated in the establishment of the Kelmscott Press, for which he designed type and borders and for which Burne-Jones made exquisite woodblock illustrations. See the Catalogue of the William Morris Centenary Exhibition at the Victoria and Albert Museum, London, 1996: *William Morris*, ed. Linda Parry (London: Philip Wilson Publishers and The Victoria and Albert Museum, 1996).

92. For a full account of the association between Rossetti, Morris, and Burne-Jones, as well as the Oxford Union project, see Mancoff, *The Arthurian Revival in Victorian Art*, Chaps. 5 and 6, esp. pp. 155–65.

93. See Mancoff, *The Arthurian Revival in Victorian Art*, Pl. III, and Scherer, p. 73. For discussions, see *Mancoff, "'Pure Hearts and Clean Hands,'" and Scherer, pp. 71–74.

94. See *Mancoff, "'Pure Hearts and Clean Hands,'" Fig. 14.7. Color plates abound; two particularly fine reproductions of "The Departure" and "The Attainment" are printed in *William Morris*, pp. 294–95 (note 91, above.).

95. For a lively discussion of the novel, see Taylor and Brewer, pp. 169–74.

96. Mark Twain, *A Connecticut Yankee at King Arthur's Court* (1889; Harmondsworth, Eng.: Penguin, 1971), p. 97.

97. See Alan Lupack, "American Arthurian Authors," pp. 165–66.

98. The apocalyptic feeling of both this poem and Robinson's *Merlin* may well derive from the poet's disillusion with World War I; see Valerie M. Lagorio, "Edward Arlington Robinson: Arthurian Pacificist," in Lagorio and Day, eds. *King Arthur Through the Ages*, II, 165–79.

99. Abbey, quoted in Scherer, p. 75.

100. Baxter, p. 20. See also O'Shaughnessy, 298–312.

101. Lanier, particularly, considered Southern chivalry a direct descendant from that portrayed in Malory: see Parins, p. 16, cited in note 74 above.

102. Alan Lupack, "Beyond the Model," 215–34.

103. See Kevin J. Harty, "*The Knights of the Square Table*: The Boy Scouts and Thomas Edison make an Arthurian Film," *Arthuriana* 4 (1994), 313-23.

104. See Beckett, Chap. 1, for an account of the evolution of Wagner's opera.

105. Jack M. Stein, *Richard Wagner and the Synthesis of the Arts* (Detroit: Wayne State University Press, 1960), pp. 203-04. *Bühnenweihfestspiel* has also been translated as "Stage Dedication Festival Play": see the translation by Andrew Porter in Nicholas John, ed. *"Parsifal": Richard Wagner*, p. 83.

106. Stein, p. 205.

107. Amfortas and Parsifal are Wagner's preferred spellings. He thought, erroneously, that Parsifal was derived from the Persian "Fal parsi,"or "pure fool" (Beckett, p. 39).

108. "Rein" can also be translated as "pure," or "blameless." This thematic term resonates through the opera, reflecting all these meanings.

109. "'Parsifal': Words and Music," in John, ed. *"Parsifal": Richard Wagner*, p. 54.

110. Shichtman, "Whom Does the Grail Serve?," p. 285.

111. See the individual entries and Richard W. Kimpel, "German Arthurian Literature (Modern)," in Lacy et al., *New Arthurian Encyclopedia.*

112. See Kevin J. Harty, "The Arthurian Legends on Film: An Overview," in Harty, ed. *Cinema Arthuriana*, pp. 3–4.

113. See Ulrich Müller, "Blank, Syberberg, and the German Arthurian Tradition," trans. Julie Giffin, in Harty, ed. *Cinema Arthuriana*, pp. 157–68; also Hans-Jürgen Syberberg, *Parsifal, ein Filmessay* (Munich: Heyne, 1982).

114. For detailed surveys, see Kimpel, "German Arthurian Literature (Modern)" and Norris J. Lacy, "French Arthurian Literature (Modern)" in Lacy et al., *New Arthurian Encyclopedia.* Recent treatments of the legend in German are also discussed by Werner Wunderlich, "The Arthurian Legend in German Literature of the Nineteen-Eighties," *Studies in Medievalism*, 3 (1991), 423–42. French novelists will be discussed in a later section of this Introduction.

115. Weston, p. 203. See pp. 203–09 for a summing up of Weston's argument.

116. *Charles Moorman, *Arthurian Triptych*, p. 144. For the concept of the "objective correlative," see Eliot's essay, "Hamlet and His Problems," first published in *The Sacred Wood* (1920).

117. I am indebted to my colleague Susan McCabe, viva voce, for this description.

118. But see *Moorman, who considers it essentially religious: *Arthurian Triptych*, pp. 146 ff.

119. "Malory and the Grail Legend," *Dublin Review*, April 1944, reprinted in *The Image of the City and Other Essays*, pp. 186–94. Other essays in the last section of this collection are also illuminating in connection with the ideas Williams developed in his poems.

120. The separate editions are *Taliessin Through Logres* (London: Oxford University Press, 1938) and *The Region of the Summer Stars* (London: Nicholson and Watson, 1944). Lewis's discussion in *Arthurian Torso* suggests the order in which the poems should be read as a continuous work. For further studies of the poems read according to Lewis's scheme, see Moorman, *Arthurian Triptych*, Chap. 3, esp. pp. 38–51; Taylor and Brewer, pp. 250–61; and *Karl Heinz Göller, "From Logres to Carbonek."

121. Williams took this sixth-century figure from the *Mabinogion*, as translated by Lady Charlotte Guest.

122. This is Williams's preferred spelling.

123. See "Notes on the Arthurian Myth," in *The Image of the City*, p. 176, also "Malory and the Grail Legend," p. 190, n. 1.

124. These symbols, taken from Wordsworth's *Prelude*, represent respectively logic or Euclidean geometry and poetry or creativity. See *Göller, "From Logres to Carbonek."

125. See also the discussion in *Göller, "From Logres to Carbonek."

126. See Anne Ridler, Introduction, *The Image of the City*, pp. lxi–lxii.

127. This was revised and reissued in 1933 as *The Holy Grail: Its Legends and Symbolism.* Waite provides detailed discussions of the many Grail texts and considers rival arguments about origins, but emphasizes, ultimately, the sacramental nature of the Grail.

128. Williams prefers this spelling.

129. Prester John is a legendary figure whose Grail connection derives from Wolfram von Eschenbach's *Parzival*, where he is born to Parzival's half-brother Fierefiz and the Grail-maiden Repanse de Schoye after they journey to India. See above, note 58.

130. Thompson, *The Return from Avalon*, p. 27.

131. It is clear that Powys read extensively in Arthurian sources, including texts such as *Perlesvaus* (the bald Mad Bet recalls the Maiden of the Cart) and the Didot-*Perceval* (his Welsh antiquary puzzles over the term *esplumoir*, which is Merlin's final abode in that text).

132. John Cowper Powys, *A Glastonbury Romance* (1933; London: Macdonald, 1955), pp. 1116–17. That the fifth shape is not revealed may be an inverted allusion to *Perlesvaus*, where Arthur sees the Grail in five forms, only the last of which is described.

133. For a full survey, see *Raymond H. Thompson, "The Grail in Modern Fiction."

134. Though *The Ill-Made Knight* was written in 1940, the whole tetralogy was not published till 1958, for reasons described by Sylvia Townsend Warner in "The Story of the Book," her Prologue to T.H. White, *The Book of Merlyn* (Austin: University of Texas Press, 1977). White's hatred of war and disillusionment about the human race may well have contributed to the note of disillusion in his account of the Quest.

135. Lancelot is barred from the Grail chamber while the three elect celebrate Mass within. White simplifies the story by conflating two separate events in Malory's "Sankgreal" and by making the priest Joseph rather than his son.

136. Note, however, that *J. Donald Crowley and Sue Mitchell Crowley, in "Walker Percy's Grail," see Percy's world as a postmodern one.

137. See Bugge, pp. 175–87, reprinted in *Lancelot and Guinevere: A Casebook*, ed. Lori J. Walters (New York: Garland, 1996), pp. 181–91.

138. For an excellent definition of the distinction between the two terms, see "Modernism and Postmodernism" in Jeremy Hawthorn, *Concise Glossary of Contemporary Literary Theory* (London: Edward Arnold, 1992).

139. See Jean Baudrillard, "Simulacra and Simulations," in *Selected Writings*, ed. Mark Poster (Stanford: Stanford University Press, 1988).

140. Donald Barthelme, *The King* (New York: Harper and Row, 1990), p. 130.

141. Sims, 42–47.

142. Julien Gracq, *The Castle of Argol*, trans. Louise Varèse (Venice, CA: Lapis Press, 1991), "Notice to the Reader," pp. 169–73.

143. Julien Gracq, *Le Roi pêcheur* (1948; rpt. Mayenne, France: Joseph Floch, 1970).

144. See Robert M. Henkels, Jr., *Robert Pinget: The Novel as Quest* (University, AL: University of Alabama Press, 1979), Chap. 8.

145. Henkels, pp. 51–52.

146. René Barjavel, *L'Enchanteur* (Paris: Denoël, 1984), p. 15.

147. Wlad Godzich argues that the Monty Python people have found an ingeniously arbitrary (and temporary) answer to the problem that the Grail cycle is itself "unfinished, and interminable" (81).

148. Shichtman, "Whom Does the Grail Serve?," p. 292.

149. The scenes were filmed at Petra, the ancient city in southern Jordan.

150. See the detailed analysis of technique by *Linda Williams, "Eric Rohmer and the Holy Grail."

151. Rider, Hull, and Smith, p. 53.

152. Rider, Hull, and Smith, pp. 42–45.

153. See *Martin B. Shichtman, "Hollywood's New Weston." For a more positive view of Boorman's film, see Lacy, "Mythopoeia in *Excalibur*," in Harty, ed., *Cinema Arthuriana*, pp. 121–34, esp. pp. 127–29.

154. See the thoughtful analysis of the film by Osberg, 194–224, esp. 208–09 for the account of the Fisher King myth.

155. Norris J. Lacy, interview in *Quest for the Holy Grail, Ancient Mysteries with Leonard Nimoy* (A &E, Phoenix, 28 Aug.1997). For the fetishizing of the Grail symbol by occultist historians and pop theorists during the Nazi regime and in recent years, see Mary Baine Campbell, "Finding the Grail: Fascist Aesthetics and Mysterious Objects," in *King Arthur's Modern Return*, ed. Debra N. Mancoff (New York: Garland, 1998), 213–25.

156. The French countered by invoking the conversion resulting from the voyage to Marseilles of Mary Magdalene, Martha, and Lazarus. See Lagorio, "The Evolving Legend," 220–23.

157. See *Felicity Riddy, "Chivalric Nationalism."

158. Helen Adolf was the first to make the historical connection between the Grail romances and the Crusaders, whose goal was the freeing of the Holy Sepulcher; the argument is provocatively developed by Stephen Knight, who argues that the whole literary tradition becomes a compensation for the loss of the holy places.

159. See Debra N. Mancoff, "Visual Arts," in Lacy et al., *New Arthurian Encyclopedia*.

160. As *Janina P. Traxler argues, even Perceval's sister has to die to get to Sarras.

161. See, for example, *Emma Jung and Marie-Louise von Franz, "The Central Symbol of the Legend: The Grail as Vessel." According to Helen Luke in "The Return of Dindrane," in Matthews, ed., *At the Table of the Grail*, pp. 91–110, Charles Williams also developed this theme in "Taliessin in The Rose Garden" and "The Last Voyage." Luke suggests that "the menstrual blood of woman is a continual reminder of the truth that after the Fall, after the split in creation [between male and female], there can be no 'return,' no healing of the split, without sacrifice, without the giving of blood. If the woman or the feminine in man does not 'bleed' there is no creation in this world" (p. 99).

162. See Rosalyn Rossignol, "The Holiest Vessel: Maternal Aspects of the Grail," *Arthuriana* 5 (1995), 52–61.

163. Shichtman, "Whom Does the Grail Serve?," pp. 283–97.

164. The chalice is open, a vessel to drink from, whereas the purpose of the ciborium is concealment of the host.

Comparative Table of Medieval Texts

Text	Language and Date	Questers	Grail	Fisher King/ Maimed King	Waste Land	Question Test
Chrétien de Troyes, *Perceval*	Old French verse, 1180–90	Perceval	Serving dish, holding a Mass wafer	Perceval's cousin, wounded in battle	Land will be in turmoil because of question failure	Perceval fails to ask the healing question
Robert de Boron, *Joseph*	Old French verse, 1191–1202	None	Vessel from Last Supper and holding Christ's blood	The Rich Fisherman (Bron)—not sick or wounded	None	None
Perlesvaus	Old French prose, 1200–10	Perlesvaus; Gauvain, Lancelot, Artus	Vessel holding Christ's blood	Perlesvaus's uncle, sick but not wounded	Kingdom is in state of war because of question failure before story began	Perlesvaus failed before story began; Gauvain fails, and Lancelot never sees the Grail
Wolfram von Eschenbach, *Parzival*	Middle High German verse, 1200–10	Parzival	A precious stone	Anfortas, Parzival's uncle, wounded in punishment for sexual sin	None	Parzival fails on the first visit, but succeeds on second visit
Peredur	Middle Welsh prose, 13th century	Peredur	Severed head on platter	Peredur's uncle, lame	Land is in state of war because of Peredur's failure to ask question	Peredur fails to ask about the head, but it is identified at end of narrative
Vulgate *Estoire*	Old French prose, 1215–35	None	Vessel ("escuele") from Last Supper and holding Christ's blood	Rich Fisherman (Alain)— not sick or wounded	None	None
Vulgate *Queste*	Old French prose, 1215–35	Chiefly Galaad, Bohort, Perceval; Lancelot	Dish (escuele) holding Paschal Lamb at Last Supper	Pellehan, Pelles's father, wounded by Lance when he tries to seize the sword on the ship	Caused by Dolorous Stroke (killing of Lambor by Varlan with sword)	None
Post-Vulgate *Queste*	Old French prose, 1230–40	Chiefly Galaad, Bohort, Perceval	Vessel, never identified	In *Suite du Merlin*, Pellehan, wounded by Dolorous Stroke (Balain)	Caused by Dolorous Stroke (Balain wielding Lance)	None
Sir Thomas Malory, "Tale of the Sankgreal"	Middle English prose, 1469–70	Galahad, Bors, Percival; Lancelot	"Dysshe" holding Paschal Lamb at Last Supper	In "Tale of King Arthur," Pellam, wounded by Dolorous Stroke (Balin)	Caused by Dolorous Stroke (Balin wielding Lance)	None

Select Bibliography

This bibliography does not list primary sources, nor does it include every title cited in notes. Articles designated by an asterisk (*) are reprinted in this volume, some in translation or revised form, as noted.

I. Useful Reference Works

Lacy, Norris J., Geoffrey Ashe, Sandra Ness Ihle, Marianne Kalinke, and Raymond H. Thompson, eds. *The New Arthurian Encyclopedia*. New York: Garland, 1991. [Hereafter Lacy et al., *New Arthurian Encyclopedia*]

Lacy, Norris J., gen. ed. *Lancelot-Grail: The Old French Arthurian Vulgate and Post-Vulgate in Translation*. 5 vols. New York: Garland, 1993–1996. [Hereafter Lacy, ed. *Lancelot-Grail*]

Loomis, Roger Sherman, ed. *Arthurian Literature in the Middle Ages: A Collaborative History*. Oxford: Clarendon Press, 1959. [Hereafter Loomis, ed. *ALMA*]

Reiss, Edmund, Louise Horner Reiss, and Beverly Taylor, eds. *Arthurian Legend and Literature: An Annotated Bibliography*. Vol I: *The Middle Ages*. New York: Garland, 1984.

II. Critical Studies

Abdoo, Sherlyn. "Woman as Grail in T.S. Eliot's *The Waste Land*." *The Centennial Review* 28 (1984), 48–60.

Adams, Alison, Armel H. Diverres, Karen Stern, and Kenneth Varty, eds. *The Changing Face of Arthurian Romance: Essays on Arthurian Prose Romances in Memory of Cedric E. Pickford*. Woodbridge, Eng.: Boydell, 1986.

Adolf, Helen. *"Visio Pacis"*: *Holy City and Grail: An Attempt at an Inner History of the Grail Legend.* Harrisburg: Pennsylvania State University Press, 1960.

Anderson, L. Flavia. *The Ancient Secret: In Search of the Holy Grail.* London: Gollancz, 1953.

Aronstein, Susan. "Rewriting Perceval's Sister: Eucharistic Vision and Typological Destiny in the *Queste del San Graal.*" *Women's Studies* 21 (1992), 211–30.

Atkinson, Stephen C.B. "Malory's Lancelot and the Quest of the Grail." In Spisak, ed. *Studies in Malory,* 129–52.

———. "'Now I se and undirstonde': The Grail Quest and the Education of Malory's Reader." In Braswell and Bugge, ed. *The Arthurian Tradition,* 90–108.

Auden, W.H. "The Quest Hero." *Texas Quarterly* 4.4 (1961), 81–93.

Baudry, Robert. "Julien Gracq et la légende du Graal." In *Actes du Colloque International sur Julien Gracq,* ed. and pref. Georges Cesbron. Angers: Press de l'Uuniversité d'Angers, 1981, 244–63.

Baumgartner, Emmanuèle. *L'Arbre et le pain: essai sur "La Queste del Saint Graal."* Paris: Société d'Edition d'Enseignement Supérieur, 1981.

———. "Les Aventures du Graal." In *Mélanges de langue et littérature françaises du Moyen Age et de la Renaissance offerts à Monsieur Charles Foulon,* ed. Michel Denis et al.. Rennes: Institut de Français, Université de Haute Bretagne, 1980, I, 23–28.

———. "From Lancelot to Galahad: The Stakes of Filiation." Trans. Arthur F. Crispin. In *The Lancelot-Grail Cycle: Text and Transformations,* ed. William W. Kibler. Austin: University of Texas Press, 1994, 14–30.

———. "*Del Graal Cui L'An Servoit*: variations sur un pronom." In *The Editor and the Text,* ed. Philip E. Bennett and Graham A. Runnalls. Edinburgh: Edinburgh University Press, 1990, 137–144.

———. "Les scènes du Graal et leur illustration dans les manuscrits du *Conte du Graal* et des *Continuations.*" In *Les Manuscrits de Chrétien de Troyes,* ed. Keith Busby, Terry Nixon, Alison Stones, and Lori Walters. 2 vols. Amsterdam: Rodopi, 1993, I, 489–503.

Baxter, Sylvester. *The Legend of the Holy Grail (as set forth in the frieze painted by Edwin A. Abbey for the Boston Public Library).* Boston: Curtis and Cameron, 1904.

Beatie, Bruce A. "The Broken Quest: The "Perceval" Romances of Chrétien de Troyes and Eric Rohmer." In Mancoff, ed. *The Arthurian Revival: Essays,* 248–65.

Beckett, Lucy. *Richard Wagner, "Parsifal."* Cambridge: Cambridge University Press, 1981.

Blank, Walter. "Die positive Utopie des Grals." In *Sprache—Literature—Kultur: Studien zu ihrer Geschichte im deutschen Süden und Westen. Wolfgang Kleiber zu seinem 60. Geburtstag gewidmet*, ed. Albrecht Greule and Uwe Ruberg. Stuttgart: Steiner, 1989, 337–53.

Bogdanow, Fanni. "An Interpretation of the Meaning and Purpose of the Vulgate *Queste del Saint Graal* in the Light of the Mystical Theology of St. Bernard." In Adams et al., eds. *The Changing Face of Arthurian Romance*, 23–46.

———. "The *Suite du Merlin* and the Post-Vulgate *Roman du Graal*." In Loomis, ed. *ALMA*, 325–35.

Bollard, John K. Introduction to "The Story of Peredur, Son of Efrog," in *The Romance of Arthur II*, ed. James J. Wilhelm. New York: Garland, 1986.

Bonney, William W. "Tennyson's Sublunary Grail." *Philological Quarterly* 72 (1993), 237–59.

Braswell, Mary F., and John Bugge, eds. *The Arthurian Tradition: Essays in Convergence*. Tuscaloosa: University of Alabama Press, 1988.

Brown, Arthur C.L. *The Origin of the Grail Legend*. Cambridge: Harvard University Press, 1943.

Bruce, J.D. *Evolution of Arthurian Romance From the Beginnings Down to the Year 1300*. Baltimore: Johns Hopkins Press, 1923.

Bugge, John. "Arthurian Myth Devalued in Walker Percy's *Lancelot*." In Braswell and Bugge, eds. *The Arthurian Tradition*, 175–87. Reprinted in *Lancelot and Guinevere: A Casebook*, ed. Lori J. Walters. New York: Garland, 1996, 181–91.

Bumke, Joachim. "Die Utopie des Grals: Eine Gesellschaft ohne Liebe?" *Literarische Utopie-Entwürfe*, ed. Hiltrud Gnug. Frankfurt: Suhrkamp, 1982, 70–79.

———. *Wolfram von Eschenbach*. Sammlung Metzler 36. 6th ed. Stuttgart: Steiner, 1991.

Burdach, Konrad. *Der Gral: Forschungen über seinen Ursprung und seinen Zusammenhang mit der Longinuslegende*. 1938. Darmstadt: Wissenschaftliche Buchgesellschaft, 1974.

Burns, E. Jane. *Arthurian Fictions: Rereading the Vulgate Cycle*. Columbus: Ohio State University Press, 1985.

———. Introduction. Lacy, ed. *Lancelot-Grail*, I, xv–xxxiii.

———. "Quest and Questioning in the *Conte du Graal*." *Romance Philology* 41 (1988), 251–66.

Busby, Keith. *Chrétien de Troyes, Perceval (Le Conte du Graal)*. Critical Guides to French Texts. London: Grant and Cutler, 1993.

Campbell, Joseph. "Indian Reflections in the Castle of the Grail." In *The Celtic Consciousness*, ed. and introd. Robert O'Driscoll. New York: Baziller; Toronto: McClelland & Stewart, 1982, 3–30.

Carley, James P., ed., and David Townsend, trans. *The Chronicle of Glastonbury Abbey: An Edition, Translation and Study of John of Glastonbury's Cronica sive Antiquitates Glastoniensis Ecclesie*. Woodbridge, Eng.: Brewer, 1985.

Cormier, Raymond J. "Rohmer's Grail Story: Anatomy of a French Flop." *Stanford French Review* 5 (1981), 391–96.

*Crowley, J. Donald, and Sue Mitchell Crowley. "Walker Percy's Grail." In Lagorio and Day, eds. *King Arthur Through the Ages*, II, 255–77.

Curtis, Jan. "Charles Williams's 'The Sister of Percivale': Towards a Theology of *Theotokos*." *Quondam et Futurus: A Journal of Arthurian Interpretations* 2. 4 (1992), 56–72.

Douchin-Shahin, Andrée. "La survivance du mythe du vingtième siècle: 'Le Roi pêcheur' de Julien Gracq." *Symposium* 40 (1986), 173–208.

Dragonetti, Roger. *La Vie de la lettre au Moyen Age: le Conte du Graal*. Paris: Editions du Seuil, 1980.

Evans, Murray J. "Camelot or Corbenic? Malory's New Blend of Secular and Religious Chivalry in the 'Tale of the Holy Grail.'" *English Studies in Canada* 8 (1982), 249–61.

Fein, Susanna Greer. "Thomas Malory and the Pictorial Interlace of *La Queste del Saint Graal*." *University of Toronto Quarterly* 46 (1977), 215–40.

Fisher, Lizette Andrews. *The Mystic Vision in the Grail Legend and in the "Divine Comedy."* New York: Columbia University Press, 1917.

Fiore, Sylvester. "Les Origines orientales de la legende du Graal." *Cahiers de Civilization Mediévale* 10 (1967), 207–19.

Frappier, Jean. *Autour du Graal*. Genève: Droz, 1977.

————. *Chrétien de Troyes et le mythe du graal: étude sur "Perceval ou Le Conte du Graal."* Paris: Société d'Edition d'Enseignement Supérieur, 1972.

*————. *Chrétien de Troyes: The Man and His Work*, trans. Raymond J. Cormier. Athens, OH: Ohio University Press, 1982. Translated from Jean Frappier, *Chrétien de Troyes: Connaissance Des Lettres*, 1968 [Ch. 7, *Perceval* or *Le Conte du Graal*, reprinted in this volume.]

Froula, Christine. "Eliot's Grail Quest: Or, the Lover, the Police, and the Waste Land." *Yale Review* 78 (1989), 235–53.

Fulweiler, Howard. "Tennyson's 'The Holy Grail': The Representation of Representation." *Renascence* 38 (1986), 144–59.

Furtado, Antonio L. "The Arabian Nights: Yet Another Source of the Grail Stories?" *Quondam et Futurus: A Journal of Arthurian Interpretations* 1.3 (Fall 1991), 25–40.

Gilson, Etienne. "La Mystique de la grace dans la *Queste del saint Graal.*" *Romania* 51 (1925), 321–47.

Godzich, Wlad. "The Holy Grail: The End of the Quest." *North Dakota Quarterly* 51 (1983), 74–81.

Goetinck, Glenys Witchard. *"Peredur": A Study of Welsh Tradition in the Grail Legends.* Cardiff: University of Wales Press, 1975.

*Göller, Karl-Heinz. "From Logres to Carbonek: The Arthuriad of Charles Williams." *Arthurian Literature* 1 (1981), 121–73 [reprinted, with deletions, in this volume.]

———. "Die Modernität von Charles Williams Arthur-Dichtung." *Inklings Jarhbuch für Literatur und Ästhetik* 3 (1985), 37–48.

Grimbert, Joan Tasker. "Testimony and 'Truth' in *Joseph d'Arimathie.*" *Romance Philology* 44 (1991), 379–401.

Groos, Arthur. *Romancing the Grail: Genre, Science, and Quest in Wolfram's "Parzival."* Ithaca, NY: Cornell University Press, 1995.

Hamilton, W.E.M.C. "L'Interprétation mystique de *La Queste del Saint Graal.*" *Neophilologus* 17 (1942), 94–110.

Harty, Kevin J. "Cinema Arthuriana: Translations of the Arthurian Legend to the Screen." *Arthurian Interpretations* 2.1 (1987), 95–113.

———, ed. *Cinema Arthuriana: Essays on Arthurian Film.* New York: Garland, 1991.

Hatto, A.T. Foreword to Wolfram von Eschenbach, *"Parzival,"* trans. A.T. Hatto. Harmondsworth, Eng.: Penguin, 1980.

Holmes, Urban T., and M. Amelia Klenke. *Chrétien, Troyes, and the Grail.* Chapel Hill: University of North Carolina Press, 1959.

Huchet, Jean-Charles. "Le nom et l'image: de Chrétien de Troyes à Robert de Boron." In *The Legacy of Chrétien de Troyes,* ed. Norris J. Lacy, Douglas Kelly, and Keith Busby. Amsterdam: Rodopi, 1988, 1–16.

Ihle, Sandra Ness. *Malory's Grail Quest: Invention and Adaptation in Medieval Prose Romance.* Madison: University of Wisconsin Press, 1983.

John, Nicholas, ed. *"Parsifal": Richard Wagner.* Opera Guide Series. London: English National Opera and The Royal Opera, 1986.

Johnson, Leslie Peter. "The Grail-Question in Wolfram and Elsewhere." *From Wolfram and Petrarch to Goethe and Grass: Studies in Literature in Honor of Leonard Forster.* Baden-Baden: Körner, 1982, 83–102.

*Jung, Emma, and Marie-Louise von Franz. *The Grail Legend.* 2nd ed. Trans. Andrea Dykes. Boston: Sigo Press; London: Coventure, 1986 [Chap. 7,

"The Central Symbol of the Legend: The Grail as Vessel," reprinted in this volume].

Kahane, Henry R., and Angelina Pietrangeli. *The Krater and the Grail: Hermetic Sources of the "Parzival."* Urbana: University of Illinois Press, 1965.

———. "Robert de Boron's *Joseph of Arimathea*: Byzantine Echoes in the Grail Myth." *Jarhbuch der Österreichischen Byzantinistik* 38 (1988), 327–38.

Kehl, D.G., and Allene Cooper. "Sangria in the Sangreal: *The Great Gatsby* as Grail Quest." *Rocky Mountain Review of Language and Literature* 47. 4 (1993), 203–17.

Keller, Joseph. "Paradigm Shifts in the Grail Scholarship of Jessie Weston and R.S. Loomis: A View from Linguistics." *Arthurian Interpretations* 1.2 (Spring 1987), 10–22.

Kelly, Thomas E. *Le Haut Livre du Graal: Perlesvaus, A Structural Study.* Geneva: Droz, 1974.

*Kennedy, Angus J. "Punishment in the *Perlesvaus*: The Theme of the Waste Land." In *Rewards and Punishments in the Arthurian Romances and Lyric Poetry of France: Essays presented to Kenneth Varty on the occasion of his sixtieth birthday*, ed. Peter J. Davies and Angus J. Kennedy. Woodbridge, Eng.: D.S. Brewer, 1987, 61–75.

Kennedy, Edward Donald. "John Hardyng and the Holy Grail." *Arthurian Literature* 8 (1989), 185–206.

*Elspeth Kennedy. "Failure in Arthurian Romance." *Medium Ævum* 50. 1 (1991), 21–32.

———. *Lancelot and the Grail: A Study of the Prose "Lancelot."* Oxford: Clarendon Press, 1986.

Knight, Stephen. "From Jerusalem to Camelot: King Arthur and the Crusades." In *Medieval Codicology, Iconography, Literature, and Translation: Studies for Keith Val Sinclair*, ed. Peter Rolfe Monks and D.D.R. Owen. Leiden: E.J. Brill, 1994, 223–32.

Kollmann, Judith. "Charles Williams' *Taliessin Through Logres* and *The Region of the Summer Stars*." In Lagorio and Day, eds. *King Arthur Through the Ages*, II, 180–206.

Lacy, Norris J. "*Perlesvaus* and the *Perceval* Palimpsest." *Philological Quarterly* 69 (1990), 263–71.

Lagorio, Valerie M. "The Evolving Legend of St. Joseph of Glastonbury." *Speculum* 46 (1971), 209–31.

———. "The Glastonbury Legends and the English Arthurian Grail Romances." *Neuphilologische-Mitteilungen* 79 (1978), 359–66.

———. "The *Joseph of Arimathie*: English Hagiography in Transition." *Medievalia et Humanistica* 6 (1975), 91–101.

Lagorio, Valerie M., and Mildred Day, eds. *King Arthur Through the Ages*. 2 vols. New York: Garland, 1990.

Leupin, Alexandre. *Le Graal et la littérature*. Lausanne: L'Age d'homme, 1982.

Lewis, C.S. *Arthurian Torso, containing the posthumous fragment of "The Figure of Arthur" by Charles Williams and a commentary on the Arthurian poems of Charles Williams*. London: Oxford University Press, 1948.

Littleton, C. Scott, and Linda A. Malcor. *From Scythia to Camelot: A Radical Reassessment of the Legends of King Arthur, The Knights of the Round Table, and the Holy Grail*. New York: Garland, 1994.

Lloyd-Morgan, Ceridwen. "Perceval in Wales: Late Medieval Welsh Grail Traditions." In Adams et al., eds. *The Changing Face of Arthurian Romance*, 78–91.

Locke, Frederick W. *The Quest for the Holy Grail: A Literary Study of a Thirteenth-Century French Romance*. Stanford: Stanford University Press, 1960.

Loomis, Roger Sherman. *The Grail: From Celtic Myth to Christian Symbol*. Cardiff: University of Wales Press, 1963.

———. "The Grail Story of Chrétien de Troyes as Ritual and Symbolism." *PMLA* 71 (1956), 840–52.

———. "The Origin of the Grail Legends." In Loomis, ed. *ALMA*, 274–94.

———. *Wales and the Arthurian Legend*. Cardiff: University of Wales Press, 1956.

Loomis, Roger Sherman, and Laura Hibbard Loomis. *Arthurian Legends in Medieval Art*. New York: MLA, 1938.

*Looze, Laurence N. de. "A Story of Interpretation: *The Queste del Saint Graal* as Metaliterature." *Romanic Review* 76 (1985), 129–47.

Lot-Borodine, Myrrha. "Les grands secrets du Saint-Graal dans la *Queste* du pseudo-Map." In Nelli, ed. *Lumière du Graal*, 151–74.

Lozachmeur, Jean-Claude. "Recherches sur les origines indo-européennes et ésotériques de la légende du Graal." *Cahiers de Civilization Médiévale* 30 (1987), 45–63.

Lozachmeur, Jean-Claude, and Shigemi Sasaki. "A Propos de deux hypothèses de R.S. Loomis," *Bibliographical Bulletin of the International Arthurian Society* 34 (1982), 206–21.

———. "Researches on the Mystery of the Grail, III: Components for a Solution to the Puzzle of the Grail." *Avalon to Camelot* 2 (1986), 37–40.

Lupack, Alan. "American Arthurian Authors: A Declaration of Independence." In Mancoff, ed. *The Arthurian Revival: Essays*, 155–73.

———. "Beyond the Model: Howard Pyle's Arthurian Books." *The Arthurian Yearbook* 1 (1991), 215–34.

Lupack, Barbara Tepa. "F. Scott Fitzgerald's 'Following of a Grail.'" *Arthuriana* 4 (1994), 334–47.

Luttrell, Claude. *The Creation of the First Arthurian Romance: A Quest.* London: Edward Arnold, 1974.

*Mahoney, Dhira B. "The Truest and Holiest Tale: Malory's Transformation of *La Queste del Saint Graal.*" In Spisak, ed. *Studies in Malory,* 109–28.

Mancoff, Debra N. *The Arthurian Revival in Victorian Art.* New York: Garland, 1990.

———. "Reluctant Redactor: William Dyce Reads the Legend." In *Culture and the King: The Social Implications of the Arthurian Legend. Essays in Honor of Valerie M. Lagorio,* ed. Martin B. Shichtman and James P. Carley. Albany: State University of New York Press, 1994, 254–73.

———, ed. *The Arthurian Revival: Essays on Form, Tradition, and Transformation.* New York: Garland, 1992.

Mann, Jill. "Malory and the Grail Legend." In *A Companion to Malory,* ed. Elizabeth Archibald and A.S.G. Edwards. Woodbridge, Eng.: D.S. Brewer, 1996, 203–20.

———. "'Taking the Adventure': Malory and the *Suite du Merlin.*" In *Aspects of Malory,* ed. Toshiyuki Takamiya and Derek Brewer. Woodbridge, Eng.: Brewer, 1981, rev. 1986, 71–91.

Marx, Jean. *La Légende arthurienne et le Graal.* Paris: Presses Universitaires de France, 1952.

———. *Nouvelles recherches sur la littérature arthurienne.* Paris: Klincksieck, 1965.

Masi, Michael. "King Arthur, the Grail Quest, and Late Medieval Spirituality." *Cithara: Essays in the Judaeo-Christian Tradition* 23 (1984), 16–24.

Matarasso, Pauline M. Introduction. *The Quest of the Holy Grail,* trans. Pauline M. Matarasso. Harmondsworth, Eng.: Penguin, 1969.

———. *The Redemption of Chivalry: A Study of the "Queste del Saint Graal."* Geneva: Droz, 1979.

Matthews, J.H. "Julien Gracq and the Theme of the Grail in Surrealism." *Romanic Review* 58 (1967), 95–108.

Matthews, John. *The Grail: Quest for the Eternal.* London: Thames and Hudson, 1981.

———, ed. *At the Table of the Grail: Magic and the Use of Imagination.* London: Routledge, 1984.

Méla, Charles. *La Reine et le Graal: la conjointure dans les romans du Graal, de Chrétien de Troyes au livre de Lancelot.* Paris: Editions du Seuil, 1984.

Meuwese, Martine. "Twelve Bleeding Tombs and Seven Flaming Hands: Text and Image in the Amsterdam *Estoire*." *The Arthurian Yearbook* 2 (1992), 135–58.

*Moorman, Charles. *Arthurian Triptych: Mythic Materials in Charles Williams, C.S. Lewis, and T.S. Eliot.* Berkeley: University of California Press, 1960 [Chap. 5, "T.S. Eliot," reprinted in this volume].

———. " 'The Tale of the Sankgreall': Human Frailty." In *Malory's Originality: A Critical Study of "Le Morte Darthur,"* ed. R.M. Lumiansky. Baltimore: Johns Hopkins Press, 1964, 184–204.

Morse, Charlotte C. *The Pattern of Judgment in the "Queste" and "Cleanness."* Columbia: University of Missouri Press, 1978.

Nelli, René, ed. *Lumière du Graal: études et textes.* Paris, 1951; Geneva: Slatkine Reprints, 1977.

Newstead, Helaine. *Brân the Blessed in Arthurian Romance.* 1939; New York: AMS, 1966.

Nitze, William A. "The Fisher King and the Grail in Retrospect." *Romance Philology* 6 (1952), 14–22.

———. "Messire Robert de Boron: Enquiry and Summary." *Speculum* 28 (1953), 279–96.

———. "*Perlesvaus*." In Loomis, ed. *ALMA*, 263–73.

Noble, James. "The Grail and its Guardian: Evidence of Authorial Intent in the Middle English *Joseph of Arimathea*." *Quondam et Futurus: Journal of Arthurian Interpretations* 1.2 (Summer 1991), 1–14.

Northcott, Kenneth J. "Seeing and Partly Seeing: Parzival's Encounters with the Grail." *Spectrum Medii Aevi: Essays in Early German Literature in Honor of George Fenwick Jones*, ed. William C. McDonald. Göppingen: Kummerle, 1983, 409–28.

Nutt, Alfred Trubner. *Studies on the Legend of the Holy Grail.* New York: Cooper Square Publishers, 1965.

O'Gorman, Richard. "Ecclesiastical Tradition and the Holy Grail." *Australian Journal of French Studies* 6 (1969), 3–8.

———. "The *Gospel of Nicodemus* in the Vernacular Literature of Medieval France." In *The Medieval "Gospel of Nicodemus": Texts, Intertexts, and Contexts in Western Europe*, ed. Zbigniew Izydorczyk. Medieval and Renaissance Texts and Studies 158. Tempe: Arizona State University, 1997, 103–31.

———. "The Prose Version of Robert de Boron's *Joseph d'Arimathie*." *Romance Philology* 23 (1970), 449–61.

Olderman, Raymond M. "The Grail Knight Arrives: Ken Kesey, *One Flew over the Cuckoo's Nest*." In *A Casebook on Ken Kesey's "One Flew Over the*

Cuckoo's Nest," ed. George J. Searles. Albuquerque: University of New Mexico Press, 1992, 67–79.

Osberg, Richard H. "Pages Torn From the Book: Narrative Disintegration in Gilliam's 'The Fisher King.'" *Studies in Medievalism* 7 (1995), 194–224.

O'Shaughnessy, Margaret. "Edwin Austin Abbey's Reinterpretation of the Grail Quest: The Boston Public Library Murals." *Arthuriana* 4 (1994), 298–312.

Owen, D.D.R. *The Evolution of the Grail Legend.* Edinburgh: Oliver and Boyd, 1968.

Pauphilet, Albert. *Études sur la "Queste del Saint Graal" attribuée à Gautier Map.* Paris: Champion, 1921.

Pickens, Rupert T. "*Le Conte du Graal (Perceval).*" In *The Romances of Chrétien de Troyes: A Symposium,* ed. Douglas Kelly. Lexington, KY: French Forum, 1985, 232–86.

Plummer, John F. "The Quest for Significance in *La Queste del Saint Graal* and Malory's *Tale of the Sankgreal.*" In *Continuations: Essays on Medieval French Literature and Language in Honor of John L. Grigsby,* ed. Norris J. Lacy and Gloria Torrini-Roblin. Birmingham, AL: Summa, 1989, 107–19.

Poag, James A. *Wolfram von Eschenbach.* New York: Twayne Publishers, 1972.

Quinn, Esther C. "Beyond Courtly Love: Religious Elements in *Tristan* and *La Queste del Saint Graal.*" In *In Pursuit of Perfection: Courtly Love in Medieval Literature,* ed. Joan M. Ferrante and George D. Economou. Port Washington, NY: Kennikat Press, 1975, 179–219.

————. "The Quest of Seth, Solomon's Ship and The Grail." *Traditio* 21 (1965), 185–222.

*Ranke, Friedrich. "Zur Symbolik des Grals bei Wolfram von Eschenbach." 1945; *Wege De Forschung* 57 (1966), 38–48 [translated in this volume].

Regalado, Nancy Freeman. "La Chevalerie Celestiel: Spiritual Transformations of Secular Romance in *La Queste del Saint Graal.*" In *Romance: Generic Transformation from Chrétien de Troyes to Cervantes,* ed. Kevin Brownlee and Marina Scordilis Brownlee. Hanover, NH: University Press of New England, 1985, 91–113.

Riddy, Felicity. "Glastonbury, Joseph of Arimathea and the Grail in John Hardyng's *Chronicle.*" In *The Archaeology and History of Glastonbury Abbey,* ed. L. Abrams and J.P. Carley. Woodbridge, Suffolk: D.S. Brewer, 1991, 317–31.

————. "John Hardyng in Search of the Grail." In Van Hoecke et al., *Arturus Rex,* II, 419–29.

Rider, Jeff, Richard Hull, and Christopher Smith. "The Arthurian Legend in French Cinema: *Lancelot du Lac* and *Perceval le Gallois.*" In Harty, ed. *Cinema Arthuriana,* 41–56.

Riquier, Martin de. *La leyenda de Graal y temas epicos medievales*. Madrid: Editorial Prensa Espanola, 1968.

Roach, William. "Transformations of the Grail Theme in the First Two Continuations of the Old French *Perceval*." *Proceedings of the American Philosophical Society* 110 (1966), 160–64.

Robinson, J. Armitage. *Two Glastonbury Legends: King Arthur and St. Joseph of Arimathea*. Cambridge: Cambridge University Press, 1926.

Roques, Mario. "Le Graal de Chrétien et la demoiselle au Graal." *Romania* 76 (1955), 1–27.

Rubin, Miri. *Corpus Christi: The Eucharist in Late Medieval Culture*. Cambridge: Cambridge University Press, 1991.

Schäfer, Hans-Wilhelm. "Wolframs *calix lapideus*." *Zeitschrift für Deutsche Philologie* 103 (1984), 370–77.

Schmid, Elisabeth. *Familiengeschichten und Heilsmythologie: Die Verwandschaftsstrukturen in den französischen und deutschen Gralsromanen des 12. und 13. Jahrhunderts*. Tübingen: Niemeyer, 1986.

Sherer, Margaret R. *About the Round Table*. New York: The Metropolitan Museum of Art, 1945.

*Shichtman, Martin B. "Hollywood's New Weston: The Grail Myth in Francis Ford Coppola's *Apocalypse Now* and John Boorman's *Excalibur*." *Post-Script: Essays in Film and the Humanities* 4 (1984), 35–48.

———. "Whom Does the Grail Serve? Wagner, Spielberg, and the Issue of Jewish Appropriation." In Mancoff, ed. *The Arthurian Revival: Essays*, 283–97.

Simes, G.R. "Chivalry and Malory's Quest of the Holy Grail." *Parergon* 17 (1977), 37–42.

Sims, Robert L. "The Quest for Happiness and the Grail Myth in Julien Gracq's *Le Rivage des syrtes* and *Un Balcon en forêt*." *Perspectives on Contemporary Literature* 8 (1982), 42–47.

Sklar, Elizabeth. "Adventure and the Spiritual Semantics of Malory's Tale of the Sankgreal." *Arthurian Interpretations* 2. 2 (1988), 34–46.

Smith, Evans L. "The Arthurian Underworld of Modernism: Thomas Mann, Thomas Pynchon, Robertson Davies." *Arthurian Interpretations* 4. 2 (1990), 50–64.

Spisak, James W., ed. *Studies in Malory*. Kalamazoo: Medieval Institute Publications, Western Michigan University, 1985.

Staines, David. "Tennyson's 'The Holy Grail': The Tragedy of Percivale." *Modern Language Review* 69 (1984), 745–56.

Starr, Nathan Comfort. *King Arthur Today: The Arthurian Legend in English and American Literature, 1901–1953*. Gainesville: University of Florida Press, 1954.

Stephenson, Will, and Mimosa Stephenson. "Proto-Modernism in Tennyson's 'The Holy Grail.'" *Quondam et Futurus: Journal of Arthurian Intepretations* 2. 4 (1992), 49–55.

Stones, Alison. "The Illustrations of BN, fr. 95 and Yale 229: Prolegomena to a Comparative Analysis." In *Word and Image in Arthurian Literature*, ed. Keith Busby. New York: Garland, 1996, 203–60.

Sturges, Robert Stuart. *Medieval Interpretation: Models of Reading in Literary Narrative, 1100–1500*. Carbondale: Southern Illinois University Press, 1991.

*Sturm-Maddox, Sara. "*Tout est par senefiance*: Gerbert's *Perceval*." *The Arthurian Yearbook* 2 (1992), 191–207 [reprinted, with added glosses, in this volume].

Szkilnik, Michelle. *L'Archipel du Graal: étude de "L'Estoire del Saint-Graal."* Geneva: Droz, 1991.

———. "*L'Estoire del Saint Graal*: réécrire la *Queste*." In Van Hoecke et al., *Arturus Rex*, II, 294–305.

Taylor, Beverly, and Elizabeth Brewer. *The Return of King Arthur: British and American Arthurian Literature Since 1900* [for 1800]. Cambridge, Eng.: Brewer, 1983.

Thompson, Raymond H. *The Return from Avalon: A Study of the Arthurian Legend in Modern Fiction*. Westport, CT: Greenwood Press, 1985.

Thornton, Ginger, and Krista May. "Malory as Feminist? The Role of Percival's Sister in the Grail Quest." In *Sir Thomas Malory: Views and Re-Views*, ed. D. Thomas Hanks, Jr. New York: AMS, 1992, 43–53.

Todorov, Tzvetan. "La Quête du récit." In *Poétique de la prose*. Paris: Editions du Seuil, 1971, 129–50.

Treharne, Reginald F. *The Glastonbury Legends: Joseph of Arimathea, the Holy Grail and King Arthur*. London: Cresset, 1967.

Tuve, Rosemond. *Allegorical Imagery: Some Mediaeval Books and their Posterity*. Princeton: Princeton University Press, 1966.

Van Hoecke, Willy, Gilbert Tournoy, and Werner Verbeke, eds. *Arturus Rex, Acta Conventus Lovaniensis 1987*. 2 vols. Leuven: Leuven University Press, 1991.

Vinaver, Eugène. "The Dolorous Stroke." *Medium Ævum* 25. 3 (1957), 175–80.

———. *The Rise of Romance*. Oxford: Oxford University Press, 1971.

Walters, Lori J. "Wonders and Illuminations: Piérart dou Tielt and the *Queste del saint Graal*." *The Arthurian Yearbook* 4 (1996), 232–78.

Weigand, Hermann John. *Wolfram's "Parzival": Five Essays with an Introduction*, ed. Ursula Hoffmann. Ithaca, NY: Cornell University Press, 1969.

Weinraub, Eugene J. *Chrétien's Jewish Grail: A New Investigation of the Imagery and Significance of Chrétien de Troyes's Grail Episode Based upon Medieval Hebraic Sources.* Chapel Hill: University of North Carolina Department of Romance Language, 1976.

Welz, Dieter. "Gedanken zur Genese des Gralsromans." *Acta Germanica* 15 (1982), 7–15.

Weston, Jessie L. *From Ritual to Romance.* Garden City, NY: Doubleday, 1957.

Whitaker, Muriel. "Christian Iconography in the Quest of the Holy Grail." *Mosaic* 12 (1979), 11–19.

———. *The Legends of King Arthur in Art.* Woodbridge, Eng.: D.S. Brewer, 1990.

Williams, Charles. *The Image of the City and Other Essays*, sel. and introd. Anne Ridler. London: Oxford University Press, 1958.

*Williams, Linda. "Eric Rohmer and the Holy Grail." *Literature Film Quarterly* 11 (1983), 71–82.

Willson, Harry B. "The Grail King in Wolfram's 'Parzival.'" *Modern Language Review* 55 (1960), 553–63.

Wolfgang, Lenora D. "Prologues to the Perceval and Perceval's Father: The First Literary Critics of Chrétien were the Grail Authors Themselves." *Oeuvres et Critiques* 5 (1980-81), 81–90.

CHAPTER 1

The Quest for Origins

GLENYS WITCHARD GOETINCK

The wonderful stories woven around the mysterious vessel that became known as the Grail have caused earnest scholars to spill oceans of ink. It is to be hoped that the following few drops will be, at least, a useful addition to the flood.

Alfred Nutt observed many years ago that the Grail romances fall into two broad categories, the Quest Versions where the emphasis is laid on the hero and his adventures, and the Early History Versions, where the emphasis is laid on the nature and history of the talismans. They cannot be neatly divided into two groups, however, for characteristics of one category overlap into romances that belong to the other category. The Quest Versions precede the Early History Versions in the development of the Grail romances, the former having a far less religious atmosphere than the latter.[1] To the author of one of the Quest Versions, Chrétien de Troyes, goes the honor of firing the interest of writers and public alike in the story of the vessel first called *graal* in his *Perceval ou le Conte du Graal*, composed between 1180 and 1190.[2]

Chrétien did not complete his romance, leaving a void which inspired four authors to compose Continuations to his work. Two of these are anonymous and composed before 1200, one is by Manessier (ca. 1225), and another by Gerbert de Montreuil (ca. 1230).[3] Yet another anonymous writer was moved to compose a prologue to the *Conte du Graal*, known as the *Elucidation*, and a further prologue was entitled the *Bliocadran* from the name it gives to Perceval's father.[4] Other romances relating varying versions of the Grail story are Wolfram von Eschenbach's *Parzival* (ca. 1200),[5] *La Queste del Saint Graal* (ca. 1220),[6] *Perlesvaus* (ca. 1230),[7]

L'Estoire del Saint Graal,[8] Robert de Boron's trilogy *Joseph d'Arimathie, Merlin,* and *Perceval* (ca. 1191-1202),[9] or the Didot *Perceval* as it became known after an owner of the manuscript, and the Welsh romance *Historia Peredur vab Evrawc.*[10] The Grail also enters into the prose *Lancelot,*[11] and a poem entitled *Sone de Nansai,* from the second half of the thirteenth century.[12] Although Chrétien's *Perceval* belongs to the Quest category, he contributed to the later christianizing of the romances by remarking that the *graal* was very holy, that it contained a Mass wafer, and that the father of *le Roi Pescheor,* the Fisher King, led a highly spiritual life.[13]

Although the various romances are known as Grail romances and they all center on the magic, or holy, vessel, and the heroes whose lives it shapes, the variety of forms in which the stories are presented and the different features they present testify not only to the talents of the romancers, but also to the wide range of materials related to this theme to which they had access. Chrétien's was the first Grail romance, but not all Grail romances are retellings of his *Perceval.* In the Welsh *Peredur* the spectators break into loud, grief-stricken lamentation when the symbolic objects are borne through the hall. *Perceval* does not contain this feature, but it does occur in *Sone de Nansai.* In *Perceval* the hero is not connected with a magic chessboard, but there is such a board in *Peredur,* in the equivalent of the Grail Castle. In *Perlesvaus* the chessboard also appears in the Grail Castle, and in the Second Continuation there is a magic chessboard, but not in the Grail Castle. In *Peredur* there is a severed head on a platter, but Chrétien makes no mention of this. In *Perlesvaus* a maiden comes to Arthur's court carrying a king's head in an *estole,* which, as Loomis showed, was a miscopying of *escuele,* which has the same meaning as *graal* and, in the Welsh romance *dysgl,* that is, a platter. In the fourteenth-century *Reductorium Morale* of Pierre Bercheur a man's head appears on a platter in an underwater castle, and in the First Continuation there is a story of a number of heads on platters. In this case they are boars' heads, but Gauvain reacts to the sight by crossing himself, which suggests that the original episode may have contained human heads. In *Peredur* the *dysgl* is borne by two maidens, in *Perceval* by one maiden, in the Didot-*Perceval* by a squire, and in *Perlesvaus* by a maiden. The Hideous Maiden, *la Demoiselle Hideuse* in *Perceval,* and Cundrie, her equivalent in *Parzival,* are not shape-shifters, but in *Peredur* the Curly Haired Maiden or the Black Maiden, as she is also called, certainly is and so is Rosete, the Ugly Maiden in the Second *Continuation.* In *Perceval* and *Parzival* the Fisher King is ill, unable to move, and he waits for the hero to ask the question that will heal him. In *Peredur* he is not ill, and his health does not depend on the hero. In the First Continuation, the *Elucidation*, and Gerbert's Continuation, the king is not ill, but his kingdom is waste and in order to restore it a certain question must be asked. In *Peredur, Perceval,* and *Parzival* a spear is carried through the hall as part of the procession of symbolic objects, but in *Parzival* it is said that the spear must be thrust into the Fisher King's wound to ease the pain, and in the *Queste* Galahad heals the king with blood from the spear. In *Perlesvaus* there is a burning lance whose flames may be extinguished only by the blood of Arthur, whom it has wounded. In *Peredur* the principal symbol is a *dysgl*, a large platter, on which lies a man's head surrounded by blood. There is no connection between the *dysgl* and food, and no detail is given concerning the dish. In *Perceval* there is a *graal*, the same type of dish as in *Peredur*, but this one is studded with precious gems, gives off a brilliant light, and is connected with marvelous food. In *Parzival* the Grail is a huge precious stone, or a dish made from an extremely large gem, also connected with food. In Robert de Boron's *Joseph* the Grail is the cup that contained the blood of the Lord, and it sustains Joseph while he is in prison. In *Perlesvaus* the Grail appears in five different forms, the last of which is a chalice. It appears before Gauvain while he is eating, but it creates a beautiful perfume rather than food. In the *Queste* the Grail is the dish of the Last Supper and also a vessel containing the Host, and yet it causes food to appear miraculously. The procession in which the talismans appear varies from one romance to another.

THEORIES OF ORIGIN

If the romances themselves are varied, so too are the opinions expressed on the origins of the material they contain. The Grail legends have been thought to originate in the initiation rituals of an ancient fertility cult, in Christian ritual, in Jewish ritual, in Celtic mythology, in Arabian tales, and in Indo-European legends. In view of the number of commentators, specialist and amateur, and the volume of material involved, it is impossible to do more than indicate certain currents of thought and provide some bibliography that may be useful.

The American scholar Jessie Weston is probably the most famous exponent of what has been called the theory of Ritual origins. She saw a link between the legends of Attis, Adonis, and Osiris, the emasculation of the Fisher King, and the connection between the nature of his wound and the desolate state of his domains. The visit to the Grail Castle was part of an initiation into an ancient fertility rite, the lance and the Grail representing the male and female organs.[14] Miss Weston's theories aroused strong opposition, but, with the passage of time and further investigation, it is clear that her views cannot be totally discounted. One of Miss Weston's supporters was the Indian scholar Ananda K. Coomaraswamy, who declared the Ritual theory to be the most satisfactory among those currently held and saw the origin of the Grail legends in an ancient vegetation cult that might be of Indian origin.[15] The religions that used to be referred to as vegetation cults are actually centered on the worship of a goddess, often termed the Great Goddess, and have been intensively studied in recent years. Where once it was sufficient to identify the cult by referring to the male divinity alone, now Cybele, Ishtar, and Isis are accorded pride of place alongside Attis, Tammuz, and Osiris. One of the best studies in this field is the one by Anne Baring and Jules Cashford.[16] Here, the various forms taken by the Grail are seen to evoke the archetype of the Feminine, which inspires the knights to their quest and provides their ultimate goal. The legends are said to show clear traces of the Bronze Age myths of the Mother Goddess and her Son-Lover, but Baring and Cashford also see influences from Gnosticism, Alchemy, and perhaps Kabbalism. Silvestro Fiore establishes strong parallels between the Grail legends and the rites and myths of Cybele and Attis, Ishtar and Tammuz, and particularly those of Isis and Osiris. Fiore maintains that the myths of Isis and Osiris enjoyed huge popularity during the first centuries of the Christian era and that the Grail was originally part of pagan rites that conferred fertility and eternal youth.[17]

The supporters of the theory of the Christian origins of the Grail legends are equally as enthusiastic in the expression of their ideas. One of the most determined and dedicated is Sister Amelia Klenke, O.P., who maintains that Chrétien composed a Christian allegory, her main sources of material being the Bible, the saints' legends which Jacobus de Voragine used to compile his *Golden Legend*, and the twelfth-century Strasbourg miniature known as the *Hortus Deliciarum*.[18] In Sister Klenke's view the Grail is the chalice of the Last Supper, *graal* being related liturgically and linguistically to the Gradual of the Mass, the Grail Bearer is Ecclesia, the Bleeding Lance is the Lance of the Passion, and the bearer of the Lance is Longinus, the first convert to Christianity, as a result of Christ's blood falling on him as he stood at the foot of the Cross. The *tailleor*, a dish used for cutting meat that is carried into the hall after the *graal*, is a communion plate used in communicating the Being in the Inner Room who subsists solely on the Blessed Sacrament. Perceval's spiritual ascent is based on the life of St. Paul, and the true meaning of the tale is that conversion is a superior alternative to religious persecution.

In his prologue to *Le Conte du Graal* Chrétien says that he is writing the romance at the request of his patron, Count Philippe de Flandres, who had given him a book containing the story. Helen Adolf considers that book to constitute a call to crusade, a call to the Christian princes and knights of the West to deliver Jerusalem and the Holy Places from the unhappy state in which they were found in 1181. Chrétien's successors used the legend to console Western Christendom for the loss of the Holy Sepulchre in 1187. The Grail represents the Tomb, and the long-standing nexus between Tomb and Eucharist allows the Grail to figure as the chalice of the Mass.[19]

Mario Roques, in a study of the Grail and the Grail Bearer, saw the Grail as the chalice of the Mass, the Grail Bearer as Ecclesia, and the bearer of the Lance as Longinus.[20] Roques proposed a synthesis of the theories of Christian and Byzantine origins, suggesting that Philippe de Flandres's book contained a description of the Byzantine rite.[21] Another supporter of Byzantine influence was W.A. Nitze, who saw the origins of the Grail theme in Celtic legends, but held that the christianization of the Grail was inspired by the Byzantine Mass described in Philippe de Flandres's book.[22]

For Leonardo Olschki, Chrétien's *Perceval* is an allegory designed, perhaps at the request of his patron, to counter the Catharist heresy and other dualist sects who were making inroads, not only in southern France, but also in the north, particularly in Champagne and Flanders. Chrétien's contemporaries had no need of explanations, for they saw their own sufferings and aspirations in the symbolism of the story. The Grail Bearer represents Supreme Wisdom and the father of the Fisher King is one of the "Perfect" of Catharism. Olschki does not consider Chrétien's orthodoxy to be in doubt.[23]

Urban T. Holmes Jr. saw the origins of the Grail theme in Hebrew tradition, reading the *Conte du Graal* as an allegory of the triumph of Ecclesia over Synagoga, the passage to the New Law from the Old. In Troyes there was contact between the Jewish and Christian communities, and Chrétien may have been a converted Jew. For Holmes the Grail Castle was a symbolic representation of the Temple of Solomon in Jerusalem and the Fisher King was Jacob, who was lamed in his struggle with the Angel of the Lord. The Tent Maiden was Esther, Gornemant was Gamaliel, the *tailleor* may have been a Seder plate used in the Passover service, and the Quest for the Grail was the conversion of the Jewish temple to Christianity.[24] Eugene T. Weinraub also turns to Judaism to explain the origins of the Grail. Chrétien may have had in mind the Haggadah, the Sephardic form of the Seder, when he described the events at the Fisher King's castle. Weinraub calls on medieval Hebrew texts, passages from the Talmud, the Bible, Midrash, and the Passover evening prayer book. He also notes the contacts between Jew and Gentile in Troyes, the fairs for which the town was famous, and the passage of traveling scholars as helping to extend the possibilities for cultural exchanges.[25]

The theory of Celtic origins seems currently to be the most widely accepted, although it, too, has been hotly debated. It is not a complete answer to the problems posed by the Grail legends, but it does provide significant parallels to many of the features occurring in the various romances. As in the Arthurian legends in general, the nomenclature of the Grail legends is clearly derived largely from Welsh or Breton sources.[26] The food-producing qualities of the Grail are seen in marvelous vessels in both Irish and Welsh literature, and there are stories in both literatures that parallel those in *Perceval*. The Maimed King appears in both literatures as does the hideous hag who transforms herself into the most beautiful maiden, known as the Sovereignty, who confers power and authority on the hero. The *enfances* of Perceval bear a strong resemblance to those of Peredur, Finn, and Cuchulainn, and the severed head, which was the object of special veneration in Celtic belief, is an important symbol in *Peredur* and is found in many episodes throughout the romances.[27]

In spite of their general agreement on the idea of the Celtic origin of the Grail legends, scholars differ in their interpretation of the various features of the legends, the degree of indebtedness to Celtic sources, and other topics great and small. Once again, one can only hope to present a sampling of the many opinions.

One scholar who consistently supported the theory of Celtic origins for both the Arthurian legends in general and the Grail legends in particular was Roger Sherman Loomis. In his many articles and books, he held firmly to his conviction that the ultimate source of the various legends was to be found in Irish myth and saga, that Wales and Welsh literature represented a transition stage between Ireland and the Continent, and that those responsible for transmitting the tales were the Breton *conteurs*.[28] While the value of his work in drawing attention to the quality and breadth of the Celtic contribution to the Arthurian and Grail legends cannot be denied, Loomis's view was too rigid and dogmatic. In fact the Welsh contribution to the legends was significant, and Constance Bullock-Davies showed quite clearly that, in addition to the Breton *conteurs*, there were others who participated in the transmission of the *matière de Bretagne* to the Continent.[29]

Joseph Campbell also supported the theory of Celtic, ultimately Irish, origin. For Campbell, the cauldron of Manannán was the vessel from which the Grail developed.[30] D.D.R. Owen designates Ireland as the ultimate source of the Grail theme but accords the Welsh *cyfarwyddiaid* a more significant role in the transmission of the material than had Loomis.[31] Although W.A. Nitze thought that the christianization of the Grail theme was inspired by the Byzantine Mass, he saw the origin of the legends as Celtic, and, for him, the figure behind the Fisher King was Nuada *Airgetlam*, Nuada of the Silver Arm, who lost his arm during the First Battle of Maighe Tuireadh (Moytura). Owing to the disability, he was forced to abdicate his position until Diancecht, physician of the Tuatha Dé Danann, made him a silver prosthesis.[32] A.G. Van Hamel also turned to Irish literature and saw numerous points of agreement between the Grail story and *Altromh Tighi dá Medar, The Fosterage of the House of the Two Goblets.*[33]

The Welsh contribution to the Grail legends was stressed by Helaine Newstead, who saw the Fisher King as originating in Brân, Bendigeidfran of the Second Branch of the *Mabinogi*. Brân was wounded in battle in Ireland, and, although the Welsh texts are not specific, it is clear that the nature of the wound is an emasculation, as it is in the case of the Fisher King. Loomis agreed with this interpretation and saw the head on the platter in *Peredur* as the head of Brân.[34] For Louis Rigaud, Celtic origins meant Welsh origins,[35] and the Welsh contribution was again stressed in my study, *Peredur: A Study of Welsh Tradition in the Grail Legends.*[36] I have already modified certain of the opinions I expressed in the latter work, and others will be modified during the course of this essay, but the main argument remains constant, that the Welsh contribution to the creation and dissemination of the Grail legends was considerable.

Three French scholars who supported the concept of Celtic origins were the Celticist Joseph Vendryes,[37] and the medievalists Jean Marx[38] and Jean Frappier. Throughout the course of his long career and his many publications, Frappier consistently defended the Celtic origins of the *matière de Bretagne* and the Grail, although he did not feel that the Celtic origins answered every question connected with them.[39]

The appearance of a man's head on a platter in *Peredur*, whereas the same type of dish in *Perceval* contains a Mass wafer, has been one of the many particular topics of discussion within the larger framework of the Grail theme. Jean-Claude Lozachmeur, while supporting the hypothesis of Celtic origins as a partial solution, proposed a series of steps whereby the head of the Welsh text became the Host in *Perceval*.[40] Although he did not offer an opinion on the Grail as such, his study of the importance

of the head in Celtic belief led the Belgian archaeologist Pierre Lambrechts to declare that he shared the position of those who believe that
the core of the Arthurian legends lies in Celtic tradition. Lambrechts
marveled at the astonishing survival of the theme of the head over a period of more than ten centuries and at the tenacious persistence of the
spiritual tradition that allowed for that survival.[41] During the long debate
over origins, scholars have rarely turned to archaeology for clarification,
yet, as we shall see later, it can be brought to bear on literary questions
with gratifying results. Archaeology and a wide-ranging knowledge of
the Celts and their beliefs also allowed another Belgian scholar, Claude
Sterckx, to investigate the passage from head in *Peredur* to Host in
Perceval.[42] The issues raised by Sterckx will be examined later.

Students of the mythology of the goddess have found the Grail stories to be of interest. Erich Neumann took the Woman-as-Vessel view of
the Grail which he saw as developing from the magic cauldron of the
Celtic priestess. The food-giving properties of the Grail derive from the
fertility symbolism of the cauldron.[43] Mary Esther Harding saw significant correspondences between the Grail legends and the mythology of
the Moon goddess. The chalice containing blood is the equivalent of the
cauldron of the Celtic Moon goddess, a vessel bestowing regeneration,
possibly immortality. As a stone (in *Parzival*) the Grail represents the
Moon goddess herself, and as a food-bearing dish it represents the goddess of Agriculture and Plenty.[44] To Edward Whitmont the import of the
Grail legend is the necessity to reverse patriarchal domination. The
wound of the Fisher King will be healed and the Waste Land restored
when due homage is paid to the great Feminine.[45] Jean Markale, a prolific writer on matters Celtic, also sees the Grail legends as a memory of
the cult of an ancient female divinity, overthrown and dominated by the
brutal strength of the male. Since the beginning of male domination, society has been seeking to redress the lost balance, and this will be
achieved when the young Son kills, castrates, or otherwise does away
with the Father and restores sovereignty to the Mother. The Grail Quest
is the glorification of the eternal, divine, shape-shifting, female power
waiting in the underworld to be restored to her status as Great Queen and
to restore balance to her sons' fractured society.[46]

One of the most interesting works supporting the Celtic origins of
the Grail legends is *Les Celtes et le druidisme* by Raimonde Reznikov.[47]
Her study emphasizes the druids' renown as astronomers and examines
Celtic mythology and its divinities in the light of ancient astronomy. The
Grail legends are the result of the christianization of traditional Celtic
themes arising from the initiation rituals of ancient mysteries. Celtic

scholars are familiar with the concept of the Other World in the depths of the earth, but Reznikov points to an Other World situated in the universe, and submits that it was by meditating on the subtle meaning of the tales of extraterrestrial and subterranean adventures that the candidates for initiation refined their concept of divinity, braved the mystery of death and resurrection, and became masters of time. The Celtic origins of the Grail legends have many supporters who argue their case with great conviction but, as we shall see, it may be wiser to think in terms of a Celtic stage in the development, rather than a Celtic origin.

Oriental origins have also been ascribed to the Grail legends, from the Middle East to India. Silvestro Fiore looked to the Middle East,[48] Coomaraswamy to India,[49] and the great Indologist Heinrich Zimmer was of the opinion that the Celts incorporated Asian mythology, brought to Britain by Phoenician traders, into their own body of belief. The Grail Castle, for Zimmer, is a Christian form of the pagan Celtic castle of the Fountain of Life, which is the source of the well-being and prosperity of the world.[50] Arabian sources are proposed by Antonio Furtado,[51] and by G. Phillips and M. Keatman, who suggest, using Wolfram's *Parzival* as evidence, that a Crusader poet, possibly a Templar, adapted an Arab legend that was later absorbed into the material of the Arthurian legends.[52] Joseph Campbell, in his "Indian Reflections in the Castle of the Grail," while retaining his belief in the Celtic origins of the Grail legends, demonstrates the extent of the material originating in the Orient that was available to Wolfram and the degree to which he incorporated that material in his work.[53] However, these are influences, not origins.

Legends of Indo-European origin have been proposed as possible sources for the Grail legends. Jean-Claude Lozachmeur, starting from the idea of Celtic origins and persuaded that this was not a sufficient explanation, saw the necessity for placing the Grail legends against a wider background. He suggested that the Grail theme is a Celtic tale, based on the story of the Vengeance of the Widow's Son, which is an initiatory myth appearing in various mythologies of Indo-European origin. The Vengeance follows the Hero's acquisition of Supreme Knowledge. There is no conflict between the esoteric side of the tales and the Celtic development.[54] The French mediaevalist Joël H. Grisward has also studied the question of Indo-European parallels and origins in the Arthurian legends and the Grail theme.[55] Grisward pursues ideas expressed earlier by Georges Dumézil, that the Grail procession should be studied as a unit rather than as a series of objects; that the talismans described correspond to objects sacred to the Scythians and detailed in an account by Herodotus; that the Celtic and Scythian legends derive from an Indo-European heritage. Perceval is the youngest of three brothers, and in the Scythian legend only the youngest brother is deemed worthy of the sovereignty. The future ruler is hidden away for a number of years. The sacred objects consigned to the care of the predestined hero/king are a cup, an axe (or a lance and an arrow in a variant version), a plow and a yoke, corresponding to the *graal*, lance, and *tailleor* in *Perceval*. The talismans represent the three cosmic and social categories, or functions, of the Indo-Europeans as formulated by Dumézil: (1) spiritual and temporal sovereignty, (2) physical force, the warrior function, and (3) fertility, wealth, prosperity. The esoteric aspect of the legends will be examined later, as will the way in which *Peredur* fits into the trifunctional scheme.

Scythian origins are proposed in a recent work by C. Scott Littleton and Linda A. Malcor.[56] The Arthurian and Grail legends are considered to originate in the heroic traditions of peoples from the northeast Iranian steppe region, who moved into Europe over a period of centuries as auxiliaries in the Roman legions or as independent groups of conquerors. In Britain, for example, a Sarmatian cavalry contingent numbering 5,500 was sent by the emperor Marcus Aurelius from Pannonia (now Hungary) to Britain. At the end of their period of service, they were settled in a *vicus*, a civilian settlement established to accommodate retired military personnel, near the modern Ribchester in Lancashire. The commander of these troops was a Roman officer named Lucius Artorius Castus, prefect of the Legio VI Victrix, and headquartered at Eboracum (York). The name of this commander is proposed as the origin of the name of King Arthur of the legends. The Nartamongae, an inexhaustible vessel (cup or cauldron) that appears at feasts, is hidden from all but the most excellent of warriors, and is the object of a sacred quest, is seen as the original Grail. That the descendants of the ancient Scythians, warrior peoples and conservative of their traditions, may have influenced the Celts with whom they came into contact as they made their way into Europe is far from improbable, but that their influence should have been as overwhelming as Littleton and Malcor suggest is difficult to accept. The Celts had a strong, vibrant, well-developed civilization, and their extensive contacts with the Scythians are well known. Far from sedentary themselves, they had pushed eastward to the Black Sea and settled in the Danube Valley. Speaking of Scythian influence on La Tène art, Henri Hubert remarked that what the artists of this period borrowed, they usually adapted and shaped according to their own ideas.[57] Pierre Lambrechts also pointed out, with regard to borrowing, that whatever is absorbed is not likely to be at variance with what already exists in the receiving culture.[58] Judging from the evidence of Welsh and Irish literature, Gaulish iconography, and the remarks of ancient commentators who wrote about them, the Celts had a highly developed religious system, comparable to that of Vedic India, and a correspondingly evolved mythology that was eventually retold in the form of heroic sagas and other traditional literature.[59] Whilst they may have borrowed from, or been influenced by, the Scythians and their descendants, it is unlikely to have been to such a degree as to virtually efface whatever was there originally.

PEREDUR, PERCEVAL AND THE BEGINNINGS OF THE TRADITION

The remainder of this study will concentrate on the two earliest and perhaps the most mysterious of the Grail romances, the Welsh *Historia Peredur vab Evrawc* and Chrétien's *Perceval, ou le Conte du Graal*. Since *Perceval* was never completed, no one has any idea how Chrétien intended to draw together the threads of the story, and *Peredur* has been a source of discussion because of the head that lies on the platter as it is borne through the hall, in contrast to the more discreet *oiste* ("host") in *Perceval*. While the degree of French influence on the extant version of *Peredur* is a matter of some dispute,[60] the origins of the material in the romance are clearly Celtic and very likely local. The earliest extant complete text of *Peredur* dates from the end of the thirteenth century, but close examination of the orthography suggests the existence of a written version probably from the early twelfth century, predating *Perceval*.[61] The strong oral tradition in Celtic culture and the nature of the material in the romance suggest that it existed in pre-Roman times, but it is not clear exactly when Peredur became the titular hero.[62] Jean Markale pointed to the fact that there are episodes in *Peredur* that do not appear in *Perceval* and that their markedly archaic character shows that the author was drawing on ancient Celtic sources.[63] He also remarked that *Peredur* takes us back to a tradition rooted in the collective unconscious of the British Celts, to the heart of the original setting in which their mythology was developed before being overwhelmed by continental influence.[64]

At this point it will be useful to outline those events in *Peredur* and *Perceval* that are pertinent to our inquiry.[65] Both romances tell the story of a youth living in the forest with his widowed mother and a few retainers. He is deliberately kept in ignorance of anything to do with the world of chivalry, but a chance encounter with a group of knights draws him into that world and, in due course, the youth becomes a paragon of knighthood. Within this framework, the romances differ considerably in the sequence of events, the characters introduced, and the relationship between them. Only those episodes having a direct bearing on our study will be related.

Peredur is sheltered, trained, and advised by two noblemen of advanced years who identify themselves as his mother's brothers and who prophesy that he will be the greatest swordsman in the land. As Peredur approaches, the first uncle is watching some youths fishing on a lake. He is later seen to walk with a limp. He advises Peredur not to remark on anything that seems strange unless someone else mentions it first. The episode in *Perceval* corresponding to this Grail scene takes place in the second uncle's castle. Neither man is named. Perceval is first welcomed, trained, and suitably clothed by Gornemant de Gorhaut, an elderly nobleman who is not related to the hero. He advises Perceval on how to conduct himself and warns him against talking too freely. Later, following the course of a river, Perceval sees two men in a boat, one of whom is fishing. The latter invites the boy to spend the night at his house. Here Perceval sees the Grail and the other talismans. His host is the *Roi Pescheor.*

While Peredur is conversing with the second of his two uncles, the two youths cross the hall carrying a huge spear with three streams of blood running from the socket to the floor. The company breaks into loud lamentation, but his uncle says nothing and neither does Peredur. Shortly afterward, two maidens enter, carrying a dish on which is a man's head swimming in blood. There is more lamentation but nothing is said by host or guest, and eventually the company retires. Similarly, when Perceval enters the castle hall, he finds his host half-lying on a bed placed in front of a blazing fire. The fire has been laid under a heavy brass canopy supported by four columns. His host gives Perceval a sword declaring that it was destined for him. A squire crosses the hall, carrying a shining Lance with a drop of blood running from the tip to the bearer's hand. Perceval says nothing. Two other youths enter, carrying golden candelabra and accompanying a maiden who bears a *graal* (a serving dish) made of gold, studded with jewels and giving off a brilliant light. Another maiden follows, carrying a silver *tailleor* (a carving dish). A splendid meal is served and the *graal* appears with every course, but Perceval says nothing. At the end of the meal the company retires.

Peredur defends a lady whose domains are under attack by the nine Witches of Gloucester. He spends three weeks at the witches' court, learning how to handle horse and arms. He later arrives at a valley crammed with mills of all kinds. He undergoes a version of the Beheading Test at the hands of the head miller, who helps him win the hand of the Empress of Constantinople. Peredur and the Empress rule for fourteen years.

In both romances the hero is present at Arthur's court when an exceedingly ugly maiden rides in on a yellow mule and castigates him for not having asked the questions that would have healed, in Peredur's case, his lame uncle, and, in Perceval's case, the *Roi Pescheor*. She is known as the Black Maiden in *Peredur*, *la Demoiselle Hideuse* in *Perceval*. Peredur leaves to seek the truth about the Lance, and Perceval to learn about the Lance and *graal*.

Peredur wanders for a year and encounters a priest who reproaches him for bearing arms on Good Friday. He stays with the priest who directs him on his way, but gives him no religious instruction. Perceval wanders for five years, and is reproached on Good Friday by a group of penitents who direct him to a hermit's cell. The hermit confesses him, instructs him, and explains the events in the Grail Castle. The *graal* serves the *Roi Pescheor's* father, whose only sustenance is the Mass wafer it contains. He is the hermit's brother, and both are brothers to Perceval's mother. Thus the *Roi Pescheor* is his cousin. Perceval stays with his uncle for two days; then the narrative returns to Gauvain, and nothing further is said of Perceval.

Peredur eventually reaches a castle in a river valley. This is *Caer yr Enryfeddodau*, the Castle of Wonders. He finds his lame uncle sitting in the hall with Gwalchmei. A squire enters and confesses to having been the Black Maiden, the bearer of the spear, the bearer of the dish with the head on it, and several other characters. The head was that of his cousin, slain by the Witches of Glouchester, who also lamed his uncle. Peredur and Gwalchmei, aided by Arthur and his men, attack the Witches who recognize Peredur as the man destined to slay them. Here the romance ends.

It has been said that the Grail legends contain an uneasy blend of two themes, a Vengeance Quest and a Question Test.[66] *Peredur* represents the first type of tale and *Perceval* the second. There is evidence in *Peredur* of attempts to connect it with the Question Test type, resulting in inconsistencies, for example, between the details of the visit to the second uncle's court and the Black Maiden's description of it, and between Peredur's stated objective as he leaves Arthur's court after the Black Maiden's visit and what he actually seeks.[67] Once the nature of the quest is changed, the nature of the hero's questions is also changed, as is the focus of the events in the Grail Castle. Instead of asking why the Lance was bleeding and whose head lay on the platter, straightforward questions that would have resulted in an explanation of the need for vengeance, the hero should have asked the question about the Lance, but also should have inquired whom the *graal* serves, which would have restored the king to health. The import of the Grail scene shifts from the head as the central symbol to the *rol méhaigné* ("maimed king") and his need to be healed, and thus the questions acquire a magical nature.[68]

The passage from severed head to Mass wafer may seem to be a question of delicacy or good taste, but there are correspondences between them that are not immediately obvious. Continuing the idea expressed by Loomis and Newstead that the head on the platter was that of Brân, the marine divinity who was wounded in the foot and subsequently decapitated in the Second Branch of the *Mabinogi*, Lozachmeur proposed that *Bendigaid Frân* was initially correctly translated into *Cor Benoit*, both meaning Blessed Raven, and later misinterpreted as *Cor Benoit*, the Blessed, or Holy, Body. The result would be the Mass wafer in the great platter. The dish in *Peredur*, which romance Lozachmeur sees as containing the earliest Grail procession, has no food-producing properties, whereas they are implied in Chrétien. The *conteur* would have made a connection between this dish and other similar food-producing *dysglau* in Welsh tradition. The transition would have been made by a French-speaking Welsh *cyfarwydd*, or an Anglo-Norman *conteur* who understood native tradition.[69] This is a more reasonable and less complicated explanation than the one proposed by Loomis, who maintained that *Cor Benoit* referred to a magical horn of plenty belonging to Brân.[70] Sterckx also shows how the transition from severed head to host could be made by considering the nature of Celtic beliefs concerning the head.[71] If the head in the platter is that of Brân, then that would represent for a Celt, quite literally, the godhead, source of life, the soul, rebirth, spiritual nourishment, equated with the Christian concept of the Body of Christ. Noting the continued presence of pagan concepts in Welsh and Arthurian literature, Sterckx points to the explicit assimilation of the severed head to the body of Christ in a gloss in the York Breviary, *caput Iohannis in disco: signat corpus Christi* ("the head of John on the dish: it represents the body of Christ").[72] Sterckx also shows that, since the Celts considered the head to be the source of sperm, which was held to reach the genitals via the spinal column, decapitation and castration were one and the same thing. In that case, transferring the emphasis from the severed head to the Fisher King and his wound would not alter the thrust of the episode.

INITIATION TALES AND THE INDO-EUROPEAN BACKGROUND

Jean-Claude Lozachmeur, investigating the possible source of the Grail theme in mythologies of Indo-European origin, compared the stories of Finn, Lug, Sigurdr, the Iranian Kai Khusrau, Yonec, Romulus and Remus,

Perseus, Jason, Krishna, and the Ossetian legend of Batraz, with those of Sir Perceval of Galles, Carduino, and Peredur. He concluded that they are all variants of the same myth concerning the goddess and her son, in which the vengeance theme occupies an important place, as do magical weapons, a royal talisman, and the acquisition of special knowledge. In short, the original story is of an esoteric nature, involving initiation and the winning of royalty.[73] The hero is hidden away from the world by his mother. He develops extraordinary physical powers at an early age. He may have to avenge his father's death or he may have to kill his father. In some versions he kills his maternal grandfather. He sometimes has a special relationship with a smith who possesses magical, or divine, powers, and he is given the knowledge that allows him to carry out his task, in mysterious circumstances, by means of a wonderful talisman.

Perceval and *Peredur* agree with the story outlined by Lozachmeur, *Peredur* more so than the French romance. In addition to the retreat of the mother, the quest for royalty, the magic weapon, and the talismans seen in the Grail Castle, *Peredur* has a clear vengeance theme, the equivalence of woman and cup in the quest for sovereignty (which is seen both in the case of Gwenhwyfar and the Empress), the two aspects of Sovereignty, fair and hideous (the Empress and the Black Maiden), and the accomplishment of the vengeance.[74] Lozachmeur notes that the reason for the vengeance is still not clear, but, as we shall see, in *Peredur* it is.

The talismans in the Grail scene in both *Perceval* and *Peredur* are easily fitted into the tripartite scheme of cosmic and social functions (categories) that Dumézil saw as being typically Indo-European.[75] Grisward shows that in *Perceval* the *graal* corresponds to the first function, magical sovereignty and heavenly administration of the universe; the Lance and the sword to the second, or warrior function, which also includes administration of the lower atmosphere; and the *tailleor* to the third function, which relates to fertility and abundance and to the administration of the earth, the underworld, and the sea. In *Peredur* the head clearly corresponds to the first function, the Lance to the second, and the *dysgl* or platter, to the third.[76]

Elisabeth Bik, while agreeing with Lozachmeur on the initiatory character of the Grail episode in *Perceval*, points out that he did not sufficiently emphasize one character who appears in Indo-European mythologies and who from early antiquity played an important role in initiatory rites: that is the Smith.[77] Trébuchet, the smith in *Perceval*, does not play a prominent role in the romance, yet Bik sees in him the same mysterious, dominant presence as the uncle in *Peredur*,[78] although her study concentrates exclusively on *Perceval*. She points out that the scene in the Grail Castle with its blazing fire and the canopy, columns, *graal, tailleor*, Lance, and sword, all made of metal, recalls a forge. The Smith in the various legends is said to make magic weapons for the hero and is often related to him. The Smith represents a powerful polyvalent divinity, having mastery over the elements, life, and death, and who is sometimes described as being lame. Trébuchet, as his name suggests, is lame, and Peredur's uncle is seen to limp. The two uncles in the Welsh romance are manifestations of the same divinity, so that the lameness of the first uncle, the proximity of his court to water, and the blazing fire in the hall, combined with the talismans, the iron column, and the sword test at the court of the second uncle create an overall image of the Smith. Bik thought that the dwelling of the Smith was probably in the Other World under the water and A.C.L. Brown also called Trébuchet a "sub-lacustrine smith."[79] When Peredur is finally directed to *Caer yr Enryfeddodau*, the Castle of Wonders, where he again finds the lame uncle, the description is ambiguous. He is told "a thi a wely lyn, a chaer o fywn y llyn" ("and you will see a lake and a fortress within the lake")[80] so that the *caer* could be in the middle of the lake on an island, or under its waters. It is possible that the lameness of Peredur's uncle may have contributed to the character of the *Roi Pescheor* in *Perceval*, since the limp may have been misunderstood as as a wound, or because, as Sterckx points out, a wound in the foot was also regarded as the equivalent of castration.[81] Originally, neither the lame smith nor the *roi mehaigné* would need to be healed, because their condition resulted from compensatory mutilations whereby the organ that would normally correspond to the god's power is sacrificed, so that the seer, like Odhin, is blind in one eye, the god responsible for contracts has no right hand, and the god responsible for bestowing fertility is castrated.[82] Thus both in *Peredur* and *Perceval* we have another figure central to the Indo-European initiation tales of the hero, the divine Smith.

It was said earlier that the characters in *Peredur* are of ancient and sometimes local origin. The romance was probably composed in the area where southeastern Wales meets southwestern England.[83] The two British Celtic tribes in that area were the Dobunni and the Silures. The Dobunni were people of importance, enjoying a high standard of living even before the Roman invasion of A.D. 43. The northern Dobunni chose not to oppose the Romans, and so their status and their prosperity continued to grow. The Silures were not as materially advanced as the Dobunni, and their opposition to the Romans was long and fierce. In both territories there are archaeological sites of major importance, and a brief comparison of the iconography of these sites with characters in *Peredur* will be useful. The Dobunni were master metalworkers in iron, copper, and bronze,[84] and in *Peredur* we have the Smith, the magical sword, and the iron column. The Miller in the romance has been shown to derive from the Celtic sky god Taranis,[85] while the Black Maiden, whose French equivalent is *la Demoiselle Hideuse*, also has roots in the area and in Celtic mythology.[86] The head cult is well attested in the region, from the glaring apotropaia on the antefixa at Caerleon (i.e., evil-averting designs on terra cotta plaques attached to the eaves of buildings), to the stone head discovered at Caerwent, the great head on the pediment of the temple at Bath (of which more will be said later), and the evidence of the headless skeletons resulting from a massacre at Bredon Hill in Worcestershire, which E.M. Clifford attributes to the Dobunni.[87] The nuns who are said to bring food to the Maiden of the Fortress, equivalent of Blancheflor, may well have been *genii cucullati*, small, hooded, male figures, clearly associated with fertility and often portrayed in twos and threes in the company of a goddess.[88] A further reflection of local mythology is found in the fact that Peredur is guided on his Quest by both male and female divinities, and, as Anne Ross has pointed out, the iconography of this region of Britain is unusual for the frequent appearance of divine couples.[89] Madrun, a local saint, is widowed and flees her enemies with her youngest surviving son, just like Peredur's mother, and, also like Peredur's mother, Madrun dies in exile.[90] Madrun is a medieval version of the goddess Matrona,[91] and, as we shall see, it is likely that Peredur's mother represents the same divinity.

Chrétien was the first to use the name *graal* for the vessel that has caused so much comment. In his day *un graal* was a normal everyday utensil used for serving food, its quality depending on the status of the household in which it was found. In the case of the *Roi Pescheor*, the *graal*'s magnificence is an indication of his wealth and importance. Helinand, abbot of Froidmont, wrote in 1225 that a *graal* was "scutella lata et aliquantulum profunda, in quae preciosae dapes divitibus solent apponi" ("a wide and fairly deep dish in which costly foods are customarily prepared for rich people").[92] Roques discussed the etymology of the word and its various dialectal forms in "Le Nom du Graal,"[93] while Reznikov sees a possible derivation from the Sanscrit *Graha*.[94] The word *graal* means exactly the same as *escuelle* ("platter"), but it has a more dignified and sonorous ring to it. If Chrétien had chosen to call his romance *Le Conte de l'Escuelle*, it would have sounded as if he were about to embark on a folktale. The *dysgl* described in *Peredur* is of exactly the same type, and Giraldus Cambrensis, writing in the same period as Chrétien, said that the Welsh ate from "scutellis latis et amplis."[95] The step from the Grail as a mysterious, wide, fairly deep dish to the holy chalice was made, quite deliberately, by Robert de Boron.[96]

THE HEAD IN *PEREDUR*

In both of these early versions of the Grail story, the author describes not a cauldron, not a chalice, not a goblet, but a large dish containing something of great significance. Because the symbol in *Peredur*, the head, is so radically different from that encountered in most of the other Grail romances, it has been said to set the Welsh tale outside the main body of Grail literature. However, it may well help to throw light on the question of origins. The head in the extant version of *Peredur* is a severed head, which may not have been the case originally, so, for the moment, we shall consider the head as being what Pierre Lambrechts called *un dieu sans corps*. Examples of this type of representation in which the head of the god stands alone, *pars pro toto* ("the part representing the whole"), are known in both Britain and Gaul.[97] Bearing in mind what has already been said about the significance of the head for the Celts, if one pictures the head in an upright position on the dish, then one has a symbol of exactly the same significance as the lingam and yoni (phallus and vagina) of Shivaite practice, the conjunction of male and female creative principles. The Celts were no strangers to phallic symbolism, frequently combining head and phallus, but as Anne Ross points out, the head takes precedence in Celtic iconography.[98] Another view of the head that will be referred to later is that it represented the sun in the sense of inner enlightenment. This brings to mind a symbol of divine power deriving from the worship of the goddess Cybele who is represented as a crescent moon in perpetual union with the sun, the solar disc resting on the crescent moon much like a globe on a dish.[99] Yet another such symbol was the *liknon*, a basket used for carrying fruit or as a child's cradle that was carried in the rites of Dionysos and contained first fruits and a phallus.[100] Alain Daniélou maintains that "the parallels between the names and legends of Shiva, Osiris and Dionysus are so numerous that there can be little doubt as to their original sameness."[101] Discussing the lingam, he quotes the *Siva Purana,* which says, "The Sun is envisaged as the progenitor of the worlds, hence its symbol is that of procreation."[102] With the Grail procession in mind, it is interesting to note that, along with the flashing spears of Celtic tradition, Shiva's favorite weapon is the spear with which he will destroy the universe.[103] The import of the two-part symbol lies not in the individual divinity of either element, but in the creative energy that is manifest at the moment of union of the two principles.

Just as Vedic Brahmanism absorbed elements of pre-Vedic Shivaism, so the Celts absorbed elements of the religion of the peoples they conquered, a religion dating from the Neolithic and Bronze Ages. It is possible that in Britain they encountered a symbol consisting of an upright phallus or a solar disc on a hollowed-out, dishlike base and, understanding the underlying significance, substituted their *dieu sans corps* for the upper part of the symbol. In view of what has already been said about *Peredur*'s links to the Severn Basin, it may be interesting to look at one more feature of the iconography of the area. The temple of Sulis-Minerva at Bath is currently world famous, and it was also known throughout the Roman empire. It was constructed possibly as early as the first century A.D. to organize the cult of Sulis along Roman lines, and to facilitate access by pilgrims, although there are signs that the Dobunni, in whose territory the sacred site lay, had made the area more accessible even in pre-Roman times.[104] One of the glories of the temple is the huge so-called Gorgon Head, centerpiece of the pediment, that serves both as an apotropaion against any evil influences that might threaten the site, and as an assurance to the devotee of the protection of Sulis. The head does have a certain resemblance to the Gorgon head *aegis* on Minerva's shield in that it has snakes among its wild locks and is set in a circle of oak leaves, but the work and the concepts are utterly Celtic.

The head is that of a male, solar divinity with a scowling face, huge glaring eyes that rivet the beholder, radiate hair (like the rays of the sun) in which are entwined a number of female snakes, huge ears, and a flowing mustache and beard, in which are entwined two male, crested snakes. Behind the head there are two great wings, and the whole picture is framed by two circles of oak leaves. Above the outer circle of oak leaves is a star and below it, on either side, is a helmet, the left one in the shape of a dolphin and the right one supporting a small owl. In each of the upper corners of the pediment is a Triton blowing a conch shell. On either side of, and supporting the outer oakleaf rim and the head, is a winged Victory whose feet rest on a globe. Richardson and Toynbee, who examined the pediment in great detail, interpret the presentation in terms of Classical mythology. They see the head, although clearly Celtic, as a version of the Medusa head on Minerva's shield; the oak leaves refer to Minerva as Jupiter's child, the owl is her bird, and the great head is that of a water divinity, set on the boss of a huge shield.[105] One should remember, however, that whereas a Roman or a Greek visitor would feel perfectly at ease with this symbolism, the site had been sacred long before the Romans arrived, presumably since humans first encountered the hot springs. The identification with Minerva was merely superficial; during the entire period of the Roman occupation, Bath was known as Aquae Sulis, not Aquae Sulis-Minerva.

The head is that of a solar divinity, all-seeing, all-hearing, and moving over his domain (indicated by his eyes, ears, and wings).[106] He is associated with the firmament (star), and the waters (Tritons), and he has chthonic associations (snakes and owl). The male snakes are crested, and, according to Ross, the crest has the same significance as the horns of bull, stag, or ram.[107] The thermal waters were a source of healing and regeneration, and divination was also practiced at the site. The picture is of a polyvalent, solar divinity, a *dieu sans corps*, a head in a huge, circular setting, supported by two young women. If we set the young women on their feet with the "shield" between them, we have the central part of the Grail scene in *Peredur*. It is likely that the Gaulish sculptors who carved the pediment were representing an important feature of regional religion and mythology in a way that would be acceptable to local Celts and foreign visitors alike.

The head on the *dysgl* in *Peredur* is a severed head, while the one on the Bath pediment is not; however, there may be an explanation. Both Peredur and Perceval's family circumstances are matrilinear, which is not an unusual situation in Arthurian literature. It is often the nephew, the sister's son, who is the important character. In this case Perceval is the nephew of the *Roi Pescheor's* father and the hermit, and Peredur also has two uncles. (The *balawc*, the Welsh priest who corresponds to the hermit, is not said to be a relative.) If the head on the platter in *Peredur* were that of his father or his cousin, then, according to the matrilinear system, either man would have been the wrong king and would have to be removed in order for the land to prosper. If the head on the platter were that of Brân, or recalled that of Brân, then it would raise the interesting possibility that the passage from *dieu sans corps* to *tête coupée* may reflect a conflict between the supporters of an older, female-centered system and a more recently introduced male-centered system. The story of Brân as it appears in the *mabinogi* of Branwen seems to describe just such a conflict. The supporters of the female-centered system are represented by Efnisien, Brân's half-brother, and the male-centered order is represented by Brân and Caswallon, son of Beli.[108]

We may have an echo of a similar situation in *Peredur*, where the head on the *dysgl* and the lameness of the uncle are blamed on the Witches of Gloucester. No reason is ever given for this enmity, but if the Witches, like Efnisien, represent the supporters of an older order trying to regain control of the system, then their attitude becomes clearer. When Peredur is sufficiently mature physically and spiritually, he calls on Arthur and his men, and the Witches are wiped out. Branwen dies, as does Peredur's mother, broken by the warrior world and the incoming power of the male. So too, does Madrun, who fled with her infant son before the advance of the Saxons. Branwen is one of the great goddess figures of Britain: behind Madrun we see the shadowy figure of Matrona, the mother goddess, and Peredur's mother probably represents the same divinity. If Beli and Brân do represent the encroaching power of the Celts over the earlier inhabitants of Britain, it is interesting that Efnisien's first reaction is to mutilate the horses belonging to Matholwch, Branwen's suitor, since the Celts greatly revered the horse in religious and temporal life. Also Cei, who is the early Celtic warrior par excellence,[109] is said to have destroyed nine witches in the same area of the world as the region in which *Peredur* was composed. The nine witches with their father and mother are reminiscent of the nine daughters of Ægir and Ran, the Norse sea divinities. It has been suggested that a closer comparison of Celtic and Norse mythology would be fruitful, and while some interesting work has been done in this area, the witches seem to have escaped attention thus far.[110]

Bik observed that Perceval is destined to be far more than the most perfect of knights, he is destined to replace the *Roi Pescheor*.[111] Lozachmeur speaks of initiation and a secret knowledge that will allow the hero to complete his task.[112] Certainly there would appear to be an esoteric level to the story. The hero is guided through his development, tested, trained, and tested again, until he is deemed fit to be brought before the sacred symbol, be it in the form of lingam and yoni, sun disc and crescent moon, or head on a great dish, which may well symbolize the fire in the water, the ultimate moment of creation. His development also includes a sacred marriage, a union with the territorial goddess, and in this part of the tale the important symbol is the cup. However, I believe that the vessel that became the Grail is not, as I had previously supposed, a sovereignty symbol, at least in any territorial sense.[113] The Irish and Welsh legends equate the land with a goddess who bestows herself on the chosen hero, and the same equation of female principle and land is shown in a tale told about Shiva. He is challenged by the tyrant Jalandhara to hand over his wife, in a story that closely resembles that of Arthur, Gwenhwyfar, and the Red Knight.[114] Perceval's search for the *graal* and the Lance and Peredur's search for the Empress and *Caer yr Enryfeddodau* reflect the adventures and trials of the heroes of the Indo-European initiation tales we have examined, and they also have much in common with the many quests of Indra, the god whose feats are celebrated in the Vedas. Jeanine Miller in her book on the Vedas analyzes the nature of the Quest and its objectives. She shows that the Quest is of a religious nature, it is always difficult, involving much effort and some violence, the hero is always alone, and, although the Quest seems to be over at the end of each adventure, it is repeated endlessly, for it is something that each individual must accomplish for himself. The object of the Quest is symbolized in many different ways, but the seeker is searching for the truth, inner enlightenment, understanding, and freedom.[115] Indra is described as seeking the sun, which he sometimes finds hidden in the waters and which is said to be the son of the waters.[116] This may be an indication of the meaning that a more evolved devotee might find in the symbolism of the great head at Bath. More than simply healing via the thermal waters, the great solar head, surmounted by a star, accompanied by Tritons, a dolphin, and an owl, and flanked by Victories standing on globes, may indicate the enlightenment, the knowledge of the mysteries of the heavens, the waters, the earth, and the regions beyond the physical cosmos, possessed by the divinities of the shrine, Sulis and her solar consort, and available to their devotees through the intermediary of the priests at the shrine. The thermal waters themselves would be a constant reminder of the creative, regenerative fire in the water. Peredur and Perceval would appear to be destined for a sacred royalty, a position combining the two aspects of Dumézil's first function, the spiritual and the temporal.

What we have come to know as the Grail theme may, then, have its origins in a myth as old as humanity, the search for the ultimate secret of creation. The story, which gives the inner search an outer form, involves the trials of the chosen ruler, his initiation into the highest mysteries, and a sacred marriage. The Smith may have been a part of the myth from the first, since the goddess, whose worship preceded the rise of the Indo-Europeans, was regarded as patroness of mines and metallurgy.[117] The Indo-European peoples developed the myth in their own way, involving kingship rituals, sacred objects, and a Vengeance Quest. In Britain, at least, the Vengeance Quest may be explained by the possibility of conflict between the incoming Celts and earlier inhabitants. In Celtic times, the central symbol became a head, a godhead, on the original great dish and still indicating a state of perfect balance. The severed head surrounded by blood, the Lance streaming with blood, indicate a state of war, of imbalance that the hero has to rectify. Peredur's family ties indicate a matrilinear situation, but his ties with his male relatives are emphasized, rather than those with his mother. Under a matrilineal system, as the sister's son, he would be the natural heir, and one would expect the Witches to be allies of the hero. However, Peredur appears to bridge both worlds; he is his mother's son, belonging to the old system, but he is also his father's son, and Efrawc seems to have been a typical Celtic warrior chief. The hero learns from the Witches, but having been instructed by his uncle, gathers together the forces of the Celtic world—Arthur and his warriors—and destroys that of the goddess. However, given the power of the Celtic goddesses, it is clear that the victory was not total.

It would appear that the original symbol was composed of two distinct parts, the dish and the phallus or sun disc, and later the head. The head was removed and the Mass wafer substituted for it in the version that Chrétien popularized. The character and role of the *Roi Pescheor* developed in such a way as to make the content of the *graal* irrelevant, so that in subsequent versions the vessel alone sufficed. Once the step to Holy Grail was taken, content was inevitably superfluous unless the vessel were said to contain the blood of Christ.

Once the emphasis had shifted from the identity of the man whose head lay on the dish and that of his killer, to the nature of the *Roi Pescheor*'s wound and the means of healing it, the Vengeance Quest lost its relevance. However, in Wales, the political situation made it extremely relevant still. The British Celts had been pushed back by Roman, Saxon, and finally Norman conquerors, creating a powerful and enduring theme of loss in Welsh literature. While *Peredur* certainly evokes memories of the sixth-century heroes of the Old North and their struggles against the Saxons, the descriptions of noblewomen in distress, nuns on the brink of starvation, and spiritual and temporal sovereignty under attack, mirror conditions in post-Conquest Britain equally well, keeping the idea of vengeance very much alive.[118]

The Grail legends appear to originate in the Celtic development of an ancient myth concerning the acquisition of spiritual enlightenment and earthly royalty. A British version of the myth, originating in the mythology of the Severn Basin, was adapted and taken to the Continent, where it was brought to the attention of Chrétien de Troyes and was subsequently blended into the rich variety of themes that constituted the *matière de Bretagne*, producing the body of literature known as the Grail romances.

NOTES

1. Alfred Nutt, *The Legends of the Holy Grail* (London: Nutt, 1902), pp. 5, 60, 125. See also R.S. Loomis, *The Grail: From Celtic Myth to Christian Symbol* (Cardiff: University of Wales Press, 1963; Princeton: Princeton University Press, 1991), p. 3.

2. *Le Roman de Perceval ou le Conte du Graal*, ed. William Roach (Geneva: Droz, 1959).

3. *The Continuations of the Old French "Perceval" of Chrétien de Troyes*, ed. William Roach, 5 vols. (Philadelphia: University of Pennsylvania Press / American Philosophical Society, 1949–83). Gerbert de Montreuil, *La Continuation de Perceval*, ed. Mary Williams (Vols. I and II) and Marguerite Oswald (Vol. III) (Paris: Champion, 1922, 1925, 1975).

4. *The Elucidation: A Prologue to the Conte del Graal*, ed. Albert Wilder Thompson (New York: Institute of French Studies, 1931). *Der Percevalroman*, ed. Alfons Hilka (Halle: Niemeyer, 1932), pp. 417–29. *Bliocadran: A Prologue to the Perceval of Chrétien de Troyes*, ed. Lenora D. Wolfgang (Tübingen: Niemeyer, 1976).

5. *Wolfram von Eschenbach, Parzival*, ed. Gottfried Weber (Darmstadt: Wissenschaftliche Buchgesellschaft, 1963). *Wolfram von Eschenbach, Parzival*, trans. Helen M. Mustard and Charles E. Passage (New York: Random House, Vintage Books, 1961).

6. *La Queste del Saint Graal*, ed. Albert Pauphilet (Paris: Champion, 1923). See also *The Vulgate Version of the Arthurian Romances*, ed. H. Oskar Sommer, 7 vols. (Washington, DC: Carnegie Institution, 1908–1916), VI.

7. *Le Haut Livre du Graal: Perlesvaus*, eds. William A. Nitze and T.A. Jenkins (Chicago: University of Chicago Press, 1932–1937).

8. *The Vulgate Version of the Arthurian Romances*, ed. H. Oskar Sommer (above, note 6), VI.

9. *Le Roman de l'Estoire dou Graal*, ed. William A. Nitze (Paris: Champion, 1927). *Merlin, roman du xiiie siècle*, ed. Alexandre Micha (Geneva: Droz, 1980). *The Didot Perceval*, ed. William Roach (Philadelphia: University of Pennsylvania Press, 1941).

10. *Historia Peredur vab Evrawc*, ed. Glenys Witchard Goetinck (Cardiff: University of Wales Press, 1976). A translation is found in Gwyn and Thomas Jones, *The Mabinogion*, Everymans Library (London: Dent, 1992), pp. 183–227.

11. *Lancelot: roman en prose du xiiie siècle*, ed. Alexandre Micha (Geneva: Droz, 1978–80); also *The Vulgate Version of the Arthurian Romances*, ed. H. Oskar Sommer (above, note 6), VI.

12. *Sone de Nansai*, ed. M. Goldschmidt (Tübingen, 1899). See also Loomis, *The Grail*, pp. 133–45 (above, note 1).

13. "Tant sainte chose est li graals. Et il, qui est esperitax Q'a sa vie plus ne covient Fors l'oiste qui il graal vient." ("The *graal* is such a holy thing. And he, himself is so spiritual that nothing more is needed to sustain his life than the host that is brought in the graal," Roach, vss. 6425–28).

14. *The Quest of the Holy Grail* (London: Cass, 1964); *From Ritual to Romance* (Garden City, NY: Doubleday, 1957).

15. In his *Yaksas*, Part 2 (New Delhi: Munshiram Manoharlal, 1971), pp. 37–47, Coomaraswamy examines Indian parallels to certain features of the Grail legends. In "On the Loathly Bride," *Speculum*, 20 (1945), 391–404, he points to Indian equivalents of the *Demoiselle Hideuse* and her ability to transform her appearance. In "Sir Gawain and the Green Knight: Indra and Namuci," *Speculum*, 19 (1944), 104–25, he examines the Beheading Test and also refers to the Grail.

16. *The Myth of the Goddess* (London: Arkana, 1991), pp. 625–53.

17. "Les Origines orientales de la légende du Graal," *Cahiers de Civilisation Médiévale*, 13 (1967), 207–19.

18. *Chrétien de Troyes and Le Conte del Graal*, Studia Humanitatis (Potomac, MD, 1981). *Chrétien, Troyes, and the Grail* (Chapel Hill: University of North Carolina Press, 1959) was written in collaboration with Urban T. Holmes Jr.

19. *"Visio Pacis": Holy City and Grail: An Attempt at an Inner History of the Grail Legend* (State College: The Pennsylvania State University Press, 1960).

20. "Le Graal de Chrétien et la demoiselle au Graal," *Romania*, 76 (1955), 1–27.

21. See his Foreword to *Perceval le Gallois ou le Conte du Graal mis en français moderne*, trans. Lucien Foulet (Paris: Delmain and Boutelleau, 1947; Paris: Nizet, 1975), pp. xix, xxii, xxxv.

22. "The Fisher King and the Grail in Retrospect," *Romance Philology*, 6 (1952), 14–22. Nitze also expressed that view in his *Perceval and the Holy Grail*, University of California Publications in Modern Philology, 28 (1949).

23. "Il Castello del Re Pescatore e i suoi Misteri nel *Conte del Graal* di Chrétien de Troyes," *Atti dell' Accademia Nazionale dei Lincei*, 10 (1961), 101–59. Further support to the theory of Christian origins is provided by Edmond Faral, "Note sur la Nature du Graal," in *Les Romans du Graal dans la littérature des XIIe et XIIIe siècles* (Paris: Editions du CNRS, 1956), pp. 59–62; Paul Imbs, "L'Élément religieux dans le *Conte del Graal* de Chrétien de Troyes," *Romans du Graal*, pp. 31–53; Myrrha Lot-Borodine, "Autour du Saint Graal: à propos de travaux récents," *Romania*, 56 (1930), 526–57; 57 (1931), 147–205; E. Anitchkoff, "Le Saint Graal et les rites eucharistiques," *Romania*, 55 (1929), 174–94.

24. *A New Interpretation of Chrétien's "Conte del Graal,"* University of North Carolina Studies in Romance Language and Literature, 8 (Chapel Hill: University of North Carolina Press, 1948); *Chrétien, Troyes, and the Grail* (Chapel Hill: University of North Carolina Press, 1959), in collaboration with Sister Klenke; *Chrétien de Troyes* (New York: Twayne, 1970).

25. *Chrétien's Jewish Grail: A New Investigation of the Imagery and Significance of Chrétien de Troyes' Grail Episode Based Upon Mediaeval Hebraic Sources* (Chapel Hill: University of North Carolina Press, 1976).

26. Rachel Bromwich, "Celtic Elements in Arthurian Romance: A General Survey," in *The Legend of Arthur in the Middle Ages* (Cambridge, Eng.: Brewer, 1983), pp. 41–55.

27. See Glenys Goetinck, *Peredur: A Study of Welsh Tradition in the Grail Legends* (Cardiff: University of Wales Press, 1975), pp. 290, 294.

28. See, for example, his *Arthurian Tradition and Chrétien de Troyes* (New York: Columbia University Press, 1952), his several contributions to *Arthurian Literature in the Middle Ages,* ed. R.S. Loomis (Oxford: Clarendon, 1959), *Wales and the Arthurian Legend* (Cardiff: University of Wales Press, 1956), and *The Grail* (above, note 1).

29. *Professional Interpreters and the Matter of Britain* (Cardiff: University of Wales Press, 1966).

30. *The Masks of God: Occidental Mythology* (New York: Penguin, 1964), p. 508; "Indian Reflections in the Castle of the Grail," in *The Celtic Consciousness,* ed. Robert O'Driscoll (Toronto: McClelland and Stewart, 1981), pp. 3–30.

31. *The Evolution of the Grail Legend* (Edinburgh: Oliver and Boyd, 1968).

32. See "The Fisher King and the Grail in Retrospect" (above, note 22).

33. "The Celtic Grail," *Revue Celtique,* 47 (1930), 340–82.

34. Helaine Newstead, *Brân the Blessed in Arthurian Romance* (1939; New York: AMS, 1966); R.S. Loomis, "The Head in the Grail," *Revue Celtique,* 47 (1930), 39–62.

35. "Naissance du Graal en Angleterre," in *Lumière du Graal: Études et Textes,* ed. René Nelli (Geneva: Slatkine Reprints, 1977), pp. 87–89.

36. See above, note 27, and Glenys Goetinck, "*Peredur*... upon reflection," *Études Celtiques,* 25 (1988), 221–32.

37. "Le Graal dans le cycle breton," *Lumière du Graal* (above, note 35), pp. 71–86.

38. "Le Héros du Graal," *Lumière du Graal,* pp. 90–100; "Le Problème des questions du château du Graal," *Romans du Graal* (above, note 23), pp. 249–74; *La Légende arthurienne et le Graal* (Paris: Presses Universitaires de France, 1956).

39. *Le Roman Breton, Perceval ou le Conte du Graal* (Paris: Centre de documentation universitaire, "Cours de Sorbonne," 1953); *Chrétien de Troyes: l'homme et l'œuvre* (Paris: Hatier-Boivin, 1957); "Le Cortège du Graal," *Lumière du Graal* (above, note 35), pp. 175–221; "Le Graal et l'hostie," *Romans du Graal* (above, note 23), pp. 63–78; *Autour du Graal,* Publications Romanes et Françaises, cxlvii (Geneva: Droz, 1977). This last work is a compilation of arti-

cles by Frappier, in two of which he argues strongly against the positions of Urban T. Holmes Jr., Sister Klenke, Helen Adolf, and Leonardo Olschki: *"Le Conte du Graal* est-il une allégorie judéo-chrétienne?" pp. 224–305, and "Le Graal et ses feux divergents," pp. 323–405.

40. Jean-Claude Lozachmeur and Shigemi Sasaki, "Researches on the Mystery of the Grail: Part II," *Avalon to Camelot*, 1 (1984), 20–23; "A Propos de deux hypothèses de R.S. Loomis," *BBIAS*, 34 (1982), 206–21; Jean-Claude Lozachmeur, "De la tête de Brân à l'hostie du Graal," in *An Arthurian Tapestry: Essays in Memory of Lewis Thorpe*, ed. Kenneth Varty (Glasgow: French Department of the University of Glasgow, 1981), pp. 275–86.

41. *L'Exaltation de la tête dans la pensée et dans l'art des Celtes* (Brugge: De Tempel, 1954), pp. 105, n. 1, 107.

42. "Perceval le Gallois, Brân le Méhaigné et le symbolisme du Graal," *Revue Belge de Philologie et d'Histoire* 62 (1984), 463–73; "Les Têtes coupées et le Graal," *Studia Celtica*, 20-21 (1985-86), 1–42.

43. *The Great Mother*, Bollingen Series XLVII, 2nd ed. (Princeton: Princeton University Press), pp. 288–89.

44. *Woman's Mysteries Ancient and Modern* (New York: Harper and Row, 1971).

45. *The Return of the Goddess* (New York: Crossroad, 1984), p. 158.

46. *La Femme Celte* (Paris: Payot, 1982), p. 292.

47. *Les Celtes et le druidisme: Racines de la tradition occidentale* (St.-Jean-de-Braye: Editions Dangles, 1994), pp. 360, 363–67.

48. See above, note 17.

49. See above, note 15.

50. *The King and the Corpse*, ed. Joseph Campbell, Bollingen series XI (Princeton: Princeton University Press, 1948), pp. 96, 98, n. 1, 129, 151, n.

51. "The Arabian Nights: Yet Another Source of the Grail Stories?" *Quondam et Futurus*, 1 (1991), 25–40.

52. *King Arthur: The True Story* (London: Century, 1992), p. 44.

53. See above, note 30.

54. "Recherches sur les origines indo-européennes et ésotériques de la légende du Graal," *Cahiers de Civilisation Médiévale*, 30 (1987), 45–63.

55. "Des Talismans fonctionnels des Scythes au cortège du Graal," in *Georges Dumézil à la découverte des Indo-Européens*, ed. Jean-Claude Rivière (Paris: Copernic, 1979), pp. 205–11; "Le Motif de l'epée jetée au lac: La mort de Batradz," *Romania*, 90 (1969), 289-340; 473-514; *Archéologie de l'epopée médiévale: Structures trifonctionnels et mythes indo-européens dans le cycle des "Narbonnais"* (Paris: Payot, 1981); "Des Scythes aux Celtes: le Graal et les talismans royaux des Indo-Européens," *Artus*, 14 (1983), 15–22.

56. *From Scythia to Camelot: A Radical Reassessment of the Legends of King Arthur, the Knights of the Round Table, and the Holy Grail* (New York: Garland, 1994).

57. *The History of the Celtic People* (1943; London: Bracken Books, 1992), pp. i, 129. See also pp. 3, 6, 38.

58. See *L'Exaltation*, p. 16 (above, note 41).

59. Françoise Le Roux noted the tendency of modern scholars to disparage the druids' intellectual sophistication due largely to their failure to reevaluate ideas based on nineteenth-century attitudes: "Le Dieu Druide et le Druide Divin," *Ogam*, 12 (1960), 379. See also Raimonde Reznikov, *Les Celtes*, pp. 11, 249, 326–27, 372 (above, note 47), and Myles Dillon, *Celts and Aryans* (Simla: Indian Institute of Advanced Study, 1975), pp. 25, 26, 95.

60. See for example Claude Luttrell, "*Le Conte del Graal* and Precursors of Perceval," *BBIAS*, 46 (1994), 291-94; B.F. Roberts, "The Welsh Romance of *The Lady of the Fountain (Owein)*," in *The Legend of Arthur in the Middle Ages*, pp. 170–82, esp. 181–82; C. Lloyd-Morgan, "Perceval in Wales: Late Mediaeval Welsh Grail Traditions," in *The Changing Face of Arthurian Romance* (Cambridge, Eng.: Brewer, 1986), pp. 78–91, esp. 79; D.D.R. Owen, *The Evolution of the Grail Legend*, pp. 179–85. For further bibliography on the relationship of *Peredur* to *Perceval* see Glenys Goetinck, *Peredur*, p. 2, n. 4 (above, note 27). I made it clear during the course of this study that French influence is evident (see pp. 204, 206, 225, 238–39, 261–63, 269), but a step-by-step, word-for-word comparison did not support heavy reliance of the Welsh text on the French.

61. Goetinck, *Peredur*, pp. 305–17; "upon reflection," 231 (above, note 36).

62. In this context it may be useful to note the warning voiced by Lozachmeur and Sasaki on the danger of confusing the date of composition and the date of transcription of a text ("deux Hypothèses," 215; above, note 40).

63. *La Femme Celte*, p. 284, n. 1 (above, note 46). Lozachmeur and Sasaki do not see *Peredur* as an adaptation of *Perceval* ("deux hypothèses," 216; above, note 40), but rather as representing an independent tradition ("Researches," 23; above, note 40).

64. *Le Cycle du Graal: Perceval le Gallois* (Paris: Gerard Watelet, 1995), pp. 18–19.

65. A detailed comparison of *Peredur* with *Perceval, Parzival, Sir Perceval of Galles*, The Second Continuation, the Didot-*Perceval*, and the legends of the Great Fool will be found in Goetinck, *Peredur*, pp. 41–128 (above, note 27). For the text of *Peredur* see Goetinck, *Historia Peredur*. Chrétien's text is edited by William Roach (see above, note 2). An English translation is to be found in Nigel Bryant's *Perceval, the Story of the Grail* (Cambridge, Eng.: Brewer, 1982). See also *Chrétien de Troyes, The Story of the Grail ("Li Contes del Graal") or Perce-*

val, ed. Rupert T. Pickens, trans. William W. Kibler, Garland Library of Medieval Literature (New York: Garland, 1990); *The Romances of Chrétien de Troyes*, trans. David Staines (Bloomington: Indiana University Press, 1990). For a modern French version, see above, note 21.

66. Loomis, *Arthurian Tradition*, p. 372 (above, note 28); Lozachmeur and Sasaki, "deux hypothèses," passim (above, note 40); Goetinck, *Peredur*, pp. 230, 259.

67. Goetinck, *Peredur*, pp. 205–06, 272, 288.

68. Lozachmeur, "origines," 47 (above, note 54).

69. Lozachmeur, "la Tête de Brân," 275–86 (above, note 40).

70. Loomis, *Wales*, p. 41 (above, note 28); *The Grail*, pp. 242–44 (above, note 1).

71. Sterckx, "Les Têtes coupées," pp. 30–34; "Perceval," pp. 468–71 (above, note 42).

72. Sterckx, "Les Têtes coupées," p. 34.

73. Lozachmeur, "origines," p. 57 (above, note 54).

74. Goetinck, *Peredur*, pp. 129–55 (above, note 27).

75. Grisward, "Talismans," pp. 206–11 (above, note 55). See also Georges Dumézil, *L'Idéologie tripartie des Indo-Européens*, Collection Latomus XXI (Brussels: Latomus, 1958).

76. For other correspondences between *Peredur* and the Indo-European tripartite system, see Glenys Goetinck, "*Peredur* and the three functions," *Zeitschrift für Celtische Philologie*, 47 (1995), 201–10.

77. Elisabeth J. Bik, "Le Forgeron lacustre, 'an inconsistent legend'?" *Cahiers de Civilisation Médiévale*, 35 (1992), 3–25.

78. Goetinck, *Peredur*, pp. 200, 203, 206–07, 220, 277, 321.

79. *The Origins of the Grail Legend* (Cambridge: Harvard University Press, 1943), pp. 445–46.

80. Goetinck, *Historia Peredur*, p. 66 (above, note 10).

81. Sterckx, "Les Têtes coupées," pp. 28–30; see also R.B. Onians, *The Origins of European Thought* (Cambridge: Cambridge University Press, 1988), p. 157, n. 1; pp. 524–43. Onians sees the Grail as symbol of fertility and he, too, feels that the long-held belief in the head as the source of procreation and fertility explains the appearance of a head on the dish in *Peredur,* "the Welsh version of the Grail."

82. For further examples see Claude Sterckx, "La Théogonie Irlandaise," *Jahrbuch für Anthropologie und Religionsgeschichte*, 4 (1982), 91.

83. Goetinck, *Peredur*, p. 35; "upon reflection," 224–25 (above, note 36). R. M. Jones, *Y Tair Rhamant* (Aberystwyth: Cymdeithas Llyfrau Ceredigion, 1960), p.xiv.

84. E.M. Clifford, *Bagendon: A Celtic Oppidum* (Cambridge, Eng.: Heffer, 1961), pp. 152–55.

85. Glenys Goetinck, "The Wheel God in Mediaeval Welsh Literature," *Ollodagos*, 7 (1994), 35–51.

86. Glenys Goetinck, "*Y Forwyn Bengrych* and her Background," *Bulletin of the Board of Celtic Studies*, 40 (1993), 83–94.

87. *Bagendon*, p. 155; see also Anne Ross, "Two Celtic Heads from Bron-y-Garth," *Archaeologia Cambrensis*, 119 (1970), 65; *Pagan Celtic Britain* (London; Routledge and Kegan Paul, 1967), p. 88.

88. J.M.C. Toynbee, "Genii Cucullati in Roman Britain," in *Hommages à Waldemar Deonna*, Collection Latomus XXVIII (Brussels: Latomus, 1957), pp. 456–69.

89. Ross, *Pagan Celtic Britain*, p. 231.

90. *The Oxford Dictionary of Saints* (Oxford: Oxford University Press, 1982), p. 255.

91. John Morris-Jones, *A Welsh Grammar* (Oxford: Clarendon, 1913, 1955), p. 97.

92. Loomis, *The Grail*, p. 29 (above, note 1); Frappier, *Chrétien de Troyes*, pp. 187–89 (above, note 39).

93. *Romans du Graal*, pp. 7–13 (above, note 23). See also F. Godefroy, *Dictionnaire de l'ancienne langue française*, s.v. *graal* and Du Cange, *Glossarium Mediae et Infimae Latinitatis*, s.v. *gradalis*.

94. Reznikov, *Les Celtes*, p. 367 (above, note 47).

95. *Opera*, ed. J.F. Dimock, Rolls Series VI (London, 1868), p. 183.

96. See Ernst Hoepffner, "Robert de Boron et Chrétien de Troyes," *Romans du Graal*, pp. 93-106, esp. p. 98 (above, note 23).

97. *L'Exaltation*, pp. 67 ff. (above, note 41).

98. "Celtic and Northern Art," in *Primitive Erotic Art*, ed. Philip Rawson (New York: Putnam, 1973), pp. 85–86.

99. Harding, *Woman's Mysteries*, pp. 133–34 (above, note 44).

100. Jane E. Harrison, *Prolegomena to the Study of Greek Religion* (New York: Meridian, 1955), pp. 518–34.

101. *Gods of Love and Ecstasy: The Traditions of Shiva and Dionysus* (Rochester, VT: Inner Traditions, 1992), p. 50.

102. *Myths and Gods of India* (Rochester, VT: Inner Traditions, 1991), p. 222.

103. Ibid., p. 217.

104. Barry Cunliffe, *Iron Age Communities in Britain* (London: Routledge, 1991), p. 174. Cunliffe has directed the excavations at Bath for many years and the major publications on the temple are to be found under his name.

105. I.A. Richmond and J.M.C. Toynbee, "The Temple of Sulis-Minerva at Bath," *Journal of Roman Studies*, 45 (1955), 97–104. See also Glenys Goetinck, "In Search of King Bladud," *Ollodagos*, 9 (1996), 177–220.

106. The wings behind the head are probably eagle wings, and whereas eagle and oak tree were sacred to Jupiter, they were also sacred to the Celtic sky god Taranis, whose main sacrificial offering was the human head. Taranis appears in *Peredur* as the Miller and threatens to behead the hero. Lleu, the hero of the Fourth Branch of the *Mabinogi*, flies off in the shape of an eagle and is discovered perched in an immense oak tree, while his unfaithful wife is transformed into an owl. For further discussion of Taranis, Lleu, eagle, oak, and owl, see Anne Ross, *Pagan Celtic Britain,* pp. 273–78 (above, note 87).

107. "Celtic and Northern Art," p. 85 (above, note 98).

108. See Glenys Goetinck, "Dioscuric and other themes in *Branwen*," *Ollodagos*, 6 (1994), 219-54, esp. 251–53.

109. See Linda Gowans, *Cei and the Arthurian Legend* (Cambridge, Eng.: Brewer, 1988).

110. Alby Stone, "Brân, Odin and the Fisher King: Norse Tradition and the Grail Legends," *Folklore*, 100 (1989), 25–38. Also see Anne Ross, *Pagan Celtic Britain*, p. 278 (above, note 87), and H.R. Ellis Davidson, *Myths and Symbols in Pagan Europe: Early Scandinavian and Celtic Religions* (Syracuse, NY: Syracuse University Press, 1988).

111. Bik, "Le Forgeron," p. 21 (above, note 77).

112. Lozachmeur, "origines," p. 57 (above, note 54).

113. Goetinck, *Peredur*, pp. 275–76, 289–90 (above, note 27).

114. See Heinrich Zimmer, *Myths and Symbols in Indian Art and Civilization*, ed. Joseph Campbell, Bollingen Series VI (Princeton: Princeton University Press, 1974), pp. 177–79.

115. Jeanine Miller, *The Vedas: Harmony, Meditation and Fulfilment* (London: Rider, 1974), pp. 33–38.

116. "Spiritual knowledge is a result of illumination and finds its full expression in the Vedic conception of the sun" (Miller, *The Vedas*, p. 86).

117. See Marija Gimbutas, *The Language of the Goddess* (San Francisco: Harper, 1989), p. 69; Mircea Eliade, *The Forge and the Crucible* (Chicago: University of Chicago Press, 1962), pp. 41–42.

118. Goetinck, "upon reflection," 225–31 (above, note 36).

CHAPTER 2

The Central Symbol of the Legend
The Grail as Vessel

EMMA JUNG AND MARIE-LOUISE VON FRANZ

It seems only natural that in the maternal domain of the unconscious—for thus we can interpret the Grail realm—Perceval should find not the personal mother but the mother *sub specie aeternitatis,* the primal image of the mother, the wondrous vessel. It is so self-evident that this is a symbol of the feminine and, as that which receives, contains and supports, of the maternal in particular that we shall not cite too many examples that bear on it but refer the reader to Jung's *Symbols of Transformation* where this aspect of the vessel is dealt with in detail.[1] Divested of the personal and viewed as an object, the vessel does not explicitly represent a human reality but rather an idea, a primal image. As such, it is of universal significance and is found in untold myths, legends and fairy-tales, of which only a few of the most appropriate will be quoted here.[2]

The symbolic meaning of the vessel goes back to the earliest of times and can therefore be termed an archetypal conception. It is one of the first manifestations of culture and as such is possessed of a magically significant, numinous character. This is apparent for example in a legend that Herodotus tells of Targilaos, the ancestor of the Scythians.[3] Four objects (ποιηματα), a plough, a yoke, an ax and a bowl (φιαλη), fall from Heaven in the presence of Targilaos' sons. Neither of the two elder brothers are able to take hold of them for when they try to the implements glow with fire. When the youngest approaches them, however, the fire is extinguished. He carries them home and is acknowledged king of the entire nation.[4] Here, four objects that distinguish the culture hero again have a numinous quality.

That the vessel is so frequently considered to be life-giving or life-maintaining is readily understandable when we realize how extremely important it must have been for earliest man to possess a receptacle in which, for instance, water, the stuff of life *par excellence,* could be transported or stored. According to Jung's definition, the archetypes represent innate predispositions to human behaviour in certain life situations and the ability to grasp their meaning. The image of the vessel could therefore correspond to such a "pattern," to a possibility inherent in the psyche of finding or producing a vessel and of discovering its uses.

Thus, in nearly all mythologies there is a miraculous vessel. Sometimes it dispenses youth and life, at other times it possesses the power of healing, and occasionally, as with the mead cauldron of the Nordic Ymir, inspiring strength and wisdom are to be found in it. Often, especially as a cooking pot, it effects transformations; by this attribute it achieved exceptional renown as the *vas Hermetis* of alchemy.

Let us begin by citing a few vessels from Celtic legends which exhibit a more or less close relation to the Grail story. Irish legend tells of Dagda's cauldron, one of the four treasures belonging to the semi–divine Tuatha De Danann; it could feed an entire army without becoming empty. In Welsh legend, too, there are many such vessels. Those who had been slain could be brought back to life in Bran's magic cauldron, merely forfeiting the power of speech in the process.[5] The cauldron of Caridwen[6] contained a beverage of wisdom and inspiration similar to the Nordic *Sinnreger.* The cauldron at Tyrnog was also one of these receptacles; when meat for a coward was put into it, it would not cook, while meat for a brave man was cooked at once. The basket of Gwyddno Gahanhir (Welsh: Mwys) [7] was one of the Thirteen Precious Things of the Island of Britain. When food for one man was placed therein, it was found on opening to contain sustenance for a hundred. According to J. Rhys, it offers the closest parallel to the Grail.[8] From the description it can be visualised as a sort of basket or chest. The word also means a measure. In Old Cornish *muis* or *moys* means table. In Irish, the charger on which John the Baptist's head lay was called *mias;* the meaning of the word is associated with the Latin *mensa* and is in fact very closely connected with the meaning of the Grail. It was said that this basket finally disappeared with Merlin when he withdrew into his house of glass on the Isle of Bardsey. According to Loomis,[9] the original model of the Grail was an Irish horn of plenty, and the word *cor* (horn) was confused with *cors* (body).[10]

Yet another vessel must be mentioned here. A poem by the Welsh bard Taliesin describes Arthur's journey to Annwn, the underworld, and the theft from that place of a vessel in many respects suggestive of the Grail. A passage from a rather obscure text,[11] a poem known as the "Preideu Annwn,"—"The Plundering (or Spoils) of the Underworld"—will indicate this similarity:

> Will fame not fall to my lot, when I let my song be heard ?
> The first word from the cauldron, when was it spoken,
> In Caer Pedryvan, which four times rotates?
> By the breath of nine maidens it was tenderly heated.
> Is it not the cauldron of the world below?
> And what is its nature?
> A round of pearls encircles its rim.
> For the coward it cooks no meat, neither for the breaker of oaths;
> A shining sword will be raised against him
> And in Lleminawg's hand will remain.
> At the gate of the Underworld the lamp did burn,
> When with Arthur we went—a splendid venture;
> None but seven from Caer Vedwyd returned.

The rim set with pearls is reminiscent of the gem-studded Grail which was also tended by young women. This vessel also did not permit the unworthy to share in the distribution of its blessed effects.

It will be useful here to make a brief survey of the meanings of the word "grail," of the forms which the vessel takes and of the peculiarities attributed to it in the various stories.

As we have already noted, the chronicler Helinandus traces the word back to the Latin *gradale* or *gradalis,* meaning a rather deep plate or dish. In F. Diez's *Etymologisches Wörterbuch der romanischen Sprachen* we find under *"Graal"*:[12] Old French *greal, grasal,* Provençal *grazal,* Old Catalonian *gresal,* a vessel, cup or bowl of wood, earthenware or metal. *Grazal, grazau, grial* are still in use today in the south of France to denote various receptacles. The French *grassale* (basin) may also be noted here. The word *grasal* (grail) is still found in certain dialects of southern and eastern France. R. Bezzola equates it with *garalis* and quotes a passage from a will of the Emperor Henry I (873), where *"garales argenteos cum binis cochleariis"* are mentioned.[13] P. Borel[14] maintains that the word must come from *grais, "Parce que ces vaisseaux sont faits de grais cuit"* ("Because these vessels are made of cooked earth"). *Vaisseau de grès* also means hard-fired earthenware crockery (stoneware). Diez considers this to be unlikely and is of the opinion that "a better case can be made for suggesting *crater,* for which Middle Latin used

the term *cratus,* from which the derivation *cratalis,* Provençal *grazal,*
French *graal,* could easily have evolved." H. and R. Kahane[15] and C.
Gossen[16] have also recently admitted to sharing this view.

Borel's questionable derivation of the word *graal* from *grès* (stone)
does, however, follow an association of mythological ideas, since in Wolfram the Grail is a *stone* which was said to have come from heaven[17] and
was called *lapsit exillis,* which was taken to mean *lapis elixir* by some,
and *lapis exilis,* meaning a small, inferior, inconspicuous stone,[18] by others. The word *grès* is closely connected with *grêle* (hailstone) and *grésil*
(hoarfrost) which, as the round white stone coming from heaven, reminds
us of manna and at the same time suggests the consecrated wafer which
was brought to the Grail from heaven every Good Friday in order to renew
its nourishing power. Conversely, *grêle* also accords with *exilis,* since it
likewise signifies *lean, thin.* Another interpretation cited by Helinandus,
but more as a popular meaning, derives *graal* or *greal* from *gratus* (pleasing, acceptable) and *gratia* (pleasantness, satisfaction, goodwill, grace,
reward), the French *agréable* (agreeable) from *gré* (wish). This interpretation is repeatedly vouched for in the works themselves. Robert de Boron's
"Joseph of Arimathea," for instance, tells us that:

> *Par droit Graal l'apelera*
> *Car nus le Graal ne verra*
> *Ce crois je, qu'il ne li agrée.*[19]

In the *Didot Perceval* we read, *"Et por ce l'appelons nos Graal,
qu'il agree as prodes hommes"* ("And this is why we call it Grail, because it please us as men"). Nascien, in the *Estoire du Saint Graal* of the
Lancelot Grail cycle,[20] says *"Car tout mi pensez sont acomplit puis ke je
voi chou que en toutes coses"* ("For all my thoughts are completed since
I see things which are in all things"). Merlin, in the poem of that name,[21]
says of the Grail:

> *Et ces gens claiment cel vaissiel,*
> *dont its ont belle grâsce—Graal.*

> All these men call this vessel
> from which they have this grace—the Grail.

In spite of the somewhat derogatory evaluation of this derivation (Helinandus describes it as popular and Nutt as punning),[22] it does not fit too

badly, since on the one hand the Grail is a wishing object, while on the other the effects of grace proceed from it. In Wolfram the wishing character is particularly clear. Of the Host, which on every Good Friday is placed on the stone (that is, the Grail) by a dove, it is said:

> *dâ von der Stein enpfaehet*
> *swaz gouts ûf erden draehet*
> *von trinken und von spîse*
> *als den wunsch von paradise:*
> *ich mein' swâz d'erde mac geberen.*

> From that the stone derives
> whatever good fragrances
> of drink and food there are on earth,
> like to the perfection of Paradise.
> I mean all things the earth may bear.

And in Book V, verse 430 ff:

> *man sagete mir, diz sage ouch ich*
> *ûf iuwex iesliches eit,*
> *daz vorem grâle waere bereit*
> *spîse warm, spîse kalt,*
> *spîse niuwe unt dar zuo alt,*
> *daz zâm und daz wilde.*

> Whatsoever one reached out his hand for,
> he found it ready
> in front of the Grail,
> food warm or food cold,
> dishes new or old,
> meat tame or game.

And verse 451:

> *môrag, wîn, sinopel rôt,*
> *swâ nach den napf iseslîcher bôt,*
> *swaz er trinkens kunde nennen,*
> *daz mohte er drinne erkennen*
> *allez von des grâles Kraft*

diu werde geselleschaft
hete wirtschaft vome grâle.

Whatever drink one held out his goblet for,
whatever drink he might name,
mulberry juice, wine, or red sinopel,
he found the drink in his glass,
all by the power of the Grail,
whose guests the noble company were.[23]

The Grail is therefore a real *Tischleindeckdich,* a horn of plenty, a wishing object or vessel such as also frequently appears in fairy-tales in the
form of pots, baskets, cups or cloths. The connection of *gratum, gratia,
grâce* with the Christian relic is obvious and accords with the concept of
the Grail as a relic of this kind. Another attempt at a derivation, which,
however, is certainly incorrect, equates *san greal* as it is often written,
with *sang real* (royal blood), meaning the blood of Christ, which was
thought to be contained in the Grail.

Yet another explanation, advocated among others by P. Paris, is that
the designation of Grail came about because the story was originally included in a gradual, a book used for church services, and so named because it contained the gradual, a hymn set to musical intervals. Actually,
the obvious and well-attested derivation from *gradale* (dish) could suffice, except that it seems to belong to the nature of the vessel that new associations to its meaning are continually being sought for. It is remarkable
how this also finds expression in speech: words present themselves as related, or as in some degree manifestly pertinent, and even if the connection cannot be proven scientifically, they do nevertheless indicate the
ambiguity of the designated object in a manner which is satisfying in a
feeling way and which allows its many facets to light up. All of this indicates that it is not simply a matter of a mere vessel but of a symbol.

W. Hertz's book, *Die Sage von Parzifal und dem Graal,*[24] gives us a
few more examples of the changes which time has brought about in the
meaning of the word. As a designation of the highest value, the word
"Grail" appears in religious songs and in *Minneliedern.* Mary is compared
to the Grail, even God himself is called "the Highest Grail." The beloved is
described as the Grail of the heart (Reinmar von Zweter), or a pure woman
is spoken of as the Grail which must be fought for.[25] With time the word
took on more and more the meaning of a banquet and an entertainment.
Thus, about 1280 a play about a young woman called Frau Feie (from

Sophia) was presented in Magdeburg, a kind of tournament in which a camp called *der Gral* was pitched. In Brunswick in the fifteenth century, the Grail was an important popular festival, taking place every seven years and held for the last time in 1481. The word *grâlen* was used to indicate loud sounds of noisy rejoicing, rather in the sense of *bawling*. In the sixteenth century, *gralisieren* or *kralisieren* (to make a cheerful noise) also came into use in High German with the substantive *Krales*. "To go to the *Grals* (or *Grollus*)" meant to go to a feast. In religious poetry, too, the Grail became a place of pleasure. In an old prayer from Bremen, for example, the eleven thousand virgins dance in the heavenly Grail before the Virgin Mary.

By degrees, the word took on a more questionable nuance. Thus, the Dutch chronicler Veldenaer wrote towards the end of the fifteenth century: "Some chroniclers assert that the Knight of the Swan (Lohengrin) came from the Grail, as the earthly Paradise was formerly thought to have been called; that, however, is not Paradise but a sinful place which is entered as the result of high adventure and is only departed from again by means of high adventures and good fortune." A chronicler of Halberstadt in Saxony says: "The historians are of the opinion that the Knight of the Swan came from the mountain where Venus lives in the Grail." In the round mountain of St. Barbara near Pozzuoli there lived, so runs the legend, a great company of bewitched men and women who were forced to spend their lives there in dancing and lechery until the Day of Judgment.[26] Among the Germans of the sixteenth century the legend and the word vanished from popular speech; in Frisch's German-Latin dictionary of 1741,[27] under *Graal* (grail) it simply says, "An old play which was performed with dancing and shouting."[28] Thus F. Locke asserts quite rightly that the symbol of the Grail is an archetypal image of polyvalent meaning.[29]

Just as the word is certainly ambiguous and as its meaning changes, so the Grail itself and the events associated with it are not everywhere the same. The impression is often clearly conveyed that with the emergence of the subject, a proliferation of fantasy set in which never tired of devising new arrangements and combinations, similar to the profusion of ornaments, flowers, animals, saints and monsters that confront us in Gothic cathedrals. The formation of such different styles and the modifications which the material underwent in the process bear witness to the fact that it possesses an inherent psychic life of its own which will not allow itself to be confined to any one specific pattern. In Chrétien it is introduced as *a* grail, not *the* Grail, for this was, as we have seen, the designation for a particular type of vessel. Further on, it is described as being of pure gold, set with precious stones and with such a brilliant light streaming from it that nearby candles lost their brightness.

It is not clearly stated here that the Grail provides food, merely that with every course the vessel is carried uncovered past those at meat. In other versions, it does provide food for those at table. In the description of Gauvain's visit to the Grail Castle, it is called *le rice Graal* and the point is made that it goes around the table serving food without being carried by anyone.

In later continuations of the romances centering around Perceval, as well as in most of the other works, the Grail is expressly referred to as the vessel used by Christ at the Last Supper which later came into the possession of Joseph of Arimathea.[30] The Grail also dispenses food in those versions which have a more religious bias. When he is in prison, Joseph of Arimathea is miraculously fed and comforted by it, as he later is during his wanderings with his family.

In the *Queste del Saint Graal,* it appears in a wondrous manner at Whitsuntide, just as King Arthur is sitting down to supper with his knights. "A clap of thunder sounded, followed by a brilliant ray of light. The Grail then entered, covered with white velvet, without being carried by anyone, and the chamber was filled with a pleasant fragrance. As it went round the table each person was served with the food he desired."

In Heinrich von dem Thuerlin's *Diû Krône,* the Grail is described as a reliquary casket containing a piece of bread, of which one third is presented to the Grail King. Besides this, a *toblier* (probably a beaker, tumbler) in which there are three drops of blood is mentioned, so that here we already have an unmistakable allusion to the Eucharistic sacrament. This finds unequivocal expression in the works of an outspokenly religious nature[31] in which the Grail, called *le Saint Vaissel,* becomes the vessel of the Mass, the chalice or ciborium, and the Grail Service the Mass. In Chrétien Perceval learns from the hermit that the Grail contains the Host which serves the Old King for food. From the vessel containing the blood of Christ to the chalice of the Mass is only a short step.[32]

In the *Perlesvaus,*[33] King Arthur attends a Grail service celebrated by a number of hermits. The story recounts that "at that time there was no chalice in King Arthur's realm. In the mystery of the Mass, the Grail appeared in five forms which, however, may not be mentioned because no one may speak of the mystery of the sacrament, excepting he who by divine grace is fitted to do so. King Arthur saw all these transformations, the last of which was into a chalice, while the hermit who had sung the Mass found on the corporal-cloth a letter saying that it was the Will of God that his body should be consecrated to his memory in that cup." We have already discussed the meaning of the blood and referred to the mysterious and numinous effect the idea of a relic of the blood of Christ must have had upon the people of that age. But it is not only in the veneration and the attempt to grasp the significance of Christ's blood that deep emotional and archaic reactions are touched; the symbol of the vessel in which it is preserved naturally causes an equally profound impression. That the "soul-substance" should be preserved in a funerary vessel conforms to a particularly archetypal concept which has its roots in antiquity and the East. At the burial of certain African chieftains, for instance, the fluids secreted by the corpse are collected in a leather bag or receptacle and buried apart as being especially "holy." According to the natives the animal that incarnates the soul of the deceased and which represents the survival of the soul of their kings comes out of this bag.[34] Similarly, in Egyptian burial rituals all of the easily corruptible parts of the body of the dead Pharoah were separately interred in four canopic vases. These, for the most part, had lids in the form of the heads of the four sons of Horus, who brought about the resurrection and ascension of their grandfather. They were the agents for the resurrection of Osiris. In later times Osiris himself was represented as a receptacle with a human head.[35] It is as if the vessel contained the magic soul-substance of the god; it does not, therefore, seem out of order to attribute a similar meaning to the Grail.

The vessel containing Christ's blood is a symbol that emerges with absolute spontaneity. It is the main motif of the story, the Grail motif.[36] It is as though it contained the living remnant of Christ and *his soul-substance, that element out of which a mystical continuation of his being is made possible.* For this reason a connection with the myth of Osiris cannot be dismissed out of hand, for there is a tradition which points in that direction, namely the *Légende de l'Abbaye de Fécamp,*[37] already referred to. In this legend it is Nicodemus who, with a knife, scrapes the dried blood from Christ's wounds and conceals it, first in his glove, then in a lead container, a small cylinder according to the description. He hides the cylinder in the trunk of a fig tree. Because of a threatened invasion of Sidon, where he is residing, and in obedience to a divine command, he entrusts the tree to the sea; it is carried to the West and washed ashore on the coast of Normandy, near Fécamp. There the trunk again takes root and puts forth leaves. Owing to the remarkable influences that emanate from the spot, a church and later a monastery are founded there, although the holy blood hidden in the trunk is not yet discovered.[38]

The similarity between this story and the Grail legend is remarkable,[39] not only in detail but also because in both the vessel containing the holy blood remains hidden for a long time and is noticed only because of the strange effects it produces. The Fécamp version clearly suggests the "myth of Osiris" reported by Plutarch,[40] in which the coffin of Osiris is washed ashore at Byblos in Phoenicia, the land of the origin of the fig tree, and is concealed in a bush of heather which grows up around it. It therefore seems probable that traces of the myth of Osiris survive in the Grail story. But even if no historical connection does exist, the same archetype appears none the less to have manifested itself once again. The aspect of the Grail as a sepulchre is very clear in Robert de Boron's version. In the Latin version of the Gospel of Nicodemus,[41] Joseph of Arimathea says to Christ, who appears to him in prison, that to prove he really is the saviour he should show him, Joseph, where he laid the body. Whereupon Christ takes him by the hand and leads him to the grave. In our version Christ delivers the cup to Joseph instead, thus hinting that the Grail is synonymous with the grave. This is the point at which the Grail story diverges from the Gospel of Nicodemus and follows its own course. At the time of the formation of the Grail legend, emotions were deeply stirred by the idea of the Holy Sepulchre, and it was this idea that imparted such inflammatory motive power to the Crusades, if it did not actually cause them. The task of freeing the Holy Sepulchre from heathen powers formed the central aim of the undertaking. This aspect of the Grail motif, and the way in which the literal freeing of the Holy Sepulchre gradually became an inner goal as well, has been brilliantly elucidated by Helen Adolf. She has also pointed out the aspect of the Holy Sepulchre as that place where the mystery of the resurrection came to pass, thereby giving the sepulchre an especially numinous character.[42]

In every age and every land, holy graves have enjoyed veneration on account of the blessed effects emanating from the remains of those buried within them. With Christ's sepulchre the case is different, in so far as Christ was resurrected and the grave consequently left empty. Furthermore, its authenticity is by no means certain, since it was said to have been choked up with rubble and only discovered as the result of a miracle three hundred years later when the Emperor Constantine had it dug for. In the intervening centuries heathen holy places had occupied the site.[43] If, in spite of this, the sepulchre was considered to be precisely the most important object of devotion in Christendom, this was because something of far greater moment was concealed behind and beyond the concrete actuality, namely a symbol or an idea. The great riddle of death has naturally occupied the human spirit from time immemorial, as is witnessed by the ideas that have attached themselves to its visible and, so to speak, its enduring expression—the grave.

The cult of the grave is one of the very earliest manifestations of religious conviction and appears among nearly all races and in the most varied stages of culture. Great significance is attributed to the graves of saints in the non-Christian worlds of China, India and Tibet, while the most holy place in all Islam is the Grave of the Prophet. The grave plays an important part not only in religion but also in popular superstition,[44] where magical powers of the most diverse kinds are attributed to it. In fairy-tales and legends, too, wonderful things come to pass in connection with graves, as in the German version of the well-known story of Cinderella, where the mother's grave possesses the power of granting wishes, and beautiful clothes or golden apples fall from the tree growing above it. For the most part the place of burial is looked upon as the home of the dead, from which either the deceased or his spirit can still exercise his influence. It was said of the Tuatha De Danann that they withdrew into the burial mounds where they live on and occasionally appear to men. As mentioned, every consecrated altar in a Roman Catholic church must contain relics, so that it is at the same time also a grave; often it is even shaped like a sarcophagus.

Like the vessel, the grave has a maternal meaning, since the mother is not only the place of birth but also, as Mother Earth, that which receives the dead back into herself. The primal image of the mother is suited for this dual aspect of life and death.[45] Both the food- and drink-imparting, life-bestowing aspect and the aspect of death and the grave are exhibited by the Grail. The mystery of coming into being and of ceasing to be is bound up with the image of the mother; this explains why Mysteries with this process as the content of their ritual were connected with the cult of mother goddesses such as Demeter and Isis. [46]

The great and genuinely vital mystery of the death and resurrection of the god also forms the central point of the Christian religion. Through the sacrificial death of Christ the believer is not only assured of the remission of sins but also of resurrection and life everlasting. The idea that new life can be produced through sacrifice, especially bloody sacrifice, is as old as mankind itself. The life-bestowing property of the Grail is therefore conditioned in a two-fold manner, on the one hand through its maternal significance and on the other through the sacrificial blood it contains. If in our story prominence is now given to the vessel in its meaning as grave, and especially the grave of Christ, this is because it is there that the mysterious transition from death to life, the resurrection, took place. Equally, the Eucharistic chalice is where the ineffable mystery of transubstantiation is consummated. Indeed, this event is represented in the Mass as eternally taking place, just as, although in a somewhat different sense, the succession of life and death is also an unending rhythm. The idea of the Communion cup as the grave of Christ and therefore as the place of his death and resurrection seems to have been familiar to the Middle Ages, as is indicated in a passage from Honorius of Autun, which reads:[47]

> When the priest says, *"Per omnia saecula saeculorum,"* the deacon comes before him and elevates the chalice. He covers a portion of it with a cloth, then returns it to the altar and covers it with the corporal, enacting the part of Joseph of Arimathea who took the body of Christ down from the cross, covered his face with a sudarium, laid the body in the grave and covered it with a stone. That which is here offered, and also the chalice, are covered with the corporal, which signifies the linen winding sheet in which Joseph wrapped the body of Christ. The chalice signifies the grave, and the paten the stone with which it was closed. [48]

In our story, the Grail vessel, as mentioned, is depicted as a prefiguration of the Communion cup and the service of the Grail as similar to the Mass. It differs from the Mass however; instead of a sacrifice another transformation takes place. The wine does not have to be transubstantiated, because the sacrificial blood is already in the vessel, nor is there anything that can be clearly recognized as a death and resurrection mystery. Perceval's assumption of responsibility for the Grail could of course denote a renewal of the Fisher King, the more so since the King dies after installing his successor in office.[49] In the version of the legend under discussion, as in most of the other versions, the sick king becomes healthy and *"toz muez de sa nature"* ("quite transformed") as soon as Perceval asks the question, only to die three days later.

This interpretation seems superficial. The type of renewal wherein the son steps into the father's shoes is far too natural and well known to be able to express the transformation that is meant by the mystery of resurrection. We must therefore try to probe the symbols more deeply and for that purpose will consider another aspect of the grave. The grave cannot be looked upon only as the place of transformation and resurrection, but must also be viewed as the state of being dead or buried. There seems to be a special significance attached to precisely this aspect of our story. In the grave life has vanished, it is not manifest but concealed. This brings us to another age-old conception, that of the hidden treasure and, in connection with it, to the following train of thought:

Hidden treasure is a preferred ingredient of legends and fairy-tales. According to popular belief[50] this treasure is imagined as being within the earth, in such places for instance as where the grass grows more luxuriantly, where the snow never lies, where a meteorite has fallen or where the rainbow touches the earth. The acquisition of buried treasure is made more difficult by its power to change location. Thus it is said that treasure moves away, it grows, rises or falls. It only comes to the surface of the earth once every seven hundred years, at which time it announces its presence by little blue flames, the so-called "treasure fire." The efflorescence of the treasure generally takes place at night and only at particular times that are propitious for excavating it. Treasure is frequently not recognised since it appears in the guise of a valueless object. The riches lying under the earth are seldom unguarded. Either a good or an evil spirit watches over them, facilitating or hindering their removal, as the case may be. Most frequently it is the Devil who is encountered as guardian, although often enough it is poor souls or little grey men who have acquired gold in a questionable manner and therefore have to atone to the treasure until it is dug up. Their salvation depends on the successful removal of the hoard. This is often reserved for a particular man of a particular age and having particular attributes. The heroes who have withdrawn into the hills, like Barbarossa or King Arthur, are also inhabitants of the treasure mountains. The typical motifs of the land of the dead can also be detected in the legends of treasure mountains; they were originally the dwelling place of the dead. The belief in treasure must therefore be rooted in the custom of burial gifts, and the earliest legends about treasure would have been stories of robbing graves. We have also seen the Grail as a treasure of this kind. For instance, it manifests itself only at a certain time and only *one person* is able to find it. Certain it is that this deeply-rooted concept of the hidden treasure contributed to the fact that the summons to liberate the Holy Sepulchre awakened such a resounding echo. It is not without reason that these ideas are the cherished children of the imagination. They are deeply embedded and should not be brushed aside as mere infantile wish-fulfilment fantasies. The treasure seeker's instinct is not directed solely towards concrete objects for, as is known, there are treasures of another kind, so that one can imagine the things in varied and different ways. The idea of being dead or in the grave as a psychic condition is sometimes reflected in philosophical views. In the *Gorgias* for instance, Plato has Socrates say: "Well, life as you describe it is a strange affair. I should not be surprised, you know, if Euripides was right when he said, 'Who knows, if life be death, and death be life ?' And perhaps we are actually dead, for I once heard one of our wise men say that we are now dead, and that our body is a tomb."[51] The same is meant in Heraclitus' dictum, "We live the death of the Immortals, they live ours."[52] Very similar is the Christian doctrine of the body as a prison. This idea was worked out in extraordinary detail in those systems of Gnostic doctrine which spoke of the descent of the soul into the physical world and of its imprisonment there, and above all in the teachings of Mani with their Zoroastrian influence. According to Mani, who accepted the opposing realms of light and darkness as existing from eternity, the entire material world, together with everything that lives in it, is the grave of the light element which has vanished or been imprisoned within it. The work of redemption consists in releasing this light element from the darkness of matter and in its reunion with the realm of light. Attention has often been called to the fact that these Gnostic ideas may be connected to the Grail stories by way of the Catharists and Albigensians.[53]

The idea of the hidden treasure finds its most far-reaching and individual elaboration in alchemy. This elaboration proceeds from the assumption that something precious, i.e. a spirit, is concealed or bound in the substance, the *prima materia* or *vilis,* and that the work of the "royal art" consists in freeing or transforming it.[54] Consequently, according to the alchemistic view, to be dead and buried—an incomprehensible state of existence—is looked upon as the primary condition and as the starting point for the *opus,* in contrast to the general view that death and burial come at the close of life.[55] From this it may be concluded that the life worked on in the *opus,* or through the Grail, was different from visible, physical existence, as Christ's empty grave also denoted the dawning of a new and differently conditioned life. This difference did not, however, appear to refer to an existence after death, but to one which would run its course during this life, though on another level.

It is natural to suppose that things buried or hidden merely refer to something unconscious which only needs to be dug up or uncovered, like a treasure raised to the light of day. The concept of an empty grave, however, seems to point further. It could be a question here of something so concealed and invisible that it is as if it had never existed at all, something which did not merely need to be uncovered but which to some extent had to come into existence first. This then would be that other life referred to above, not the natural, bound-to-nature life of the body but the life of the inner man, transcending nature, that encompassing personality which Jung has called the Self.[56] In the dreams and fantasy pictures of modern man this hidden, invisible something is occasionally depicted as a meaningful and numinous void. There is one picture in which an egg-shaped void, from which rays stream forth, forms the centre of a world or of a mandala with an empty centre.[57] The words of Meister Eckhart beautifully express what is meant by this image: "Everything must be lost, the soul must exist in unhampered nothingness," or "Whosoever would come to God must come as nothing."[58] Or, expressed in Eastern imagery: "In the purple hall of the city of jade dwells the God of Utmost Emptiness and Life."[59] The Confucians call it "the centre of the void." A nothingness, a void, is therefore the inescapable condition for the emergence of the Self.[60] The Self is not already present from the beginning in a comprehensible form, but manifests itself only through the outer and inner realizations of a life lived to its end. For this reason Jung has likened it to the crystal lattice[61] present as a potential form in a solution but which first becomes visible in the process of crystallisation, although crystallisation does not necessarily take place. The Self is therefore not complete, but is present in us as a potentiality which can become manifest only in the course of a specific process. Certainly, the Self is not invariably realized through the unfolding of the natural biological life processes. There appear to be many lives where this does not come to pass.

Then how and by what means can the Self become manifest? It is realized to that extent in which it is lived in the experience of daily life. It is not achieved, however, when it appears in symbolic form in dreams and inner images, nor is it when consciousness acquires a specific degree of clarity, nor yet when a psychological function has attained a high degree of differentiation. Important as consciousness undoubtedly is—and rightly utilized consciousness is an invaluable means of help for the realization of the Self—it is not by itself the determining factor. For it does not depend so very greatly on knowledge and ability or upon some degree of intelligence, but rather upon the use which is made of these attributes and above all, on the psychic attitude a person adopts in the face of the various circumstances of his life and fate. As the threads of fabric are woven into a pattern, so the Self as the living garment of divinity is woven out of the many decisions and crises, in themselves possibly insignificant, by which we are affected in the course of our lives. Such occasions present themselves at every level of life and intelligence and in every milieu. Whether or not they lead to a manifestation of the Self depends solely on our own response. Many of us have observed that children, even small children, when faced with some difficulty, possess an attitude which many adults could only envy. That "something," the lack of which we experience as soullessness, is a "someone," who takes a position, who is accountable and who feels committed. Where this higher, responsible ego is lacking there can be no

Self. Ethos and the Self are therefore mutually interdependent. For this reason, too, an attitude of "beyond good and evil," such as has been commended in many quarters in modern times and especially since Nietzsche, is the best way to prevent the emergence of the Self.

From the foregoing we can see that a fascination can emanate from something empty. It longs for completion like an invisible form which calls out for substance; the individual is conscious of the existence of this summons and of the growth of this attraction, but without knowing what it is that calls to him. The influence emanating from the hidden Grail could be likened to such a summons.

A further characteristic of the Grail is that it distinguishes between good men and sinners, in that its beneficial effects are perceived only by the former. A vessel possessing a similar discriminating function also appears in Celtic mythology. Manawyddan, son of Lir, a divinity of the sea, owned, among other precious objects, a cup which broke whenever a lie was told. The same trait is found in an old Irish tale, "The Vessel of Badurn" (from *Irish Ordeals):*

> Badurn is the name of a king. His wife went to the fountain on one occasion, and there saw two women, carrying a bronze chain between them, come out of the fairy hills. When they saw the woman coming towards them they vanished into the fountain. She followed them in and in their home she saw a wonderful method of ordeal. This was a crystal vessel or cup that had the peculiarity that when someone spoke three lying words it divided itself into three parts in his hand, and when anyone uttered three true words the pieces united again. Badurn's wife begged for the vessel, which Badurn then kept in order to discriminate between truth and falsehood.[62]

Through *disintegration* the vessel indicated that a lie was being told, and through *unification* it bore witness to the truth, as though to illustrate the way an individual's soul is similarly affected by his words. He who lies deceives himself and disintegrates in the process, whereas he who tells the truth "heals" his soul and makes it whole. It is a temptation at this point to think of that vessel filled with νοῦς (understanding and consciousness) which is mentioned in the *Corpus Hermeticum* and which, as Hermes taught his pupil Thoth, was sent from heaven to earth so that men, plunging into it, might understand the purpose for which they were created.[63] A vessel of this kind also played a part in the Gnostic mystery celebrations of late antiquity. In Hans Leisegang's study, "The

Mystery of the Serpent," [64] an illustration is given of a bowl that appears to have originated in an Orphic community.[65] On it sixteen naked men and women, in reverential and worshipping attitudes, stand around a coiled and winged serpent, the symbol of the Redeemer and Son of God in the Orphic Gnosis. The serpent leads them towards the development of consciousness. A text of the Perates[66] says: "Now no one can be saved and rise up again[67] without the Son, who is the serpent. For it was he who brought the paternal models down from above, and it is he who carries back up again those who have been awakened from sleep and have reassumed the features of the Father." In this bowl the Logos-serpent is clearly being worshipped by the initiates. According to the views of the Gnostic Naassenes, another vessel, known as the cup of Anacreon, mediated a similar gnosis (knowledge) of God. This sect believed that there was an androgynous original being who had to be redeemed from matter. The Greeks called him "the heavenly horn of the moon" and in a state of ecstasy declared:

> Bring water here, boy, bring wine.
> Immerse me in stupor and frenzy.
> My tankard tells me
> Speaking in mute silence
> What I must become.[68]

Probably the Persian-Arabic legend of the cup of Jamshyd, in which all the mysteries of the world could be perceived, and the stories of Solomon's miraculous cup can be traced back to just such Gnostic sources.[69] The writer Ibn Malik recounts a vision of Mohammed's which the latter commanded Malik to describe as follows: "On the night when I ascended to Heaven I glimpsed, under a canopy, a goblet of such penetrating brightness that all the seven heavens were illuminated by it. Around the goblet was a prayer written in green characters. [According to a second manuscript[70] the goblet itself was green.] . . . A voice declared, 'Oh, Mohammed, the All Highest God has created this goblet for thine enlightenment.'"[71] That Gnostic traditions survived into the early Middle Ages is proved by the *coffrets gnostiques,* boxes found in Provence on which are portrayed naked initiates.[72] Gnostic cult objects, presumably through the agency of Arabic and especially Sabean culture, reached into Sicily, Spain and the south of France. It is therefore not beyond the bounds of possibility that certain influences which affected the Grail legend could have originated there. The vision of the Gnostic alchemist Zosimos of Panopolis in Egypt (third century A.D.), in which he saw a cosmic altar in the form of a bowl,[73] is related to the vessel mentioned in the *Corpus Hermeticum* in which men acquired νοῦς (consciousness). In a dream Zosimos saw an altar in the form of a shallow bowl in which men in torment were being cooked and thereby sublimated into a state of spirituality. In another of his works, Zosimos mentions the *krater* (mixing bowl) of Poimandres[74] in which he advises his *soror mystica* to immerse herself. "The *krater*," says Jung, "is . . . a font or piscina, in which the immersion takes place and transformation into a spiritual being is effected. It is the *vas Hermetis* of later alchemy . . . uterus of spiritual renewal or rebirth."[75] In this *krater*, which is the subject of the books of the *Corpus Hermeticum,* Henry and Renée Kahane even see the actual source of Wolfram's idea of the Grail. They assume that this book came to Spain via the agency of the Sabeans and thus to the notice of the mysterious Kyot—Wolfram's source.[76]

In alchemy the vessel is at times identical with its contents. The *Rosarium,* a fifteenth-century text, says: "One is the stone, one the medicine, one the vessel, one the procedure, and one the disposition,"[77] and the *Aurora consurgens,* another text of the same period, declares that the vessel is the *aqua permanens,* the arcane substance itself.[78] The "Liber quartorum," a Latin translation of a Sabean text, emphasises that the vessel is "like the work of God in the vessel of the divine seed *(germinis divi),* for it has received the clay, moulded it, and mixed it with water and fire."[79] "This," says Jung, "is an allusion to the creation of man, but on the other hand it seems to refer to the creation of souls, since immediately afterwards the text speaks of the production of souls from the 'seeds of heaven.' In order to catch the soul, God created the *vas cerebi,* the cranium."[80] Thus, the symbol of the vessel is also applied to the soul. Caesarius of Heisterbach gives an excellent example of this: "The soul is a spiritual substance of spherical nature, like the globe of the moon, or like a glass vessel that is furnished before and behind with eyes and 'sees the whole universe.' "[81] In this case the vessel or soul thus has a relation to the whole cosmos and its creation.

The emergence of human consciousness can be compared to the Genesis story of creation. On the first day God divided the light from the darkness and called the light day and the darkness night. Psychologically translated, this would mean that on the same day the light of consciousness emerged from the chaos of undifferentiation, night, the unconscious, also came into being as an absolute and independent opposite to consciousness. "Unconscious" is the negative of "conscious," which is

there, presupposed to exist. Small children have no individual unconscious because they have no corresponding consciousness. They have
their being in a dreamlike, twilight state out of which, with increasing
consciousness, they awaken into an ever higher, more consolidated consciousness, oriented towards the outer world. With consciousness, the
unconscious therefore also comes into existence. If we follow the Genesis story further we read that on the fourth day, after the firmament which
separates the waters above from those below has been created and when
the lower waters have been collected together to form the seas so that the
dry land can appear and bring forth vegetation, God speaks: "Let there be
lights in the firmament of the heaven to divide the day from the night;
and let them be for signs, and for season, and for days, and years: And let
them be for lights in the firmament of the heaven to give light upon the
earth: and it was so. And God made two great lights; the greater light to
rule the day, and the lesser light to rule the night: he made the stars also."

The great light of day, the sun, may be compared to the mind, the
lesser light which rules the night to the soul.[82] After the earth, as solidity
and consciousness, had been separated from the sea, the surging, fluctu-
ating unconscious, the soul came into being as if arising from the water.
Is it not her whom the ancients worshipped as Aphrodite, the foam-born,
and who is still called upon today as Stella Maris? Morgane, the sea-
born, is the name given to the fairy, skilled in magic and healing, who
holds sway in the world of the Breton stories, the same otherworldly we
experience as the realm of the unconscious and of dreams. It was also
she, the Lady Soul, whom those heroes of chivalry saw and sought behind the real woman. In truth, service and worship were offered her without it always being known that such was the case.

In a quite particular sense the winning of the soul was the problem of
that age. If we keep to the analogy of the Genesis story, the soul, the light
of night, makes its first appearance after the creation of a world which it
can assimilate. Mankind, or at any rate Western man, had obviously
reached this stage at the rise of Christianity. The growing consciousness
of the soul coincided with this phenomenon, indeed the highest value was
attributed to the soul in the Christian religion. The part played in Christianity by suffering and the Passion clearly indicates (in contrast to some
other religions) that a *feminine element* is included and is of importance,
and that the soul could be described as the organ of suffering. Tertullian's
saying, *"Anima naturaliter christiana"* ("The soul is Christian by nature"), can also be understood in this sense. The process of realizing or becoming conscious of the soul was greatly intensified in the Middle Ages

and was manifested not only in religion but also in the secular *Minne-dienst,* to which, moreover, a pronouncedly religious character adhered, so that the process finally came round again full circle to its true foundation, the soul.

Adam de Saint Victor's beautiful song, written during the time the Grail stories were being produced, also harmonizes with this spirit:

> *Salve Mater salvatoris*
> *Vas electum, vas honoris*
> *Vas caelestis gratiae*
> *Ab aeterno vas provisum*
> *Vas insigne, vas excisum*
> *Manu sapientiae.*

> Chosen vessel, vase of honour,
> Vase of heaven's grace
> From eternity foreseen,
> Noted vessel, vessel carved
> By wisdom's hand.

In a special sense, therefore, the soul is that wondrous vessel which is the goal of the quest and in which the life-giving power inheres, whose final secret can never be revealed, but must ever remain hidden because its essence is a mystery. In that age the alchemists, who sought it in the "soul in matter," were also devoting themselves to this same mystery.

NOTES

Reprinted from Chapter 7, *The Grail Legend,* trans. Andrea Dykes, 2nd. ed. (Boston: Sigo Press, 1986), pp. 113–41, with permission from the C.G. Jung Foundation. Bibliographical references have been incorporated in the Notes.

1. Carl Gustav Jung, *The Collected Works of C.G. Jung* (London and New York, 1953–67), *Symbols of Transformation,* Vol. 5 (1956), pars. 298, 450 and 407; cf. also *Psychology and Alchemy,* Vol. 12 (1953), par. 338.

2. It has already been mentioned in Chapter I (Introduction) that in the Vedic scriptures the sun and moon appear as divine vessels, the sun as a pap bowl, the moon as a vessel for soma, and an attempt has been made to see in them the archetype behind the Grail vessel. Cf. L. von Schroeder, "Die Wurzeln der Sage vom heiligen Graal," *Sitzungberichte der Kais. Akad. Der Wiss. Phil. -hist. Klasse,* Vol. 166 (Vienna, 1910), pp. 8 *ff.*

3. *Historiae,* Book IV, Ch. 5.

4. Cf. O. Glaser, *Skythenkörige als Wächter des heiligen Goldes,* Archiv für Religionswissenschaft, 34, 3/4, p. 277.

5. See *The Mabinogion,* ed. J. Rhys, transl. Lady Charlotte Guest (Everyman Library), the Mabinogi of "Branwen the Daughter of Llyn," p. 37.

6. *Ibid.,* Mabinogi of "Taliesin," pp. 263 *ff.*

7. *Ibid,* notes, p. 328.

8. *The Arthurian Legend* (Oxford, 1891), pp. 312 *ff.*

9. Roger Sherman Loomis, *The Arthurian Tradition and Chrétien de Troyes* (New York, 1949), p. 172.

10. For a contrary view, see W.A. Nitze, "The Fisher King and the Grail in Retrospect," *Romance Philology,* 6; also Urban T. Holmes and Amelia Klenke, *Chrétien de Troyes and the Grail* (University of North Carolina Press, 1959), p. 177.

11. Cf. J. Rhys, Introduction, *Le Morte d'Arthur* (Everyman Library), p. xxxiii; and T.W. Rolleston, *Myths and Legends of the Celtic Race* (London, 1911), p. 410.

12. *"Grada"* in original, p. 602.

13. *Le sens de l'aventure et de l'amour* (Paris, 1947), p. 254, note 18.

14. *Recherches,* p. 242, quoted in Diez, *Etymologisches Wörterbuch der romanischen Sprachen,* 5th ed. (Bonn, 1887), p. 602.

15. "Wolframs Gral und Wolframs Kyot," *Zeitschrift für deutsches Altertum und Literatur,* 89 (1959).

16. "Zur etymologischen Deutung des Grals," *Vox Romanica,* 18, 2. Cf. also Herbert Kolb, *Monsalvaesche: Studien zum Kyotproblem,* (Munich, 1964), pp. 140 *ff.*

17. According to another tradition it is considered to have been a precious stone which fell out of Lucifer's crown when he was cast out of heaven.

18. In one passage in Arnaldus de Villanova the *lapis philosophorum* is described as *lapis exilis.* Cf. Johannes Jacobus Mangetus, ed., *Bibliotheca Chemica Curiosa . . .* (Geneva, 1702), Vol. II, p. 88, where it says:

> *Hic lapis exilis*
> *extat precio quoque vilis*
> *spernitur a stultis*
> *amatur plus ab edoctis.*

19. W.A. Nitze, ed. *Le Roman de L'Estoire dou Saint Graal* (Paris: Champion, 1927), Verse 2659.

20. E. Hucher, ed., *Le Saint Graal ou Josef d'Arimathie* (Le Mans, 1874–78), Vol. II, p. 306.

21. G. Paris and J. Ulrich, eds. *"Merlin," Roman en prose du XIIIe siècle,* SATF (Paris, 1886).

22. A.T. Nutt, *Studies on the Legend of the Holy Grail* (London, 1888), p. 76.

23. *Parzival*, ed. K Bartsch (Leipzig, 1927–29), Book IX.

24. (Breslau, 1882), pp. 33 *ff.*

25. J. Fischart mentions it as being synonymous with the Venusberg in the *Gargantua*.

26. Cf. A. de la Sale, *Le Paradis de la Sibylle*, p. lxxxv.

27. *Deutsch-lateinischem Wörterbuch*.

28. Quoted from Hertz, p. 36 (above, note 24).

29. *The Quest of the Holy Grail* (University of California Press, 1960), pp. 3 and 7.

30. According to another version, Joseph had had it made.

31. Especially in the *Lancelot-Grail*, the *"Queste"* and the *Perlesvaus*.

32. The Grail was thus actually interpreted as the Eucharistic chalice. See Holmes and Klenke, p. 172 (above, note 10), and the literature there cited; also Mario Roques, *Studies in Philology*, 44, pp. 413–14. Sometimes the Grail was identified with the ciborium or the chalice.

33. W.A. Nitze and T. Jenkins, eds., *Le Hant Livre du Graal, Perlesvaus* (Chicago, 1932), Verses 7220 *ff.*

34. Cf. Leo Frobenius, *Erythräa, Länder und Zeiten des heiligen Königsmordes* (Berlin, 1931), pp. 128 *ff.*

35. Cf. H. Bonnet, *Reallexikon der ägyptischen Religionsgeschichte* (Berlin, 1952), under "Kanopus."

36. Certainly, in the poems of Chrétien and Wolfram, the Grail is depicted either as a precious vessel that is not described in any greater detail, or even—in Wolfram—as a stone, but in Robert de Boron it is unequivocally a vessel containing Christ's blood. In the Continuations the Grail is generally understood in this sense.

37. Cf. A. Langfors, ed., *Histoire de l'Abbaye de Fécamp*, Annales Acadeemiae Scientiarum Fennicae, 22 (Helsinki,1928), *passim;* and Bodo Mergell, *Der Gral in Wolframs Parzival* (Halle, 1952), pp. 100 *ff*, and the literature cited there, as also pp. 107–8.

38. According to the legend this first happened in 1171 during the rebuilding of the burned-out church. Actually a scroll was said to have been found earlier, on which it was written that *"le prix del mont"* ("the prize of the world") that had come from Jerusalem was in this church but without its being known where.

39. The similarities of expression may also be compared. The opening of Book One of the Fécamp story reads as follows:

Cel qui de contes s'entremeit
Celui sa cure et s'entente meit
A rimer la plus heute estoire
Mande salus premièrement.

A tout cheny qui parfaitement
Jhesu Crist emoient et servent
Et qui la sou amour deservent.

And the *Roman de Perceval* opens with these lines:

Chrétien qui autant et . . .
à rimoier le meilleur conte
per le commendement le conte
qui soit conté cort real.

40. T. Hopfner, ed., *Über Isis und Osiris* (Prague, 1940).

41. W.C. von Tischendorf, *Evangelia Apocrypha* (Leipzig, 1876), p. 382.

42. *Visio Pacis, Holy City and Grail* (Pennsylvania State University, 1960), *passim.*

43. Cf. article entitled "Heiliges Grab," in *Die Religion in Geschichte und Gegenwart*, 1910.

44. B. Bächtold-Stäubli, ed., *Handwörterbuch des deutschen Aberglaubens* (Berlin/Leipzig, 1936), under *"Grab."*

45. More precise information on this matter may be found in Jung's "Symbols of the Mother and of Rebirth," *Symbols of Transformation, Collected Works*, Vol. 5 (1956), pars. 300–418, and also in his "Psychological Aspects of the Mother Archetype" in *The Archetypes and the Collective Unconscious, Collected Works*, Vol. 9 (1959), pars. 148–98. Cf. Erich Neumann, *The Great Mother* (New York, 1953).

46. Prof. Kerényi brought out this connection very skillfully in a series of lectures, "Seele und Griechentum," Psychotechnischen Institut, Zurich, 1943–44.

47. *"Dicente sacerdote: Per omnia saecula saeculoram, diaconus venit, calicem coram eo sustollit, cum favone partem eius cooperit, in alteri reponit et eum corporali cooperit praeferens Joseph ab Arimathia, qui corpus Christi deposuit, faciem eius sudario cooperuit, in monumento deposuit, lapide cooperuit. Hic oblate, et calix cum corporali cooperitur, quod sindonem mundam significat, in quam Joseph corpus Christi involvebat. Calix hic, sepulchrum; patena lapidem designat, qui sepulchrum clauserat."*

48. *Gemma Animae*, Book I, Chap. XLVII; J.P. Migne ed., *Patrologia. Latina* (Paris, 1844-64), Vol. 172, quoted by B.A. Birch-Hirschfeld, *Die Sage vom Graal* (Leipzig, 1877), p. 221. This same point is also independently emphasized by Helen Adolf in *Visio Pacis.*

49. J.L. Weston, *From Ritual to Romance* (Cambridge University Press, 1920), supports the view that the Grail legend is a relic of pagan Oriental cults,

especially that of Adonis, therefore of the dying and resurrecting god. She corroborates her theory with numerous examples from Frazer's *Golden Bough*. It is, however, more a question of an analogue. On the other hand there does appear to be a real connection with the Osiris legend via the story of the Abbaye de Fécamp.

50. Cf.B. Bächtold-Stäubli, ed., *Handwörterbuch as deutschen Aberglaubens*, under *"Schatz"* and *"Schatzhüter."*

51. "Gorgias," in The *Collected Dialogues of Plato*, pp. 274–75.

52. Vide H. Diels, *Fragmente der Vorsokratiker*, 6th ed., p. 164.

53. As mentioned, specific traces of these views may be detected in the Grail legend, for which reason O. Rahn makes the suggestion, in *Der Kreuzzug gegen den Graal* (Fribourg, 1933) that the Grail should be looked upon as a Manichaean or Catharistic relic, and the Grail legend interpreted as a veiled description of the Manichaean-Catharistic mysteries. This, however, seems questionable, even though Catharistic ideas were very widely disseminated at that time, especially in the south of France (E. Anitchkof, *Joachim de Flore et les milieux courtois* [Collezione Meridionale Editrice. Rome,1931] *passim*) and, as the crusade against the Albigenses showed, were considered to be so heretical that a disguising of the same might well have been desirable.

54. Cf. Jung, *Psychology and Alchemy, Psychology and Religion,* and *Mysterium Coniunctionis, Collected Works*, Vols. 12, 11, and 14 (above, note 1).

55. Cf. Jung, "The Relations between the Ego and the Unconscious," in *Two Essays on Analytical Psychology, Collected Works*, Vol. 7 (1953).

56. Cf. *ibid.,* par. 399.

57. Cf., for instance, *Psychology and Religion, Collected Works*, Vol. 11 (1958), par. 136.

58. H. Büttner, ed., *Meister Eckeharts Schriften und Predigten* (Jena, 1909), pp. 202 *ff*, 206.

59. *The Secret of the Golden Flower,* trans. Cary F. Baynes, with commentaries by Richard Wilhelm and C.G. Jung (London and New York, 1931; rpt. 1962), p. 22.

60. Indian Yoga teaching also speaks of a void (the void of consciousness) that must be established before the Self can be perceived. Cf. Heinrich Zimmer, *Der Weg zum Selbst* (Zurich,1964); and J.W. Hauer, *Der Yoga als Heilsweg* (Stuttgart, 1932), pp. 29 and 129.

61. *Psychology and Alchemy, Collected Works*, Vol. 12 (1953), par. 325.

62. Quoted by A.W. Thompson, *The Elucidation: A Prologue to the Conte del Graal* (New York, 1931), p. 41.

63. W. Scott, *Hermetica* (Oxford, 1924), Vol. 1, p. 151. With this compare Jung, *Alchemical Studies, Collected Works*, Vol. 13 (1967), par. 96.

64. In *The Mysteries,* Vol. 2 of the Papers from the Eranos Yearbooks (New York, 1955).

65. In the possession of Jacob Hirsch, Lucerne, until 1957. In the auction catalogue it figures as "Important work of art from the estate of the late Dr. J. Hirsch, A. Hess AG, Lucerne, No. 105." I do not know who bought the bowl or where it is now.—*M.-L. von F.*

66. Hippolytus, *Elenchos,* V, 17, 8; quoted by Hans Leisegang, *Die Gnosis,* 2nd ed. (Jena), p. 230.

67. From the abyss of the world.

68. Cf. Leisegang, *Die Gnosis,* p. 126; and Jung, *Psychology and Alchemy,* par. 550.

69. For the part played by a mystical cup in the legend of Solomon, in general, cf. F. Kampers, *Das Lichtland der Seelen und der heilige Gral* (Cologne, 1916), pp. 81 *ff.*

70. The Dresden Library.

71. Quoted from Kampers, p. 85 (above, note 69).

72. J. de Hammer, *Mémoire sur deux coffrets gnostiques du moyen âge* (Paris, 1832), described and illustrated in *Psychology and Alchemy,* par. 184 and Fig. 70.

73. Interpreted and commented on by Jung in *Alchemical Studies, Collected Works,* Vol. 13, pars. 85 *ff.*

74. *Ibid.,* pars. 96 *ff.*

75. *Ibid.,* par. 97.

76. "Proto–Perceval und Proto–Parzival," *Zeitschrift fürromanische Philologie,* 79, 3/4 (1963), and the further literature there cited.

77. "Unus est lapis, una medicina, unum vas, unum regimen, unaque dispositio." 1550 edition, fol. AIII; quoted by Jung, *Alchemical Studies,* par. 113.

78. (Part II) *Artis Auriferae* (Basel, 1593), I, p. 203; quoted by Jung, *Alchemical Studies,* par. 113. Cf. the numerous passages on the identity of the vessel and its contents from the texts there quoted.

79. *Theatrum Chemicum* (Ursellus, 1602–1661),Vol. V, p. 148; quoted by Jung, *Alchemical Studies,* par. 113.

80. *Ibid.*

81. *Dialogus miraculoram,* IV:34, and I:32; quoted *ibid.*

82. Cf. *Mysterium Coniunctionis, Collected Works,* Vol. 14 (1963), Ch. III, "The Personification of the Opposites," pars. 104 *ff.*

CHAPTER 3

Perceval or *Le Conte du Graal*

JEAN FRAPPIER

Translated by Raymond Cormier

Chrétien's last romance, left unfinished, was dedicated to Philippe of Alsace, count of Flanders, who died at Acre on the Third Crusade, in June 1191. The poet was doubtless truthful in his assertion that he followed his great patron's "command" and that he had received from him (around 1179–82) a *livre*, containing some version of the Grail story.

Whether the gift itself was spendid or not matters little, for from Philippe's gracious hand came an admirable subject whereby Chrétien "acquits himself" well, as he says, so that without realizing it he created a myth: with Chrétien's last work, born of a fusion, coalesces the inspiring story of the Grail.

Many have wondered what the "book" contained.[1] The answers to this question tend to be influenced by theories concerning the origin of the Grail legend. Some have surmised that it was written in Latin, that it set forth some type of ritual about the Grail as a Christian relic or liturgical vessel; others have plausibly argued that it was a "tale of adventure" filled with Celtic marvels. Yet further disagreement exists as to whether the story of Perceval was already linked to the legend of the Grail. The two stories could have existed independent of each other: in *Erec*, Perceval le Gallois is listed among the knights of Arthur's court and he reappears in *Cligés* where he is dubbed a "man of great fame"—a rather nondescript hint of the hero-to-be (Micha ed., *Cligés*, vv. 4773–74). The Middle English romance (ca. 1370) *Sir Perceval of Galles (Sir Percyvelle)* has not a word of the Grail or the Fisher King. Even though the question has been much disputed, it seems most probable that Sir Perceval derives from a "tale of adventure" relating stories of Perceval's childhood (*enfances*), independent

175

of the Grail. These indications suggest that Chrétien's *Conte du Graal* is the result of a synthesis, although it still remains undetermined whether there existed an earlier amalgamation in the "book," or whether it may be attributed to Chrétien's own initiative.

But the dedication to the count of Flanders stands firm. The praise Chrétien bestows on his Maecenas, however grandiloquent, reaches a higher level than mere flattery. Filling nearly the whole prologue, its accent is such that it may very well accord with the *sen* of the romance: it celebrates the chivalric ideal by which worldly glory gives way to Christian humility and divine love. The panegyric is made up mainly of paraphrases and quotations from the gospels and contrasts the ostentatious largess of Alexander the Great with another largess, i.e., inner piety and spirituality, "charity" in the strictly religious sense of the word. In point of fact, there is a correspondence between this prelude and the Good Friday and hermitage episodes, which appear late in the romance, because the religious ideal predominates at the consummation of Perceval's ascent. Chrétien's goal seems to have been this: to direct, across a series of initiatory experiences, through naive bravery and half understood lessons, a noble adolescent, ignorant of everything and most of all of himself, yet essentially generous and good, to comprehension of his duties and the discovery of the divine.

As in the proem of *Lancelot*, Chrétien again indicates discreetly his own efforts to assure the literary quality of the work: "Chrétien . . . strives to put into rhyme the best tale which may be told in a royal court" (vv. 62–64). We sense here his confidence, the felicitous probity of a maestro in full array. We may infer that his thoughts were turned not only to the beauty of the style but also to the structure of the narrative, for his conception of the genre included improvisation, however controlled by the sources.

The *Story of the Grail* is not a well-organized narrative since Chrétien did not finish the work. But enough of the redaction survives (9234 lines) to suggest that certain internal inconsistencies were unplanned. Most striking is Gawain's considerable role: at l. 4747 he moves to center stage, and the rest of the poem, utterly unrelated to the central theme, is given over to his adventures, with the single exception of a critical episode of some 300 lines, when Perceval reaches his uncle's hermitage. This duality of interest has seemed to certain critics so gross a flaw in composition as to justify exculpating Chrétien entirely for it. Becker would reduce his authentic work to the first 3427 lines (up to Perceval's departure from Grail castle); Hofer more generously would assign to him all Perceval's adventures, but those of Gawain to an awkward continuator—even though Gawain's "romance" is written in Chrétien's most brilliant and inimitable manner. Hoepffner adjudged that two independent works, both unfinished, were unscrupulously stitched together after Chrétien's death.

Be that as it may, there are good reasons to believe that it was the poet's own intention to give Gawain a minor but still significant role. Nowhere is it written that Chrétien could not change his artistic style. With *Perceval* his conception of the romance form could have broadened to permit greater allusion. This dual interest was not a novelty: already in *Lancelot*, Chrétien maintained a sort of parallelism between the roles of Gawain and the hero. In *Perceval*, he causes Gawain to undertake a secondary quest for the bleeding lance (vv. 6158–98), thus paralleling Perceval's search for the castle of the Fisher King.

The direction of the narrative is not always clear, for the marvelous tale included some strangeness and mystery, wisely retained by Chrétien. These amusing, seductive qualities are enduring in his work: already in *Lancelot*, the extraordinary is deftly bound to his narrative manner— suspenseful, enigmatic—and now the *chiaroscuro* will truly whet our curiosity. The *Conte du Graal* is also characterized by a more subtle and original method of composition: by progressions, Chrétien relates almost everything through Perceval's eyes. This mode of presenting facts as they happen and as they are gradually explained in part for the hero results logically in a psychological *and* artistic impressionism. Here is another reason for the uncertainty and obscurity in the romance, yet neither its impressionistic style nor the author's smiles, nor even his apparent inattention, should lead to a misunderstanding of its concerted structure.

Perceval's silence at the Fisher King's is closely related to his naivety, or simplicity, a trait especially nurtured by his loving and fearful mother. His initiations unfold gradually: once again Chrétien traces in story the evolution of the hero's personality, but never before was his program so extensive, for the young Perceval is at first a quasi-primitive creature, "the young fool." Nothing reveals more the existence of an elaborate structure than Chrétien's two explanations of Perceval's silence: the first says it arises from excessive docility, a too-strict obedience to warnings against loquacity (vv. 3202–12, 3243–53, 3290–303); but, according to the hermit, if Perceval did not ask the question—an error—it was because of a "sin against his mother," his heartless desertion of her when she swooned and died in sorrow (vv. 3591–606 and 6392–414). These two explanations are complementary, rising in stages, each valid on its own plane. The second offers a spiritual perspective,

changing the Grail adventure to a drama of conscience. The lack of judgment which, in psychological and more worldly terms, kept him from
asking the liberating question, corresponds to the absence of grace in the
religious order. Only let the hero feel the weight of his sin, let his heart be
moved by charity, and grace will do its work, leading him to a third, yet
higher, plane. We may suppose that if Chrétien had completed his poem,
his hero would have returned to the Grail castle to accomplish the miracle. Thus, Perceval's adventures would harmonize with the spirit of the
prologue.

These different levels and this progressive development suggest already the great depth and breadth of *The Story of the Grail*. But surely
Chrétien was aware that, in order to embellish his subject with charm,
there must remain tantalizing concealments, in a way unfocused mysteries, unlike the interpretations found in so many later romances of the
Grail and of the Holy Grail. Rather, Chrétien was to hint at merely probable or possible meanings. If so, the refusal to explain clearly, the narrative ambiguity (notably in the procession scene at the Grail castle),
implies a deliberate symbolism: he has freely allowed ancient myth to
subsist, yet around it he creates an atmosphere of Christian spirituality.

One received opinion makes of the *Conte du Graal* a *Bildungsro-
man*—a kind of twelfth-century *Telemachus*—presenting models of behavior; it would be grouped then in the category of simple didactic
literature. This view is not altogether false, only incomplete, for at a certain point Perceval rises above the didactic stage to seek his personal
path through inner suffering. It is then that he truly begins to be himself.
Thus one may judge better the sense of Gawain's adventures in relation to
Perceval's. For those who see the "Grail Story" solely in terms of its didac-
ticism, the explanation is simple: Chrétien presented Gawain as a noble
and elegant model which Perceval must ever strive to match. But this interpretation takes no account of artistic lengthening in the romance. In the
first part the uncouth manners and laughable blunders of the youthful
"fool" brought up in the Welsh forest contrast with the refined savoir vivre
of Gawain. Yet the two personages are almost equal, even in courtesy, in
the poetic episode of the blood drops on the snow. But then their adventures and destinies diverge: Perceval, the only Perceval at the Round Table,
chooses to undertake the difficult quest for the Grail, while the chivalrous
Gawain lets himself be carried along in a whirlwind of frivolous, worldly
adventures or misadventures. Henceforth, they are no longer on the same
level of excellence, and within the organic spatiality of the *Conte du Graal*,
Gawain is presented as a counterpoint—not antithesis—to Perceval.

Clearly, it cannot be maintained that Chrétien intended to oppose the two, like a clumsy sketch next to a consummate model. The one, after protracted confusion and despair, arrives at the hermitage, enters the path of repentance, and becomes a new man before leaving again for parts unknown (since the romance is unfinished); yet we suspect that he somehow found the Fisher King's castle again. But Arthur's nephew remains unchanged: ever courteous, tactful, preoccupied with mundane glories and chivalric honor, Gawain's grandeur is not diminished, although, upon closer examination, he comes through as a static character, one whose prestige is indeed tarnished, someone destined for some kind of debasement. But let us now give a brief sketch of the poem.

Perceval's mother, in perpetual mourning over the death of her two older sons and her husband, raises her youngest in a remote forest dwelling, ignorant of chivalry and its perils.[2] But one spring morning (stunningly described), the Welsh youth, so far unnamed, meets five knights, and his inner destiny is awakened. He decides immediately to go to Carduel, where Arthur dwells, "the king who makes knights."

The poor mother obtains from her stubborn son only a three-day delay. Consenting reluctantly, she makes him a cumbersome outfit "à la mode de Galles," and gives him some parting advice, in haste, about his behavior with damsels, about seeking the companionship of gentlemen (*prodomes*), and about entering churches to pray to the Lord (though Perceval has never yet seen a church!). She also reminds him of Christ's passion, of the mysteries of the Eucharist and of the Redemption (vv. 567–98).

As Perceval goes off, he turns for a moment only to see his mother fallen at the end of the bridge, "as if she had dropped dead." But he whips his mount and gallops forth "through the great dark forest" (vv. 622–30). That is his sin.

Mistaking a splendid tent for a church, he enters and, recalling his mother's counsel, kisses exuberantly a damsel lying within. After the youth leaves, her jealous lover returns and, convinced of her infidelity, forces her to ride forth in sad array. In the meantime, at Arthur's court Perceval makes a heroicomic entrance, is insulted by the sarcastic Kay, but is greeted as the best knight in the world by a laughing maiden. Then, by throwing a javelin in the eye, he kills the Red Knight who had insulted King Arthur and Guenevere, and with help strips him of his arms and charger. In the castle of the friendly and benevolent Gornemant de Gohort, the "young fool" learns the correct way to hold a lance and shield, how to manage the charger and handle a sword. He receives the order of knighthood, and Gornemant instructs

him in the moral principles of chivalry, also warning him about courteous
discretion, for loquacity is a sin.

But Perceval cannot put aside thoughts of his mother who had fallen
from the end of the bridge. Is she dead or alive? At least he does know that
she swooned because of his departure (vv. 1580–92). Thus he refuses to
tarry with Gornemant de Gohort, whose niece, Blancheflor, will detain
Perceval a little longer. This beautiful maiden is beseiged in her castle of
Beaurepaire, threatened by famine, because of a cruel enemy, Anguingueron, seneschal of a knight, Clamadeu des Iles, who covets her land and
her person. Perceval's arrival saves her. He vanquishes the enemies and
sends them as prisoners to Arthur. The hero now has a mistress and begins
to be courteous, stirred by love, by its emotions, mixed with forthright
sensuality and tender pity for the defenseless woman. Heretofore purely
instinctual, the hero now acquires a sense of moral autonomy and inner
freedom. At Beaurepaire, he continues to enjoy the embraces of Blancheflor, and though she seeks to keep him, and though he promises to return, he leaves her, being haunted by the image of his swooning mother.

Moving to another level, Perceval will go to experience the Grail adventure. All day, lance at the ready, he has ridden in solitude, continually
hoping in God to find his mother alive. In prayer he comes to a deep river
of the Fisher King, "the wounded one." Directed to his castle nearby,
Perceval is received in the hall by his magnificent and sickly host, already arrived, and he obtains from the "blond maiden" a sword "destined" for him (v. 3168). Then he witnesses the enigmatic procession of
the bleeding lance, candelabra, the gold-encrusted vessel called a *graal*,
and the silver carving platter (*tailloir*).

Through the octosyllables flows the charming scene—noble, graceful, and mysterious—of visual artistry. However extraordinary, nothing
mars the impression of harmony. There is beauty and youth, and especially beautiful is the one carrying the *graal* in the center of the procession; there is an unpeculiar indication of distinctive gestures: the lance
grasped in the middle, the *graal* held between the two hands; there is a
painstaking progression of the effects of light, with the prodigious luster
of the *graal* twice told: first the strange brightness emanating from it,
then the splendor of its gold and jewels, before and after the passage of
the platter. Hardly less brilliant are the contrasting colors of the precious
metals, the red blood and white lance—all expressive of a startling visu-
alization elegantly accomplished.

Though fascinated by this cortege as it passes again to enter another
chamber, and though amazed, for he would like to know why the lance

bleeds and whom one serves with the *graal*, Perceval controls himself, recalling Gornemant's injunction against too many words, and asks no question. Then an exquisite meal is served, and, with his host, Perceval partakes of the abundant food. With each course, he sees the *graal* in all its splendor, again crossing the room, but still he masters his curiosity. When he wakes in the hall the next morning, he finds the castle deserted. Perceval accoutres himself unaided, finds his horse already saddled and the castle bridge lowered; he rides off on his steed, just crossing the drawbridge as it is raised up rapidly. He is nearly upended.

Riding on across the forest without a hint of his recent humiliation, he sees a young woman lamenting and grasping her dead friend. He greets her, and, when she learns that he spent the night with the rich Fisher King, she submits him to a detailed interrogation.[3] She upbraids him violently for his silence about the bleeding lance and about the *graal*. The maiden then asks his name and the hero "guesses," by a kind of divination, that he is Perceval of Wales (vv. 3573-77). Rather, Perceval "the wretched," she answers, and she informs him in detail that if he had spoken he would have healed his infirm host, causing great rejoicing. She says that his silence is the consequence of his sin in leaving his mother. (She knows all this since she is no other than his first cousin.) At the news of his mother's death Perceval is saddened, but he controls himself, putting aside sterile regret and refusing filial anguish: "'I must now take another road. . . . The dead to the dead, the living to the living'" (Roach ed., v. 3625). His other way will be one of action, the easiest form of illusory freedom. Perceval's conduct will remain chivalrous and generous, but will neither open his eyes to repentance nor lead him to the spiritual life.

He next meets the maiden of the tent, mounted on a wretched palfrey, her face worn by tears, and followed by her jealous lover, the Proud Knight of the Glade. In reparation, the hero forces him in combat to admit the girl's innocence. Some days later, after a fall of snow, Perceval sees a flock of wild geese, pursued by a falcon. One is wounded and blood falls on the white field. Perceval hastens, his hunting instinct awakened, but the wild goose has flown off again: there remain only three drops of blood on the snow. The bright red contrasts with the white, and Perceval, leaning on his lance, falls into a prolonged reverie on the fresh color of his love Blancheflor.[4] This amorous ecstasy, almost involuntary, is his first sign of introspection.

Now Arthur's court, in quest of the hero, was camping nearby. The strange attitude of the contemplative invites Sagremor to interrupt and lead the dreamer to the king, but in his brashness he is unseated. The seneschal Kay goes to threaten him, but he too is knocked out of his saddle, breaking his arm in the fall. But Gawain, the model knight, alone understands that worthy thoughts preoccupy the unknown youth. He alone succeeds, through courtesy, in bringing the love-smitten hero to Arthur's camp. Thus the two noble knights become companions. Because of the report of Perceval's deeds, the widow's son is deemed worthy to sit at the Round Table. Queen Guenevere speaks for the whole court when she greets him: "'You are most welcome, as a knight whose high and noble prowess has been well proved'" (Roach ed., vv. 4593–95). Thus closes, seemingly, a cycle. Were it Perceval's fate only to match Gawain, the story could end here. But such is not the case.

After the court returns to Carleon for a two-day celebration, a damsel of fantastic ugliness rides in on a mule and accuses Perceval for his muteness at the Grail castle. The devastating consequences for the Fisher King and his land are irremediable. The infirm king will continue to suffer, unable to govern, and in his wasted kingdom women will become widows, damsels will remain orphans, scores of knights will die. Before going off she mentions two high adventures to tempt the valiant: that of Castle Orgulous and the more difficult liberation of the Maid of Montesclaire. These are at once undertaken by Gawain and other knights. But Perceval alone vows that he will not sleep two nights in the same spot, that he will in fact not rest until he repairs his error by finding the *graal* and bleeding lance and by comprehending their mystery.

The episode (vv. 4603–746) is brief but crucial if we would grasp the general structure of the romance, such as Chrétien seems to envisage it. The narrative pivots at this point and dilates unexpectedly; as in the *Erec* and *Yvain*, a crisis causes the action to rebound. Perceval's role is enriched with new meaning as he is directed away from the involvements of the other Knights of the Round Table.

The Loathly Damsel continues to pour out curses and scorn on the unworthy hero, implacably proclaiming his responsibility for all to hear: "'All these calamities will befall because of you.'" Most disastrous of all—something his cousin had not mentioned in the forest—is that his error is unforgivable, that once missed, the opportunity will never knock again. Perceval is at a crossroads—one way will be the easier, more orderly path, gaily embellished with worldly glory; the other seems to lead nowhere. Perceval chooses to undertake the impossible adventure, the conquest of the Grail. In this sublime moment, the hero's liberty is proven, for Perceval refuses fate, refuses to despair over the irreversible.

Indeed, the revelation by the loathsome messenger that the Fisher King would never be healed was a most cunning trap. Neither Gawain nor the others have a mind to replace Perceval on the quest for the Grail and lance. The Loathly Damsel offers adventures within their reach, dangerous, bestowing "supreme glory" (line 4708), but merely chivalrous. She even seems to snigger a bit as she sees false hopes glimmer in their eyes. Thus an antithesis between Gawain and Perceval is established in this episode, although Chrétien shuns the obvious and direct, expressing it discreetly with a very simple, pregnant line to underscore the contrast: "*Et Percevaus redit tot el*," "But Perceval spoke otherwise" (v. 4727).

This autonomous, willful decision, made by a hero of inner freedom, distinguishes Perceval from the brilliant court to which he belongs. Yet he still has in view no other battles or trials but chivalric adventures, no other concerns of a spiritual nature. And he manifests no repentance. There has been no mention of his mother, and Perceval is unmindful of God.

For five years he performs magnificent acts of chivalry, but has not yet found the way to the Grail. Morally confused, he has never entered a church and has forgotten God (vv. 6217–37). He has not grasped the religious significance of the adventure, for his soul remains unrepentant.

A graphic and remarkable event causes him great agitation and awakens his conscience: the sight of penitent knights and ladies in a deserted forest on Good Friday. At their direction, he reaches a hermitage where he falls to his knees weeping at the chapel door. The good hermit hears his confession and Perceval acknowledges his fall in the Fisher King's castle, reproaching himself for his failure in the Grail adventure, for he has forgotten God. Hearing his name, the hermit sadly explains to him that his tongue had been tied at the Grail castle because he had left his mother in a swoon. Perceval here learns, moreover, of his whole ancestry: the Fisher King is his cousin; the Fisher King's father (Perceval's maternal uncle) has been an invalid for fifteen years and has not left the chamber where the glorious procession passes. But he is of so pure a spirit that a single Mass wafer brought to him in the *graal*, "so sacred a thing" (line 6425), suffices to keep him alive. Thus the ascetic and mystical background is revealed, something Perceval has not fully understood since his visit to the Fisher King's castle.

For his penance, the hermit (another maternal uncle) gives Perceval counsels of piety and charity which the nephew sincerely promises to follow. For two days Perceval must share the hermit's frugal food; he attends Good Friday services, adores the cross, and feels peace arising within his soul. He receives Communion on Easter Sunday. The narrative then returns to Gawain, telling nothing more, ending abruptly.

Never before had Chrétien set forth a structure of such complexity. According to our summary, at least three "well-organized narratives" (*conjointures*) and three meanings are superimposed. In the first stage of Perceval's growth he serves an apprenticeship as the "young fool." The treatment is racy and supple, though its natural acceleration cannot conceal the gradually concerted tableaux bundled in narrative segments, to mark turning points in the life of the hero. These episodes are filled with human truth both for Perceval and for us, each of them representing the different phases of human existence. The first level, then, is psychological, during which Perceval's "naivety" explains his error of judgment in failing to ask the fateful question at the castle of the Fisher King.

A second stage, a moral drama, is revealed when the progressive development of the adventures reaches a climax. It is characterized by a problem of continual interest to Chrétien, that of the hero's awareness of his duties and inner freedom. In Perceval's case, these are asserted, even though the Loathly Damsel predicts failure, when he sets out to undo the wrong he has done.

The third is a spiritual experience, depicted as a slowly dawning consciousness of his mother's suffering and death. This is the cause of Perceval's muteness. Previously uncommitted to grace or repentance, he is redeemed spiritually on Good Friday.

Understood as a symbol, the Grail corresponds to each of these stages. The passing of the cortege illustrated Perceval's amusing but tragic naivety (*niceté*) as well as his fervor, completely spent on the enjoyment of prestigious marvels found in chivalry. Then he undergoes a glimmering awareness of his own inner freedom roused by the vision of the Grail. And finally, the image of the eucharistic Grail brings a full illumination and purification of the hero.

Thus interpreted, the romance must be confronted with the complex legend, to which the Grail is integral, in that it furnished the title of the work. But this is only half of the story. For the legend also comprises the Fisher King, his castle, and his pathetic kingdom; it includes the fateful questions which, if asked during the procession (Why is the lance bleeding? Whom does one serve with the *graal*?), would heal the king and bring joy to his land. But whence comes the strange tale? Is there a connection between it and the rest of Perceval's adventures? For this complicated problem, the most diverse opinions have been held. It is most difficult of all because, to examine it properly, one should consider all medieval traditions of the Grail and compare the various versions. One single fact is unquestionable in the *Conte du Graal*, one guiding truth, namely, the heterogenous character of a highly elaborated legend. Christian notions mingle with magical marvels of paganism, grafted in such a way as nearly to compromise the narrative coherence.

According to the theory of Christian origins, the bleeding lance is no other than the Holy Lance of Longinus, and the grail, containing the Mass wafer (perhaps a consecrated host), supposedly designates a liturgical vessel, or ciborium, or chalice, or ciborium-chalice, or perhaps even a pyx, thus somehow related to eucharistic ritual. Whatever its variants, this religious interpretation is in harmony with the spiritual cast of Perceval's experience on Good Friday and is in essential conformity with the late and partial revelations by the hermit (although he says only that for fifteen years the repeated service of the *graal* is a host borne like food to the Fisher King's father, but gives no explanation for the bleeding lance). Yet the most knotty problem of all is to determine whether the liturgical, Christian theory—which nearly coincides with what might be called a revelation of the *sen* in the hermitage episode—suffices to explain the whole legend. For the fact is that it does not agree in many details with the text.

To designate a liturgical vessel as a *graal* is surprising in itself, and certainly no more appropriate for a ciborium or chalice. As evidenced by a number of citations, a *graal* (similar to the carving platter or *tailloir* carried by the second damsel in the cortege), is a part of a vessel unattested except in the service of a profane meal of delicacies. In his Latin chronicle dating from the beginning of the thirteenth century, Helinandus of Froidmont has significantly defined the contemporary meaning of a graal: "*Gradalis autem sive gradale gallice dicitur scutella lata et aliquantulum profunda, in qua pretiosae dapes cum suo jure divitibus solent apponi gradatim, . . . et dicitur vulgari nomine* 'graalz.'" ("The Grail is the French name for a broad and somewhat deep dish in which delicacies are often set before the rich in different rows. . . . It is also called in the vernacular, '*graalz.*'")

One must then imagine the Grail as a dish (*scutella*) in the medieval sense of the word: a plate or dish, with no hint of vulgarity, of a particular form notable for its width, not for its depth: *lata et aliquantulum profunda*, "broad and somewhat deep," but most likely much wider than deep (*aliquantulum* is not *aliquantum*). Helinandus specifies also that a *graal* was used to bring exquisite food to the table of the wealthy and that it was silver or of some other precious material. Thus the presence of a *graal* in the Fisher King's castle at first would normally call to people's minds an aristocratic usage, with the exception of the fact that the golden object which fascinates Perceval is exceedingly bright and splendid. Other occurrences of the word—both earlier and later than Chrétien's romance—do not controvert Helinandus's definition. Within a brief description of a knightly meal in the epic poem *Girart de Roussillon* (ca. 1136–80) are cited grails with gold spangles—*greaus ab aur batuz*—beside goblets, basins, and vases (*orçols*) both large and small; "goblets, grails, candelabra" is found in the same poem, in an enumeration of precious objects (W.M. Hackett, ed., vv. 1622, 6370). A more interesting example, suggesting clearly that a *graal* is to be distinguished from a small cup or bowl, occurs in the decasyllabic version of the *Roman d'Alexandre* (ca. 1170): when a pilgrim sat down as a guest at a seneschal's table, two passages specify that he "drank from his bowl of pure gold" and that he "ate with him from his *graal*."[5] Finally a passage in the *First Continuation of Perceval* relates that a *graal* is wide enough to allow a boar's head to be brazed upon it, a characterization in agreement with the epithets used by Helinandus, *lata et aliquantulum profunda*.[6]

Nothing authorizes us to believe that Chrétien imagined the *graal*, carried across the "hall" in the Fisher King's castle, in any other way except as a wide and hollow dish.[7] Even if it were not so for authors who followed in his wake, Chrétien gave the word a precise, technical meaning, one it perhaps had among the twelfth-century nobility. Moreover, one passage, paramount for the understanding of the story, implies that the enigmatic and sumptuous *graal* was large enough to hold good-sized fish. Thus Chrétien, through the hermit, explains to Perceval whom one serves with the *graal*: " 'And believe me that the rich Fisher is the son of the king who causes himself to be served with the grail [*del graal*]. But do not think that he takes from it [*qu 'il ait*] a pike, a lamprey, or a salmon.' The holy man sustains and refreshes his life with a single Mass wafer' " (vv. 6417–24). This allusion to fish by which the father of the Fisher King is perhaps nourished must be associated with the origins of the legend. So too, when the fish are replaced by a host with no apparent correlation to the new and startling revelation in meaning, the significance is obscure. A dropped stitch, an awkward change is noticeable here. Does the mention of the pike, lamprey, and salmon, as has been claimed, have anything to do with the Grail service? The immediate context and manner of the passage imposes the view that the *graal* could be used to carry large fish to the "holy man." The expressions used by Chrétien ("And believe me," "do not think") would be absurd if the eventuality mentioned was altogether improbable or contradictory to the form and size of the Grail. It is the better part of wisdom, then, to keep to Helinandus's definition when considering the *graal* in Chrétien's romance. Critics have attempted, more or less ingeniously and laboriously—always without success—to transform this wide and hollow dish into a bowl similar to a ciborium or chalice. Does this suggestion mean that the Grail borne ceremoniously—yet without a single pious gesture—to the Fisher King's father carries no religious value? Obviously not, for each time it holds a wafer and is qualified by the hermit as "so sacred a thing." In Christian tradition there is in fact a supremely sacred vessel that easily conforms to the "broad and somewhat deep dish," a single one, the dish used at the Last Supper. However odd it may seem, we must recognize the equivalence, even if purely symbolic, between this holy *paropsis* ("small dish") and the Grail of the mysterious castle, although the evangelical simplicity of the one cannot match the obviously amazing allusiveness of the Grail, which itself turns our eyes always to other horizons.

Before he saw the *graal*, Perceval watched a young squire carry, "grasping by the middle," a bright white lance. There is no accompanying light. Its special feature is that from its white point of iron a drop of blood oozes down to the hand of the squire. This is the "lance which bleeds," as Chrétien calls it, and the expressions he uses in this regard imply that a drop of blood continually reappears at the tip before dripping down the length of the handle: "the lance of which the point bleeds, though there is no flesh or vein there" (vv. 3549–50); "Sin cut off your tongue when you saw before you the bleeding point which never has been staunched . . ." (vv. 4656–58); ". . . the lance of which the point continually bleeds; and never can it be wiped enough to keep a new drop of blood from forming again at the tip" (vv. 6113–15); "the lance of which the point cries tears of bright blood."[8] This last usage seems altogether conclusive: the dripping or oozing of the lance is continuous, tear after tear, drop after drop, intermittently, or perhaps rapidly or slowly, whereupon each drop, once formed at the point, oozes down the shaft. No medieval author ever conceived of the "lance which bleeds" as not bleeding. It even happens that in certain Grail romances the effusion of blood is almost a violent hemorrhage. Though Chrétien is more tasteful and discreet in his poem, nothing in the text justifies the supposition that he limited the marvel of the lance to an indelible trace of a single drop. Now is this "lance which bleeds" simply the Holy Lance? One detail suggests Chrétien's intention to connect the two lances: at the Fisher King's the blood flows down to the squire's hand; and, according to the legend of Longinus, from the wound in the crucified Christ's side, blood and water flowed the length of the lance down to the blind centurion's hand, who then regained his sight by rubbing his bloody hand over his eyes. But this faintly recondite analogy does not dispose of the whole mystery. Explore as one may the complex history of the origin of the Holy Lance or of the relic's peregrinations, nowhere is any miracle chronicled about blood flowing from its point. As far as we can determine, it is only after Chrétien de Troyes and his narrative tradition that the Holy Lance emerges as the lance which bleeds. Here again is an apparent mutation in the *Conte du Graal*, and, if so, it must be taken either as a personal religious meditation that compelled the poet to invent alone this splendid ornament of ever-flowing blood, or else his lance which bleeds derives from a source other than religious literature on the Holy Lance; thus, somehow considering the latter, he naturally associated two different concepts.

One motif seems to substantiate the second of these hypotheses, the devastation of the kingdom of Logres by the lance which bleeds: "It is written that the day will come when the whole kingdom of Logres . . . will be destroyed by this lance" (vv. 6168–71). It is quite doubtful that this destructive role can be reconciled with the Holy Lance, instrument of the Passion and the Redemption. And for what reason would the usually indulgent author of *The Story of the Grail* decide that the Saviour's vengeance must now strike down Arthur's realm through the Holy Lance? The kingdom of Logres is already Christianized, as the Good Friday episode demonstrates. If its prestige and enchantment endure side by side with religion as in most Arthurian romance, there is no justification for a divine chastisement as harsh as the *destruction* of an entire country. Thus, it is all the more likely that in this motif survive some mythical features relative to the marvels of Britain. The lance which bleeds is apparently a compound of pagan and Christian elements.

There is no question of attributing a religious significance to the cortege of the lance and *graal*, yet we cannot determine the amount of significance in relation to other elements. Does the procession represent Holy Communion given to one dying? In this view, it is in an emergency that the holy viaticum, contrary to the liturgy, is administered by a woman. But the Fisher King's father is not sick as such, only an ascetic, who for fifteen years has sustained his life solely by being served with the Grail. Other critics have suggested further the Great Entrance Rite of the Greek church, a Byzantine interpretation even less substantiated than the preceding, for with each of these opinions we are forced to admit that Chrétien somehow ingeniously travestied the liturgy.

More preferable are the nonliturgical definitions advanced by Roques:[9] it is the lance of Longinus that bleeds, reminiscent of the eternal and ever-renewed sacrifice of the Redemptor. The *graal* is the eucharistic vessel "in

which the Church visibly and symbolically gathers the blood of Christ."
The procession viewed by Perceval would be "like an animated, living
tableau of the immobile symbols of the crucifixion," and thus closely related to a frequent iconographic theme in late twelfth- and thirteenth-century religious art. For example, a miniature from the *Hortus deliciarum*
(*Garden of Delights*) represents, on the right and left below the cross, two
contrasting allegorical female figures, *Ecclesia* and *Synagoga* (the "church"
and the "synagogue"). The latter is blindfolded, but *Ecclesia*, wearing a
crown, gathers in a chalice the blood flowing from the wound in Christ's
body, made by the lance of Longinus, who, in fact, stands next to *Ecclesia*,
and holds his weapon slightly tilted, while exending his other hand toward
Christ's face. There is no good reason to doubt that this scene influenced the
elaboration of the cortege, and the notion that a summary image of Christian dogma was observed by Perceval is easily assimilable to the spiritual
character of his adventure.[10] This theory is persuasive also because, according to it, *Ecclesia* can be the "legitimate bearer of a sacred vessel," thus
solving with elegant simplicity the insoluble problem which the role of the
Grail damsel presented to liturgical theorists. Nevertheless, certain curious
anomalies subsist if we assume that Chrétien used no other source but this
allegory.

But we must go on to point out the striking differences between textual evidence and the miniature in the *Hortus deliciarum: Ecclesia* at the
foot of the cross gathers the divine blood in a chalice held up with a single
hand. The damsel in the procession grasps the *graal* "in her hands"; blood
from the lance cannot flow into it (the Grail) because it bears the single
Mass wafer which sustains the Fisher King's father. All other Grail romances that represent the mystic and graphic vision of the redeeming
blood gathered in the eucharistic vessel post-date Chrétien. If, on the
other hand, the dogmatic meaning connected with the succession *both* of
the lance *and* of the *graal*, taken solely as Christian symbols, were inherent and indispensable to Chrétien's elaboration of the cortege, is it not odd
that the *graal* alone crosses the room with each course-change of the meal
(vv. 3291, 3299–301), but without any mention of the lance? Nor must we
forget that Perceval was a visitor there for only a single night, while one
has served with the *graal* for some fifteen years. But is it a service that includes *Ecclesia* or not? Are we really certain that *Ecclesia* is to be unques-
tionably identified with the "beautiful, gracious, splendidly-garbed"
damsel? Appeals to personifications or allegorical readings are not usually Chrétien's style.[11] But let us concede (putting aside for the moment
the second damsel of the processsion) that the poet made an exception in

favor of *Ecclesia*. Then we must also allow that he took great pains to disguise her, for indeed, why is her crown gone, why is there no cross, no "cross-shaped standard," which is held in her left hand in the *Hortus* miniature? And especially why not leave her the title of *dame*, "lady," suitable to the spouse of Christ, rather than designate her with the merely honorific *demoiselle* ("damsel"), *pucelle* ("maiden"), and finally with *on* ("one"). This indefinite pronoun is only used by the hermit as he relates that with the *graal* the Fisher King's father is served: ". . . the Mass wafer which comes [literally that one brings to him] in the grail."[12] It seems that Chrétien did not consider this feminine character as *Ecclesia*, or else he has in no way hesitated to alter her form. Another important fact shows that no medieval author after Chrétien considered the damsel of the *graal* as an allegory of *Ecclesia*. For instance, in the *Didot-Perceval*, she is replaced by a "squire"; in the *Prose Lancelot* she falls in love with Lancelot and becomes Galahad's mother. It will be noted that her latter-day development in Grail literature did not exactly inspire thoughts similar to the scene in the *Hortus deliciarum*.

Certainly Chrétien's refined style might confuse us enough to miss his hidden intentions. But would he allow himself to use an unwieldy mystification to distort a religious allegory, if *indeed* it produced his vision of the cortege? And would this effort then be art or illusion? In matters of artistic creation the opposite seems more poetic and more natural, if, that is, we consider the whole narrative and its tone within the whole legend. Rather than depicting a travesty of religious mystery, our author raised, it would seem, a magical and primitive tale to the level of inviting Christian phenomena.

The culminating interpretation of the *Conte du Graal* must include a religious meaning, but one that should not conceal the text, which, in fact, clearly reflects the original theme: service from the Grail involves food. The wafer brought to the Fisher King's father is defined as a food that nourished because of the supernatural power of the dish in which it comes: he "sustains and refreshes his life" (line 6424); it is "sustenance" for "twelve years" (vv. 6427, 6429) for the old man. Service from the *graal* is first of all a miracle of food, a fundamental legendary feature that survives in all, even the most Christian, versions.

The impression one has when considering the cortege and *graal* scenes is not so much one of dogmatic symbolism but rather of its romantic religious character, in harmony with the legendary atmosphere with which Chrétien imbued his romance of adventure and chivalry—in spite of certain rationalizations or a few hidden winks about the marvelous.

Chrétien's supposed remembrance of some precise liturgical tableau or of some allegorized theological conceptions cannot explain fully the easily seductive ambiguity floating around the lance and *graal*. A magic is there, fitting for the free play of imagination and subtle compromise, favoring more poetic symbolism than matters of orthodoxy. The two realms—the nimbus of Christianity that seems to illuminate the damsel of the Grail, and the marvels of Britain, with a surfeit of damsels of Arthurian fiction— are not necessarily mutually exclusive.

Moreover, it is audacious and arbitrary under any circumstances to isolate either lance or *graal* from the other formants of the legend. But whence derive the rich Fisher King and his castle? Whence comes the Loathly Damsel? Certainly she does not appear in Christian tradition. To what beliefs are related the power of the question which would cure the infirm king, restore his sovereignty, establish happiness and prosperity in his kingdom? The function of this theme is essential, for it creates a psychological and dramatic link between the passing of the two objects and the destiny of both the Fisher King and Perceval. If suppressed, all is mutilated. And if the theme can indeed be reconciled with a Christian interpretation of the romance (we note that it has been eliminated from the narration in the *Quest of the Holy Grail—Queste del Saint Graal*), who would venture to affirm that its origin is neither primitive nor magical? One must ask then what would have been the primordial meaning of the question in relation to the eucharistic mystery.

This does not mean that to search for a non-Christian origin of the legend will solve all the problems. For the legend, or variants of it, is known in folklore and mythology the world over. It has been connected with vegetation cults; with ancient oriental mysteries, such as the cults of Attis, Osiris, and Adonis; and even with various myths whose common feature is the seasonal alternation of death and resurrection. The "waste land" (which is more latent in Chrétien's romance than in other versions of the Grail story) conjoins the sterility of the land to the infirm king's wound and to the return of fertility when he is healed. Perceval's visit to the castle of the Fisher King (the "maimed") has been seen perhaps provisionally as broadly analogous to an unsuccessful initiation to a fertility rite.

But the most interesting parallels have been drawn with Celtic traditions—not surprising, generally speaking, in an Arthurian context. From this angle, the *graal* would go back to one of the marvelous containers mentioned in many Irish and Welsh tales—caldrons, baskets, drinking horns, bowls, dishes, plates of plenty—all of which emanate some degree of magic insofar as they freely dispense drink and food. These objects, symbols of wealth and fertility, most often belong to otherworld treasures and talismans of kingship; sometimes they were won on journeys or raids by heroes. Now the food-producing function of the *graal* is not as evident in Chrétien's work as in the later romances. For Wolfram von Eschenbach it grants to each guest his fill of food and drink; in the *First Continuation of Perceval* and the *Quest of the Holy Grail*, circulating without support from table to table, it distributes one's choice of food automatically. But in Chrétien's work the nutritive feature of the *graal* is not suppressed, only attenuated or oriented toward a religious meaning. The reiterated passings of the *graal* in the hall, at each course-change during the knightly feast, may possibly have some sort of relationship with the un-ending profusion of delicacies. With discretion, Chrétien specifies merely a simultaneity of the two events, though he customarily diminishes the marvelous without completely effacing it. He seems to be performing with both the real *and* the supernatural in the two scenes, so that the strange goings and comings of the *graal* perhaps represent a survival of its magical powers.

A "lance which bleeds" (or at least a bleeding lance) also exists in Celtic mythology and literature. An otherworld talisman like the dishes and bowls of plenty, it is a divine, royal weapon, alternately a lance of fire and a lance of blood red, a terrible instrument of vengeance and de-struction. For example, the intense heat of Celtchar's burning warrior lance may be cooled only by plunging it into a caldron of poisoned blood, whereupon blood flows profusely from it, then drips, then the lance turns back slowly to flames. Obviously, the image of the lance in Chrétien's harmonious, imposing description does not correspond to such mythical primitivism. But Chrétien was an artist, and as such was doubtless capable of reworking and refining any raw material impinging upon him, and could, for the flowing blood, substitute a single, recurrent drop. In this way, he might effect a mystical protraction toward the no-tion of *the* Holy Lance and the eternal Redemption. Nevertheless, the lance which bleeds will bring the fall of the kingdom of Logres; thus it retains some kinship with the mythical Celtic lance, though Chrétien's intention was clearly not to designate two different lances in an identical way, as has been conjectured.

The only plausible origin so far advanced for the mysterious, wealthy, and infirm Fisher King also brings us to Irish and Welsh leg-ends. It remains quite problematic to trace out the whole apparent pedi-gree, so that we hesitate to single out one mythological ancestor for this character. Among various possible progenitors—all somewhat inter-

changeable—the hero Bran, Bran the Blessed, seems the least uncon-
vincing since part of his legend suggests parallels with the story of the
Fisher King. Bran, a marine divinity or one associated with the sea, or, in
certain adventures, an otherworld king, possesses a marvelous caldron
and a horn of plenty. Renowned for his luxuriant hospitality, he suffers
from a battle wound made by a lance in his foot, so that he must give up
his throne. By comparison, Robert de Boron calls the Fisher King both
Hebron and Bron, the latter name considered by several scholars as related to Bran. Granted that these are thematic, not identical, analogies,
between the two characters, yet, as is known, the transmission of Celtic
mythology to Arthurian romance involved a certain rupture or mutilation
of the mythical schemata. Just as the legendary Irish oceanic circumnav-
igations (*immrama*) were reduced, as Philipot noticed, to the crossing of
a river or of a castle moat, a marine deity might be transformed into a
fisherman. Thus, the Fisher King's castle in Chrétien's romance emanates the marvelous aura of an otherworld palace: at first invisible to
Perceval, it suddenly arises, near a river of deep rapids, from nowhere
(vv. 3466–82), and its inhabitants mysteriously disappear. It has also
been observed that the disposition of the hall in which the Fisher King receives Perceval is mindful less of a medieval castle than of the royal
palace of Tara in Ireland, with its banquet hall (*bruiden*) presided over by
an otherworld deity. There we find the hearth in the middle of the room,
the warriors seated around it on couches, with the king's place situated in
front of the fire. The exact form of *the* tale known to Chrétien, or more
probably that of the *tales* he synthesized, is lost, but nevertheless certain
correspondences between various Celtic myths and the character of the
wealthy Fisher King must be recognized. For, in fact, the epithet *wealthy*
is apt for a master of a marvelous castle in which circulates, at each meal,
a golden *graal* encrusted with precious stones, the most beautiful gems
"that exist in the sea and in the earth." Nor does it seem inappropriate to
associate the epithet with the theme of abundance and perhaps with the
enigmatic name Fisher King. Chrétien's explanation of the name, by the
way, that he fishes because he can no longer hunt, typically does not reflect a primitive notion, but does demonstrate a kind of secondary rationalization often associated with the processes of mythology.

Other parallels have been drawn concerning the cortege, the waste
land theme, Perceval's silence which presumably was the result of an ancient *geis* ("taboo," "injunction"). Further parallels deal with the meaning of the questions (apparently related to the surrender or restoration of
kingship), with the Loathly Damsel (conversant with Perceval's error),

and with the damsel of the Grail. The latter two perhaps have an affinity with a mythical figure, the "Sovereignty of Ireland," whose two-fold aspect was manifested either as a radiant maiden or a monstrous witch. In each case it is possible to note both the analogies and the dissimilarities. In a word, the major themes of the Grail romances may be found within the body of Celtic mythology, but nowhere in the extant medieval narratives are these themes organized or disposed in any way, except in the form of a scattered, disjointed puzzle.

It is possible, however, that a general schema, or a kind of mythical Celtic archetype formed a nadir for disparate tales. In his study, *La Légende arthurienne et le Graal*, Jean Marx has endeavored in particular to reconstruct its fundamental schematic coherence, basing his ideas on both Irish and Welsh materials and on the corpus of Grail literature. The pattern, then, would be that the quest for the Grail departs from the terrestrial court in response to a call from the otherworld, threatened with sterility and death. The realm surrounding the magical castle of the otherworld king, or Grail castle, was once extraordinarily fertile but now has become the waste land because the king was dealt a "dolorous stroke" by some magic weapon—lance, javelin, or sword—that is, one of the marvelous, talismanic objects of the otherworld kingdom. There would thus be at the outset a close relationship between the lance which bleeds and the wound which caused the Fisher King's infirmity. The king has been killed, crippled, or maimed especially in his virile parts by the dolorous stroke, a catastrophe with repercussions or near-repercussions in the whole terrestrial court. The hero, the chosen one, will then penetrate the Grail castle, overcome obstacles, vanquish the effects of the dolorous stroke, heal the infirm king, restore fertility to the earth, and will himself then become king of the Grail and of the otherworld. All these motifs—the dolorous stroke *and* its abrogation, the maimed king, the waste land, the quest for the Grail, and the talismans of sovereignty—together form a transparent and grandiose mythical structure, a provocative reconstruction which, in fact, is not altogether fanciful, even if it has been severely criticized for injecting themes properly belonging to twelfth- and thirteenth-century Arthurian romance into Celtic mythology. Yet between the two areas certain fundamental patterns seem unquestionable, and it would only be logical to attribute precedence to the mythological conceptions. Still, the very spine of the primitive, hypothetical schema remains just that, conjectural, even though the proposed hypothesis is ingenious and at times convincing.[13]

Today *The Story of the Grail* has become an adventure especially for erudite critics anxious to explain the origins of the mysterious and intriguing legend. Their own quest is strewn with enigmas, pitfalls, and temptations, difficulties arising mostly from the far too fragmentary documentary lacunae. To research the Grail legend, Arthurian scholars have to face the ever-diminishing mythical framework, must own their ignorance of Chrétien's immediate sources, must reckon with the unfinished state of his poem, and must recognize the scintillating subtleties of his narrative, all of which deterrents aggravate our doubts and incertitudes. But it has also happened that overly systematic critical attitudes or exclusively biased views regarding a single theory have perverted or complicated the possibility of open debate.

One fact, however, is in no way subject to doubt: the *Conte du Graal* as we know it amalgamates Christian elements with those emanating the marvelous and the magical. Every attempt to interpret the romance according to only one of the two great antagonistic theories, the Christian and the Celtic (or at least the primitive), any attempt to deny the work any contact with the *matière de Bretagne* and Celtic mythology, is doomed forthwith to reveal its shortcomings because textual anomalies will always crop up in the process. But for the Grail and for the lance which bleeds, a unilateral explanation cannot suffice. The blend of pagan marvel and Christian supernatural calls forth the logical alternative that either the *Conte du Graal* paganizes the Christian input or it Christianizes pagan input. To choose one or the other can remain a matter of personal preference, but the first option runs counter to the history of literary ideas. With the second we can more easily embrace the strange and equivocal nature of narrative.

It would really not be difficult to disclose briefly how the pagan primitive tale was Christianized. Even though we still have to accept the problem of working within the probable, all the marks of a seam between the primitive myth and its Christian reorientation have not worn away. The terms *graal* and *tailloir* ("paten," "carving platter") simply do not harmonize with the word "Mass wafer," and, in my opinion, when the hermit reveals that instead of the pike, lamprey, or salmon, the *graal* serves, for his only nourishment, the Fisher King's holy father with a "host" (*oiste*), this is a most crucial passage in every sense of the word. If, on the other hand, we consider the nutritive power of the host as a consequence of the sacred nature of the *graal*, and that its presence *in* the *graal* cannot be explained by any kind of outside intervention, we may presume that the magical power of the receptacle of plenty survives in the *graal* of Chrétien's romance, just as it apparently survives in subsequent versions. In other words, Chrétien would have drawn from the mythical concept the notion of a receptacle that regenerates boundless nourishment. But, mindful also perhaps of certain hagiographic legends in which an angel or a dove brings a nourishing host to a saintly anchorite, he might have substituted a small wafer for the theme of abundance, represented, it seems, by the enumeration of large fish that the *graal*, in an earlier version, may very well have served the rich Fisher King. In this way, Chrétien would have achieved, in addition to a spiritualization of the theme, a kind of dilation—from quantity to quality; the transmutation of the fish into the wafer would parallel the change of the primitive *graal* into a Christianized one: "Do not believe" (to paraphrase the hermit's words), "in a *graal* with multiple fish; the true one is that of the single wafer." Here is uncovered the *new sen* by which the tale waxes, and the shift effects a double surprise: first the contrast between what *was* believed and what *is* learned, then the disparity between the size of the receptacle and the meagerness of the miraculous nourishment. The modification is also a modulation: the *graal*, "so sacred a thing," now a transcendent one, adumbrates *the* Holy Grail. Even unexplained, the transfusion evokes, at a distance, the mystical image of the Last Supper dish, yet without overstepping the limits of symbolic suggestion. But the Christian interpretation of the marvelous dish remains nevertheless bolstered by the magic given.

It is also possible that the Fisher King's father was invented to enhance the Christian meaning of the tale. Rather curiously, this personage is missing in several versions; perhaps the original legend told only of the Fisher King. In any case, the invisible ascetic, chronologically confined to his chamber, serves to create the enigma of the cortege. Over and above the profane and brilliant feast in the castle hall, the character represents the spiritual plane, a notion veiled until the moment when Perceval's conscience awakens to contrition.

Is there anything unusual about our author's Christianization of a pagan tale? To such a question there can be only one resounding answer: a multiplicity of examples exists that demonstrate the medieval tendency to "moralize" pagan fables, once their latent power of converging toward religious truths was understood. The kind of prevalent mental attitude and the method involved in the systematic reinterpretation of Virgil and Ovid through adumbration and symbolism should be considered as equally operative for all legendary fiction, not just for that of Graeco-Roman antiquity. Now it is true that Chrétien hardly betrays a "moralizing" tendency in his earlier romances, although he was always careful to enhance the *matière* with an original *sen*. But his *Conte du Graal* marks a change in direction: the evangelical interest of its prologue and the hermitage episode have no equivalent in *Erec and Enide, Cligés, Lancelot,* or *Yvain.* Nevertheless, a pristine "moralization" of the Grail remains comparatively diffuse and poetically buoyant.

If he raised a tale of fancy to the threshold of Christian interpretation and elicited the idea of Redemption by the passing of the lance which bleeds and of the *graal,* this may enable us to explain the ambiguous atmosphere, the *chiaroscuro* ("light-dark") of sacred and profane that bathes the scene surrounding the cortege. This very ambiguity, adhering to the narrative structure, whereby, in fact, two different levels are juxtaposed or rather superimposed, is at once indicative of a rational, prudent, and suggestive style. But it also becomes, either because of Chrétien's perfected talent or because of the splendid subject, a form of poetic invention. A symbolism of marvelous objects emerges from this ambiguity; it illuminates the miraculous sustenance in the enchanted abode of the rich and infirm Fisher King, and it throbs with thoughts of Christian mystery.

Like filigree, a *conjointure* binds the texture of the narrative to successive images of the ambiguous and symbolic *graal.* The creative continuity, whereby profane manifestations are elevated to religious ones, parallels, in part, Perceval's own development from a near-savage and quasi-heathen (he has some inkling of Christian dogma, but lacks charity) to knighthood, courtesy, and spirituality.[14]

Perceval is indeed the true hero of the romance. Gawain's adventures belie the deliberate contrast indicated in the "Loathly Damsel" episode, and they reveal that he could not be the definitive model set before the "widow's son." Yet his mode of action remains patently exemplary in many circumstances. Gawain indeed possesses the merits of faultless prowess, scrupulous attachment to chivalric honor and tact, elegance and politeness, but this varnish hides a basic frivolity, a preoccupation with earthly glories, and an incurable weakness for casual amours. In spite of his sympathy, is there not a muffled irony in Chrétien's treatment of a model knight, the brilliant nephew of King Arthur, that leads Gawain to one disappointment after another?

Let us recall one episode when Gawain was about to liberate the Maid of Montesclaire and is deflected from it. A certain Guingambresil appears and, before the court, challenges Gawain, accusing him of treachery in the death of his father, the king of Cavalon. The customary single combat is to take place in forty days. Gawain departs, anxious to keep the rendezvous with Guingambresil. But on the way he does not fail to become interested in the "Maid with Little Sleeves," younger daughter of Tiebaut of Tintagel. It is a zestful situation to find the great champion and veteran lover risking his honor by delay, all for a very young, very innocent girl. But in the course of the journey, he breaks a promise made to himself, thus risking his honor and good name simply for the sake of a mischievous but interesting sweet thing with beautiful eyes. In the keep of Cavalon castle, he is trading sweet nothings and ardent kisses with a charming damsel, the king's sister, when suddenly they are interrupted by the attack of rioting townsmen. After a heroicomic battle, he only manages to escape the impasse by swearing to quest for the bleeding lance. But, in fact, Gawain does none of that and his adventures become ever more curious. Beyond the "Pale of Galloway" he steps into a heteroclite universe of reality and otherworld fantasy. Half-caught in the "evil maiden's" trap, he survives quite well a series of insults, until a new adventure, faintly analogous to that of the Grail, hints of his return to prestige. Crossing a river, he enters an impressive castle and spreads joy among its melancholic inhabitants after a successful test with the "marvelous bed." But he liberates no one. Surrounded by feminine entities, among whom he is surprised to find his grandmother, Ygerna, the hoary queen, with his mother, wife of King Lot, and his sister, Clarissant, Gawain himself is left condemned to become the prince of a courtly gynaeceum and forever a prisoner of enchantment.

Chrétien's account ends shortly after alluding to other episodes: the love between Clarissant and Gawain's enemy, Guiromelant, the proximate arrival of Arthur's court, warned by a message, and so on. We shall never know what continuation he had in mind. But he had sufficiently progressed with his narrative to give a clear feeling of contrast between the adventures of Gawain and of Perceval. It is not an accidental, witty insight. The first, yearning for no other equilibrium but his own, more a tourist than quester of worldly prowess, always led on by his love of universal praise, ends up by lowering himself. The second, dissatisfied with himself, tormented by the unfulfilled desire of a new ideal, enters the path of repentance, thus holding out a more austere, nobler, and purer message.

The right interpretation of the *Conte du Graal* will always remain at once difficult and problematic because of its symbolism and because of its unfinished state. But, in the final analysis, its incompleteness is its special beauty, its mystery, its charm. Like a splendid fragment that evokes dreams of the whole statue, we might say that, had Chrétien brought it to a final conclusion, his romance might not have stirred to the same degree the immense fires of imagination which have prolonged for centuries the effulgence of the Grail.

NOTES

Reprinted from *Chrétien de Troyes: The Man and His Work*, Chapter 7, trans. Raymond J. Cormier (Athens: Ohio University Press, 1982), pp. 127–55, Notes, pp. 187–89. Translated from Jean Frappier, *Chrétien de Troyes: Connaisance Des Lettres*, 1968. Permission to reprint granted by the translator. Bibliographical references have been incorporated into the Notes.

1. The word "book" does not necessarily mean a work written in Latin, for Chrétien himself called his Lancelot a "book," line 25. The following editions are cited in the text: *Cligés* edited by A. Micha, CFMA 84 (Paris, 1957); *Der Percevalroman (Li Contes del graal)*, ed. A. Hilka (Halle, 1932).

2. The theme of Perceval's mysterious *enfances* may be compared to traditions in both Irish (in the heroic narratives, the "boyhood deeds" of Cú Chulainn and of Finn) and Welsh (those of Pryderi).

3. The young girl is precise (vv. 3507–27) about the fact that, during a battle, the Fisher King was wounded by a javelin "through the two hips" (variants: "through the two legs," "through the two thighs"), and that since then he has been unable to walk or ride, so that for diversion, unable to hunt, he has himself placed on board a "ship" and físhes with a hook: "Therefore he is called the Fisher King."

4. The conjunction of snow, of blood, of the bird, and of the beloved appears to be a motif of Celtic origin, but it has been artfully reworked by Chrétien.

5. *Girart de Roussillon, chanson de geste*, edited by W. Mary Hackett, 3 vols. SATF (Paris, 1953-55); *The Medieval French Roman d'Alexandre, III. Version of Alexandre de Paris, Variants and Notes to Branch I*, edited by A. Foulet (Princeton, 1949); cf. p. 91, lines 601, 611, and commentary, p. 92.

6. W. Roach, ed. *Perceval ou Le Conte du Graal*, TLF 71 (Geneva, 1956; 1959), 1: 9648–50, 2: 13430–32, 3: 1.268, 269.

7. Whether the *graal* is mounted on a pedestal or not cannot be determined. Nor is it clear how the damsel in the procession holds it "between her two hands" (line 3220), an expression which is ambiguous, although "between" suggests more or less that the damsel's hands are parted to hold the *graal* at opposite ends.

8. Cf. "*La lance dont la pointe lerme/Del sanc tot cler que ele plore*" (vv. 6166–67); "*la lance dont la pointe verse des larmes de sang*" is L. Foulet's version. Would Chrétien have used the expression "*lerme del sanc*" and a collective verb like *plorer* if he meant that the dripping of the lance was caused solely by a "tear of blood"? And the use of the singular elsewhere (*une gote, cele gote*, "a drop," "this drop") may be explained by reference to the single drop which flowed when Perceval observed the lance.

9. Quotations from Mario Roques, "Le Graal de Chrétien et la demoiselle au Graal," *Romania* 76 (1955):1–27.

10. Yet it must be noted that a corollary of the interpretation under discussion is the idea that Britain was not yet truly Christianized, a notion nevertheless controverted by several passages. The same objection can be made to the hypothesis which claims that the procession would merely be "an imaginary vision granted to Perceval."

11. The allegorical maze misled U.T. Holmes, *in A New Interpretation of Chrétien's "Conte del Graal"* (Chapel Hill, 1948), to discern in *The Story of the Grail* a *figura* of the ancient Mosaic law and of the prophecy that it would be superseded by the new law of Christ, that is, a *figura* for the conversion of the Jews. The theory claims that the *graal* contains manna; the lance represents Aaron's rod; the Grail castle is to be identified with Solomon's temple; the Fisher King is no other than Jacob. Holmes maintains that Chrétien himself may have been a converted Jew. Sister M. Amelia Klenke, O.P., in *Liturgy and Allegory in Chrétien's "Perceval"* (Chapel Hill, 1951), goes even farther: the father of the Fisher King would be the prophet Elias, or rather Melchisedech; the hermit is Saint John the Baptist; the damsel of the tent would be the Virgin Mary; Blancheflor personifies chastity. Sister Klenke also believes the damsel of the Grail to be *Ecclesia*.

12. To choose only one example, the Church is always designated as *dame* in the *Queste del Saint Graal (Quest of the Holy Grail)*, ed. A. Pauphilet (Paris: Champion, 1923), pp. 168–85, while *Synagoga*, usually also a *dame*, is nevertheless named once with the less dignified title "damsel ," ibid ., p .173, line 4.

13. Jean Marx, *La Légende aurthurienne et le Graal* (Paris, 1952). On the Celtic hypothesis, see Helaine Newstead, "Recent Perspectives on Arthurian Literature," in *Mélanges Frappier* (Geneva, 1970), pp. 877–83; R.J. Cormier, "Tradition and Sources: The Jackson-Loomis Controversy Re-Examined," *Folklore* (London), 83 (1972): 101–21. (Translator's Note.)

14. One stylistic detail expresses discreetly the progressive symbolism of the *graal*: in the procession the damsel bears *a* grail (line 3220); later the hermit declares, " 'So sacred a thing is *the* grail'" (line 6425). This grammatical slip from the indefinite to the definite article carries us from the secular to the spiritual plane. The definite article used by the hermit doubtless refers to *this grail* (line 6423) in which one brings the wafer to the old king; however, it confers upon the object in addition an exceptional and unique value (this grail, no other, is a *sacred* thing), thus making the somewhat sententious line, though here latent and unspecific, almost prophetic of the later fixed expression: *the* Holy Grail.

CHAPTER 4

Tout Est par Senefiance
Gerbert's *Perceval*

SARA STURM-MADDOX

In the opening scene of Chrétien de Troyes's *Conte du Graal*, the Perceval who encounters knights for the first time in his native forest is much preoccupied with questions. During the naive exchange that affords his initial acquaintance with the practice and the accoutrements of chivalry, one chivalric interlocutor complains of this youth that he can do nothing but ask questions:

> "C'a rien nule que li demant
> Ne me respont il ainc a droit,
> Ains demande de quanqu'il voit
> Coment a non et c'on en fait." (238–41)[1]

> ("No matter what I ask him, he doesn't give me a straight answer, but asks, about whatever he sees, what it's called and what its use is.")

Thereafter, however, answers are repeatedly supplied to critical questions that have *not* been asked: what are the hero's familial ties? what indeed— and here the answer is not afforded by an interlocutor or informant but "deviné" by the subject himself—is his name? All of these are ultimately accessory to the questions that remain unasked at the castle of the Fisher King, where Perceval follows scrupulously the advice of his chivalric mentor against asking too many questions and thus occasions the disastrous consequences that haunt the rest of his story; at the end of Chrétien's unfinished romance, resolved to rectify his omission, he has not made his way back to that privileged place.[2]

The text generally known as the *Perceval Continuation,* by a certain
Gerbert, perhaps of Montreuil, is framed by the questions at the Grail
castle and their answers.[3] Its point of departure in both of the two manuscripts that contain it is a second visit by Perceval to the castle, where he
at last asks the questions, an episode that affords the point of suture of
this text with the Second Continuation which immediately precedes it; it
closes upon yet another visit to the Castle, a third sojourn that concludes
with the anticipation of his receiving those answers—which are indeed
provided in the opening of yet another Continuation, that of Manessier,
which immediately follows.[4] In the manuscripts that lack this interpolation, the questions asked on the second visit to the Fisher King's castle
are followed almost at once by their answers; in this sense, Gerbert's
contribution might better be termed a supplement than a continuation,
forming a loop in the linear progression of Perceval's story.

The immediate and obvious consequence of the refusal of the answers to Perceval at the opening of Gerbert's Continuation is one of deferral: between the questions and the answers is introduced a long and
richly varied series of adventures once again, as in Chrétien's romance,
involving both Perceval and Gauvain. But it is not merely deferral: because of the nature of its insertion, we are invited to read Perceval's adventures in this text in a special light. The issue is defined, in fact, by
pronouncements by the Fisher King in both the opening and the closing
scenes written by Gerbert. As Gerbert takes up the thread, the Fisher
King sets forth the condition that Perceval is not to learn the Grail secrets
"devant ce qu'il avra / Cel pechié et autre amendé" ("before he shall have
made amends for that sin and another . . . ," Gerbert, 52–53), and in the
final scene he confirms the hero's worthiness:

> "Amis, fait il, la vostre paine
> avez vous bien guerredonee,
> quant Diex vous a l'onor donee
> que dignes estes de savoir
> de ces affaires tot le voir." (Gerbert, 17076–80)

> ("Friend, he said, your striving is well rewarded, for God has granted
> you the honor of being worthy to know the whole truth of these
> matters.")

Framed in this way, Gerbert's interpolation implicitly invites us to seek
in Perceval's adventures an account of his qualification, denied at its

beginning and confirmed at its close, to receive the answers to the questions concerning Lance and Grail. It also suggests that Gerbert is not merely embarking upon the venture that is frequently attributed to Chrétien's various continuators, sending the well-known Perceval out once again *en aventure* to capture an audience for retelling or inserting new episodes into Chrétien's story. Both the issue of Perceval's sin and that of "making amends" alter the premises of Chrétien's romance, and the attempt to distinguish the two accounts in regard to these fundamental issues may help to define the particularity of Gerbert's Continuation in the series of texts that continue the story of Perceval.

Chrétien's unfortunate Perceval is given no opportunity to "make amends," for the rebuke by a Hideous Damsel who intrudes upon the celebration of his chivalric renown at Arthur's court appears to preclude the possibility of changing the outcome of his failure at the Grail castle: enumerating the disasters that followed upon that failure, she denies any further opportunity to heal the Fisher King, who would have held in peace the lands "dont il ne tendra point jamais" ("which he shall never hold," Chrétien, 4674). But already at the beginning of Gerbert's text the devastation of which this Perceval is inculpated has been rectified by the formulation of the questions recounted in the end of the Second Continuation: while the Fisher King has not been healed, the wasted lands have been transformed into lands of plenty, and the communal woe turned to joy and productivity (Gerbert, 312–515).[5] The issue of his incapacitating sin, however, remains. In the opening scene of this text, as Perceval is deep in thought in an attempt to discover "par quel pechié, par quel desfense / Que il ne set du Graal l'oevre" ("because of what sin, or what prohibition, he may not know the workings of the Grail"), his host acknowledges his grief at the "pechiés / ... / De sa mere qui chaï morte / Al pié del pont devant la porte / Quant il de li se desevra" ("sin ... concerning his mother, who fell dead at the foot of the bridge before the door when he took his leave of her," Gerbert, 39–51), affording the necessary identification with Chrétien's account where the knight's failure to ask the questions at the Grail castle is later attributed both by his cousin and by his hermit uncle to the sin unwittingly committed in his abrupt departure from his native forest, leaving his mother to die of sorrow (Chrétien, 3593–95, 6392–98). In Gerbert's text, however, the Fisher King speaks of "cel pechié et autre"; and while the nature of this "autre" is never to be specified, the issue is repeatedly renewed for the reader as Perceval continues to consider himself in a state of sin and to interrogate himself concerning the nature of the sin that remains undisclosed.

In the course of his self-interrogation, Gerbert's Perceval happens upon one possible answer, that of another failed obligation incurred in Chrétien's romance. Finding himself once again in the company of Gornemant, he attempts to narrate to his chivalric mentor the critical events that have occurred since his earlier visit in Chrétien's poem, and he protests his ignorance concerning what sin has rendered him unworthy: "'si en sui en doutance / Que ne sai par quel mesestanche / Ne par quel pechié ce me vient'" ("I am in a state of doubt because I don't know through what misdeed or what sin this is happening to me . . . ," Gerbert, 5125–27). He can recall no sins that he has not confessed, none for which he has not done penance, save one: his failure to keep his solemn promise to return to Blancheflor, whom he had left, rescued but enamored, to seek his mother, only to learn of the latter's death. "'Or m'en membre,'" he exclaims, "'c'est li pechiez / Dont je quit plus estre entechiez'" ("Now I recall, it is the sin by which I think I am most stained," 5147–48), and Gornemant urges him to rectify this omission at once: "'aiez em penser / Que la dame irez espouser / Tantost con partirez di chi'" ("Keep in mind to go and wed the lady as soon as you leave here," 5153–55). Soon, Perceval will indeed make this reparation: returning to Blancheflor's realm, he weds his still-willing hostess, although the marriage will remain unconsummated by mutual consent of the couple, following a vision in which Perceval receives a lecture on the superior merits of virginity.

Thus Perceval "makes amends" of sorts to Blancheflor, and so too he makes amends of sorts concerning the "pechié sa mere." Prompted by a heavenly voice, he returns to his mother's *manoir* to find his sister, accompanies her to visit a saintly hermit with whom their mother had formerly taken refuge, then leaves her in the care of a religious community presided over by their maternal aunt. While the encounter with his sister is already recounted in the Second Continuation, Gerbert's episode represents a deliberate rewriting of the scene of Perceval's departure in the *Conte du Graal*. Again sorrow is occasioned by leave-taking, now the sorrow of those who have cared for his sister far from society as Perceval had been cared for by his mother, and like the mother, they fall in a deathlike faint on this new occasion, but now the pious sympathy of Perceval's sister affords a positive contrast to the oblivious youth that Perceval had been (Gerbert, 2856–61). While Perceval himself again appears to ignore the sorrow around him, the motivation for his determined departure undergoes a positive modification, for whereas Chrétien's young rustic had left in precipitous haste to find "li roi qui fait les chevaliers," this Perceval departs in quest of the Grail:

A poi ne sont de doel parti
Quant d'aus se depart Perchevaus
Qui si a empris grans travaus
Con du Graal que il va querre. (Gerbert, 2852–55)

("They were almost overcome with grief when Perceval took leave of them, he who had undertaken the great task of seeking the Grail.")

His careful and devout disposition of his sister, moreover, affords for that female relative the positive resolution that he had hoped in vain to achieve with regard to his mother in Chrétien's poem, to establish her as a "nonain velee" ("veiled nun," Chrétien, 2962–71).

Are Gerbert's rewritings of Perceval's incomplete or failed adventures in Chrétien's romance thus so many *épreuves qualifiantes* that make his hero at last worthy to learn the mysteries of Lance and Grail? On the contrary: both episodes occur early in this very long Continuation, and while both are conducted according to divine promptings, neither in Perceval's own self-interrogations nor in the large number of narratorial interventions that guide the reader of this text is there an indication that this is the case. Just as Perceval's success in asking the questions has not resulted in his obtaining the answers, at no point in his subsequent adventures before the Fisher King's final assurance will his qualification to receive those answers be explicitly affirmed. The nature of his necessary qualification remains as much shrouded in mystery as the fate of the hero in Chrétien's romance, where the reader's anticipation of his return to the Grail castle is frustrated by the incomplete nature of the text.

What "happens," then, between the two visits to the Fisher King's castle to make of Gerbert's Perceval, apparently unworthy on the first occasion, the sanctioned addressee of the Grail answers on the second? The answer may be suggested by another element adapted from Chrétien's romance. On the occasion of Perceval's visit to the Grail castle in the *Conte du Graal,* we recall, a sword is presented to the Fisher King as the youth sits in conversation with his noble host. It is a precious sword, "worth a treasure," sent by the Fisher King's niece, who wishes him to bestow it. It is also a wondrous sword, one of only three by its forger, as the bearer explains. The Fisher King at once bestows it upon Perceval, for whom, he declares, it is "voee et destinee" ("pledged and destined," Chrétien, 3167–68). It is immediately following Perceval's acceptance and first *maniance* of this arm that the Grail procession first appears: and

while the Fisher King has seen where it was forged—for it is engraved
on the sword itself—and perceived too that it would break upon a single
peril known only to its forger, this information is not shared with Perceval. It is only later, following his departure from the Grail castle, that
Perceval is to learn from his cousin that the sword's forger is named Tri-
boet, and that the sword, when broken, is to be entrusted to him alone, for
he alone will be able to repair it (Chrétien, 3654–85).

And indeed the sword will break, as the Fisher King had understood
and the cousin foretold, at a moment of great peril. Although Perceval
has been engaged in mortal combat on earlier occasions, he employs this
sword apparently for the first time against the fierce knight known as
Orgueilleus de la Lande, "por che qu'il le volt ensaier" (Chrétien, 3926
a–g). When it breaks into two pieces as he strikes a great blow, a much-
distressed Perceval carefully replaces the pieces in his scabbard before
continuing the combat; fortunately, he has another sword to draw, that
which he had conquered from the Chevalier Vermeil in his first encounter
with a chivalric adversary on his initial visit to Arthur's court, and with it
he will bring the present encounter to a successful completion.

The repair of the sword that Perceval receives from the Fisher King
remains, like his possible return to the Grail castle, unrealized in the incomplete *Conte du Graal,* and perhaps almost forgotten by the reader.
Chrétien's early continuators, however, effect a significant modification:
they include a magnificent broken sword among the objects in the Grail
procession, and make the resolution of the enigma of Grail and Lance dependent upon its repair, to be effected only by the most perfect of knights.
In the First Continuation, where it is Gauvain who witnesses the appearances of the Grail, the hero is twice encouraged to undertake the mending
of the sword, and twice he fails; on the second occasion his host informs
him that the accomplishment of the feat awaits the arrival of another.[6] In
the Second Continuation, that other, Perceval, is almost successful, but
not quite. Here, however, that failure is productive for Gerbert's own
poem, which it both differentiates and makes possible.[7] In the manuscripts lacking Gerbert's interpolation, the comfort afforded Perceval by
the Fisher King for his disappointment at his failure to mend the sword
completely, recounted at the close of the Second Continuation, is followed by the answers to the Grail questions with which Manessier opens
his Continuation. In Gerbert's opening, on the contrary, Perceval is told
that he will not receive answers to those questions until—or unless—he
can mend the sword entirely, and that that deed is contingent upon rectification of his state of *pechié.* Gerbert's Continuation closes some 17,000

verses later with yet another return to the Fisher King's castle, yet another Grail procession, and again the appearance of the broken sword: now Perceval again takes up the sword, and it is miraculously whole, to the great joy of his host, who confirms that he is now worthy "'de savoir / de ces affaires tot le voir'" ("to know the whole truth of these matters," Gerbert, 17079–80).[8]

Thus, in Gerbert's Continuation, the sword assumes a particular significance quite different from that in Chrétien's poem. Chrétien's Perceval takes possession of the sword, first examining it and then passing it to a servant charged with the care of his arms before returning to his seat beside its donor to witness the passing of the Grail procession (Chrétien, 3180–86). In Gerbert's version, where the already-broken sword figures in the Grail procession, it is not conferred upon Perceval by the Fisher King. The eventual warning to Chrétien's Perceval concerning the repair of the sword given him by the Fisher King, moreover, is replaced in Gerbert by a discourse about sin that anticipates its "reforging" by the most perfect of knights. Here, upon Perceval's failure, the bearer of the sword returns to wrap it and take it away; while Perceval will repeatedly recall that his receiving the answers to the Grail questions is contingent upon his repair of this damaged sword,[9] the object itself will not reappear until the end of the interpolation, when he at last effects its mending at the Grail castle.

How then is the sword related to Perceval's qualification? The answer, never explicit in the text, is suggested in the account of his first adventure upon leaving the castle, where we learn that, like Chrétien's hero, this Perceval has another sword, his own.[10] And now this sword will break. Hearing the sweetest of music behind a closed gate and receiving no response to his insistent calls, Perceval attempts to force the gate with his sword. It is not to be forced: the sword breaks into two pieces, and a venerable gatekeeper appears to observe pointedly that "Vos brans a mestier de refaire, / Car je le voi brisié par mi" ("The blade of your sword needs repairing, for I see that it is split in two," Gerbert, 192–93). The significance of this doubling is underlined by the fact that while the repair of the first sword by Perceval remains contingent upon his rectification of his sinful state, the knight's own sword breaks as a result of a sinful action: the gatekeeper informs him that his striking the door has been a "grans pechiez" inspired by the "anemis." The connection with his earlier failure is confirmed in the admonition that follows, which duplicates that of the Fisher King: Perceval is not to see again the Bleeding Lance or learn the secrets of the Grail until he has rid himself of all sin through confession, due repentance, and penance (Gerbert, 199–205).

Thus the emphasis changes from the sins committed by Perceval before the poem's opening, those that impede his learning the answers to the Grail enigmas, to a sin committed within the text. While this is only one of several occasions on which he is enjoined to repent, confess, and do penance, its particular structural importance is due to the fact that it accounts for the prolongation of his period of questing, as the gatekeeper informs him: "Set ans entirs et un demi / En avez alongié vo paine . . ." ("You have extended your travail by seven full years and a half . . . ," Gerbert, 194–95).[11] Now the gatekeeper's reply to Perceval's anxious question, recalling Chrétien's poem in the expectation of the breaking and mending of the Fisher King's sword, combines the observations of that ruler and Perceval's cousin:

> "Cil qui le fist set le peril
> Par coi ele est brisie et fraite;
> Portez li, si sera refaite:
> Nus autres n'en venroit a chief." (225–29)

> ("He who made it knows by what peril it has been broken and split. Take it to him and it will be repaired; no one else will be able to do it.")

Yet while the reference to the mysterious "peril" known only to the forger of the sword directly echoes the phrasing of the model text, the nature of that peril is here quite different: the gatekeeper refers, not to a future unspecified occurrence, but to that which has just occurred, and this sword, unlike that conferred by the Fisher King in Chrétien's poem, has not broken in combat. The similarity of phrasing of the two texts heightens the contrast: what then is this peril? It is indeed the forger of his sword, to whom Perceval returns, who will identify it:

> "Vassal, fait il, par grant pechié
> Avez vostre brant pechoié,
> Que je fis passé a mains dis:
> A le porte de Paradis
> Le brisastes, tres bien le voi." (851–55)

> ("Vassal, he said, through a great sin have you shattered your sword that I made some time ago. You broke it on the gate of Paradise, I see that clearly.")

Perceval, then, has attempted, quite literally albeit unwittingly, to "take Paradise by force." Already the gatekeeper had sermoned him concerning his quest for the "chose tant sainte":

> "Mais li malvais de nient s'esforce
> Qu'il quide a le joie celestre
> Venir par la joie terrestre.
> Ne por grant pris ne por proece,
> Por hardement ne por richece,
> Nenil! ce ne puet avenir
> Qu'il puist a la gloire venir
> Que nous arons al jugement." (268–75)

("The wicked man wastes his effort thinking that he can attain to heavenly joy through earthly joy. Neither through great outlay nor through prowess, through boldness or riches, in no way! it cannot happen that he attain the glory that shall be ours at Judgment Day.")

Those within the walled enclosure are preparing themselves for Paradise, and the gate of Paradise, like that of the enclosure, cannot be forced by the sword, which becomes the emblem of that renown, prowess, daring, and wealth through which secular gain is achieved and measured. The opposition of spiritual glory to earthly glory upon which the gatekeeper insists—

> "Perchevaus tout apertement
> A veu Paradis terrestre;
> De cestui arons le celestre
> La ou la gloire est si tres grans" (276–79)

("Perceval has openly seen the earthly Paradise; we shall have the heavenly one, there where glory is great indeed.")

—will be repeated for Perceval by the hermit whom he visits in the company of his sister, who assures him that "'Mescreans est et ypocrites / Cil qui quide par vaine gloire / Avoir l'amour Dieu et sa gloire'" ("He is an unbeliever and a hypocrite who thinks through vainglory to have God's love and His glory," 2752–54). This formulation resonates not only with biblical language but with the praise Chrétien offers in the prologue of the *Conte du Graal* to Philippe de Flandres, the exemplary patron who is said to "aime droite justise / Et loiauté et sainte eglise" ("love true justice and loyalty and Holy Church") and to avoid "la vaine gloire / Qui vient de fausse ypocrisie" in favor of an unostentatious charity. Much later, Gerbert's Perceval will encounter another religious figure who will perform the sacred rituals, hearing his confession and offering him communion. His request for counsel receives this reply concerning the chivalric life in which he has incurred some of the sins he has just confessed:

> Li preudom dist que fors du sens
> est hom qui maine tel usage:
> "Je ne tieng pas celui a sage
> qui en sa vie tant desert
> que le cors use et l'ame pert.
> Dix ne fist mie chevalier
> por gent tuer ne gerroier,
> mais por tenir droite justise
> et por desfendre Sainte Eglise,
> car Dix n'ama onques beubanche.
> Biax dols amis, de cele enfance
> vous gardez, si ferez savoir,
> se l'amor Dieu volez avoir." (15814–26)

("The wise man says that a man who behaves this way is out of his mind: 'I do not consider him wise who in his life acts in such a way that he wears out his body and loses his soul. God did not make the knight to kill people or make war, but to uphold true justice and defend Holy Church, for pridefulness was never pleasing to Him. My dear friend, preserve yourself from this childishness, you will do well to do so if you wish to have God's love.'")

"'Dix n'ama onques beubanche'": the lesson concerning the besetting sin of this secular chivalry is so pervasive in this text that Jean Larmat identifies in "vaine gloire" comprehensively the "other" sin of which Perceval is inculpated.[12]

Chrétien's Perceval too attempts to realize his quest through chivalric prowess, as he promises in his vow in response to the Hideous Damsel's rebuke: he will not sleep two consecutive nights in a single place,

> Ne n'orra d'estrange passage
> Noveles que passer n'i aille,

Ne de chevalier qui miex vaille
Qu'autres chevaliers ne que dui
Qu'il ne s'aille combatre a lui,
Tant que il del graal savra
Cui l'en en sert, et qu'il avra
La lance qui saine trovee
Et que la veritez provee
Li ert dite por qu'ele saine;
Ja nel laira por nule paine. (Chrétien, 4730–40)

(Nor will he hear news of a forbidding passage without going to pass through it, nor of a knight who is worth even two others without going to fight him, until he learns who is served by the Grail and until he has found the bleeding lance and learned the real truth of why it bleeds; he will not give up whatever the cost.")

He pledges, that is, to take up all the challenges of chivalric adventure until he has learned the secrets of Grail and Lance, and he will fail utterly: when the text returns to Perceval following its attention to a series of Gauvain's adventures, we find that while he has passed five years "a requerre chevalerie" ("in chivalric pursuits"), his constant success in chivalric exploits has not resulted in success in his quest nor bettered his state. Indeed, he has been forgetful both of God and of the Grail questions, as he tells his uncle: ". . . rien n'en demandai. / Onques puis, certes, n'amendai" ("I didn't ask anything about it; certainly I never made amends for it. . . I did nothing that was not bad . . . ," 6377–78). More explicitly, he adds that during that protracted period of his alienation from God "puis ne fis se mal non," and it is in these terms that he sorrowfully avows his failure:

"Que Damedieu en oblïai,
Ne puis merchi ne li crïai
Ne ne fis rien, que je seusse,
Por coi jamais merchi eusse." (6383–86)

("For I forgot the Lord God, nor did I thereafter beg for mercy, nor do anything that I was aware of through which I might obtain it.")

In the critique of chivalric violence in the *Conte du Graal* the bearing of arms becomes the vehicle for an opposition of spiritual to worldly values. The single scene in which Chrétien's Perceval participates in the ritual of repentance, confession, and penance is introduced by his encounter on Good Friday with penitents who reproach him for bearing arms on such a day, just as Gerbert's gatekeeper opens in response to his violent assault to find a Perceval in full armor, "de fer covert" ("covered with iron," Gerbert, 184). To the brutality and presumption of Perceval's blow upon the gate the gatekeeper opposes faith, in an image that recalls the biblical mustard seed:

> "Si te dirai en bone foi
> Que s'en toi avoit tant de foi
> Come est uns petits grains de sel
> Que tu porroies un et el
> Savoir et faire tot sans force." (263–67)[13]

> ("I will tell you in good faith that if you had as much faith as a tiny grain of salt, you could know both one and the other, and do it all without show of force.")

Gerbert, however, points his own lesson by reinstating the motif of armed struggle through his appropriation of the common agonistic biblical metaphors that cast man's earthly life as a perpetual combat against sin, the lesson later to be repeated by Perceval himself to a vanquished adversary: "'Cist siecles est une bataille. . .'" ("this world is a battle," 9926).[14] Paradise is indeed to be conquered, and by arms, but these arms are the forms of religious devotion and observance. And if all Christians may be said to be part of Christ's "militia," the metaphor is particularly appropriate for the chivalric class.[15] A hermit will make the application explicit: "'De tels armes se doit armer / Chevaliers qui Dieu velt amer, / S'il velt estre preus et vaillans'" ("with arms such as these must the knight who seeks to love God arm himself, if he wishes to be upright and valiant," 2761–63). Yet more specifically, he now redefines for Perceval the principal arm of the chevalier in God's service: it is a double-edged sword to serve the defense of Sainte Eglise on the one hand, and on the other to afford "droite justice terriene" to "la gent crestïene" ("true earthly justice to the Christian people"). This mission, that would engage the rededication of an abusive secular chivalry, is already urged upon the Perceval of the *Conte du Graal*.[16] In Gerbert's interpolation it repeatedly takes the form of a theologically oriented discourse, defining a mission that the hermit proclaims unfilled by a rapacious chivalric class that wields instead a secular sword:[17]

"Chascuns chevaliers taut et taille
Les povres homes et raeint
Sans che qu'il ne lor mesfont nient.
De cele part est trop trenchans
L'espee et cil est Dieu trichans
Qui tele espee avec lui porte.
De Paradis li est la porte
Fermee, s'il ne s'en amende.
Biaus dols amis, Dieus vous desfende,
Dist l'ermites, de tele espee
Dont vostre ame soit encorpee." (2776–86)

("Each knight oppresses and cuts down and afflicts the poor folk without having suffered any harm from them. On that side the sword is too sharp, and he wrongs God who bears such a sword. The gate of Paradise is closed to him, if he does not make amends. Fair dear friend, said the hermit, God protect you from such a sword by which your soul would stand accused.")

In this text this is not mere metaphor: armed with such a secular sword, we have seen that Perceval has indeed found the "door of Paradise"—or rather its gate—closed to him.

Returning at last to the Fisher King's castle, Perceval responds to his host's request to recount his adventures by evoking two dramatic *épreuves*. The first constitutes as it were a composite analogue to the disposition of the two principal figures in the Grail castle: a wounded knight seen within a chapel is identified as one who, converted long ago by Joseph of Arimathea, had attempted unbidden to approach the Grail and been told that as a consequence his wounds were to remain always fresh—but his death to be deferred—until the advent of the Grail Knight, in whose arms, his wounds now healed, he will die (Gerbert, 10547–51). Chrétien's maimed Fisher King, who awaits the destined knight for his healing, and the old king sustained only by the Grail are combined in this figure, who through the centuries has been nourished only by the host, the "pain de vie." Perceval is not ready, not yet fully "sanz pechié vrais confés" ("truly confessed and without sin"), for he is unable to enter the chapel, bring the *aventure* to its end, and heal the king. In the second adventure, after being first deceived by a demonic "anemis," he succeeds in effecting its reimprisonment in a rock, but not before he has heard from this knowledgeable adversary the story of the angels' fall and of the Fall in Eden that is repeated through individual human history—and in particular his own, and specifically in the episode that resulted in the breaking of his sword and the prolongation of his quest—as a story of temptation. Finally, he evokes an adventure from near the end of the Second Continuation, in which a child in a tree spoke enigmatically concerning what he was to learn at the Mont Douloureux where he was to be instructed concerning his return to the Grail castle.

And now, having left that castle at the beginning of Gerbert's text without the answers to his questions about Lance and Grail, Perceval returns to it with new questions, questions about the knight in the chapel and the demon in the stone and the child in the tree, that he puts now to the Fisher King:

> "De che savoir ai grant desir,
> sire, s'il vous vient a plaisir;
> et de l'enfant que vi soz l'arbre,
> qui tant me fist le cuer esmarbre,
> car onques rien ne m'en volt dire,
> s'en ai al cuer dolor et ire
> si me vient a molt grant merveille,
> car ce n'est pas chose pareille.
> Sire, volentiers en orroie
> la novele, se Diex me voie,
> et que on m'en seüst conter." (16999–7009)

> ("I greatly desire to learn of that, Sire, if it please you; and about the child I saw in the tree, who chilled my heart so, because he refused to tell me anything about it; I feel pained and angry about that, and I marvel greatly, for it is unprecedented. Sire, I would gladly hear the news of it, so help me God, if someone could explain it to me.")

In these new questions, we find confirmation that while the textual points of entry and exit of Gerbert's interpolation in the manuscripts are identical, Perceval's adventures in the course of this Continuation afford more than a simple deferral of the anticipated revelation of the secrets of Lance and Grail. Just as the breaking of Perceval's sword in his armed assault on the gate of Paradise leads to a reconception of that chivalric arm as the double-edged sword that defines the proper but neglected mission of chivalry, the "vaine gloire" sought by a secular chivalry has been replaced by celestial glory, and that which he must "conquer" redefined as

Paradise itself. Perceval will not forget: defending his virginity against the invitation of a seductive damsel by reminding himself of his quest for the Grail, he in turn sermons his hostess: "'Mais bien doit redouter pechié / Li hom, et en fais et en dis, / Qui conquerre velt Paradis'" ("The man who would conquer Paradise must beware of sin in both word and deed," 642–44). The Grail castle, whose secrets he had sought in vain to learn and to which he seeks to return, is doubled by a second, equally mysterious locus of secrets, the walled enclosure from whose secrets he is also excluded, a sort of Paradise-on-earth, an Earthly Paradise that is at the same time the gateway to the celestial Paradise. Now Perceval is to learn the answers, not only to the Grail questions, but to his new questions as well, "de ces affaires tot le voir" ("the whole truth of these matters"). If we have not learned the precise nature of his qualification to receive the answers concerning Lance and Grail, his objective is no longer merely the receiving of those answers; the anticipated answers to the Grail questions, long deferred, have been recontextualized through his initiation as participant in a quest for a larger *senefiance*.

NOTES

Reprinted with permission from *Arthurian Yearbook* 2 (1992), 191–207. Translations by the author have been added.

1. Citations are from *Le Roman de Perceval ou le Conte du Graal*, ed. W. Roach (Geneva: Droz, 1959), cited as Chrétien, translations mine.

2. For the importance of the issue in the romance as a whole, see E. J. Burns, "Quest and Questioning in the *Conte du Graal*," *Romance Philology*, 41 (1988), 251–66.

3. The author names himself in the text only as Gerbert. Citations are from the CFMA edition: Gerbert de Montreuil, *La Continuation de Perceval* (Paris: Champion), vol. I, ll. 1–7020, and II, ll. 7021–14078, ed. M. Williams, 1922, 1925, vol. III, ll. 14079–end, ed. M. Oswald, 1975, all cited in the text as Gerbert.

4. For the passage that opens this Continuation and recurs at its end, see *Perceval le Gallois ou le Conte du Graal*, ed. Ch. Potvin, 6 vols. (Mons: Dequesne-Maquillier, 1867–72), V, 34930–33, cited in Williams's edition of Gerbert.

5. The verb "amender," frequent in this text, is used twice in the passage, with regard to Perceval's query concerning the Grail, "par coi amendé somes," and concerning the Lance: "Biaus sire, quant le demandastes, / Tot cest païs en amendastes" (490–91, 497–98).

6. For the episode see *The Continuations of the Old French Perceval of Chrétien de Troyes*, ed. W. Roach, Vol. I: The First Continuation (Philadelphia, 1949, rpt. Philadelphia: The American Philosophical Society, 1965), pp. 364–65.

7. A. Leupin observes that "la brèche qui marque la lame lui permet d'insérer la continuation de Gerbert"; see "La faille et l'écriture dans les Continuations de *Perceval*," *Le Moyen Age*, 88 (1982), p. 260.

8. There is no mention here of the vengeance motif, introduced in the First Continuation and repeated in the Second, that associated the mending of the sword and the qualification to receive answers to the Grail questions with a dead knight; for the motif, see W. Roach, "Transformations of the Grail Theme in the First Two Continuations of the Old French *Perceval*," *Proceedings of the American Philosophical Society* 110 (1966), pp. 163–64.

9. Thus, he recalls it in the long interior monologue in which he summarizes his failure as he leaves the Grail Castle behind: "'Et l'espee que j'ai ajointe / Fors l'osque qui est a sauder, / De tant i a a amender'" ("and my sword, that is well made except for the break that must be mended, to that extent amends must be made," 128–30); thus, too, he will recall it to the saintly lady who reveals herself to be his mother's cousin: "'Mais il me dist que si pecheres / Estoie que riens ne saroie / Du Graal devant que j'aroie / L'osque de l'espee soldee'" ("But he told me that if I were a sinner, I would learn nothing of the Grail before I had mended the break in the sword," 3074–77).

10. Leupin (above, note 7) observes that "il faut voir qu'ici le symbole lui-même est soumis à un incessant principe dédoublement, où se marque, de façon impérative, la logique de la faille" (p. 259).

11. L. Cocito notes a suggestive parallel with the episode in Dante's *Commedia* where the angelic gatekeeper of Purgatorio proper inscribes with his sword seven letters "P," signs of sin, on the brow of the pilgrim; these are to be removed in his laborious ascent before he may enter the Earthly Paradise at the top of the mountain. See *Gerbert de Montreuil e il poema del Graal* (Genoa: Bozzi, 1964), pp. 115–16.

12. "Tout permet de croire qu'il s'agit de l'orgueil et de la vaine gloire, le péché majeur selon la théologie chrétienne, le péché majeur de l'aristocratie féodale." See "Le péché de Perceval dans la *Continuation* de Gerbert," in *Mélanges d'Histoire littéraire, de linguistique et de Philologie Romanes offerts a Charles Rostaing*, ed J. De Caluwé et al. (Liège: Marche Romane, 1974), I, pp. 542, 549–50.

13. When Perceval's hermit uncle learns his name after his later sermon on chivalry, he exclaims "'C'est damages que tiex vassax / est atornez a tel mestier; / mix devez amer le mostier'" ("It's a pity for such a youth as yourself to follow such a calling; you should prefer the Church," 15832–34)—revealing rather di-

rectly the bias of the poet concerning the chivalric versus the religious vocation in the question of the "redemption of chivalry."

14. For the biblical metaphors of spiritual "arming" see Cocito (above, note 11), who cites as well the lesson pronounced by a hermit in the *Queste:* "Si ne devez mie cuidier que ces aventures que ore avienent soient d'omes tuer ne de chevaliers occirre; ainz sont des choses esperituex, qui sont graindres et mielz vaillanz assez" ("You must not believe that the adventures that are occurring now are those of killing men or destroying knights; they are instead of spiritual things, which are far greater and of greater worth," pp. 94–95).

15. As E. Köhler observes, "La règle donnée aux Templiers par Bernard de Clairvaux en 1128 scellera la mutation de la 'militia secularis' en militia Christi.'" See *L'aventure chevaleresque: idéal et réalité dans le roman courtois* (Paris: Gallimard, 1974), pp. 133–34.

16. See S. Sturm-Maddox, " 'Tenir sa terre en pais': Social Order in the *Brut* and the *Conte du Graal,*" *Studies in Philology,* 81 (1984), 28–41.

17. For this evident predication, see Larmat (above, note 12), pp. 556–57.

CHAPTER 5

Punishment in the *Perlesvaus*
The Theme of the Waste Land

ANGUS J. KENNEDY

The physical blighting of Arthur's Kingdom as a form of collective punishment imposed for a variety of reasons (an individual's misdeeds,
vengeance, or the miraculous act of devastation wrought by the so-called
Dolorous Stroke) constitutes one of the most characteristic and memorable
ingredients of the Grail Legend as it developed in France between c. 1180
and c. 1240. Occurring as it does in nearly all of the Grail texts composed
over this period (notably, Chrétien's *Conte du Graal,* the *Elucidation* prologue, the *First* and *Fourth Continuations,* the *Estoire* and *Queste* sections
of the *Vulgate Cycle,* the *Perlesvaus,* the Balaain section of the *Suite du
Merlin,* and also in the much later Grail-related *Sone de Nansai*),[1] the
Waste Land theme has naturally attracted fairly frequent critical attention
and discussion over the years.[2] Much of this discussion has tended to concentrate on the question of origins rather than on the literary handling of
the theme in individual texts. Jessie L. Weston, for example, taking as her
starting-point the sympathetic relationship that seemed to exist in Grail romance between the vitality of the king and the life-forces of his kingdom,
and conversely the maiming of the king and the wasting of the land, devoted all her energies to relating her findings in Arthurian romance to oriental nature-rituals, while Loomis, Nitze, Newstead and others, working
on more concrete evidence and with more positive results, pointed to fairly
clear parallels to and echoes of the Waste Land in the literature and lore of
Ireland and Wales, and used these as part of their general argument for the
ultimate Celtic provenance of the Arthurian cycle.[3] This kind of approach
to the Waste Land theme is best summed-up in the title of Jessie Weston's
now famous book *From Ritual to Romance,* of Nitze's article "The Waste

Land: a Celtic Arthurian Theme," or of the chapter "Irish *echtrai:* the Waste Land and the Bleeding Lance" in Loomis's *The Grail. From Celtic Myth to Christian Symbol.*[4] Not all studies of the Waste Land, however, have been presented within the framework of theories about ultimate origins—though these still attract, and are likely to continue to attract, scholarly attention (see, for example, the interesting articles on the Maimed King by O'Sharkey and Riemschneider).[5] Invaluable studies by Nitze, Vinaver, Bogdanow, Kelly and Cor, among others, have concentrated less on origins and more on the creative adaptation of material in each successive text, attempting to journey along what Vinaver referred to as "the steep and adventurous path of creation";[6] and more recently, in an article entitled "Waste Land and Round Table: the Historical Significance of Myths of Dearth and Plenty in Old French Romance," Bloch has perceptively explored how the Waste Land theme may reflect or project issues of contemporary reality.[7] These studies still leave scope, however, in my view, for a more detailed examination of the Waste Land as it is presented in the *Perlesvaus.*[8] It is the purpose of this article to approach the Waste Land in the *Perlesvaus* from both a literary and historical point of view (though no reference will be made to questions of origins), in order to bring out more clearly than has been attempted to date something of the author's originality with regard both to the way in which he handles the theme and the "senefiance" he attaches to it. Given the overtly propagandist nature of the *Perlesvaus,* it is impossible to separate literary and didactic intentions. A useful, overall perspective for this discussion is provided by Vinaver's analysis of the basic ingredients that can occur in various combinations in the presentation of the Waste Land: a miraculous weapon, a wound inflicted upon a knight or king (the Dolorous Stroke), the wasting of the land, the healing of the wound.[9] As will be shown, not all of these motifs are applicable to the *Perlesvaus,* but they do provide a general focus within which the author's priorities can be judged. This survey will examine, firstly, the development of the Waste Land at the level of plot or narrative; secondly, the textual indications that guide us towards interpreting the Waste Land in a certain way; thirdly, the Waste Land as part of a complex pattern of related, criss-crossing themes that all point towards a similar if not identical "senefiance."

1. THE WASTE LAND AT THE LEVEL OF PLOT

When the story opens, Perlesvaus' first visit to the Grail Castle has already taken place. We learn through a number of retrospective allusions woven into the opening sections of the romance that Perlesvaus has been to the Castle of the Fisher King, that he has seen the Grail and the Bleeding Lance, but has failed to ask what purpose the Grail served and whom it served, and that, as a result of this, the Fisher King has fallen ill, disaster has overtaken the whole of Arthur's Kingdom and all the adjacent islands. Now what the author is at pains to do throughout the rest of Part I of the romance (i.e. up to 1. 6271) is to bring these consequences constantly before the reader's attention, and it is in executing this design that he develops his own conception of the Waste Land theme. What strikes the reader as perhaps the most immediately obvious consequence of Perlesvaus' disastrous silence is the physical blighting that overtakes not the Grail Country but Arthur's Kingdom itself. Brief but telling descriptions of the landscape, emphasising above all its bleakness and sterility, are carefully introduced, at all times confronting us and the knights of Logres with the fact of the Grail hero's failure. For example, Gauvain enters into "la plus orrible forest e la plus hideuse que nus veïst onques; e sanbloit qu'onques verdeur n'i eüst eüe, ainz erent totes les branches nues de fueille e seches, e tuit li arbre noir ausi comme brullé de feu, e la terre par desoz arsice e noire e sanz verdeur e plainne de granz crevaces" (ll. 737–42). At another point Gauvain comes to "une terre seche et povre et sofraiteuse de toz biens. Et trove un povre chastle et entre dedenz, et le trove molt agasti . . ." (ll. 2529–31). In the course of one of his adventures, Lancelot finds himself in "une terre gaste et un païs grant et large, ou il n'abitoit ne beste ne oisiax, car la terre estoit si seche et si povre q'il n'i trovoient point de pouture. Lanceloz esgarde devant lui en loig, et voit une cité aparoir, si chevauche cele part grant aleüre, et voit que la cité est si grant q'il senble q'ele porpraige un païs. Il voit les murs qui dechïent environ, et les portes enclinent de vellece. Il entra la dedenz et trove la cité tote voide de gent, et voit les granz palés deschaüz et gastes, et trove les marchiez et les changes toz voiz, et volt les granz cemetires toz plains de sarqex et les iglises totes gastes" (ll. 2857–65). Perlesvaus, passing through "un païs qui li senbloit estre gastez, car il estoit tot voit de gent" (ll. 4906–07), is told by a hermit that this desolate terrain marks the beginning of the Kingdom of Logres: "Ceste terre gastee en son ceste forest par ont vos venistes est li conmencemenz dou roiaume de Logres' (ll. 4920–21). Equally indicative of this widespread desolation is the proliferation of the word "gaste' in the titles assumed by the knights and ladies of the Kingdom: the Chevalier de la Gaste Meson, the Povre Chevalier dou Gaste Chastel, the Seigneur dou Gaste Chastel, or the Dame dou Gaste Manoir.

This concrete picture of the blighting of the land is itself only part of the author's development of the Waste Land theme: the depiction of the blighted land proceeds apace with a description of the moral and spiritual decline of Arthur and his court after Perlesvaus' failure, in such a way that the one is made to reflect and constantly reinforce the other. The theme of Arthur's decline is developed throughout Part I (e.g. in Gauvain's and Lancelot's visits to the Grail Castle or in Perlesvaus' numerous encounters with his sister), but it is presented most clearly of all in the prologue, then in a hermit's severe censure of Arthur during his pilgrimage to a chapel in Wales, and in Arthur's first encounter with the Damoisele du Char. In the prologue the author states: "par molt poi de parole qu' il (i.e. Perlesvaus) delaia a dire, avindrent si granz meschaances a la Grant Breteingne que totes les illes e totes les terres en chaïrent en grant doleur . . . "(ll. 18–21) . . . "une volentez delaianz li (i.e. to Arthur) vint, e commença a perdre le talent des largesces que il soloit fere. Ne voloit cort tenir a Noël, ne a Pasques, ne a Pentecoste. Li chevalier de la Table Reonde, qant il virent son bienfet alentir, il s'en partirent e commencierent sa cort a lessier. De trois .c. e .lxx. chevaliers q'il soloit avoir de sa mesniee, n'avoit il ore mie plus de .xxv. au plus. Nule aventure n'avenoit mes a sa cort. Tuit li autre prince avoient leur biensfez delaiez por ce q'il veoient le roi maintenir si foiblement" (ll. 69–76). Then, in the course of his pilgrimage to Saint Austin's Chapel in Wales, Arthur is vigorously upbraided by a hermit for this transformation that has taken place in himself and at his court: 'Car vos estes li plus riches rois du mont e li plus poissanz e li plus aventurex, si devroit a vos toz li mondes prendre essanple de bien fere e de largesse e d'oneur: e vos estes li essanples de vilenie fere a toz les riches homes qui ore sont. Si vos en mescharra molt durement, se vos ne remetez vostre afere o point o vos l'aviez commencié; car vostre corz estoit la sovrainne de totes les corz, e la plus aventureuse; or est la pis vaillanz" (ll. 333–9). Arthur himself is then given, for the first time, an explanation for this decline in terms that clearly recall those of the prologue: 'Mes une granz doleurs est avenue novelement par un chevalier qui fu herbergiez en l'ostel au riche roi Pescheeur, si s'aparut a lui li sainz Graauz e la lance de coi la pointe de fer saine, ne ne demanda de coi ce servoit, ne cui on en servoit; por ce qu'il ne le demanda, sont totes les terres de guerre escommeües, ne chevaliers n'e[n]contre autre en forest q'il ne qeure sus e ocie s'il puet, e vos meïsmes vos en perceveroiz bien ainz que vos partez de ceste lande" (ll. 349–56). And finally, in his encounter with the Damoisele du Char, Arthur (and the reader) is reminded yet again: 'por ce que cil ne volst demander cui on en servoit, totes les terres en furent commeües de guerre;

chevaliers n'encontra onques puis autre en forest ne en lande, o il n'eüst contenz d'armes sanz resnable achoison; vos meïsmes vos en poez bien estre perceüz, car vos en avez delaié vostre bienfet grant piece, de coi vos avez esté molt blasmez e tuit li autre baron qui pris ont garde a vos, car vos estes li mireoirs au siecle de bien fere o de mal" (ll. 640–46). It is worth pointing out too that the Damoisele du Char, who speaks these words, seems to embody the decline that each of these passages underlines: once the Grail bearer at the Court of the Fisher King, she is now forced to wander over the face of the earth, her right hand (which she once used to carry the Grail) slung in a gold stole about her neck, her head once adorned with luxuriant tresses now "tote chauve e sans chevex" (ll. 648–9) as a result of Perlesvaus' failure. For the Damoisele du Char, as for Arthur and his court, Perlesvaus' silence has wrought a dramatic reversal in their fortunes.

Arthur and his court, however, as the Damoisele du Char reminds us in one of the passages just quoted, represent "li mireoirs au siecle de bien fere o de mal" (ll. 645–6). As part therefore of his development of the Waste Land theme, the author goes on to show us in detail how the woes and calamities that beset Arthur's court are reflected on a much larger scale throughout the whole kingdom. Now the way in which the author chooses to do this is to show us Arthur's kingdom exposed to the ravages of war, both from without and within. This involves him and his readers in a very long and at times highly complicated series of adventures to do with warfare and copious blood-letting, ranging from the Sire des Mares' repeated attacks on the estates of Perlesvaus' mother (e.g. ll. 461, 513, 1076–7), the King of Chastel Mortel's attacks on the Grail Castle (e.g. ll. 1081–5, 2486, 3929–31, 4986), through Perlesvaus' feud with the family of the Red Knight (e.g. ll. 512, 1077, 3046–7) to the conquest of the Chevalier au Dragon Ardant (l. 5913) and the Tor de Cuivre (l. 5960), and the story of Keu's treacherous murder of Loholt, Arthur's son (ll. 4010–12). The inherent complexity of these adventures at times puts additional demands on the reader in that the adventures are not developed in a straight, narrative sequence, but are interlaced with one another in such a way that we are left waiting for the reappearance of some theme held temporarily in suspense whilst already following a second or a third. Yet, however intricate the complexities of the plot or narrative technique, however easy it is for us to lose sight of the central threads amidst all the detail with which the author presents us, it is clear that there is one overall consideration running right through this section, giving shape and coherence to what on the surface may appear to be a meaningless patchwork of bigger and better battles: namely, the cause-effect relationship between Perlesvaus' silence at the

Grail Castle and *all* the disasters that overtake the land. Indeed, it is notable that on a few occasions, even when immersed in the detail of some
particular feud or battle, the author has taken the trouble to help the reader
keep this central consideration in mind. For example, when describing the
Sire des Mares' assaults on the estates belonging to Perlesvaus' mother,
the author reminds us that it is precisely because of Perlesvaus' failure in
the Grail adventure that his mother has no-one available to defend her
land (ll. 1076–85): Perlesvaus has withdrawn to a hermitage to recover
from the humiliation of his first visit to the Grail Castle, while the Fisher
King, who is related to Perlesvaus and his mother and who therefore
could be expected to come to her aid, cannot help because he has fallen
into languishment, again as a direct result of Perlesvaus' silence. It is evident, therefore, that the account of how Arthur's Kingdom is exposed to
the ravages of war is part and parcel of the wasting of the land that results
from Perlesvaus' failure at the Castle of the Fisher King.

Considered solely from the point of view of narrative or plot, then, the
Waste Land theme is composed of a number of interwoven, criss-crossing
strands: the physical blighting of the land, the decline of Arthur's chivalry,
the proliferation of war and dissension throughout his Kingdom. The already considerable impact which the reappearance of these various strands
must have on the reader, at the level of plot, is deepened by an additional
element introduced and highlighted by the author, namely, the striking antithesis which he develops between Arthur's Waste Kingdom and the fertile country of the Fisher King. As was touched upon earlier, although the
Fisher King falls into languishment as a result of Perlesvaus' failure, his
land escapes the punishment inflicted upon Arthur's territories, and his
country is as fertile and plenteous as Arthur's is poor and sterile. When
Gauvain arrives at the Fisher King's country, he finds it to comprise "une
terre molt bele e molt ri[ch]e e molt plenteïve" (ll. 1689–90). . . "la plus
bele terre du mont et les plus beles praeries et les plus beles rivieres que
nus veïst onques, et forez garnies de bestes sauvaches" (ll. 2255–7) . . . "[li
chastiax] est avironé de granz eues et plenteüreuses de toz biens" (ll.
2267–8). A similar description is given on Lancelot's arrival at the Grail
Castle: . . . et trouva .i. molt bele praerie qui tote estoit chargie de flors, et
coroit une molt grant riviere qui molt estoit clere et large, et avoit forest
d'une part et d'autre, mes que les praeries estoi[en]t granz et larges entre la
riviere et la forest" (ll. 3627–30). Additional details, pointing to the same
abundance and fruitfulness, are provided when Arthur arrives at the castle
after it has been reconquered by Perlesvaus: "Li rois . . . esgarda la richoise
e la grant habundance qui eu chastel venoit, car il n'estoit riens ou monde

qui i faillist, qui covenist a cors de bone gent . . . Il avoit derier le chastel .i. flun, ce tesmoigne l'estoire, par coi toz li biens venoit ou chastel. Icil flun estoit mout beaus e mout plentious. Josephez nos tesmoigne que il venoit de Paradis Terrestre, e avironnoit tot le chastel, e coroit dusqu'en la forest chiés .i. prodom hermite. Iluec perdoit son cors e entroit en terre, mais tot la o il s'espandoit estoit grant la plenté de toz les biens" (ll. 7193–5, 7198–203). The contrast thus established between drought and fertility, dearth and plenty, poverty and wealth, sterility and fruitfulness serves to highlight the seriousness of Perlesvaus' failure and the punishment it has imposed on the whole Arthurian world.

It remains now to look briefly at the Waste Land theme at plot-level in Part 2 of the text (l. 6272–end). After the languishment and death of the Fisher King (l. 5145) and Perlesvaus' reconquest of the Grail Castle (l. 6252), one would have expected the author to orchestrate fully the transformation of the Waste Land to a land of fruitfulness and plenty: the articulation of this theme would have neatly counterbalanced the depiction of the blighting of the kingdom in Part 1 and would have served to underscore the redemptive nature of Perlesvaus' mission and his atonement for his original transgression. Rather surprisingly, however, the theme of the restoration of the land is somewhat muted: it occurs, as will be seen, in Lancelot's regeneration of the Waste City, but there is no general depiction of the land suddenly regaining its fruitfulness. In addition, even after the Grail conquest and Arthur's pilgrimage to the castle, one still finds echoes of the Waste Land theme reverberating throughout the text. Lancelot, for example, approaching Carduel, finds "la terre gaste e essilliee" (l. 7635). Similarly, Arthur "trove sa terre gastee en plusors lex, de quoi il est molt dolenz" (7811). The risk of war bringing dissension and ruin is still ever-present: "Sa[g]ramors, fait Briens, meuz vendroit le roi que il congeast Lancelot un an que il fust por lui gerroiez dis, ne que sa terre fust gastee ne maumise" (ll. 8093–5). Perlesvaus, whose life as a knight is never "sanz travaill e sanz paine en tant com il vesqui chevaliers" (ll. 8983–4), at one point on his various journeys "passe .iii. roiaumes e plus, e trove isles gastes e desertes, [d'une part]e d'autre part la mer, quar la nef coroit assez pres de terre" (ll. 9825–7), and later comes across the forest of Noir Hermite once visited by Gauvain: "[La forest] tent est lede e hideuse qu'il n'i a fueille ne verdeur en iver ne en esté, ne chanz d'oisel n'i fu onques oïz, ainz est la terre lede e arsice e les crevaces granz" (ll. 9942–5). Even the Grail Castle itself eventually crumbles away, with only the Grail Chapel being left intact: ". . . commença li manoirs a deschaoir e les sales a agastir, mes onques la chapele n'enpira, ainz fu adés en son buen point, e est encore" (ll. 10167–9). All of these examples are clearly not directly related to the Waste Land theme as developed in Part 1: there, as has been shown, there was a cause–effect relationship between Perlesvaus' silence and all the calamities that befall the Kingdom. That said and allowed for, these allusions nonetheless constitute an important continuation and echo of the Waste Land throughout Part 2, confronting the reader with the spectacle of a land that (despite Perlesvaus' redemptive mission and Lancelot's restoration of the Waste City) never quite manages to free itself from dissension and the threat of further devastation.

At the level of plot or narrative, then, it can be seen that the author of the *Perlesvaus* has made a highly original use of the material familiar to him, exploiting it as he does to depict the Arthurian world in its collective death–throes, no more than a "heap of broken images" (to borrow Eliot's phrase from *The Waste Land*), morally and spiritually wasting away as the result of Perlesvaus' failure at the castle of the Fisher King. His handling of the Waste Land reflects too an attempt to simplify and rationalise inherited motifs. For example, he has rejected the Dolorous Stroke as the cause of the Waste Land (as we find it in the *First Continuation*, the *Suite du Merlin* and the later *Sone de Nansai*)[10] he has rejected too as unnecessary a distinction that some texts make (e.g. Chrétien's *Conte du Graal*) between the cause of the Fisher King's malady and the cause of the wasting of the land. In Chrétien's romance, as in the *Perlesvaus*, the calamities that befall the land are explained by the hero's failure: but in Chrétien the illness of the Fisher King is antecedent to and not explained by the hero's first visit to the Grail Castle—we learn in ll. 3509–15 of the *Conte du Graal* how Chrétien's Fisher King came to be wounded in battle. In the *Perlesvaus*, by contrast, the author seems to have regarded this distinction as an unnecessary extra, and in his text it is the hero's failure to ask the appropriate Grail questions that explains both the illness of the King and the wasting of the land. These modifications, together with the fact that there is no healing of "The Maimed King" (in *Perlesvaus* the Fisher King languishes and eventually dies), reflect a consistent design to highlight the seriousness of Perlesvaus' failure and the punishment that this imposes on the whole Arthurian world. This overall design explains not only the rejection of the Dolorous Stroke and the attribution of the wasting of the land and the illness of the Fisher King to a single cause but also the reason why the author excludes altogether an account of Perlesvaus' first visit to the Grail Castle—he began instead, as was shown earlier, by concentrating on the consequences, i.e. the wasting of the land. All of this confers on the Waste Land in the *Perlesvaus* the status of a major and coherent theme, designed to reflect the moral and spiritual wilderness into which Perlesvaus has brought himself and the rest of the Arthurian world, and worked out with a consistency and seriousness of purpose found rarely in the other texts. That said, there still remains a number of unanswered questions at the level of plot or narrative: the exact nature of Perlesvaus' sin that causes the wasting of the land is left unspecified; Perlesvaus' failure brings disaster not so much on the Grail Country as on Arthur's Kingdom; the author refrains from giving a full articulation to the theme of the restoration of the land, and instead confronts the reader with the contrast, not between the Waste Land and its regeneration, but between the Waste Land and the rich country of the Fisher King—a contrast echoed in the concluding section of the text in the opposition between the Isle Souffroitose and the Isle Plenteureuse (ll. 9631, 9633); after Perlesvaus' conquest of the Grail Castle, the inhabitants of Arthur's country are not granted the "reward" of a definitive regeneration of the land: there is evidence to suggest that Arthur's Kingdom is still exposed to the twin evils of physical blighting and devastation caused by warfare. Answers to these problems will emerge when we turn to examine the "senefiance" that the author has conferred on his theme.

2. THE "SENEFIANCE" OF THE WASTE LAND

When one turns now to the task of interpreting the Waste Land theme, it is important to stress at the outset that the *Perlesvaus* belongs to a type of romance that is self-avowedly symbolic, the author's design being to recall or bring to mind the spiritual truths of the New Law of Christianity: ". . . ce nos trete en senefiance li bons hermites por la Novele Loi, en la quele li plusor ne sont pas bien connoissant, si en volt fere remenbrance par essanples" (ll. 2184–6). What is particularly important about this statement is not just its suggestion that more is meant in *Perlesvaus* than meets the eye, or even the clear pointer it provides as to the general lines of interpretation we should follow, but rather the warning it contains against making excessive claims for symbolical analysis. All that the author claims he is doing is using the Arthurian material to recall or bring to mind certain truths of the Christian faith: he makes no claim that certain parallels he proposes are precisely worked out in every detail, or that certain identifications made at one point in the narrative need be applied throughout the text.[11] This technique confers on the romance what Tuve calls "a flickering intermittent clarity of the double senses"[12] or, as Kelly puts it, "an intermittent allegorical significance."[13] With this general point in mind, let us look now at the "senefiance" which the author suggests for the Waste Land theme: through it he tries first of all to direct the reader's mind to the Christian doctrine of the Fall and the consequent legacy of suffering and death it bequeathed to mankind. Through Perlesvaus' failure at the Grail Castle the author brings to mind Adam's first disobedience, while the wasting of the land becomes representative of the punishment and misery which the human race brought upon itself as a result of Original Sin. It must be emphasised that not all of this is explicitly stated by the author, nor at any point does he suspend narration to insert an explanation of the Waste Land; but if the Waste Land is not directly interpreted for us, there are other episodes which are, and it is in the light of these that its significance begins to emerge. Two such episodes will be looked at: Gauvain's adventure at the Castle of Noir Hermite (1. 736 seq.), and Perlesvaus' reconquest of the Grail Castle (1. 6095 seq.), the adventure whereby he redeems himself and makes up for his initial failure. In what follows, no claim is made for any originality in the understanding of the "senefiance" of the *Perlesvaus* as a whole, or of individual episodes—this has been admirably established by the works on *Perlesvaus* already referred to, particularly Kelly's monograph. What the analysis is designed to bring out is the obliqueness of the author's approach in his handling of the Waste Land, and the quite subtle way in which he works into it a number of overlapping meanings.

During his quest for the Grail Castle and the Fisher King, Gauvain encounters the Damoisele du Char who asks him to conduct her safely past the Castle of Noir Hermite (ll. 716–17). By this point in the narrative the Damoisele du Char has already become a familiar figure to the reader: she first appeared at Arthur's court (1. 596 seq.), robed in silk and gold, attended by two damsels and followed by a richly ornamented cart drawn by three white deer. In her hand she carries the head of a king, sealed in silver and crowned in gold, while one of her attendants carries the head of a queen who, it appears, betrayed not only the king but also 150 knights whose heads, sealed in gold, silver or lead, are in the cart which accompanies her everywhere. When Gauvain begins his task of escorting this strange company past the Castle of Noir Hermite, they are attacked by 152 knights clad in black, exactly the right number, since the assailants can then carry off one head each and bring it back with them into the castle. At a later stage in the narrative, the author gives a detailed interpretation of this adventure (ll. 2173–86): the heads of the king and queen are those of Adam and Eve, while the other 150 represent the souls of the rest of mankind, the Castle of Noir Hermite represents Hell, Noir

Hermite is Lucifer, the account of the heads being carried off by the black knights represents the peopling of Hell with the souls of mankind after the Fall. Now this deliberate inclusion on the part of the author of an adventure designed to remind the reader of Adam's first disobedience and its legacy of suffering and death, carefully introduced in the midst of an account of Perlesvaus' sin at the Grail Castle and the consequent misfortunes that overtake the land, positively invites us to see a parallel in the two events, to see in Perlesvaus' sin a representation of the Fall and therefore to see in the wasting of the land a reminder of the consequent punishment inflicted on the whole of mankind. It is this design that best explains why the author does not specify the exact nature of Perlesvaus' sin or point out precisely where his guilt lies. We are left to deduce that his original transgression is representative of Original Sin. This parallelism would perhaps be all the more apparent to an audience versed in the detail of scripture: God's cursing of Cain in Genesis 4:12 ("when thou tillest the ground, it shall not henceforth yield unto thee her strength") would make a link between the Waste Land theme and the Fall all the more readily discernible.

Perlesvaus' reconquest of the Grail Castle from the hands of the King of Chastel Mortel points in exactly the same direction (1. 6095 seq.). The meaning that the author wishes to attach to this, the central event of the whole romance, is quite unmistakable, and there is no need to extract it, as Carman does,[14] by over-rigid attention to detail. There is enough evidence supplied by the author himself that points to a broad parallel between Perlesvaus' victory over the King of Chastel Mortel and Christ's victory over death and sin at the crucifixion: throughout the adventure Perlesvaus wears on his head a Cercle d'or, in his hand he carries a shield with a red cross whose boss contains "del sanc Nostre Saignor et de son vestement" (1. 5851); in addition to being known as le Bon Chevalier or le Chevalier au Cercle d'or, Perlesvaus also enjoys the name of Par-lui-fez (1. 1647), which seems to be a clear enough reference to the Self-Begotten Son and the Incarnation; and finally, just as Perlesvaus wins his victory over Chastel Mortel and reestablishes the New Law of Christianity, so Christ won his victory over death, thus releasing humanity from the bondage of mortality. Now if Perlesvaus is represented as a figure of Christ at the moment when he redeems himself at the Grail Castle, it is not difficult for any reader familiar with Saint Paul to see him as a figure of Adam at the moment of his failure, and therefore to see the Waste Land as a symbol of humanity punished as a result of man's first disobedience. Further to help the reader establish this link, the author has provided one other important signpost: the contrast already referred to between the Waste Land of Arthur's Kingdom and the rich country of the Fisher King. Given that the river surrounding the Grail Castle comes from the Earthly Paradise (ll. 7200–1), that the names of the castle are Eden, Joy, Souls (ll. 7205–6), one is led to see the Fisher King's rich and plenteous country as a projection of Eden/Paradise, and to see in the contrasting Waste Kingdom a symbol of fallen humanity, as yet unredeemed. The fact that after Perlesvaus' reconquest of the Grail Castle there is no definitive or generalised restoration of the land presents one final problem, best solved by a suggestion put forward by Kelly: the work of redemption and the extension of the New Law are to be seen as representing a slow, gradual process. As he points out, the unspelling of the Waste Land is "presented as a slow process which, although well under way as the story closes, remains to be completed. By depicting the regeneration of the Waste Land as an unfinished process, our author reveals a keen sense of the reality of Salvation history which is the progressive transmission and extension of the effect of Christ's victory over Sin, His setting aright the disorder caused by the Original Fault."[15] The Waste Land theme, therefore, is developed in a quite original way as part of a parable illustrating the Fall and progressive redemption of man.

3. THE WASTE LAND AND RELATED THEMES

This central "senefiance" conferred on the Waste Land is further reinforced and enriched by the fact that the Waste Land itself is only part of a very intricate pattern of closely interrelated themes, each one echoing and intensifying the other. Two examples will suffice: Lancelot's participation in the Beheading Game at the Waste City, and the author's treatment of the Coward Knight story. Like the Waste Land, these are themes which the author of the *Perlesvaus* inherited from his predecessors, and then adapted and remodelled to suit his own didactic purposes.[16] Given that the Beheading Game is played out within the setting of the Waste City, it enriches the general theme of the Waste Land, inevitably echoing the parable of the Fall and Redemption. The Coward Knight story points to an overlapping but somewhat different "senefiance": when we view it in conjunction with the Waste Land we are led to see in the latter a representation not just of the punishment mankind had to endure after the Fall, but of what is in the author's eyes the sterility and inferiority of the Jewish faith: and we are led to see in the contrast between the Waste Kingdom and the rich country of the Fisher King a contrast between two faiths, the Jewish and the Christian, between the Synagogue and Holy Church. In addition to bringing to mind the parable of the Fall, the Waste Land becomes indeed the projection of a collective punishment that awaits all those who remain blind to the true rewards of Christ's redemptive death. As it is handled in the *Perlesvaus,* the Waste Land theme is made to form part of a militant, not to say aggressive and intolerant, statement of the overall supremacy of the Christian faith.

The adventure involving Lancelot, the Beheading Game at the Waste City (ll. 2860–923, 6657–733), is one version of a story made familiar to English readers in *Sir Gawain and the Green Knight.* When Lancelot arrives at the Waste City (1. 2860), he is received by a young knight carrying a large axe and is invited to take part in a "geu-parti": Lancelot will cut off the knight's head with the axe, on condition that one year later, on the same day, at the same place, and at the same hour, Lancelot will submit himself to the same test. Lancelot strikes off the knight's head, departs from the Waste City, keeps his covenant by returning in order to receive the blow, but fortunately emerges unscathed (1. 6705), is spared, and the adventure is brought to an end. Although in itself this episode has no inherent connection with the Grail theme, what makes it relevant is, firstly, the author's description of the transformation which the Waste City undergoes as a result of Lancelot's exploits, and secondly, the key position or positions which this episode is given within the narrative as a whole. When the adventure is completed, the Waste City's empty streets are filled with thronging people, rejoicing at this long-awaited deliverance from grief and sorrow: "Sire, font les damoi[seles], or poez oïr la joie de vostre venue . . . Lanceloz . . . voit popler la cité de la plus bele gent dou mont, e emplir les granz sales, e venir clers e provoires a grans processions, qui loent Deu e aorent de ce qu'il ont pooir de revenir a lor iglises, e donent beneïchon au chevalier par qui il ont pooir de repairier" (ll. 6726–32). When one adds to this the fact that the author has deliberately chosen to divide the Beheading Game into two parts, the first occurring before Perlesvaus' conquest of the Grail, and the second, after, it becomes apparent that the author's account of the desolation and misery prevailing at the Waste City, its deliverance by Lancelot and its return to happiness and prosperity, not only highlights Perlesvaus' achievements but also echoes the central theme: the wretchedness of man after the Fall, Christ's deliverance of mankind, the consequent reconquest of its lost prosperity.

Like the Waste Land and the Beheading Game, the Coward Knight story is brought to bear on the theme of regeneration and deliverance. It is used, however, not so much to contrast the Fall and Redemption (though it does that as well) as to oppose two conflicting sets of belief, the Old Law and the New, the Jewish and the Christian. Apart from his cowardice, the most striking thing about the Coward Knight is his strange appearance: the armour which he wears is in complete disorder, his shield upside down, his spear the wrong way round, his hauberk and greaves strung round his neck, and he rides backwards on his horse (ll. 1354–7). By forcing him to defend two damsels against the attack of a robber-knight (1. 5581), Perlesvaus gives the Coward Knight a taste for action that he had never experienced before, the latter acquitting himself so well that at the end of the exploit he is dubbed the Hardi Chevalier (1. 5616). This transformation had been hinted at, and its significance already glossed, in an earlier episode in which a hermit had explained to Gauvain that the Coward Knight represents the inferiority, confusion and blindness of the Old Law which was "bestornee devant le crucefiement Nostre Saignor, et tantost comme il fu crucefiez si fu remi[s]e a droit" (ll. 2217–18). It is worthy of note too that the Coward Knight story is itself reinforced by a number of parallel episodes all proclaiming the superiority of Holy Church over the Synagogue, for example, the Damoisele du Char's recovery of her tresses once the New Law is established (ll. 9946–8), or the conversion of the heathen queen Jandree, an immediately recognisable representative of the Old Law in that she is blind, but recovers her sight as soon as she is prepared to be baptised (1. 9216). Given that each of these episodes is, like the Waste Land, a *type* of the theme of regeneration, and perhaps more importantly, given that at plot level all of these themes are closely interlaced with one another, the Waste Land comes to represent in our eyes not just the Fall but all the imperfections that the author associates with the Jewish faith. It is clear, then, that, in the light of what has been said, an appreciation of all the overtones of meaning which the author has obliquely worked into his material requires us to see the Waste Land not in isolation but as part of a rich and intricate pattern of related themes, all pointing in similar but not necessarily identical directions.

The author of the *Perlesvaus,* then, has elaborated a quite distinctive, subtle and original approach to the Waste Land, adapting basically secular material to suit his Christian priorities and preoccupations. The foundations of the "senefiance" are firmly laid at plot level: what may appear initially to constitute rather puzzling modifications to his basic theme (e.g. the rejection of the Dolorous Stroke, the fact that the Fisher King is never healed but is allowed to languish and die, the contrast developed between the Grail Country and the Waste Land, the latter's partial restoration and the continuing, ever-present threat of further devastation) is seen on reflection to be part of a deftly articulated, interlaced structure designed to prove the wretchedness and misery of man when he turns his back on God. In the execution of this design, the author's talent, like the country of the Fisher King, could be said to be "rich and plenteous" and "garnished with all things good." With regard to the "senefiance," perhaps the author's most original contribution is his perception that the Waste Land is not so much a geographical location as a dark country of the soul into which, through sin or blindness, man is ever-likely to stray. Through the Waste Land, projected as it is as a form of collective, self-imposed punishment, the author tries to inspire in his readers the conviction that the central event of human history is represented by the crucifixion and resurrection of Christ. This conviction of course forms part of his wider, militant affirmation of the overall supremacy of the Christian faith, whose enduring quality is underscored in the concluding pages of the text when we are told that, amidst the decay that ultimately overtakes even the Grail Castle, the chapel of the New Law alone survives (ll. 10168–9). As I have pointed out elsewhere,[17] whether one prefers, with Nitze, to relate this militancy to Cluny, with Helen Adolf to the Albigensian Crusade, or with Margaret Schlauch to the disputes between Church and Synagogue, there is little doubt that *Perlesvaus* reflects the aggressive, intolerant Christianity of the crusading era. The author's handling of the Waste Land thus reveals considerable literary talent put at the service of the militant advancement of the New Law.

NOTES

Reprinted with permission from *Rewards and Punishments in the Arthurian Romances and Lyric Poetry of France: Essays Presented to Kenneth Varty on the Occasion of his Sixtieth Birthday,* ed. Peter J. Davies and Angus J. Kennedy (Woodbridge, Eng.: D.S. Brewer, 1987), pp. 61–75.

1. Chrétien de Troyes, *Le Roman de Perceval ou le Conte du Graal,* éd. par W. Roach, Geneve: Droz, 1956 (Textes Littéraires Français, 71), ll. 3583–90, 4469–83; *The Elucidation, A Prologue to the Conte del Graal,* ed. by A. W. Thompson, Geneve: Slatkine, 1982 (Reprint of New York ed., 1931), ll. 26–33, 89–98, 383–400; *The Continuations of the Old French Perceval of Chrétien de Troyes,* ed. by W. Roach, Philadelphia: University of Pennsylvania Press, 1949, Vol. I, ll. 13560–88; Gerbert de Montreuil, *La Continuation de Perceval,* ed. by M. Williams, Paris: Champion, 1922 (Classiques Français du Moyen Age, 28), Vol. I, ll. 312–24, 363–9, 492–501; *Vulgate Version of the Arthurian Romances,* ed. by H.O. Sommer, Washington: Publications of the Carnegie Institution of

Washington, 1908-16, Vol. I, p. 290, Vol. VI, p. 147; *La Queste del Saint Graal,*
éd. par A. Pauphilet, Paris: Champion, 1949 (Classiques Français du Moyen Age,
33), p. 204; *Le Haut Livre du Graal, Perlesvaus,* ed. by W. A. Nitze and T. A.
Jenkins, New York: Phaeton, 1972, 2 Vols. (Reprint of Chicago University Press
ed., 1932–37); all subsequent references will be to lines of this edition; *Merlin,*
éd. par G. Paris et J. Ulrich, Paris: Firmin-Didot, 1886 (Société des Anciens
Textes Fr.), Vol. I, p. 212- Vol. II, p. 60, cp. also *Le Roman de Balain,* ed. by M.
D. Legge, Manchester: University Press, 1942 (French Classics); *Sone von
Nausay,* hgg. von M. Goldschmidt, Tübingen, 1899 (Bibliothek des Litter-
arischen Vereins in Stuttgart, 216), ll. 4841–56.

    2. For bibliographical details, see C. E. Pickford and R. Last, *The Arthurian
Bibliography,* Woodbridge: Brewer, 1981, 2 Vols.; E. Reiss, L.H. Reiss, B. Taylor, *Arthurian Legend and Literature. An Annotated Bibliography,* Vol. I, *The
Middle Ages,* New York and London: Garland, 1984 (Garland Reference Library
of the Humanities, 415), *sub.* Waste Land.

    3. Jessie L. Weston, *From Ritual to Romance,* New York: Doubleday, 1957
(Reprint of Cambridge University Press, 1920); R.S. Loomis, *The Grail. From
Celtic Myth to Christian Symbol,* New York: Columbia University Press, 1963;
Perlesvaus, ed. cit., Vol. II; H. Newstead, *Bran the Blessed in Arthurian Litera-
ture,* New York: Columbia University Press, 1939 (Columbia University Studies
in English and Comparative Literature, 141).

    4. For Weston and Loomis, see Note 3 above; Nitze, *Modern Philology,*
XLIII (1945–46), pp. 58–62.

    5. E. O'Sharkey, "The Maimed Kings in the Arthurian Romances," *Etudes
Celtiques,* VIII (1958–59), pp. 420–8; M. Riemschneider, "Li rois mahaignies,"
Romanistisches Jahrbuch, IX (1958), pp. 126–38.

    6. E. Vinaver, *The Rise of Romance,* Oxford: Clarendon, 1971, p. 67; *Per-
lesvaus,* ed. cit. Vol. II; F. Bogdanow, *The Romance of the Grail,* Manchester: University Press, 1966; T.E. Kelly, *Le Haut Livre du Graal: Perlesvaus. A Structural
Study,* Geneve: Droz, 1974 (Histoire des Idées et Critique Littéraire, 145); M.A.
Cor, "Structure and Theme in the *Perlesvaus";* Ph.D., University of North Carolina
at Chapel Hill, 1979 (available through University Microfilms International).

    7. *New Literary History,* Xl (1980), pp. 255–76.

    8. For bibliography of *Perlesvaus,* see works by Kelly (pp. 194–8) and Cor
(pp. 139–49) cited in Note 6 above.

    9. Vinaver, op. cit., pp. 56–7.

    10. For editions, see Note I above.

    11. For a good discussion of technique, see Kelly, op. cit., pp. 91–102.

    12. R. Tuve, *Allegorical Imagery,* Princeton: University Press, 1966, p. 401.

    13. Kelly, op. cit., p. 92.

14. J. N. Carman, "The Symbolism of the *Perlesvaus*," *PMLA*, LXI (1946), pp. 42–83.

15. Kelly, op. cit., p. 178.

16. *Perlesvaus*, ed. cit., Vol II, pp. 129 seq.

17. *Romania*, XCV (1974), p. 69; *Perlesvaus*, ed. cit., Vol. II, pp. 86–8; H. Adolf, "Studies in the *Perlesvaus*, the historical background," *Studies in Philology*, XLII (1945), pp. 723–40; M. Schlauch, "The Allegory of Church and Synagogue," *Speculum*, XIV (1939), pp. 448–64.

CHAPTER 6

A Story of Interpretations
The *Queste Del Saint Graal* as Metaliterature

LAURENCE N. DE LOOZE

It is well known that in the Grail-Prose Cycle of the Arthurian romances the *Queste del Saint Graal* poses a system of signification different from that of the *Lancelot*.[1] While maintaining the paradigm of the quest, the *Queste* weaves a new web of celestial signifieds for the signifiers long canonized by knightly romances: forking paths, castles with strange customs, seduction tests, wandering knights, anonymous challenges to arms, mysterious ships— "adventures," in short. Terrestrial signifieds are disinherited and replaced by celestial ones, and in this respect the *Queste* is a fundamental reinterpretation of the romances' system of signification.

The *Queste* is also a consistent privileging of the signified over the signifier. The "essential" quest of the work takes place at the level of the signified. The master interpreter Nascien makes this clear in his well-known pronouncement: "les auentures qui ore sont & qui ore auienent si sont les senefiances & les demonstrances del saint graal" (VI, 115). Adventures are no longer an end but a means; their only *raison d'être* is demonstrative. The real quest is always *ailleurs*, at the plane of the signified.

To decode these new "senefiances" one must learn to read anew. Hence the *Queste* posits a new mode of reading suited to the novel relationship of terrestrial signifier to celestial signified.[2] That the Queste begins with the first utterances of a new scripture—the "lettres nouelement escrites" (VI, 5) which herald Galahad—is altogether fitting. The scripture and the knight totally fluent in it appear at the same time, two enunciations of the same code. Language and action are both demonstrations (*demonstrances*) of the new signified. Equally telling is the fact that Lancelot—whose interpretation of the quest paradigm according to the rules of *fin'amor* is about to be overthrown by the "celestial" semiotics of his son—is thrown into such consternation by this new scripture that he immediately covers it up rather than trying to interpret it.

Since Galahad inaugurates and embodies the new semiotics, it is no surprise that examples abound of his extraordinary fluency in the new language of the Grail quest. Let us consider one which illustrates not only the disparity between Galahad and other knights but also the way in which the Grail quest recuperates and reinterprets the traditional enunciations of the knightly quest. Shortly after Galahad has acquired all his armature for the Grail quest, he meets an eager young squire named Melian and dubs him knight, then takes the new knight along in quest of the Holy Grail at the novice's request. At a fork in the road they come upon a cross on which they

> trouerent lettres qui erent entaillies el fust · & disoient les lettres · os tu cheualiers qui vas auenture querant voi ci · ij · voies lune a destre lautre a senestre · cele a senestre te desfen ie que tu ni entres · Car trop couient estre preudome celui qui i entre & nus en puet issir sans mort · & se tu en cele a destre entres tost poras perir. (VI, 30)

To the reader familiar with knightly romances, as to any Arthurian knight, this situation seems quite standard at first glance. Hector, for example, meets with an almost identical challenge in the middle of the *Lancelot*. Traveling along with Gauvain, he comes upon

> j · chemin forkie · ou il auiot lettres escriptes sor · j · perron qui disoient · Os tu cheualiers errans · qui auentures uas querant · vois chi · ij · voies lune a destre lautre a senestre · mes garde si chier com tu as ton cors · que tu ne tachemines en celui a senestre · quar bien saches que tu ne ten partiras ia sans honte se tu y entres · mez de cele a destre ne di iou pas quil ni a mie tel peril. (IV, 341)

Hector and Melian both have the same reaction. Each resolves to enter the left path in hopes of glory (Hector states he'll take it precisely "pour chou que lez lettres le defendant" (IV, 341). According to the old system of signification this is the correct response. Indeed Hector acquits himself magnificently; he defeats a knight of a bridge (IV, 350), and delivers the castle "oruale de guindoel" where he is consequently hailed as "la flor de cheualerie" (IV, 351–353). In the *Queste* the flower of chivalry, Galahad, abstains from taking the path to the left because of what it signifies (earthly pride). Melian, by contrast, acts as Hector did, but with a very different outcome; he suffers failure and humiliation and is half-dead when Galahad appears unexpectedly to rescue him. The difference in success is precisely the difference in the two types of quest, terrestrial and celestial. Melian fails to read for celestial signifieds and acts before interpreting. "Car li escris," a hermit tells Melian afterwards, "parloit de la cheualerie celestiene & tu entendis de la seculer · par coi tu entras en orguel." Melian's failure is a failure in hermeneutics; the sign spoke correctly but Melian misunderstood. What was once the flower of chivalry according to a terrestrial system of signification is now become significant of pride although the signifiers have hardly changed.[3] The inability to see the new nature of the signified in the Grail quest—which is a total failure of the hermeneutic process—proves disastrous for Melian as it will for most other knights, including Lancelot.

Why this disaster? We have said that the *Queste* disinherits the code of *fin'amor,* and proposes to replace it with a celestial code whose promise is salvation.[4] But what may be excellent theology proves to be an absolute failure as a social program. Only four knights (if we include Lancelot) actively embrace the new system; the rest reject it outright or fail to understand it at all. Rather they cling doggedly to old codes of action—to chivalry of *fin'amor*—apparently ignorant that these modes are not suited to the Grail quest. The result is that most knights are unable to find any adventures—that is, they do not even discover the signifiers of the quest.

Since the *Queste* never achieves consensus for its theory of the sign,[5] what we witness throughout most of the work is a tension between the usurping and usurped systems of signification. For every signifier there are two competing signifieds—one celestial and one terrestrial—as in the scene of Melian at the forking paths. What reads as honor according to the old system becomes dishonor in the new, an inversion best personified by Lancelot who becomes the most wretched knight after, and because, he has been the most honored according to the old code. The two systems propose diametrically opposed readings of the same signifiers as moral right is cloven from knightly convention.

Yet the tension between competing signifieds for particular signifiers is hardly unique to the *Queste.* The *Mort Artu* will take up the problem of a society collapsed back upon itself with no integral system of signification and in which vestiges of old codes compete to interpret the world.[6] The *Lancelot,* too, contains labyrinthian examinations of the relationship between signifier and signified. It dramatically poses the problem of two signifiers competing for the same signified[7] as well as of multiple signifieds in a situation where only one of them can correspond to a particular signifier.[8]

Furthermore, the substitution of the *Queste's* celestial signification for terrestrial signification actually begins in the *Lancelot*.[9] Well before the *Queste* Lancelot is told that certain adventures surpass him, and his status is carefully qualified.[10] With the birth of Galahad the two sets of signifieds begin to come into conflict and the initial tilts are taken at the old code and its chief representative, Lancelot.

What then distinguishes the *Queste* from the *Lancelot* if the tension between signifieds is not unique to the Grail quest? One answer which has been put forward is that the *Queste* is to be read typologically. In a recent book Pauline Matarasso argues that the *Queste* is "a biblical-type allegory with three levels of meaning."[11] In her view the knights' adventures are the signifiers to which the hermits' interpretations provide the signifieds.

Tempting though this argument is as one uncovers the many passages that echo biblical or mystical writings, the allegorical approach is methodologically unsound. Although implicitly acknowledging the fact that the Queste contains its own gloss, this view forgets that the hermits' interpretations are not treatises outside the text but scenes within it—integral parts of the fiction. Hence Matarasso's interpretation does not treat the *Queste* as allegory, as she claims, but only certain episodes within it which the work already reads allegorically.

That the *Queste* is self-interpreting was noted by Albert Pauphilet.[12] More recently Tzvetan Todorov has considered this "récit double" and observed that

> la *Quête du Graal* met les deux types d'épisodes [terrestrial episodes, scenes of interpretation] les uns à coté des autres; l'interprétation est incluse dans la trame du récit. Une moitié du texte porte sur des aventures, une autre sur le texte qui les décrit. Le texte et le méta-texte sont mis en continuité.[13]

We are here at the very definition of metaliterature and can distinguish two levels or generations of the narrative, the first purely *eventual* ("adventures"), the second explicative (encounters with interpreters) which expounds or glosses the first. The *Queste*, we would argue, privileges this explicative level; the work is essentially a story of interpretations—a metafiction—and in this respect is distinct from other portions of the Vulgate. The scenes of explication which organize the whole narrative (Todorov, p. 138) are *événements*, simply of a kind different from knightly adventures.[14] These explicative events not only reveal the signified behind the eventual encounters, but they are themselves the most important encounters in this new type of quest. The explicative level is a kind of adventure in hermeneutics. To take the chivalric adventures as the main narrative events is to commit the capital mistake in priorities made by Gauvain (see below, p. 248). Just as the knights must drop the prideful code of terrestrial chivalry, so the reader must recognize that the *Queste* proposes a series of adventures in interpretation. [15]

If the *Queste del Saint Graal* takes interpretations as its object of study, the introduction of a new theory of the sign is the catalyst that makes possible their investigation. Because the *Queste* examines systems of signification in tension with each other and in transition from one to another, it is vitally concerned with the relationship between the individual and knowledge—that is, with the hermeneutic process. The hermeneutic act informs every facet of the work—knights' deeds (to act is to act hermeneutically in the Grail quest) as much as hermits' interpretations. The *Queste* thematizes, in a manner consonant with the uniquely linguistic epistemology of the Middle Ages, the three functions implied by the Greek verb *hermeneuein*: telling, explaining, and translating.[16]

We must distinguish at this point between the *Queste* as text and the quest as the story it tells. The former, as we shall consider shortly, is a metatext, overtly concerned with individuals' recovery, transmission, and translation of meaning. But what—or for what—is the quest itself?

The quest is for the Holy Grail, of course, but such a response only invites the equally perplexing question: what is the Holy Grail? Answers to this latter query have indeed been numerous: "la manifestation romanesque de Dieu" (Pauphilet), the "Grace del Saint Esprit" (Gilson, quoting the *Queste*), the Holy Ghost itself (Lot-Borodine), "la personnification du Saint Sacrement" (Hamilton).[17] As Matarasso rightly observes in her review of these theories (pp. 180–182), the Grail is polysemic. The Grail—or more precisely what it contains, for the Grail is but a vessel—is ineffable and *innarrabilis*;[18] it transcends language and this material world. The telos of the quest is that which terrestrial eyes cannot see, nor human language become: pure signification, immanent and direct, experienced without the intermediary of the signifier.[19] Only one knight can look into the Grail, can see Truth revealed. But even he cannot speak what he saw and he quits the world almost immediately.

If Galahad achieves the Holy Grail quest when he peers into the Grail, then the quest must be for the divine revelation he experiences. His is a quest to arrive at the signified—to see it openly and not through any signifiers. In its "celestial" telos the quest of the *Queste* contrasts with the *Lancelot*'s quest which is begun by Galehot who has an insatiable thirst for knowledge of *this* world (*scientia*).[20] The *Queste* is championed by the celestial knight who seeks the other world which mortal eyes cannot see.

Gauvain, who first announces the quest, vows that "ne revendrai a cort . . . devant que je l'aie veu [the Grail] plus apertement qu'il ne m'a ci esté demostrez" (Pauphilet, p. 16).[21] Flawed though Gauvain is, his statement implies an "opening," a revelation and clarification of what has been "demostrez"—that is, shown and demonstrated/explicated—by the appearance of the Grail at the Round Table.[22] He seeks an aperture: the disclosing and unveiling of the Grail object.

Galahad, who formulates the precise terms of the questers' sermon, refines Gauvain's vow by shifting the emphasis from the Grail object itself to the truth it houses; the knight who will transcend speech wields it best. Galahad vows that he "ne revendroit devant qu'il la verité savroit del Saint Graal . . ." (Pauphilet, p. 23). Gauvain, trapped in iconicity, cannot conceive of the Grail as anything beyond the precious object it appears to be; thus he wishes simply to see the Grail-object better. Galahad's desire adds a hermeneutic dimension: he wishes to see Truth itself. Yet that truth, when he sees it, proves *innarrabilis*, ineffable. Upon gazing into the vessel Galahad exclaims, "Car or voi iou tout apertement ce que langue ne poroit dire ne cuers penser" (VI, 197). What Gauvain wishes revealed more manifestly (expressed as a comparative: *plus apertement*) Galahad experiences as an absolute state (*tout apertement*). Having glimpsed immanence, Galahad desires only that he "trespasse de ceste terriene vie en la celestijel" (VI, 197), a wish that is soon granted.

The *Queste* narrative, then, establishes an impossible goal for itself. Unable to narrate the un-narratable, it can only commemorate Galahad's achievement through signification of every event of the quest except its completion, at which crucial point language (which must pass by way of signification) fails. The narrative signifies precisely the *absence* of the moment of the quest's completion, and the Grail once more eludes both Arthurian world and literary audience—is deferred, if you will. For the *Queste* the aperture becomes a *trou* in the text; its language can signify only the inability of language to make present the achievement of the Grail adventures. Disclosure becomes, at the textual level, its contrary: exclusion, denial, *blocage*.

In seeking to narrate what transcends speech the *Queste* reveals its fundamental concern with the limits of language and the relationship between divine utterance and human understanding. With the exception of Galahad it is only by means of a process of linguistic indoctrination that members of the Arthurian world can be initiated into the *Queste's* new theory of the sign. Through its scenes of interpretation the *Queste* poses for itself a problem that haunted Christian epistemologists throughout the Middle Ages—that of the relationship between signification, however divine, and man's understanding of that signification.

The process of making the quest intelligible to its knights and to the reader of the *Queste* narrative is hermeneutic. At the textual level (the first hermeneutic concern is the transmission of the narrative) the *Queste* effects the best resolution it can. Fully aware of the "trou" it cannot fill, it reconstructs nevertheless the purest possible narrative of the Grail quest, namely the account dictated by Bors (the quest's highest remaining representative) to the scribes.[23] The *Queste's* final task is to commemorate and enshrine the genesis of its *hypotext*:[24]

> Quant il ot mangie li rois fist venir les clers qui metoient en escrit les auentures as chevaliers de laiens · Et quant bohort ot contees les auentures del saint graal teles comme il auoit veues · si furent mises en escrit & gardes en labeie de salesbieres dont maistre gautiers map les traist a faire son liure del saint graal por lamor del roi henri son signor qui fist lestoire translater du latin en franchois · Si se taist atant li contes que plus nen dist des auentures del saint graal · Expliciont les auentures des saint graal. (VI, 198–199)

The narrative which began with the "lettres nouelement escriptes" of divine revelation ends with the *mise en écrit* of the *Queste*. In delineating the origin, preservation, and transmission of the quest-as-narrative, the text incarnates the movement from quest to *Queste*. Every recension of the manuscript is accounted for,[25] of which the first and last recensions effect two of the three distinct functions inherent in hermeneutics: telling (Bors' account) and translation (Walter Map). The third function—explaining—is the stuff of the scenes with the hermit-decoders.

The *Queste* poses the new axiom that knights must become hermeneuticians. To take part in the adventures is a hermeneutic act as much as is to tell them, for which the highest remaining participant (Bors) is also the seminal narrator. Only one knight, Galahad, has the requisite pre-understanding to see signifieds instinctively. For the others the sign retains a certain opacity. This opacity not only gives rise to a precise hierarchy of knights but also occasions the investigation of hermeneutics through "tutorials" in which master hermit-decoders offer the highest knights— Perceval, Bors, Lancelot, Galahad, and Hector—readings of their roles in the Grail quest.[26]

Reaction to these tutorials is hardly uniform, however. Perceval, Bors, and Lancelot undergo active initiation into the new semiotics of celestial chivalry. Of these three, Perceval and Bors become adept enough at decoding the new relationship of signifier to signified that they merit seats at the Holy Grail table at Corbenic. Lancelot, by contrast, never becomes proficient enough to understand the new code except as it is explicated for him after each of his successive failures. Finally Gauvain and, more passively, Hector prove to have no interest in learning the code. By adhering to the old relationship of earthly signified for earthly signifier they continue to dwell in the "Old Testament" of knightly romances and disqualify themselves from the Grail quest.

Let us consider Galahad first. The perfect knight, Galahad alone needs no explanation of his role in the Grail quest. He performs his deeds according to what Todorov has called "logique rituelle" (Todorov, p. 140 ff.), whereby the outcome is never in doubt and Galahad's successes are merely affirmations of his perfection, of the fact that he is chosen for these adventures. He instinctively knows what adventures are due him; he sees the signified of his quest. For example, his explanation for why all knights but he have failed to withdraw the sword found stuck in marble the day he arrives at Arthur's court is "marvelously" simple: "Sire fait galaad ce nest pas merueille · car lauenture nest pas lor ains est moie" (VI, 10).

It is fitting, then, that Galahad needs no explication of his role in the quest; such explanations, in his case, would only distance him from his goal. As a result, his sole appeal to the hermit-interpreters is limited to requesting an explanation of a more technical sort. After the successful completion of his first major adventure—the "adventure of the tomb" (VI, 27)—Galahad asks an old friar "porcoi tent de merueilles en sont auenues" (VI, 28), prompting the friar to tell the "grant senefiance" of the tomb which, he says, "senefie la durte de cest monde." The friar also comments on the history of the tomb and specifically designates Galahad as the postfiguration of Christ. In contrast to all other knights, Galahad needs lessons neither in how to read the semiotics of which he is the herald nor in how to interpret his own role in the quest.

Perceval is second in perfection to Galahad. He is close to reading signifiers wholly in terms of their celestial signification. When, for example, he is nearly drowned by a black horse (VI, 66–67), he makes recourse to the *Queste's* truth-guarantee—he crosses himself—upon which the steed disappears.[27] Afterwards Perceval quite rightly reads the scene according to the *Queste's* system of exegesis: he recognizes that the apparition "estoit li anemis." On the island where he finds himself the following morning he comes to the conclusion that "proece de cheualerie" is for naught (VI, 67).

The subsequent testing of Perceval and the explication of the test's significance guide Perceval in interpreting his quest—and in interpreting interpretations of the quest. Adventures and interpretations merge as interpretations themselves become adventures, new signifiers which in turn must be explicated. Perceval's dream of being visited by two women (VI, 69–71) is the first "text" to be explicated by a "preudome . . . en semblance de prestre" who arrives on a marvellous boat and "bien sambloit sains hom" (VI, 71). But the old man glosses the dream as a commentary on events to come, suggesting that event and commentary/ interpretation are inextricably joined. Reading the two women typologically, he says:

> cele qui sor le lion estoit montee senefie la nouele loy • si senefie chi endroit ihesu crist qui i prist pie . . . [and] cele dame que tu veis en ton soigne cheuachier sor le serpent senefie la vielle loi • li serpens qui le porte cest lescriture maluaisement entendue. . . . (VI, 73–74)

As scripture wrongly understood, the serpent is false hermeneutics, a fallacious theory of knowledge that perverts interpretations and tests/ tempts Perceval subsequently.

Next to visit Perceval is a beautiful damsel in another marvellous ship. In contrast to the old man, the maiden exploits the discourse of the traditional Arthurian quest in an effort to return signs to their pre-*Queste* conventions of signification. She represents herself as a noble girl disinherited by a rich lord and enlists Perceval's help through use of the rash boon topos. According to the Arthurian code of terrestrial chivalry Perceval is obliged to aid her:

> sui ie cha venue a vous por aide · & vous le deues faire por ce que vous estes compains de la table roonde · Car nus qui conpains en soit ne doit faillir a damoisele desiretee por quele le requiere daide & vous saues ore bien se ie di voir. (VI, 77)

She not only insists on the old way of reading disinheritance, she also (mis)reads readings. She interprets the old priest-decoder of the first boat as a false interpreter, an *enchanteres*. She lures Perceval away from the celestial quest by harnessing to her ends the literary commonplaces of wine, the bed, the pavilion, and the seduction scene. Indeed Perceval is on the point of succumbing to her when he inadvertently crosses himself; this sign of salvation immediately reveals the scene to be false significa- tion. The damsel is a mis-interpreter, a false hermeneutician; her expla- nations are only rhetoric, designed to sway and convince but which in no way instruct.[28]

The priest misinterpreted by the maiden now returns and interprets the mis-interpreter typologically as the serpent-riding woman of Perce- val's initial dream. Perceval's encounter with false-hermeneutics is thus interpreted as the signified of the dream which preceded it. The customary order of adventure followed by exegesis, of event before interpretation, is reversed, or rather the two components have become self-reflexive. Text and gloss are reciprocal, and the signified meaning of each becomes a new signifier at a second generation of signification. Perceval is first given a vision of events to come (presented *mise-en-abyme* fashion), then the dream is expounded exegetically, and only after all this does he "experi- ence" the events the dream signified. That experience is itself an en- counter with false-interpretation which the old priest subsequently reads as the signified of the dream, implying through his two readings the equa- tion of Old Law with false hermeneutics. The crucial test for a knight has evolved from consisting in eventual encounters to being encounters with (mis)interpretation (explicative adventures).

The hermit-hermeneuticians give Bors, next in the hierarchy of knights, similar tutoring in the new hermeneutics. Again it is not enough simply to read for celestial signifieds; one must also learn to recognize false interpretations of signs. Like Perceval, Bors is already aware that there are celestial signifieds behind the signifiers he sees. This knowl- edge (and his chastity) earns him his seat at Corbenic, just as his inability to dispense with the level of the signified excludes him from the experi- ence of pure signification, enjoyed by Galahad.

Bors' fluency in reading for celestial signifiers that are impossible for human eyes to see is dramatically revealed when he takes commu- nion from an old priest. After having sung mass, the priest calls Bors forth and, holding up the *corpus domini*, asks, "bohort vois tu ce que ie tieng[?]" Bors responds:

> le voi que vous tenes mon salueor & ma redemption en semblance de pain Et en tel maniere nel veisse ie mie • Mais mi oeil sont si terrien quil ne peuent veoir les espirituels choses ne il nel me laissent autrement veoir ains me tolent la vraie samblance. (VI, 120)

The aspect of the sign Bors actually sees is the wafer (the *samblance de pain* already identified by the text as indexical of the body of Christ, the *corpus domini*), yet he reads it in terms of its "vraie samblance," as symbolic of his salvation and redemption.[29] That Bors names the wafer immediately in terms of its celestial signification, even though he cannot know the signified except by means of a hermeneutic act of explication, is evidence of his interpretive skills.

After Bors leaves the priest, he sees a marvellous event: a bird revives its dead offspring with the blood it pecks from its own breast. This *troueure*, as an abbot later calls it, is by its very nature an object of meditation.[30] Bors instantly recognizes it as something more than an iconic sign; although "il ne set quel chose pust auenir de ceste semblance . . . [nevertheless] tant connoist il bien que cest samblance merueilleuse" (VI, 120). And indeed he is correct: the *troueure* is later explicated for him as a *mise-en-abyme* of Christ, sent Bors by God (VI, 131–132). Here again, then, is a reciprocity of event and interpretation. A marvelous adventure is itself a gloss on Biblical events; an abbot's interpretation is itself an adventure.

Bors' adventures with King Amans' daughter (VI, 122–125) recall, of course, Perceval's adventure on the island, although the test given Bors is not quite as rigorous as that given Perceval. Rather than being solicited by the dispossessed older sister, as was Perceval, Bors is sought out by the younger sister who has supplanted the elder. His acceptance of her suit reverses the traditional discourse of knighthood and, as explicated typologically afterwards, is quite correct since the younger sister signifies New Law on whom disinherited Old Law makes war. Bors' response implicitly acknowledges that the adventure is to be read as the supplantation of the Old Testament by the New, of terrestrial chivalry by celestial chivalry, and of one semiological system by another.

More importantly, Bors must learn to interpret interpretations of events and his test, like Perceval's, addresses this issue. After having dreamed of two birds, one black and one white, both of whom seek him as their champion, Bors asks the next "home de religion" he meets to explain the "senefiance" (VI, 128). The priest's interpretation of the dream reads the white bird as the "grant pechie" Bors will commit when he will refuse her love in order to remain chaste. Is this then the same pattern Perceval followed: exegesis before event—or better, exegesis as event?

Not quite. Bors is led to the maiden who kills herself out of love for him. At this point Bors crosses himself, as did Perceval, and the adventure is revealed to be pure illusion, the work of the devil (VI, 129–130).

An abbot Bors then meets reads his dream anew and reinterprets the "home de religion" as a false-interpreter. Thus an eventual adventure is sandwiched this time between two explicative ones, one of falsehood and one of truth. The false-hermeneutician masquerades as a priest but is in fact the devil, the same "hypocrite" as the white bird of Bors' dream (a swan) who is beautiful without but foul within. Like the serpent of Perceval's dream, the hypocrite writes false scripture in attempting to pervert the relationship between revealed truth and its signifiers in the material world.

Both Perceval's and Bors' tests are thus adventures in the hermeneutic process. Both knights are assaulted by systems of false signification; the interpretation of events, and even the interpretation of interpretations of events, are their most important adventures. Both knights are given *exempla*, true and false, of the decoding process, and both make appeal when in doubt to Truth via the sign of the cross. Finally, having passed their trials, they meet and tell one another their adventures (VI, 139). This movement towards enunciation (narration) is indicative of their progress as hermeneuticians.

If Bors and Perceval are the exemplars of a receptivity to hermeneutics, lesser knights do not fare as well. Melian, as we have noted, has his mishap explained to him (VI, 32–34), after which we hear of him no more. Gauvain and, less obviously, Hector represent the outright rejection of the new code of chivalry and the hermeneutics necessary to it. After having disturbing dreams, they seek Nascien for an explanation. According to the hermit, they have clung obstinately to terrestrial chivalry and thus the semiotics they have shunned excludes them, in turn, from the Grail quest (VI, 111–115). When they have left and "sont j poi eslongie," Nascien recalls (*rapele*) Gauvain and suggests that he cease serving the devil and turn to God (VI, 115–116). But Gauvain, the *mise au point* of terrestrial chivalry, not only brushes off Nascien's suggestion but does so in a most "courtly" manner, claiming he has not the leisure (*loisir*) to discuss the matter. Failing to recognize the significance of being (re)called—which is both recall and reminder, the anamnesis that is also the road back to knowledge—Gauvain chooses the mode of terrestrial signification.

Between the extraordinary receptivity of Bors and Perceval and the outright rejection of a new semiotics is Lancelot, the middle figure and eternal outsider, included among neither the celestial knights nor the terrestrial knights (for which he is rightly the most wretched). Lancelot's encounters with the hermit-decoders differ from those of Perceval and

Bors. Rather than being given readings of readings or taught to interpret the interpreters, Lancelot must first be taught to recognize semiological systems as such. Thus the hermeneuticians encode for Lancelot the events of his own quest in language constructs which can be explicated both typologically (Biblical exegesis) and within the specific context of the Grail quest. For Lancelot, knowledge of how language signifies becomes a primary step towards perceiving that the terrestrial signs are merely signifiers whose values are celestial and unspeakable. The specific language construct used to gloss Lancelot's quest is the Biblical parable which, by its very nature, has a meta-literary aspect in that its commentary on events analogous to the story it actually relates is more important than the particulars of its narrative. In other words the parable-narrative exists solely to be decoded as an interpretation/ explication of an exterior set of events.

The encoding and decoding of Lancelot's adventures via Biblical parables first occurs after his misadventures at the Grail Chapel where, having had a vision of the Holy Grail, Lancelot is admonished by a voice which labels him, "lancelot plus durs que piere plus amer que fust & plus despris que figuiers" (VI, 44). This riddling voice alerts us to the difficulty of language to encompass Lancelot. The hermit Lancelot seeks for an explanation avails himself of divine scripture to explicate Lancelot and his quest. Reminding the knight of the four gifts the Lord has given him, the hermit then recalls the parable of the talents (Matthew 25:14–30) in which the servant who has received the fewest talents from his master returns only as much as he has been given (VI, 45–46). Lancelot immediately sees that the parable commemorates his own life-story, for which the narrative discomforts him greatly,

Car ie sai bien que ihesu crist me garni en menfance de toutes les boines graces que nus hons pooit auoir • & por ce quil me fu larges de prester & ie li ai si malement rendu ce quil mot preste & baillie sai ie bien que ie serai iugies comme le maluais serians qui le besant reponst en terre . . . (VI, 46–47)

In fact, Lancelot, even more than the servant of the parable, has hidden his "talents" in the terrestrial world. His guilt has a superlative quality of the kind suggested by the voice of the Grail Chapel. Just as he was described as a comparative of an absolute state—harder than what is hardest, etc.— at the Grail Chapel, so now Lancelot actually surpasses the bounds of the parable applied to him. The guilty servant of the Bible receives the *fewest* talents from God yet still renders as much as he has received; Lancelot, by contrast, has received far more than other men yet renders even *less* than the servant who was least endowed.

What concerns us here is that Lancelot reads the Biblical parable tropologically, as a commentary on his own life and worldly quest. He recognizes himself in the narrative precisely because he begins to read according to his son Galahad's semiotics. Indeed Lancelot is so moved by the experience that he confesses his love affair with Guenevere. One commemorative narrative produces another: the parable causes him to confess precisely the narrative which, according to the disinherited code of *fin'amors*, is to remain ineffable. Lancelot's first hermeneutic act is to enunciate the secret love which, once overthrown, may be replaced with a new, equally ineffable love, *caritas*.

The second parable applied to Lancelot is that of the wedding feast (Matthew 22:1–14). A hermit recounts the story of the ill-dressed man turned out of the wedding to which "many are called, but few are chosen." Then the holy man invites Lancelot to read the parable as analogous to the Holy Grail quest:

> Car la queste nest pas de terrienes coses mais de celestienes • Et qui el ciel ueult entrer ors & vilains il en est tresbuchies si felenessement quil sen sent tos les iors de sa vie • Aussi est il de chaus qui en ceste queste sont entre ort & conchie des uices terrienes . . . si est ore auenue la samblance dont li ewangille parole. . . • (Vl, 91)

Only an exegetical interpretation can comprehend that Holy Grail quest and Biblical parable are equivalent at the level of their signified: "Cele samblance dont li ewangille parole poons nous veoir en la queste del saint graal . . . " (VI, 91). The wedding feast and the Holy Grail narrative are two, mutually commemorative enunciations of the same invitation. In the Bible the parable is presented as a *mise-en-abyme* of Christ's mission in the world.[31] In the hermit's discourse this standard typological reading becomes a *mise-en-abyme* of the quest's invitation to the knights of the Round Table: the signified becomes a new signifier in its own right. The *Queste* once more defines two levels of narrative, the eventual and the explicative, privileging the latter. And again Lancelot is profoundly affected (he "ploroit durement") and utters a confessional narrative which consists of both events and interpretations: "si li conte de son estre & toutes les paroles que cil [the first hermit] auoit dites & la senefiance des · iij · paroles qui li auoient este dites en la chapele" (V1, 92).

Like the *Queste* as a whole, Lancelot's narrative becomes primarily a story of explanations and interpretations.

Does this mean Lancelot is becoming a hermeneutician? This encounter with the hermit refuses to deliver a clear answer. In applying the parable of the wedding feast to the Holy Grail quest, the hermit has apparently encoded Lancelot's role in the quest as that of the soiled guest cast out from the feast (hence dropped from the Grail quest, hence denied salvation); indeed this is how Lancelot reads the parable. But if the logic of the *mise-en-abyme* then holds, should we not conclude that Lancelot will not be redeemed, and the hermit's injunction to do penance, confess regularly, and observe a strict diet is for naught? Perhaps it is to avoid closing any such fatalistic circle around Lancelot that the hermit does not explicitly state the correspondence that both reader and Lancelot infer between knight and wedding guest. At this point we can conclude only that Lancelot has been called—but may not be chosen.

The final *mise-en-abyme* applied to Lancelot's quest makes clear his exclusion from the ranks of the chosen;[32] the commemorative structure becomes a time-loop, suggesting that the failure of Lancelot it signifies is a never-ending, unredeemable process.[33] Salvation in the *Queste* depends upon not only reading one's past actions for their celestial significance, but upon reading events celestially as they arise and before selecting a course of action, as the adventures of Perceval, Bors, and Melian clearly demonstrate. When confronted with the adventure of the tournament, however, Lancelot again adheres to the paradigm of "Old Testament" knighthood. Unlike Perceval and Bors who reject the claims of dispossessed Old Law, Lancelot readily takes up the cause of the weaker party besieged in a castle. The result is that he loses, and when the adventure is explicated by a recluse, Lancelot learns that the tournament was a kind of parable of the Grail quest thus far. That is, the tournament pitted "li chevalier terrien" against "li chevalier celestial," so that the tournament and Lancelot's role in the Grail quest were mutually commemorative.

With this ready equation of tournament and quest, the recluse traces Lancelot's fortunes in the tournament as signifying his actions up through the tournament episode. She translates, as the hermit figures are wont to do, the terms of one enunciation into those of another with supreme ease:

> Quant li tornoiemens fu commenchies · cest a dire quant la queste fu emprise tu regardas les pecheors & les preudomes · si te fu auis que li pecheor furent vencu Et por ce que tu estoies de la partie as pecheors

cest a dire que tu estoies en pechie mortel si te tornoies deuers els & te
mellas as preudomes. (VI, 103)

In the narrative of the *Queste* the moment of Lancelot's relapse is, of
course, when he is tested by the tournament. But here Lancelot becomes
trapped between the logic of the *mise-en-abyme* and the demands of the
Grail quest, for the tournament must function as a *mise-en-abyme* of the
narrative sequence of which it is also the last increment. As *mise-en-
abyme* the tournament must incarnate the wrong path taken by Lancelot
at the beginning of the quest; that is, for the tournament to signify
Lancelot's role in the *Queste* thus far he *must* join the terrestrial knights,
else the tournament would not commemorate his tainted quest. Yet as a
narrative event subsequent to his meetings with the first two hermits, the
tournament would seem to offer Lancelot a chance to adopt the new code
of celestial chivalry, and it is precisely because he doesn't help the celestial knights that Lancelot is guilty of remission.

Partaking of two structures which have conflicting demands, the
tournament episode effectively sacrifices Lancelot and his quest. Lancelot
cannot win grace unless he helps the heavenly knights, yet his role in the
tournament cannot function as a *mise-en-abyme* unless he sides with the
earthly knights. In the end it is the commemorative structure—the *mise-
en*-abyme—that wins this contest. The commentary on events proves
powerful to the point of determining eventual adventures. Exegesis will
out, even when the fate of an individual hangs in the balance.

That narrative sequence should be sacrificed to commemoration,
though tragic for Lancelot personally, is perfectly consonant with the
Queste's privileging of interpretation and explication over eventual encounters. It is a final proof that the *Queste* is primarily a story of interpretations of the events of its own narrative. The *Queste's* thematization of the
interpretive process (itself a quest) allows the work to accommodate a rigid
system of celestial semiotics to the difficulty of apprehending and transmitting meaning (hermeneutics). What is, for the hermits, self-evidently
conveyed by the systematic relationship of signifier to signified is obscure
to the knights for whom the meaning of "quest" and the process by which
they interpret actions are in transition. The master hermeneuticians exemplify the metatextual, glossing function of the narrative in which they
move; they bridge between semiotics and hermeneutics and thus do not
themselves submit to any convenient allegorization, unlike the events they
so smoothly explicate. Evaluating the hermits—which implies evaluation
of the *Queste* as metaliterature—implicates the reader in the hermeneutic
act of translating or explicating interpreters and their interpretations.

The reader thus reproduces the hermeneutic process thematized within the literary work. Indeed the temptation to label the *Queste* as allegory is testimony to the fact that the insistence within the work that characters read every event for its celestial significance is keenly felt by the reader as well. Reader-critics have even supplied the appropriate exegesis where the text does not. In enunciating these explications, the reader also projects himself into the role of hermit-decoder. Should these interpretations ignore the potential of the *Queste's* explicative scenes to signify, they defer, in effect, the very hermeneutic function they assume. For the critic continues the process of explaining the Holy Grail quest, of making it more intelligible—a process that begins with the hermits, passes by way of Bors (where it becomes associated with the authorial role) and Walter Map (our immediate intermediary) to the reader. The annexation of the reader to this chain of (re)telling and (re)interpreting is the final (re)enactment of the interpretive strategy thematized within the *Queste del Saint Graal* itself. In a sense the reader becomes the final quester and the last hermit-decoder, subsuming both functions in the effort to explain and (re)establish celestial semiotics once and for all within the world of the Grail quest.

NOTES

Reprinted by permission from *Romanic Review,* 76, no. 2 (1985), 129–47. Copyright by the Trustees of Columbia University in the City of New York.

1. The limitations of *The Vulgate Version of The Arthurian Romances*, ed. H. Oskar Sommer, 8 vols. (Washington: The Riverside Press, 1909–1916), are well known. Nevertheless references for the *Lancelot* and the *Queste del Saint Graal* will be to Sommer's edition unless otherwise noted, the volume cited in Roman numerals and the pages in Arabic numbers. I also follow Sommer's division of the cycle into component romances. For the *Queste* I will also make reference as needed to Albert Pauphilet's edition of *La Queste del Saint Graal* (Paris: Champion, 1923), designated hereafter as "Pauphilet." All references to *La Mort le Roi Artu* are to the edition of Jean Frappier (Geneva: Droz, 1964), hereafter "Frappier." I am grateful to the Fulbright-Hays Commission for their generous grant which aided in the preparation of this article.

2. This semiotics is, to be sure, only new in the fictional world of the *Queste.* Such a reading of the world is central to Christian epistemology and was first— or at least most forcefully—formulated by Saint Augustine. For a discussion of Augustine's semiotics, see Marcia L. Colish, *The Mirror of Language: A Study in the Medieval Theory of Knowledge* (New Haven: Yale University Press, 1968), chapter 1. Hereafter, "Colish."

3. Upon rereading, of course, one notices subtle differences that suggest the change in semiological systems. The Melian passage forbids (*desfen*) entrance and warns of death and perishing (*mort, perir*) to him who flaunts the warning. The terminology has charged meanings for the Christian. The vocabulary in the *Lancelot* is less acute: Hector risks shame (*honte*) and danger (*peril*).

4. The motif of disinheritance which runs through the Vulgate Cycle becomes, in the *Queste*, theological and linguistic as well as feudal and economic. The New Law disinherits the Old, one semiotics overthrows another, and celestial chivalry replaces terrestrial knighthood—all to the good of Christians everywhere. This is a dramatic reinterpretation of the kind of disinheritance characterized by Claudas' betrayal of king Ban and the infant Lancelot: (III, 6–12). A small aspect of the disinheritance motif is discussed, pp. 245–46, 251.

5. The conventional nature of the sign is one of the fundaments of semiotics and is best known through the pronouncements of Ferdinand de Saussure in his *Cours de linguistique générale* (Paris: Payot, 1965). This axiom, however, has a long history in Western thought and is prominent in the thinking of Saint Augustine's *De doctrina christiana*, ed. Iosephus Martin and K.-D. Daur, *Corpus Christianorum*, series latina, 32 (Turnholt: Typographi Brepols Editoris Pontifici, 1962). In the *Queste* the problem is precisely that this convention has never been "signed," as it were. One may in fact argue that the *Queste* has no theory of the sign in the strict sense of a social contract concerning specific relationships.

6. The *Mort Artu* can be read as a clash of codes; one character's actions, performed according to one code, are read in terms of another code, giving rise to paradoxes. Thus Lancelot is most loyal according to the code of *fin'amors*, but most traitorous according to the feudal chivalric code. Agravain is precisely the inverse. The "demoisele d'Escarlot" manipulates various codes masterfully to entrap Lancelot (Frappier, pp. 9–11). A similar conflict of codes undermines any sure determination of guilt in two key episodes concerning the Queen. Since no code achieves consensus (due to the fragmentation following the "social failure" of the *Queste's* new code) in the *Mort Artu*, different codes are adhered to by different characters, and even by a single character at different points in the work.

7. For example, the episode of the False Guenevere (IV, 10 ff.). The *Lancelot* also considers the production of false signifiers. Morgan the enchantress, mistress of false signs, creates whole "theatrical sets" to manipulate misreadings of events; one such decor leads Lancelot to perceive a signified meaning (Guenevere's infidelity to him) which is wholly false (IV, 151).

8. This is best illustrated when a cleric reveals to Galahot "li termes" of his life (IV, 23–24, 31–35). The cleric discerns that Galahot has forty-five units of time left—signified as planks on a bridge—but doesn't know which of four possi-

ble signifieds is the correct one: do the planks stand for days, weeks, months, or years? (IV, 32: "Sire vees chi la senefiance des · xlv · planches et par ce saures vous par coi elles sont senefies · ou as ans ou as mois ou as semaines ou as iors ·").

9. The damsel who heals Lancelot after he has drunk poisonous water explicitly substitutes *amor caritas* for terrestrial love when she demands that he love her and be her knight (V, 79–84).

10. Lancelot learns that the adventure of the tomb of Symeu (IV, 175–177) is not for him and will be reserved for the knight who achieves the Grail adventures. At Symeu's grave Lancelot declares that he is no longer a good knight (*bons cheualiers*). When thrown down a well Lancelot calls himself a *cheualiers maleureus* (V, 157) and after having engendered Galahad he is often qualified as the greatest knight "of this century" (*del secle*). At the end of the *Lancelot*, Lancelot has taken to fighting knights under the name of "li cheualier mesfais" (V, 403 ff.).

11. Pauline Matarasso, *The Redemption of Chivalry: A Study of the Queste del Saint Graal* (Geneva: Droz, 1979), p. 11. Hereafter, "Matarasso."

12. Albert Pauphilet has a short section on "la glose" in his *Etudes sur la Queste del Saint Graal* (Paris: Champion, 1921). He observes that most episodes are followed by exegetical explications and calls the latter "une véritable glose du roman, tout à fait analogue à celle que le Moyen Age écrivit en merge des Livres saints" (p. 171). Hereafter, "Pauphilet, *Etudes*."

13. Tzvetan Todorov, *Poétique de la prose* (Paris: Seuil, 1971), p. 132. Hereafter, "Todorov."

14. By a narrative "event" we mean a narrative sequence as defined by Roland Barthes: "une suite logique de noyaux, unis entre eux par une relation de solidarité" ["Introduction à l'analyse structurale des récits," *Communications*, 8 (1966) reprinted in *Communications*, 8: *L'analyse structurale du récit* (Paris: Seuil, 1981), p. 19]. A formal definition is necessitated by the ambiguous meaning attached to the word in much criticism on the *Queste*. We maintain that the opposition, which persists at times even in Todorov's perceptive discussion, between "events" and "interpretations" is a false one and treats the scenes with the hermits as though they were at a different level of diegesis than the knightly adventures, which they are not. They are simply translations and explications. Although we agree with Todorov that "l'organisation du récit se fait au niveau de l'interprétation et non à celui des événements-à-interpréter" (Todorov, p. 138), it cannot be stressed enough that the scenes of interpretation are equally events or sequences within the *Queste*. We must, therefore, speak of events to be interpreted and events of interpretation. We have called these the "eventual" and the "explicative," respectively. Explicative events tend to reproduce the same sequence each time: arrival, confession, explication, departure. In the case of the

Gauvain episode (discussed below, p. 248) this sequence is expanded slightly by Gauvain's being "recalled"—itself a mini-sequence of which the telling feature is Gauvain's elision of the usual confession and explication, reducing the event to (re)arrival and (re)departure. "Eventual events" (inelegant as the redundancy may be) underscores the fact that these narrative sequences may vary substantially and cannot be resumed under any heading except one which calls attention to their essentially sequential/eventual nature. Eventual episodes correspond roughly to what medieval romances typically call "adventures."

15. The *Queste* does not hesitate to pass over long periods of eventual episodes which are not worth recording. Adventures of Galahad's are skipped over when they have no great significance (for example, VI, 140), and we are even told that Galahad and Lancelot spent half a year together during which "il trouerent auentures merueilleuses quil menerent a fin" (VI, 177) —adventures which, marvellous though they may be, do not merit narration.

16. Richard E. Palmer, *Hermeneutics: Interpretation Theory in Schleiermacher, Dilthey, Heidegger, and Godamer* (Evanston: Northwestern University Press, 1969), pp. 12–32.

17. Pauphilet, *Etudes*, p. 25; Etienne Gilson, *Les Idées et les Lettres*, pp. 62–63, 63, n. 1; M. Lot-Borodine, "Les Grands Secrets du Saint-Graal" in *Lumière du Graal*, ed. René Nelli (Paris: Les Cahiers du Sud, 1951), p. 173; W.E.M.C. Hamilton, "L'interprétation mystique dans la 'Queste' du pseudo-map," *Neophilologus* 27 (1942), 106.

18. Cf. Matarasso, pp. 182–183. Along with underscoring the materiality of the grail object itself, as Matarasso does, it should be noted that the quest, as Galahad describes it, is not for the Grail itself but the truth it contains.

19. The many associations of the Grail with the Eucharist miracle and the Holy Ghost are very *à propos* in that both the Eucharist and the appearance of the Holy Ghost at Pentecost are examples of language surpassing the limits of language, the first through the incarnation of the Word in Jesus Christ, the second as the expression of the Inexpressible in language intelligible to each listener (the resolution of Babel).

20. Jean Frappier has called attention to Galehot's extraordinary thirst for knowledge in "Le Personnage de Galehaut dans le *Lancelot en prose*," in *Amor courtois et Table Ronde* (Geneva: Droz, 1973), pp. 199–202.

21. Sommer's edition reads, "ne ne revenrai encore a cort por chose qui mauiegne deuant quil ne ma ci este moustres apertement sil puet estre. . . ." (Vl, 14). Since "apertement" is Sommer's own editorial addition to Add. MS 10294's lesson, it would appear preferable to follow Pauphilet's edition here which has the additional advantage of making a clearer distinction between Gauvain's and Galahad's definitions of the quest.

22. Old French *demostrer*, like Modern French *démontrer* and Modern English *demonstrate*, connotes both the idea of showing or revealing and that of explaining or interpreting. Cf. Tobler-Lommatzsch, *Altfranzösisches Wörterbuch*, II (Berlin: Weidmann, 1936), 1390–1391.

23. As Frederick W. Locke has shown in his book, *The Quest for the Holy Grail: A Literary Study of a Thirteenth-Century French Romance* (Stanford: Stanford University Press, 1960), every event of the *Queste* had to be known to Bors and Bors alone (see especially pp. 20–25). This relative order contrasts with the *Lancelot* which evidences a more tortuous history of its narrative elaboration which must include collation of knights' accounts as well as corrections (for example, of Lancelot's lying, V, 191); it also contrasts with the *Mort Artu* which makes no attempt to show its sources. Are we to believe that Walter Map again worked from documents or that he made up the story of the *Mort Artu* to satisfy King Henry's desire for closure and completion? The text (Frappier, p. 1) is silent on this point. For a more complete discussion (and contrasting view) of the *Queste's* authority and a consideration of the Vulgate Cycle's fictive manuscript history in each of the component portions, see Alexandre Leupin's article, "Qui parle? Narrateurs et scripteurs dans la 'Vulgate Arthurienne,'" *Diagraphe* 20 (1979), 83–109, especially pp. 105–106.

24. In using the term *hypotext* I follow Gérard Genette in *Palimpsestes: la littérature au deuxième degré* (Paris: Seuil, 1982), pp. 11–14. If I have any hesitation with the term, as applied to medieval literature, it is that *hypotext* makes no distinction between the ancestral text which has spawned a whole genealogy of recensions and variations and the immediate parental text from which the particular version we are reading descends. This distinction is important in medieval literature because it is frequently kept by the literary works themselves. The Vulgate Cycle, quite typically, cites its immediate predecessor as *li contes* ("ce dit li contes") and in no way confuses its immediate parent with the original narrative from which both descend. My own use of the term *hypotext* is therefore more restricted than Genette's. I use it to refer solely to the ancestral, original text.

25. The recensions are very few. After the commission of Bors' account to parchment, there is only Walter Map's translation which must be the *conte* continually cited by the *Queste* as its immediate predecessor (we are, of course, speaking of a fictive history of manuscript transmission). The *Queste's* reconstruction of its genealogy would seem to make Walter Map responsible for the *entrelacement* technique—for the translation from first person narrative to novel as well as from Latin to French. Is this the sense behind the act of "faire son livre"? Also, from the point of view of fictive manuscript history, Salisbury has importance not only as a religious center but also as a means of conveniently disposing of 800 years of manuscript history while limiting manuscript recensions to zero during

that time (the written adventures stored after Bors' death are presumably the same ones Walter Map withdraws). No other portion of the Vulgate can account as smoothly for the gap between the fifth century and the thirteenth century.

26. Melian is also given an explication of his failure in the episode already discussed, pp. 238–39, which functions as a prelude to the series of explicative scenes with the hermits. It should be noted that I do not distinguish in my discussion between the various roles of the hermit-figures within the Church hierarchy: friars, "men of religion," priests, recluses, etc. I am concerned with their role as hermeneuticians vis-à-vis the questers, not with their particular religious status.

27. This scene, like that of the suicidal maiden in love with Bors (see p. 247, below) dramatically illustrates the canonical view of evil as being merely the perversion of good and thus having no real substance, a view vociferously expounded by Saint Augustine. See his *Confessions* 7.12–7.13, ed. Lucas Verheijen, in the *Corpus Christianorum*, series latina, 27 (Turnholt: Typographi Brepols Editoris Pontifici, 1981), 105: "Itaque uidi et manifestatum est mihi, quia omnia bona tu fecisti et prorsus nullae substantiae sunt, quas tu non fecisti. Et quoniam non aequalia omnia fecisti, ideo sunt omnia, quia singula bona sunt et simul omnia ualde bona, quoniam fecit deus noster omnia bona ualde . . . Et tibi omnino non est malum, non solum tibi sed nec uniuersae creaturae tuae, quia extra te non est aliquid, quod inrumpat et corrumpat ordinem, quem imposuisti ei."

28. For the Christian view of rhetoric which does not convey Christian truth, see Saint Augustine, *De doctrina christiana*, book 4 (CCL 32, 116–167).

29. Bors' response is in perfect accord with the theology of the sacraments. In *De civitate Dei* 10.5, ed. Berhardus Dombart and Alphonsus Kalb, *Corpus Christianorum*, series latina, 48 (Turnholt: Typographi Brepols Editoris Pontifici, 1955), 276–277, Saint Augustine defines *sacramentum* in the following manner: "Sacrificium ergo visibile invisibilis sacrificii sacramentum, id est, sacrum signum est." For Augustine's own definition and discussion of *signs (signa)* see *De doctrina christiana* 2.1.1 and ff. (CCI 32.32 ff.).

30. In fact, *trouere* connotes a meditation of a writerly sort. Its first meaning is a literary composition; only secondly does it mean a *trouvaille*—something found, discovered, a "Godsend" (cf. Tobler-Lommatzsch, *Altfranzösisches Wörterbuch*, X (Wiesbaden: Franz Steiner Verlag, 1976), 699. Bors' Godsend is a divine Scripture, a gloss written in the book of the world.

31. The most exhaustive study of the *mise-en-abyme* is Lucien Dällenbach's *Le Récit spéculaire:essai sur la mise en abyme* (Paris: Seuil, 1977). I understand *mise-en-abyme* according to Dällenbach's "pluralistic" definition: "est mise en abyme tout miroir interne réfléchissant l'ensemble du récit par réduplication simple, répétée ou spécieuse" (p. 52). In the Bible parables are simple *mises-en-abyme* of Dällenbach's first type: *réduplication simple* or "reflexion de l'énoncé"

(p. 61), though never of the whole of biblical narrative. Thus the wedding parable reflects the mission of Christ in the world as "product" or *énoncé;* it is an interrogation on neither the agent of enunciation nor the code which structures Christ's mission. The *Queste*, in turn, adopts this same type and makes the wedding parable a *mise-en-abyme* of the *Queste* while keeping intact—by exploiting, in fact—the usual *mise-en-abyme* relationship of wedding parable to Christ's mission. What is novel in the *Queste's* exploitation of the *mise-en-abyme* is the rigor with which it maintains the logic of the *abyme*. As Dällenbach shows himself aware (in his section, "La Logique de l'Abyme," pp. 143–148) this logic, rigorously maintained, would oblige "une véritable compulsion de répétition" and produce an endless "prolifération des mise-en-abyme figures à l'intérieur de la figure" (p. 143) as the degree of analogy slid from similarity (*similitude*) to mimesis (*mimétisme*). In its application of the wedding parable the *Queste* does not make clear the degree of analogy; even a relation of similarity would suggest Lancelot's expulsion from the quest/wedding. Yet he continues to seek after the grail, hence that part of the *mise-en-abyme* which expels him is either prospective or the similitude is weak enough to suggest possibilities which are not of fatalistic certainty (Dällenbach does not discuss it *per se*, but there are many *mises-en-abyme* where the analogy is more suggested than established. This is particularly true in the *nouveau roman*. In Alain Robbe-Grillet's *Le Voyeur*, for example, the successive *mise-en-abyme* movie posters reflect Matthias' doings, but since we never know in absolute terms whether Matthias has committed a crime the *mise-en-abyme* is as speculative as it is *spéculaire*.)

32. There is one meeting with a hermit (VI, 95–99) which intervenes between the parable of the wedding feast and the episode of the tournament and in which a dream Lancelot has had is explicated as a *mise-en-abyme* of his genealogy. The vision once again suggests Lancelot's failure in the quest and prepares the way for the tournament episode's complete denial of redemption.

33. The tournament episode puts new pressure on the *mise-en-abyme* logic and moves closer towards Dällenbach's second type of *mise-en-abyme*, based on mimesis (p. 142), by establishing a more exact correspondence between *mise-en-abyme* and the narrative it reflects. In order for the demands of the *mise-en-abyme* to mesh with the syntagm of the story of which it also partakes, Lancelot must be effectively denied any possibility of redeeming himself in the tournament episode.

CHAPTER 7

Dying to Get to Sarras
Perceval's Sister and the Grail Quest

JANINA P. TRAXLER

"Ce vos mande par moi Nascienz li hermites que nus en ceste Queste ne maint dame ne damoisele qu'il ne chiee en pechié mortel" (QSG, 19) ("Nascien the hermit sends you word by me that none may take maid or lady with him on this Quest without falling into mortal sin," QHG, 47).[1] With these words, Nascien's messenger defines the Grail quest, the greatest adventure in Arthurian literature, as an all-male story, even more male than chivalric adventure already was. Thus, discussing women and the Grail story as it is told in the Vulgate *Queste* seems almost too easy: no women can *go* on the quest, and most female figures who appear during the quest are incidental messengers or agents of temptation. Perceval's sister, however, plays a role significant enough to warrant our attention. Despite her strongly stereotypical portrait—she is virginal and self-sacrificing—she nevertheless dominates the episode of the Miraculous Boat, one of the most important passages of the romance, and thus causes us to wonder at this apparent violation of the rule imposed by the hermit Nascien. In particular we should ask two questions: (1) Why does a man not carry these responsibilities, as in the rest of the romance, and (2) why must Perceval's sister die rather than disappear quietly or survive to receive the heavenly reward appropriate to her worth? In the following pages I attempt to answer these questions by arguing that the author of this Grail quest both needs a female figure the caliber of Perceval's sister and needs to dispose of her before the quest can conclude.

In the *Queste*, Perceval's sister has no history, not even the meager history we find for her in the *Perlesvaus*[2]—no highly active role, no rounded personality, not even a name; she simply appears at the appropriate moment and performs tasks defined by the needs of the Grail story.[3] Given the prohibition against women joining the quest and given the degree to which she is depersonalized, we might wonder why Perceval's sister appears at all and whether her place could not be occupied just as well by a male like the many others who appear at key moments to facilitate the progress of the Grail heroes. Before trying to answer this question, let us examine what Perceval's sister does.

Personalized or not, Perceval's sister is unique among the women in the romance: she actually plays an important role. Females in the *Queste* are most notable for their insignificance. They are nameless and occasional; they appear only briefly then disappear into a narrative void after they have fulfilled their specific functions of providing information, tempting the Grail seekers, or needing to be rescued. Examples of these three normal roles for women abound: Perceval's aunt provides information; the she-devil on the island tempts Perceval; the maidens at the castle of Carcelois all need to be rescued, to mention but a few. By contrast, Perceval's sister not only interacts meaningfully with the Grail triad but actually joins it. She dominates the material from the appearance of the Miraculous Boat to her death at the leper's castle, about one-sixth of the romance. In addition she posthumously affects the narrative to the very end: the rudderless boat that bears her body also receives Lancelot and Galaad for their last reunion and later arrives at Sarras as she predicted, so her body can be buried in the Spiritual Palace beside Perceval. Ironically, in a story that contains a prodigious number of people who should have been dead for centuries, she dies young and becomes the most mobile corpse in the story! Only the Grail seems to wander farther and more mysteriously than she does.

The features just noted distinguish Perceval's sister from other females and many males. If in addition we examine both her deeds and their meaning, we notice that her role, rather than being marginal, is complex and essential to both Galaad's portrayal and the development of the romance's major themes. At her first appearance she reunites Galaad, Perceval, and Bohort after a separation that occupies 60 percent of the romance. Clearly an agent of divine will, she finds Galaad and instructs him to go with her immediately: "je voil que vos vos armez et montez en vostre cheval et me sivez. Et je vos di que je vos mostrerai la plus haute aventure que chevaliers veist onques" (QSG, 198) ("I want you to arm and mount your horse and follow me. And I declare to you that I will show you the highest adventure that ever knight was witness to," QHG, 210). When she and the three Grail heroes arrive at the Miraculous Boat, she notes "en cele nef la est l'aventure por coi Nostre Sires vos a mis en-semble" (QSG, 200) ("in that ship yonder is the adventure to be found for which Our Lord has gathered you together," QHG, 212). Once they are on the Miraculous Boat, Perceval's sister further demonstrates her divine function through the information she gives. After introducing herself, she warns the Grail knights that they risk death if they board this boat without having perfect faith: "que se vos n'estes parfetement creanz en Jhesucriz, que vos en ceste nef n'entrez en nule maniere, car bien sachiez que maintenant i peririez" (QSG, 201) ("on no account to step aboard this ship if you have not perfect faith in Jesus Christ, for in so doing you would bring about your death forthwith," QHG, 213). Next, she supervises the knights' discovery of the precious objects on the boat—the inscribed sword of David and its scabbard, the bed with its spindles of three colors, and Solomon's crown. As the men look at each object, either Perceval's sister or the narrative voice provides its history.

Even more important, Perceval's sister has special deeds to perform. In order to finish becoming the Bon Chevalier, Galaad must put on the Sword of the Strange Belt, David's sword preserved by Solomon. But before he can do this, two things must happen, and both require Perceval's sister. The sword and the scabbard bear inscriptions that guarantee that only the rightful owner can safely possess the sword but that also seem so menacing as to dissuade Galaad from trying. Inscriptions, like swords, can be double-edged. The one on the scabbard announces that no harm will come to the one who wears the sword but that only a virgin princess can replace the unsuitable straps:

> Car li cors de celui a qui costé je pendrai ne puet estre moniz en place tant come il soit ceinz des renges a quoi je pendrai. Ne ja nus ne soit si hardiz qui ces renges, qui ci sont, en ost por rien: car il n'est pas otroié a home qui or soit ne qui a venir soit. Car eles ne doivent estre ostees fors par main de feme et fille de roi et de reine. Si en fera tel eschange que ele i metra unes autres de la riens de sus li que ele plus amera, et si les metra en leu de cestes. Et si covient que la damoisele soit toz les jorz de sa vie pucele en volente et en oevre. (QSG, 205–06)

> (But if he keep me cleanly he shall be safe wherever he shall go for no bodily hurt can come to him at whose side I shall hang, while he is girded with the belt that shall support me. Let none be so bold as to remove this present belt on any grounds: this is not granted any man now living or to come. It must not be unfastened save by a woman's hand,

and she the daughter of a king and queen. She shall exchange it for another, fashioned from that thing about her person that is most precious to her, which she shall put in this one's stead. It is essential that this maiden be throughout her life a virgin both in deed and in desire. QHG, 217)

Though a virgin, Galaad is not a princess, so this inscription prevents him from unfastening the straps of the sword we know he deserves. Moreover, the reverse side of the sword complicates the situation by announcing that "a celui a qui je devroie estre plus debonere serai je plus felonesse. Et ce n'avendra fors une foiz, car einsi le covient estre a force" (QSG, 206) ("to him to whom I should be kindest I shall show myself most cruel. This will occur but once, for so it is ordained," QHG, 217). Quite apart from the problem of the straps, Galaad must wonder whether it is even safe to claim the sword. Perceval actually encourages Galaad not to touch it.

Thus Perceval's sister has two tasks: (1) to validate that Galaad is the intended bearer of the sword, and (2) to change the straps so he can wear it. She accomplishes the first because she possesses essential unwritten knowledge. As Robert Hanning notes, since the maiden is the only one on the boat who knows the sword's history, she alone can inform Galaad that its daunting prophecy has already been fulfilled and that Galaad can safely wear it.[4] Perceval's sister, the requisite virgin princess, accomplishes the second task by replacing the shabby straps on the sword's scabbard with the requisite worthy straps, made of material only she can provide—her hair. She then underscores the significance of her acts by adding: "Certes, sire, or ne me chaut il mes quant je muire; car je me tiegn orendroit a la plus beneuree pucele dou monde, qui ai fet le plus preudome dou siecle chevalier. Car bien sachiez que vos ne l'estiez pas a droit quant vos n'estiez garniz de l'espee qui por vos fu aportee en ceste terre" (QSG, 228) ("Truly, Sir, it matters no more to me when death shall take me; for now I hold myself blessed above all maidens, having made a knight of the noblest man in the world. For I assure you, you were not by rights a knight until you were girded with the sword which was brought to this land for you alone," QHG, 237).

This last statement by Perceval's sister signals that Galaad's dubbing and arming in the early lines of the romance were only partial, provisional. Galaad acquired his sword by drawing it from the block of red marble that floated to Camelot, an act demonstrating that he is "the best knight in the world" (QHG, 35; QSG, 5). This sword's appearance and Galaad's success in drawing it are both marvelous events, but there is nothing particularly holy about them; they resemble many other purely unusual happenings in Arthur's realm and signal Galaad's special chivalric character without announcing his quasi-divine nature. Galaad left Camelot only partially equipped; he found his shield later at a Cistercian abbey. Unlike the sword in the stone, this shield has a sacred history. It marks Galaad as "the finest knight in Christendom" (QHG, 55; QSG, 29) and links him to his New Testament ancestor, Joseph of Arimathea.[5] Now on the boat, Galaad receives an even more remarkable sword; its inscription proclaims that Galaad is the best knight of all time (QSG, 203; QHG, 214), and its history links him to his Old Testament ancestor, King David (QSG, 223; QHG, 232).[6] Clearly Galaad must come to the Miraculous Boat in order to finish becoming the Bon Chevalier. This episode completes his evolution from superior knight (surpassing his father Lancelot) to servant of God, destined to accomplish the nonworldly adventure to end all adventures; from a new Arthurian knight to the long-awaited descendant of David; from a figure whose sword is marvelous yet without name or history to one whose shield and new sword demonstrate his nature and heritage and place him beyond comparison with all other humans. Galaad thus becomes a fully equipped "serjant de Dieu" through a three-stage process that, like the romance, begins in Arthur's realm and ends in the world of the Grail mystery, here represented by the Miraculous Boat; what Lancelot begins, Perceval's sister concludes.

These events illustrate why *someone* must do what Perceval's sister does, but they do not reveal why a female should play this role. The episode on the Miraculous Boat contains other information that makes the author's logic clear, however. Before Perceval's sister changes the straps on David's sword, we learn the history of the wondrous bed with its spindles of white, green, and red. This material extends the historical underpinnings of the Grail quest back to Adam and Eve and links Genesis to Galaad. The Vulgate *Queste* takes the traditional Christian understanding of the human condition—that the first couple's disobedience condemned us to a state of sin until Mary and Christ provided the means for redemption—and enlarges this vision to include Arthur's reign as the conclusion to human spiritual history.[7] The stories of the sword and scabbard, the bed, and the boat clearly lay out three important stages in this history: Genesis, Solomon's reign, and the Arthurian present. The material about Adam and Eve contributes the Fall (and thus human need for redemption) and the wood of three colors from successive mutations of the Tree of Life. Next comes Solomon's reign, which produces the sword (including David's blade) with its unusual straps, the bed with its spindles of three different colors from the offshoots of the Tree of Life, Solomon's crown, and the boat destined to convey these objects through time and space to Solomon's last heir. Though references to Mary (QSG, 221; QHG, 231) remind us of Christ's story, the Arthurian present receives greater emphasis as the third stage of the history. As Solomon learns from the Holy Spirit, his line does not end with Mary and Christ. They are simply one act in a drama that concludes only with Perceval's sister and Galaad: "Et tant encercha et enquist que li Sainz Esperiz li demostra la venue de la glorieuse Virge, et li dist une voiz partie de ce qui li ert a avenir. Et quant il oï ceste novele, si demanda se ce estoit la fins de son lignage: 'Nanil, fist la voiz; uns hons virges en sera la fins, et cil sera autant meillors chevaliers de Josué ton serorge come cele Virge sera meillor de ta fame'" (QSG, 221) ("He sought so diligently that the Holy Ghost revealed to him the coming of the glorious virgin, and a voice told him in part what was to be. When Solomon learned of this he asked whether this maid was to mark the end of his lineage. 'No,' said the voice, 'a man, himself a virgin, shall be the last: one who shall pass in valour Josiah, thy step-brother, by as much as that Virgin shall surpass thy wife," QHG, 231). This prophecy about the future of Solomon's line retains the Virgin Mary's importance, but displaces to Galaad and the Arthurian period the parallel importance we would expect to see accorded Christ, who is surprisingly absent from this material.[8] The Miraculous Boat, which Solomon and his wife launch into a vaguely defined future, bypasses Christ and Mary to arrive in Arthurian Logres. Here, it reaches the virgin princess who will supply the definitive straps for the sword and present all these articles to the most worthy knight ever, Galaad, who cannot alone fulfill the prophesies announced to Solomon and his wife.[9] Perceval's sister is thus not only important but *necessary* to this event; she is the character who assures that essential information and objects from Biblical history reach Galaad.

The marvelous features of this entire passage signal a fascinating characteristic of the *Queste*: the author blends elements of theology and romance in a combination that keeps the narrative from falling comfortably (or mundanely) into one mode or the other.[10] This restatement of the medieval Christian vision of redemption in a way that is *both* Catholic and Arthurian also helps us understand why there should be a woman to accomplish the tasks of Perceval's sister. The episode of the Marvelous Boat underscores a theme that is present from the beginning of the romance: purity, both physical and moral, is at the heart of the story, and specific male/female pairs provide the structure in which this theme develops. Thus while no women may go on the Grail quest, the story succeeds artistically and theologically because the author uses Perceval's sister as his Arthurian Virgin Mary. The Grail adventure requires someone both virginal and messianic[11] to continue in Arthurian time the story of redemption which begins with the disaster in Genesis, continues with the Passion of Christ, and is expected to conclude at the Second Coming. Galaad fits into this scheme perfectly. Less obvious but equally important, the story requires a female equivalent, not only at the end but at each step of the history. In the account of the Fall, Adam plays his customary role, but the *Queste* author expands the story from Genesis by adding pseudepigraphal and legendary material that gives Eve an active role in the story of redemption.[12] Eve carried the branch from the Tree of Life as she left Eden and planted it outside the Garden. Why was Adam not given this important task? Because "par fame estoit vie perdue et par fame seroit restoree" (QSG, 213) ("through a woman life was lost, and through a woman life would be regained," QHG, 224). Later Solomon knows that he needs to send a message into the future, but his wife figures out how to do it. She suggests that Solomon have a boat built and that he refashion his father's sword and put it in the boat. She also devises the original straps and the three colored spindles. She completes Solomon's "grant sens" (great wisdom) with her "grant subtilité" (great ingenuity, QSG, 222; QHG, 231). Ever present in the background is Christ's role; he is of course inconceivable without Mary. At each of the important moments that lead up to this episode on the Miraculous Boat, a carefully balanced couple—male and female—together do what is necessary to further the story of the items on the boat. This pattern continues when the Marvelous Boat arrives in the Arthurian present: the virgin prince cannot find it or claim its objects without the help of the virgin princess. This narrative therefore requires that a *female* do what Perceval's sister does and that she be flawless like Galaad, that she be a Mary-like figure to the Christlike Galaad.

Perceval's sister serves not just as a Mary, however; she is an *Arthurian* Mary. As Esther Quinn notes, Perceval's sister also displays many of the characteristics of the Arthurian fairy female.[13] Like typical fairy females, she appears out of nowhere, unannounced, and summons the man she has come to help. Her rudderless boat, driven by forces unseen and unexplained, goes where it must and when it must. It bears objects whose special properties are tied to the specific identity and destiny of the hero. Marie de France's *Guigemar* and other stories that exploit Celtic fairy motifs often feature a magical boat that carries people to another world; in the Grail romance, this boat is incomplete without Perceval's sister. She transports Galaad and his fellows on one boat in order to put them on another, the Nef de la Joie, where she performs her essential tasks. Their removal from the "real" world of Logres to an unanchored Otherworld, a boat outside of Arthurian time and space, coincides with Galaad's passage from secular Arthurian knighthood, symbolized by the sword he drew from the stone, to celestial knighthood, symbolized by the marvelous sword of David and Solomon.[14]

Clearly the story needs a male/female pair and the female must be an Arthurian Mary. Let us turn now to the second question: why this important character must subsequently disappear, specifically why she must die. By making Perceval's sister a significant player in the Grail drama, the author furthers the development of his theological message but also causes himself some difficult narrative and structural problems. Emmanuèle Baumgartner observes that in the *Queste*, the Arthurian world provides a third era to human history, transforming the Christian dualistic vision into a ternary vision which combines strictly Christian with Breton otherworldly elements.[15] This ternary structure is less stable than it might appear, however, because it does not *replace* the dualistic structure so much as overlay it. The triplet Old Testament / New Testament / Arthurian era can also be expressed as the four periods of Eden, Solomon, Christ, and Arthur. The first two eras feature fallen men and women, whereas the latter two feature the redemptive virgins (male and female).

Particularly important for this discussion, this shift from a familiar dualistic vision to a more unstable and complex one is related to the presence of Perceval's sister. Along with the dualistic vision just recalled, an equally familiar symbolism of three informs the narrative, and the presence of Perceval's sister disturbs this tidy balance. The Grail quest exploits the traditional symbolism of three in various ways: for example, the Round Table is the final of three great tables,[16] there are three Grail knights, the marvelous bed is surmounted by a structure in three colors made from spindles of three different generations of the Tree of Life, and the history of the bed emphasizes the triads Adam / Solomon / Galaad, as well as Eve / Solomon's wife / Perceval's sister.[17] By her presence Perceval's sister causes the symbolism to waver between pairs and triplets, between elements of two (especially two plus two) and three. Thus the Grail triad really becomes an unstable three plus one, with different pairs forming within the group of three: Galaad and Perceval's sister for their link to the biblical tradition; Perceval and his sister for their royal blood relationship; Perceval and Galaad as the male virgins who merit burial in the Spiritual Palace. Indeed, in this light *Bohort*, rather than Perceval's sister, is the odd character, less essential to the group than the other three, so one wonders why Bohort does not disappear.[18]

Perhaps more important than confusing the number symbolism, the role of Perceval's sister clashes with medieval theological assumptions about woman. The narrative is built upon the dominant perspective that all women are a threat to men's souls, that all women are Eve. Nascien's messenger states this clearly: whether virgin or not, virtuous or not, "dame ne damoisele," every female is barred from the quest. Furthermore, all men who go on the quest must first cleanse their hearts and souls: "ne nus n'i entre qui ne soit confés ou qui n'aille a confesse, car nus en si haut servise ne doit entrer deant qu'il soit netoiez et espurgiez de totes vilanies et de tox pechiés mortex. Car ceste Queste n'est mie queste de terriennes choses, ainz doit estre li encerchemenz des grans secrez et des privetez Nostre Seignor" (QSG, 19) ("nor shall anyone set out unless he be shriven or seek confession, for no man may enter so high a service until he is cleansed of grievous sin and purged of every wickedness. For this is no search for earthly things but a seeking out of the mysteries and hidden sweets of Our Lord," QHG, 47). The message is clear: women cannot be allowed even to be near these most holy marvels. This prohibition becomes ironic when we realize that it excludes women like Perceval's sister from the quest but allows such corrupt knights as Gauvain to participate. By excluding all women, virgin or not, the Cistercian monk suggests that Galaad, Perceval, and Bohort really must not be around Perceval's sister for long, even though she is necessary to their success.[19] In a context governed by the ideas of Tertullian, Ambrose, and Augustine, any woman—by the simple fact of being female—was Eve incarnate and therefore dangerous and unclean.[20] Thus, despite the perfection of Perceval's sister, medieval theology would not permit her (or any woman) to participate in the Grail liturgy at Corbenic and the removal of the Grail from Corbenic to Sarras. Nevertheless, she cannot simply leave the Grail knights and go off on her own; the thought of a virgin princess wandering unescorted through Logres would be completely unacceptable for the same reason the Cistercians adamantly opposed the establishment of mendicant women's orders.[21] Clearly she posed a problem for the theological vision behind the quest.

The needs of romance do not offer Perceval's sister significantly better options than those of theology. Maureen Fries points out that Arthurian women have only a limited number of roles available. Whether we put Perceval's sister into the categories Fries defines as "heroine" or "female hero," in neither case does she act on her own behalf.[22] Rather she furthers the male hero's accomplishments in a male-centered narrative. Given her divine mission and the emphasis on her physical and spiritual purity, Perceval's sister cannot be a love object; neither can she be a damsel in distress, since she sought the knights and furthered their mission. Furthermore, she cannot reasonably join the heroes as an equal, since she is a mere female. To use Rosemary Morris's words, Perceval's sister becomes a "superfluous lady" after the episode on the boat, and as such she must be disposed of. Morris adds, "whether or not they win our sympathy, superfluous ladies are always seen by Arthurian heroes as a threat: sometimes to their already pledged honour, but always to their freedom. On this ground, all Arthurian ladies are ultimately a threat."[23] Perceval's sister thus becomes problematic from the standpoint of both theology and chivalric adventure.

Even if we can agree that Perceval's sister is a threat (either moral or chivalric) to the Grail knights, we should still wonder why the *Queste* author does not simply make her disappear as all the other women do, perhaps stay on the Marvelous Boat when the heroes leave it. The episode of her death contains elements not already featured in her portrayal but important to answering this question. After the episode on the Miraculous Boat, the four return to *terra firma*, if Logres might be called that, and soon come to a nameless castle where the local evil custom requires all passing virgins to give a bowl of their blood to try to heal the châtelaine's leprosy. Not just any virgin will do; they need Perceval's sister specifically: "Au derreain nos dist un hons sages que se nos poions avoir pleine escuele dou sanc a une pucele qui fust virge en volonté et en oevre, por quoi ele fust fille de roi et de reine et suer Perceval le vierge, si en oinsist l'en la dame, et ele garroit errannment" (QSG, 239) ("Finally a wise man told us that if we could obtain a basin filled with the blood of a maiden who was a virgin both in fact and in intent, still more if she were the daughter of a king and queen and sister to Perceval the chaste, and if we anointed our mistress with it she would be speedily cured," QHG, 247). Though she knows she will die from this ordeal, she agrees to do it for the honor it will bring her and her lineage: "se je moroie por ceste garison, ce seroit honors a moi et a tot mon parenté" (QSG, 240) ("should I die to give her healing, honour would accrue to me and mine," QHG, 248).[24] The bleeding occurs, Perceval's sister dies as expected, and the afflicted woman is completely cured. The Grail knights then honor the maid's dying request: they send her body off in a boat that will bring her to Sarras to join them. Thus Perceval's sister wins a consolation prize in the Grail quest—admission to Sarras, albeit dead.

We would not be surprised if the episode ended there, with the Grail knights disencumbered of their female and ready to move into the conclusion of the quest. That evening, however, a horrible storm destroys the castle and all its inhabitants. The Grail knights learn that the storm represents divine vengeance for the sacrifice of the good virgins: "as bones puceles, qui çaienz a esté espanduz por la terrienne garison d'une desloial pecheresse" (QSG, 244–45) ("the blood of the innocent maidens which was spilled here for the earthly weal of a wicked and sinful woman," QHG, 252). The death of Perceval's sister is thereby avenged and the wicked custom ended, but we wonder why divine anger did not simply strike a day earlier and spare Perceval's sister. Our wonder increases when Perceval and Galaad explore the ruins of the castle and find the graves of twelve other virgins who were unnecessarily martyred.[25] There is a misogynistic sort of economy in the sacrifice of one maiden to abolish an evil custom which would have continued to take others' lives. Yet in a romance which places so much emphasis on virginity, it seems a shame to waste it!

I think the author, having paired Galaad with Perceval's sister as he linked the Biblical pseudo-history to the Grail quest, created a character whose role does not fit the narrow parameters of romance or theology. Neither the court nor the Church could imagine a holy virgin princess ranging freely and pursuing adventures of her own; she is problematic because she does not need the knights whose story she joins. The knights need her only for specific parts of their adventure, yet they have no way to be rid of her. To abandon her in mid-story would destroy the elaborate Mary-like role the author had built for her. The author's only real option was to have her remain with the Grail knights until she met a thematically logical demise. What better end to an exemplary life than an exemplary death? Martyrdom seems the perfect thing for Perceval's sister.[26]

Once we realize that the author intends at least in part to make the Grail quest a sort of Arthurian saint's life, we can see that whereas Galaad is the star, the portrayal of Perceval's sister forms a well-contained subplot that displays many of the dominant traits of thirteenth-century hagiography. Brigitte Cazelles discusses the relationship between hagiography and romance in the thirteenth century, emphasizing that both were the products of authors who were most commonly men, formed in a Church-dominated intellectual tradition and writing for an audience whose tastes were largely defined by male-dominated institutions, whether the Church or the family. In this context, similar content and rhetorical techniques recurred in sacred and non-sacred intellectual forms.[27] As Cazelles notes, the female saints' lives typically "[exalt] virginity as a prerequisite for female salvation, but through narratives whose main story line puts the heroine's virginal status in constant jeopardy."[28] Admittedly, the integrity of Perceval's sister is not constantly in jeopardy, nor is the *Queste* purely hagiographic or primarily centered on the life of Perceval's sister. Her virginity is, however, the one factor that endangers her after she has performed the duties for which she was created, and therefore Cazelles's analysis can help us understand the bizarre and seemingly senseless death the maiden endures.[29]

Although the *Queste* does not go to quite the gruesome extremes of well-known female saints' lives (those of Saints Agnes, Agatha, Elizabeth, Catherine, to name but a few),[30] the martyrdom of Perceval's sister nevertheless reflects the intellectual environment of the thirteenth century, especially the religious misogyny that excludes her from the Grail mysteries and defines her as a threat to the Grail heroes' virtue.[31] Her death solves both the narrative and the theological complications of the story. In particular, it offers the knights a way to dispense with a lady who has become extraneous. The foursome leave the Miraculous Boat and soon thereafter meet with a "normal" adventure: they come to a castle whose local evil custom demands that they surrender the woman. At last Perceval's sister fits a role these knights can understand—she needs to be defended. And they defend her in full chivalric order, stopping only because night falls and an elderly man persuades them to hear the story of the horrible custom (QSG, 238–39; QHG, 246–47).

When Perceval's sister agrees to sacrifice herself, however, the pattern changes and hagiographic needs take over. If this story were based on medieval realities and common superstitions, significant details would be different. The châtelaine would be isolated socially, probably confined to a leper colony and ostracized, rather than being the free occupant of her castle. Furthermore, even gory medieval superstition did not demand that a virgin bleed to death to cure a leper; normally a certain amount of child's blood would do the trick.[32] Hagiography, however, has its own demands. Virtuous women do not simply die of old age; they are martyred, often in a way related to their virginity, as is clearly the case here. By shedding her blood for a sinner, Perceval's sister becomes even more saintly than before. Indeed, in his enthusiasm for creating an Arthurian female saint, the author nearly made her too admirable: though her role is at times parallel to that of the Virgin Mary, Perceval's sister is more highly qualified to complete the tasks of the Miraculous Boat than even Mary, who is merely virginal rather than both virginal and royal. Even more shocking, despite all the indications that he is a Christ figure, Galaad does not lose a drop of his blood. Perceval's sister thus wins her admission to Sarras at a higher price than do the Grail knights.

Despite these bothersome details, the death of Perceval's sister solves the author's literary and theological dilemma. By her virginity and selfless dedication to their cause she ranks among the Grail elect. If only she were a man, she would be the perfect woman.[33] But as a woman she is also a potential temptress, and in retrospect we can see that from Pentecost evening onward, the *Queste* author has progressively neutralized her, making her sublimely harmless—like Mary. As she states, she sacrificed her stunning hair, the most beautiful anyone knew, to make the new straps for Galaad's sword: "Sachiez, fet ele, que je les fis de la chose de sus moi que je avoie plus chiere, ce fu de mes cheveus. Et se je les avoie chiers ce ne fu mie de merveill, car le jor de Pentecoste que vos fustes chevaliers . . . avoie je le plus bel chief que fame dou monde eust. Mes si tost come je soi que ceste aventure m'estoit apareilliee et q'il le me convenoit rere, si me fis tondre erranment et en fis ces treces tels com vos les poez veoir" (QSG, 227) ("I made it of the most precious thing I had, which was my hair. Nor was it any wonder that my hair was dear to me, for on the feast of Pentecost when you, Sir, . . . were knighted, I had the finest head of hair of any woman in the world," QHG, 236). Furthermore, in order to cure the leper, Perceval's sister must bleed to death. Relieved of her hair and her blood (and by extension her beauty and her sexuality), Perceval's sister becomes at once ill-suited to romance and well-suited to the only role thirteenth-century theology would allot her—sainthood, won in the messy, voyeuristic style frequently used for women saints. Then like the Virgin Mary, with whom the romance pairs her symbolically, Perceval's sister goes to join her male counterpart (Galaad) in heavenly bliss after death.

Perceval's sister is thus a mixture of stereotype and innovation, of romance and hagiography. Though she is essential to the success of the Grail Quest, she also clashes with the male-dominated vision of the romance's author and the audience. Unnamed, identified only with respect to her brother, she is nevertheless the only significant woman who appears on the quest, and she alone can complete Galaad's investiture as the Grail hero. She is the only woman allowed to arrive in Sarras, but she must die in order to do so. She alone can provide the blood that cures the leper, but God destroys the woman and her castle that very night, which renders the sacrifice of Perceval's sister at best superfluous, perhaps ludicrous. In this jumble of mixed messages, we see a narrative effort that strains the themes on which it is built, a character who threatens to break free of the space allowed her. In order to accomplish the two things that she must do and that she alone can do (equip Galaad and cure the leper), she must be stripped of her symbols of female temptation and reduced to an almost stereotypical safe, nameless, and self-sacrificing figure. In the world of the Grail Quest, not only is the best woman a dead woman, but the best woman is a dead virgin.

NOTES

1. In this chapter I will regularly cite the standard edition and translation of this romance: Albert Pauphilet's *Queste del Saint Graal* (Paris: Champion, 1921, 1975) and Pauline M. Matarasso's *Quest of the Holy Grail* (Harmondsworth, Eng.: Penguin, 1969), abbreviated respectively as QSG and QHG.

2. In one sense Perceval's sister is so unremarkable that we are tempted to overlook her. Though she occurs elsewhere in Arthurian literature, her appearance here is so different from her other appearances that they do not help us understand her. She appears in the Wauchier Continuation of Chrétien's Grail romance, the Didot-*Perceval*, and the *Perlesvaus*. She does, however, have a name in the *Perlesvaus*: Dandrane (var. Dondroine, Dardane, Dandrenor). For more on Perceval and his sister, see Jessie L. Weston, *The Legend of Sir Perceval; Studies Upon Its Origin, Development and Position in the Arthurian Cycle*, 2 vols. (London: Nutt, 1906, 1909).

3. In "Rewriting Perceval's Sister: Eucharistic Vision and Typological Destiny in the *Queste del San Graal*," *Women's Studies*, 21 (1992), 211–30, Susan Aronstein argues that Perceval's sister actually decides to accept the ordeal, against the arguments of her brother and Galahad, and that this decision causes her to be killed as punishment for her independence. See esp. p. 224. I disagree somewhat with this position; Perceval's sister seems like Galaad to follow a script even as she decides to sacrifice herself.

4. Robert W. Hanning, "Arthurian Evangelists: The Language of Truth in Thirteenth-Century French Prose Romances," *Philological Quarterly*, 64 (1985), 347–65, ref. p. 361.

5. This shield was destined for "Galahad, the Good Knight, the last of Nascien's line" and its red cross was painted from the blood of Josephus, son of Joseph of Arimathea (QHG, 60; QSG, 34).

6. The sword's history likewise links the Old Testament elements with Arthurian legend, since this sword also caused the Maimed King's wound (QSG, 209; QHG, 220–21).

7. Here, as on so many other points, the Vulgate *Queste* contrasts with Malory's version, where the role of Perceval's sister in the fulfillment of Old Testament hopes and prophecies has been minimized if not completely removed. See Sandra Ness Ihle, *Malory's Grail Quest; Invention and Adaptation in Medieval Prose Romance* (Madison: University of Wisconsin Press, 1983), esp. pp. 110–19.

8. Nancy Freeman Regalado discusses this aspect of the Vulgate *Queste*, noting how unusual this treatment of the material is. In speaking specifically of

Fig. 9.2. New Haven, Yale University, Beinecke Library 227, f. 12 (photo: Alison Stones)

Fig. 9.4. Amsterdam, Bibliotheca Philosophica Hermetica 1, f. 6v (photo: Alison Stones)

Fig. 9.6. Paris, Bibliothèque Nationale de France, fr. 344, f. 26 (photo: Bibliothèque Nationale de France)

Fig. 14.1. William Dyce, *Piety: The Knights of the Round Table Departing on the Quest for the Holy Grail* (1849). Watercolor, 9 1/8"x 17 3/8". The National Gallery of Scotland.

Fig. 14.3. Dante Gabriel Rossetti, *How Sir Galahad, Sir Bors, and Sir Percival Were Fed with the Grael, but Sir Percival's Sister Died by the Way* (1864). Watercolor, 11 1/2" x 16 1/2". The Tate Gallery, London / Art Resource, NY.

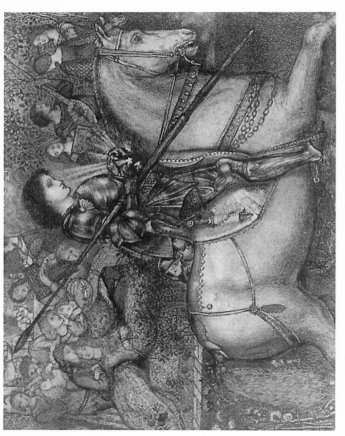

Fig. 14.5. Edward Burne-Jones, *Sir Galahad Riding Through a Mysterious Wood* (1858). Pen and ink, 6"x 7 1/2". Courtesy of the Fogg Art Museum, Harvard University Art Museums, Bequest of Grenville L. Winthrop.

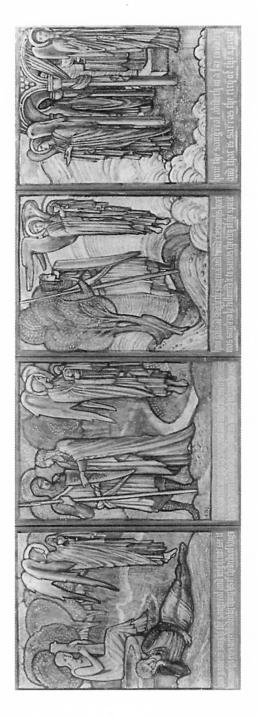

Fig. 14.6. Edward Burne-Jones, Cartoon for *The Story of the Quest for the Holy Grail* (1886). Ink, sepia, and gouache, 17 7/8" x 132 7/8''. William Morris Gallery, London.

Fig. 14.7. Edward Burne-Jones, "The Attainment of the Grail," from *The Quest of the Holy Grail* (1891–94). Wool and silk on cotton warp, 96"x 273 1/2". Birmingham Museum and Art Gallery.

Galaad's destiny as final member of Solomon's lineage (QSG, 221; QHG, 230–31) she adds, "We must not gloss over such an astonishing disparity between religious orthodoxy and the *Queste's* representation of Christian history and doctrine that has embarrassed religiously oriented *Queste* critics from Pauphilet to Matarasso" (104). She also notes "The *Queste* is filled with typological narratives from the Christian tradition which are made to prefigure the very events of the Arthurian story itself" (103). See "La Chevalerie Celestiel [sic]; Spiritual Transformations of Secular Romance in *La Queste del Saint Graal*," *Romance: Generic Transformation from Chrétien de Troyes to Cervantes*, ed. Kevin Brownlee and Marina Scordilis Brownlee (Hanover, NH: University Press of New England, 1985), pp. 91–113.

9. The reader is left to wonder about the details of this genealogical link between Solomon and Galaad! After all, Galaad's genealogy is traced through Joseph of Arimathia, who is not linked with Solomon's line.

10. Matarasso notes that "The *Queste del Saint Graal* despite its Arthurian setting is not a romance, it is a spiritual fable" (QHG, 9). I do not necessarily agree with her assessment, but in this discussion I will avoid defining romance too narrowly. Instead, by romance I will imply the fictional literature that includes Chrétien's works and the Vulgate cycle; by contrast, saint's lives and primarily didactic works belong in other categories. As the reader will see, I eventually note that this story seems to blend traits from more than one genre.

11. Pauphilet and Quinn have both examined aspects of this issue. See Albert Pauphilet, *Études sur La Queste del Saint Graal attribuée à Gautier Map* (Paris: Champion, 1921). See also Esther Casier Quinn, "The Quest of Seth, Solomon's Ship and The Grail," *Traditio*, 21 (1965), 185–222. For a more general study of the history of the concept of original sin and the misogyny which developed from that, see Elaine Pagels, *Adam, Eve, and the Serpent* (New York: Random House, 1988).

12. Quinn studies these influences in her article.

13. Quinn, 196–98.

14. Quinn, 210–12. It is probably not accidental that the central symbol of Galaad's role should be a marvelous sword. We recall Christ's statement that he came not to establish peace but rather to bring a sword (Matthew 10:34–36).

15. *L'Arbre et le pain; essai sur La Queste del Saint Graal* (Paris: SEDES, 1981), pp. 92–94.

16. The table of the Last Supper is the first; next is the table of the Holy Grail, associated with Joseph of Arimathea and early Christianity in Britain; and finally there is the Round Table, which has the same association with Galaad that the first table had with Christ (QSG, 74-78, esp. 77–78; QHG, 97–100).

17 Baumgartner, p. 94 (above, note 15); Quinn 198 (above, note 11).

18. Myrra Lot-Borodine notes this implication: "Il est tout à fait significatif, à notre avis, que la soeur de Perceval remplace ici Bohort, se substitue en quelque sorte à ce dernier membre de la triade élue. Après la fin édifiante de ses compagnons, Bohort rentre dans le siècle, revient à la cour d'Arthur pour lui apprendre les merveilleuses aventures du Graal. Seuls demeurent en la Jérusalem céleste, unis dans la mort et dans la béatitude, les trois êtres vierges, également purs, diversement parfaits: Perceval, le chevalier du Christ, qui, douloureusement, à travers la 'gaste' forêt d'épreuves s'est frayé une voie jusqu'aux sommets de la vie spirituelle; le Christ-chevalier, Galaad, et sa blanche dame, montée d'un seul élan à l'état de grâce. A côté de deux hommes: une femme. Relevons aussi le fait si curieux que ce soit précisément la femme qui seule ait scellé par la mort volontaire—le martyre rédempteur—sa mission ici-bas." ("We find it significant that Perceval's sister in a sense replaces this latter member of the chosen triad. After the edifying death of his companions, Bohort returns to the secular world, goes back to Arthur's court to recount the marvelous adventures of the Grail. The only ones who remain in the heavenly Jerusalem, united in death and beatitude, are the three virginal figures, equally pure, diversely perfect: Perceval, Christ's knight who painfully and through the 'Waste Land' of trials forged his path all the way to the heights of spiritual life; the Christlike knight Galaad, and his fair lady, who ascended in one bound to the state of grace. Beside two men: one woman. We should also note the curious fact that it is specifically the woman who alone concluded her mission on earth by voluntary death—by redemptive martyrdom.") See *De l'amour profane à l'amour sacré; Études de psychologie-sentimentale au Moyen Âge* (1961; rev. ed. Paris: Nizet, 1979), p. 156, n. 17.

19. The belief that *any* woman poses a threat, by her very nature, to every man is so deep-seated in patristic theology that it crops up in forms as varied as sculpture, literature, and sermon practice during the Middle Ages. In the debate over whether to allow religious women to join religious men, the resistance stemmed from the "certainty" that even a nun was a threat to a man, monk or otherwise. For more on this topic, see Eleanor Commo McClaughlin, "Equality of Souls, Inequality of Sexes: Woman in Medieval Theology," *Religion and Sexism*, ed. Rosemary Radford Ruether (New York: Simon and Schuster, 1974), pp. 213–66; ref. pp. 242, 252–57. Mary Daly also analyzes the misogyny of the medieval church in *The Church and The Second Sex* (New York: Harper and Row, 1968).

20. Patristic theology generally casts every woman as Eve and therefore the source of all human problems. Tertullian's words are among the most famous: "Do you not know that every one of you is Eve? The curse God pronounced on your sex weighs still on the world. Guilty, you must bear its hardships. You are the Devil's Gateway, you desecrated the fatal tree, you first betrayed the laws of God, you softened up with your cajoling words the man against whom the devil

could not prevail by force. The image of God, Adam, you broke him as if he were a plaything. You deserved the death and it was the Son of God who had to die!" (*De Cultu Feminarum* I, 12; quoted in Pagels, p. 63 [above, note 11]).

21. See Brenda M. Bolton, "Mulieres Sanctae," *Women in Medieval Society*, ed. Susan Mosher Stuard (Philadelphia: University of Pennsylvania Press, 1976), pp. 141–46.

22. Maureen Fries, "Female Heroes, Heroines and Counter-Heroes: Images of Women in Arthurian Tradition," *Popular Arthurian Traditions*, ed. Sally K. Slocum (Bowling Green, OH: Bowling Green State University Popular Press, 1992), pp. 5–17. In summarizing her analysis, Fries states "Arthurian heroines are conservative, passive, instrumental non-actors, useful for provoking, renewing and rewarding the actions of their knight-agents. Arthurian female heroes may, indirectly and for a specified time, consciously play female parts to effect transformation of their male-dominant world, but they always act only for knightly benefit" (15).

23. Rosemary Morris, "The Knight and the Superfluous Lady: A Problem of Disposal," *Reading Medieval Studies*, 14 (1988), 111–24, quoted p. 121. Roberta Kreuger's observation also comes to mind here: women who appear in early texts are not representatives of women's reality. They are male constructs, developed to speak for male purposes to a largely male audience. See "Double Jeopardy: The Appropriation of Women in Four Old French Romances of the 'Cycle de la Gageure,'" *Seeking The Women in Late Medieval and Renaissance Writings: Essays in Feminist Contextual Criticism*, ed. Sheila Fisher and Janet E. Halley (Knoxville: University of Tennessee Press, 1989), pp. 21–50. Brigitte Cazelles develops a similar position in the commentary of her anthology, *The Lady as Saint: A Collection of French Hagiographic Romances of the Thirteenth Century* (Philadelphia: University of Pennsylvania Press, 1991), pp. 43 ff.

24. This is somewhat ironic, since Perceval and his sister are the last survivors of this family and neither will bear children to carry on the lineage.

25. There is something else odd about this passage. The castle's inhabitants state clearly that they need Perceval's sister, which implies that people who are not Perceval's sister need not worry. Presumably the martyred virgins knew they were not Perceval's sister. Why did they not simply note this fact and save themselves?

26. In discussing St. Cyprian's attitudes toward women, R. Howard Bloch summarizes thus: "the only proper adornment for the virgin are the wounds of the martyr" (246). See "The Arthurian Fabliau and the Poetics of Virginity," *Continuations: Essays on Medieval French Literature and Language in Honor of John L. Grigsby*, ed. Norris J. Lacy and Gloria Torrini-Roblin (Birmingham, AL: Summa, 1989), pp. 231–49.

27. Cazelles develops three arguments for comparing the women of hagiography and romance: both types of characters are essentially fictional; the story line in female saints' lives focuses on "the relationship between genders" and dwells more on the woman's physical attributes than her spiritual ones, features which recall courtly lyric and romance; and the woman's increased prominence results in loss of freedom and voice, in contrast to what happens to male heroes (pp. 43–44 [above, note 23]).

28. P. 44. See also Kathryn Gravdal, *Ravishing Maidens: Writing Rape in Medieval French Literature and Law* (Philadelphia: University of Pennsylvania Press, 1991).

29. In *Ravishing Maidens*, Gravdal studies the prominence of rape in hagiography. She notes, "The Church fathers are well known for calling women to a virginal life. Most patristic thinkers propounded the idea that woman is the objective correlative both of the sexual body and of human sinfulness. A woman could be saved from her inferior female nature only by renouncing sexuality and becoming like a man, *vir*, through virginity. A woman accedes to sanctity by prizing her chastity so highly that she dies for it" (p. 22).

30. For English versions of many well-known examples, see Jacobus de Voragine, *The Golden Legend*, trans. Granger Ryan and Helmut Ripperger (New York: Longmans, 1941). Cazelles also provides English versions of several women saints' lives from Old French sources, plus a good deal of basic bibliographic material.

31. Others have studied the relationship between women and the Church in the thirteenth century. For various aspects of this question, see the following: Caroline Walker Bynum, "Women Mystics and Eucharistic Devotion in the Thirteenth Century," *Women's Studies,* 11 (1984), 179–214; Mary Daly, *The Church and the Second Sex* (New York: Harper and Row, 1968); Michael Goodich, *Vita Perfecta: The Ideal of Sainthood in the Thirteenth Century*, Monographien zur Geschichte des Mittelalters 25 (Stuttgart: Hiersemann, 1982).

32. For a detailed study of how medieval literature represents leprosy, see Paul Rémy, "La lèpre, thème littéraire au moyen âge," *Le Moyen Âge*, 52 (1949), 195–242.

33. Aronstein recalls Saint Jerome's statement of this attitude: "she who wishes to serve Christ more than the world . . . she will cease to be a woman and will be called a man" (215 [above, note 3]).

CHAPTER 8

Failure in Arthurian Romance[1]

ELSPETH KENNEDY

"Failure and the Unattainable in Medieval Literature" was once chosen as the theme for a series of seminars in Oxford. It was found to be a remarkably rich topic for discussion and was particularly interesting in relation to romance, that genre so notoriously difficult to define. In a way, as they appear in Arthurian romance failure and the unattainable could be described as two sides of the same coin: the impossibility of achieving some aim in totality and definitively can be presented in two different ways. On the one hand, an emphasis may be laid on what has not been achieved, on the inability of a character to attain a goal or to maintain a standard appropriate to a good knight, to a lover, to a king; hence failure of a particular character or set of characters. On the other hand, an emphasis may be placed on what is to be striven for, on the special nature of the ideal, the aim always beyond one's grasp; hence an incentive for constant striving, for endeavouring to rise above ordinary human limits to something more heroic or more refined or more spiritual. The quest for an elusive object like the Grail would be a perfect embodiment of the second type of approach. Thus failure to complete a task, to keep a promise, to maintain an ideal will be an important element in Arthurian romance, but it will have a different function within the structure according to the role of the character who fails, the stage in the text at which the failure occurs, the nature of the failure, the way it is presented, its relationship to the central theme and to the expectations of the mediaeval reader of romance.[2]

The establishment of the position of the hero within the hierarchy of Arthurian knights is always an important element in any Arthurian romance; it would have its parallel in the importance given to the establishment of a hierarchy based on achievement in other times and contexts. Battles must therefore be lost by lesser characters in order to enhance the stature of the hero; hence the series of jousts, of single combats, and of competition for the main prize in tournaments. More particularly Arthurian, however, is the relationship between the marvellous adventures presenting themselves to a knight and his quality as the hero set apart to fulfil a great destiny. That he is chosen over all other knights may be demonstrated by their failure at a task and his success: for example, the hero's achievement, where others have failed, can be underlined by the presence of vast numbers of prisoners delivered by him from a place whose enchantments they have tried vainly to bring to an end. In the *Lancelot-Grail* cycle (also known as the Vulgate cycle) Lancelot (through his quality as knight and lover) frees many knights entrapped in the Val sans Retour because they have been false to their beloved, even if only in thought.[3] The hero's success may be highlighted by the inability of another well-known Arthurian knight to complete a task. In the *Lancelot-Grail* cycle, it is the damsel bringing Lancelot and Yvain to end the enchantments at Escalon le Tenebreus who insists that Yvain, not Lancelot, should try the adventure first, for she knows that Lancelot will succeed if anyone does. If Yvain is tested first and cannot complete the adventure and then Lancelot achieves it, the greater will be the honour and joy the latter will win by it.[4] Needless to say, Yvain fails and Lancelot succeeds. Sometimes the perils surmounted by the hero, by contrast to those who have preceded him, may be made manifest in a more final form: for example, by the severed heads which Erec sees as he embarks on the Joie de la Cort adventure in *Erec et Enide.* Another way of distinguishing the chosen from the unchosen will be the absence of adventures presenting themselves to the less worthy knights. In Lancelot's early adventures in the prose romance,[5] only Lancelot and Gauvain encounter adventures which contain a strong element of the marvellous. In the *Queste,* when Gauvain and most of the other Knights of the Round Table have persistently failed to understand the spiritual nature of the Grail Quest, they no longer encounter the adventures to which they are accustomed, whereas Galahad has so many that there is no space to recount them all (a variation on the usual formula for exclusion from the tale being told):

> Si trova laienz mainte aventure qu'il mist a fin, dont li contes ne fet mie mencion, por ce que trop i eust a fere s'il vousist chascune dire par soi;
> (*Q,* p. 195)

to be contrasted with:

> Or dit li contes que quant messires Gauvain se fu partiz de ses com-
> paignons, qu'il chevaucha mainte jornee loign et pres sanz aventure
> trover qui face a amentevoir en conte. Et ausi faisoient li autre com-
> paignon, car il ne trovoient mie de dis tanz tant d'aventures come il
> souloient; et par ce lor ennuia plus la Queste. Messires Gauvain
> chevaucha des la Pentecoste jusqu'a la Magdaleine sanz aventure tro-
> ver qui a conter face; si s'en merveilla, car en la Queste del Saint Graal
> cuidoit il que les aventures forz et merveilleuses fussent plus tost tro-
> vees que en autre leu. (*Q*, p. 147)

Gauvain himself comments on this when Hector tells him of his lack of
adventures:

> Par foi, fet messires Gauvain, de ce me voloie je plaindre a vos: car, se
> Diex me conseut, puis que je me parti de Camaalot ne trovai je aven-
> ture nule. Si ne sai coment ce est alé: car por aler par estranges terres et
> en loingtains païs et por chevauchier de jorz et de nuiz ne remest il pas.
> Car je vos creant loiaument come a mon compaignon que por aler sole-
> ment, sanz autre besoigne fere, ai je puis ocis plus de dis chevaliers
> dont li pires valoit assez, ne aventure ne trovai nule. (*Q*, p. 147)

The destructive irrelevance of the activities of Gauvain in this Grail
Quest is related to two other important points, linked with the function of
failure in Arthurian romance: namely, lack of understanding and the connection between failure and the nature of the central theme—aspects
which will be pursued further later.

The quality of the knight who fails may also be an important element in the enhancement of the principal hero's achievement and may
again be linked with the main theme. A good example of this is Gauvain's fruitless attempt to cross the underwater bridge into the land of
Gorre in Chrétien's *Chevalier de la Charrete*. Gauvain's established reputation as the leader of Arthur's knights is used to underline both the
stature of the hero Lancelot, who succeeds in crossing the sword bridge,
and the importance of love as a source of inspiration for great deeds, an
aspect of the *sen* of the romance. Gauvain, nephew of Arthur and great
knight, fails, where Lancelot, loyal lover of Guinevere, succeeds—although this success may be followed by frustration.

The failure of a king to cope with the responsibilities of kingship can provide a challenge for the knightly hero (again a question of failure in judgement or understanding, here on the part of the king), and this may motivate a series of adventures or a quest, as, for example in Chrétien's *Chevalier de la Charrete,* where Arthur's rash promise to Kay enables Meleagant to abduct the queen without an adequate challenge. Another instance of this is to be found in the *Conte del Graal,* where the king's passivity opens the first series of Perceval's adventures. In *Lancelot do Lac,* Arthur's failure to avenge the death of Ban and disinheritance of his son, when Lancelot is a child, and the king's dependence on the hero after his knighting are again important in relation to one of the main themes, the inspirational and positive power of a love such as that of Lancelot and Guinevere as presented in the text common to both non-cyclic and cyclic romances. Through the recurring references to Arthur's inability to fulfil his obligations[6] a contrast between passive king and active knight is also provided, one which has been linked to the aspirations of a class of nobility in contemporary society.[7]

The examples of defeat and inadequacy so far cited tend to enhance the achievement of the main hero, but I now propose to look at examples of failure more central to the structure of the romance in that they involve the character whose adventures are the principal subject of the text. The characteristic pattern of a Chrétien romance contains a crisis point at its heart: the hero's achievement, at the moment of apparent triumph, is revealed to be flawed. This flaw usually involves a lapse in judgement, a wrong choice of priorities, a lack of awareness. Lancelot only hesitated before getting into the cart, but this brings a public rejection by the queen when he has just achieved the impossible in crossing the Sword Bridge. Yvain broke a promise to return to his wife Laudine within the allotted term. Perceval did not make the right response to an experience of the marvellous with religious resonances which he should have been able to perceive. The failure is made apparent through criticism in public and is usually linked to a central theme such as the exploration of an ideal of love, a quest for identity and for a role in society, the meaning of chivalry at a deeper level, or perhaps a questioning or playing with literary form and with the expected conventions of romance. The usual structure is a journey leading to the accomplishment of perilous adventures, a success which is acclaimed by a court, followed by revelation before others of the imperfect nature of the achievement; this gives rise to a second journey leading to a revindication of the knight's reputation, rediscovery of himself, redemption from his former fault through the new adventures he has undertaken, and the attainment of a greater understanding through his experiences.

In Chrétien's finished romances, therefore, it is never a question of the retaking of the same test, the successful achievement of an adventure at a second attempt, for this would not fit in with the nature of the hero's failure. The usual pattern is for the romance to end with a final success, now not followed by a criticism in public; but of course in Chrétien's work nothing is cut and dried: the form which the final success takes may still leave unanswered on one level some of the questions raised by the earlier point of crisis. Yet perhaps the most interesting and tantalizing failure of all is to be found in Chrétien's last, unfinished romance, the *Conte del Graal*. Here the link between the hero's failure and the religious significance of the Grail vision, a theme central to the romance, brings up the relationship between failure and the unattainable. By that I mean the enhancement of the mysterious nature of the adventure undertaken, for here the failure is associated with a quest for a holy vessel, or rather for some understanding of its mysteries. This is no object which can be brought back as a trophy; nor is it a form of enchantment which can be laid bare; so that to see it *apertement* is to bring it to an end. The fact that the first Grail romance was unfinished, and as a result the failure of the hero left unresolved, has been important for the development of the Grail tradition, and, in a way, this lack of an ending seems peculiarly appropriate to the theme. It might therefore be interesting to explore further the problem of enclosing the Grail theme within a traditional romance pattern of failure and success.

How should we approach this first Grail romance, which has no end? On the one hand, we have the speculations of modern scholars as to how Perceval might have made good his silence before the Grail, a silence which left the Fisher King unhealed and his land laid waste. On the other, we have the contemporary reaction to this uncompleted quest as revealed in the attempts of the continuators to pursue the adventures to a satisfactory conclusion according to their terms. Is it fruitless to ask how Chrétien would have finished the romance, given the subtle complexity of his art? The difficulty which confronts scholar and continuator alike is that by the end of the fragment Perceval and the reader already know the answers to most of the questions the hero should have asked. Significantly, considering the clear link made in the romance between Grail and Eucharist, Perceval discovers the path to the answers in response to a question he does ask when he sees the barefoot knights and ladies in procession on Good Friday.[8] The answer they provide leads him to the hermit who explains to him the deeper reason for his silence before the Grail and tells him what it contains and who is served by it, thus making explicit the connection with the mystery of the Eucharist already implied in a number of passages within the text. From the pattern of Chrétien's other romances, it would seem likely that Perceval would have had to go through another, different test in order to complete the task he was destined to achieve. The ugly damsel's prediction that he would never repair his omission would correspond to the apparently irrevocable nature of the disaster at the moment of crisis in another Chrétien romance, caused by the hero's negligence or lack of understanding: in *Yvain* the erring husband is eventually reconciled with his wife in spite of the message of final dismissal brought to him when he has failed to return. For Perceval the way of expiation must be a different journey from that undertaken by the hero in the first part of the romance, although there may well be meaningful parallels between the two.

Was Gauvain to be associated with this setting-right and making-good? There are perhaps some indications in Chrétien's romance that this might have been the plan: for example, Gauvain is given the task of seeking the bleeding lance. These are picked up in the First Continuation, where a new task and a new test are introduced—vengeance against an unknown knight and the joining-together of the fragments of a sword; but the asking of questions is also retained, here in relation to a different hero. Gauvain's failure at the Grail Castle is not complete: he achieves part of the task—the land is restored, for he asks about the lance—but he then falls asleep and learns nothing of the Grail; nor has he been able to join the pieces of the sword. The presentation of the failure receives a different kind of emphasis from that given to Perceval's silence. It is no longer that the hero destined to achieve the adventure has shown a lack of awareness through sin, and therefore does not pass the test and complete the task, but rather that Gauvain, for all his qualities, can only achieve part of the adventure—with the implication that Gauvain fails not through some sin which prevents him from accomplishing his destined role, but because he is not the hero born to achieve the adventure. Of course, each failure makes it possible to prolong the story, to bring in more adventures. In the Second Continuation, after much straying from the direct path to the Grail Castle, Perceval achieves partial success in the new task set—the joining of the sword—but to his great disappointment a small crack remains: he is not yet a perfect knight.

A work particularly interesting in its treatment of failure is the *Perlesvaus*, a continuation of Chrétien's romance in that it takes Perceval's silence at the Grail Castle in the *Conte del Graal* as its starting-point. Two factors in particular affect the pattern of failure and achievement within the work: the use of allegory and the integration of this Perceval Grail Quest into the wider Arthurian tradition and the history of the kingdom. Not only does the romance take as its point of departure events already related in Chrétien's romance; it also makes connections with Robert de Boron through the hero's ancestry (which fits in with that of Joseph of Arimathea) and through the linking of the Grail with the vessel which received the blood of Christ. The unifying theme of the romance is that of a Grail associated with Eucharistic visions and with the opposition between the Old and the New Law (Sinagoga and Ecclesia) presented on both an allegorical and a literal level. The text moves in and out of allegory in a sometimes rather disconcerting way. The destined Grail-winner, Perlesvaus, has a past with its roots in Chrétien's fallible hero, but a very different present within the narrative, where some of his achievements are presented as being from a certain point of view of the same type as those of Christ, much as certain happenings in the Old Testament can be interpreted as prefiguring events in the life of Christ. How is this transformation made? The author of the *Perlesvaus* does not, like the author of the *Lancelot-Grail*, take a completely new, pure and chaste Grail hero without a previous record: he keeps Chrétien's hero Perceval (in the form Perlesvaus). However, he transforms him by putting the failure in the past; the knight is even given a new name, *Par lui fait*, by his hermit uncle.[9] After the Prologue,[10] apart from a rapid reference (at the beginning of branch VII)[11] to his distress after the visit to the Grail Castle, this failure is only referred to indirectly through allusions by some of the characters to past events not related within the text, but only in Chrétien's romance.[12] These tend to dissociate the early achievement of a good knight, identified as son of the Veuve Dame and member of the Grail lineage, from the fateful silence of an unnamed knight in the presence of the Grail. The mother only recognises that silent knight and good knight are the same after the death of the Fisher King,[13] when Perlesvaus comes to save her land. There is no mention in the text of the rather comic mishaps and misunderstandings alongside achievement characteristic of Perceval's adventures in Chrétien. In the *Perlesvaus* no one succeeds in asking the questions, including the main hero; however, he redeems the past with a new achievement, a victory by arms, but one invested with allegorical significance. The inaccessible nature of the spiritual mysteries represented by the Grail and the idea that the struggle in defence of the New Law is never finally won in this life are illustrated by the double sequence: defeat of the Lord of the Castel Mortel (enemy of the Fisher King) in the first sequence has to be followed by defeat of the Noir Hermite (also an enemy of the Grail Guardians) in the second sequence. This is paralleled in adventures operating on an earthly level, the wars against Claudas, Brian des Illes, Arthur's rival lords and rebellious barons, which are not finally resolved within the romance.

The wars against Claudas bring us back to the effect of the integration of the Grail theme into the history of Arthur's kingdom and into the wider Arthurian tradition. This involves two levels of adventures, one set working on the allegorical level, the other on the literal. I mean by this that the defence of the New Law is linked with the maintenance of order and harmony in Arthur's kingdom through earthly means, by the sword. There are two levels of time: the eternal, and the historical, temporal. A wider range of characters than in Chrétien or the first two Grail Continuations becomes involved with the Grail theme in terms of the physical maintenance of the New Law in Logres. These do not succeed in achieving the main Grail adventure, but more than one at least achieve something positive. Lancelot fails totally at the Grail Castle because he refuses to renounce his love for Guinevere, a refusal which the hermit who urges him to repent of his love has to accept with sad resignation.[14] The Grail does not appear at all while he is at the castle, because of his sin, but he is honoured there:

> Mes li contes tesmoigne et dit que li Graax ne s'aparut mie a cel mangier. Il ne demora mie por ce que Lanceloz ne fust .i. des trois mellors chevaliers dou monde, mes por le pechié de la roïne que il amoit sanz repentir, car il ne pensoit onques tant a nule rien comme a li, ne n'en pooit son cuer oster. (*Perl*, p. 171)

But after the death of Guinevere, as T. E. Kelly has pointed out,[15] he can use the inspiration of his love for her (now of necessity purified of carnal desire) to achieve great feats with the sword in defence of the New Law. At the beginning of the romance, Arthur, to heal himself and his kingdom of apathy, undertakes the perilous journey to the Austin Chapel, sees a Eucharistic vision, is admonished by a hermit and returns home to re-establish the New Law, and he and his kingdom recover their former glory. Later Arthur is led astray again by false counsellors, but has another vision, sees the Grail, and is once more involved in the defence of the New Law. Gauvain too has his share of failure and success. He wins John the Baptist's sword and takes it to the Fisher King, but does not ask the question because he is so overcome by thoughts of God. Here are to be found parallels with the First Continuation but a contrast to the causes of Perceval's silence in Chrétien: Gauvain fails not through sin or blindness but because he is not the hero destined to achieve this adventure.

The very structure of the romance, with its exclusion of the beginning of the main hero's story relating his failure, is matched by the openended nature of the conclusion to the romance. Perlesvaus is told by a heavenly voice in the Grail Chapel that he is soon to depart, and that the Grail will no longer appear there:

> E li Sainz Graaus ne s'aparra plus ça dedenz, mes vos savroiz bien desq'a cort terme la o il iert. *(Perl,* p. 407)

He sets off for an unknown destination; over the years the castle falls into ruins, but the chapel remains miraculously intact, and those who dare to enter it take up a holy life; but the Grail has disappeared from the narrative without further explanation; nor are the earthly wars brought to a final end. This lack of conclusion to events is made even more explicit in the Brussels manuscript, with the colophon which postpones until another time the relating of further wars involving Brian des Illes, Claudas and Galobrus.[16] Thus neither failure nor definitive success is contained within the romance, and the Grail remains mysterious and elusive.

There is a different pattern of failure and success in the *Lancelot-Grail* cycle. In the first stage in the development of the Prose *Lancelot,* the noncyclic romance,[17] there are no failures on the part of the protagonist, Lancelot. He achieves the marvellous and perilous adventure of the Dolorous Guard, which has gained its name because "nus chevaliers erranz n'i venist qui n'i morist o qui n'i fust enprisonez au mains, si tost com l'an an venoit au desus."[18] He raises the slab which could only be raised by the conqueror of the castle whose name was inscribed beneath it.[19] Gauvain himself tries in vain to raise it later, in order to discover the name of the knight who had conquered the castle.[20] Lancelot is also the only knight who can bring to an end the enchantments of Dolorous Guard. He, as the main hero of the romance, is never defeated in single combat or in general battle although sometimes forced to withdraw after a battle to heal the wounds which he has received during his exploits. He may be diffident as a lover, but he is invincible as a knight. Gauvain, leader of Arthur's men, who cedes the role of greatest knight to Lancelot, would have been defeated by the latter in one single combat if the fight had not been interrupted,[21] but in all his other adventures he maintains his reputation as a great knight, second only to Lancelot. It is Arthur, rather than Lancelot or Gauvain, who has his menacing dreams, his moments of crisis, and who is publicly demonstrated to be a flawed king. This is done first by the *rendu* who, before the knights assembled at table, condemns Arthur's failure to avenge the death of Ban, father of Lancelot.[22] The king later again admits his fault with his explanation of his gloomy abstraction when the presence of Ban's godson at court reminds him of the unpunished death of his vassal.[23] The smallness of his army in comparison to that of Galehot (a great prince who invades Arthur's lands and wins the friendship of Lancelot) is also a sign that he has lost the hearts of his men and has not been fulfilling his duty as king; he is severely criticized by a visiting *preudomme* for his inadequacies,[24] although such condemnations are balanced elsewhere by praise of his qualities as monarch presiding over the Round Table and by allusions which remind the reader of his achievements as recorded in the Arthurian chronicles.[25] Galehot too receives warnings: in spite of his power to summon great armies, and in spite of the favourable description given of him by one of Arthur's own knights,[26] the emptiness and vanity of his achievements are suggested by the supernatural manifestations and dreams which prepare the way for his death and give signs of God's disapproval of his attempt to conquer Arthur.[27] By contrast, Lancelot's progress towards the winning of Guinevere's love and a seat at the Round Table is interrupted by no setback. He achieves everything he attempts; his periodic withdrawals for captivity, for wounds or illness (as, for example, when he goes mad in a Saxon prison) are the nearest approach to a crisis, and these do not arise from any manifest fault on the part of the hero. Only the shadow of Galehot's death disturbs the triumph of his final integration into Arthur's court as deliverer of king and kingdom, vindicator of the queen's name.

There is a transformation of this pattern of unwavering success on the part of the hero once the last part of this first prose *Lancelot* is rewritten to prepare the way for the incorporation of a Quest for the Holy Grail into the story of Lancelot. The first allusions to failure on the part of the hero occur in the cyclic version of the "False Guinevere" episode (in which a damsel tries to prove that she is the true Guinevere), during the interpretation by Helie, Arthur's wise clerk, of Galehot's dreams and the collapse of his castles. Lancelot is still the greatest knight, but is now destined to be surpassed by another:

> Je sai bien de voir k'il est li mieldres chevaliers de cels qui orendroit sont. Mais il en sera uns mieldres de lui . . . Je le sai bien, fet li mestres, que cil qui achevera les aventures de Bretaigne sera li mieldres chevaliers de tot le monde et remplira le deerain siege de la Table Reonde, et cil a en escripture la senefiance de lion. (*LM*, iv, 35)

For the first time we hear the prophecy of Merlin that Lancelot will not achieve an adventure, the greatest of all, that of the Grail:

> Je sai, fet li mestres, vraiement que ce ne puet avenir, kar il est tels qu'il n'avendroit pas a l'aventure del Graal, ne a l'achievement des aventures, ne a acomplir le siege de la Table Reonde ou onques chevaliers ne sist qui n'emportast ou la mort ou le mehaing. *(LM,* iv, 36)

Galehot also learns that Lancelot would have achieved this adventure if he had remained chaste,[28] and that the knight who is to surpass him will be descended from him.[29] There is a contrast here to the account of Lancelot's early adventures, as well as a change in the identity of the Grail-winner. In the narration of Lancelot's childhood there is an allusion to Perceval (Perceval in twelve manuscripts, Perlesvaus in ten) as the knight who has achieved the adventure of the Perilous Seat.[30] Now that the Grail is to be brought into the romance, the theme is linked closely to the story of Lancelot through the introduction of a new, chaste and faultless Grail hero, son of Lancelot. There is also a change in the attitude to love. The inclusion of the Grail leads to a reassessment of Lancelot's earlier achievement and of the role of love as an inspirational force, but the past (where love was a source of strength) is not cut off totally at this point. There is a series of adventures coupling success and failure at a series of tombs; those which emphasize the positive power of love look towards the past, while those which emphasize the destructive side of love foreshadow the future. In the Charrete episode, in the perilous cemetery there are two tomb-slabs; each of these is linked to a different adventure and a different type of hero, but the heroes themselves are connected as father and son—a relationship which is to have an important thematic and structural significance. In the first of these tombs lies Galaad, the younger son of Joseph of Arimathea. According to the inscription of the tomb, the slab will be raised by the knight who will free the prisoners of the Roialme sans Retor.[31] This has a double resonance: it evokes both the scene in Chrétien's *Chevalier de la Charrete,* and the raising of the slab in the cemetery of the Dolorous Guard,[32] itself setting off echoes in the reader's memory of Chrétien's Lancelot, lover of Guinevere, and thus interlacing the theme of love with that of the making of a name. In the prose romance version of the *Charrete* story Lancelot, as the greatest living knight, and lover of Guinevere, is destined to free the prisoners of Gorre, as is appropriate for the man who, in his own view, has achieved the rank of the best knight under the inspiration of love. He succeeds at this tomb and raises the slab. In the same cemetery, however, is the tomb of Symeu, of which the slab is destined only to be raised by the knight "qui abatroit les enchantemens del Roialme Aventureus et metroit fin as aventures et acompliroit le siege de la Table Reonde."[33] Lancelot experiences fear at the sight of the flames coming from the tomb and fails to raise the slab. He is immediately plunged into gloom and laments: "Ha Diex, com grant damage!" He is deeply ashamed of his fear and of what it implies for his position as the greatest knight. He explains his lament to a voice coming from the tomb:

> Certes, fet li chevaliers, jel dis por ce que je ai le siecle trop vilement traï et deceu, kar il me tienent al meillor des buens chevaliers: or sai je bien que je nel sui mie, kar il n'est pas buens chevaliers qui poor a.
> *(LM,* xxxvii, 37)

The voice (that of Symeu) tells Lancelot that he is still the greatest knight: "Kar cil qui sera buens chevaliers n'est pas encore avant venus et molt est sa venue pres." Lancelot learns that he has all the prowess and worth which can be found "en home corrumpu," but will be surpassed in his adventure by someone who will be of his lineage and so full of virtue that as soon as he enters the chamber where the tomb is the flames will be extinguished. The intertwining of the theme of the two tombs with Lancelot's name and with that of his descendant serves to highlight the contrast between Lancelot's present status at the pinnacle of chivalry and his future displacement. Both achievement and condemnation are combined in the episode in which Gauvain and Hector find a red marble tomb; the only knight who should enter the cemetery where the tomb is to be found is "li chaitis chevaliers qui par sa maleurose luxure a perdu a achever les merveilloses aventures del Graal, celes ou il ne porra jamés recovrer."[34] This knight is identified in another inscription as the son of *roïne dolerose*[35]—a name, in the form *Reine as Granz Dolors,* used to designate the mother of Lancelot in the account of his childhood at the beginning of the romance.[36]

Passages such as these, which give more emphasis to what cannot be achieved than to the lesser adventure in which Lancelot will succeed, are balanced by others which stress Lancelot's present greatness. The court does not believe that anyone except Lancelot can bring the Grail adventures to an end. He shows his quality as the greatest knight and lover when he puts an end to the *carole,* a magic dance into which are drawn those who love or have loved, and which can only be stopped by the arrival of "li plus leaux chevaliers . . . et li mieldres et li plus biaux."[37] He is also successful in a chess game which can only be won by a knight "gracieuz et desirrez et amez sor touz autres."[38]

These achievements, however, look backwards rather than forwards, and as the beginning of the *Queste* approaches there is increasing emphasis on the destructive side of Lancelot's love: it is shown to bar his future progress and to threaten the kingdom of Logres with dissension. It even begins to throw a shadow over his past achievement, however strenuously Lancelot protests against this. It is only within the *Queste* itself that he is prepared to accept that his love for Guinevere has damaged his quality as a knight. Lancelot's experiences at the tomb of his grandfather (Lancelot) combine achievement, failure and a link with the identity theme. Because he is still the best knight in the world, he is able to take his grandfather's head, raise the tomb-slab and lay the bodies of both his grandparents in the same grave; but he is not able to cool a boiling fountain or to restore light to the castle, for he is "chauz et luxurieux," as a hermit explains to him when he tells him that it is only his sin with Guinevere that will prevent him from achieving the adventure of the Grail which he had once been meant to achieve. His adventures during his first visit to Corbenic illustrate his triumphs (linking with the past) and his future displacement as the greatest knight. He is able to save a damsel from a tub of hot water, an adventure which Gauvain[39] was unable to achieve; he then raises the slab on a tomb of which the inscription reads as follows:

> Ja ceste tombe ne sera levee devant que li lieparz i mestra main, de qui li granz lions doit issir, et cil la levera legierement, et lors sera engendrez li granz lions en la bele fille au roi de la Terre Forainne. (*LM*, lxxviii, 46)

When Lancelot achieves this adventure, he reveals himself to be the leopard who is to engender the hero destined to surpass him. All these adventures prepare the way for Lancelot's loss of the position of greatest knight once Galahad appears at court.

In the *Queste* the pattern of achievement and failure is determined by the significance given to the search for the Grail. We have here adventures functioning on a consistently allegorical level (as opposed to the intermittent allegory of the *Perlesvaus*) but within a cyclic romance functioning elsewhere on a literal level. A large number of Arthur's knights are involved: they fail in varying degrees because they are incapable of operating at the spiritual level required but persist in behaving according to the normal conventions of Arthurian romance. The Quest concerns the search for the vision of God and can be pursued through different stages of revelation to the final vision, where no sensorial images are interposed. This last stage is only attained by Galahad, who alone looks into the Grail and sees *apertement*. Progress can be made solely under the inspiration of divine grace. Gauvain fails because he does not seek help outside himself (that is, from God), but relies on his own resources, on his own prowess, as he had done in the past (unlike Lancelot, who had drawn strength from love, although the wrong kind of love). Thus Gauvain continues to behave according to the rules governing knightly behaviour in the earlier branches of the romance—rules which are just as inappropriate to the Grail adventures as Alice found her accustomed ways of behaviour to be once she had entered the Looking-Glass world. It is necessary that it should be the best knight after Lancelot—that is, the courteous, considerate and valiant Gauvain— who has to retire totally unsuccessful from the Quest, in order to bring out the contrast between the *choses espirituelles* of the search for revelation of the Grail mysteries and the ordinary adventures of Arthurian romance. The nature of Lancelot's failure in the supreme achievement of the Quest and the limited kind of revelation which he receives are linked to one of the central themes of the cycle, the winning and loss of a name. In the early adventures in the romance, the hero's discovery of the *sorenon* Lancelot at the Dolorous Guard is presented as the winning of a glorious name through an adventure which is of service to others. In the part of the cycle that leads up to the *Queste,* this theme is already being transformed with the inscriptions and prophecies condemning Lancelot's love for Guinevere, in his eyes the motivating force behind his knightly exploits. The begetting of Galahad explicitly transforms the use of the hero's *sorenon* rather than his baptismal name into a loss, not a gain—a loss which has to be made good through Lancelot's son, who by his purity and virtue re-establishes the name Galahad.[40]

Lancelot's decline in status is made clear at the beginning of the *Queste.* A traditional test for the hero presents itself: the sword to be drawn from the stone only by the best knight. Lancelot refuses to attempt the adventure; Gauvain is forced to do so by the king and fails, as does Perceval. When Galahad appears, he achieves the adventure of the Perilous Seat and then draws the sword from the stone. At that point a damsel appears and speaks to Lancelot:

"Ha, Lancelot, tant est vostre afere changiez puis ier matin!" Et quant il ot ce, si li dist: "Damoisele, coment? Dites le moi." "Par foi," fet ele, "je le vos dirai voiant toz çax de ceste place. Vos estiez hier matin li mieldres chevaliers dou monde; et qui lors vos apelast Lancelot le meillor chevalier de toz, il deist voir: car alors l'estiez vos. Mes qui ore le diroit, len le devroit tenir a mençongier: car meillor i a de vos, et bien est provee chose par l'aventure de ceste espee a quoi vos n'osastes metre la main. Et ce est li changemenz et li muemenz de vostre non, dont je vos ai fet remembrance por ce que des ore mes ne cuidiez que vos soiez li mieldres chevaliers dou monde." Et il dist qu'il nel cuidera ja mes, car ceste aventure l'en a mis tot fors del cuidier. (*Q*, pp. 12–13)

Thus the *Queste* begins with the public demonstration of failure on the part of the two knights up till then acknowledged to be the greatest. The evidence of and reasons for the failure of these two are made clear at intervals throughout the text. For example, Lancelot helps the Black Knights against the White; he loses, and is very disconcerted by such an unaccustomed defeat. Visions, heavenly voices and hermits make manifest the cause of his wrongful choice and failure: his adulterous love for Guinevere. When he renounces his love for a heavenly love of God, he receives a fragmentary vision of the Grail. Gauvain is warned by hermits that he is not engaged on earthly adventures and that he must seek help from God, but he is so anxious to pursue his quest that he does not stay for Mass; hence, as was explained earlier, his actions become irrelevant to the goal which he strives for because he misunderstands the nature of it. Perceval and Bohort have a better though still imperfect perception of the requirements of the Grail Quest and attain to a high degree of revelation. Only Galahad reaches the ultimate and inexpressible ecstasy, passing briefly beyond the limits of the human senses, but such a revelation cannot be prolonged in this life and he dies shortly afterwards.

Once again, both failure and the pattern of the chief Grail Hero's achievement serve to emphasize the unattainable nature of the object of the Quest, its spirituality and immateriality. Noteworthy too is the fact that in this cyclic romance whose subject is the story of Lancelot, as references to the tale frequently point out, the main hero fails at the greatest adventure and never surmounts this failure, as does Perlesvaus for example, but is displaced for the Grail branch by another hero, his son. Once Galahad is knighted, Lancelot loses his position as greatest knight until Galahad dies, and even then he never again has the chance to undertake the kind of adventures at which he had made his name, because with the achievement of the Grail Quest the marvels of Logres have been brought to an end. Lancelot's great stature as a knight is still made clear in the

Mort le roi Artu, but mainly in terms of the disastrous consequences of his *absence* in the final battle, both battle and absence arising from the chain of events set off by his passionate love for the queen.

We have, therefore, in the *Lancelot-Grail* cycle a hero of romance who fails and never redeems this failure. The failure is linked in the *Queste* to a questioning of a fundamental theme of romance: the inspirational power of earthly love. Lancelot's setback in the *Queste* is followed by the tragedy of the *Mort Artu,* another form of questioning of the value of a love such as that of Lancelot and Guinevere. Thus the introduction of the Grail theme and the final failure in relation to it of the central hero of the cycle bring a new dimension to the story of Lancelot and a questioning of the values given expression in his early adventures—a questioning not to be found in the non-cyclic romance, which does not include the Grail theme within it. The pattern of success and failure in the *Lancelot-Grail* cycle should be compared with that of the *Perlesvaus,* where the Fisher King dies, but the resonances of a Harrowing of Hell on an allegorical level in the victory achieved by Perlesvaus against the Noir Hermite[41] mean that he transcends this early failure, recounted in another text. However, the open-ended final episode of the romance makes it clear that the Grail cannot be won in ordinary human terms. The other characters' failures on the supreme, spiritual level in the *Perlesvaus* are balanced by achievements on a literal level, but these are linked with the triumph of the New Law, central to the romance. No such compensation for failure is to be found in the *Queste,* where all the adventures have meaning solely on the allegorical level and attempts to work on the literal plane can only lead to frustration and defeat. The lack of comprehension which such attempts imply recalls the failure in understanding characteristic of the crisis points in the careers of Chrétien's heroes, although the drawing of this parallel does not imply an allegorical interpretation of Chrétien. However, as I suggested earlier, failure has a particular function in the Grail romances: it can serve to enhance the mystic quality of the central theme. In the *Lancelot-Grail* it is associated with a turning-upside-down of the conventions of romance, so that the traditional episodes and vocabulary of romance are given a new meaning. Some of the characters within the romance never fully understand this and hence make mistakes.

A last point to be explored is whether a questioning or testing of established conventions of romance is to some degree involved in the failure of the main hero in other romances. The way that failure is experienced and made public and the place in the romance where this occurs may be of interest with regard to this. It is at Arthur's court that a knight's name is

made and that success and failure will be reported. Usually, the testing itself takes place outside the court: for example, Perceval's failure at the
Grail Castle and success at other adventures in the *Conte del Graal.* In the
Queste, the trial of the sword in the stone takes place at court, but news of
the knights' failures on the Grail Quest are brought back by the individuals concerned, if still alive, for it is made clear from an early stage in the
Prose *Lancelot* that knights must swear an oath to tell the truth on their return,[42] and it is on the basis of these reports that the whole narrative is
founded. Arthur's clerks record the knights' accounts of their adventures,
and this record is presented as the authentic source for the romance.[43] The
court has certain expectations: adventures are in one sense unpredictable,
but they are also part of the inherent pattern of events in the Arthurian
world, and the court would anticipate that they would accord with their
accustomed experience and with the kind of events previously set down in
the clerks' big book, however marvellous they might be. Prediction of
failure on the part of established heroes would disconcert and might be
greeted with incredulous astonishment. An example of this is to be found
in Arthur's reaction to Lancelot's refusal to attempt to put his hand to the
sword which can only be drawn from the stone by the best knight in the
world.[44] In both verse and prose romances, the public accusation by a
messenger (such as the ugly damsel in the *Conte del Graal)* that a hero
who has just been acclaimed at court has failed irretrievably may force
hero and court to question the validity of the praise just given; but if the
denunciation occurs in the middle of the romance, this may give the hero
a chance to disprove the prediction of irretrievability, at least in terms of
narrative events (see Y*vain,* for example). If the knight has to return home
and report lack of achievement and damage done, as Gauvain has to do at
the beginning of the *Mort le roi Artu* in relation to his actions in the
Queste, there may be both self-condemnation and royal condemnation for
what cannot be undone. Gauvain recognizes his *pechié,*[45] but shows no
clear understanding of the nature of it, in conformity with his role in the
Grail adventures, and because he has never been able to detach himself
from the conventions of romance turned upside-down in the *Queste.* In *Sir
Gawain and the Green Knight* the hero also has to report a degree of failure back to court. His insistence on self-condemnation, where the court is
more lenient in judgement, suggests that on one level a failure at the end
of an adventure may still enhance the stature of the hero through a final
self-questioning, which may also be paralleled in the ways that the conventions of romance are presented and, one might say, played with in the
work. In Chrétien too, as I mentioned earlier, the manner in which at the

end of the romance problems are left resolved on one level but perhaps unresolved on another may also involve a subtle and shifting alternation of conventional expectations fulfilled or unfulfilled. A Grail romance such as the *Perlesvaus* gives no clearcut, comfortable ending. Although Perlesvaus has replaced the fallible Perceval, the theme cannot be confined within a rigid framework of success or failure neatly rounded off. The *Lancelot-Grail* cycle sets the hero's successes and setbacks within the context of both Grail Quest and history of Arthur's kingdom. In so doing, it includes within a romance a set of opposing values; here too, although in a different way, hero and reader are brought to question their interpretation of earlier events in terms of success and failure, to reconsider their expectations in relation to the knightly hero in the Arthurian world.

NOTES

Reprinted with permission from *Medium Ævum*, 50, no. 1 (1991), 16–32.

1. Abbreviations used for texts cited:

Continuation: *The Continuations of the Old French Perceval of Chrétien de Troyes*, ed. by W. Roach, 6 vols. (Philadelphia, Pa., 1949–83). First Continuation: Vol. III; Second Continuation: Vol. IV.

LM: Lancelot: roman en prose du XIIIe siècle, ed. by A. Micha, 9 vols. (Paris; Geneva, 1978-83). The roman numerals refer to chapters, the arabic to paragraphs; the references are to the long version. Part of the *Lancelot-Grail* cycle or Vulgate cycle.

MA: La Mort le roi Artu: roman du XIIIe siècle, ed. by J. Frappier, 3rd edn (Paris; Geneva, 1964).

Perc: Chrétien de Troyes: Le Roman de Perceval ou le Conte del Graal, ed. by W. Roach, Textes littéraires français (Geneva; Lille, 1956).

Perl: Le Haut Livre du Graal. Perlesvaus, ed. by W. A. Nitze and T. Jenkins, 2 vols. (Chicago, 1932-7).

PL: Lancelot do Lac: The Non-Cyclic Old French Prose Romance, ed. by E. Kennedy, 2 vols. (Oxford, 1980).

Q or Queste: La Queste del Saint Graal, ed. by A. Pauphilet, Classiques français du moyen âge (Paris, 1949).

2. "Reader" would, of course, also include listener to the reading aloud of a romance.

3. *LM*, xxii–xxiv.

4. *LM*, xx, 12.

5. *PL; LM*, Vols. VII and VIII.

6. *PL*, pp. 56, 137–8, 285.

7. See E. Köhler, *L'Aventure chevalresque. Idéal et réalité dans le roman cortois* (Paris, 1974); F. Wolfzettel, "Idéologie chevaleresque et conception féodale dans *Durmart le Galois:* l'altération du schéma arthurien sous l'impact de la réalité politique du Xllle siècle," in *Actes du 14e Congrés International Arthurien* (Rennes, 1985) pp. 668–86.

8. *Perc,* line 6264.

9. *Perl,* p. 139.

10. "Mes, par molt poi de parole qu'il delaia a dire, avindrent si granz meschaances a la Grant Breteingne que totes les illes e totes les terres en chaïrent en grant doleur; mes puis les remist il en joie par la valor de sa buenne chevalierie" *(Perl,* pp. 23–4).

11. *Perl,* p. 139.

12. A hermit tells Arthur: "Mes une granz doleurs est avenue novelement par un chevalier qui fu herbergiez en l'ostel au riche roi Pescheeur, si s'aparut a lui li sainz Graauz e la lance de coi la pointe de fer saine, ne ne demanda de coi ce servoit, ne cui on en servoit; por ce qu'il ne le demanda, sont totes les terres de guerre escommeües, ne chevaliers n'encontre autre en forest q'il ne qeure sus e ocie s'il puet, e vos meïsmes vos en perceveroiz bien ainz que vos partez de ceste lande" *(Perl,* pp. 37–8). See also *ibid.,* pp. 67–8,117.

13. *Perl,* p. 230.

14. *Ibid.,* pp. l67–9.

15. T. E. Kelly, *Le Haut Livre du Graal: Perlesvaus, a Structural Study* (Geneva, 1974), pp. 171–2.

16. Brussels, Bibliothèque royale, MS 11145 adds the following reference to the tale not to be told in this book: "Aprés iceste estoire conmence li contes si conme brians des illes guerpi li rois artus por lanc' que il namoit mie et conme il laseura li rois claudas qui le roi ban de benoic toli sa terre. Si parole cist contes conment il le conquist et par quel maniere et si com galobrus de la uermeille lande uint a la cort le rois artus por aidier lanc'. Quar il estoit de son lignage. Cist contes est mout lons et mout auentureus et poisanz. Mes li liures sen tera ore atant trusqua vne autre foiz" *(Perl,* p. 409).

17. This non-cyclic version *(PL)* brings the story to an end with the death of Galehot. It contains no quest, but there are allusions outwards to the Grail as to an adventure told elsewhere. It is to be found in the early thirteenth-century Paris, Bibliothéque nationale, MS f. fr. 768 (where the last folio is missing), in Rouen, Bibliothéque municipale, MS 1055 (06) and in Florence, Biblioteca Laurenziana, MS 89 inf. 61; it is also found in part in twelve other manuscripts. The cyclic romance presents the same version of Lancelot's adventures up to his installation as a Knight of the Round Table, but rewrites the episodes leading up to the death of Galehot (the journey to Sorelois and the False Guinevere episode) in

order to prepare the way for the inclusion of the great twelfth-century Arthurian themes of the abduction and rescue of Guinevere (recounted by Chrétien in *Le Chevalier de la Charrete*), a Grail Quest and a *Mort Artu*. See *PL*, II, 39–41; E. Kennedy, *Lancelot and the Grail: a Study of the Prose Lancelot* (Oxford, 1986).

18. *PL*, p. 183.

19. *Ibid.*, p. 194.

20. *Ibid.*, p. 240.

21. *Ibid.*, pp. 535–7.

22. *Ibid.*, pp. 54–7.

23. *Ibid.*, pp. 136–8.

24. *Ibid.*, pp. 283–92.

25. For a more detailed study of Arthur's role in the romance, see E. Kennedy, "Etudes sur le Lancelot en prose, II: Le roi Arthur dans le *Lancelot* en prose," *Romania*, CV (1984), 46–62, and *Lancelot and the Grail*, pp. 72–4, 79–89, 224–31.

26. *PL*, p. 264.

27. *Ibid.*, p. 582.

28. *LM*, iv, 41.

29. *Ibid.*, iv, 42.

30. The allusion to the adventure of the Perilous Seat occurs in a passage in which the daughter of Pellés is presented as one of the two women whose beauty could be compared with that of Guinevere: "Et l'autre fu fille au roi mehaignié, ce fu li rois Pellés qui fu peres Perlesvax, a celui qui vit apertement les granz mervoilles del Graal et acompli lo Siege Perilleus de la Table Reonde et mena a fin les aventures del Reiaume Perilleus Aventureus, ce fu li regnes de Logres. Cele fu sa suer, si fu de si grant biauté que nus des contes ne dit que nule qui a son tens fust se poïst de biauté a li apareillier, si avoit non Amide en sornon et an son droit non Heliabel" *(PL,* p. 33). The reference is clearly in conflict with the *Queste*, where Galahad achieves the adventure, and with the *Perlevaus*, but would fit in general terms in the context of Chrétien de Troyes and Robert de Boron. See *PL*, II, 89–90; Kennedy, *Lancelot and the Grail*, pp. 150–1.

31. *LM*, xxxvii, 29.

32. *PL*, p. 194.

33. *LM*, xxxvii, 29.

34. *Ibid.*, lxv, 25.

35. *Ibid.*, lxv, 32.

36. *PL*, p. 16.

37. *LM*, lxxxiii, 8.

38. *Ibid.*, lxxxiii, 12.

39. *Ibid.*, lxvi, 4–8.

40. *Ibid.*, lxxviii, 58.

41. *Perl*, p. 109.
42. *PL*, pp. 298, 406.
43. *Ibid.*, p. 571; *LM*, lxxxiv, 69–73, and ci, 1–11.
44. *Q*, pp. 5–6.
45. *MA*, pp. 2–3.

CHAPTER 9

Seeing the Grail
Prolegomena to a Study of Grail Imagery in Arthurian Manuscripts

ALISON STONES

> *Or as veu ce que tu as tant desirré aveoir, et ce*
> *que tu as convoitié*[1]

The Quest for the Holy Grail is one of several significant themes in the courtly culture of the Middle Ages, a search for purity and perfection, for personal fulfillment and collective aspiration, in which only a chosen few of King Arthur's knights will succeed.[2] The Grail itself—a potent, mysterious, life-giving object, providing food, healing the wounded, bestowing sight, both physically and metaphorically, on the deserving few, yet blinding the unworthy—is never fully described in the texts that transmit its legends. Rather, it is reified by a word or phrase evoking some kind of receptacle: "vessel," in the *Perceval* of Chrétien de Troyes (ca. 1175), the verse *Estoire* of Robert de Boron, and the prose *Joseph* (Modena version), "vessel" or "escuelle" in the prose *Lancelot-Graal* (early thirteenth century), or something more elemental, like the stone of Wolfram von Eschenbach's *Parzival* (ca. 1200–1210).[3] Its pictorial presence in the illuminated manuscripts that transmit its legends is equally spare. Often it is excluded altogether in otherwise fully illustrated manuscripts. When it is depicted, its shape and degree of visibility follow several different patterns, whose other cultural referents offer visual clues beyond the words of the text as to how the Grail was perceived by those makers and patrons who felt its legends were worth copying and illustrating, selling and buying, reading, looking at, and owning, between the thirteenth and sixteenth centuries.

By far the greatest number of Grail depictions occur in the manuscripts of the *Lancelot-Graal* or Vulgate Cycle of Arthurian romances in French prose.[4] Composed soon after the turn of the thirteenth century, this five-part cyclical romance includes two branches, the *Estoire* and the

Queste del Saint Graal, in which the early history of the Grail and its quest
by King Arthur's knights are the primary focus. Although these were not
the first romances to emphasize the Grail in their texts, the illustrations devised to show it are particularly significant in the development of illustrated vernacular manuscripts: illustrated copies of the *Lancelot-Graal*
cycle emerge early (by ca. 1220),[5] last late (to the end of the fifteenth century),[6] and survive in very large numbers (close to 200 copies),[7] and their
chronological and geographical distribution can be plotted with a fair degree of accuracy. By contrast, there is only a single Grail depiction in surviving copies of the *Perceval* of Chrétien de Troyes (composed ca.
1189)—Paris, BNF fr. 12577, f. 18v—although the late thirteenth- and
early-fourteenth-century copies of the Continuations added by later writers
include more Grail depictions.[8] Illustrated copies of Wolfram's *Parzival*
(composed ca. 1200–1210) are few, and those that have survived rarely
show the Grail.[9] Robert de Boron's verse Grail romance (ca. 1200) is unillustrated.[10] The special prose version in Modena has historiated initials,
but includes no depiction of the Grail.[11] The Spanish and Galician/Por-
tuguese Arthurian romances are also unillustrated, while texts in French
copied in Spanish are rare, and do not include the Grail. Arthurian texts in
English or made in England are sparsely illustrated and have no Grail illustration. In Italy the illustrative Arthurian tradition occurs predominantly in
copies of romances in French—with the important exception of the *Tavola
Ritonda*, a special case that I consider below. The Perceval casket in ivory
similarly lacks depictions of the Grail.[12] Although there are illustrated
copies of *Peredur, Perlesvaus, Tristan*, and *Palamède*, they do not, to the
best of my knowledge, depict the Grail. The *Lancelot-Graal* cycle, then,
provides the corpus of Grail illustrations discussed here.

As text scholars and liturgists have long recognized, the legends of
the Grail related in the *Estoire* and the *Queste* are permeated with Christian Eucharistic associations, which are particularly explicit in the Grail
liturgies described at the beginning of the *Estoire* and at the end of the
Queste. Christian liturgical and devotional practices relating to the transubstantiation of the Eucharistic elements—especially the elevation, veneration, and reservation of the Host,[13] and the celebration of Eucharistic
miracles, including the cult of the Holy Blood—inform the texts' descriptions of how the Grail is perceived by the few knights who are privileged
to see it. References to transubstantiation in the Fourth Lateran Council of
1215, for instance, show that such liturgical and devotional practices as
these were already widespread,[14] while the reservation of the Eucharist
and the celebration of the feast of Corpus Christi emerged in the second
half of the thirteenth century and became standard by the early fourteenth.

Not surprisingly, liturgical vessels and containers for the celebration of the Mass and for the veneration and reservation of the Eucharistic elements are significant models for the depiction of the Grail. But they are not the only models. We shall see that Grail depictions often reflect Old Testament imagery instead of or as well as Eucharistic models, while concerns about the visibility of other sacred objects, especially the relics of saints and the relics of the Passion of Christ, also bear on the question of whether, and how, the Grail was revealed or concealed. Similarly, the depiction of liturgical vessels, in pictures of the Mass or as symbols in other contexts—especially at the Crucifixion of Christ—may be additional referents that inform the meaning of the shapes chosen to illustrate the Grail. We shall also see that this Holy Vessel is treated in a variety of ways in copies produced by the same craftsmen.

I outline here the major appearances of the Grail as they were depicted in *Estoire* and *Queste* manuscripts, in the order of the texts, and comment briefly on some of the major variants in the treatment of the Grail itself and on some of the chief pictorial sources and related receptacles that may have informed the depictions. At the end of this chapter, I attach a working list of the illustrated *Estoire* and *Queste* manuscripts as a preliminary step towards a comprehensive study of Grail illustration, which I reserve for more extensive treatment elsewhere. Limitations of space allow me to reproduce only a small selection of the illustrations I discuss here.

Just how the cycles of pictures in the *Lancelot-Graal* were selected,[15] how the individual scenes were treated, what each manuscript tells us about its patrons and makers, how these manuscripts relate to what else the patrons owned and the makers made, are questions that are just beginning to be investigated in detail.[16] Elsewhere I have used selected subjects in *Lancelot-Graal* cycle manuscripts, and a few particular copies of that version, to suggest some approaches to these questions.[17] Here I lay the basis for a comparative study of the iconography of the Grail as a means to assess some medieval attitudes toward this symbol whose quest held so high a place in the medieval—and the modern—imagination.[18]

THE GRAIL DEPICTED IN THE *ESTOIRE*

Christ and the Hermit

The opening scene in the *Estoire* usually shows Christ appearing to the hermit, handing him the book that relates the story of the Grail. Off to one side there is often an altar with a chalice—sometimes draped with a cloth, at other times undraped—upon it. Nothing suggests directly that this chalice *is* the Grail, since it is only after the hermit has opened the book that the Grail appears in the story. Furthermore, given the number of times in the Vulgate Cycle that visits to hermits by penitent knights include confession, it is most probable that the hermit himself, here and elsewhere, was also a priest, making the presence of a Eucharistic chalice upon an altar a commonplace. But it is also the case that the Grail is often given the shape of a chalice or goblet-shaped vessel, and so the depiction of this Eucharistic chalice could also be read as a visual anticipation of the Grail, whose story will follow.

It is in the form described above that Christ's appearance to the hermit is treated in the badly rubbed historiated initial that opens the text in

Fig. 9.1. Rennes 255(148), f. 1 (photo: Alison Stones)

the earliest extant copy, Rennes 255, made in Parisian royal circles ca. 1220 (Fig. 9.1), and a similar version of this subject can still be found in the mid-fourteenth-century copy written by Jean Deloles of Hainaut (?) in 1357, Yale 227 (Fig. 9.2).[19] During the intervening 125 or so years, *Estoire* manuscripts show many variants on this subject, for instance, whether there is one scene or more, whether the chalice is present or not, and whether or not it is veiled with a cloth or corporal, whether the hermit is asleep in bed, sitting up, or kneeling in prayer, and whether the divine messenger is Christ or an angel.

An alternative opening illustration is simply an image of the Trinity by itself. One of the very earliest manuscripts, Paris, BNF fr. 748, f. 1, shows a "B" initial with what may be a multi-Person Trinity at the top, and Christ blessing and holding an orb below, while BNF fr. 95 shows a Throne of Mercy (Gnadenstuhl) type of Trinity, where God the Father holds the crucified Christ on the cross, with the Dove between.[20] Occasionally both subjects are combined, so that in BNF fr. 749, f. 1, there is a Two-Persons and Dove Trinity as well as Christ appearing to the hermit (Fig. 9.3) and in Brussels, BR 9246, f. 2,[21] the book is flown in by the Holy Ghost as dove, watched from the sky by God the Father and God the Son. The purpose of Christ's appearance to the hermit is to dispel his fears about the mystery of the Trinity, and there is more explanation and discussion of the Trinity

Fig. 9.2. New Haven, Yale University, Beinecke Library 227, f. 12 (photo: Alison Stones). (See insert for greater detail.)

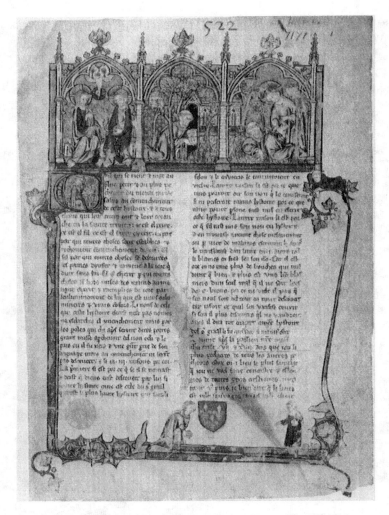

**Fig. 9.3. Paris, Bibliothèque Nationale de France, fr. 749, f. 1
(photo: Bibliothèque Nationale de France)**

farther on in the text as well, so the depiction of a Trinity image here, rather
than a scene of Christ and the hermit, has considerable textual justification.[22] The subject would have been familiar to artists from a variety of
liturgical contexts, such as the opening of the canon of the Mass in Missals,
as the illustration of Psalm 109, "Dixit Dominus" ("The Lord said unto my
Lord"),[23] or at the opening of the hours of the Holy Ghost;[24] for a medieval

audience, a Trinity image in the *Estoire* would have resonated with allusions to these liturgical and devotional contexts—and perhaps vice-versa.

The Grail at the Crucifixion

The story goes on to relate how, after the Crucifixion, Joseph of Arimathea visited the room in which Christ celebrated the Last Supper with the disciples[25] and took the vessel Christ used, the "escuelle,"[26] in order to collect Christ's blood in it at the Entombment. Often, what is depicted here in *Estoire* manuscripts is a standard Crucifixion, without Joseph, no doubt because the Crucifixion is by far the commonest subject of the Passion of Christ in art, and medieval artists would certainly have been called upon to depict it. It is also a subject in which, as early as the late ninth century, a vessel was often depicted at the foot of the cross, in which the blood of Christ could fall.[27]

Nothing is said in the *Estoire* of Joseph collecting the blood of Christ at the Crucifixion itself, although his presence at it, narrated in the Gospels, is confirmed in *Estoire*. It is surprising, then, that two groups of manuscripts show him holding the Grail at the cross: the Additional, Royal and Amsterdam group of ca. 1315, and the two early-fifteenth-century manuscripts sold in Paris by Jacques Raponde, one of which was owned by Jean de Berry and inherited by Jacques d'Armagnac. In the

Fig. 9.4. Amsterdam, Bibliotheca Philosophica Hermetica 1, f. 6v (photo: Alison Stones). (See insert for greater detail.)

copy now in Amsterdam (Fig. 9.4), Joseph is shown seated on the ground at the foot of the cross, holding the "escuelle," with Mary and John also present. The other two early-fourteenth-century copies show a similar depiction, including Joseph holding the "escuelle," and the two thieves as well as Mary and John (Add. 10292, f. 3v and Royal 14. E. III, f. 7). The fifteenth-century books show the Grail as a chalice.

The shallow bowl used by Joseph in the Add./Roy./Amsterdam group corresponds in shape to the "escuelle" of the *Estoire* text, but is a shape that carries other resonances as well. A shallow bowl is also the vessel depicted in Old Testament illustration for collecting the blood of sacrificial animals, or other hallowed liquid, like the water Moses produced by striking the rock.[28] Pertinent parallels for the "escuelle" in Old Testament imagery produced by the artists of Add./Roy./Amsterdam/Ryl./Douce have not so far come to light, despite the prolific artistic output of these illuminators,[29] but this vessel can be found in biblical illustration of the second quarter of the thirteenth century, in manuscripts stylistically related to the Rennes *Estoire*. Made ca. 1220, this is the copy that contains the earliest depiction of a Grail whose interpretation is certain.[30] The Rennes manuscript lacks an image of Joseph at the Crucifixion, and so I return to it below, in my discussion of Josephe's journey to Norgales, the one place in the illustrations of the Rennes manuscript where the Grail makes an appearance.

In the other illustrated manuscripts that include Joseph at the Crucifixion, the vessel he holds is shown as a chalice. The versions in Paris, Ars. 3480, f. 483, and BNF fr. 120, f. 520, both made in Paris soon after 1400 (the latter owned by Jean de Berry), show a simpler Crucifixion with Mary and Joseph, and Joseph of Arimathea as a much smaller figure robed in a long mantle kneeling on the left, a chalice in his outstretched hands. The Crucifixion is not depicted in Jacques d'Armagnac's copy of *Estoire* of ca. 1475 (BNF fr. 113), but it is interesting to note that the opening miniature of the *Queste* part of the same set of volumes (BNF fr. 116, f. 607) is a Crucifixion where five angels catch the blood of Christ in chalices, following a model common in crucifixion iconography, and Joseph is not present.

The Entombment

Only occasionally is Joseph shown actually collecting the blood of Christ at the Entombment, and in the "escuelle." Both the Bonn manuscript made in 1285 and the closely related and possibly earlier manuscript, Paris, BNF fr. 19162, f. 6[31] include this as the final scene in the composite arrangement of images that opens the *Estoire*—in Bonn 526 the arrangement is six square miniatures grouped two deep across the three columns of the text and in BNF fr. 19162 there are three miniatures arranged vertically in the first of two columns and one at the top of the second column. To my knowledge, the only other manuscript to include this motif is the set made for Jacques d'Armagnac, Paris, BNF fr. 113, f. 7, ca. 1475, where the Grail is a flat, paten-like receptacle (Fig. 9.5).[32]

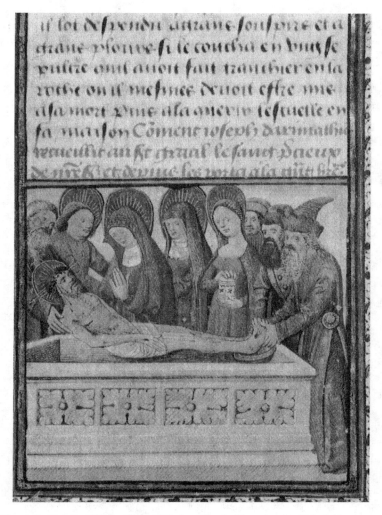

Fig. 9.5. Paris, Bibliothèque Nationale de France, fr. 113, f. 7 (photo: Bibliothèque Nationale de France)

Fig. 9.6. Paris, Bibliothèque Nationale de France, fr. 344, f. 26 (photo: Bibliothèque Nationale de France). (See insert for greater detail.)

The Ark

Joseph builds a wooden ark to house the Grail.[33] Representations of the ark in *Estoire* manuscripts are again rare, and there are interesting links between the various depictions of the Grail-ark in *Estoire* and the ark of the Covenant in Old Testament iconography, of which north French and Flemish manuscripts offer some interesting depictions in the second half of the thirteenth century.[34] In BNF fr. 344, f. 11v (made in Lorraine, ca. 1300) it is shown as a pink chest on four legs, with a lock, its contents not revealed until later (f. 26) when Joseph's son, Josephe, outside the ark, shows King Eualach and Queen Sarracinte what is within—a gold "escuelle" and three gold nails (Fig. 9.6).[35] In the Le Mans manuscript, Josephe, at Christ's invitation, enters the ark and sees Christ Himself surrounded by five angels: in the image, the structure of the ark is dispensed with, and we see Josephe surrounded by what he sees. The text says the angels hold three bleeding nails, a bleeding Lance, a red cloth, a bloody sponge held upright, and a bleeding scourge, and describes these objects as "les ames par coi li gugieres qui chi est, uainqui la mort et destruist" ("the arms with which the judge of the world conquered and destroyed death").[36] The illustration shows four angels, not five, and only the cross (not mentioned in the Le Mans text version), nails, and Lance are shown, while a man on horseback holding a white shield and raising his sword against a snail provides an inverted play on the notion of "arms."[37] Even so, as I have noted elsewhere,[38] both text and picture represent an extremely early[39] version of the "arma Christi," the devotional image based on emblematically depicted Instruments of the Passion that only in the early fourteenth century came to be widespread, often with accompanying prayers, as a focus for private prayer and meditation.[40] A different, in some ways simpler, view of the ark and its contents is shown in BNF fr. 105, f. 19 (a Parisian product of the 1320s–40s),[41] where Josephe stands outside and looks into the ark, here painted gold and resting on silver (or tin) legs, seeing Christ crucified flanked by two seraphim inside it (Fig. 9.7).

We shall see that the exterior/interior views in BNF fr. 344 and 105 are significant in relation to other ways artists found to screen the Grail from view, while the more fully developed vision of the interior shown in the Le Mans manuscript also finds echoes in the depiction of the liturgy in other manuscripts. The screen functions as a protection for the viewer as well as for the Holy Vessel. Looking into the ark is perilous. Nascien is so bold as to try to see what is in the Holy Vessel itself, having removed the "platine" which covered it—and is blinded.[42] An angel restores his sight

Fig. 9.7. Paris, Bibliothèque Nationale de France, fr. 105, f. 19 (photo: Bibliothèque Nationale de France)

by anointing his eyes with blood, collected in a "boiste" (box), from the Holy Lance.[43] The blinding, so far as I know, is not included in the visual tradition, and the curing is also rare. The Bonn manuscript, however, includes the latter (f. 16v), showing the angel's "boiste" as a round container with a round finial on the lid; the presence of the Grail, shown as a chalice, in the top right corner of the miniature behind Nascien serves as a reminder of what caused his blindness in the first place (Fig. 9.8).

Fig. 9.8. Bonn, Universitätsbibliothek 526, f. 16v (photo: Alison Stones)

The Grail Liturgy

The liturgy of the Grail follows, celebrated at great length in the text by Josephe, son of Joseph of Arimathea and first Christian bishop, according to the *Estoire*. Particularly notable about the text of *Estoire,* composed at least as early as ca. 1220 (because of the likely date of Rennes 255 made at about that time), is the extremely detailed description of the elevation and transubstantiation, including explicit mention of the "cors autre tel comme d'un enfant" ("actual body like that of a child") that Josephe finds in his hands, and that Christ orders him to tear apart.[44] As we shall see, this is also a feature of the Grail liturgy in the *Queste*, probably composed at about the same time or shortly before the *Estoire*, and depictions of the transubstantiation in *Queste* illustration are considerably more literal than those that accompany the Grail liturgy in *Estoire*.

At the time of the composition of these texts, the elevation of the Host during the Mass was a relatively recent phenomenon, decreed at the synod of Paris between 1205 and 1208, under Bishop Eudes de Sully, and surrounded by considerable debate about the precise moment of transubstantiation in relation to the two elements of the Eucharist.[45] Debate about transubstantiation as such was already under way very much earlier, as shown in the opposing positions taken by Berengar of Tours (d. 1088), in favor of the symbolic presence of Christ, and Lanfranc of Bec, advocate of the real presence, whose view prevailed.[46] The illustrations in an eleventh-century copy of the Life of St. Aubin of Angers (a text composed in the Merovingian period), show an early depiction of a Eucharistic miracle. The Life includes scenes where the saint is compelled to bless unconsecrated wafers (*eulogia*) that are to be given to an excommunicate, who then dies at the sight of the objects. The illustrator has shown a transformation that goes beyond the text, to reflect the contemporary Eucharistic debate, by inscribing the eulogia with the letters IHS and XPC, the Name of Christ, transforming them thereby into transubstantiated Hosts.[47] We shall see that the Host at the Grail liturgy in *Estoire* manuscripts is sometimes similarly inscribed, carrying similar liturgical connotations.

The appearance of Christ as a Child in the Host, described unambiguously in both *Estoire* and *Queste* liturgies, also has parallels in earlier accounts of Eucharistic miracles and in their depiction. Among the earliest accounts is the one given by Guibert de Nogent (d. 1124),[48] and among the earliest depictions is a miracle witnessed by St. Edward the Confessor.[49] A generation later, growing devotion to the Eucharist was marked by the founding of a feast of Corpus Christi in the diocese of

Liège in 1246. By the early fourteenth century, the reservation of the Eucharist had become a general practice and Corpus Christi had become a universal feast, and by 1337-1339, the Bolsena miracle of the Bleeding Host, and the commissioning of the Corpus Christi liturgy (once attributed to Thomas Aquinas) had been depicted in a series of eight scenes on the reliquary made by Ugolino di Vieri in 1337–1338 to house the relic of the corporal (cloth) on which the Host bled;[50] and three explicit renderings of the transubstantiation, also by Ugolino, had been painted on the walls of the reliquary chapel.[51] The Host is shown as Christ in the form of a small naked boy, holding (in two of the three images) a cross staff and facing frontally, visible to viewers both within the scene and outside it, unlike the side-on view presented in the Life of St. Edward, which limits the perception of the event to those in the composition who witness it. Both the *Estoire* and the *Queste* must be read against this background, which is also significant in relation to the illustrations devised for them.[52] We shall see that illustrations of the Grail and the liturgy of the Grail in *Queste* manuscripts sometimes include a depiction of transubstantiation that is just as explicit as it is in the Life of St. Edward and in Orvieto, and there are even a few instances where, conversely, aspects of Grail iconography based on the *Estoire* or the *Queste* seem to find reflection in devotional or liturgical depictions of the Last Supper and the Mass.[53]

Each of the manuscripts that depict the Grail liturgy in *Estoire*—and only a few of them do—shows a slightly different aspect of the events described, and emphasizes a position in relation to the elevation and transubstantiation to a greater or lesser degree. They are perhaps rather reticent by comparison with the Life of St. Edward and the Bolsena reliquary and frescoes, but at least one illustration datable in the middle of the thirteenth century clearly suggests a link between the growing cult of the Eucharist and the Grail, and by the end of the century, several ways of depicting the Grail liturgy had been developed.

Probably the earliest representation—since the earliest surviving manuscript, Rennes 255, does not illustrate the liturgy, or the ark, at all—is the small historiated initial made perhaps in Paris about 1250, in UCB Berkeley 106, f. 126, where Josephe stands before an altar on which is a draped chalice. A golden Host hovers in midair, and the head of God looks down from a cloud above. This is a depiction that certainly suggests the veneration of the Eucharist, and perhaps alludes also to its reservation—neither of which is depicted in liturgical illustration at a comparable date. But not all *Estoire* depictions herald these new trends in contemporary liturgical practice. Much more commonplace is the illustration in BNF fr. 770, f. 19v (made on the Artois-Flanders border, ca. 1280), which simply depicts an altar with a chalice on it and a group of figures kneeling before it. But by the end of the century, *Estoire* illustration shows several parallels with the iconography of transubstantiation. In BNF fr. 95, f. 18 (made in the diocese of Thérouanne, ca. 1290) the Grail liturgy illustration is similar to that of BNF fr. 770, but what is shown is the moment of the elevation of the Host, with Josephe bareheaded and his followers kneeling on the ground behind,[54] a depiction similar to what is commonly shown at the beginning of the canon of the Mass in missals.[55] Josephe elevates a Eucharistic wafer, not the human figure, but the Host is inscribed with the letters IHS of the Name of Jesus, and so contains a cryptographic reference to the transubstantiation. On the altar is the partly veiled Grail, shown as a chalice. The right-hand part of the opening miniature of *Estoire* in Yale 227 (Fig. 9.2), is similar: Josephe, in the presence of three kneeling knights, celebrates Mass at an altar on which are a draped chalice and a large Eucharistic Host with a cross between dot motifs inscribed on it. But at the place in the text where the liturgy is described, there is no corresponding illustration.

The most extensive pictorial treatment of Josephe's liturgy in the *Estoire* occurs in the Amsterdam and Royal copies, both made in Flanders by the same craftsmen ca. 1316.[56] Both manuscripts include two scenes of Josephe's liturgy, but the third manuscript made by this team, Add. 10292, omits illustrations of the liturgy altogether. The first image in Amsterdam, f. 18, shows Josephe in the ark, robed as a bishop, accompanied by an angel holding a silver ewer and two more angels kneeling to the left of the ark, one holding an incense-boat and swinging a thurible. As his father Joseph looks into the ark, shown as a Gothic church,[57] he sees a small altar, covered with a white cloth and a red cloth of "samit" (special fabric, of uncertain translation, omitted in the miniature); on the altar are three bleeding nails and the top of a bleeding Lance (held, in the text, by hands which are omitted here),[58] a silver chalicelike vessel on a stem with a lid, mostly covered by a cloth painted red in the miniature but described as white in the text, and partially veiled from our sight but revealed to Joseph; and the silver bowl-shaped "escuelle"—the Grail. The presence of both the "escuelle" of the text and also a ciborium suggests a conflation of sacred objects to include both what is called for in the text and what was familiar from contemporary liturgical practice; at the same time this image is reminiscent of the depiction of Josephe in the ark as shown in the Le Mans manuscript. The Royal 14. E. III version is

similar but much simpler in treatment, omitting the elaborate architectural ark, reducing the censing angels to two busts in the top corners, also
omitting the hands holding candles and the Lance and nails; but it does
include a red cross held by a hand above the altar (Fig. 9.9), and so is not
merely a simplification of the Amsterdam image.

**Fig. 9.9. London, British Library, Royal 14. E. III, f. 15v (photo:
British Library)**

The hands holding the instruments of the Passion (the three nails and Lance) are rarely shown in *Estoire* illustration: one isolated example occurs in a later manuscript, BNF fr. 113, f. 18v, one of those made for Jacques d'Armagnac. There, the hands holding cross and candle emerge from the reredos behind the altar, on which rest the three nails and the tip of the Lance, a round ciboriumlike vessel, and a flat, dishlike paten. Is the Grail the ciborium or the paten? The more elaborate vessel is undoubtedly the ciborium, yet in the rare depiction of the collecting of Christ's blood at the Entombment found earlier in this manuscript, Joseph used a shallow dish that is remarkably similar to the paten shown on this altar. So this time the proliferation of sacred vessels is not simply based on the multiple vessels of the Eucharist, but also links back to Joseph's pious act earlier in the story. Josephe, wearing civilian clothes and bareheaded, kneels, alone, before the altar; back in the doorway behind him stand four wingless angels, one of whom holds a situla (bucket) and aspergillum (holy-water sprinkler), while another holds a processional cross. In BNF fr. 113, f. 18v, both picture and rubric focus on Josephe contemplating the Grail in a chapel "C(i) iosephez estoit devant le saint Graal a genoulx" ("Here Josephe knelt before the Grail"). Four angels stand behind him in the doorway, one of whom holds a situla and aspergillum; and on f. 21v, three angels administer the communion to Joseph and his company.[59]

The second miniature in Amsterdam, BPH 1, on f. 21, shows Christ and Josephe administering the sacrament—a Eucharistic Host, to the kneeling assembly. Although Christ is present in the text, and is described as wearing priestly robes, the communion is administered, in the text, by Josephe alone.[60] Undoubtedly Christ's actions as shown in this image can be explained by reference to the Grail liturgy and its illustrations in the *Queste*, in which it is Christ, not Josephe, who distributes the Host to the knights, as I show below; but the addition of Christ here is all the more interesting as none of these three manuscripts includes an illustration to the liturgy in the *Queste*.[61] The Royal 14. E. III version is simpler, showing the altar draped with a cloth on which are a gold chalice and wafers; Christ holds the Grail, shown as a gold bowl-shaped vessel, and blesses a kneeling man, probably Joseph, while Josephe, robed as bishop, administers the Host to the rest of the assembly.

Josephe's Journey to Norgales

The Grail is subsequently taken by Josephe to Norgales, a journey miraculously accomplished on the hem of his garment.[62] It is in this context, surprisingly, that the earliest depiction of the Grail is found, in the Rennes mansucript, made probably in Paris, ca. 1220.[63] The journey is simply depicted in Rennes 255, where Josephe, wearing a round-crowned skullcap-style Jewish hat rather than a mitre, carries the silver (?) "escuelle" in his hands (no depiction of the hem of the garment is included).[64] In BNF fr. 749, f. 98, the silver "escuelle" has been endowed with a gold cover with a round finial on the top.[65] In BNF fr. 344, f. 65v (Fig. 9.10), the Grail is borne in procession, much like the ark of the covenant (a link with the ark shown earlier in BNF fr. 344 and a few other manuscripts), or a reliquary, and even more like a monstrance (a vessel for the display of the consecrated Host), since a circle has been lightly sketched within the tabernacle-like shrine that is carried on rods on the shoulders of two men. The earliest surviving example (second quarter of the thirteenth century?) of a monstrance for the reservation of the Eucharist is the one preserved in the treasury of the church of Notre-Dame at St.-Omer, from the Cistercian abbey of Clairmarais near St.-Omer (diocese of Thérouanne). It is a vessel on a stem in which the Eucharistic element could presumably be seen through the horizontally disposed openings around the perimeter.[66] But, as with the "Arma Christi," the depiction of a Corpus Christi procession with the Host in a monstrance would seem not to appear in liturgical manuscripts for another generation or so.[67] The version of Josephe's miraculous journey shown in Amsterdam BPH 1 reverts to the depiction of the Grail found

Fig. 9.10. Paris, Bibliothèque Nationale de France, fr. 344, f. 65v (photo: Bibliothèque Nationale de France)

elsewhere in this manuscript, and shows Josephe, robed as a bishop, carrying the "escuelle," and the assembled company traveling on the hem of Josephe's alb; this is also included in mirror image in Add. 10292. In Royal 14 E III (f. 66v), the journey is depicted, showing Joseph holding the alb on which stand the traveling figures, but no Grail is shown.

The Grail Transmitted by Josephe to Alain

Thereafter, shown again as the "escuelle," the Grail is handed by the dying Josephe to his follower Alain.[68] What Josephe hands to Alain in BNF fr. 344, f. 78v, is a veiled vessel with a cross on top of the veil and, as in the procession to Norgales, a circle lightly drawn on the veil, suggesting again the analogy between the Grail and a monstrance for the display of the Host (Fig. 9.11).[69] BNF fr. 770, f. 117v, Amsterdam BPH 1, i, f. 114v, and BNF fr. 105, f. 122,[70] show the Grail again as the "escuelle," whereas in Royal 14. E. III, and Add. 10292, f. 73, it has become a covered ciborium with a stem, painted entirely in gold, as also in Yale 227. In Le Mans 354, this might be the episode represented as the last of

Fig. 9.11. Paris, Bibliothèque Nationale de France, fr. 344, f. 78v (photo: Bibliothèque Nationale de France)

the scenes in the composite opening miniature on f. 1, although the curious hand gesture of the standing figure holding the "escuelle" and the presence of a companion suggests that this is a curing scene rather than the transmission of the Grail, and I return to it below. One variation on the transmission theme occurs in BNF fr. 749, where it is the shield *argent a cross gules*,[71] rather than the Grail, which is handed by Josephe to his followers.

King Alphasem

The final episodes in *Estoire* include miraculous acts performed by the Grail concerning King Alphasem: the cure of his leprosy, effected by the Grail after his baptism, and his wounding in the groin, as punishment for having presumed to sleep in the Grail Castle.[72] Neither is commonly illustrated, ceding place rather to concluding incidents about the tomb of King Lancelot, ancestor of King Arthur's knight of the same name,[73] or Nascien and King Mordrain at Josephe's tomb,[74] or Celidoine defeating his enemies,[75] or Celidoine and his son bidding farewell to Nascien.[76] None of these other episodes involve the Grail.

A few exceptional miniatures do depict the cure of King Alphasem or his wounding: Bonn 526, Royal 14. E. III, and Add. 10292 all combine the baptism and cure of the king into a single scene, in which the Grail is present, shown in Bonn as a chalice (without an accompanying cross) and in Royal and Add. as a covered ciborium. The wounding alone is shown in Amsterdam BPH 1,[77] where a cleric stands by the king's bed, wearing a maroon cope over his alb, holding in his left hand the Grail—shown as the usual silver bowl—and in the other a Lance; in the corresponding miniature in Add. 10292, f. 74, a bearded man wearing a hooded robe and painted orange (to represent flames), pierces the king through the bedclothes with a spear, but the Grail is not present,[78] while in BNF fr. 113, f. 113v, an angel hovers above the wounding scene, holding the Grail.[79] Neither picture quite corresponds to the text, where the Grail has disappeared before the appearance of "vns hons ausi comme tous enflammes" ("a man as if all in flames") who does the wounding, and there is nothing in the text that justifies the representation of this figure as a cleric. The previous scene in BNF fr. 113, on f. 112v, shows King Alphasem and his followers standing before Alain, having been cured, without the Grail depicted. One further image might be interpreted as showing a combination of the Grail's appearance and the wounding, again not quite justified by the text: in Le Mans 354, f. 1, an uncrowned figure in bed is admonished by two men who stand behind the bed raising accusing index fingers at him; one of them holds the Grail, shown as a bowl, and the other, taller, is clad in an orange tunic, corresponding somewhat to the "hons tout enflammes" of the text. An alternative interpretation, proposed above, is the transmission of the Grail from the dying Josephe to Alain.

It is worth noting the contrast between the paucity of illustrations of the healing of King Alphasem in the manuscript tradition as a whole, and the prominence accorded it in popular twentieth-century studies of Arthurian legend, such as the much-read *Ritual to Romance* by Jessie L. Weston.[80] The healing episode was allusively drawn upon by T. S. Eliot in *The Waste Land*, as his notes to the poem indicate.[81] Harvard's copy of the 1920 edition of Weston's book is inscribed by T.S. Eliot: "This is the copy I had before writing The Waste Land. T.S.E."[82] We shall see that the parallel event in the *Queste*, the curing of the Roi Mehaignié, enjoyed an equally spare iconographic tradition.

THE GRAIL IN *QUESTE* MANUSCRIPTS

In the *Queste del saint Graal*, depictions of the Grail are in general even less numerous than they are in the illustrations of the *Estoire*. They occur in just a few key scenes, shown in a small selection of otherwise quite fully illustrated manuscripts.

The Appearance of the Grail at Arthur's Court

Towards the beginning of the *Queste*, the Grail makes its first appearance before King Arthur and his knights as they sit at table. Emitting marvelous odors, it miraculously refreshes them with whatever meat ("del tel viande") each knight desires.[83] Five manuscripts depict this episode, with differences in pictorial emphasis. In the two versions commissioned by Jacques d'Armagnac, BNF fr. 112, vol. II, f. 5 (ca. 1470), and BNF fr. 116, f. 610v (ca. 1475), Arthur and the knights sit at the Round Table (shown as annular), contemplating the Grail, which appears in the open circular space at the center of the table. Shown as a ciborium, it is surrounded by rays of light and supported by two angels; this is also how the scene is shown in BNF fr. 120, f. 524.[84] In the Rylands manuscript and in the closely related copy Royal 14. E. III (ca. 1315), Queen Guinevere is also present,[85] sitting with King Arthur and his knights behind a rectangular table, in front of which is the Grail, painted gold and shaped like a ciborium with a closed lid. It is borne by a figure who stands on the near side of the table, a monk/cleric who is encircled by a wavy cloud motif—

so that he is visible to us, but not to Arthur and his court, while the Grail
that he holds out before the assembled company lies beyond the perimeter of the cloud. This paradox of visibility and invisibility is suggested by
the text, "mes il n'i ot onques nul qui poïst veoir qui le portoit" ("but
there was not a soul who could see who carried it")[86] and the cloud motif
also refers back visually to the opening scenes in *Estoire* where, in these
two manuscripts and in the related Add. 10292, Christ hands the book to
the hermit. Curiously, however, this Grail-scene at the beginning of the
Queste is omitted in Add. 10294.[87] The other book that shows it is the
one made in 1319 in Avignon, Florence, Laur. Ash.121, f. 6 (Fig. 9.12),[88]
where the Grail, without a Grail-bearer, and depicted as a veiled chalice,
is poised on a rod (the Holy Lance?) high above the heads of the diners,
who (without Queen Guinevere) sit behind a rectangular table. The elevated placing of the Grail here may allude to another important liturgical
practice concerning the Eucharist that can be traced to the early thirteenth century—that of its reservation (as opposed to its open display in
a monstrance), which was accomplished by suspending the ciborium
containing the Host above the altar by means of pulleys.[89]

**Fig. 9.12. Florence, Biblioteca Mediceo-Laurenziana, Ash. 121(48),
f. 6 (photo: Alison Stones)**

Lancelot Sleeps While a Wounded Knight Is Cured by the Grail

Lancelot, because of his sin of adultery, is denied entry to the Grail chapel and sleeps outside by a cross, while a wounded knight is cured by the Grail.[90] This episode is a second instance where a Grail-scene is depicted (by two different painters) in Royal 14. E. III and Rylands, but omitted altogether in the related manuscript, Add. 10294.[91] The setting of this miraculous cure, in both text and pictures, is described and depicted in these two manuscripts in great detail. On the left is the chapel, from which the six-branch candlestick with lighted candles, the silver Grail Table, and the Grail itself (shown as a gold ciborium) have emerged into the open air. The wounded knight (wearing a knotted headscarf in Ryl) kisses the altar. In the background is his litter, drawn by two horses. Lancelot is shown asleep. In the illustration in BNF fr. 342 (whose text was copied a generation earlier, in 1274, by a female scribe),[92] the Grail itself is omitted altogether,[93] whereas in Bonn 526 (written in 1286), it is given particular visual emphasis by being shown as a chalice with a cross inside, hovering in midair. Since the scribe of the Bonn manuscript, Arnulphus de Kayo, tells us in his colophon that he was in Amiens at the time of writing ("qui est ambianis," as though he were not normally there), it is interesting to note the presence of a closely similar chalice with cross in it, shown on a shield held by the virtue "Faith" among the virtues carved on the west façade of the Cathedral of Amiens.[94] In other ways, however, as I have shown elsewhere, the style of Bonn 526 has more to do with manuscripts associated with Thérouanne or Cambrai than it does with Amiens books.[95] The chalice-with-cross motif can occasionally be found elsewhere, as in the early twelfth-century psalter made in England for the anchorite Christine of Markyate and commonly known as the St. Albans Psalter,[96] or, ca. 1250, on the cover of the Sainte-Chapelle Gospels, Paris, BNF lat. 17326, where the chalice and cross, placed on the right of Christ, symbolize Ecclesia, a parallel for the Tablets of the Law on His left.[97] Other examples are rare.[98]

This episode is also prominent in the special version made in Lombardy, ca. 1380, BNF fr. 343, f. 18, where Lancelot sits off to the left, separated from the healed knight by the litter, placed in the center of the composition, while the knight, now cured, kneels on the right in the chapel where the Grail is depicted on the altar.[99] The Grail is shown as a gold chalice with a round cup and a polygonal base, and has a paten, also in gold, covering the top. In Paris, B. Ars. 3479 and BNF fr. 117, both made in Paris ca. 1405, this episode is given unprecedented prominence. Lifted out of its narrative context, it is the last of four key events in the life of Lancelot that are placed in a four-part composite miniature at the very beginning of the set of three volumes that transmit the five-part cycle complete. Florence, Laur. Ash. 121, the Avignon copy, also gives considerable emphasis to this subject, showing it (at the normal place in the text) in two separate scenes, ff. 20v, 21v. Jacques d'Armagnac's manuscripts, BNF fr. 116, f. 621, and BNF fr. 112, vol. II, f. 15v, both include this curing scene in the body of the text, elaborating upon the treatment of the Grail, which in these books has been transformed into a highly ornamented and bejeweled ciborium.[100]

The Grail Liturgy[101]

The depiction of the Grail liturgy that occurs toward the end of the story is relatively rare,[102] being limited to just a few examples, which I examine below. Other manuscripts depict one or more alternative scenes at the end, instead of the Grail liturgy or in addition to it: the death of King Mordrain,[103] Galaad joining together the broken sword with which Joseph had been wounded,[104] Galaad curing the Roi Mehaignié,[105] the three knights Galaad, Perceval, and Bohort, kneeling before the Grail,[106] the three knights together with a cripple, carrying the Grail Table at Sarraz, or the crowning and death of Galaad.[107] Some of these alternative scenes also include a depiction of the Grail, and I return to them below. But most manuscripts of *Queste,* including Jean de Berry's and Jacques d'Armagnac's manuscripts, leave the climactic Grail liturgy to the imagination—a deliberate ploy, also used in the illustration of the manuscripts of Chrétien de Troyes's *Perceval* and its Continuations, the other great story about the Grail.[108]

Identified in the context of the two earlier Grail episodes as "li Sainz Graal" or "li Sainz Vessel" (or a variant thereupon), it is only in the context of the liturgy that the Grail, in the *Queste,* is defined more precisely: "Ce est, fet il [Christ], l'escuele ou Jhesucriz menja l'aignel le jor de Pasqes o ses deciples. Ce est l'escuele qui a servi a gré toz çax que j'ai trovez en mon servise; ce est l'escuele que onques hons mescreanz ne vit a qui ele ne grevast molt. Et por ce que ele a si servi a gré toutes genz doit ele estre apelee le Saint Graal" ("This is, he [Christ] said, the bowl from which Jesus Christ ate the Pascal lamb with his disciples. This is the bowl which has satisfied all those in my service; it is the bowl which no unworthy man set eyes upon without it doing him grievous harm. And because it has so served the desires of all people it should be called the Holy Grail").[109] From this description one would expect that depictions of the Grail in *Queste* illustration would show it looking just like the "escuelle" that is so common in *Estoire* illustration. But we have seen that the Grail in *Estoire* illustration also takes other forms, derived from Christian liturgy, and those liturgical forms have so far been the ones preferred for Grail depiction in *Queste* scenes as well. None of the depictions of the Grail in the context of the *Queste*'s Grail liturgy follow these words. Nor is there any parallel in *Queste* illustration for the "escuelle" mentioned here in the text and illustrated in the *Estoire* manuscripts.

A sacred liturgy is enacted several times in the text of *Queste*: The first could be considered a proto-Grail liturgy, since the Holy Vessel is not explicitly part of the episode. The three Grail knights, Galaad, Perceval, Bohort, and Perceval's sister, see, as a priest celebrates mass of the Holy Ghost, the miraculous white stag transformed into Christ in Majesty, and the four accompanying lions become the symbols of the four evangelists, the man, eagle, lion, and ox.[110] Two illustrations depict this in the Avignon manuscript, one showing the four companions kneeling behind the priest and acolyte at an altar on which is a partially veiled chalice; the second is a historiated initial Q enclosing Christ in Majesty and the four evangelist symbols. While the stag and lions are depicted at this spot in Add. 10294 and the Udine manuscript (f. 91),[111] and several manuscripts show two knights in a chapel,[112] there is, to my knowledge, only one parallel for the illustration of this episode in the Avignon copy—in the special version of the *Queste* made in Lombardy ca. 1380, BNF fr. 343. There, the two scenes are combined, to show the three knights—without Perceval's sister—outside a chapel, addressed by a priest; inside the chapel, Christ is enthroned on the altar, sitting on a beige wooden throne decorated with ebony and ivory inlay, surrounded by the four evangelist symbols. At Christ's feet are two cushions and a book. This is a second instance of a rare subject illustrated in the Avignon and Lombard manuscripts, and only there, so far as I know.[113]

Next, the Grail liturgy is viewed through the open door of the Grail chamber by Lancelot, who has been forbidden to enter the room: it is almost an antiliturgy, comparable with and referring back to Lancelot's presence at, but exclusion from, the Grail's healing miracle related and illustrated earlier.[114] Only one manuscript includes a depiction of what Lancelot sees as he witnesses the Grail liturgy from afar: it is the Avignon copy. There is no attempt to render the doorway through which Lancelot looks, although the entire scene takes place under an arched frame. Lancelot is shown standing to the left, next to the two figures whom the text says handed the priest a third person whom the priest elevated before the assembled company. The two figures—positioned, according to the text, above the priest, "desus les mains au preudome en haut"—are here shown standing on the ground, on Lancelot's side of the altar, with the third person raised above the chalice-Grail on the altar, while the priest and two onlookers are on the right of the altar. This is an allusion to the Trinity, linking thereby with the opening of the *Estoire*—although the Avignon manuscript transmits only the *Queste* and *Mort Artu* branches and no companion volumes have survived. By including the transubstantiation, this miniature also anticipates the much longer passage describing the liturgy that the three chosen knights will witness later. The miniature in the Avignon manuscript has been severely defaced, as have several other illustrations, or parts of illustrations, in the manuscript. Perhaps in this instance someone felt it was inappropriate to show Lancelot seeing the transubstantiated Host.

The earliest surviving *Queste* manuscripts do not depict any liturgy at all, so the earliest illustration we have of the major climactic liturgy in the *Queste* is the one in Yale 229, made ca. 1295 in the diocese of Thérouanne, perhaps for one of the sons of Guy de Dampierre, whose iconography I have analyzed elsewhere.[115] Several of its notable features do not depend on the text: the presence of five knights (not just Galaad, Perceval, and Bohort), the celebrant shown as Bishop Josephe, wearing a mitre (not Christ), and the extraordinary shrinelike, or tabernacle-like, container, painted in gold, which conceals the Grail from the viewer.[116] According to the text, Josephe disappears, and Christ emerges from the Grail and Himself administers the sacrament to the knights:[117] the artist (or planner) has misinterpreted the text.

Josephe and Galaad are also the major participants, though shown without an audience of other followers, in the illustration showing the liturgy in the late-thirteenth-century Italian copy, Udine, Bibl. Archivescovile 177, illustrated with the tinted line drawings that characterize a large number of French manuscripts copied probably in Genoa for Italian patrons in the late thirteenth and early fourteenth centuries.[118] There is only one Grail scene, showing Josephe, mitred and holding a cross staff, borne on a throne by four angels before a single knight wearing civilian dress who stands beside a table on which is placed the Grail, shown as an amazing pear-shaped vessel with a wide rim and a shallow base and two huge rounded handles. This depiction of the Grail is without precedent: it reminds one of the vessels common in Early Christian mosaics from which flowering plants and fruit grow as Paradise motifs; two-handled vessels of this sort also figure among the vessels at the foot of the cross in ninth- and tenth-century Crucifixion scenes.[119] Possibly associations like these were intended.

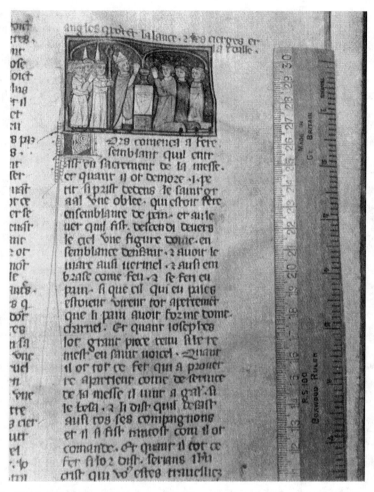

Fig. 9.13. Florence, Biblioteca Mediceo-Laurenziana, Ash. 121(48), f. 86 (photo: Alison Stones)

In the copy made in Avignon in 1319, Florence, Laur. Ash. 121 (48), the Grail liturgy is treated as a single-column miniature (Fig. 9.13) showing Josephe raising his hands in prayer as he celebrates Mass at an altar with a chalice-shaped vessel on it; on the left, behind Josephe, stand angels with two candles behind them; one of the angels holds the Lance, resting its foot on the floor. On the other side of the altar kneel three knights.

It is in Pierart dou Thielt's famous depiction in Paris, Bibl. de l'Arsenal 5218, f. 88, made in Tournai in 1351,[120] that the emphasis on transubstantiation corresponds most precisely to the textual description of the Host transformed into a child—for which Eucharistic miracles like that of Edward the Confessor and those painted on the walls of Orvieto cathedral are parallels.[121] Placed earlier in the text, at the spot where the Yale manuscript and others show the death of King Mordrain, it combines the Grail procession with the transubstantiation.[122] The central pivot of the miniature is the figure of Christ in the chalice-shaped vessel, which floats in midair, between the two kneeling, candle-bearing angels, in front of the horizontal bleeding Lance; both Lance and chalice stand out against the white cloth on the table, behind which are grouped the eleven knights. Josephe sits, holding his crozier, on a throne at the left short end of the table, and the space on the right of the composition is occupied by two standing angels, one of whom carries an object draped with a red cloth, while the other holds a Lance. The composition is ingeniously arranged so that the narrative climax, the transubstantiation, is enclosed within the rest of the pictorial depiction of the procession, as though the preceding action were taking place around it.[123]

In one long image, Pierart dou Thielt has apparently rearranged the items carried by the angels so that the Grail, covered by the "touaille de vermeil samit"("cloth of red fabric"), is carried by one of the angels on the right, while the Lance is borne separately by the other, and does not drip into the vessel. In the middle of the same image is another depiction of the Grail, shown as a chalice with the figure of Christ inside it, and the Lance is again placed so that the Grail does not receive the dripping blood—this time it is horizontal, as if floating, a position perhaps governed by the desire to make it stand out against the long horizontal white of the tablecloth. The floating effect (not in the text) may at the same time underline its supernatural quality.

Both Italian manuscripts, the special French version of the *Queste* made in Lombardy, BNF fr. 343, and the Italian compilation based on the *Queste*, and known as the *Tavola Ritonda*, Florence, BN, Pal. lat. 556,[124] include a depiction of the Grail liturgy: as a single, unfinished, scene in BNF fr. 343,[125] and as a series of no fewer than nine tinted drawings in Pal. lat. 556. The scene in BNF fr. 343, f. 103v, shows Christ, standing on a table, holding a closed cylindrical pyx (vessel for consecrated Hosts) with a round finial on its lid in His left hand, while handing a Host inscribed with a cross to a large group of kneeling knights (Fig. 9.14). The drawing was left uncolored and the head of Christ, which is surrounded by rays of light, remains featureless.

Figure 9.14. Paris, Bibliothèque Nationale de France, fr. 343, f. 103v (photo: Bibliothèque Nationale de France)

Produced in 1446 by two craftsmen from Cremona, the scribe or editor (or both ?) Zuliano di Anzoli,[126] and, in all likelihood, the artist Bonifacio Bembo,[127] the Mantua manuscript now in Florence depicts nine different stages in the enactment of the liturgy, a phenomenon remarkable as an unprecedented number of Grail images in general, and as a pictorial concentration of images extraordinary within this manuscript.[128]

The Grail liturgy begins on the lower half of f. 147v with the appearance of Josephe, in bishop's robes, holding a crozier and supported by three angels, before the knights. The Grail procession enters on f. 148 (upper miniature), passing alongside Josephe: the first angel carries two candles, the second a cloth with a band of decoration and a fringe at the end; the third holds the Lance, held at an angle over the angel's shoulder, so that its tip is poised directly above the Holy Grail, which the fourth angel raises high in veiled hands in order to catch in it the blood of the Lance. The Grail is extraordinary in shape: like a huge round ceramic pot with a heavy torus molding at the rim and base, each decorated with a band of small circles; the rounded body of the vessel is patterned with a ring of cinqfoil flowers, matching in shape and size the ones on the walls of the room !![129] The lower miniature on the same page shows the angels kneeling beside and behind Josephe, two of them now holding the candles, while the Grail rests on the table with the Lance standing vertically inside it; the knights watch the moment of transubstantiation as Josephe holds up high the small blessing figure of Christ.[130]

Then Josephe, having replaced the transubstantiated bread in the vessel (in which the Lance still stands), bends over to give Galaad the Kiss of Peace (f. 148v, top), which Galaad should then transmit to the other knights; the four angels stand behind Josephe, two holding candles, the other two holding their arms crossed over their chests like the knights. As in the *Queste*, Josephe then disappears (not represented in the illustration), and Christ appears and administers the sacrament to the knights. Here (f. 148v, bottom) Christ, lifesize, revealing the wounds of the Passion, actually stands on the table next to the Grail (no Lance in the Grail this time), and blesses the knights. After that (f. 149, top) Christ leans over, his hand on the rim of the vessel, about to lift it up for Galaad to drink from it; Galaad bends over the vessel, still with crossed arms. Then (f. 149, bottom) Christ flies up toward the window. Outside, Lancelot, not permitted to witness the events, sits on the ground by the door.

The scene shifts altogether to the outside of the Grail palace on f. 149v (bottom) as Lancelot, still seated on the ground facing the closed door, looks up at Christ, now transformed into a seated stag, who has emerged from the window above the door and is borne away on a cushion by three angels.[131] In the next scene (f. 150) Lancelot sees the four angels carry away the two candles and the Lance, still dripping blood into the Grail, which is borne by the last angel who is still emerging through the window above the door of the castle.

Although Josephe consecrates the bread in the *Tavola Ritonda*, the substance that is meted out to the knights is not flesh, as in the *Queste*,[132] but blood. As Breillat pointed out, much more attention is given to blood as an underlying motif throughout the *Tavola Ritonda*. Not only does the description of the Grail liturgy make clear that the blood of the Lance actually falls into the vessel, as is also shown in the illustrations, but the Christ is the Christ of the Passion, revealing his wounds in both text and picture much more explicitly than in the *Queste*.[133]

Bloodletting and the Element of Blood

In the *Tavola Ritonda* as in the *Queste*, Perceval's sister dies from donating her blood to cure a maiden with leprosy. But in the *Tavola Ritonda* version of this episode, the leper is cured by drinking the blood, not by having it splattered on her breast as in *Queste*.[134] Only three manuscripts illustrate the bloodletting and curing: the Avignon manuscript of 1319, Florence, Laur. Ash. 121, the Bonn manuscript of 1286,[135] and the special version made in Lombardy ca. 1380, BNF fr. 343. In the Bonn manuscript's version, the tourniquet, wound, blood, bowl, and supporting staff lend an air of medical reality to the depiction, while striking a discordant note. For the scrupulously supervised bloodletting is the sacrifice that will lead to death, whereas the simultaneous application of the blood to the breast of the leper—a symbolic act—is what will lead to a miraculous cure. The Avignon version shows the surgeon making the incision as Perceval's sister holds the bowl to catch the blood, watched by three standing figures; the leper (her face rubbed out—because it was disfigured?) lies on a patterned bed in front of the scene. BNF fr. 343, f. 59v, shows the assembled company watching Perceval's sister swooning in a chair, supported by the hooded physician, her right arm resting on a cushion, bared to show the incision, a silver "escuelle"-shaped bowl placed at the edge of the red-and-gold cushion to catch the blood. The cured damsel stands to the right, accompanied by a knight.[136]

Although these bloodletting scenes occur in the text without the accompaniment of the Grail, the illustrations in Bonn 526 and the Avignon and Lombard copies may allude to its healing powers through the shape of the bowl in which the donated blood is collected—the same as the Grail so common in the *Estoire* tradition, occasionally in the Last Supper,[137] and the blood of Old Testament sacrifice or of healing water.[138] In *Queste* illustration the Grail itself is always depicted as a chalice or a ciborium, the former shape evoking the Eucharistic blood, the other the Host. I would suggest that the occasional depiction of a chalice to represent the Grail in *Estoire*—as in its one appearance in the illustrations of BNF fr. 770—seems merely to reflect the Eucharistic connotations of the Grail in general, while the consistent use of a chalice to represent the Grail in the Avignon manuscript—where the Grail as such is shown more times than in any other manuscript—does suggest a particular desire on the part of those who devised the illustrative program to place special emphasis on the element of blood. This emphasis on the element of blood links this manuscript thematically with the text and the images of the *Tavola Ritonda*.

The cult of the Holy Blood at Mantua, one of the earliest documented in Western Europe,[139] was a governing factor in the Gonzaga's choice of an Arthurian subject about Bohort, the only one of the Grail heroes to produce any progeny, for the painting by Pisanello in their castle at Mantua.[140] The Florence *Tavola Ritonda*, whose illustrations have been attributed to

Bembo, is thought to belong to the same artistic current as the Camera paintings, and Benedetti has identified the *Queste* manuscript of Italian manufacture, Udine Bibl. Arcivescovile 177, discussed above, in the Gonzaga inventory of 1407.[141] Although Yale 229 has no known medieval provenance, apart from what can be deduced stylistically and from the heraldry in its decoration,[142] it has been suggested that it or another copy from the same workshop might well have also been in the Visconti-Sforza library (where many Arthurian manuscripts are listed in terms too general for particular copies to be identified) and could have been available to Bembo during one of his visits to Milan to work for the dukes of Milan. There he might also have seen BNF fr. 343, made ca. 1380 for someone in the circle of the Visconti dukes of Milan and identifiable in their fifteenth-century inventories.[143]

Some of the French manuscripts with particularly interesting depictions of the Grail were also made in regions that were also important for the cult of the Holy Blood. I have argued that BNF fr. 95 and Yale 229 were most likely made in the region of the diocese of Thérouanne.[144] Boulogne-sur-Mer, in the diocese of Thérouanne, and Bruges, in the neighboring diocese of Tournai,[145] also boasted Holy Blood relics; and Ars. 5218 was made in Tournai. The Bruges relic was allegedly acquired by Thierry of Alsace from the Patriarch of Jerusalem in 1148, in appreciation of his valor in the Second Crusade, and housed in a crystal cylinder with late-thirteenth-century metal terminations;[146] the Boulogne relic is a piece of cloth supposedly donated to his native Boulogne-sur-Mer by Godefroi de Bouillon in 1101 and now preserved under rock crystal in the splendid translucent enamel disk made to house it in the last decade of the thirteenth century, its workmanship attributed to the Parisian goldsmith Guillaume Julien, and its patron Philippe le Bel, king of France.[147] BNF fr. 95 and Yale 229 were made at about the same time as this reliquary.

In the *Queste,* the Grail cult is essentially based on the bread of the Eucharist rather than on the wine-blood. In the *Estoire,* both the elements are present, though the emphasis on transubstantiation gives greater weight to the bread than to the wine.[148] In the *Tavola Ritonda* the more important element is the blood, an emphasis that is anticipated visually in the illustrations of the *Queste* made in Avignon and in Italy (there are no surviving copies of *Estoire* from Italy), where the Grail is consistently shown as an open chalice—a vessel to be drunk from—rather than a closed ciborium, a vessel for reservation and concealment.

The Healing of the Wounded King

Even in the *Queste*, the conclusion to the liturgy of the Grail emphasizes the element of blood, since Christ's final instructions to Galaad are that he cure the Roi Mehaignié by anointing his wound with the blood of the Lance.[149] A parallel to the wounding of King Alphasem in *Estoire*, the healing of the Roi Mehaignié by Galaad is depicted considerably less frequently than one might expect. Only a single manuscript includes a scene of it, the special version in French made in Lombardy, BNF 343, f. 103 (Fig. 9.15), and the illustration depicts a shift of emphasis in the healing element. Rather than use the holy Lance dipped in blood to heal the king, as the *Queste* text says, Galaad effects the cure by placing the Grail itself, shown as a chalice which he holds in the middle of the stem, at the groin of the seated king, suggesting that the vehicle of healing is the vessel itself, regardless of which element of the sacrament it contains.[150] This healing scene is anticipated in BNF fr. 343 by an earlier episode, showing an emaciated King Mordrain, sitting on an invalid's bed on wheels, receiving the Host from a priest who holds a chalice covered by a folded corporal (cloth).

Fig. 9.15. Paris, Bibliothèque Nationale de France, fr. 343, f. 103 (photo: Bibliothèque Nationale de France)

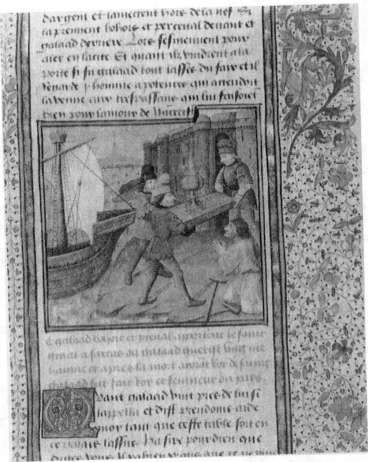

Fig. 9.16. Paris, Bibliothèque Nationale de France, fr. 116, f. 672 (photo: Bibliothèque Nationale de France)

The Grail at Sarraz

The final healing episode in the *Queste* also links the cure with the Holy Vessel. After a miraculous sea voyage in the boat on which they had earlier found the sword with the mysterious hangings ("estranges renges"), where now they find the silver Grail table and the Grail itself, the three knights Galaad, Perceval, and Bohort arrive at the city of Sarraz and are instructed to carry ashore the silver altar and the Grail.[151] Finding the table heavy, Galaad asks a cripple to assist them, pronouncing him cured of his affliction. Illustrated in all three early-fourteenth-century Flemish manuscripts, Add. 10294, Royal 14. E. III, and Rylands Fr. 1, this scene is also in Ars. 3482, f. 537, and in BNF fr. 112, f. 181, but none of these illustrations shows the Grail on the table. In the Avignon manuscript, Florence Laur. Ash. 121, f. 88v, the Grail is shown, as a chalice, on the table which the three knights carry, while the standing cripple occupies a separate compartment to the right.[152] In Jacques d'Armagnac's copy, BNF fr. 116, f. 672, the knights carry the table on which is the Grail, shown as a multilobed circular ciborium with a knop and tall spirelike finial, while the cripple is shown rising, his hands in prayer (Fig. 9.16).[153]

The Final Events: The Knights Before the Grail, The Crowning of Galaad, The Last Grail Liturgy, The Death of Galaad and The Disappearance of the Grail

In the final appearance of the Grail in the *Tavola Ritonda* (f. 151), the nails of the Passion and the Crown of Thorns are also included; they all accompany the dead body of Perceval's sister on the boat (bottom) and are transferred by the knights to the altar in the Grail chapel, before which Perceval's sister is buried (top) and where Galaad, having ruled as king for a year, will also be buried (a scene not illustrated in Pal. 556).[154] In the story as the *Queste* relates it, Galaad, Perceval, and Bohort, having buried Perceval's sister (an episode not illustrated in any of the surviving manuscripts), are imprisoned by King Escorant. In prison they are succored by the Grail (shown in the Avignon manuscript). At the death of King Escorant—an episode illustrated in the Avignon copy, now badly rubbed, showing the king on his deathbed with figures behind—the three are released from prison and Galaad is crowned as successor to Escorant,[155] again illustrated in the Avignon copy (f. 89v). Galaad builds a tabernacle ("arche") of gold and precious jewels to cover the Holy Vessel, a textual link with the ark in which the Grail is seen by Josephe in the *Estoire*, and a cross-media link with the shrinelike Grail tabernacle shown in the Yale manuscript's depiction of the liturgy. But neither the Yale copy nor any other includes an image of this ark at this point in the text. After this comes the final Grail liturgy, celebrated for the three knights by Josephe, followed by the death of Galaad and the return of the Grail to heaven, transported by a miraculous hand.

There is sometimes ambiguity in the illustrations as to which of these episodes is intended in the picture, as the placing of the final miniatures in the text is often far removed from the event shown in the image.

In BNF fr. 342, f. 145v, there is a rather generic final scene of knights before a table, with no Grail present;[156] while in the final scene in Bonn 526, f. 451v, Galaad, Perceval, and Bohort stand behind a laden table, Galaad (presumably) holding a chalice with a cross in it, like the one before which, in this manuscript, Lancelot is shown sleeping earlier in the story.[157] The Avignon manuscript unequivocally shows the three knights in prison receiving communion from Christ, who holds the Grail, shown as a large chalicelike vessel,[158] while Josephe's final appearance is not shown. In Ars. 3482, f. 538v, the final image shows Galaad, alone, receiving the sacrament from Josephe, robed as a bishop. Jacques d'Armagnac's special version, BNF fr. 112, f. 179v, shows the knights kneeling, their backs to the viewer, before an altar on which rests a spectacular jeweled polygonal ciborium-like Grail with a knop in the center of the stem and surmounted by a polygonal turret with a jeweled cross on top.[159] As Galaad dies before the Grail (f. 181v, Fig. 9.17]), supported by Perceval and Bohort, the vessel in BNF fr. 112 has become a round ciborium on a splayed stem, with scalloped motifs on bowl and cover, and beading on the rim of the foot, the base of the lid, and the top of the lid below a finial of four balls supporting another ball on top of which is a cross. As described in the text,[160] a hand appears and miraculously carries off the Grail and the Lance. The Avignon manuscript has a simpler version: Galaad, crowned, lies beside the altar on which is the chalicelike Grail from which the Lance projects vertically. The miniature is badly rubbed, like many in this manuscript, and one cannot be sure whether Galaad has a halo or whether his head rests on a cushion.[161]

CONCLUSION

As befits its mysterious nature, the depiction of the Grail does not reflect a single direction or trend, nor is it depicted in a single way in the illustrations of *Estoire* and *Queste*. Manuscripts produced by the same team of craftsmen show inconsistencies as to which Grail scenes are included and how the Grail is treated, suggesting that the rules were flexible at best, and that there was no single line of development.[162] The complexities of the iconography of each branch of the *Lancelot-Graal* suggest that painters—or, more likely, their patrons and/or the directors of operations—took upon themselves either to exclude or include the subject on an ad hoc basis, and, if the latter decision was made, to be guided by what seems to have been quite a complex network of factors, the rationale for which is not altogether clear.

Fig. 9.17. Paris, Bibliothèque Nationale de France, fr.112, f. 181v (photo: Bibliothèque Nationale de France)

The adaptation of models from the context of Christian art was an obvious route to follow, since the events surrounding the Crucifixion, Deposition, and Entombment are directly narrated in *Estoire*, and since Christ Himself plays a mystical part in the Grail liturgies in the *Queste*. In both texts the Grail liturgy explicitly includes consecration, elevation, transubstantiation, and communion, which link it directly to the Christian sacrament of the Mass. But the vessel used to depict the Grail depends only partially on parallels drawn from Christian liturgy, deriving its pictorial form not only from the chalice and paten used in the celebration of the Eucharist, but also from the ciborium and monstrance that during the thirteenth century came to be used in its reservation and veneration.

Certain iconographic patterns do emerge: the predominance of the Grail as a shallow bowl, the "escuelle," in the first century of *Estoire* illustration (Rennes, Le Mans, Add. Royal, Amsterdam); the displacement of the "escuelle" in *Estoire* and its replacement by the chalice or the paten in the manuscripts of the fifteenth century (BNF fr. 117-20, BNF fr. 112, BNF fr. 113–16); a preference for the chalice as the Holy Vessel in *Queste* illustration in the thirteenth and fourteenth centuries (Bonn, Avignon, Ars. 5218), the emergence of the ciborium as Grail in *Queste* manuscripts of the early fourteenth century (Add. Royal, Rylands) and the displacement of the chalice by the ciborium in the fifteenth century (Ars. 3479–80, BNF fr. 117–20, BNF fr. 112, BNF fr. 113–16).

At the same time there are instances where the shape of the Grail seems to reflect particular interests and present isolated solutions to the question of how to depict it—notably the presence of the Host shown ca. 1250 in UC Berkeley 106, the cross-in-chalice in Bonn 526 in 1286, the tabernacle-shrine in Yale 229 (ca. 1295), the allusions to Corpus Christi processions and the depiction of the Host in BNF fr. 344 (ca. 1310-1320), and to the reservation of the Eucharist and the emphasis on the element of blood in the Avignon manuscript of 1319, the presence of the Child in the chalice in Ars. 5218 in 1351, the peculiar urnlike shapes given to the Grail in the Udine (ca. 1300) and Florence manuscripts (1446), and the paten shown in BNF fr. 113 (ca. 1475). Some of these are cases where representations of the Grail and its liturgy in the *Estoire* and the *Queste* keep pace with, perhaps even anticipate, what is shown in contemporary liturgical and devotional books. There are also some instances where a model drawn from Christian iconography is inappropriate to the context: the Grail-bearing Joseph included at the Crucifixion; Josephe robed and mitred distributing the sacrament rather than Christ, and the corollary of this scene: Christ as well as Josephe administering the sacrament.

Although the Christianization of the Grail plays such an important part in the development of its iconography, the healing and nourishing properties of the Holy Vessel itself are an aspect of the Grail that have no parallel in the theology of the Eucharist. From this point of view, the most interesting depictions are those that illustrate the Grail itself, rather than its contents, functioning as the instrument of healing and nourishing—in the curing of King Alphasem in the *Estoire*, and of the Roi

Mehaignié in the *Queste*; the nourishing of the knights at the Round Table, the curing of the wounded knight in the presence of Lancelot, and of the cripple who assists Perceval, Bohort, and Galaad in carrying the Grail Table. Yet the illustrative tradition—if such it can be called— makes no distinction among the various types of vessel depicted, so that, depending on which manuscript and which text is concerned, these nourishing or healing aspects of the Grail's supernatural power are effected either by the Grail as "escuelle," or as chalice, or as ciborium—and, in the case of the curing of the Roi Mehaignié in BNF fr. 343, the power of the Holy Vessel itself, shown as a chalice, displaces that of the blood it contains.

NOTES

Parts of this essay were presented at the Lancelot conference in Austin, Texas, in March, 1992, and at the 17th International Arthurian Congress held in Bonn in 1993. I am especially grateful to Elspeth Kennedy and Martine Meuwese for helpful discussion, and to Dhira Mahoney for her patient and pertinent editing.

1. ("So you have seen what you so desired to see, and what you coveted"). Albert Pauphilet, *La Queste de Saint Graal* (CFMA) (Paris: Champion, 1965), pp. 270–71. I warn the reader that the pagination in previous and subsequent editions is not the same.

2. The classic studies are Jessie L. Weston, *The Quest of the Holy Grail* (London: Bell, 1913; London: Cass, 1964) and Roger Sherman Loomis, *The Grail: From Celtic Myth to Christian Symbol* (Cardiff: University of Wales; New York: Columbia University Press, 1963).

3. The textual sources—Matthew 27: 57–61, the Pseudo-Gospel of Nicodemus (6th C.), *Vindicta Salvatoris* (based in part on a manuscript of the 8th C.), Chrétien's *Perceval*, Robert de Boron's verse *Estoire*, the prose *Joseph*, the *Estoire*, and the *Queste*—are most conveniently drawn together in Guilio Bertoni, *Materiali per la storia della leggenda del San Gral in Francia*, Testi Romanzi 1 (Rome: Maglione, 1930). The most recent text edition of Chrétien is by Keith Busby, *Chrétien de Troyes, "Le roman de Perceval, ou, Le conte du Graal," édition critique d'après tous les manuscrits* (Tübingen: Niemeyer, 1993). For Wolfram, see Wolfram von Eschenbach, *Parzival und Titurel*, ed. Karl Bartsch, 2nd ed. (Leipzig: Brockhaus, 1875–1877); Joachim Bumke, *Die Wolfram von Eschenbach-Forschung seit 1945: Bericht und Bibliographie* (Munich: Fink, 1970).

4. Heinrich Oskar Sommer, ed., *The Vulgate Version of the Arthurian Romances, edited from Manuscripts in the British Museum*, 8 vols. (Washington:

Carnegie Institution, 1909–1916). For Joseph, see Richard O'Gorman, ed., *Robert de Boron, "Joseph d'Arimathie," Critical edition of the verse and prose versions* (Toronto: Pontifical Institute of Mediæval Studies, 1995). For the manuscript tradition, see Brian Woledge, *Bibliographie des romans et nouvelles en prose française antérieurs à 1500* (Geneva: Droz, 1975), nos. 93, 96, 114, and id., *Supplément 1954–1973* (Geneva: Droz, 1975), nos. 93, 96, 114.

5. Probably the earliest surviving *Lancelot-Graal* manuscript with cyclical illustration is the *Estoire, Merlin*, and beginning of *Lancelot*, Rennes, BM 255, ca. 1225, see Alison Stones, "The Earliest Illustrated Prose *Lancelot* Manuscript?" *Reading Medieval Studies* 3 (1977), 3–44. This antedates the earliest surviving manuscripts of Chrétien de Troyes that contain narrative illustrations, which are datable only in the third quarter of the thirteenth century: see *Les Manuscrits de Chrétien de Troyes*, ed. Keith Busby, Terry Nixon, Alison Stones, Lori Walters, 2 vols. (Amsterdam: Rodopi, 1993), particularly the Catalogue of Manuscripts by Terry Nixon, II, 18–86, and the chronological sequence of illustrations, particularly figs. 103–435. Other "early" French vernacular manuscripts with a single historiated initial at the beginning of each text are the Guiot manuscript of Chrétien's works, Paris, BNF fr. 794, and the prose *Lancelot do Lac*, Paris, BNF fr. 768, the *manuscrit de base* of Kennedy's edition, Elspeth Kennedy, *Lancelot do Lac*, 2 vols. (Oxford: Clarendon, 1983); see *Les Manuscrits* for full references and especially Patricia Stirnemann, "Some Champenois Vernacular Manuscripts and the Manerius Style of Illumination," *Les Manuscrits*, I, 195–226, at pp. 204–05 and fig. 22 (Guiot), and p. 207 and fig. 24 (*Lancelot*). These two manuscripts also exclude illustrations of the Grail or related subjects. Early examples of the sporadic use of the historiated initial as such can also be found in the *Roman de Troie*, Paris, Bibl. de l'Arsenal 3340, copied in 1237, on which see Charles Samaran and Robert Marichal, *Catalogue des manuscrits en écriture latine portant des indications de date, de lieu ou de copiste*, 7 vols. (Paris: CNRS, 1959–84), I, 159, pl. 12. Latin manuscripts offer some early examples of the presence of historiated initials, such as the classical Latin compilation, Paris, BNF lat. 7936, on which see François Avril, "Un manuscrit d'auteurs classiques et ses illustrations," in *The Year 1200: A Symposium*, ed. Jeffrey Hoffeld (New York: Metropolitan Museum of Art, 1975), pp. 261–82, and the possibly related compilation in Edinburgh University Library, MS 20 (D.b.VI.6), described in Catherine R. Borland, *A Descriptive Catalogue of the Western Mediaeval Manuscripts in Edinburgh University Library* (Edinburgh: Edinburgh University Press, 1916), pp. 30–31. To my knowledge no scholarly opinion has so far been expressed about the likely date of BNF fr. 748, mentioned below for its interesting opening initial; it is possible that it may also be included among these "early" books.

6. See Elizabeth Burin, "The Pierre Sala Manuscript," in *Les Manuscrits*, I, 323–30 (above, note 5). The unillustrated *Estoire*, BNF fr. 1427, was written in 1504, see Woledge, *Bibliographie*, p. 74 (above, note 4). See also the editions of the *Lancelot, Queste,* and *Mort Artu* and the *Tristan* printed by Antoine Vérard from 1488 onward, discussed in C.E. Pickford, "Antoine Vérard: Éditeur du *Lancelot* et du *Tristan*," in *Mélanges de langue et de littérature françaises du Moyen Âge et de la Renaissance offerts à Charles Foulon*n, 2 vols. (Rennes: Institut de français, Université de Haute-Bretagne, 1980), pp. 280–84; see also R.S. and L.H. Loomis, *Arthurian Legends in Medieval Art* (London: Oxford University Press; New York: Modern Language Association, 1938), pp. 140–44; Woledge, *Bibliographie*, p. 75; *Creating French Culture: Treasures from the Bibliothèque Nationale de France* (exhibition catalogue), ed. Marie-Hélène Tesnière and Prosser Gifford (New Haven: Yale University Press, 1995), no. 53.

7. A precise count depends on whether multiple volumes of the same set are counted separately or as part of the same cycle; see the Working List of Illustrated Manuscripts at the end of this chapter. For approximate numbers of manuscripts per branch, see Alison Stones, "The Illustrations of BN, fr. 95 and Yale 229, Prolegomena to a Comparative Analysis," in Keith Busby, ed., *Word and Image in Arthurian Romance* (New York: Garland, 1996), pp. 206–63, at note 23, cited hereafter as Stones, "BN, fr. 95 and Yale 229." The most important survey is still Loomis, *Arthurian Legends* (above, note 6). See also Alison Stones, "Arthurian Art Since Loomis," in *Arturus Rex II* (Acta Conventus Lovaniensis 1987), ed. W. van Hoecke, G. Tournoy, W. Verbeke (Leuven: Leuven University Press, 1991), pp. 21–78; Muriel J. Whitaker, *The Legends of King Arthur in Art* (Woodbridge, Eng.; Rochester, NY: Brewer, 1990); and the articles on "Manuscripts, Illuminated," by Alison Stones and Marilyn Stockstad in Norris J. Lacy, *The New Arthurian Encyclopedia* (New York: Garland, 1991), pp. 299–308. Most of the manuscripts discussed here were included somewhere in my unpublished Ph.D. dissertation, "The Illustrations of the French prose *Lancelot*" (University of London, 1970–71), cited hereafter as Stones, "The Illustrations." Two other unpublished dissertations have been devoted to the iconography of the *Estoire* in two related Franco-Flemish manuscripts of the early fourteenth-century: Elizabeth M. Remak-Honef, "Text and Image in the *Estoire del Saint Graal*, A Study of London, British Library MS Royal 14. E. iii" (Ph.D., University of North Carolina, 1987), and Martine Meuwese, "*L'Estoire del Saint Graal*, Een studie over de relatie tussen miniaturen en tekst in het eerste deel van de Vulgaatcyclus uit de Biblioteca Philosophica Hermetica te Amsterdam" (Doctoraalscriptie, Rijksuniversiteit Leiden, 1990). Lists of the subjects in BNF fr. 112, 113–116, 117–120, together with comparative iconography charts of the *Lancelot, Queste,* and *Mort Artu* branches of the cycle, are given in another dissertation, by Susan A. Blackman, "The Manuscripts and Patronage of Jacques

d'Armagnac" (Ph.D., University of Pittsburgh, 1993), cited hereafter as Blackman, "The Manuscripts." The charts are also reproduced in ead., "The Arthurian Manuscripts of Jacques d'Armagnac: A Pictorial Synopsis," in *Word and Image,* pp. 3–57, cited hereafter as Blackman, "Pictorial Synopsis."

8. See Emmanuèle Baumgartner, "Les scènes du Graal et leur illustration dans les manuscrits du *Conte du Graal* et des Continuations," in *Les Manuscrits,* I, 489–503 (above, note 5). A more general study of Grail iconography is Konrad Burdach, *Der Graal* (Stuttgart: Kohlammer, 1938; reprint, Darmstadt: Wissenschaftliche Buchgesellschaft, 1974), pp. 415–49; and, for Chrétien, see (with reservations) Sandra Hindman, "King Arthur, His Knights, and the French Aristocracy in Picardy," *Contexts: Style and Values in Medieval Art and Literature,* ed. Daniel Poirion and Nancy Freeman Regalado, Special Issue, *Yale French Studies* (New Haven, 1991), 114–33. The relation between the chalice/attribute of Ecclesia and the Grail, overplayed in much of the popular literature, cannot be dealt with here.

9. In the late–thirteenth-century copy, Munich, Bayerische Staatsbibliothek, Cgm 19, f. 50v, the bottom register shows the Grail twice, each time borne by the Grail Queen who holds it at Feirefitz's baptism and again, before him. In both instances she holds it in a huge cloth in such a way that her hands are veiled by the cloth. This is a device to emphasize the holiness of the Grail that is borrowed from Christian iconography, where, from Early Christian times, holding something precious (such as a crown of martyrdom, as in the apse mosaic of San Vitale, Ravenna, mid–6th C.) in veiled hands was a sign of reverence. See Loomis, pp. 131–32, fig. 358 (above, note 6); *Parzival, Titurel, Tageliede: Cgm 19 der Bayerischen Staatsbibliothek Munchen,* facsimile, text ed. Gerhard Augst, Otfried Ehrismann and Heinz Engels, essay on the manuscript by Fridolin Dressler (Stuttgart: Muller and Schindler, 1970); the four other illustrated manuscripts are summarily described in K.J. Benziger, *Parzival in der deutschen Handschriften des Mittelalters. Eine Vergleichende Darstellung des gesamten vorhandenen Bildmaterials unter besonderer Berücksichtigung der Berner Handschrift Cod. AA 91* (Studien zur deutschen Kunstgeschichte 175) (Strassburg: Heitz, 1914), and Bernd Schirok, *Wolfram von Eschenbach: "Parzival." Die Bilder der illustrierten Handschriften* (Litterae 67) (Göppingen: Kümmerle, 1985). See also Lieselotte E. Stamm-Saurma (Saurma-Jeltsch), "Zuht und wicze: Zum Bildgehalt spätmittelalterlicher Epenhandshcriften," *Zeitschrift des deutschen Vereins für Kunstwissenschaft,* 41 (1987), 42–70, and Michael Curschmann, "Der Berner 'Parzival' und seine Bilder," *Probleme der Parzival-Philologie,* ed. Joachim Heinzle (Marburger Kolloquium 1990) *Wolfram-Studien* XII (Berlin: Schmidt, 1992), 153–71. Paradoxically, the Grail is not a major feature of the illustrations of these manuscripts.

10. Edited from the only surviving manuscript, Paris, BNF fr. 20047, by William A. Nitze, *Le roman de l'Estoire dou Graal* (Paris: Champion, 1927). See also Bertoni, *Materiali*, pp. 30–47 (above, note 3), and Burdach, *Der Graal*, pp. 450–502 (above, note 8).

11. It may well be that the special prose version of Arthurian romance transmitted in the Modena manuscript, Biblioteca Estense alpha 930 (E. 39), containing *Joseph*, *Merlin*, and *Perceval*, illustrated with fifteen small historiated initials, dates sometime between 1190 and 1210, as William Roach surmised for its *Perceval* section: see *The Didot Perceval, According to the Manuscripts of Modena and Paris*, ed. William Roach (Philadelphia: University of Pennsylvania, 1941), p. 130. See also Woledge, *Bibliographie*, no. 1213, pp. 90–91, and *Supplément*, pp. 70–71 (above, note 4).

12. For the one surviving example, see Raymond Koechlin, *Les Ivoires gothiques françaises* (Paris: Picard, 1924), I, 513–16; II, no. 1310, 3, pl. CCXXIII–IV; *Images in Ivory: Precious Objects of the Gothic Age*, ed. Peter Barnet (Detroit: Detroit Institute of Arts; Princeton: Princeton University Press, 1997), no. 62 (entry by Danielle Gaborit-Chopin).

13. Cf. OED: the action or practice of retaining or preserving a portion of the Eucharist.

14. See Norman P. Tanner, S.J., *Decrees of the Ecumenical Councils*, 2 vols. (London: Sheed and Ward; Washington, D.C.: Georgetown University Press, 1990), I, 227–303.

15. A useful survey of how medieval books were made and illustrated, and by whom, is Jonathan J.G. Alexander, *Medieval Artists and their Methods of Work* (New Haven: Yale University Press, 1992). See also Alison Stones, "Indications écrites et modèles picturaux, guides aux peintres de manuscrits enluminés aux environs de 1300," *Artistes, artisans et production artistique* (Actes du colloque, Rennes, 1983), ed. X. Barral I Altet, 3 vols. (Paris: Picard, 1986–1990), III, 321–49.

16. I have investigated these questions in relation to some particular cases. For Rennes 255, see Stones, "The Earliest" (above, note 5). For London, BL Add. 10292–94 and Royal 14. E. III, together with Amsterdam, BPH 1/Manchester, Rylands Fr. 1/Oxford, Bodl. Douce 215, see ead., "Another Short Note on Rylands French 1," in *Romanesque and Gothic, Essays for George Zarnecki*, ed. N. Stratford (Bury St. Edmunds: Boydell and Brewer, 1987), pp. 185–92. For Paris, BNF fr. 95/New Haven, Yale 229, see ead., "BN, fr. 95 and Yale 229." See also my analysis of artistic contexts in relation to the manuscripts of Chrétien de Troyes, "The Illustrated Chrétien Manuscripts and their Artistic Context," *Les Manuscrits*, I, 227–322 (above, note 5).

17. For the Death of Arthur, see Stones, "Aspects of Arthur's Death in Medieval Illumination" in *The Passing of Arthur: New Essays in Arthurian Tradition*, ed. Christopher Baswell and William Sharpe (New York: Garland, 1988),

pp. 52–101; for the depiction of the adulterous love between Queen Guinevere and Arthur's valorous knight Lancelot, see Stones, "Arthurian Art Since Loomis," at pp. 38–41 (above, note 7); ead., "Images of Temptation, Seduction and Discovery in the Prose *Lancelot*: a Preliminary Note," *Festschrift Gerhard Schmidt, Wiener Jahrbuch für Kunstgeschichte*, 46–47 (1993–94), pp. 725–35, and ead., "Illustrating Lancelot and Guinevere,' in *Lancelot: A Casebook*, ed. Lori Walters (New York: Garland, 1996), pp. 125–57. A few other episodes— Lancelot finding the head of his ancestor, the Magic Carole, the liturgy of the Grail— are discussed in Stones, "BN, fr. 95 and Yale 229" (above, note 7). For an earlier note on the Grail, see ead., "Sacred and Profane Art; Secular and Liturgical Book-Illumination in the Thirteenth Century," in Harald Scholler, ed. *The Epic in Medieval Society: Aesthetic and Moral Values* (Tübingen: Niemeyer, 1977), pp. 100–12 at pp. 102–03. For the iconography of bloodletting, see Stones, "Indications écrites," pp. 322–23 (above, note 15), and for the hermit in the tree see ibid., pp. 323–24, and "Arthurian Art Since Loomis," pp. 39–41 (above, note 7).

18. Surprisingly few studies have directly addressed the issue of how the Grail was depicted. Among the recent popularizing studies (to be read with caution) are Gerhard von dem Borne, *Der Gral in Europa: Wurzel und Wirkungen* (Stuttgart: Urachhaus, 1976); John Matthews, *The Grail: Quest for the Eternal* (London: Thames and Hudson; New York: Crossroad, 1981); L. Bouyer and Mireille Mentré, *Les lieux magiques du Graal* (Paris: OEIL, 1984); Danielle Buschinger, Anne Labia, and Daniel Poirion, eds., *Scènes du Graal* (Paris: Stock, 1987), and Michel Roquebert, *Les Cathares et le Graal* (Toulouse: Privat, 1994).

19. The colophon on f. 31 reads, "Cis livres fu par escript l'an mil.ccc.lvii. le premier samedi de guillet et le fist Jean Deloles escriven nes de hainnaut (de haumaut ?) pries pour lui et ce que vous endires puissiez." See Barbara A. Shailor, *Catalogue of Medieval and Renaissance Manuscripts in the Beinecke Rare Book and Manuscript Library, Yale University*, 2 vols., Medieval and Renaissance Texts and Studies, 34, 48 (Binghamton: SUNY, 1984, 1987), I, no. 227.

20. Reproduced in Stones, "BN, fr. 95 and Yale 229," fig. 8.16 (above, note 7). Tenth-century wall-paintings in Norfolk (whose recent discovery is noted in the Newsletter of the International Center of Medieval Art, Spring 1997), apparently include a Gnadenstuhl Trinity that is among the earliest examples to have survived.

21. Reproduced in Loomis, *Arthurian Legends*, fig. 299 (above, note 6), and in color in Matthews, *Grail: Quest*, p. 37 (above, note 18).

22. Sommer, I, 4, lines 18–20 and 7, lines 17 and 36 (above, note 4); a Gradenstuhl Trinity also occurs toward the beginning of *Estoire* in Paris, BN fr. 344, f. 9, at the words, "Cil sains esperiz" (Sommer, I, 25, line 6).

23. See Günter Haseloff, *Die Psalterillustration im 13. Jahrhundert* (Kiel: n. p., n. d. [1938]); Victor Leroquais, *Les psautiers manuscrits des bibliothèques publiques de France*, 3 vols. (Paris: Protat, 1940–1941).

24. Victor Leroquais, *Les livres d'heures manuscrits de la Bibliothèque nationale*, 3 vols. (Paris: Protat, 1927).

25. For a rare instance of what I think is the influence of Grail imagery reflected in Last Supper iconography, see Alison Stones, "Madame Marie's Picture-Book: a precursor of Flemish Painting around 1400," in *Flanders in a European Perspective*, ed. Maurits Smeyers (Leuven: Peeters, 1995), pp. 429–43. See also note 53 below.

26. Sommer, I, 13, line 27 (above, note 4).

27. The most comprehensive study is the unpublished dissertation by Linda A. Malcor, "The Chalice at the Cross: A Study of the Grail Motif in Medieval Europe" (Ph.D., University of California, Los Angeles, 1991), which, as the title implies, includes many dubious Grails. The earliest depiction of a vessel in association with the crucifixion is in the Stuttgart Psalter, made in northern France in the early ninth century, and the subject was also popular in Anglo-Saxon England, Ottonian Germany, and Mozarabic Spain; I reserve a detailed examination for another occasion.

28. Illustrations abound, particularly in the Moralised Bibles of the second quarter of the thirteenth century: see Alexandre de Laborde, *La Bible moralisée, conservée à Oxford, Paris et Londres: reproduction intégrale du manuscrit du XIIIe siècle accompagnée d'une notice par le comte Alexandre de Laborde*, 5 vols. (Paris: Société française pour la reproduction de manuscrits à peintures, 1911–1927); Reiner Haussherr, *Bible moralisée. Faksimile-Ausgabe im Originalformat des Codex Vindobonensis 2554 der Österreichischen Nationalbibliothek* (Graz: Akademische Druck- u. Verlagsanstalt, 1973), with reference to many articles by the same author; Gerald Guest, *Bible moralisée: Codex Vindobonensis 2554, Vienna, Österreichische Nationalbibliothek* (London: Miller, 1995). A Moses example is reproduced from Bodl. Bod. 270b, f. 50, in Stones, "Sacred and Profane," p. 1972 (above, note 17), fig. 8.

29. Discussed in Stones, "Another Short Note" (above, note 16).

30. For mention of earlier depictions of sacred vessels which eager writers have interpreted as "Grails," see note 27 above.

31. This is stylistically closer to the miscellany, Paris, Bibl. Sainte-Geneviève 2200, part of which was written in 1277, than to Bonn 526, made a decade later (Stones, "The Illustrations," p. 459; above, note 7). It is interesting that neither of the two other *Lancelot-Graal* manuscripts that these craftsmen also made—BNF fr. 110, close to Bonn 526, and BNF fr. 24394, close to BNF fr. 19162—includes a picture of this scene. Indeed, neither shows the Grail at all.

32. See Blackman, "The Manuscripts," p. 505 (above, note 7).

33. Sommer, I, 20, lines 33–34, "de cest bois feras tu a mesculele une huche" ("from this wood you will make an ark for my vessel"; above, note 4).

34. Again, examples abound in the Moralised Bibles, on which see note 28 above. There are also several notable examples in the Old Testament Picture Bible, New York M 638 with leaves in the BNF, Paris, and the J. Paul Getty Museum, reproduced in full in *Old Testament Miniatures*, ed. Sydney C. Cockerell (New York: Braziller, 1969); other examples are in the Psalter of St. Louis, Paris, BNF lat. 10525, reproduced in *Le psautier de saint Louis*, ed. Marcel Thomas (Graz: Akademische Druck- und Verlagsanstalt, 1970), and the hours with a calendar of Arras in the Musée de Lille, SA 367, reproduced in Stones, "BN, fr. 95 and Yale 229," fig. 8.40 (above, note 7). Bibles provide another obvious source of comparisons, a topic too large to outline here. Some provocative examples are reproduced in Helen Rosenau, *Vision of the Temple: The Image of the Temple of Jerusalem in Judaism and Christianity* (London: Oresko, 1979), to which Martine Meuwese kindly drew my attention. For more on links between the Grail chapel and the Temple, see note 57 below.

35. Not in Sommer.

36. Eugène Hucher, *Le Saint Graal*, 3 vols. (Le Mans: Monnoyer, 1877–78; Geneva: Slatkine, 1967), is a complete edition based on this manuscript. This passage, in Hucher, II, 174–75, corresponds with some variants to Sommer, I, 32. For related manuscripts, see note 39 below. For a reproduction, see Stones, "BN, fr. 95 and Yale 229," fig. 8.20 (above, note 7).

37. For other examples of the motif of knight fighting snail, see Lilian M. C. Randall, "The Snail in Gothic Marginal Warfare," *Speculum*, 37 (1962), 358–67.

38. "BN, fr.95 and Yale 229," p. 224 (above, note 7).

39. For discussion of Le Mans 354 in relation to BN fr. 342 of 1274 and BN fr. 770, see Stones, "The Illustrations," 1971, ch. 3 (above, note 7). The same scribe, Walterus de Kayo, signed his name and the date 1282 in a copy of the *Image du Monde*, Paris, BN fr. 14962, a discovery made by Terry Nixon and cited in A. Stones, "The Illustrated Chrétien manuscripts and their artistic context," in *Les Manuscrits* (above, note 5), I, 237–38. BN fr. 770 and BN fr. 342 are included in Andreas Brähm, "Ein Buchmalereiatelier in Arras um 1274," *Wallraf-Richartz Jahrbuch*, 54 (1993), 77–104, which omits Le Mans 354 and numerous other books I have identified as part of this stylistic group; and the attribution to Arras is certainly open to challenge since the use of the liturgical and devotional books is of Douai (in the diocese of Arras, though not Arras itself). I think Le Mans 354 was probably made ca. 1285.

40. For "Arma Christi," see Rudolph Berliner, "Arma Christi," *Münchner Jahrbuch der bildenden Kunst*, 3e ser. 6 (1955), 35–152; Robert Suckale, "Arma

Christi: Überlegungen zur Zeichenhaftigkeit mittelalterlicher Andachtsbilder," *Städeljahrbuch,* n.s. (1977), 177–208; and my summary in Wace, *La Vie de sainte Marguerite* (Beihefte zur Zeitschrift für romanische Philologie 229) (Tübingen: Niemeyer, 1990), pp. 195–96. See also Lucy Freeman Sandler, "Jean Pucelle and the Lost Miniatures of the Belleville Breviary," in *Art Bulletin* 66 (1984), 73–96. The lance, nails, and crown of thorns appear earlier in monumental art, together with the cross, in the context of the Last Judgment, for instance in the sculpture of the west facade at Saint-Denis (1137–1140), which had relics of the Passion given in the eleventh century but quickly claimed to be a donation of Charles the Bald. See Paula Lieber Gerson, "Suger as Iconographer," in *Abbot Suger and Saint-Denis, A Symposium,* ed. P.L. Gerson (New York: Metropolitan Museum, 1986), pp. 183–98, especially notes 28 and 31, with references to Beaulieu and Conques. The Apocalyptic Vision tympanum of 1186 at Santiago de Compostela has been linked with Grail iconography and an interest in Perceval: see Serafín Moralejo, "Entre el Grial y la Divina Commedia," in *Diario de Galicia* (Santiago de Compostela, 1.vi.88), pp. 44–45.

41. It is illustrated throughout by a painter closely related to, if less competent than, the Master of the *Roman de Fauvel,* Paris, BNF fr. 146, made ca. 1316 in Paris. I call him the Sub-Fauvel Master, and discuss his artistic personality in "The Artistic Context of *le Roman de Fauvel* and a Note on *Fauvain,*" in *Fauvel Studies,* ed. Margaret Bent and Andrew Wathey (Oxford: Oxford University Press, 1998), pp. 529–67. Interestingly, the iconographic selection in BNF fr. 9123, illustrated in part by the same artist, is different, and omits this scene of Joseph and the ark.

42. Sommer, I, 79 (above, note 4).

43. Ibid., I, 80.

44. Ibid., I, 40.

45. See V.L. Kennedy, "The Moment of Consecration and the Elevation of the Host," *Mediaeval Studies* 6 (1944), 121–50, esp. 146–47, and Édouard Dumoutet, *Le désir de voir l'hostie et les origines de la dévotion du Saint-Sacrement* (Paris: Beauchesne, 1926), noting also the critical analysis of Dumoutet in André Wilmart, *Auteurs spirituels et textes dévots du Moyen Age latin* (Solesmes: Bloud and Gay; Paris: Études augustiniennes, 1971), p. 371, n. 2. See also Michele Maccarone, "Innocenzo III teologo dell'Eucharistia," in *Studi su Innocenzo III* (Italia Sacra, Studi e documenti di storia ecclesiastica 17) (Padua: Antenore, 1972), pp. 341–431, and Peter Browe, S.J., *Die Verehrung der Eucharistie im Mittelalter* (Rome: Herder, 1967), esp. pp. 70–88. The custom of elevating the Host was already attested by Hildebert of Le Mans (d. 1133), cited by Magdalena Carrasco, "Notes on the Iconography of the Romanesque Illustrated Manuscript of the Life of St. Albinus of Angers," *Zeitschrift für Kunstgeschichte*

47 (1984), 333–48, at 339, with reference to J.-P. Migne, *Patrologiæ cursus completus: seu bibliotheca universalis, integra, uniformis, commoda, economica, omnium SS. Patrum, doctorum scriptorumque eccelesiasticorum, sive latorum, sive græcorum, qui ab ævo apostolico ad tempora Innocentii III (anno 1216) pro Latinis et concilii Florentini (anno. 1439) pro græcis floruerunt . . . series Latina. In qua prodeunt patres, doctores scriptoresque ecclesiæ Latinæ a Tertulliano ad Innocentium III*, 221 vols. (Paris: Garnier, 1878–90).

46. See Jean de Montclos, *Lanfranc et Bérenger: La controverse eucharistique du XIe siècle*, Spicilegium sacrum Lovaniense, Études et documents, 37 (Louvain: Spicilegium sacrum, 1971), cited by Carrasco, 338.

47. Carrasco, 337–41. A second eucharistic miracle depicted in an eleventh-century manuscript is the final communion of St. Denis, in which the host is given the saint by Christ, in Paris, BNF lat. 9436, f. 106v. This is reproduced and discussed in Maurice Vloberg, *L'Eucharistie dans l'art*, 2 vols. (Paris: Arthaud, 1946), II, 186, and also cited by Carrasco, 339 . Further depictions of Eucharistic miracles cited by Carrasco are listed in Charles Rohault de Fleury, *La Messe: Études archéologiques sur ses monuments*, 8 vols. (Paris: Morel, 1883-89), IV, 1–36; G. de Boom, "Le culte de l'eucharistie d'après la miniature du moyen âge," *Studia Eucharistica: DCCI anni a condito festo Sanctissmi Corporis Christi, 1246–1946* (Antwerp: Nederlandsche Boekhandel, 1946), pp. 326–32; Victor Elbern, "Über die Illustration des Messkanons im frühen Mittelalter," in *Miscellanea pro Arte: Festschrift H. Schnitzler*, ed. P. Bloch and J. Hoster (Düsseldorf: Schwan, 1965), pp. 60–67. To these lists may be added the miracle in which Guillaume d'Aquitaine is reconciled to the church by a consecrated Host held out before him by St. Bernard of Clairvaux, depicted in the pair of illustrated antiphonaries probably made for the Cistercian abbey of Cambron (diocese of Cambrai), and now divided between the J. Paul Getty Museum, MSS 83.ML.99 (Ludwig VI. 5) and MS 44, and the Hill Monastic Manuscript Library, Collegeville, Minnesota, MS 8 (Bean MS 3), with fragments in Stockholm, New Mexico, and elsewhere: see Alison Stones and John Steyaert, *Illuminations, Glass and Sculpture in Minnesota Collections* (Minneapolis: University of Minnesota Gallery, 1978), no. 4; Anton von Euw and Joachim Plotzek, *Die Handschriften der Sammlung Ludwig*, 4 vols. (Cologne: Schnütgen Museum, 1979-1985), I, 280–84; "Acquisitions/1992," *The J. Paul Getty Museum Journal* 21 (1993), 111. The only other known representation of this subject is in the early fourteenth-century Hungarian Legendary divided between the Morgan Library, the Vatican, and Berkeley, see *Magyar Anjou Legéndarium*, éd. Ferenc Levárdy (Budapest: Magyar Helikon, 1973), *Ungarisches Legendarium, Vat. lat. 8541*, éd. Giovanni Morello, H. Stamm et Gero Betz (Stuttgart: Belser, 1991); *Vaticana: Liturgie und Andacht im Mittelalter*, ed. Joachim Plotzek (Stuttgart: Belser, 1992), no. 48.

48. Cited by Carrasco, 339 (above, note 45), with reference to *De pignoribus sanctorum*, 1.2: PL 156: 616, and by Dumoutet, *Le désir*, pp. 46–47 (above, note 45). Browe, *Die Verehrung*, pp. 100–01 (above, note 45), cites a ninth-century miracle described by Paschasius Radbertus (d. 864). For other textual accounts see Jules Corblet, *Histoire du sacrament de l'Eucharistie*, 2 vols. (Paris: Librairie catholique, 1885), I, 447–515. See also Maurice Vloberg, "Les miracles eucharistiques. Histoire et iconographie d'hosties miraculeuses," *Sanctuaires et pèlerinages* 2 (1955), 7–26.

49. He witnessed Christ's real presence in the consecrated host; the miracle had been depicted by ca. 1250 in *La estoire de seint Aedward le rei*, Cambridge, UL Ee.3.59, p. 37. See Miri Rubin, *Corpus Christi: The Eucharist in Late Medieval Culture* (Cambridge: Cambridge University Press, 1991), pp. 118–42, and the full description of the manuscript in Nigel J. Morgan, *Illuminated Manuscripts Made in the British Isles, Gothic Manuscripts*, II (London: Miller, 1988), cat. no. 123.

50. The reliquary is preserved in the Cappella del Corporale, situated off the north side of the north transept in the Cathedral of Orvieto, whose rebuilding on a grand scale appears to have been closely associated with the occurrence of the miracle close by at Bolsena and its authentication in Orvieto by Pope Urban IV. The miracle and surrounding events are also depicted on the east wall of the chapel, in frescoes by Ugolino di Prete Ilario (1357–64), including a scene showing the pope commissioning the office of Corpus Christi. The corporal reliquary is fully reproduced in Paolo Dal Pogetto, *Ugolino di Vieri, Gli Smalti di Orvieto* (Forma e colore) (Florence: Sadea, 1965); see also Pierluigi Leone de Castris, "Il reliquiario del corporale a Orvieto e lo smalto senese di primo trecento," in *Il duomo di Orvieto e le grandi cattedrali del duecento* (Atti del Convegno Internazionale di Studi, Orvieto, 12–14 novembre 1990), ed. Guido Barlozzetti (Turin: Nuova ERI, 1995), pp. 169–91, and the not very scientific study by Giusi Testa, *La Cattedrale di Orvieto, Santa Maria Assunta in Cielo* (Orvieto: Libreria dello Stato, 1990), pp. 80–83. Another famous example of the miracle of Bolsena coupled (indirectly, since they are in different *stanze*) with the transubstantiation (showing the Host in a monstrance) is among the frescoes by Raphael and followers, commissioned by Pope Julius II ca. 1507–17, for the Vatican *stanze*. See George Hersey, *High Renaissance Art in St. Peter's and the Vatican* (Chicago: Chicago University Press, 1993), pp. 129–76 (accepting the institution of the feast in 1264 as a result of the miracle, p. 150). I thank David Wilkins and Matthew Roper for these references and for helpful discussion of depictions of transubstantiation in Italy.

51. Although these frescoes were completely repainted between 1855 and 1860, the sinopia, discovered during the restorations of 1977–1978, clearly

shows that the details of transubstantiated Host as Christ/boy holding a cross are accurate in the restoration (Testa, pp. 198–99). One of the transubstantions of Orvieto is reproduced (but not actually mentioned in the text) in Piero Camporesi, "The Consecrated Host: A Wondrous Excess," in *Fragments for a History of the Human Body*, ed. Michel Feher et al. (New York: Zone, 1989), I, 220–37, which focuses on perceptions about the swallowed transubstantiated Host assimilating and being assimilated by the human body during the process of digestion.

52. See particularly Édouard Dumoutet, *Corpus domini: aux sources de la piété eucharistique médiévale* (Paris: Beauchesne, 1942), and Eugène Anitchkof, "Le saint Graal et les rites eucharistiques," in *Romania* 4 (1929), 174–94. Other critics have emphasized the rôle of a Cistercian ethic (Albert Pauphilet, *Études sur la Queste del saint Graal* [Paris: Champion, 1921]), or the concept of grace (Étienne Gilson, "La mystique de la grâce dans la *Queste*," *Romania* 51 [1925], 321–47, and id., *Les Idées et les lettres* [Paris:Vrin, 1932], pp. 59–91).

53. A case in point is a depiction of a celebration of mass in the early–fourteenth-century Breviary of the Cathedral of Saint-Lambert, Liège, Darmstadt, Hessische Landes- und Hochschulbibliothek 394, which I shall return to elsewhere. Another case is the Last Supper miniature in the Livre d'images de Madame Marie, cited in note 25 above.

54. Reproduced in Stones, "BN, fr. 95 and Yale 229," fig. 8.15 (above, note 7).

55. Victor Leroquais, *Les sacramentaires et les missels manuscrits des bibliothèques publiques de France*, 2 vols. (Paris: Protat, 1924).

56. They are reproduced and discussed in Stones, "BN, fr. 95 and Yale 229," figs. 8. 18 and 8. 19 (above, note 7).

57. This is quite different from the centrally planned "Grail Temple," based on the Temple of Jerusalem, described in Albrecht's *Jüngere Titurel*, composed in Middle High German ca. 1270, which is the starting point for Ringbom's wide-ranging study: Lars-Ivar Ringbom, *Graltempel und Paradies, Beziehungen zwischen Iran und Europa im Mittelalter* (Stockholm: Wahlström and Widstrand, 1951). See also Rosenau, *Vision* (above, note 34).

58. Sommer I, 33–34 (above, note 4).

59. Blackman, "The Manuscripts," p. 505 (above, note 7). No image of the liturgy is in BNF fr. 112 or BNF fr. 117–20, the other Vulgate Cycle manuscripts owned by Jacques d'Armagnac. BNF fr. 112 is the special version he commissioned; BNF 117–20 is the set he inherited from his great-grandfather, Jean de Berry.

60. Sommer, I, 34. See Stones, "BN, fr. 95 and Yale 229," fig. 8.19 (above, note 7).

61. Illustrations of the *Queste* liturgy in other manuscripts are discussed below.

62. Sommer, I, 211 (above, note 4).

63. See Stones, "The Earliest" (above, note 5), where the date is argued on the basis of stylistic parallels with royal manuscripts of ca. 1220. The carrying of the Grail to Norgales is fig. 3a.

64. BNF fr. 770, f. 98, and BNF fr. 9123, f. 79 show a very similar, non-text-specific, depiction. UCB Berkeley 106, Le Mans 354, BNF fr. 95, and Yale 227 have no illustration of this; it is in BNF fr. 113, f. 88, but without the Grail. See Blackman, "The Manuscripts," p. 506 (above, note 7).

65. This manuscript has a large number of marginal notes for the illumina-tor: the one on this page says "Josef q(ui) enporte le sent vaisel (et) gens avec lui." It is by the same painters as London, BL Harley 4979, discussed in my "Notes on Three Illuminated Alexander Manuscripts," in *The Medieval Alexan-der Legend and Romance Epic*, ed. Peter Noble, Lucie Polak, and Claire Isoz (Millwood, N.Y., London, and Nendeln: Kraus, 1982), pp. 193–254.

66. Marie-Madeleine Gauthier, *Les routes de la foi* (Fribourg: Office du Livre, 1983), no. 66, in the treasury of the church of Notre-Dame, St-Omer (Pas-de-Calais); see also *Trésors des églises de l'arrondissement de Saint-Omer* (Saint-Omer: Musée Sandelin, 1992), no. 3, pp. 42–45, where it is identified as a pyx, a type of vessel that is not normally perforated. Another pertinent example is the fully visible lunar stand, made to support the Host, within rock crystal sur-rounded by an architectural framework, seen on the monstrance made in Paris for another Cistercian house, the nunnery of Herkenrode (near Hasselt, province of Limburg, diocese of Liège) in 1286. An inscription indicates it was commis-sioned for Herkenrode by prioress Adelheid von Diest in 1286, and it bears the earliest dated Parisian silver stamp. See Michel Andrieu, "Aux origines du culte du Saint-Sacrement: Reliquaires et monstrances eucharistiques," *Analecta Bol-landiana* 68 (1950), 379–418, and *Schatz aus den Trümmern* (exhibition cata-logue), ed. Hiltrud Westermann-Angerhausen (Cologne: Schnütgen Museum, 1996), no. 27. It now belongs to the church of Saint-Quentin in Hasselt (Bel-gium) but is on loan to the Stellinwerff-Waerdenhof Museum in Hasselt.

67. For Christ as priest, and the Host displayed in a monstrance, see François Avril, "Une curieuse illustration de la Fête-Dieu: l'iconographie du Christ prêtre élevant l'hostie et sa diffusion," in *Rituel: Mélanges offers à Pierre-Marie Gy, o. p.*, ed. Paul de Clerck and Eric Palazzo (Paris: Cerf, 1990), pp. 39–54, cited in Stones, "BN, fr. 95 and Yale 229," note 118 (above, note 7). See also the Eucharistic miracles referred to in note 47 above.

68. Sommer, I, 286 (above, note 4). The Rennes manuscript shows Alain weeping at Josephe's deathbed, but no Grail is shown.

69. Not according to Loomis, *The Grail* (above, note 2), p. 280, where Josephe hands Alain an "escuelle."

70. It is worth noting that in this manuscript Josephe is shown standing, not lying on his deathbed as in the other depictions of this episode.

71. These are standard heraldic terms: argent=silver (here white is used as a substitute), gules=red.

72. Sommer, I, 288-89 (above, note 4).

73. As in Amsterdam, BPH 1 and Royal 14. E. III.

74. Rennes 255, f. 98v; Tours 951, f. 156v.

75. Add. 10292, f. 74v; Yale 227, f. 138.

76. Rennes 255, f. 98v; Yale 227, f. 131v.

77. Sommer, I, 289 (above, note 4). In the parallel miniature in Add. 10292, f. 74, the wounding is also shown but the Grail is omitted.

78. Reproduced in Matthews, *Grail: Quest*, p. 76 (above, note 18).

79. Blackman, "The Manuscripts," p. 508 (above, note 7).

80. Jessie L. Weston, *From Ritual to Romance* (Cambridge: Cambridge University Press, 1920; Princeton: Princeton University Press, 1993).

81. T.S. Eliot, *Collected Poems 1909–1935* (New York: Harcourt, Brace, 1936), p. 91.

82. I thank Oliver Benjamin for discussion of this point.

83. Pauphilet, p. 15 (above, note 1).

84. See Emmanuèle Baumgartner, "La couronne et le cercle: Arthur et la table ronde dans les manuscrits du *Lancelot-Graal*," *Texte et image* (Actes du colloque international de Chantilly, 13-15 octobre 1982) (Paris: Belles Lettres, 1984), pp. 191–200, all illustrated; Matthews, *Grail: Quest*, pp. 81, 84 for reproductions; Blackman, "Pictorial Synopsis," p. 38 (above, note 7).

85. Not according to Pauphilet p. 15 (above, note 1), nor in the previously described episodes at the beginning of the *Queste* where Arthur and his knights are at table.

86. Pauphilet p. 15.

87. Nor is this Grail-scene illustrated in Brussels, BR 9627–8, Paris, BNF fr. 339, Oxford, Bodl. Digby 223, Paris, BNF fr. 342 (a banquet scene is shown at the beginning of the *Queste*, but without the Grail), BNF fr. 344, Bonn 526, BNF fr. 110, BNF fr. 123, Yale 229, Paris, BNF fr. 1422–4, Oxford, Bodl. Rawl. Q.b.6, Douce 199, Paris, B.Ars. 3482.

88. See Pierre Breillat, "La *Quête du Saint-Graal* en Italie," *Mélanges d'archéologie et d'histoire de l'École française de Rome* 54 (1937), 262–300, esp. 296–300; Stones in "BN, fr. 95 and Yale 229," pp. 213–19 (above, note 7); and Lori Walters in "Wonders and Illuminations, Pierart dou Tielt and the *Queste del saint Graal*," in *Word and Image*, 1996, pp. 339–72 (above, note 7).

89. The tabernacles on pulleys cited in Rubin, p. 47 (above, note 49), are English and date between the late fourteenth and sixteenth centuries; so also the

hanging tabernacle depicted on a triptych of the sixteenth century at Arras Cathedral, reproduced in Vloberg, *L'Eucharistie*, I, 73 (above, note 47). Several considerably earlier (early thirteenth century) French examples are extant, made of Limoges enamel and taking the form of a dove; see Vloberg, I, 72 and, most recently, *Enamels of Limoges 1100–1350* (New York: Metropolitan Museum, 1996), ed. John P. O'Neill, no. 106, Paris, Musée du Louvre, Département des Objets d'art (OA 8104), catalogue entry by Elisabeth Taburet-Delahaye, with full bibliography. There is no reflection of this form in *Estoire* or *Queste* iconography. See Joseph Braun, *Das christliche Altargerät* (Munich: Hueber, 1932), for chalices: figs. 2–144; patens (non–bowl-shaped), figs. 145–164; pyxes (three of them stemless), figs. 165–178; ciboria figs. 179–197, of which figs. 186, 187, 192, 193, 194 are fifteenth-century examples; monstrances: 226–296.

90. Pauphilet, p. 59 (above, note 1). A few examples are illustrated in Stones, "Sacred and Profane," pp. 100–12 (above, note 17), figs. 4, 5, 6.

91. This scene is also omitted in Brussels, BR 9627–28, Paris, BNF fr. 339, 110, 123, Oxford, Bodl. Digby 223, Rawl. Q.b.6, Douce 199, Yale 229, BNF fr. 344, Ars. 3482.

92. The colophon says, "pries pour ce li (not "celui") ki l'escrist," cf. M.K. Pope, *From Latin to Modern French* (1952; Manchester: Manchester University Press, 1961), p. 325, para. 845.

93. The Grail is also omitted in the Avignon copy of 1319, Florence, Laur. Ash. 121 (48).

94. Reproduced in Vloberg, *L'Eucharistie*, II, 232 (above, note 47).

95. See Stones, "The Illustrations," ch. 5 (above, note 7), and ead., "Sacred and Profane," 108–10 and fig. 5 (above, note 17). See also the image of the knights at the Grail Table with chalice and cross in the Bonn manuscript, discussed below.

96. Preserved at the church of St. Godehard, Hildesheim. See *The St. Albans Psalter*, ed. Francis Wormald, Otto Pächt, and Charles Reginald Dodwell (London: Warburg Institute, 1960), pl. 25 and 26, illustrating pages 39 and 40 of the manuscript, the Agony in the Garden and Christ waking the sleeping apostles (the manuscript is paginated, not foliated). The commentary on pp. 61 and 69 recognizes that the inclusion of the "cup of bitterness" in these scenes is unusual, but makes no mention of the still less common presence of the cross in the chalice.

97. For a reproduction, see *Art and the Courts*, ed. Marie Montpetit (Ottawa: National Gallery, 1972), no. 37, pl. 55. I thank Adelaide Bennett for suggesting this and the examples mentioned in the following note.

98. Very few other examples show the combination cross and chalice: a painted panel of ca. 1400, now in the Staedelmuseum, Frankfurt, shows an angel

holding a cross descending toward a chalice containing a wafer, before which Christ kneels. A similar scene is included in the *Belles Heures* of Jean de Berry at the Metropolitan Museum, The Cloisters, New York, acc. no. 54.1.1, f. 123, illustrating Matins of the Hours of the Passion. A painting attributed by Henk van Os to Taddeo di Bartolo at the Thorvaldsenmuseum, Copenhagen, shows an angel holding a cross-surmounted chalice, descending toward the kneeling Christ: see *Simiolus* 7 (1974), 82 (no reproduction given).

99. Reproduced in Loomis, *Arthurian Legends*, fig. 333 (above, note 6). See also the brief catalogue entry in François Avril, *Dix siècles d'enluminure italienne, Vie–XIVe siècles* (Paris: Bibliothèque Nationale, 1984), no. 84, pp. 98–99. I thank Marie-Thérèse Gousset for her generous assistance with this manuscript.

100. Blackman, "The Manuscripts," p. 23, and "Pictorial Synopsis," 39 (above, note 7).

101. The Grail liturgy is discussed in more detail in Stones, "BN, fr. 95 and Yale 229," pp. 213–21 (above, note 7).

102. Pauphilet, pp. 269–72 (above, note 1).

103. Pauphilet, p. 263: illustrated in BR 9628, BNF fr. 339, 123, 342, Yale 229, Oxford, Bod. Rawl. Q.b.6, BNF fr. 1424, Add. 10294, Royale 14.E.III, Rylands Fr. 1, Florence, Laur. Ash. 121 (48), BNF fr. 111, 112, 116.

104. Pauphilet, p. 266: illustrated in BNF fr. 342, Add. 10294 (but not in Royal 14. E. III or Rylands Fr. 1); BNF fr. 112 (but not BNF fr. 116).

105. Pauphilet, p. 271, discussed below.

106. Pauphilet, p. 277, discussed below.

107. Pauphilet, pp. 277–79. The crowning and death are illustrated as two separate scenes in Florence, Laur. Ash. 121(48); just the death, as a single scene, in BNF fr. 112 (but not BNF fr. 116, see Blackman, "Pictorial Synopsis," 42; above, note 7).

108. For Chrétien's *Perceval* see Baumgartner, "Les scènes du Graal" (above, note 8).

109. Pauphilet, p. 270.

110. Pauphilet, pp. 234–35. Standard elements of Christian iconography, the association of the evangelists with these creatures, which emerged in the Early Christian period as man=Matthew, lion=Mark, ox=Luke, eagle=John, is based on the Visions of Ezekiel (Ezek.1, 4–28) and of St. John in the Apocalypse (Apoc. 4, 7–9), and on commentaries on those passages.

111. Guiseppe Bergamini and Gian Carlo Menis, *Miniatura in Friuli* (Udine: Instituto per l'enciclopedia del Friuli Venezia Giulia, 1985), no. 22, p. 79, and the facsimile edition, *La grant Queste del Saint Graal: la grande Ricerca del Santo Graal, Versione inedita della fine de XIII secolo del ms. Udine, Biblioteca Arcivescovile, 177*, ed. Gianfranco d'Aronco et al. (Tricesimo [Udine]: Vattori, 1990).

112. Oxford, Bodl., Digby 223, Paris, BNF fr. 110, BL Royal 14. E. III, BNF fr. 116, f. 643v, Florence, Laur. Ash. 121(48). The white stag also features in the major Grail liturgy in the Florence *Tavola Ritonda*, discussed below.

113. The other such scene occurs just before this, and shows Bohort seeing a Pelican in her Piety, a symbol of Christ drawn from the Bestiary tradition and a common iconographic motif (Pauphilet, p. 168). The Florence example is reproduced in Stones, "BN, fr. 95 and Yale 229," as fig. 8. 5 (above, note 7).

114. Pauphilet, p. 255.

115. See Stones, "BN, fr. 95 and Yale 229," pp. 214–15, 219–20.

116. Numerous parallels with shrines and tabernacles of the late thirteenth century can be drawn: see ead., "BN, fr. 95 and Yale 229," pp. 225–27.

117. Pauphilet, pp. 269–70.

118. For the attribution to Genoa, see *La grant Queste*, pp. 31–47 (above, note 111), and François Avril, Marie-Thérèse Gousset, and Claudia Rabel, *Manuscrits enluminés d'origine italienne, II, XIIIe siècle* (Paris: Bibliothèque nationale, 1984), pp. 25, 32–52. The Udine manuscript would seem to be the only surviving illustrated copy of *Queste* from this workshop, whereas there are several copies of the *Lancelot* proper: see Daniela Delcorno Branca, "Tradizione italiana dei testi arturiani. Note sul Lancelot," in *Medioevo Romanzo* 17 (1992), 215–50. An Italian artist participated in the illustration of Tours 951 (E, J, M), but neither he nor his French collaborator included the Grail. See Jaroslav Folda, *Crusader Manuscript Illumination at St. Jean d'Acre, 1275–1291* (Princeton: Princeton University Press, 1976), pp. 122–23. The Italian *Joseph* and *Merlin*, in Florence, Bibl. Riccardiana 2759, is unillustrated, and the Italian *Queste*, Oxford, Bodl. Rawl. D. 874, is minimally illustrated and does not include a depiction of the Grail.

119. See note 27 above.

120. For the artistic context see François Avril in *Fastes du Gothique, le siècle de Charles V*, exhibition catalogue (Paris: Musées de France, 1981), no. 301, pp. 348–49, and for the iconography, Walters, "Wonders" (cited in note 88 above). This was also reproduced in Loomis, *Arthurian Legends*, fig. 341, and in Stones, "Sacred and Profane," fig. 7, and, in color, in Matthews, *Grail: Quest*, pp. 52–53, and on the cover of Weston, *Ritual*.

121. See notes 50–51 above.

122. Pauphilet, pp. 269–70 (above, note 1).

123. Pauphilet, p. 269.

124. Edmund Garrett Gardner, *The Arthurian Legend in Italian Literature* (New York: Dent-Dutton, 1930; reprint, New York: Octagon, 1971), p. 153, reproductions facing pp. 2, 112, 122, 174, 180, 190, 208, 268, 272, 286; Loomis, *Arthurian Legends*, p. 121, figs. 337–39 (above, note 6); *Mostra dei codici romanzi delle Bibliotheche fiorentine* (Florence: Sansoni, 1957), pp. 119–20. For

the text, see *La Tavola Ritonda o L'Istoria di Tristano, Testo di lingua,* ed. Filippo-Luigi Polidori, I, *Testo* (Bologna: Romagnoli, 1864); Daniela Branca, *I Romanzi italiani di Tristano e la "Tavola Ritonda"* (Florence: Olschki, 1968), esp. pp. 204–07; see also Christopher Kleinhenz, "Tristan in Italy: The Death and Rebirth of a Legend," in *Studies in Medieval Culture* 5 (1975), 145–58; Marie-José Heijkant, *La tradizione de "Tristan" in prosa in Italia e proposte di studio sul "Tristano Riccardiano"* (Nijmegen: Sneldruck Enschede, 1989).

125. Many of the illustrations in BNF fr. 343 remain as drawings, including the opening portrait of the patron on f. 1, although the miniature on the same page was completed in color, and others sporadically throughout the manuscript are also unfinished. There appears to have been more than one painter at work, and perhaps more than one draftsman, a question I cannot pursue here.

126. His name and the date are in the colophon; he is known as a Cremonan from his *Filocolo,* see D. De Robertis, "Centesimo dei manoscritti delle Rime di Dante," *Studi Danteschi* 38 (1961), 276, cited by Delcorno Branca, "Tradizione italiana" (above, note 118) at 243, n. 78.

127. For the attribution to Bembo, see Niccolò Rasmo, "Il Codice palatino 556 e le sue illustrazioni," *Rivista d'arte,* ser. 2–11 (1939), 245–81; Mario Salmi, "Nota su Bonifacio Bembo," *Commentari* 4 (1953), 7–15; Germano Mulazzani, *I tarocchi viscontei e Bonifacio Bembo: il mazzo di Yale* (Milan: Bocca, 1981); Joanna Woods-Marsden, *The Gonzaga of Mantua and Pisanello's Arthurian Frescoes* (Princeton: Princeton University Press, 1988), pp. 28, 184, n. 81; see also L. Stephani, "Per una storia della miniatura italiana da Giovanni de' Grassi alla scuola cremonese della 11a metà del Quattrocento: appunti bibliografici," *La miniatura italiana tra Gotico e Rinascimento* (Atti del II Congressi di Storia della Miniatura Italiana, Cortona 24–26 settembre 1982), ed. Emanuela Sesti (Storia della Miniatura, Studi e Documenti 6), 2 vols. (Florence: Olschki, 1985), II, 823–81, esp. 859. A useful summary of the problems is Daniela Delcorno Branca, "Rassegna sulla letteratura arturiana in Italia (1985–1992)," *Lettere italiane* 44 (1992), 465–97. I thank Daniela Delcorno Branca, Marie-José Heijkant, Christopher Kleinhenz, and Joanna Woods-Marsden for their generous assistance with the manuscripts of the Italian tradition.

128. Pierre Breillat, "Le manuscrit Florence Palatin 556 et la liturgie du Graal," *Mélanges d'archéologie et d'histoire de l'École française de Rome* 55 (1938), 342–73. Other aspects of the iconography are equally unusual, see Stones, "Aspects of Arthur's Death," p. 71 (above, note 17).

129. The closest parallel is the two-handled urn-shaped Grail shown in the single Grail illustration in the Udine manuscript (see notes 111 and 118 above).

130. This corresponds to Polidori, *La Tavola Ritonda,* p. 473–74 (above, note 124). For the citations, see Stones, "BN, fr. 95 and Yale 229," pp. 216–19 (above, note 7).

131. Reproduced in Matthews, *Grail: Quest*, p. 89 (above, note 18).

132. "la piece en semblance de pain," Pauphilet, p. 270 (above, note 1).

133. Cf. Pauphilet, p. 270: "un hom ausi come tout nu, et avoit les mains saignanz et les piez et le cors"; there is no mention of the wounds as such.

134. Pauphilet, pp. 240–41; Polidori, p. 472.

135. For connections with medical illustrations of this subject, see Stones, "Indications écrites," 322–23, figs. 1–3 (above, note 15). One of Jacques d'Armagnac's manuscripts, the special version, BNF fr. 112, has on f. 172 a scene showing the three knights Galaad, Bohort, and Perceval fighting the knights who want a dishful of blood from Perceval's sister. This scene is not otherwise represented, and BNF fr. 112 does not include the bloodletting scene itself. See Blackman, "The Manuscripts," p. 238, and "Pictorial Synopsis," p. 41 (above, note 7).

136. Reproduced in Loomis, *Arthurian Legends*, fig. 329 (above, note 6), and, in color, in Matthews, *Grail: Quest*, p. 49 (above, note 18). The miniature is rubbed in the area around Perceval's sister's arm, and the bowl is unclear in black-and-white reproductions, although it is perfectly distinct in the original and can be seen in the color reproduction.

137. See note 25 above.

138. See note 28 above.

139. Discovered in 804 in a vessel contained in a chest of leather inscribed *Jesu Christi Sanguis*, noted in *Annales Regni Francorum*, ed. G.H. Pertz and Fridericus Kurze, Scriptores rerum germanicarum in usum scholarum ex Monumentis Germaniae historicis recusi 6 (Hanover: Hahn, 1895), p. 119, also mentioned in Jonathan Sumption, *Pilgrimage, an Image of Medieval Religion* (London: Faber, 1975), pp. 46–48. Pope Sixtus IV granted indulgences in three briefs of 1475 to Lodovico Gonzaga and Barbara of Brandenburg and their descendants: see Woods-Marsden (above, note 127), pp. 54, 63–64, 212, n. 126, citing I. Donesmondi, *Dell'istoria ecclesiastica di Mantova* (Mantua: 1612), pp. 4–12 (which was not available to me); R.J. Peebles, *The Legend of Longinus, Its Ecclesiastical Tradition in English Literature and Its Connection with the Grail*, Bryn Mawr College Monographs 9 (Baltimore: Furst, 1911); Marita Horster, "Mantuae sanguis preciosus," *Wallraf-Richartz Jahrbuch* 25 (1963), 151–71. The relic is in the crypt under the dome at the church of San Andrea in Mantua, but the crypt is not accessible to the public. In the main church, an enormous bronze polygon, containing explanatory inscriptions and surrounded by a marble railing, marks the spot below which the relic is preserved. Part of the Mantua relic came in 1055 into the hands of Emperor Henry III, then at his death the following year to Count Baldwin of Flanders. It was taken by Baldwin's daughter Judith to the Welf court at her marriage in 1071 to Duke Welf IV, and came at her death to the abbey of Weingarten. The story is recounted on an altarpiece of 1489 now at the Württembergisches Landesmuseum, Stuttgart. See

Norbert Kruse, *Die Weingartner Heilig-Blut-Tafel von 1489* (Kleinode 1) (Ravensburg: Sparkasse, 1994).

140. What is shown is the victory of Bohort over King Brangoire in a tournament, followed by his deception, thanks to a potion, by the king's daughter, which resulted in the conception of Helain le Blanc, future emperor of Constantinople, see Woods-Marsden, *The Gonzaga*, pp. 13–20 (above, note 127).

141. Roberto Benedetti, "'Qua fa' un santo e un cavaliere . . . .' Aspetti codicologici e note per il miniatore," in *La grant Queste del Saint Graal*, pp. 32–47, cited by Daniela Delcorno Branca, "Sette anni di Studi sulla Letteratura arturiana in Italia. Rassegna (1985–1992)," *Lettere Italiane*, 44 (1992), 465–97 at 470.

142. See Stones, "BN, fr. 95 and Yale 229," pp. 232–33 (above, note 7).

143. See note 124 above. In addition to the unfinished state of the portrait initial at the beginning, perhaps intended to show the patron, there is no Visconti-Sforza heraldry. It did however enter the Visconti-Sforza library, where Pellegrin identified it with inventory no. A 908 (see Elisabeth Pellegrin, *La Bibliothèque des Visconti et des Sforza* [Paris: CNRS, 1955], p. 274), and Delcorno Branca suggests that it can also be identified with an entry in the Sforza inventory of 1488. See Delcorno Branca, "Tradizione italiana"(above, note 118), 241, n. 69, citing A.G. Cavagna, "'Il libro desquadernato: la carta rosechata dai rati.' Due nuovi inventari della libreria Visconto-Sforzesca," *Bollettino della società pavese di storia patria*, n.s. 41 (1989), 29–97, item no. 617.

144. Stones, "BN, fr. 95 and Yale 229," pp. 229–30 (above, note 7).

145. The most reliable maps are the ones in Édouard de Moreau, *Histoire de l'Église en Belgique*, 5 vols. (Brussels: Édition universelle, 1945–1952); see also Laurent Henri Cottineau, *Répertoire topo-bibliographique des abbayes et prieurés*, 2 vols. (Mâcon: Protat, 1939); *Supplément*, ed. Gregoire Poras (Mâcon: Protat, 1970).

146. Jacques Toussaert, *Le sentiment religieux en Flandre à la fin du Moyen Age* (Paris: 1963), pp. 259–67.

147. It is housed today at the church of St-François-de-Sales in Boulogne-sur-Mer. See Marie-Madeleine Gauthier, *Les émaux du moyen âge occidental* (Fribourg: Office du Livre, 1972), no. 158; *Trésors des Églises de France*, ed. Jean Taralon (Paris: Hachette, 1966), no. 42, pl. 111. The reliquary was a gift from Philippe le Bel to Notre-Dame de Boulogne in commemoration of the marriage in 1308 of his daughter Isabelle to Edward II of England. Vloberg, *L'Eucharistie*, II, 149 (above, note 47), refers to Monseigneur Malou, *Du culte du Saint Sang de Jésus Crist et de la Relique de ce Sang qui est conservé à Bruges* (1851; Bruges, 1927), which was not available to me. Vloberg, II, 149–51, also discusses the Fécamp relic of the Holy Blood, allegedly contained in a vial and hidden in a hollow fig tree by Isaac, nephew of Nicodemus, then carried by water to Fécamp (Fici Campus).

148. Sommer, I, 40 (above, note 4).

149. Pauphilet, pp. 271–72 (above, note 1).

150. The scene is reproduced in Loomis, *Arthurian Legends*, fig. 334 (above, note 6), and Matthews, *Grail: Quest*, p. 59 (above, note 18). Perhaps BNF fr. 343 is the copy that inspired the thinking of Jessie L. Weston; one wonders whether she saw the manuscript itself or perhaps Loomis's photographs of the manuscript. There is one other possible example: although unlikely given the absence of this episode elsewhere in the French illustrative tradition, it may be that the scene on f. 525 in Ars. 3482, showing a knight and a servant before a king who stands in front of a throne, depicts this episode. What is going on is not clear, and another explanation is that this might depict the death of King Mordrain. It is also worth noting that BNF fr. 112, f. 281, has a blank space for an illustration of Perceval and the Roi Mehaignié.

151. Pauphilet, pp. 273–75.

152. The miniature is partially rubbed, and the cripple erased, as was the case with Lancelot observing the Grail liturgy from the doorway, discussed above. Here, however, there is no obvious reason why the cripple's presence should have been objected to.

153. See Blackman, "The Manuscripts," p. 239, and "Pictorial Synopsis," p. 42 (above, note 7).

154. Polidori, pp. 475–76 (above, note 124). This corresponds to Pauphilet, p. 276.

155. Pauphilet, p. 277.

156. The miniature has been placed at Pauphilet, p. 268.

157. Reproduced in Ringbom, *Graltempel und Paradies* (above, note 57), fig. 132, p. 473 (where the manuscript is wrongly identified as a "*Parzival*-Handschrift"), and in von dem Borne, *Der Gral* (above, note 18), fig. 16. This scene is placed at Pauphilet, p. 262, at a point where most illustrated manuscripts show King Mordrain dying in the arms of Galaad.

158. Placed at Pauphilet, p. 276.

159. Not in Jacques d'Armagnac's other manuscripts, BNF fr. 116 and BNF fr. 120: see Blackman, "The Manuscripts," p. 239, and "Pictorial Synopsis," p. 42 (above, note 7).

160. Pauphilet, p. 279.

161. Pauphilet, p. 278.

162. The major groups are: Le Mans 354 and BNF fr. 770, to which BNF fr. 342 is also related; BNF fr. 95 and Yale 229; Amsterdam/Rylands/Douce, Royal 14. E. III, Add. 10292–4; BNF fr. 105, 9123, Ars. 3482; BNF fr. 117–120, Ars. 3479–80; BNF fr. 112, 113–116; for the approximate dates, see the Working List of Illustrated Manuscripts at the end of this chapter.

WORKING LIST OF ILLUSTRATED MANUSCRIPTS OF THE *ESTOIRE* AND THE *QUESTE*

This list was initially drawn from Brian Woledge, *Bibliographie des romans et nouvelles en prose française antérieurs à 1500* (Geneva: Droz, 1975), pp. 50, 69, 71–79, 82–83, 99–100, and id., *Supplément 1954–1973* (Geneva: Droz, 1975), pp. 48–59, 64–65, 80–82, and the lists in Alexandre Micha, "Les manuscrits du *Lancelot* en prose," *Romania* 81 (1960), 145–87; *Romania* 84 (1963), 28–60, 478–99; "La tradition manuscrite du *Lancelot* en prose," *Romania* 85 (1964), 293–318, 478–517. Revisions to the chronology and dating proposed by Woledge and Micha are in Stones, "The Illustrations" (1970–1971) (above, note 7), "The Earliest" (1977) (above, note 5), pp. 42–44, and "Aspects of Arthur's Death," at 87–101 (above, note 17). These branches are rarely transmitted alone, so I include reference to the others where they are in the same volume as *Estoire* or *Queste*: *Joseph* (J), *Merlin* (M), *Lancelot* (L), *Mort Artu* (MA). I omit from the list that follows those manuscripts which do not have *Estoire* or *Queste*. Common titles of other texts that accompany *Estoire* or *Queste* are written out in full.

ESTOIRE MANUSCRIPTS

a) Manuscripts with One Illustration, or One for Each Branch, or Gaps

Bourg-en-Bresse, BM 55	E	illustrations cut out
Chantilly, Musée Condé 643 (307)	EM	spaces left blank
Darmstadt, 2534	EML	
Oxford, Bodl. Douce 303	E	
Paris, BArs.2997	EM	
Paris, BN fr. 98	EMLQMA	

b) Manuscripts with Cycles of Illustrations

Numbers of illustrations are approximate (the count depends on whether or not composite miniatures, and miniatures accompanied by historiated initials, are counted as one or more)

Amsterdam BPH 1 (ex-
Phillipps 1045/7[numbering
problematical], 3630)/Oxford,

Bodl. Douce 215/Manchester, Ryl.fr.1	EMLQMA	189
Berkeley, UCB 106 (ex-Phillipps 3643)	EM	21
Bonn, UB 526	EMLQMA	346
Brussels, BR 9246	E in Guillaume de la Pierre's adaptation (1480)	52
Geneva-Cologny, Bodmer 147 (ex-Phillips 1046)	EMLQMA	167
London, BL Add. 10292–4	EMLQMA	748 [sic]
London, BL Roy. 14. E. III	EQMA	116
Manchester, see Amsterdam		
Le Mans MM 354	E	17
Modena, BEstense E 39	special version	15
New Haven, Yale, Beinecke 227	EM (1357)	164
Paris, BArs.3349	E	
Paris, BArs.3350	E	
Paris, BArs.3479–80	EMLQMA	130 ?
Paris, BN fr. 95	EM *Sept sages, Pénitence Adam*	163
Paris, BN fr. 96	EML	
Paris, BN fr. 105	EM	127
Paris, BN fr. 110	EMLQMA	99
Paris, BN fr. 112	special version	258
Paris, BN fr. 113–16	EMLQMA	209
Paris, BN fr. 117–20	EMLQMA	131
Paris, BN fr. 344	EMLQMA	344 [sic]
Paris, BN fr. 748	JM	15
Paris, BN fr. 749	EM	126
Paris, BN fr. 769	E	
Paris, BN fr. 770	EM *Prise de Jerusalem*	140
Paris, BN fr. 1426	E	

Paris, BN fr. 1427	E (1504)	no illus-trations
Paris, BN fr. 9123	EM	167
Paris, BN fr. 12582	E	
Paris, BN fr. 19162	EM	83
Paris, BN fr. 24394	EM	71
Paris, Private Collection (ex-Phillipps 1047)	EM	129
Rennes BM 255	EML	64
St Petersburg SSL Fr. F.v.XV.5	E	43
Tours, BM 951	EJM	133
unidentified private collection (ex–Phillipps 1047)	EM	129

c) French Manuscripts Copied and Illustrated in Italy

Oxford, Bodl. Douce 178	EM

QUESTE MANUSCRIPTS

a) Manuscripts with One Illustration, or One for Each Branch, or Gaps

Berkeley, UCB 73 (ex-Phillips 4377)	QMA	
London, BL Roy. 19. C. xiii	LQMA	
London, BL Roy. 20 C. vi	LQMA	
London, BL Add. 17443	QMA	
Lyon, BM PA 77	LQMA	illustrations cut out
Oxford, Bodl. Rawl. D. 899	LQMA	
Paris, BArs. 3347	LQMA	
Paris, BN fr. 98	EMLQMA	
Paris, BN fr. 751	LQMA	
Paris, BN fr. 758	*Tristan*, QMA	
Paris, BN fr. 771	LQ	
Paris, BN fr. 12580	LQMA	

Paris, BN fr. 12581	Q	
Paris, BN n.a.fr. 1119	LQMA	
Ravenna, BClassense 454	Q	illustrations cut out

b) Manuscripts with Cycles of Illustrations

Numbers of illustrations are approximate (the count depends on whether or not composite miniatures, and miniatures accompanied by historiated initials, are counted as one or more)

Amsterdam BPH 1 (ex-Phillipps 1045/7[numbering problematical], 3630)/Oxford, Bodl. Douce 215/Manchester, Ryl.fr.1	EMLQMA	189
Bonn, UB 526	EMLQMA	346
Brussels, BR 9627-8	QMA	37
Florence, Laur. Ash.48 (121)	Q (1319)	62
Giessen, BU 93, 94	LQMA fragments	?
Geneva-Cologny, Bodmer 147 (ex-Phillips 1046)	EMLQMA	167
Geneva-Cologny, Bodmer 105	LQMA	45
London, BL Add. 10292–4	EMLQMA	748 [sic]
London, BL Roy. 14. E. III	EQMA	116
Manchester, see Amsterdam		
Modena, BEstense E 39	special version	15
New Haven, Yale, Beinecke 229	LQMA	166
Oxford, Bodl. Digby 223	LQMA	12
Oxford, Bodl. Douce 199	LQ	32
Oxford, Bodl. Douce 215, see Amsterdam		
Oxford, Bodl. Rawl. Q. b. 6	LQMA	212
Paris, BArs. 3479–80	EMLQMA	130 ?
Paris, BArs. 3482	MLQMA	136
Paris, BArs. 5218	Q	3
Paris, BN fr. 110	EMLQMA	99

Paris, BN fr. 111	LQMA	50 in QMA
Paris, BN fr. 112	special version	258
Paris, BN fr. 113–16	EMLQMA	209
Paris, BN fr. 117–20	EMLQMA	131
Paris, BN fr. 122	LQMA (1344)	120
Paris, BN fr. 123	LQMA	90
Paris, BN fr. 339	LQMA	120
Paris, BN fr. 342	LQMA (1274)	92
Paris, BN fr. 344	EMLQMA	344 [sic]
Paris, BN fr. 1422–4	LQMA	73
Paris, BN fr. 12573	LQMA	78

c) French Manuscripts Copied and Illustrated in Italy

Chantilly, MCondé 649 (1111) (1288)	QMA	4
Paris, BN fr. 343 special version	Q*Tristan*MA	119
Udine, Bibl.Arcivescovile 177	Q	34
Florence, BN Pal. 556 in Italian	*Tavola Ritonda*	

AN APPROXIMATE CHRONOLOGY AND GEOGRAPHICAL DISTRIBUTION OF *ESTOIRE* AND *QUESTE* MANUSCRIPTS

I use the symbol + to indicate manuscripts which I consider were made by the same craftspeople or are closely related to each other stylistically. Justification of the stylistic groupings of thirteenth- and early-fourteenth-century manuscripts can be found in Stones, "The Illustrations"(above, note 7); for the fifteenth-century ones see Blackman, "The Manuscripts" (above, note 7), and François Avril and Nicole Reynaud, *Les manuscrits à peintures en France 1440–1520* (Paris: Bibliothèque Nationale-Flammarion, 1993).

c. 1220	Paris	Rennes BM 255 (EML)
c. 1220 ?	? north	Modena Bibl. Estense E 39 (special version: JM*Perceval*)
c. 1250	Paris	Brussels, BR 9627–8 (QMA)
	Paris ?	BNF fr. 339 (LQMA)

	Paris ?	UCB Berkeley 106 (ex-Philipps 3643) (EM)
1274	Douai ?	BNF fr. 342 (LQMA)
c. 1285	Douai	Le Mans 354 (E)+BNF fr. 770 (EM *Prise de Jerusalem*)+Oxford, Bodl. Digby 223 (LQMA)
	Ghent ?	BNF fr. 749 (EM)
	Thérouanne	Paris, BNF fr. 19162 (EM) + Paris, BNF fr. 24394 (EM) + (1286)
	or Cambrai ?	Bonn UB 526 (EMLQMA) + BNF fr. 110 (EMLQMA)
c. 1290	Acre, Italy, or Cyprus ?	Tours BM 951 (EJM)
	Thérouanne	Paris, BNF fr. 95/Yale 229 (EM *Sept sagesAgravain* QMA)
c. 1295–1300	Thérouanne or Cambrai ?	Paris, BNF fr. 110 (EMLQMA) + Bonn UB 526, see above
	Metz	
	or Verdun	Paris, BNF fr. 344 (EMLQMA) + ex-Phillipps 1047 (Paris, Private Collection) (EM)
c. 1300–1310	Paris	St Petersburg Fr. F.v.15.5 (E) + Oxford, Bodl., Rawl. Q.b.6 (LQMA)
c. 1300	Genoa	Udine, Bibl. Arcivescovile 177 (Q in French)
1319	Avignon	Florence, Laur. Ash. 121(48) (Q)
c. 1316	Saint-Omer, Tournai, or Ghent	London, BL Add. 10292–4 (EMLQMA) + Royal 14. E. III (EQMA) +Amsterdam, BPH 1/Manchester, Rylands Fr. 1/Oxford, Bodl. Douce 215 (EMLQMA)
c. 1315–35	Paris	Paris, BNF fr. 105 (EM)+BNF fr. 9123 (EM)+B.Ars. 3482 (MLQMA)
c. 1330–50	Tournai or Ghent	Paris, BNF 1422-4 (LQMA)

1344	Tournai	Paris, BNF fr. 122 (LQMA)+
1351		Paris, Ars. 5218 (Q)
1357	Paris ?	Yale 227 (EM)
c. 1380	Lombardy	Paris, BNF fr. 343 (Q*Tristan*MA, special version in French)
c. 1400–1410	Paris ?	Tenschert (ex-Geneva-Cologny, Bodmer 147 and ex-Newcastle 937 (EM)
1405	Paris	Paris, Ars. 3479–80 (EMLQMA)+
c. 1404 and c. 1465		Paris, BNF 117–20 (EMLQMA)+
c. 1450–60	Paris and La Marche	Paris, BNF fr. 96 (EM)+
1446	Mantua	Florence, BN Pal. 556 (*Tavola Ritonda*, in Italian)
1470		Paris, BNF 112 (special compilation)+
c. 1475		Paris, BNF 113–16 (EMLQMA)
1480–82	Geneva	Guillaume de la Pierre's adaptation: BR 9246 (E) and BNF fr. 91 (M).

CHAPTER 10

The Symbolism of the Grail in Wolfram von Eschenbach

FRIEDRICH RANKE

Traditional studies of the Grail show a predilection for its embryology, dealing with the question of what it was before it entered literary history in the works of Chrétien, Robert, and Wolfram. In contrast to these studies, I would like to deal exclusively with the extant work of Wolfram, which, like any true literary work, must be self-explanatory. I will try to answer the following question: What did Wolfram have in mind as he was writing about the Grail? By using a philologist's methods, i.e. by providing a closer reading of several passages from the *Parzival*, I hope to provide a better answer to this question and to penetrate more deeply into the meaning of this profound epic poem.

Let me briefly recall the unambiguous facts: in contrast to Chrétien's golden vessel and Robert's "bowl," the Grail in Wolfram's poem is a *stein*, a term which, according to Middle High German usage, can be safely translated as "precious stone." We are told only that the stone was *vil reine* ("of purest kind," 469,4).[2] There is no information whatsoever about the outer characteristics of this stone, neither about its size nor about its shape or its color. We may assume that it was not very big, because the Grail King's sister bears the object, placed on a green silk cloth, into the hall with her own hands. Let me note at this point already that Wolfram also fails to mention that the Grail, unlike many other precious stones in the Middle Ages, gives off a gleam. On the contrary, as Wolfram expressly states, the light spreading in the hall as the Grail enters comes from the numerous candles and lamps accompanying it as well as from the beauty radiating from the Grail-bearer's face. This piece of information is all the more striking because it differs markedly from Chrétien's clear statement that the precious stones on the *graal* gave off such a bright light that the candles lost their luster just as stars do when the sun or the moon rises. Let us keep in mind that Wolfram dropped this detail from Chrétien's poem, certainly not without a purpose.

Wolfram's statements with regard to the mystical powers and qualities of the Grail stone are much more detailed than in Chrétien's text, however. First, Wolfram's Grail is a miraculous dispenser of food. As it is borne into the hall and placed on the table in front of the king, who has gathered his Grail knights for a banquet, it provides the whole community with abundant food and drink according to each person's desire. The servers only need to distribute on the tables what they receive from the Grail. In fact, the Grail's miraculous power is evident not only on exceptional occasions at special festive banquets, but also at quite common meals: "sie lebent von einem steine" ("they lived from a stone," 469,3), i.e., they live from the Grail. Every year on Good Friday, on the day of the Holy Eucharist, the miraculous strength of the Grail is renewed by a dove descending from heaven and placing a host in the Grail.

Furthermore, the Grail also has the power to bestow a blooming youthful appearance on the beholder. Just as, in the Middle Ages, a person who had received the host during High Mass was believed to be spared from death that week, a person who saw the Grail would not die the following week. This proves to be a misfortune for the Grail King who, tortured by pain, seeks death in vain. The life-giving power of the Grail is symbolically expressed in the statement that it is also the source of renewal for the phoenix.

Another miraculous feature of the Grail is its weight. The person who wants to lift it must be of immaculate chastity, as is the case with Repanse de Schoye, the bearer of the Grail; otherwise "wiget er sô swære, daz in diu falschlîch menscheit nimmer von der stat getreit" ("it is so heavy that all of sinful humanity cannot move it from its place," 477,16).

Likewise, the Grail knights are required to lead chaste lives. Like the members of the spiritual orders of knights, the Grail knights must remain celibate, while the Grail King is allowed to marry, but must abstain from extramarital love. Feirefiz, a pagan, cannot see the Grail before he has been baptized.

Another miraculous feature of the Grail is the fact that it can be "hunted" only by an individual designated by God. The person who is granted this special grace finds his name and kin inscribed on a stone. As soon as the inscription has been read, it disappears.

So far, Wolfram's report about the Grail is mysterious, but also un-ambiguous and indisputable. Fabulous and magic elements of fantasy are mixed with elements of Christian mysticism and symbolism. As I indi-cated above, I do not want to address, in this context, the literary histori-cal issue of how this mixture came about. There are, however, a few details in Wolfram's account that, I think, require and deserve a new in-terpretation.

Let me first make a negative observation. Most of the critical studies of the Grail legend maintain that Wolfram's Grail is descended from heaven. This statement can already be found in Birch-Hirschfeld's semi-nal work on the Grail (1877), admittedly toned down by the phrase "it seems." In his literary history, Scherer adopts the same view, also using the phrase "seemingly." Nowadays, most scholars accept the heavenly provenance of the Grail as an undeniable fact. Thus, for example, Ehris-mann writes in his handbook (1927): "A choir of angels (the so-called neutral angels) brought it from heaven to earth." Let me cite a few of the most recent critical studies. In the chapter on Wolfram in Burdach's com-prehensive book on the Grail (1938), Hans Bork maintains that "the Grail was brought to the earth by the neutral angels"; Hermann Schneider, in a review of Burdach's work in GGA (1939), accepts this view, as does Benedikt Mockenhaupt in his otherwise outstanding essay on the theme of piousness (1941) in Wolfram's *Parzival*. In contrast to the studies cited above, Bodo Mergell's excellent book on the *Parzival* (1943) contains the cautious phrase "it might be difficult to prove that Wolfram invented the general motif that the Grail was brought to the earth by angels" (p. 200). This remark should set us thinking. In the following we will take a look at what Wolfram actually says about the relations between the Grail and the neutral angels.

The first passage, a quotation from the mysterious writings of Flege-tanis, a "pagan" astrologer, says: "er jach, ez hiez ein dinc der grâl. des namen las er sunder twâl in dem gestirne, wie der hiez. ein schar in ûf der erden liez: diu fuor ûf über die sterne hôch, ob die ir unschult widerzôch" ("He said there was a thing called the Grail whose name he had read clearly in the constellations. A host of angels left it on the earth and then flew away up over the stars. Was it their innocence that drew them away?" 454,21 ff.). A host (what kind of a host is meant in this context is specified in the second passage: the angels who remained neutral in the battle between Lucifer and Trinitas) left it on the earth. It rose high above the stars (i.e., to God), if their innocence allowed them to rise again. The poem continues: "Since then baptized men have had the task of guarding it, and with such chaste discipline that those who are called to the service of the Grail are always noble men." I dare not decide whether being "noble" is a requirement for or a consequence of the Grail service. Being designated to serve the Grail is a permanently valid patent of nobility, and it is not important in this context. What is important, though, is the sentence: "ein schâr in ûf der erden liez." This phrase is ambiguous: rising up to heaven again, the host of angels "left it on the earth." One possible interpretation, so far the most commonly accepted one, is that the angels had previously brought the Grail from heaven to the earth and then left it behind. The phrase can also be interpreted as meaning only that they left it alone, left it on the earth where they had been guarding it so far (*lân* = "to leave", e.g., in the song "Innsbruck I must leave you" and in innumerable instances in Middle High German texts). Thus, the provenance of the Grail is not specified.

The second passage, which refers to the neutral angels, proves that only the second interpretation can be correct. Wolfram has his Trevrizent retell the same event in greater detail: "di newederhalp gestunden, dô strîten begunden Lucifer und Trinitas, swaz der selben engel was, die edelen und die werden muosen ûf die erden zuo dem selben steine" ("Those who took neither side when Lucifer and the Trinity fought—these angels, noble and worthy, were compelled to descend to earth, to this same stone," 471,15 ff.). There is no ambiguity in this passage: the angels who did not join any party when Lucifer and Trinitas were beginning to fight each other, all the noble and high-ranking angels had to go to *this stone on the earth*; consequently, in those days, before the creation of man, the stone was already on the earth. If the angels had previously brought it from heaven to the earth, the text would say: "muosen ûf die erden *mit* dem selben steine" ("were compelled to descend to the earth *with* this same stone.") The poem continues: "der stein ist immer reine" (the stone is always pure); it is pure, remains pure, and demands purity. I am not sure whether God pardoned them or *fürbaz verlôs* them, destined them to perish after they had served the Grail. He allowed them to live in his presence again, if His justice permitted Him to do so. This is precisely the meaning of the lines "diu vuor ûf über die sterne hôch, ob die ir unschult wider zôch" in the first passage. Thus, at that time, "liez diu schar den grâl ûf der erden."

Ever since that time, Trevrizent continues, it has been guarded by persons who were designated by God and to whom He sent His angel (this angel is not mentioned again in the text. He is probably the one who engraves the mysterious inscription in the Grail stone that serves to designate the keepers of the Grail). In any case, both passages deal with exactly the same event, and in the second passage, Wolfram's idea is unambiguously clear: the Grail was already on the earth when, after Lucifer's descent into hell, the neutral angels were sent down to the earth to the place where it lay. Mergell rightly observes that Wolfram's text does not support the assertion that the Grail is descended from heaven. It is indeed surprising that, so far, scholars have unanimously ignored this obvious fact. Even a philologist is occasionally blinded by prejudices, until his eyes are suddenly opened and he reads what the text actually says.

This realization causes a great many of the sources from which the Grail may have been derived to collapse suddenly (Wolfram's Grail is in no way related to the kaaba, some other meteorite, the table from heaven, or the precious stone that fell from heaven into the chalice used by St. Lupus for the sacrifice of the mass). At the same time, we also have to discard one of the most wide-spread interpretations of the mysterious and confusing Latin term for the Grail in Wolfram's poem. In his account of the Grail, Trevrizent includes the well-known phrase: "er heizet *lapsit exillis*" ("It is called *lapsit exillis*," 469,7). Manuscript D (g), the best manuscript, has this spelling; variant spellings are *erillis* (G) and *exilis* (g); the occurrence of the variants *exillix* and *exilix* can be explained by the fact that the second *x* serves to rhyme this word with the normal version of the word for phoenix, which, in Wolfram's text, appears in the unusual form *fênîs* (or *fênis* ?). In the best manuscripts, the first word is identically spelled *lapsit*; the Latin variants *jaspis* and *lapis* in more recent texts are certainly idiosyncratic emendations of the barbaric form of the original manuscript.

As long as critics started out from the assumption that the Grail was descended from heaven, it made indeed some sense for them to accept *lapis ex celis* as a conjecture for *lapsit exillis*. Until recently, I myself have supported this conjecture as the most likely interpretation of the mysterious term. Now we know that it is untenable. For it is, of course, methodologically unacceptable to use a rather bold conjecture in order to smuggle in through the back door an interpretation that cannot be supported by the text. The fact that one hates to give it up is not a sufficiently good reason.

If, however, *lapis ex celis* is untenable (to my mind, the conjecture *lapis elixir* and the identification of the Grail with the alchemical philosophers' stone is totally unfounded), a second attempt at an interpretation suggested by Gustav Ehrismann some twenty years ago gains more and more weight. In 1928 (in a brief note in the *Zeitschrift für deutsches Altertum*), Ehrismann drew attention to the fact that, in the medieval legend of Alexander, the famous miraculous stone from earthly paradise is given the attribute *exilis* ("thin, inconspicuous") in the Latin text of the "Iter ad paradisum." In the Middle Ages, the "Iter ad paradisum" was one of the best-known episodes of the Alexander legend, and it was often mentioned especially in German poetry. At the gate of paradise, the porter gives to Alexander's messengers a precious stone whose size and appearance resemble a human eye. "Give this stone to your king," he says; "after he has understood its meaning, he will be cured of his ambitious desire." Subsequently, Alexander turns back and, in Susa, sends for the wise men of his realm. But no one is able to tell him what the meaning of the stone is, until, finally, an old Jew provides the explanation: "lapis hic modicæ quantitatis est sed immensi ponderis" ("This stone is of modest size but immense weight"). He orders a pair of scales to be brought in, places the stone in one of the scales and more and more gold in the other scale. But the stone is heavier than all the gold. Eventually, the old man covers it with a thin layer of earth. Suddenly it becomes so light that a feather in the other scale is sufficient to raise it. Then he gives his interpretation: like the human eye, human greed and excessive ambition cannot be satisfied by all the goods that this world has to offer; but a handful of earth thrown on the human body puts an end to all ambition: "te mundi dominum *lapis iste* præfigurat, te monet, te increpat, te substantia *exilis* compescit ab appetitu vilissimæ ambitionis" ("this stone is a symbol for you, lord of the world, it warns you, rebukes you, the thin substance restrains you from the desire for worthless pomp"). Alexander meditates on these words and is cured of his ambition to conquer the world.[3]

Thus Ehrismann interprets the *lapsit exillis* of the Parzival tradition as *lapis exilis*, assuming that Wolfram used this term with reference to Alexander's miraculous stone. As a matter of fact, this interpretation has a good deal to commend it, and several critics have already supported it. Compared to all the other attempts at an interpretation, this one has the advantage that it corresponds most closely to the extant manuscripts (*lapsit* is misspelled at any rate and requires a conjecture; I will leave it open whether or not the misspelling results from the *lapis iste* of the "Iter," as Ehrismann assumes). Moreover, there are also certain factual parallels that should not be overlooked. First, the weight of both stones changes miraculously. Furthermore, the German version of this episode in the Alexander legends of Strassburg (it can be proved that Wolfram was familiar with this text) contains the phrase "er gibit . . . den alden di jugint"

("he gives . . . youth to the old," 7105). It may also be more than a coincidence that, when mentioning the Grail the first time, Wolfram calls it "den
wunsch von pardîs"; Alexander's stone also comes from paradise (there is
a possibility, however, that "wunsch von pardîs" means only "the most
precious object").

In my opinion, however, we may and must go even farther. According to Ehrismann, Wolfram's choice of the term *lapis exilis* for the Grail is
just one more proof of the poet's well-known "predilection for far-fetched
knowledge." Ehrismann thinks that Wolfram used the term "mainly because of its strange, exotic sound, not because of its inherent meaning."
Our question is: is it really true that Wolfram, a man known for his brood-
ing disposition, did not attribute any meaning to such a term? If we pay
closer attention to the meaning of Alexander's miraculous stone, we discover another aspect. As we have seen above, the stone in the Alexander
legend is a symbol of transitoriness or, from a subjective point of view, a
symbol of man's humble self-knowledge. In the Alexander legend of
Strassburg, the old man at the gate of paradise says explicitly: "ob er wille
genesen, sô sal er ôtmûte wesen" ("if he wants to recover, he must become humble"). The realization of this meaning of the stone causes
Alexander, the immoderate conqueror of the world, to become a *rex jus-
tus*; his pride is transformed into humility.

These observations make us realize the significance of humility and
its opposite, *hôchvart*, in Wolfram's poem. Parzival's mother, Herzeloyde,
is a model of humility: "diemuot was ir bereit" ("humility was her way,"
113,16); she was "ein wurzel der güete und ein stam der diemüete" ("a
root of goodness she, and a branch of humility," 128,28). Moreover,
Gurnemanz teaches young Parzival: "vlîzet iuch diemüete" ("strive for
humility," 170,28). Furthermore, in Trevrizent's remarks regarding the
demands that the Grail makes on the Grail King, humility and pride play a
decisive role. After Parzival has stated that if the Grail can be sought "mit
schilte und ouch mit sper" ("with shield and spear"), the marks of knighthood, he would like to be designated by God, he is warned by the hermit:
"ir müest aldâ vor hôchvart mit senftem willen sîn bewart. . . . hôchvart ie
seic unde viel" ("A humble will would have to guard you against pride. . .
. Pride has always sunk and fallen"). With these words he is not referring
to Lucifer, who is mentioned a few lines earlier, and his descent into hell,
but to his brother Anfortas, the Grail King, and the "herzebære nôt, die
hôchvart im ze lône bôt" ("his grief of heart, which pride gave him as reward"). Anfortas's misery was a result of his youth, his wealth, and "daz
er gerte minne ûzerhalb der kiusche sinne. der site ist niht dem grâle reht."

dâ muoz der rîter und der kneht bewart sîn vor lôsheit: *diemüet ie hôch-vart überstreit*" ("his desire for love beyond all restraint and bounds. Such ways are not fitting for the Grail. There both knight and squire must guard themselves against incontinence. Humility has conquered their pride," 472,13 ff.). Later, he refers once more to the guilt of Anfortas who in-dulged in extramarital love: "Amor was sîn krîe. der ruoft ist zer *diemuot* iedoch niht volleclîchen guot" ("Amor was his battle cry. But that cry is not appropriate for a spirit of humility," 478,30 ff). Trevrizent subsumes Anfortas's indulgence in extramarital love, which doomed him to pro-longed suffering, under the more comprehensive concept of pride, be-cause it represents a violation of humility. Anfortas speaks of his guilt in the same terms: "des grâles krône ist alsô guot, die hât mir hôchvart ver-lorn: nu hân ich diemuot mir rekorn" ("The Grail crown is just as rich. I lost it through pride, but now I have chosen humility," 819,18 ff). *Hôch-vart* has made him unworthy of the Grail kingship. After greeting Parzival as his lord and praising God for the miracle of designating Parzival for the Grail quest, Wolfram's Trevrizent concludes his speech most effectively with the exhortation to practice humility: "sich hât gehoehet iur gewin. *nu kêrt an diemuot iuwern sin*" ("your gain has been increased. Now turn your mind to humility," 798,29). Then he sends his nephew forth to seek the Grail. The last words that he addresses to the young Grail King con-tain the quintessence of the qualities required by his high office. The Grail, the *lapis exilis*, is the stone of humility.

Let us put our findings to the test. If we accept this interpretation of the *lapis exilis*, some puzzling questions that hitherto appeared to be unanswerable seem to answer themselves. A minor one first: as we saw above, Wolfram omits the bright radiance of the Grail that he found in Chrétien's poem. According to Hans Bork, it is "not clear" why he did this. As soon as we know that the Grail is the *lapis exilis*, there is no longer any need for this question. The stone of humility, which is incon-spicuous but rich in inner strength, cannot possibly have a radiant outer appearance. A second, more important question: what of the neutral an-gels? Wolfgang Golther wrote in 1925: "It is impossible to determine what Wolfram had in mind when he had the neutral angels serve the Grail as its first keepers." With the results of our previous discussion in mind, it is not difficult for us to understand why the angels who refused to take sides in a battle in which pride rebelled against God should be sent to the stone of humility. It seems to make a great deal of sense that those who had been saved from the danger of pride should be sent to the stone of humility for some time, so that they could be tested and "re-educated" and eventually learn *diemüete*. It is unclear, however, why Trevrizent later has to give up the previously expressed kind hope that, after this period of trial, God in His mercy will allow the neutral angels to return to heaven. The only possible explanation is that the neutral angels will also face final damnation because they failed to take God's side against pride right from the beginning. But this is a separate issue, which I cannot address in this context.[4]

In conclusion, the *lapis exilis* as a symbol of man's humility before God harmoniously fits in with the system of ideas in Wolfram's great poem in which he traces the spiritual and intellectual development of his characters. Parzival's development ultimately leads to a synthesis of the two main ideas of courtly culture, the harmony of Christian and chivalrous ideas that, as the following lines demonstrate, Wolfram felt to be in serious conflict with each other: "Swes leben sich sô verendet, daz got niht wirt gepfendet der sêl durchs lîbes schulde, und der doch der werlde hulde behalden kan mit werdekeit: daz ist ein nütziu arebeit" ("A life so concluded that God is not robbed of the soul through fault of the body, and which can obtain the world's favor with dignity, that is a worthy work," 827,19 ff.). He aims at achieving a synthesis. The one indispensable prerequisite for this synthesis is, however, that the knight must overcome the original sin of pride, which in his particular case represents the most immediate danger, and learn to glorify and love God, his lord and savior, with humility and gratitude. Even before meeting with his uncle, the hermit, Parzival has taken the first steps in this direction. He gives up his own willfulness and asks God to guide his horse: "nu genc in der gotes kür!"("Now go, whichever way God chooses!" 452,9). The first words that he addresses to Trevrizent are: "hêr, nu gebt mir rât: ich bin ein man der sünde hât" ("Sir, now give me counsel. I am a man who has sinned," 456,29). Realizing his own sinfulness, Parzival has fought the hardness of his soul and softened his self-will to such a degree that he has become amenable to the *süezen mœre* of the hermit, under whose wise spiritual guidance his inner transformation is completed.

It seems to me that our theory has passed the test and is valid. To the poet who chose the term *lapis exilis* for the Grail, this term was more than a word with an exotic sound. It was rather a term with a profound symbolic significance. The two details in which Wolfram's account differs from its source (he leaves out the radiant gleam of the Grail stone and has the neutral angels serve as its first guardians) are meaningful in so far as he condenses, in this one term, the essence of what he has to say about the religious and moral problems that he addresses in his poem.

According to the poet, man can achieve the longed-for harmony between God and the world only by practicing Christian humility. Let me mention in passing that, in my opinion, this poet must have been Wolfram and no one else.

Finally there remain, perhaps, some objections to be addressed. Is it possible that Wolfram, who was illiterate, understood the Latin term?[5] My answer to this question is that this is only one of the many cases in which Wolfram shows a surprisingly high level of education. He must have had at least one or two well-educated advisers who taught him, for example, the names of the planets in Arabic. In the same way he may have learned the list of scholarly terms for precious stones from Marbod's book about stones as well as the names of various peoples from Solin's Polyhistor. It is possible that a scholarly adviser, with whom he had talked about the miraculous stone in the legend of Alexander and who remembered the use of this relatively unusual term in the Latin text, mentioned and explained to him the Latin *lapis exilis*. If we assume, however, that Wolfram understood the meaning and the symbolism of the term the way it was used in the Latin text, should we not expect him to emphasize this meaning more clearly? Whoever asks such a question fails to recognize the special characteristics of Wolfram's poetry. Such an objection would be justified with regard to his great opponent, Gottfried von Strassburg, who, as his allegory of the grotto of love demonstrates, discusses such a significance at great length. Wolfram is different. He does not think in abstractions. He thinks, or rather he writes *in symbols*. Moreover, he is not interested in making himself clearly understood. As a result, his work is characterized by a certain mysteriousness on which he prides himself: "er mac mir lîthe sîn ze tump, den ichs niht gâhs bescheide" ("someone may well be left in the dark if I don't set him straight," *Willehalm*, 237,13). Therefore, he needs to provide, as Gottfried observes in a mockingly reproachful tone, "*mære tiutære*" ("a guide to his story"). But, at the same time, this mysteriousness accounts for the immense depth of his poetry, which continually tempts us to take fresh approaches to his work.

NOTES

Published as "Zur Symbolik Des Grals bei Wolfram von Eschenbach," *Wege der Forschung*, 57 (1966), 38–48. Translated by Adelheid Thieme. Permission given by Dr. Karl Heinrich Ranke.

1. This essay is based on a paper read on September 23, 1945, at the Fourth Annual Conference of the Academic Society of Swiss Germanists in Lucerne. [*Editor's note*: It was subsequently published in *Trivium*, 4 (1946), 20–30.]

2. [*Translator's note*: Middle High German translations are from *Wolfram von Eschenbach, Parzival*, trans. and introd. Helen M. Mustard and Charles E. Passage (New York: Vintage Books, 1961)].

3. For the Latin text, see K. Kinzel, *Lamprechts Alexander* (1884), p. 357 ff. [Translations are provided by the editor.]

4. Mergell's interpretation of the neutral angels' fate in connection with the role of *zwîfel* in *Parzival* (p. 198 ff.) does not contradict my explanation.

5. [*Editor's note*: scholarly opinion no longer considers Wolfram illiterate.]

CHAPTER 11

The Truest and Holiest Tale
Malory's Transformation of
La Queste del Saint Graal

DHIRA B. MAHONEY

Sir Thomas Malory tells us that his Tale of the Sankgreal, "breffly drawyn oute of Freynshe . . . ys a tale cronycled for one of the trewyst and of the holyest that ys in thys worlde."[1] Despite the reverence of this assertion, there has been much disagreement among scholars about Malory's fidelity to his French source, the thirteenth-century *La Queste del Saint Graal.* Although no critic denies that he reduced it considerably, with many omissions and small alterations, many insist that what remains is still a close translation of the source romance. Eugène Vinaver calls the Tale "the least original of his works" *(Works,* p. 1534), and Terence McCarthy describes it as "slavishly, indeed thoughtlessly faithful."[2] Yet Mary Hynes-Berry has shown in her recent studies that Malory's simpler paratactic style has resulted in a very different kind of prose from the patterned, rational French of the *Queste:* Malory translated "his French book not just into another language but into another idiom."[3] The chief argument, however, has been not over style, but *sens:* to what extent did Malory understand the theology of his source, and did he successfully transmit its message or meaning? Hynes-Berry claims that he did not: "the *Sankgreal* is a case study in how one man read the *Queste del Saint Graal* two centuries and a culture later." She also endorses P. E. Tucker's view that Malory did not understand its theology. Vinaver also maintained that, despite his fidelity to the original *matière,* Malory's "one desire seems to be to secularize the Grail theme as much as the story will allow" *(Works,* p. 1535), and Larry D. Benson agrees that "he drastically alters its thematic meaning." On the other hand, Charles Moorman asserts that Malory "always preserves the core of the French book's doctrinal statements, no matter how great his deletions," and Charles Whitworth, while taking issue with many of Moorman's points, claims that Malory did understand the Grail legend and was "able to adapt it without denaturing it."[4] I propose to thread my way through this thicket of conflicting opinions by suggesting that what Malory does to his source is not so much secularize it as anglicize it. He faithfully transmits the central dichotomy of the *Queste* between worldly and spiritual chivalry, whereby the traditional chivalric standards are reinterpreted in the light of spiritual values. However, at the same time, by cutting much of the doctrinal exegesis of the French he shows that he is not sympathetic to its typological method. The result is the expression of the thirteenth-century spiritual message in language and thought that is characteristic of the religious temper of fifteenth-century England, where secular and spiritual pursuits could be considered complementary rather than competitive elements of a knightly life.

That Malory belongs firmly in the fifteenth century has been demonstrated effectively by the criticism of the past two decades. His choice of chivalric subjects was not, as once was thought, an exercise in nostalgia. Arthur B. Ferguson and Benson have shown that chivalric ideals were taken extremely seriously in fifteenth-century England, even if they were beginning to have little relationship to the actual facts of political and social life.[5] The line between romance and reality was shifting and faint; real tournaments and passages of arms imitated literary ones, and literary descriptions echoed the rules and rituals of real ones. Kings and knights consciously reenacted the vows, battles, and disguises of romance heroes, the actual deeds becoming interchangeable with those of romance as models of knightly behavior.[6] The audience for these exploits, fictional or actual, was, of course, aristocratic, the comparatively limited agrarian and military class for whom jousting, hunting and the rules of war were not merely leisure activities but living and urgent concerns. When young John Paston III writes to his mother in 1468, describing the nuptials in Bruges of Princess Margaret and Charles, Duke of Burgundy, he falls easily into the language of romance:

> And as for the Dwykys coort, as of lordys, ladys, and gentylwomen, knytys, sqwyirs, and gentyllmen, I herd never of non lyek to it save Kyng Artourys cort. By my trowthe, I have no wyt nor remembrans to wryte to yow halfe the worchep that is her.[7]

Yet it was not John III but his elder brother John II who loved tournaments and chivalric romance, and was sometimes rebuked for it.[8] Though the main preoccupations of the Paston family were the acquisition and administration of property, the language of romance was neither remote nor unfamiliar to them. Like John II, Malory must have delighted in chivalric literature, and considered tournaments and knightly training significant and worthwhile activities. The world of his Arthurian knights is one in which horses and armor are not only the trappings but also the symbols of knightly life. When Palomides falls "oute of his wytt," the mark of his changed state is that he has put his horse out to pasture (423.19–23), and during the Quest, when the Grail knights disembark from the Ship of Solomon, Malory is quick to remind his readers that "they had no horse in that contrey, for they lefft their horsys whan they toke their shippe" (996.27–29). At the end of the *Morte* a tiny detail suffices to indicate renunciation of the knightly life by Lancelot's seven companions when they follow him into the cloister: "And soo their horses wente where they wolde, for they toke no regarde of no worldly rychesses" (1255.8–9).

The significance of the outward trappings lies in the fact that the primary motivation for action in the world of the *Morte Darthur* is the search for earthly glory, for "worshyp" and a name. "Name" comes to mean, in this context, not only a knight's identity and rank, but also his lineage and past exploits. "Worshyp" is more than reputation; it is a man's worth-ship, his self-worth, captured in his "name," or what is publicly known about him—the battles he has won, the great knights he has defeated. For this is a society in which self-worth is exclusively bound up with the public recognition of it. Action is validated by public recognition, and values are externally apprehended. A great knight has a role to maintain, and it is his duty to maintain it. In the episode of the Poisoned Apple, when the Queen has banished Lancelot from the court in a jealous fury, he considers returning to his own country, but is counseled not to do so by Bors: "ye muste remembir you what ye ar, and renomed the moste nobelyst knyght of the worlde, and many grete maters ye have in honde" (1047.16–18). Similarly Isolde urges Tristram not to stay away for her sake from the great tournament and feast at Pentecost: "ye that ar called one of the nobelyste knyghtys of the worlde and a knyght of the Rounde Table, how may ye be myssed at that feste?" (839.31–33). The pursuit of worship is essentially agonistic, and the desire for it informs the actions of Malory's knights. "Hit is oure kynde to haunte armys and noble dedys" (810.6–7), says young Percival to his mother when she begs him to stay at home.

Given such chivalric predilections, it would not be surprising to find Malory secularizing the Grail story when he came to translate what is, after all, primarily a theological treatise on salvation, in which innumerable hermits and recluses explicate the visions and adventures "in [the] bitterest detail," as E. K. Chambers puts it.[9] Yet Malory's colophon shows that he held the story in great reverence, and he seems to have chosen the Vulgate version in preference to the more secular version that he is likely to have known from the prose *Tristan,* his source for the Tale of Tristram.[10] The prose *Tristan* contains a post-Vulgate version of the *Queste* in which the adventures of non-Grail knights such as Tristan, Erec, Kaherdin, and Palamède are so interlaced with the traditional ones that the spiritual message of the *Queste* is entirely dissipated.[11] One might argue, if one were following McCarthy's contention that the Tale of the Sankgreal was the first to be written, that Malory had not yet come upon the prose *Tristan* version of the Grail, but Edward D. Kennedy has shown that it is very likely that Malory knew other secular versions as well, such as that in Hardyng's *Chronicle.*[12] Apparently Malory's choice of the Vulgate *Queste* was deliberate, perhaps because this earlier version of the story was purer, less adulterated by the wider chivalric narrative of the prose *Tristan.*

La Queste del Saint Graal is a tightly woven interlaced romance, which progresses by a series of deepening revelations. The controlling metaphors of the narrative are finding one's way and seeing. At the first appearance of the Grail at the Arthurian court, there is only mystery and marvel. It is Gauvain's oath not to give up till he sees the Grail more openly that precipitates the Quest, and the knights set out on individual paths which converge and diverge until the narrative narrows its focus to the three Grail knights and Lancelot.[13] The Grail knights achieve the highest stage of revelation, but even they have to progress by stages. In the first half of the romance they are purified by trial and temptation, until they come together on Solomon's ship, where they are brought in touch with the whole range of Old Testament tradition that has prefigured the Quest. Arriving at the castle of Corbenic, they celebrate a Mass in which Josephus, the son of Joseph of Arimathea and the first Bishop of Christendom, descends from Heaven to conduct the service, and the crucified Christ himself issues from the Grail to administer the sacrament to the knights. Yet, marvellous though this is, it is not the ultimate revelation. Galaad does not see as openly as he will see. The three knights must take the Grail, with its table and bleeding lance, to the holy city of Sarras. Here, after imprisonment and further tribulation, Galaad is granted the supreme Vision: celebrating Mass, he looks into the Grail, and, trembling with ecstasy, asks to pass over into the next world. Perceval also dies in holy orders, and only Boort returns to tell the court the story of the *Queste*.

Albert Pauphilet was the first to identify the religious order featured in the *Queste* as Cistercian, and to study its narrative technique. "Sous l'apparence chevaleresque," writes Pauphilet, "c'est la grande adventure de l'homme qui est ici exposée: c'est un tableau de la vie chrétienne telle que pouvait l'observer ou la rêver une conscience du treizième siècle."[14] Throughout the narrative a constant dichotomy is built up between the worldly, chivalric values of the Arthurian knights and the spiritual values by which their actions must now be interpreted. What each knight has to learn is that this is a totally new order of adventure: to succeed in this quest, unlike so many previous ones, it is not enough that a knight should improve his life; he must learn to think in a new way, to abandon his traditional values and adopt a new ethic. The different levels of achievement among the knights reflect their capacity to understand this, or to act upon it once understood. Gauvain never does understand it; he gets bored and discouraged, and finally returns to the court. Lancelot is the repentant sinner who is granted a partial, corporeal vision of the Grail: at the castle of Corbenic, he looks into the room where Mass is being celebrated. However, his impulsive entrance to help the celebrant apparently struggling to raise a human figure above the altar shows that he is still, in Pauline Matarasso's words, "interpret[ing] in physical terms an experience purely mystical."[15] His punishment is to be knocked down by a burning wind and lie unconscious for twenty-four days. The three Grail knights do achieve the penitential vision, but even among them there is a hierarchy: Boort is the deliberate saint, the type of those who win salvation by the sweat of their brows; Perceval is the innocent, ingenuous type, saving himself by instinct rather than conscious thought; and Galaad is the perfect hero, the figure of Christ, redeemer and deliverer.[16]

It is not surprising that the lesser knights take so long to understand the nature of the new quest, for the language in which the adventures are announced is the traditional chivalric language. Galaad is "cil qui metra a fin les aventures de la Grant Bretaigne" (he who will bring the adventures of Britain to a close, p. 10), and he will prove by his achievements that Lancelot is no longer "li mieldres chevaliers dou monde" (the best knight of the world, p. 12). In his first adventure, the new-made knight Melyans chooses the left-hand fork to prove his courage because of a warning sign that forbids entry to all except one who considers himself a "preudome" (p. 41). This term can mean an exceptionally wise or a valiant man, and Melyans is clearly interpreting it as the latter. After he has narrowly escaped death, his error is explained to him: "li escriz parloit de la chevalerie ce-lestiel, et tu entendoies de la seculer" (the writing referred to spiritual chivalry, and you understood it as worldly chivalry, p. 45).

This constant tension between the familiar chivalric terms and their new meanings, the usurpation of the old values by the new, is best exem-plified in the temptations of Boort and Perceval. Perceval's major test oc-curs when he is alone on a rocky island and told in a dream:

> demain te covendra combatre encontre le champion dou monde qui
> plus fet a redouter. Et se tu ies vaincuz, tu ne seras pas quites por un de
> tes membres perdre, ainz te menra len si mal que tu en seras honiz a toz
> jorz mes. (p. 97)[17]

When a beautiful lady arrives on a barge and asks his help to regain her lost inheritance, invoking his duty as a companion of the Round Table, Perceval is easily deceived. She persuades him to come into her silken pavilion to eat and drink, and almost entices him into her bed, but just in time he catches sight of the pommel of his sword and instinctively crosses himself. There is a cloud of black smoke and the lady and barge vanish in flames on the water. Only later does Perceval learn the full sig-nificance of the encounter: the lady was the devil and this was the battle with the champion that he was due to fight. Boort's major test forces him to choose between saving his brother Lyonel from certain death and a virgin from equally certain dishonor. It is a terrible dilemma: by tradi-tional chivalric standards, his first duty should be to his brother, but he is also aware of his duty to save defenseless virgins. In anguish, he calls on God to look after his brother and saves the virgin. Although his torment is increased when he is shown what appears to be Lyonel's corpse, he later discovers that his choice was the correct one, for he had put behind him "toute naturel amor por amor de Jhesucrist" (p. 187). Brotherly love has no place in the *Queste*. Its doctrine demands total absorption, total detachment from worldly ties. "L'attachement au monde est chose d'en-fer," explains Pauphilet.[18] Not surprisingly, Lyonel does not see it that way, and when next he meets Boort he accuses him of treachery and tries to kill him.

The technique of the *Queste* is not allegorical so much as typological, or, as Erich Auerbach would call it, figurative. Whereas modern history views events chronologically, interpreting their significance according to cause and effect, the figurative approach interprets an event by projecting it vertically onto the plane of providential design. The victory of Joshua, for instance, prefigures Christ's, and the victory of Christ is a fulfillment of Joshua's. "Both entities in the figurative relationship are equally real and equally concrete," explains Auerbach; "the figurative sense does not destroy the literal, nor does the literal deprive the figured fact of its status as a real historical event."[19] Tournaments in the *Queste* are real, but when Lancelot goes to help the weaker party he is also proving his kinship with those who cannot shake off worldly values;[20] the city of Sarras is real, concrete, but at the same time it prefigures the city of God, Jerusalem. The Table of the Last Supper, the Table of the Grail, and the Round Table are all linked: each is a figure of the next or an echo of the last, yet each is a separate table, belonging to a different occasion and era. The whole patristic exegetical tradition is evoked in these links and correspondences, which use an imagery always public, not secret, yet which flows from abstract to concrete and back, never quite identifiable by a charted system. The Grail itself appears sometimes as a cup, sometimes a dish, sometimes on the table, sometimes without it, sometimes carried by an unseen agency, sometimes accompanied by angels. As Frederick Locke observes, "at the end of the *Queste* we cannot define the Grail with any greater precision than when we first saw it or when we continued to see it in the development of the narrative."[21]

In conventional allegory one event is pure sign, but in the figurative technique neither the prefigured nor the prefiguring event loses its literary and historical reality. As Locke explains, Galaad does not "stand for" Christ, but acts like Christ at times, reminds priest and hearers of Christ, then "emerges from his temporary analogical immersion and stands alone once more—a knight confined by time and space to the fifth century" (p. 35). Thus the *Queste* is not a *Pilgrim's Progress*. Bunyan uses allegory to present a concrete realization of what is actually a spiritual and moral journey. The *Queste* is also a journey, but one which takes place on different planes of experience simultaneously. It is a journey back to the primal innocence, or its recreation in the Divine Union. Virginity is extolled as a primal virtue because it denotes a state as far removed as possible from the corruption of the flesh. The narrator, or rather "li contes," even distinguishes between "virginitez" and "pucelages." "Pucelages" is the condition of those who have never experienced carnal companionship, but virginity is the condition of those who would never desire it, who have no knowledge of its existence—the state of absolute purity before the Fall.[22] Thus the "archetypal movement" of the *Queste,* as Locke puts it, is "from obscurity and darkness to light and vision" (p. 9), and, because obscurity is the condition of the flesh, from the carnal to the spiritual. The vision of the Host is a reward for Lancelot, but one in accord with his stage of development, his limited capacity for seeing. The ultimate achievement is Galaad's—he looks into the vessel of the Grail and is translated.[23] After his apotheosis the Grail is removed from Logres, from England, because most men are not capable of the search. Galaad's vision, however, foretells the Beatific Vision at the end of time, the face-to-face vision of God which St. Paul tells us will be granted to the whole Church.

It is this theological view, the doctrinal significance of the Quest in the context of the history of the human race, that Malory chooses not to transmit, perhaps because it is alien to the temper of his time. He cuts long sections of doctrinal explication, as in the Ship of Solomon episode,[24] and, above all, he cuts the "senefiances"—the cobweb of doctrinal significance that structures the *Queste,* the subtle and beautiful correspondences that link disparate elements and show the action taking place on many planes at once. He omits, for instance, the explanation of the link between the three Tables, of the Last Supper, the Grail, and the Round Table (pp. 74–78); and while he retains the heat which provides an excuse for the devilish lady to invite Percival into her pavilion (917.32), he cuts the subsequent explanation that the sun is a figure of Christ's grace, which would have melted the ice of the fiend, and which she therefore feared and tried to avoid (p. 114). Similarly, Malory modifies the figurative imagery of the *Queste.* The ambiguous, shifting image of the French Grail becomes in his hands a constant image of a miraculous vessel filled with Christ's blood, though it still has the power to heal, to feed, to beautify, to make happy. His treatment of Gawain's dream points up the difference most clearly. The French Gauvain dreams of a meadow full of bulls, all but three of whom have stained and speckled skins (p. 149). The bulls represent the Arthurian knights, whose mortal sin and carnal enslavement appear outwardly, as stains on the skin (p. 156). The French author uses the image once only. Malory turns the scene of the dream into a meadow full of proud black bulls, among whom are three white ones, one with a black spot (942, and 946). He has also used the image previously. Where the French author categorized the three companions who would achieve the Grail as "li dui virge et li tierz chastes" (p. 77), Malory shows that he is already thinking of the dream: "There sholde be three whyght bullis sholde encheve hit, and the two sholde be maydyns and the thirde sholde be chaste" (906.31–33). The single, delicate image of the French has become for Malory a recurrent moral sign to distinguish the Grail knights from the rest of the Questers.

Yet, though he may eliminate much of the doctrine, Malory does not fail to understand or to transmit the central dichotomy of the *Queste* between worldly and spiritual values. Apart from a few minor details he translates Perceval's temptations and Boort's dilemma faithfully and effectively,[25] though one can imagine that he sympathized strongly with Boort's anguish at having to abandon his brother. He even adds a passage to the Tale of Tristram, which is not authorized by the source, warning Lancelot that, although "of all worldly adventures he passyth in manhode and proues all othir, . . . in this spyrytuall maters he shall have many hys bettyrs" (801.31–33).

Indeed, Lancelot is the key figure in both French and English Quests. Though he is not the hero, he is the doctrinal pivot, for it is in his partial success or partial failure that the Quest is defined. Most of the critical discussion has been over Malory's treatment of Lancelot's role, and whether it is classed as a success or a failure seems to depend on each critic's attitude to the *Morte Darthur* as a whole. Vinaver claims that Malory, in accord with his desire to secularize the story, attempts to "rehabilitate" his favorite knight, by underlining that he is the best of all earthly knights (*Works,* pp. 1536–37). Tucker and Moorman maintain that Malory emphasizes Lancelot's failure, because of his adulterous relationship with the Queen.[26] It is true that Malory does accentuate Lancelot's superiority among earthly knights more than the French text, but he is always careful to qualify that praise. On the other hand, those critics who are obsessed with the theme of adultery do not seem to notice that neither in the French nor in the English Quests is adultery the main issue.

The French Lancelot is told by a hermit that he had, initially, five great virtues: virginity, humility, patience, rectitude, and charity. The devil, casting about for a means to destroy him, hit on the idea of woman and, entering into the Queen Guenievre, caused her to eye Lancelot with desire. Through her seduction of him his virtues were corrupted and transformed into lust and pride, "luxure" and "orgeuil." The description of the effect on Lancelot shows the intimate relationship between these two vices:

> Car si tost come tu eus tes eulz eschaufez de l'ardor de luxure, maintenant enchaças humilité et atresis orgeuil et vousis aler teste levee ausi fierement come un lyon, et deis en ton cuer que tu ne devoies riens prisier ne ne priseroies ja mes, se tu n'avoies ta volenté de cele que tu veoies si bele. (p. 126)[27]

Pauline Matarasso's exhaustive discussion of the passage shows that the desire for possession is linked with the desire for self-aggrandizement:

both are forms of concupiscence in which the main object is self-gratification instead of the service of God. Lancelot's love for Guenievre is indeed idolatrous; he has seen her as the source of his prowess and must learn that the true source is God.[28] Idolatry rather than adultery is the issue. When Lancelot confesses his sin to a hermit in the early stages of the romance, he is told to promise never again to offend his Maker "en fesant pechié mortel de la reine ne d'autre dame ne d'autre chose dont vos le doiez corrocier" (in committing mortal sin with the queen nor with another lady nor doing anything else by which you are bound to anger Him, p. 67). It is not the extra-marital relationship but the abandonment to the flesh, the enslavement by the world, that is the sin by Cistercian standards. The devil tempted Lancelot through woman, as he did Adam, Solomon, Samson, and Absolom (p. 125). Lancelot thus becomes a figure of Adam, the fallen sinner; Guenievre is also a type, of "Eve la pecheresse." Her opposite and redeemer is Perceval's sister, the virgin who gives her blood to save another, the figure of Mary, the new Eve.[29] Although Malory modifies the interpretation of Lancelot's character, cutting out the long description of the provenance of Lancelot's sins, he does not travel far from the implications of the French. Since the figurative view is foreign to him, he refashions Lancelot's imperfections. Lust and pride, which in the French are the result of Lancelot's initial corruption by the flesh, become in Malory's version Lancelot's main sins. In his confession to the hermit Lancelot admits that all his battles in the past were motivated by the desire to win worship and be better loved, "and litill or nought I thanked never God of hit" (897.21–22). Whereas the French Lancelot erred in thinking the source of his valor was the Queen, Malory's Lancelot errs in believing that the source of his valor is himself; both Lancelots have to learn that the true source is God.

Indeed, this is Lancelot's chief lesson throughout the Tale of the Sankgreal. In one of his dreams, God appears to him in the form of an accusing old man: "thou hast ruled the ayenste me as a warryoure and used wronge warris with vayneglory for the pleasure of the worlde more than to please me" (928.34–929.1). Much has been made of the "wronge warris,"[30] but they are surely just an attempt to render the idea of the French: "tu ne m'as mie esté comme sergans, mais comme guerroiers; tu ne m'as mie esté comme fieulx, mais comme fillastre" (You have not acted towards me like my soldier, but like my opponent; you have not been to me like a son, but like a stepson).[31] The wars were wrong because of their motivation by personal pride rather than the desire to serve God. When Lancelot instinctively joins the weaker party in the tournament, thinking to "[increse] his shevalry" (931.25), he is again in error; he is told later that he "enclyned to that party for bobbaunce and pryde of the worlde, and all that muste be leffte in that queste" (933.31–934.1). Even after many sermons, penances, and humiliations, when he comes to the castle gate of Corbenic and finds it guarded by lions, Lancelot still instinctively draws his sword, and has it struck from his hand while a voice from above rebukes him: "O, man of evylle feyth and poure byleve! Wherefore trustist thou more on thy harneyse than in thy Maker?" (1014.21–22). The source of his strength is God, not himself, and that Malory considers he has finally learned the lesson is proved by the episode of the healing of Sir Urry, after the Quest is over. When all the Arthurian knights at court have failed to heal the wounded knight, Lancelot succeeds, because he prays secretly to be given the power to do so "by the grete vertu and grace of The, but, Good Lorde, never of myselff" (1152.23–25).

Though pride is his major sin, lust is a close second. Lancelot never denies to others or to himself that it is his love for Guenevere that prevents him from achieving the full vision of the Grail, as he tells her at their last meeting: "in the queste of the Sankgreall I had that tyme forsakyn the vanytees of the worlde, had nat youre love bene" (1253.13–14). As in the French, the fault is not so much that the love is adulterous, as that it exists at all. It is enslavement by the flesh that prevents Lancelot from forsaking the vanities of this world and pursuing perfection.

The central issue to most arguments by the critics who emphasize Lancelot's failure is Malory's introduction of the concept of stability in connection with the evaluation of Lancelot's achievement. In a speech that has no parallel in the French, a hermit explains to Gawain, using the familiar opposition between worldly and spiritual values, why Gawain will see no adventures in this Quest. He is a sinner, but Lancelot

> hath takyn upon hym to forsake synne. And nere were that he nys nat stable, but by hys thoughte he ys lyckly to turne agayne, he sholde be nexte to encheve hit sauff sir Galahad, hys sonne; but God knowith hys thought and hys unstablenesse. (948.23-27)

"Stable" is usually glossed as steadfast, constant, and it is certainly a common doublet with "steadfast" in Middle English. Tucker interprets Lancelot's instability as emotional weakness, a fault of character that prevents him, despite his best resolve, from pulling free of the adulterous liaison (pp. 87–89). However, I believe Tucker, and those who follow him, are missing the specific context the term is being given in this tale. Malory uses the adjective form of the word a few pages later, in connection with Bors: "And thys good man founde hym in so mervales a lyffe and so stable that he felte he was never gretly correpte in fleyshhly lustes but in one tyme that he begat Elyan le Blanke" (956.1–4). Bors is so stable that he only once yielded to the desires of the flesh (he was the bull with one spot in Gawain's dream). The corresponding term in the source passage is "religieuse" (p. 166), which meant pious, honest, good, and was frequently used as a doublet with "bone" or "sainte" in Old French.[32] Malory's translation of the adjective by "stable" suggests that the latter term had a significant religious connotation at the time. The suggestion is confirmed by reference to other Middle English works and to the *OED*. A person is "stable" in faith or virtue, and stability is frequently invoked in the context of perseverance in the religious or monastic life.[33] A novice promises "de stabilitate sua perseverantia" in the first stage of acceptance into the Benedictine Order.[34] Caxton's translation of this phrase in his Abstract of the *Rule* reads: "And yf he promyse to contynwe and to be stable in his purpoos, thenne after two monethes the rule shall be red hole by ordre unto hym."[35] In similar vein, the writer of the devotional treatise *The Pilgrimage of Perfection,* printed in 1526, urges his readers to be strong on the difficult journey to the heavenly Jerusalem: "Therfore let us be stable and never loke backwarde agayne to the worlde, lest it happen to us as it fortuned to the wyfe of Loth, whiche (as scripture sheweth) for ones lokynge backwarde was turned into a salte stone."[36]

Thus Malory is not simply confusing stability with holiness, as Vinaver suggests (*Works,* p. 1536, n. 5). In the context of his Sankgreal, stability means perseverance in the pursuit of holiness, and connotes withdrawal from the world. It is not surprising, then, that Lancelot should forget his promise to take himself to perfection after the Quest. For when he returns to the Arthurian world, he returns to public life, and, moreover, to his role in it: the best of all earthly knights, and the lover of the Queen. "Ye muste remembir you what ye ar" (1047.16), Bors had told him when he was thinking of returning to his own country. Lancelot's fault is less a weakness of character than a failure of his whole being, his self-integrity. He cannot renounce the world because his love is too great; and he cannot remain in the world and not love. Only when Guenevere herself renounces it is he free to do so. As he says to her at their last meeting, "I take recorde of God, in you I have had myn erthly joye" (1253.19–20). Arthur's death and Guenevere's rejection release him from his final ties to his old life. Public values are no longer given shape in action: there is no longer any necessity to maintain his "name"—indeed, once the world in which he had a name is gone, there is no longer any meaning to that name. Lancelot turns hermit and dies of grief, but at his death his corpse lies smiling. His relatives go to fight in the Holy Land, where they die "upon a Good Fryday for Goddes sake" (1260.15). When the public world which gave their lives meaning has gone, they too can turn to private redemption.

Benson and Ferguson have shown us that withdrawal from the world was an acceptable alternative to the knightly life in fifteenth-century England.[37] The two avenues of action were equally valid, but not to be led concurrently; one was a recognized successor to the other. Malory's hermit Sir Bawdwyn of Bretayn tells us, "sometyme I was one of the felyship, but now I thanke God I am othirwyse disposed" (1075.22–23). Real as well as literary knights turned hermit in their old age. Malory's contemporary, Sir Stephen Scrope, suggests that knights whose physical strength has failed them because of old age should occupy their time "in gostly chevallrie off dedes of armes spirituall."[33] The attitude is not unlike the Hindu view of life, which teaches that a man's duties are divided into four stages: first childhood and education, then marriage and procreation, then establishment in world affairs, and finally renunciation of the world and retreat into asceticism. The last stage does not invalidate the others.

Here, then, lies the essential difference between the two Quests. For the French author the "chevalerie celestiel" was to replace the "terriene," to invalidate and supersede it. For Malory it is a separate pursuit, of equal validity, in which success is fully achievable only by withdrawal from the world, either into the reclusive life, like Percival and the hermits at the end of the *Morte,* or into death, like Galahad. The contrast is pointed up most clearly in the two scenes of Galahad's death. Malory's Galahad, seeing the Grail openly at last, prays, "Now, my Blyssed Lorde, I wold nat lyve in this wrecched worlde no lenger" (1034.25–26), and asks Bors to greet his father Lancelot and "bydde hym remembir of this worlde unstable" (1035.11–12). "Wrecched worlde," "worlde unstable," "thys unsyker worlde" (1036.28)—these phrases ring of the homiletic tradition which surfaces so often in late medieval English literature, that particularly Boethian contrast between this fickle, unreliable, "corrumpable" world with the perfection and "perdurability" of the next.[39] It is a note which is not struck in the French. When the French Galaad finally sees the full mystery of the Grail, he sends greetings but no message to his father and prays that he be allowed to "trespasse de ceste terriene vie en la celestiel" (p. 278). He is not asking to be released from this wretched world, or what Chaucer would call "this foule prisoun of this lyf" (A 3061), for he has already achieved on this earth the highest kind of vision, that which the heart cannot conceive nor the tongue describe, the intellectual vision of God. He prays for death simply to sustain that vision forever. In Charlotte Morse's words, "he passes from the shadow of the heavenly banquet, the sacrament of the Mass, to the reality of its eternal celebration, a passage from time to eternity without any division between the two conditions."[40]

The controlling image of Galaad's journey in the *Queste* is a progression into more and more refined revelation, till the vision of the ineffable in this world shades imperceptibly into union in the next. The controlling image of the journey of Malory's Galahad is also a progression into greater spirituality, but one which culminates in his translation from one world into the next, with a sharp awareness of the division between them. Malory presents the spiritual pursuit of perfection as complementary to rather than competitive with the pursuit of earthly glory. Matarasso has shown that the function of the *Queste del Saint Graal* in the Vulgate Cycle as a whole is to redeem earthly chivalry by presenting a new way of life that negates and exposes the old one.[41] To Malory, however, the Grail quest is a digression rather than an exposure: "the Rounde Table shall be brokyn for a season" (793.33–34).[42] For his knights the "ghostly chivalry" is an alternative that is only emotionally available after the earthly chivalry has been relinquished, after the fellowship that gave it meaning has gone. Malory is not, therefore, turning the Grail Quest into just another earthly adventure, as Vinaver averred (*Works*, p. 1535); it is still the truest and holiest tale in the world. However, he is, inevitably, transforming it in the light of his own culture and his native literary tradition. Just as the Boethian ending of *Troilus and Criseyde* does not negate the passionate earthly drama that precedes it, but puts it in perspective, so the Tale of the Sankgreal does not negate the heroic-chivalric values of the *Morte Darthur* as a whole. Only in the perspective of eternity is the greatest of all earthly institutions seen as fragile and finite, doomed inevitably to fall.

NOTES

Reprinted with permission from *Studies in Malory*, ed. James W. Spisak (Kalamazoo, MI: Medieval Institute Publications, 1985), pp. 109–128.

1. *The Works of Sir Thomas Malory*, ed. Eugène Vinaver, 2nd ed., 3 vols. (Oxford: Oxford University Press, 1967), 1037.9–11. All quotations and references are to this edition.

2. Terence McCarthy, "The Sequence of Malory's Tales," in *Aspects of Malory*, ed. Toshiyuki Takamiya and Derek Brewer (Cambridge: D.S. Brewer; Totowa, N.J.: Rowman and Littlefield, 1981), p. 117.

3. Mary Hynes-Berry, "Language and Meaning: Malory's Translation of the Grail Story," *Neophilologus,* 60 (1976), 318.

4. Hynes-Berry, "Malory's Translation of Meaning: *The Tale of the Sankgreal," Studies in Philology,* 74 (1975), 257; P. E. Tucker, "Chivalry in the *Morte*," in *Essays on Malory,* ed. J. A. W. Bennett (Oxford: Oxford University Press, 1963), p. 83; Larry D. Benson, *Malory's* Morte Darthur (Cambridge, Mass: Harvard University Press, 1976), p. 210; Charles Moorman, *The Book of Kyng Arthur: The Unity of Malory's* Morte Darthur (Lexington, Ky.: University of Kentucky Press, 1965), p. 33; Charles Whitworth, "The Sacred and the Secular in Malory's *Tale of the Sankgreal," Yearbook of English Studies,* 5 (1975), 19.

5. Arthur B. Ferguson, *The Indian Summer of English Chivalry* (Durham, N. C.: Duke University Press, 1960), p. 222; Benson, p. 201, and Chs. 7–9 generally; see also *Chivalric Literature: Essays on Relations between Literature and Life in the Later Middle Ages,* ed. Larry D. Benson and John Leyerle, Studies in Medieval Culture, 14 (Kalamazoo: Medieval Institute Publications, 1980).

6. Benson, pp. 196–97.

7. *Paston Letters,* ed. Norman Davis (Oxford: Oxford University Press, 1958), no. 50, p. 66.

8. See, e.g., *Paston Letters,* no. 49.

9. E. K. Chambers, *Sir Thomas Wyatt and Some Collected Studies* (London: Sidgewick and Jackson, 1933), p. 32.

10. Fanni Bogdanow has shown that the *Queste* section of the prose *Tristan* is derived from the First redaction of the post-Vulgate *Queste,* which, together with an extended *Suite du Merlin* and a post-Vulgate *Mort Artu,* formed what may be called the *Roman du Graal;* see *The Romance of the Grail: A Study of the Structure and Genesis of a Thirteenth Century Arthurian Prose Romance* (Manchester: Manchester University Press; New York: Barnes and Noble, 1966), Ch. 4. Since the *Suite du Merlin* was Malory's source for his opening Tale, it is likely he knew this version of the *Queste.* Furthermore, a reference in Malory's colophon to the "Tristram" to a division between a second and third book of the French work is reflected in certain MSS of the prose *Tristan* (see *Works,* pp. 1531–32), which suggests that Malory's source MS contained the *Queste.*

11. See Emmanuèle Baumgartner, *Le "Tristan en Prose": Essai d'interprétation d'un roman médiéval* (Geneva: Droz, 1975), pp. 199–200.

12. Terence McCarthy, "Order of Composition in the *Morte Darthur,"* *Yearbook of English Studies,* I (1971), 18–29; also "The Sequence of Malory's Tales," in *Aspects of Malory,* pp. 107–24; Edward D. Kennedy, "Malory and His English Sources," in *Aspects,* pp. 44–47.

13. Suzanne Greer Fein discusses this aspect in "Thomas Malory and the Pictorial Interlace of *La Queste del Saint Graal," University of Toronto Quarterly,* 46 (1977), 214–40.

14. Albert Pauphilet, *Etudes sur "la Queste del Saint Graal" attribué à Gautier Map* (Paris: H. Champion, 1921), p. 26.

15. Pauline Matarasso, trans., *The Quest of the Holy Grail* (Harmondsworth: Penguin Books, 1969), p. 301, n. 73.

16. Albert Pauphilet, ed., *La Queste del Saint Graal, roman du Xllle siècle,* CFMA 33 (Paris: H. Champion, 1921, rpt. 1967), p. xi. Subsequent quotations from the *Queste* are from this edition; the glosses are my own.

17. "Tomorrow you must fight against the most dreaded champion of the world. And if you are vanquished, you will not escape with the loss of a limb, but it will go so badly with you that you will be shamed for ever after. "

18. *Etudes,* p. 44. Love between spiritual "brothers," those who are united in the common pursuit of the mysteries of the Grail, is a very different matter. The Grail questers frequently show affection to one another, embracing joyfully in welcome and tearfully in farewell, e.g., pp. 194, 245–46, 250, 252. It is, however, an exclusive brotherhood, limited to those who are "compainz de la Queste" (p. 268).

19. Erich Auerbach, "Typological Symbolism in Medieval Literature," *Yale French Studies,* 9 (1952), 4.

20. See *Queste,* p. 143; also see Eugène Vinaver, *Malory* (Oxford: Oxford University Press, 1929; rpt. 1970), p. 185, for a partial edition of MS. B.N. fr. 120, which is in some respects closer to Malory's translation than Pauphilet's base text (see Vinaver's explanation in *Works,* pp. 1534–35).

21. Frederick Locke, *The Quest for the Holy Grail: A Literary Study of a Thirteenth Century Romance* (Stanford: Stanford University Press, 1960), p. 95. See also Pauline Matarasso, *The Redemption of Chivalry: A Study of the* Queste del Saint Graal (Geneva: Droz, 1979), pp. 182–83.

22. *Queste,* p. 213, and Pauphilet, *Etudes,* pp. 39–40.

23. Locke explains this very persuasively, pp. 95–100.

24. Hynes-Berry discusses some of the major alterations to the *Queste* in "Malory's Translation of Meaning," especially pp. 245–48.

25. Malory does expand the virgin's appeal to Bors with a reference to King Arthur and "the hyghe Ordre of Knyghthode" (961.7–11), and adds the sentence "he ys a murtherer and doth contrary to the Order of Knyghthode" (968.11–12) to the hermit's description of Lionel's character. However, this particular criticism may well have been suggested by the French text, where Lyonel represents the "type" of anger, just as Hector does of pride. See Pauphilet, *Etudes,* pp. 125–27.

26. Tucker, p. 85, and Moorman, pp. 36–37.

27. "For as soon as your eyes were inflamed by the fever of lust you chased away humility and welcomed pride and wished to carry your head as proudly as a lion, and said in your heart that you should not nor never would value anything

unless you had your desire of her whom you saw as so beautiful." Cf. the corresponding passage in Vinaver's *Malory*, pp. 165–66.

28. Matarasso, *Redemption of Chivalry*, pp. 145–49.

29. See Locke, pp. 74–77.

30. Tucker, for instance, argues that Lancelot's love for Guenevere has obscured his sense of right and wrong, p. 85; Hynes-Berry endorses his view in "Malory's Translation of Meaning," pp. 248–50.

31. *Malory*, p. 171, which is closer here; cf. *Queste*, 131:14–15.

32. See *relïgios, Altfranzösisches Wörterbuch*, ed. Tobler-Lommatzch, 9 vols. (Wiesbaden: Franz Steiner Verlag, 1969–73), which cites "mout sainz hon et religïeus," *Perceval*, H. 1912; also *religios, Dictionnaire de l'ancienne lange française*, ed. F. Godefroy, 10 vols. (Paris, 1881, 1902), which cites "saint homme et de religieuse vie," *Livre du Chevalier de la Tour Landry*.

33. See *OED*, *stable*, 6. a, b; *stability*, 3. a, b.

34. See *RB 1980: The Rule of St. Benedict, in Latin and English with Notes*, ed. Timothy Fry, OSB (Collegeville, Minn.: Liturgical Press, 1981), p. 266, 58:9. "Stability" is usually taken to mean a vow of loyalty to the house in which the novice is professed, but in his Commentary on the passage Fry shows that the early promise, made either after a few days or after two months, "simply means that the candidate . . . has decided to stay and wants to persevere through the novitiate to profession. The second promise, at the end of the year, means that he wants to make profession and bind himself permanently to all the obligations of the monastic life" (p. 445); see also pp. 463–65.

35. *Three Middle English Versions of the Rule of St. Benet*, ed. Ernst A. Kock, E.E.T.S., 120 (1902), 135:28–30; see also the Lansdowne ritual for the ordination of nuns, 141:27–142:3.

36. William Bonde, *A Devout Treatyse in Englysshe Called the Pilgrymage of Perfeccyon*, printed by Wynkyn de Worde (1531), STC 3278, fol. 86b (my own punctuation); for the earlier printing by Richard Pynson (1526), STC 3277, see fol. 24b (repaginated from Book 3 onwards).

37. Ferguson, pp. 52–56, and Benson, pp. 194–95.

38. Stephen Scrope, Preface to Sir John Fastolf, *The Epistle of Othea, trans. from the French Text of Christine de Pisan*, ed. Curt F. Buhler, E.E.T.S. 264 (1970), p. 121.

39. The *locus classicus* is Theseus' speech in Chaucer, *Knight's Tale*, A 2994–3010, *The Complete Works of Geoffrey Chaucer*, ed. F. N. Robinson, 2nd ed. (Boston: Houghton Mifflin, 1957); but see also the Balade, "Lak of Stedfastnesse" (p. 537), and *Boece*, 2, m3, lines 16–23, and 4, p6, lines 42–47; also *OED*, *unstable*, 3, *unstableness*, 1.b. As in the *Knight's Tale*, 2995, "wrecched" is fre-

quently associated with the sinfulness of this temporal world. For evidence that the association persists through the fifteenth century, see *OED, wretched,* 2.y, *wretchedly,* 2, *wretchedness,* I.a, 2: a good example is the citation, c. 1450, of Lovelich, "For more they loven wrechednesse Thanne hevenely thing," *Grail,* xliii, 413. Note also that the alliterative *Morte Arthure,* which is Malory's source for the Tale of Arthur and Lucius, begins with a prayer to God to guide us "here / In this wrechyd werld, thorowe vertuous lywynge," *The Alliterative Morte Arthure,* ed. Valerie Krishna (New York: Burt Franklin, 1976), ll. 4–5.

40. Charlotte Morse, *The Pattern of Judgment in the* Queste *and* Cleanness (Columbia and London: University of Missouri Press, 1978), p. 128.

41. *Redemption,* pp. 92–95.

42. "For a season" is not in Caxton's edition.

CHAPTER 12

Chivalric Nationalism and the Holy Grail in John Hardyng's *Chronicle*

FELICITY RIDDY

I

In a European football competition held in the summer of 1996, England found itself playing Germany for a place in the final. The match provoked intense and often crude national feeling in the English popular press, which represented it as a rerun of World War II (which that kind of newspaper, of course, chooses to see as an English rather than an Allied victory). Many English supporters expressed the jingoistic mood of the moment by going to the match as icons of patriotism, with their faces painted white and superimposed with the red cross of St. George, England's patron saint, from ear to ear and from forehead to chin, like actors in some chauvinistic *commedia dell'arte*. Their use of the red cross as a signifier of an aggressive and warlike national identity was not new, of course, or even modern; it goes back to the fifteenth century. After the capture of Rouen by the English in 1419, it is reported that Henry V raised banners at each of its gates, including the sign of the red cross: "at Porte Martuyle he vp pight / Of Seint George a baner bright."[1] Only four years earlier, after the English victory over the French at Agincourt, the saint's feast day had been declared a major festival on which he was to be honored "as the nation's patron and special protector."[2] St. George had been the patron saint of the Order of the Garter since it was founded by Henry V's great-grandfather, Edward III, in 1348; by the fifteenth century he had become the patron saint of England.

At about the same time, King Arthur seems to have become St. George's secular equivalent. Arthur, as is well known, had been used by

English kings to enhance ideas of kingship from the thirteenth century on; Arthurian ceremonial, feasting, and tournaments provided a vocabulary of monarchy drawn on by several kings, and most notably Edward III in the mid-fourteenth century.[3] As ruler over the lesser kings of Britain, Arthur was truly emperor in his own kingdom in a way that late medieval kings found useful to emulate. By the fifteenth century, however, the Arthurian story had come to sustain a specific discourse not only of kingship but also of Englishness, and Arthur was part of a way of representing the political interests of that section of society whose function was, traditionally, to fight. He occurs very frequently in chronicle histories written on the model initiated by Geoffrey of Monmouth's *Historia regum Britanniae* in the twelfth century: histories of the kings of Britain and, after the Anglo-Saxon invasions, of England, in which the past is conceived of as the scene of chivalric activity. The most widely read late-medieval example is the prose *Brut*, which I have already quoted; originally composed in the late thirteenth century, it was continually brought up to date until well into the fifteenth. The *Brut* survives in nearly 200 manuscripts and is the nearest England has to a national history in the period.[4] It begins with the founding of Britain by Brutus in the aftermath of the Trojan War and traces the line of kings, including Arthur, up to the time of writing. History of this kind is secular and public: it is about kingship, governance, and the transmission of power. Moreover, in the fifteenth century, Arthur had by various sleights of hand become an English, not a British, king. In one *Brut*-style chronicle from the mid-fifteenth century, for example, Arthur's father, Uther Pendragon, "a gode knyght and a worthi" marries a "faire lady" called Ingerne,

> and at that tyme was a great abbicion [disagreement] for the londis
> name. Some did call hit Brettayne, and some called hit Engelonde; and
> for the love that Uter had to his wyfe, and for the gentill blode that she
> came of, he named this londe after hir name Ingerne, Englonde.[5]

This renaming takes place just in time for their son Arthur to be born an Englishman.

Writing about Arthur in mid-fifteenth-century England was thus almost inevitably a way of exploring some of the senses of Englishness that had been sharpened by the Hundred Years' War and complicated by what many felt to be its humiliating outcome.[6] Caxton saw clearly enough the connection between Arthur and Englishness, and one of the reasons he gives in his preface for publishing Malory's *Le Morte Darthur* is that "many noble and dyvers gentylmen of thys royame of England" have told him that he ought to print a book about Arthur, rather than the one he had already printed about Godfrey of Boulogne, because Arthur "was a man born wythin this royame and kyng and emperour of the same . . . Kyng Arthur . . . ought moost to be remembred emonge us Englysshemen tofore al other Cristen kynges."[7] Arthur, like George, is part of a complex of ideas out of which a masculine and martial sense of national identity was formed.

One fifteenth-century writer—possibly the only one—who brings Arthur and George together is John Hardyng, the author of a verse chronicle which he wrote and then rewrote between the early 1440s and 1464.[8] Hardyng's model is the *Brut*, and his chronicle includes an extended life of Arthur whom he links to George through the story of the Holy Grail. He is able to do this because in the French Vulgate *Estoire del Saint Graal* and *Queste del Saint Graal*, both probably composed in the second quarter of the thirteenth century, the red-cross symbol appears on the shield of the Grail knight, Galaad, Lancelot's perfect son. Galaad's red-cross shield has its origins in both these texts in the story of Joseph of Arimathea, the keeper of the Grail. Joseph of Arimathea figures in the New Testament and the apocryphal *Gospel of Nicodemus* as the owner of the tomb in which Christ's body rested after the Crucifixion. By the twelfth century the story had developed that Joseph kept the cup from which Jesus drank at the Last Supper—the Holy Grail—and collected in it some of Jesus' blood at the deposition from the Cross. Then he and his followers, including his saintly son, Josephus, who was believed to be the first bishop, later brought the Grail to England, where Joseph instituted the table of the Holy Grail in memory of the Last Supper and converted some of the pagan Britons. In the *Estoire*'s sensationally embellished account of these fictional events, which are much more briefly told in the *Queste*, Evelach, king of Sarras (where the Saracens come from), is given a shield by Josephus; later, converted to Christianity and baptized as Mordrains, Evelach brings the shield to England where the dying Josephus inscribes it with a cross in his own blood, saying,

> whenever you hold the shield you will remember me, for the cross I made will always last, as fresh and new as it is now, as long as the shield lasts. And it will last a long time, because henceforth any knight who hangs it round his neck will repent of it, until Galaad, the very good knight . . . comes and hangs it round his neck.[9]

All this was believed to have happened in the first generation after the death of Christ. Several hundred years later, according to the *Queste del Saint Graal*, Galaad received the red-cross shield at the outset of the Grail quest from monks at the abbey where it had been kept, we are told, ever since Mordrains's death; thus the red cross became Galaad's sign and remained so in later Arthurian heraldry.[10] The thirteenth-century *Queste* and the *Estoire* were both, of course, composed long before the red cross came to represent Englishness. At the time at which they were written, the symbol had a number of meanings, including that of the crusade,[11] which was particularly relevant given the focus of both these texts on the Holy Land; at the end of the *Queste* Galaad leaves Logres and sails to Sarras, where he becomes king for a year and then dies after seeing the mysteries of the Grail.

The French authors of these two works were only hazily interested in the Grail story as part of a specifically English history. They were certainly not concerned with the problems of chronology that the story of Joseph of Arimathea's arrival in England with the Holy Grail presented to English chroniclers, problems caused by the fact that authorities such as Bede or even Geoffrey of Monmouth placed the conversion period much later than the generation after Christ. Nevertheless, more than one late-medieval English chronicler overcame these problems, including John of Glastonbury in the fourteenth century and John Hardyng in the fifteenth, both of whom use the French Vulgate Grail texts as historical sources.

John of Glastonbury, who wrote a history of Glastonbury Abbey in the 1340s, says that in the reign of the British King Arviragus, who was supposedly a first-century contemporary of the Roman emperor Vespasian, Joseph of Arimathea came to Glastonbury, or Avalon, bringing "two white and silver vessels, full of the blood and sweat of the prophet Jesus."[12] He preached the faith and founded a wattle church there, where he lies buried. This account was given wide credence, especially since Glastonbury was one of the richest and most powerful abbeys in England in the later Middle Ages. In 1191 the Glastonbury monks had claimed to have discovered the tombs of Arthur and Guinevere there, so the abbey already had persuasive Arthurian connections. John of Glastonbury's interest in Joseph of Arimathea is part of an attempt to claim a particular antiquity for his abbey, and although Galaad's miraculous shield is mentioned, the red cross on it is not, because it is irrelevant to John's concerns.[13] The Holy Grail, as cup of the Last Supper containing Christ's blood, was evidently too dangerous in its Eucharistic implications to be incorporated comfortably into the history of the abbey, and so it has dwindled to a relic—the phials containing Christ's blood and sweat—of a kind that the abbey had in abundance. The relic lists that John of Glastonbury incorporates into his chronicle include, for example, some of Christ's hair, part of the sponge from which he drank the wine mixed with myrrh on the cross, part of the hole where the cross was placed on the hill of Calvary, and many other relics of Christ.[14] John of Glastonbury's version of the Grail shows how flexible it was as a symbol, and thus how widely differing interest groups were able to rewrite it to serve their own purposes.

A century later, John Hardyng read the Vulgate Grail texts in another way. He was much more interested in the red-cross arms than in the Holy Grail, which barely features in his account of Joseph's mission to England. He knew the Glastonbury version of history, and when he first wrote his chronicle, Hardyng followed it in making Joseph bring with him "two fyols, full of the swete to sayne / Of Ihu Cryste, as red as blode of bayne."[15] The blood is now only a figure of speech, and the phials are not identified as the Holy Grail. When he rewrote it, even the phials of sweat are not mentioned in the text, although a marginal gloss, which must derive from one of the Vulgate Grail texts, reads:

> Also this Joseph brought into Britayne with hym parte of the blode of Criste / whiche is called Seyntgraal / the true sayinge is Sank Roiall / Also this Joseph made a Rounde Table for hym and for hys fellows in remembraunce of xii Apostolles / whiche Rounde Table kynge Arthure honoured and held.[16]

By marginalizing the Grail in the way he does, Hardyng is able to focus on other things. As an Agincourt veteran, he knew that the red cross stood for England and St. George, and the red cross with which Josephus marked Mordrains's—later Galaad's—shield must have leapt off the page at him. He uses it to develop an episode of his own invention, Joseph of Arimathea's gift of a shield to King Arviragus after the latter's baptism:

> And gaue hym than a shelde as siluer white,
> A crosse endlonge and ouerthwerte full parfite
>
> Of his own blode whiche from his necke did rynne.
> He made that crosse in signyficacioun
> Of Cristes blode that ranne oute fro withynne

Vpon the crosse at his expiracioun;
He bore on hym in feldes of werre alwaye
And in his baners and cote armour gaye.

The armes were used in all Bretayne
For comoun signe eche man to knowe his nacioun
Fro his enemyse, which we nowe call certayne
Seynt Georges armes, by Mewyns informacioun;
Which armes here were hade after Cristes passioun,
Full longe afore Seynt George was generate
Were worshipped here of mekell elder date.[17]

For Hardyng the red cross is a national emblem, a "comoun signe
eche man to knowe his nacioun." It is British rather than English because
for Hardyng England is Britain: one of the most powerful themes in his
chronicle is that England was rightfully sovereign over Scotland (Wales
was not an independent kingdom and therefore not an issue).[18] Moreover,
he suggests here that the red cross had been a national symbol as early as
the reign of King Arviragus, long before St. George was born. I have already mentioned that the red cross was used in a number of contexts in the
later Middle Ages, including that of the crusade, and that St. George had
been officially claimed for England only during Hardyng's own lifetime.
Even by the mid-fifteenth-century there must still have been ambiguity as
to what the symbol meant; the process whereby it and St. George settled
down to represent Englishness was a gradual one.[19] Outside England, St.
George continued to be regarded as an epitome of chivalry rather than of
Englishness: the Holy Roman Emperor Sigismund had a particular devotion to St. George, and had founded his own Order of the Dragon around
1413, while in Germany the Brotherhood of St. George's Shield flourished
in the fifteenth century, as did the confraternity of St. George, founded in
Franche-Comté in the 1430s.[20] Hardyng's treatment of the red-cross symbol sounds like an attempt to appropriate it: just as the English church in
the fifteenth century claimed to be the oldest in Europe because it had been
founded by Joseph of Arimathea,[21] so England—according to Hardyng—
could lay claim to ownership of the red-cross symbol because it derived
from the shield which Joseph made for one of the early British kings. In
fact Hardyng claims that the red cross is even more anciently British than
this: it had also been the armorial bearing of Brutus, Britain's legendary
founder, and it turns up again not only in the reign of Arviragus, but in the
later reigns of Lucius, Constantine, and Uther Pendragon, Arthur's father:

The armes als of Troye that Brutus bere,
The armes also of goode kynge Lucius
Which after bapteme his armes alway were,
The same armes that kyng Constantynus
At his bataile ayenst Maxencius,
He [Uther] bore alway, that seynt Georges armes we call
Whiche English men nowe worship ouer all.[22]

The red-cross arms bring together the secular genealogy that Geoffrey of Monmouth developed when he linked Britain, through Brutus, to Troy and the religious genealogy of the Vulgate Grail texts that linked Britain, through Joseph, to Jerusalem.

II

Hardyng's chronicle survives, as I have already said, in two versions, the first of which was completed by 1457 and the second by 1464. It was dedicated to three successive kings or would-be kings: Henry VI who was deposed in 1460; Richard, duke of York, who was briefly heir to the throne between October 1460 and his death two months later, and York's son, who assumed the throne as Edward IV in 1461. Hardyng originally wrote his chronicle for Henry VI and presented it to him in 1457.[23] He then opportunistically rewrote it in a shortened form, initially for presentation to the duke of York, possibly at the instigation of a Yorkist patron. York was killed, however, while Hardyng was in the throes of composition. Apparently unfazed, Hardyng went on working and dedicated this new version to Edward IV and his queen, Elizabeth Woodville, in 1464. By this time Hardyng was well into his eighties and he probably died soon afterwards.[24]

The chronicle has two unusual elements: one is that, at the climax of the episode of the Roman war, Arthur actually reaches Rome, where, in the earlier version, he is crowned emperor. Traditionally in the chronicles and in chronicle-based poems deriving from Geoffrey of Monmouth—in Layamon's *Brut*, for example, or the alliterative *Morte Arthure*—the news of Mordred's treachery comes from England just as Arthur is on the brink of driving home his triumphs, but he does not actually conquer Rome. The other unusual element is the Grail quest which is not included, as far as I know, in any other chronicle version of the life of Arthur.

To deal briefly with the first: Hardyng is not the only fifteenth-century writer to improve on Geoffrey of Monmouth's account in allowing

Arthur to conquer Rome, since Malory does the same thing in "The Tale of King Arthur and the Emperor Lucius." Hardyng had lived through the English successes in France under Henry V—he had fought at Agincourt, as I have already noted—and then watched England failing to maintain its hold on its French territories from 1435 on. Malory belonged to a younger generation that must have heard its elders' boasts of the old victories turn into acrimonious national self-castigation. When Hardyng began the first version of his chronicle in the 1440s, the outcome of Henry's peace policy was still not clear; by the time Hardyng finished the second version in the 1460s, all France, apart from Calais, had been lost. Small wonder that these men should invent the comforting myth of England's great imperial past. Hardyng has Arthur ride in triumph in an extraordinary procession through the streets of Rome; psychologically it seems to be at one with the grandiose claim made in the epilogue to the later version of the chronicle that Edward IV is true heir to the thrones of England, Scotland, Wales, Ireland, France, Spain, Portugal, and Jerusalem.

The Grail episode serves different but related purposes. There was plenty of interest in late-medieval England in the Grail history and in the Joseph of Arimathea legends. The *Estoire del Saint Graal* was used by John of Glastonbury in his chronicle and was translated into English verse in the 1420s by the London skinner, Henry Lovelich, along with the prose *Merlin*. The post-Vulgate *Suite du Merlin* was translated into English prose at around the same time, and Pynson printed a life of Joseph of Arimathea in 1520. Nevertheless, Hardyng's Grail is not like any of these: his version of the Grail quest in Arthur's reign harks back, via the red-cross shield, to the reign of King Arviragus and Joseph of Arimathea's mission, but it also takes an entirely new direction.

It begins, apparently drawing on the *Queste del Saint Graal*, with Galaad coming to court and sitting in the "sege perilouse." He is acknowledged as Lancelot's son and in the later version is even legitimized, being described as one

> Whom Launcelote gote in verie clene spousage
> On Pelles daughter, that kynge full longe had been
> Of Venedoce, that Northwalis now is, men wene.[25]

Lancelot figures occasionally elsewhere in Hardyng's life of Arthur, but with the supernumerary presence to which he is condemned in works drawn from the chronicle tradition. In this tradition he is not Guinevere's lover; she betrays Arthur only with Mordred, and the great adultery story of the Vulgate *La Mort le Roi Artu* has no place. So when Lancelot appears in chronicle-based works such as the Alliterative *Morte Arthure*, for example, he functions only as one of Arthur's best knights. Released from the tie to Guinevere, which is the source of so much narrative complication in the romance tradition, Lancelot is free to marry, as he does here. Hardyng's decision to make the Grail maiden his wife is skillful; it eliminates at a stroke all the jealousy and madness of the Vulgate *Lancelot* and the prose *Tristan*. Nevertheless with Galaad's origins made so thoroughly domestic and respectable, much of his otherworldly aura is lost. Hardyng's account of the Grail itself, though, is hardly otherworldly anyway.

It arrives at a feast, as in the *Queste*, accompanied by a great flapping of doors and windows, and flies three times around the room at top speed before disappearing:

> And with that noise the Seynt Graale preciouse
> Flewe thries abowte withyn the hall full ofte
> Fletherynge full faste above high on lofte.[26]

"Fletherynge" may be intended to link the flying Grail to the symbolism of the Holy Ghost as a dove.[27] In the source—assuming it was the *Queste*—the Grail circles the hall and furnishes all who are there with whatever food they desire. Arthur's knights are struck dumb; it is one of those moments of intense religious experience that the French text habitually expresses through speechlessness. In Hardyng's version, by contrast, the knights all press forward with drawn weapons "to see and wytt what thynge that it myght be;"[28] the Grail is an object of curiosity, perhaps even a threat, but not a religious mystery. It is a "thynge," intractably material in a world of things.

Hardyng follows the *Queste* in making Galaad set off in search of the Grail without a shield. In the French text he is given the red-cross shield at an abbey of white monks, or Cistercians. In Hardyng's chronicle the white monks become black: Galaad goes to Avalon or Glastonbury, which was a Benedictine house, and collects the shield that Joseph of Arimathea had left there in Arviragus's reign. In both versions of the chronicle the central part of the Vulgate *Queste*, which is devoted to the separate journeyings of Lancelot, Bors, Percival, Gawain, and the rest, is omitted. The early version summarizes it thus:

> With that Galaad rode forthe so with his route;
> At euery way he made a knyght departe,

To tyme thay all seuerally so were gone oute,
And none lefte than, so had echone thaire parte.
And iff on mette an other in any arte,
His reule was so he shold his felawe tell
His auenturs, what so that hym befell.

And also sone as thar way lay sondry wyse,
Thay shulde departe and mete no more agayne,
Bot auenture it made thurgh exercyse
Of grete laboure that thaym did so constrayne,
By dyuerse stretes whiche togedire layne.
And whan he had his felawes all convayed
He chese his way, full lyke a knyght arayed.[29]

These stanzas seem to record the experience of reading the *Queste del Saint Graal* and reveal one reason why Hardyng treats the Grail Quest as apparently cavalierly as he does. This is the response of the narrator of a strictly linear narrative to the complexities of interlace, with its ways that lie "sondry wyse" and its "dyuerse stretes," which converge apparently by a mixture of chance and the strenuous agency of the characters. Interlace is a digressive and in some sense uncentered narrative mode that is incompatible with the chronicle's more narrowly sequential forward drive. Malory's unpicking of the interlace that he found in the sources for Book 7 of *Le Morte Darthur* seems to confirm this: he simplifies the narrative line of "The Poisoned Apple" and "The Maid of Astolat" into a chronological sequence that helps to create the tragic pressure of the end. Malory does not, though, unpick the interlace of the *Queste* in Book 6; the fact that its focus wavers between Galahad and Lancelot (and to a lesser extent the other knights) serves his purpose of exploring the tension between competing values. In Hardyng's chronicle the tensions are located elsewhere: they are between Englishmen and foreigners, especially Scots, and not between Arthur's knights, at least until the treachery of Mordred that brings Arthur's reign to an end.

The Quest itself is completed in only four lines in the later version of the chronicle, in which Hardyng simply says of Galaad that

when he hade so laboured foure yere
He founde in Walis the Sanke Roiall full clere.

Then rode he furth vnto the Holy Londe
Thorowe gode and holy inspiracioun . . . [30]

In the earlier version, the Welsh leg of the quest had been ignored entirely, and Galaad had made straight for the Holy Land, where he was crowned king of Sarras. It is possible to see another reason why the Vulgate *Queste* had to be gutted in this way: it is caught between the mighty opposites of the chronicle account of Arthur's reign and the romance elaborations of it. If Lancelot is not Guinevere's lover, then the story of his penitence for their adultery, with which so much of the *Queste* is concerned, is simply irrelevant. Nor do the adventures of Gawain, the impenitent sinner, have any place in a story in which he is simply Arthur's heroic nephew. All that simply has to go. But Hardyng's treatment of his source is not merely a matter of a preference for uncomplicated narrative or the plot functions of his characters. Throughout the chronicle Hardyng's emphasis is public and social, not internal and private. That is why he writes history and not romance. Malory, for all his demystification of the Grail, has a much stronger awareness than Hardyng of the inwardness of the religious experience that it represents and the spiritual meanings it might be made to bear.

For Hardyng, the Grail of the Quest is not a religious symbol but a heraldic emblem that harks back through history to Joseph of Arimathea, binding together the past rather than transcending history in the Eucharist. It becomes the insignia of the chivalric Order of the Holy Grail that Galaad founds at Sarras, with Joseph of Arimathea as its exemplar if not its patron saint:

> Sir Bors with hym went and Sir Percivale,
> And other moo of the Table Rounde,
> Whome knightes he made of the Sanke Riale,
> Which order so he ordeyned so and founde
> At Sarras, that to Egipte londe doth bounde,
> Forto leue chaste and mayntayne Cristiante,
> Liche as Ioseph dide of Aramathe.[31]

Although Hardyng specifically links Galaad's Order of the Holy Grail with the military orders of the Templars and the Hospitallers, nevertheless Galaad in the Holy Land is not a crusader but a just king with a vision of a good society, in a book addressed to kings. The rule of Galaad's Order is more fully elaborated in the early version of the chronicle than in the late:

> Whose reule was this by Galaad constytute:
> To leue evermore in clennesse virginall;
> Comon profyte all way to execute;

All wronges redress with batayll corperall
Where law myght nought haue course iudiciall;
All fals lyuers his londe that had infecte
For to distroy, or of thair vice correcte.

The pese to kepe, the laws als sustene,
The fayth of Criste, the kyrke also protecte;
Widows, maydyns, ay whare fore to mayntene
And chyldre yonge, vnto thar age perfecte
That they couthe kepe thaym selfe in all affecte.
Thus sette it was in hole perfeccioun,
By gode advise and full cyrcumspeccion.[32]

This rule is similar to the terms of the Pentecostal oath sworn by Arthur's
knights in Malory's *Le Morte Darthur*, but both are also reminiscent of
the statutes of the secular orders of chivalry that were founded all over
Europe in the course of the fourteenth and fifteenth centuries: Edward
III's Order of the Garter, Philip the Good's Order of the Golden Fleece
(1431), and René of Anjou's Order of the Crescent (1448) are only the
most famous.[33] With their princely leaders, their restricted numbers, their
commitment to chivalric ideals, their avowed ethos of brotherhood, and
their recording of their own deeds of valor, they are very like Galaad's
Order of the Holy Grail, or rather, Galaad's Order is very like them.
Maurice Keen has pointed out that Arthur's Round Table, which is given
by Merlin and modeled on the Table of the Last Supper and Joseph of
Arimathea's Table of the Grail, provided an archetype for many of the
elite curial orders of the period.[34] In Hardyng's account of the Order of
the Holy Grail we can see a second stage in the process Keen describes,
whereby aristocratic social practice, itself fed on chivalric literature, provides a new model for the rewriting of Arthurian history.

Galaad's death is, equally, a rewriting in which contemporary events
are inscribed. In the Vulgate *Queste*, which Malory follows quite closely
in his version, Galaad dies at Sarras after being vouchsafed a final version of the Grail mysteries during the solemn part of the mass. Hardyng,
of course, has nothing to do with such things. In both versions of the
chronicle Galaad's death is not a visionary moment but a pious conclusion to a life spent in virginity and good works. Percival, who in the
Queste has accompanied him to the Holy Land and dies at Sarras,
here takes Galaad's heart, encased in gold, back to Arthur's court with
Bors:

But after longe upon the Witsonday,
Sir Bors and Percivale come to the kynge
With knyghtes all that leuynge were that day
At Caerlion, but Percivale dide brynge
Oute of Sarras, withoute any lettynge,
Sir Galaades herte enclosed all with golde.[35]

It has been suggested that this detail may come from the fourteenth-century story of the heart of King Robert the Bruce of Scotland, which was also encased in gold and was being taken to the Holy Land by Bruce's lieutenant Sir James Douglas, on Bruce's dying instructions, when Douglas was killed in Spain. Hardyng could have read this story in Barbour's *Bruce* when he was in Scotland, or in Froissart, or he may even have heard it from Sir James Douglas's grandson, who was taken prisoner by Henry Percy at Homildon in 1402, when Hardyng was a member of Percy's household.[36] Another and closer analogue, though, and one that Hardyng must have known about through his "good lord," the Garter knight Sir Robert Umfraville, is St. George's heart, which was presented to Henry V by the Emperor Sigismund on the occasion of the latter's admission to the Order of the Garter in 1416. The occasion is included in the Beauchamp Pageants, a pictorial record made in the 1470s of the achievements of Richard Beauchamp, earl of Warwick, himself a Garter knight, where St. George's heart is depicted in an elaborate reliquary.[37] Sigismund presented it to Henry at Windsor, after the installation ceremony in St. George's Chapel, where other relics of the saint were kept.[38] It was a gesture whose graceful appropriateness related not only to the Garter but also to Henry's victory at Agincourt and the recent adoption of George as patron saint of England.

Whereas Robert the Bruce's heart was being taken to the Holy Land, Galaad's, like St. George's, comes home; home, what is more, to Glastonbury where Joseph of Arimathea already lies and where, according to Hardyng, Arthur himself is to be buried. Nor, unsurprisingly, is the redcross shield forgotten; Percival brings it back also and asks Arthur to place it over the tomb that Galaad shares with Joseph:

And there to set his sheld that Iosep made,
Which was the armes that we saynt Georges call,
That aftir thare full many yere abode
And worsshypt were thurgh out this reme ouer all,
In so ferre forthe that kynges, in especiall,

Thaym bare alway in batayle whare thay wente
Afore thaym euere, for spede in thare entente.[39]

The complex of meanings Hardyng gives to the red cross—Christian,
English, ancient and royal—shapes his interpretation of the story of
Galaad and provides its closure. The Grail hardly signifies, despite the
fact that it plays so large a part in Hardyng's sources, and his younger contemporary, Malory, devotes a whole book to it. The difference between
the ways in which these two English writers treat the Grail Quest is revealing. Malory's interest in the Grail may be related to his interest in
Lancelot, since the story of the Vulgate *Queste*, which Malory follows, is
part of Lancelot's biography rather than Arthur's. Nevertheless the difference between Hardyng's Grail narrative and Malory's may also be gener-
ational. Malory was probably born after Agincourt and was only a child
when Henry V died. Englishness for his generation, at the tail end of the
Hundred Years' War, must have been altogether less glamorous than for
Hardyng's. Hardyng, born between thirty and forty years earlier, grew to
manhood fighting the Scots on the northern borders of England, and
served under Henry V against the French in a battle—Agincourt—that
was to become a legend. Looking back on history in old age, he saw a past
peopled with warrior heroes, Arthur, Henry, his own master Robert Umfraville—true Englishmen, all dead—and a country in which armed men
now ruled in every shire.[40] In 1452, in the last months of the Hundred
Years' War, while Hardyng was writing the first version of his chronicle,
Richard, duke of York, argued against the terms of the peace that Henry
V's son was negotiating with the French. York compared the "worship,
honour and manhood . . . ascribed of all Nations unto the people of this
Realm whilst the Kingdom's Sovereign Lord stood possessed of his Lord-
ship in the realm of France," with the "derogation, lesion of honour and
villainy [which] is said and reported generally unto the English nation for
the loss of the same."[41] No one, it seemed, cared enough to act. Within a
year the war was over, within a decade York himself was dead, and only
old men like Hardyng could remember and celebrate the red-cross days of
England's greatness.

NOTES

1. *The Brut or The Chronicles of England*, ed. F. Brie, 2 vols, EETS o.s. 131,
136 (London: Oxford University Press, 1906–8), II, 421.

2. Quoted by E.C. Williams, "Mural Paintings of St. George in England,"
Journal of the British Archaeological Association, 3rd ser., 12 (1949), 19–36, at 20.

3. Edward III held a Round Table tournament at Windsor in the early 1340s, and his foundation of the Order of the Garter in 1348 was, according to contemporary chroniclers, modeled on Arthur's Round Table.

4. For edition, see note 1. For an up-to-date account of the text and manuscripts, see E.D. Kennedy, *XII. Chronicles and Other Historical Writings*, in *A Manual of the Writings in Middle English 1050–1500*, ed. A.E. Hartung (New Haven, CT: Archon Books, 1989), VIII, 2629–37 and 2818–33.

5. J.A. Gairdner, ed., "A Short English Chronicle," in *Three Fifteenth-Century English Chronicles*, Camden Soc., n.s. 28 (London: Camden Society, 1880), p. 10. In Geoffrey of Monmouth's *Historia regum Britanniae* Arthur is presented as king of Britain, and his reign is set in the period preceding the arrival of the Anglo-Saxons, from whom England took its name.

6. This is true of Malory's *Le Morte Darthur*; see my "Contextualizing *Le Morte Darthur*: Empire and Civil War," in *A Companion to Malory*, ed. Elizabeth Archibald and A.S.G. Edwards (Cambridge, Eng.: D.S. Brewer, 1996), pp. 55–73.

7. *The Works of Sir Thomas Malory*, ed. Eugène Vinaver, 2nd ed. (Oxford: Oxford University Press, 1971), p. xii.

8. John Hardyng was born in 1378, presumably into a northern gentry family since there are traces of northern dialect in the language of the chronicle. He was placed at the age of twelve in the household of Sir Henry Percy—Shakespeare's Hotspur in *Richard II*—and fought on the Scottish border. After Percy was killed at the battle of Shrewsbury in 1403, Hardyng entered the service of another northerner, Robert Umfraville, who became a Garter knight and with whom Hardyng fought at Agincourt in 1415 and in Scotland in the reign of Henry V. Hardyng was for a time constable of Warkworth Castle in Northumberland and later of Umfraville's Lincolnshire castle of Kyme. Robert Umfraville died in 1436, but Hardyng remained in Lincolnshire. He held a corrody at the Augustinian priory at Kyme in 1440, which might have provided the books from which he compiled his chronicle. He was still living at Kyme in 1457 and probably died there in 1464. For the circumstances of writing both versions of the chronicle, see my "John Hardyng's Chronicle and the Wars of the Roses," in *Arthurian Literature XII*, ed. James P. Carley and Felicity Riddy (Cambridge, Eng.: D.S. Brewer, 1993), pp. 91–108.

9. *The History of the Holy Grail*, trans. Carol J. Chase, in *Lancelot-Grail: The Old French Arthurian Vulgate and Post-Vulgate in Translation*, ed. Norris J. Lacy, 5 vols. (New York and London: Garland Publishing, 1993–96), I, 157.

10. See, for example, Lisa Jefferson, "Tournaments, Heraldry and the Knights of the Round Table: A Fifteenth-Century Armorial with Two Accompanying Texts," in *Arthurian Literature XIV*, ed. James P. Carley and Felicity Riddy (Cambridge, Eng.: D.S. Brewer, 1996), pp. 75, 145.

11. St. George was associated with the First Crusade at the end of the eleventh century, and the red cross was the standard badge of crusaders (known as "cruciferi" or bearers of the cross) throughout the Middle Ages. In the fourteenth century there were disputes between English crusaders and the Teutonic Knights, both engaged in the Baltic crusade, over the right to bear the banner of St. George. See Christopher Tyerman, *England and the Crusades 1095–1588* (Chicago and London: Chicago University Press, 1988), pp. 14, 272. Tyerman's chapter on "National Crusades?" (pp. 324–42) is helpful for showing how the vocabularies of crusade and of patriotism come together in the fifteenth century, creating a context for Hardyng's curious, eclectic cult of Joseph, Galaad, Arthur and George.

12. James P. Carley, ed., *The Chronicle of Glastonbury Abbey: An Edition, Translation and Study of John of Glastonbury's Cronica sive Antiquitates Glastoniensis Ecclesie*, trans. David Townsend (Woodbridge, Eng.: Boydell Press, 1985), p. 55.

13. Ibid., p. 53.

14. Ibid., p. 23.

15. London, British Library, Lansdowne 204, fol. 39v. This, the earlier version of the chronicle, has not been published.

16. London, British Library, Harley 661, fol. 27r. All quotations from the later (short) version of the chronicle are from this manuscript. The short version has been edited by H. Ellis, *The Chronicle of Iohn Hardyng* (London: F.C. and J. Rivington et al, 1812). This gloss does not occur in any of the other manuscripts and is probably not authorial. See my "Glastonbury, Joseph of Arimathea and the Grail," in *The Archaeology and History of Glastonbury Abbey*, ed. Lesley Abrams and James P. Carley (Woodbridge, Eng.: Boydell Press, 1991), pp. 317–31, at 329, n. 35, where I suggest that these sentences have been added to Harley 661 or its exemplar by a "knowledgeable scribe."

17. Harley 661, fol. 28r. For "Mewyn," sometimes identified with "Melkin the bard," see my "Glastonbury, Joseph of Arimathea and the Grail" (above, note 16), pp. 317–31, at 319–25; also James P. Carley, "Melkin the Bard and Esoteric Tradition at Glastonbury Abbey," *The Downside Review* 99 (1981), 1–17. The episode described in these lines plays havoc with the received view of the history of Christianity in England, which was that the first Christian king was Lucius, Arviragus's great-grandson, who invited Christian missionaries to Britain and was converted by them. Even John of Glastonbury respected this chronology and did not suggest that Joseph converted King Arviragus, but merely that he received a grant of land from Arviragus on which to build his church. I have not found any other chronicler before Hardyng who makes Arviragus a Christian.

18. See Edward D. Kennedy, "John Hardyng and the Holy Grail," in *Arthurian Literature VIII*, ed. Richard Barber (Cambridge, Eng.: D.S. Brewer, 1989), pp. 185–206, for a good discussion of this aspect of the chronicle.

19. The red cross is still ambiguous, of course. Today it is much more widely known as a humanitarian symbol than as an English one.

20. See Maurice Keen, *Chivalry* (New Haven and London: Yale University Press, 1984), pp. 179,188–89.

21. Valerie Lagorio has shown how Joseph's mission was used by the English delegates at four church councils between 1409 and 1434 to buttress their claims for the status and antiquity of the English church; see "The Evolving Legend of St. Joseph of Arimathea," *Speculum* 46 (1971), 209–31.

22. Harley 661, fol. 42r.

23. Lansdowne 204 is probably the presentation manuscript made for Henry VI.

24. See my "John Hardyng's Chronicle and the Wars of the Roses" (above, note 8), for a fuller discussion.

25. Harley 661, fol. 48v.

26. Harley 661, fol. 49r.

27. Compare Margery Kempe's account of a transubstantiation miracle which she witnessed: "On a day as þis creatur was herynge hir Messe, a zong man and a good prest heldyng up þe Sacrament in hys handys ouyr hys hed, þe Sacrament schok & flekeryd to & fro as a dowe flekeryth wyth hir wengys." See *The Book of Margery Kempe*, ed. S.B. Meech and H.E. Allen, EETS, o.s. 212 (London: Oxford University Press, 1940), p. 47.

28. Harley 661, fol. 49r.

29. Lansdowne 204, fol. 77r.

30. Harley 661, fol. 49r.

31. Harley 661, fol. 50v.

32. Lansdowne 204, fol. 78r.

33. See Malcolm Vale, *War and Chivalry* (London: Duckworth, 1981), pp. 32–62; Keen, *Chivalry* (above, note 20), pp. 179–99.

34. Keen, *Chivalry*, p. 190. Galaad's Order of the Holy Grail adopts the same model: ". . . than he made twelue knightes of the ordure / Of the Sanke Roiall, in full signyficacioun / Of the Table which Ioseph was the foundoure, / At Aualone, as Mewyne maketh relacioun, / In tokyn of the Table and refiguracioun / Of the brotherhode at Cristes soper and maunde, / Afore his deth, of higheste dignyte"; Harley 661, fol. 50v.

35. Harley 661, fol. 50v.

36. See Kennedy, "John Hardyng and the Holy Grail" (above, note 18), 204–05.

37. See *Pageant of the Birth, Life and Death of Richard Beauchamp, Earl of Warwick, K.G. 1389–1439*, ed. Viscount Dillon and W.H. St. John Hope (London: Longmans Green, 1914), pp. 69–70.

38. "At Windsor they had only one of the saint's bones, a piece of his arm, and part of his skull;" see James Hamilton Wylie and William Templeton Waugh, *The Reign of Henry the Fifth*, 3 vols. (Cambridge: Cambridge University Press, 1929), III, 14.

39. Lansdowne 204, fol. 78r.

40. The long version of the *Chronicle*, completed in the 1450s, includes a eulogy to Sir Robert Umfraville, who died in 1436, that contrasts Umfraville's commitment to "comoun profit" with the lawlessness of nowadays: "In euery shire with jakkes and salades clene / Missereule doth ryse and maketh neyghbours were / The waykere goth be nethe as ofte is sene / The myghtyest his quarell wyll preferre" (Lansdowne 204, fol. 221v). Galaad's exemplary rule in Sarras can be read as a similar commentary on the current situation.

41. Quoted in Ralph A. Griffiths, *The Reign of Henry VI* (London: Ernest Benn), p. 694, from *Original Letters Illustrative of English History*, ed. Henry Ellis, 1st ser., 3 vols. (London: Harding, Triphhook and Lepard, 1825), I, 11–13.

CHAPTER 13

Scandals of Faith and Gender in Tennyson's Grail Poems

LINDA K. HUGHES

Medievalists accustomed to the reverent spirituality of the Grail episode in Malory or his French sources might well express incredulity about the fate of the Grail quest in Tennyson's *Idylls of the King* (1859–85). In "The Holy Grail," Percivale's sister becomes a victim of unrequited love who enters a nunnery on the rebound, as it were. She is first to see the Grail, and the poem hints that her vision may be a hallucination resulting from unremitting fasting and prayer, if not hysteria. Percivale strives to mirror Galahad's heroic faith but produces only a weak imitation, nor can Percivale understand the king who discourages the Quest. As for Sir Bors's unsought but welcome vision of the Grail, Tennyson suggested in a footnote that this "might have been a meteor." Such wholesale reworking of literary tradition, however, may be less significant for botching Arthurian tradition than for transforming Arthurian materials into an acute register of ideological formations and anxieties in Tennyson's day. Tennyson published three poems related to the Grail Quest over a forty-three-year period: "Sir Galahad," published in 1842; "The Holy Grail," the title poem in the second installment of *Idylls of the King*, published in 1869; and "Balin and Balan," a final idyll published in *Tiresias and Other Poems* in 1885. From the beginning these three poems were viewed in relation to Victorian religious controversy, especially that surrounding the Oxford Movement. I wish to revisit the poems' relation to the Oxford Movement to suggest that the lineaments of the Grail Quest assumed in each work were prompted in part by scandals of faith and gender associated with the Oxford Movement and its aftermath.

FAITH AND GENDER IN THE OXFORD CONTROVERSY

Like the Arthurian or Medieval Revival, the Oxford Movement looked to
the past as a source of value and guidance amidst the heady change that
characterized the nineteenth century. The two principal doctrines of the
movement were a conception of the Anglican Church as the via media between Calvinism and the Roman Catholic Church with which Henry VIII
had broken in the sixteenth century,[1] and an unbroken apostolic succession dating back to the church fathers, a view premised upon St. Augustine's founding of a bishopric in England late in the sixth century. Both
tenets were crucial because the Oxford Movement arose in reaction to the
secularizing of church governance in 1833 when a Whig-controlled Par-
liament suppressed ten Irish bishoprics as part of a reform program, implicitly asserting the precedence of temporal over spiritual power. The
movement began on 14 July 1833, when John Keble preached a sermon at
Oxford on national apostasy.

Keble and his circle, which included John Henry Newman (then a fellow of Oriel College), jointly began to issue a series of tracts on church history, ritual, and related matters in the 1830s, hence the movement's
alternate name of Tractarianism. Tractarianism gathered momentum and
adherents from the 1830s until 1841, a period coincident with Tennyson's
composition of "Sir Galahad." If Keble led the Oxford Movement, he did
so from a quiet country curacy outside Oxford, and Newman, a gifted
writer and vicar of St. Mary's Church in Oxford, became its leading publi-
cist. Early in 1841, however, Newman argued in Tract 90 that the Thirty-
Nine Articles of the Anglican Church were consistent with Catholicism[2]—
a stance that seemed to collapse one church into the other and thus rocked
Anglican orthodoxy. Oxford divines responded by censuring Newman
publicly.[3] When Newman himself left Oriel College and was received into
the Roman Catholic Church in 1845, shock waves ensued in the Victorian
religious community. Amidst this scandal the Oxford Movement quickly
foundered.

This episode in Victorian religious history provides a context for Tennyson's Grail poems in numerous respects. "Sir Galahad" was composed
soon after Keble's 1833 sermon and, as discussed below, clearly bears the
impress of the idealism and some of the imagery associated with the early
years of the Oxford Movement. No additional Grail poem followed for
over thirty years, even after the immense success of the 1859 *Idylls* and the
urging of Emily Sellwood Tennyson that the poet undertake the subject.[4]
One reason Tennyson hesitated, I suggest, was the scandal attached to me-

dievalized religious aspirations and artifacts of ritual in the wake of New-man's conversion to Catholicism. The situation was particularly delicate because Tennyson had dedicated the *Idylls* to the memory of the Prince Consort shortly after Albert's death in 1861; and as poet laureate Tennyson himself held a court appointment that aligned him with the State to which the Anglican Church was wedded. Moreover, the controversy, or at least memory of the controversy, associated with the Oxford Movement would have been re-established as a context for the reception of Tennyson's sec-ond volume of idylls. Newman converted to Catholicism almost fifteen years before the 1859 *Idylls*, but in 1864 Charles Kingsley revived the issue by attacking Newman's veracity in print; in turn Newman began issu-ing the pamphlets known as *Apologia Pro Vita Sua*. Four years later, in 1868, Tennyson began composing "The Holy Grail."

The scandal of Newman's conversion resulted from entrenched anti-Catholic sentiment in England reinforced by (Anglican) historical memo-ries of the disastrous reigns of Queen Mary and James II and exacerbated by the reestablishment after some four hundred years of a Catholic see of Westminster in 1850. But as is true in the late twentieth century as well as in the mid-Victorian era, religious issues are often gender issues and a form of gender politics. One issue crucial to differentiating Anglicans from Roman Catholics was also crucial to constructions of heterosexual-ity: the issue of celibacy. Both churches endorsed chastity, but only the Roman Catholic Church demanded that its priests remain celibate. Angli-can clergymen like John Keble and Edward Pusey could and did marry, enfolding notions of religious rectitude into practices and representations of domesticity. Newman, on the other hand, practiced celibacy first as an Anglican, then as a Roman Catholic priest. This distinction allowed for a troubling ambiguity regarding male sexual activity. Refraining from het-erosexual activity might be construed as manly self-suppression, but it could also be a mark of effeminacy—an absence of "proper" sexual desire evident in the exclusive resort to men; at its worst it might even suggest desire for men.

To juxtapose the doctrine of priestly celibacy with Eve Kosofsky Sedgwick's work on homosocial relations between males is to underscore the highly problematical nature of celibacy in Victorian religious debate. Sedgwick notes the crucial role of "obligatory heterosexuality" and the re-currence of "homophobia [a]s a *necessary* consequence of such patriarchal institutions as heterosexual marriage."[5] One "consequence of this [social] structure," Sedgwick asserts, "is that any ideological purchase on the male

homosocial spectrum—a . . . set of discriminations for defining, controlling, and manipulating these male bonds—will be a disproportionately
powerful instrument of social control" (p. 86). She notes as well the "tendency toward important correspondences and similarities between the
most sanctioned forms of male-homosocial bonding, and the most reprobated expressions of male homosexual sociality. . . . For a man to be a
man's man is separated only by an invisible, carefully blurred, always-al-
ready-crossed line from being 'interested in men'" (p. 89).

In both Protestant and Catholic communities of the Victorian era,
homosocial priesthoods regulated doctrine about sexuality and the status
of women. But in Protestant communities the practice of a celibate
priesthood was viewed with a certain horror and anxiety. David Hilliard
cites a revealing instance from the 24 September 1864 *Norfolk News*,
which averred that "The 'suppression or perversion of natural love' by
monastic vows led inevitably to 'corruption' and 'defilement.'"[6] With
celibacy, no empirical—no genital—evidence of heterosexuality was
available. Thus the spectacle of Protestant conversions to Catholicism
was interpreted not only as a form of national scandal (an un-English
form of submission to a foreign power), but also as a scandalous transgression of gender norms.

Both Charles Kingsley's attack on Newman and Newman's response illuminate this relationship between gender and religious institutions. The debate between Kingsley and Newman was ostensibly about
veracity. Yet, curiously, the first example from Newman's sermons discussed by Kingsley in his pamphlet *"What, Then, Does Dr. Newman
Mean?"* turned on the issue of celibacy for men and women:

First, as to the sermon entitled "Wisdom and Innocence." It must be remembered always that it is not a Protestant, but a Romish sermon. It is
occupied entirely with the attitude of "the world" to "Christians" and
"the Church." By the world appears to be signified, especially, the
Protestant public of these realms. What Dr. Newman means by Christians, and the Church, he has not left in doubt; for in the preceding sermon . . . he says: "But, if the truth must be spoken, what are the humble
monk, and the holy nun, and other regulars, as they are called, but
Christians after the very pattern given us in Scripture?". . . This is his
definition of Christians. And in the sermon itself he sufficiently defines
what he means by "the Church" in two "notes" of her character, which
he shall give in his own words . . . : —"What, for instance, though we
grant that sacramental confession and the celibacy of the clergy do

tend to consolidate the body politic in the relation of rulers and subjects, or, in other words, to aggrandize the priesthood? . . ."
     Monks and nuns the only perfect Christians; sacramental confes-
sion and the celibacy of the clergy notes of the Church. . . . What more?
                                   (Newman pp. 28-29; see also p. 57)

Kingsley was also quick to seize on Newman's remark that the "strict
self-restraint" which "religious men exercise" is "the first thing which
makes holy persons seem wanting in openness and manliness" (Newman, pp. 30–31) and to use Newman's phrasing to vilify him (p. 34).
     If we might expect emphasis on the scandal of celibacy from Kings-
ley, a proponent of muscular Christianity and joys of the marriage bed,[7]
Newman himself, in a private letter early on in the controversy, also singled out the issue of celibacy (as indicated by his reference to "purity").
He wrote on 8 January 1864:

> Truth is the same in itself and in substance to Catholic and Protestant;
> so is purity: both virtues are to be referred to that moral sense which is
> the natural possession of us all. But when we come to the question in
> detail, whether this or that act in particular is conformable to the rule of
> truth, or again to the rule of purity; then sometimes there is a difference
> of opinion between individuals, sometimes between schools, and some-
> times between religious communions. I, on my side, have long thought,
> even before I was a Catholic, that the Protestant system, as such, leads
> to a lax observance of the rule of purity; Protestants think that the
> Catholic system, as such, leads to a lax observance of the rule of truth.
>   (Newman, p. 11)

Newman goes on to say how egregious it would be if he were to accuse
all Anglicans of insufficient chastity, just as Charles Kingsley had suggested that all Catholics were insufficiently veracious in the January
1864 book review in *Macmillan's Magazine* that initiated the entire exchange.
     But if Newman was quick to pinpoint celibacy as a fracture line in the
debates between Protestants and Catholics when he penned private letters,
he shifted the emphasis in the *Apologia* exclusively to the issue of
truthtelling. Only in an appendix titled an "Answer in Detail to Mr. Kingsley's Accusations" did Newman return to the celibate monks and nuns
Kingsley began by citing. In the first section of the appendix, Newman
defended the practice of celibacy;[8] significantly, however, he suppressed

this section in 1865 and allowed to stand only the second section of the appendix, which minimized the importance of celibacy to Catholicism.[9] Both his and Kingsley's documents, then, suggest the degree to which norms of gender and sexuality underlay the public debate over doctrine and truth, even when mention of those norms and the gender roles they endorsed was suppressed.

This linking of religious and gender issues, I suggest, also informs Tennyson's three Grail poems. The course of the Oxford Movement helps to explain the sequence of representations of the Quest Tennyson shared with his public over a forty-year period. As has often been remarked, Tennyson shifted from apparently straightforward and honorific presentation of the quest in 1842 to distinctly ambiguous and even skeptical treatment of the search for the Grail in later years. His wavering commitment to celebrating a cup associated with medieval communion and mystery is coincident with the declining influence of the Oxford Movement (as well as, it should be stressed, direct assaults on traditional religious institutions through such works as Darwin's *Origin of the Species*, published in 1859). It may also be relevant that in writing the first poem, "Sir Galahad," Tennyson was himself unmarried, most likely celibate, and socialized into a homosocial group, the Cambridge Apostles. In 1868, when he wrote "The Holy Grail," he was the married laureate and father of two. That "homosexual panic" is part of the subtext of Tennyson's Grail poems cannot be established with certainty, but it is clear that the celibate and homosocial world of "Sir Galahad" in 1842 was followed by a deliberate inscription of heterosexuality into the Grail quest in the 1869 poem. By the time of "Balin and Balan" in 1885, Tennyson represents celibacy and wanton carnality as polar yet mutually constituent opposites, with duly regulated matrimony the implied via media.

"SIR GALAHAD"

"Sir Galahad" is usually given short shrift in twentieth-century commentaries, relative to Tennyson's other Arthurian poems. Yet the poem was a favorite of Victorians, even a form of credo for the likes of Edward Burne-Jones and William Morris during their undergraduate days, when they contemplated founding a celibate brotherhood.[10] Debra Mancoff has established the lingering impact of Tennyson's "Sir Galahad," along with Kenelm Digby's *Broadstone of Honour* (1822) and William Dyce's frescoes, on the construction of Victorian manhood and nationalist ideals.[11] Mark Girouard notes the link between "Sir Galahad" and discussions of virginity precipitated by the Oxford Movement in the 1830s.[12] For Mancoff and Girouard, Galahad's chivalric rather than religious virtues—his staunch dedication to his quest, fearless confidence, and sexual purity—formed the core of his appeal in the middle decades of the century. The poem's relation to religious issues, however, merits revisiting.

As part of the attempt to conserve sacred authority from the past (evident in the emphasis on unbroken apostolic succession), participants in the Oxford Movement looked back to older forms of ritual, including those associated with the Gothic churches that were viewed as a distinctive English legacy (Mancoff, pp. 4, 9–10). But the movement was reformist as well as conservative. As Owen Chadwick remarks, "it was more a movement of the heart than of the head. . . . It always saw dogma in relation to worship, to the numinous, to the movement of the heart, to the conscience and the moral need, to the immediate experience of the hidden hand of God" (p. 1). Its aims in this respect were greater sanctity and a commitment to a sacramental view of the universe. An April 1869 article on John Keble in *Blackwood's Edinburgh Magazine* indicated, some thirty-five years after the fact, the profound influence of this spiritual reform in its early days:

> the authors of the movement had, by their lives and conversations, effected the greatest moral revolution in Oxford itself which modern times have witnessed. The tone of society, especially among the younger Fellows, and, through them, among a very large section of the undergraduates, became elevated to a pitch never before attained. Chapel ceased to be regarded as a bore. . . . They studied the requirements also of the Church, and endeavoured to act up to them—even to the keeping of saints' days and the observance of Lent.[13]

Nor, according to the article, was the impact restricted to the university, for the movement had a beneficial influence on the clergy as well: "Self-sacrifice—earnest devotion to duty—the Church's wellbeing rather than their own advancement—has taken the place of that miserable self-seeking which was almost universal among the clergy sixty years ago" ("Keble," 414).

The idealism and ritualism emphasized in the *Blackwood's* article characterize Tennyson's poem as well. Tennyson's exemplar of virtuous manhood is strong, pure, visionary, and resolutely oriented toward women as subordinate warrants of heavenly approval, as vehicles by which Galahad might be returned to an exclusive relationship with his (male) God. But this last is no cause for anxiety or ambivalence in the poem. Galahad, who speaks *in propria persona*, seems to begin with a boast of strength but quickly subordinates this power to purity rather than to carnality:

> My good blade carves the casques of men,
>   My tough lance thrusteth sure,
> My strength is as the strength of ten,
>   Because my heart is pure.
>   (ll. 1–4)[14]

What seems unavoidably sexual discourse to late-twentieth-century readers ("My tough lance thrusteth sure") is likewise shifted to the discourse of abstinence and self-restraint.

In the second stanza Galahad acknowledges the beauty and allure of maidens and seems to underwrite heterosexual desire, but the love of women is quickly subordinated to the greater love of God. Thus the virgin knight modulates from the rituals of court (bowing to ladies) to the rituals of worship (bowing in prayer):

> How sweet are looks that ladies bend
>   On whom their favours fall!
> For them I battle till the end,
>   To save from shame and thrall:
> But all my heart is drawn above,
>   My knees are bowed in crypt and shrine:
> I never felt the kiss of love,
>   Nor maiden's hand in mine.
> More bounteous aspects on me beam,
>   Me mightier transports move and thrill;
> So keep I fair through faith and prayer
>   A virgin heart in work and will.
>   (ll. 13–24)

Women's status as instruments by which a man can achieve greater rewards is articulated amidst the medieval setting of "crypt and shrine." In subsequent stanzas the trappings of medieval worship are given even more prominence, here functioning to aestheticize the supernatural. When Galahad passes by secret shrines, for example,

Fair gleams the snowy altar-cloth,
 The silver vessels sparkle clean,
 The shrill bell rings, the censer swings,
 And solemn chaunts resound between.
  (ll. 33–36)

Galahad is a religious version of Wordsworth's solitaries who experience rapturous transports only when they are removed from contact with the social world, though strength and privileged loneliness are defining elements of the romantic quest in medieval literature as well as Wordsworthian Romanticism. Galahad first resorts to "lonely mountain-meres," then abandons even the shore for the indeterminate middle of the lake where he alone is given exalted visions of the Grail. The poem concludes with Galahad's leaving the plain and enduring fierce storms amidst inhospitable terrains, until he achieves contact with heaven itself. The earthly and heavenly fuse in all he sees, does, and is, clear evidence that he is the "knight of God" (l. 79):

A maiden knight—to me is given
 Such hope, I know not fear;
 I yearn to breathe the airs of heaven
 That often meet me here.
 I muse on joy that will not cease,
 Pure spaces clothed in living beams,
 Pure lilies of eternal peace,
 Whose odours haunt my dreams;
 And, stricken by an angel's hand,
 This mortal armour that I wear,
 This weight and size, this heart and eyes,
 Are touched, are turned to finest air.
  (ll. 61–72)

The dissolving materiality Galahad experiences as a result of the grace of God has its counterpart in the poet's substitution of "mortal" for steel armor (l. 70); the "mail" that earlier repelled the tempest (l. 54) now dissolves and reveals the body underneath, itself a permeable and perishable armor encasing the transcendent soul. So confident is the poet of Galahad's virtuous male knighthood that he can appropriate the term "maiden"—earlier a signifier of female bodies (l. 20) —as an adjective for the virtuous male knight.

The poem thus has a double significance. On one hand (if the evidence of *Blackwood's* essay on Keble may be accepted),[15] the tone and atmosphere of the poem exemplify those of the early Oxford Movement, with which the composition of the poem was roughly contemporary. The poem celebrates a religious quest, the ideal of purity, a sacramental landscape, and the evocative beauty of implements associated with medieval religious ritual. And since the Grail was associated both with the cup in which Joseph of Arimathea caught Christ's blood during the Crucifixion and the cup from which Christ drank at the Last Supper, the poem, like the Oxford Movement, helped link conceptions of high spiritual quests with ancient Christian lore and tradition.

On the other hand, the poem serves as a perspective on gender roles in the early 1840s. The poem's configuration of gender relations suggests an untroubled presentation of homosocial male roles consistent with Sedgwick's model, in which women function as a form of subordinate exchange to confirm masculine power from which they are firmly excluded. Abstaining from sexual contact with women, in this poem, is an expression of virginity, not necessarily of celibacy (since Galahad is not a priest); here it ensures rather than problematizes power.

"THE HOLY GRAIL"

"Sir Galahad" was eagerly embraced by many of Tennyson's readers, for whom the poem apparently posed few problems in doctrine or gender ideology.[16] If the poem received little attention in reviews of the 1842 volume, the imagery of the poem was adopted as part of a visual vocabulary seen, for example, in Burne-Jones's 1858 pen-and-ink *Sir Galahad*, which depicted Galahad much as Tennyson had in 1842 (see Mancoff, pp. 164–65, 149–52).

But when after the success of the first four idylls ("Enid," "Vivien," "Elaine," "Guinevere") in 1859 Tennyson wished to continue *Idylls of the King*, he confronted a number of problems. As noted above, the Oxford Movement had by then become a form of scandal, especially insofar as it was linked with the Roman Catholic Church. The same *Blackwood's* article of 1869 that lauded the profound idealism wrought by the early Oxford Movement continued, "On the other hand, Keble and his friends did the Church, and the cause of the Church, great damage too. They carried further than truth will allow dogmatic teaching, which is not the teaching of the primitive Church, but the results of one superstition after another, accumulated in ages subsequent to the first" ("Keble," 415). The essay judged Newman "one whose fate it has been to work more of good and more of evil to the Church of England than, perhaps, any other individual of his age and country" ("Keble," 406).

By the 1860s this perception of harm was enmeshed with anxieties about gender that surfaced in debates over the role of ritual in Anglican worship. As David Hilliard observes, the vogue of ritualism in the 1860s was an afterglow of the Oxford Movement (189), a second-generation development after theological debate had been quelled by the logical outcome to which Newman's conversion pointed as inevitable. More than ritual itself, the vestments associated with its priests caused unease, especially after *Punch*, the comic magazine noted for social satire, entered the fray. As W.S.F. Pickering remarks,

> Something of the female dress, or certainly male dress of an exotic kind, is to be seen in eucharistic vestments, lace cottas, cassocks. . . . In 1865 *Punch* had the caption: "Parsons in Petticoats" (10 June 1865). It was a *double entendre*, whether intended or not. Were Anglo-Catholic clergy accused of dressing up in peculiar ecclesiastical garments or of being effeminate? Perhaps both.[17]

Nor was such anxiety short-lived, for until the end of the century "the conflict between Protestantism and Anglo-Catholicism within the Church of England was still regularly depicted by Protestant propagandists as a struggle between masculine and feminine styles of religion" (Hilliard, 190). A poem with a medieval setting and descriptions of medieval ritual, then, would in the late 1860s have implicitly invoked Roman Catholicism, Newman's conversion, and the controversial practice of ritualism in selected congregations of the Anglican Church.

Moreover, as poet laureate Tennyson could not afford to seem too hospitable to Roman Catholicism, particularly after he had dedicated the 1859 *Idylls* to the memory of Prince Albert. Queen Victoria was herself antagonistic to Newman and the like-minded, as suggested by S.L. Ollard:

> . . . in October 1850 Lord J. Russell wrote to the Queen: "The matter to create national alarm is, as your Majesty says, the growth of Roman Catholic doctrine within the bosom of the Church. Dr. Arnold said very truly, 'I look upon a Roman Catholic as an enemy in his uniform. I look upon a Tractarian as an enemy disguised as a spy.' It would," he added, "be very wrong to do as the Bishop of Oxford proposed, and confer the patronage of the Crown on any of the Tractarians." So later the Queen

wrote to her uncle, King Leopold, in the same year, of "the very alarming tendency of the Tractarians, which was doing immense harm," and in 1852, when Lord Derby took office, "the Queen expressed to him her sense of the importance not to have Puseyites . . . recommended for appointments in the Church as bishops or clergymen."[18]

Such attitudes prohibited the straightforward exploration of the Grail Quest Tennyson had undertaken in 1842. Yet a wholesale repudiation of the idealism of "Sir Galahad," a favorite with many (and frame of reference for numerous reviews of the 1869 work), was also undesirable. All these factors helped shape the technical and ideological contours of the poem Tennyson eventually wrote.

In part Tennyson solved the dilemma of how to avoid extremes of endorsement or repudiation of the Quest by resorting to the technical device of the dramatic monologue, a means by which Tennyson could avoid allocating full poetic authority to any one position. As well, he constructed a narrative that allowed for nonironic as well as skeptical response, the mystery of religious revelation as well as naturalistic demystification.[19]

His success is suggested in contemporary reception of the poem, which reflected the work's complicated social and historical context. The 22 December 1869 Church of England *Guardian*, which as a high church periodical had links to the Oxford Movement, saw in the poem an uncomplicated treatment of the Grail: "In searching for the cup from which our Lord drank at the last supper . . . [t]he good and the evil show symptoms of separating. . . . The Holy Grail itself is as a test distinguishing between man and man" (1439). Yet responsiveness to the sanctity of the Quest did not preclude very different reactions. The 14 December 1869 *Daily Telegraph* immediately noticed the departure from the earlier Grail poem:

> Mr. Tennyson had already given evidence, in his "Sir Galahad," that the spiritual significance of the Quest had deeply impressed him. The Idyll is scarcely equal to the lyric, nor, indeed, in the nature of things would it be reasonable to expect that it should; we lack the especial and appropriate charm of the lyric—its picture of calm, stately, absorbed purity, in, but not of, the world. . . . But the perturbation, the disappointment, the jarring of worldly levity and selfishness, that we encounter in the Idyll, are proper to the poet's description of an eager and fanatical quest, undertaken in a moment of irresponsible rapture, by men of many natures. . . . (p. 5)

Other papers went even further. The 25 December 1869 *Spectator*, for example, emphasized the representation of superstition in terms that seem to refer to Tractarians: "[Tennyson] paints with the richest possible colouring the visions of enthusiasts seeking for a restoration of the age of miracle and of an opened heaven. The picture is full of skilfully disguised 'modern touches'" (1532). Thus, in moving from the 1842 to the 1869 Grail poem, Tennyson effected a shift from the impassioned idealism of "Sir Galahad" to a poem that allowed readers to affirm the same sense of high spiritual purpose suggested by the earlier poem or to discern a deeply skeptical telling of the Quest and the legend with which it was associated.

But if the scandals associated with the Oxford Movement caused Tennyson to proceed so carefully (and deftly) in his second Grail poem, the contours imposed by gender norms are even more intriguing, and account for some of the most striking departures from medieval Arthurian tradition. All suggest that the poem inscribes a "*compulsory* heterosexuality"[20] in reaction to the celibacy associated with Roman Catholic priesthoods and conventual life. And since celibate brotherhoods that prohibited heterosexual activity could become aligned with the absence of heterosexual desire,[21] the poem may also reflect homosexual panic as defined by Sedgwick: "Because the paths of male entitlement, especially in the nineteenth century, required certain intense male bonds that were not readily distinguishable from the most reprobated bonds, an endemic and ineradicable state of what I am calling male homosexual panic became the normal condition of the male heterosexual entitlement" ("Beast," p. 151).

The three figures that most strongly reflect the inscription of heterosexuality into the 1869 Grail Quest are Percivale's sister, the monk Ambrosius, and Percivale himself. In Malory the sister is a gentlewoman who appears suddenly while Galahad, Bors, and Percivale are on the Quest; she possesses the store of wisdom which can narrate and explicate the miraculous trappings of the boat into which all four enter. In "The Holy Grail" she is a nun, a shift that at once foregrounds the issue of celibacy and, potentially, of Anglo- and Roman Catholicism (since a number of Anglican nunneries were founded in the aftermath of the Oxford Movement). The 1842 "Sir Galahad" implied that Galahad's virginity was grounded in spiritual purpose that transcended (and repudiated) the carnal, but the 1869 "Holy Grail" suggests that the nun's celibacy is grounded in heterosexual desire. His sister, Percivale avers, is,

> "if ever holy maid
> With knees of adoration wore the stone,
> A holy maid; though never maiden glowed,

> But that was in her earlier maidenhood,
> With such a fervent flame of human love,
> Which being rudely blunted, glanced and shot
> Only to holy things; to prayer and praise
> She gave herself, to fast and alms."
>   (ll. 70–77)

Even in her remote convent the force of heterosexuality impinges upon her: "'the strange sound of an adulterous race, / Across the iron grating of her cell / Beat, and she prayed and fasted all the more'" (ll. 80–82). When her Father Confessor tells her of the Holy Grail, she so intensifies her devotions to effect the Grail's appearance that "'she prayed and fasted, till the sun / Shone, and the wind blew, through her'" (ll. 98–99). Only when she has become anorexic, perhaps even hysteric, does the Grail appear to her (ll. 108–23).

It is fascinating to turn from this passage in "The Holy Grail" to Charles Kingsley's 1864 pamphlet against Newman, *"What, Then, Does Dr. Newman Mean?,"* and see a very similar configuration among religion, desire, and hysteria. Though Kingsley's pamphlet is unlikely to have influenced Tennyson to depict the nun as he did, the two representations together suggest the anxieties aroused by groups of celibate women removed from heterosexual contact with (and control by) men.[22] As noted earlier, Kingsley's distrust of Catholicism reflected his own gender anxieties, sexual obsessions, and earlier "rescue" of his wife from her decision to enter a nunnery. Because the passage from Kingsley is so pertinent, I quote it in its entirety. It occurs as part of Kingsley's discussion of Newman's sermon entitled "The Religious Character of Catholic Countries No Prejudice to the Sanctity of the Church."

> [There] follows a passage—of which I shall boldly say, that I trust that it will arouse in every English husband, father, and brother, who may read these words, the same feelings which it roused in me; and express my opinion, that it is a better compliment to Dr. Newman to think that he did not believe what he said, than to think that he did believe it: —
> "You turn to go home, and in your way you pass through a retired quarter of the city. Look up at those sacred windows; they belong to the Convent of the Perpetual Adoration, or to the poor Clares, or to the Carmelites of the Reform of St. Theresa, or to the Nuns of the Visitation. Seclusion, silence, watching, adoration, is their life day and night. The Immaculate Lamb of God is ever before the eyes of the worshippers; or, at least, the invisible mysteries of faith ever stand out, as if in

bodily shape, before their mental gaze. Where will you find such a realized heaven upon earth? Yet that very sight has acted otherwise on the mind of a weak sister; and the very keenness of her faith and wild desire of approaching the object of it has led her to fancy or to feign that she has received that singular favour vouchsafed only to a few elect souls; and she points to God's wounds, as imprinted on her hand, and feet, and side, though she herself has been instrumental in their formation" (Lecture IX. 237, 238).

There are occasions on which courtesy or reticence is a crime, and this one of them. A poor girl, cajoled, flattered, imprisoned, starved, maddened, by such as Dr. Newman and his peers, into that degrading and demoralising disease, hysteria, imitates on her own body, from that strange vanity and deceit which too often accompany the complaint, the wounds of our Lord; and all that Dr. Newman has to say about the matter is, to inform us that the gross and useless portent is "a singular favour vouchsafed only to a few elect souls." And this is the man who, when accused of countenancing falsehood, puts on first a tone of plaintive and startled innocence, and then one of smug self-satisfaction—as who should ask, "What have I said? What have I done? Why am I upon my trial?" On his trial? If he be on his trial for nothing else, he is on his trial for those words; and he will remain upon his trial as long as Englishmen know how to guard the women whom God has committed to their charge. If the British public shall ever need informing that Dr. Newman wrote that passage, I trust there will be always one man left in England to inform them of the fact, for the sake of the ladies of this land. (Newman, pp. 51–53)

Kingsley's agitated prose, itself hysteric by twentieth-century standards, helps identify through its extremism the undercurrents of Tennyson's far more subtle treatment of celibacy, hysteria, and the immuring of the female with a Catholic priest. Kingsley's work (along with Sedgwick's) also helps clarify why Tennyson is anxious to recover and reposition the figure of the nun under the rubric of heterosexuality. Thus when the nun meets Galahad, she presents him with the swordbelt made of her own hair in such a way that the discourse can be equally that of religious mystery or of heterosexual courtship:

> "[She] saw the bright boy-knight, and bound it on him,
> Saying, 'My knight, my love, my knight of heaven,
> O thou, my love, whose love is one with mine,
> I, maiden, round thee, maiden, bind my belt.'

. . . .
She sent the deathless passion in her eyes
Through him, and made him hers, and laid her mind
On him, and he believed in her belief."
    (ll. 156–59, 163–65)

The movement of "Sir Galahad" was transcendental, from the allure of women to the glorious love of God. The movement in "The Holy Grail" is descendental, as the ostensible language of religious worship keeps returning to the passions and desires of the heterosexual body. Since Percivale's sister is moreover the first to see the Grail here—a clear departure from Malory—one might say that the entire Quest becomes grounded in the heterosexual passions that, once thwarted, led her to the nunnery.

Ambrosius might seem a figure fraught with even more anxieties about gender than is the nun. He is part of the celibate brotherhood to which Percivale retreats after the quest, and the poem expressly states that Ambrosius loved Percivale:

And one, a fellow-monk among the rest,
Ambrosius, loved him much beyond the rest,
And honoured him, and wrought into his heart
A way by love that wakened love within,
To answer that which came. . . .
    (ll. 8–12)

Such directness complicates any attempt to reduce Tennyson's work to pat ideological categories even though he at times seems to endorse them at their crudest.[23] Still, alongside this deliberate refusal to engage homosexual panic is a reinscription of it. For on one hand Ambrosius assumes the role of bohemian bachelor as defined by Sedgwick; on the other he emerges as one who suffers compulsory celibacy and remains a passionate advocate of heterosexuality. This last contrasts strongly with the Galahad of 1842. Galahad was a knight, not a priest, who celebrated the power of virginity; Ambrosius is a celibate monk who preaches the virtue of heterosexual marriage.

One reaction to homosexual panic, Sedgwick argues, was the bohemian bachelor found, for example, in the novels of Thackeray:

Most obviously, in the increasingly stressed nineteenth-century bourgeois dichotomy between domestic female space and extrafamilial, political and economic male space, the bachelor is at least partly feminized by his attention to and interest in domestic concerns. (At the same time, though, his intimacy with clubland and bohemia gives him a special passport to the world of men, as well.) Then, too, the disruptive and self-ignorant potential for violence in the Gothic hero is replaced in the bachelor hero by physical timidity and, often, by a high valuation on introspection and by (at least partial) self-knowledge. Finally, the bachelor is housebroken by the severing of his connections with a discourse of genital sexuality. ("Beast," p. 156)

The monastery is a kind of parallel to the club, especially since it too features all-male dinners, as we see in Ambrosius's memory of the presence of Sir Bors at a monastic meal (ll. 696–704). But Ambrosius accords most fully with Sedgwick's model in his role as parish priest, in which his exclusion from "genital sexuality" is paired with warm "interest in domestic concerns":

"These ancient books—and they would win thee—teem,
Only I find not there this Holy Grail,
With miracles and marvels like to these,
Not all unlike; which oftentime I read,
Who read but on my breviary with ease,
Till my head swims; and then go forth and pass
Down to the little thorpe that lies so close,
And almost plastered like a martin's nest
To these old walls—and mingle with our folk;
And knowing every honest face of theirs
As well as ever shepherd knew his sheep,
And every homely secret in their hearts,
Delight myself with gossip and old wives,
And ills and aches, and teethings, lyings-in,
And mirthful sayings, children of the place,
That have no meaning half a league away:
Or lulling random squabbles when they rise,
Chafferings and chatterings at the market-cross,
Rejoice, small man, in this small world of mine,
Yea, even in their hens and in their eggs. . . ."
        (ll. 541–60)

Ambrosius, however, exceeds the asexual bachelor who moves between exclusive male domains and domestic interiors, since Ambrosius desires the heterosexual contact prohibited by vows enforced upon him as a small child ("'For never have I known the world without, / Nor ever strayed beyond the pale'" [ll. 20–21]). He consistently assigns heterosexual rather than religious motives to Percivale, first asking if Percivale has come to the monastery because of "'earthly passion crost'" (l. 29), later inquiring after Percivale's initial recital of the Grail quest, "'Came ye on none but phantoms in your quest, / No man, no woman?'" (ll. 562–63). When he learns that during the quest Percivale had been reunited with, then abandoned, an earlier love, he expresses incredulity and yearns for the "double life":

> "O the pity
> To find thine own first love once more—to hold,
> Hold her a wealthy bride within thine arms,
> Or all but hold, and then—cast her aside,
> Foregoing all her sweetness, like a weed.
> For we that want the warmth of double life,
> We that are plagued with dreams of something sweet
> Beyond all sweetness in a life so rich, —
> Ah, blessed Lord, I speak too earthlywise,
> Seeing I never strayed beyond the cell,
> But live like an old badger in his earth,
> With earth about him everywhere, despite
> All fast and penance."
> (ll. 618–30)

A monk, Ambrosius is credited with an insistent and inherent heterosexuality; as with the nun, removal into a celibate religious house does not preclude the stirrings of heterosexual desire. His carnal weakness ("I speak too earthlywise") is thus his badge of virtuous masculinity.

Only Percivale endorses and fully chooses the celibate life, and within the poem he is (aside from Gawaine, an irreligious rake whose heterosexuality flouts the regulation of marriage) presented as the least sympathetic character.[24] This celibate who has abandoned fighting for the nonaggressive, contemplative life of a monk is indicated to be dead from the poem's beginning:

> From noiseful arms, and acts of prowess done
> In tournament or tilt, Sir Percivale,
> Whom Arthur and his knighthood called The Pure,

> Had passed into the silent life of prayer,
> Praise, fast, and alms; and leaving for the cowl
> The helmet in an abbey far away
> From Camelot, there, and not long after, died.
>> (ll. 1–7)

The sole male eager to embrace celibacy, then, is permitted only a ghost's voice. Even in retrospect Percivale fares badly relative to others. He is rather shocked when Ambrosius suggests that he left the Round Table because of unrequited passion. And unlike the 1842 Sir Galahad (ll. 10–14), whom he echoes only to oppose, Percivale asserts that fighting and faith are mutually exclusive:

> "Nay," said the knight; "for no such passion mine.
> But the sweet vision of the Holy Grail
> Drove me from all vainglories, rivalries,
> And earthly heats that spring and sparkle out
> Among us in the jousts, while women watch
> Who wins, who falls; and waste the spiritual strength
> Within us, better offered up to Heaven."
>> (ll. 30–36)

Appropriately, one of the mirages Percivale sees on the Quest is that of domestic life. He perceives a woman spinning—"'And kind the woman's eyes and innocent, / And all her bearing gracious'"—but when she opens her arms to embrace him, she and her cottage and even the baby in the vision all crumble to dust (ll. 391–400).

Percivale again expresses horror of contact with women when Ambrosius inquires whether he saw any but phantoms while on the Quest: "'All men, to one so bound by such a vow, / And women were as phantoms. O, my brother, / Why wilt thou shame me to confess to thee / How far I faltered from my quest and vow?'" (ll. 564–67). Even when he relates his encounter with the woman he thought he once loved Percivale seems allotted, at best, a quiescent heterosexual drive. He and his supposed beloved, now a widowed queen, had not so much as kissed or touched hands during their youth, though resident in the same house. When the kiss at last comes, it is because the adult woman has taken the initiative and offered both the embrace and marriage:

> "The Princess of that castle was the one,
> Brother, and that one only, who had ever

Made my heart leap; for when I moved of old
A slender page about her father's hall,
And she a slender maiden, all my heart
Went after her with longing: yet we twain
Had never kissed a kiss, or vowed a vow.

. . . .

                              one fair morn,
I walking to and fro beside a stream
That flashed across her orchard underneath
Her castle-walls, she stole upon my walk,
And calling me the greatest of all knights,
Embraced me, and so kissed me the first time,
And gave herself and all her wealth to me."
     (ll. 577–83, 590–96)

The reluctant fiancé quickly abandons the woman when he remembers
his vow and is happy only when back in the exclusive company of men:
"'I rose and fled, / But wailed and wept, . . . / Then after I was joined with
Galahad / Cared not for her, nor anything upon earth'" (ll. 607–8,
610–11). Though Percivale's monologue can be, and has been, read
straightforwardly (or queerly), it also seems coded to suggest to Tennyson's contemporaries that Percivale and his homosocial desires are im-
poverished compared to the imperative of heterosexual desire.

    Only one married man figures in the narrative of the Grail Quest,
and he is given the privileged perspective of truth and power: Arthur.
Arthur opposes the Grail Quest, expresses no desire to see the Grail.
While the homosocial group of bachelor knights, having prayed and
fasted, assemble in Arthur's hall and experience some form of religious
wonder, Arthur, the married man, has left to save "An outraged maiden"
(l. 208). He is dismayed when he learns of the vows the knights have
sworn to seek the Grail. And when all is over, he again indicates displea-
sure (through silence) at Percivale's wish to join a monastery:

"So when I told him all thyself hast heard,
Ambrosius, and my fresh but fixt resolve
To pass away into the quiet life,
He answered not, but, sharply turning, asked
Of Gawain, 'Gawain, was this Quest for thee?'"
     (ll. 733–37)

Like Victoria in her repudiation of Tractarianism and Roman Catholicism, King Arthur distances himself from monastic aims and visions; he also models the superiority of marriage vows to celibate ones. And unlike proponents of the Oxford Movement, who emphasized unbroken Anglo-Catholic tradition, Arthur articulates staunch Protestant belief in the primacy of individual religious experience: "Blessed are Bors, Lancelot and Percivale, / For these have seen according to their sight" (ll. 870–71). Vision is true relative to the individual, not the Church or mediating priests.

Note, however, that the married Arthur indeed blesses Percivale. This penultimate passage blurs the binarisms of heterosexuality and celibacy before the poem moves once more to contain Percivale's appeal, since his response to Arthur's impassioned declaration of religious vision (ll. 899–915) is one of dumbfounded perplexity in the poem's closing line: "'So spake the King: I knew not all he meant'" (l. 916). Arthur likewise insists that Percivale's sister is genuinely holy, and that Galahad's Quest is a true one:

> "'Ah, Galahad, Galahad,' said the King, 'for such
> As thou art is the vision, not for these.
> Thy holy nun and thou have seen a sign—
> Holier is none, my Percivale, than she—'"
>   (ll. 293–96)

The poem's regulation of compulsory heterosexuality, then, is decidedly uneven.[25] Yet in comparison to the 1842 poem, representations of the Grail Quest in "The Holy Grail" function to inscribe compulsory heterosexuality into this Arthurian episode. An important factor in this shift, I suggest, is the Oxford Movement and its own entanglement with issues of gender.

"BALIN AND BALAN"

"Sir Galahad" and "The Holy Grail" remain Tennyson's most important Grail poems, but Tennyson returned to the subject once more, at least tangentially, in "Balin and Balan," written between 1872 and 1874 (though not published until 1885). When he did so, he again made issues of celibacy and religion central to his treatment. If, as J. Phillip Eggers argues (p. 180), Pellam's celibacy echoes Percivale's in "The Holy Grail," Tennyson's third treatment of the Grail quest was also enwound with the discourses of Victorian anthropology, shifting the emphasis from a critique of Anglo-Catholicism to an identification of Roman Catholicism with superstition and primitivism.

In Malory, Balin establishes the pretext for the Grail quest: after Balin unwittingly strikes the Dolorous Stroke within Pellam's castle, King Pellam is maimed and his lands laid waste until the Grail is achieved by Galahad. Earlier Pellam holds a feast and decrees that no one can attend who does not bring a wife or paramour.[26] But in Tennyson, Pellam serves to indicate the link between pagan primitivism and the medieval Catholic Church to which the Oxford Movement had harkened back in its heyday. Pellam is a married man who, after a sudden conversion from paganism, has adopted the religious extremism of asceticism and isolated himself from all heterosexual contact. As Arthur's emissary remarks,

> "seeing that thy realm
> Hath prospered in the name of Christ, the King
> Took, as in rival heat, to holy things;
> And finds himself descended from the Saint
> Arimathaean Joseph; him who first
> Brought the great faith to Britain over seas;
> He boasts his life as purer than thine own;
> Eats scarce enow to keep his pulse abeat;
> Hath pushed aside his faithful wife, nor lets
> Or dame or damsel enter at his gates
> Lest he should be polluted."
> (ll. 95–105)

Hence Pellam not only insists on celibacy but also surrounds himself with artifacts associated with medieval—and Catholic—superstition:

> "This gray King
> Showed us a shrine wherein were wonders—yea—
> Rich arks with priceless bones of martyrdom,
> Thorns of the crown and shivers of the cross,
> And therewithal (for this he told us) brought
> By holy Joseph hither, that same spear
> Wherewith the Roman pierced the side of Christ.
> He much amazed us. . . ."
> (ll. 105–12)

Yet again Tennyson's revision of Malory needs to be set within the context of the particular historical moment in which it occurred. In 1870 the doctrine of papal infallibility was promulgated, not only an encroachment on British sovereignty but also, if viewed within the framework of Protestant individualism and the rising prestige of empirical science in Victorian England, a scandalous superstition. That same year Benjamin Disraeli, formerly active in the Young England movement that supported the chivalric revival (Girouard, pp. 82–85), published a preface to his collected novels in which he criticized those in the Anglican Church who had " 'sought refuge in mediaeval superstitions, which are generally only the embodiments of pagan ceremonies and creeds.' "[27] Here one detects the language of Victorian anthropology and its interest in comparative religion as an index of cultural development.

The scenario of "Balin and Balan" is in many ways consistent with the views of sociocultural evolutionists described by George Stocking in *Victorian Anthropology*. These included the notion that human spirituality and religious belief were subject to the same forces of evolution as physiological development, and that in some cases "survivals" from earlier phases of primitive development could underlie (and even contaminate) later stages of civilization.[28] As E.B. Tylor remarked in *Primitive Culture: Researches into the Development of Mythology, Philosophy, Religion, Language, Art, and Custom*, published in London in 1873, the question was " 'how far are modern opinion and conduct based on the strong ground of soundest modern knowledge, or how far only on such knowledge as was available in the earlier and ruder stages of culture where their types were shaped.' " Hence one function of ethnography was " 'to expose the remains of crude old culture which have passed into harmful superstition, and to mark these out for destruction' " (quoted in Stocking, p. 194). Notably, for Tylor as for his colleagues, J.F. McLennan and John Lubbock, religion and marriage were the two central institutions by which the rise from primitivism to higher civilization was gauged (Stocking, p. 197), with Victorian bourgeois marriage functioning as the standard of higher civilization (Stocking, p. 204). In this context the value center offered by "Balin and Balan" is the image of Arthur and Guinevere enthroned, side by side, Christian husband and wife, the wife subordinate to king and silent when he speaks:

And Arthur, when Sir Balin sought him, said
"What wilt thou bear?" Balin was bold, and asked
To bear her own crown-royal upon shield,

Whereat she smiled and turned her to the King,
Who answered "Thou shalt put the crown to use.
The crown is but the shadow of the King,
And this a shadow's shadow, let him have it,
So this will help him of his violences!"
        (ll. 194–201)

If one threat to Arthur's kingdom is represented by Pellam, the former pagan who has now renounced conjugal ties for the celibacy that is
simply one more superstition, another threat is Balin himself. As in Malory Balin's full appellation is Balin the Savage. In Tennyson, however,
the name bears its full anthropological weight, and the question is how
far a savage with a veneer of civilization upon him—a colonized savage,
as it were—can be assimilated into the highest order offered by civilization. At the outset of the idyll Arthur, the "spirit of youth returned" upon
him (l. 19), rides disguised to the fountain where Balin and Balan challenge all comers. Arthur easily overthrows the brothers, then announces
that, a member of Arthur's hall, he is "rather proven in his Paynim wars /
Than famous jousts" (ll. 36–37). A savage pure and simple offers no
threat to Arthur. Harm instead occurs when Balin attempts to become
one of Arthur's court and thus emerges as a source of instability and self-
destruction. Though worshipping Arthur and himself well-intentioned,
Balin's hold upon civilization is tenuous, always on the brink of breaking
up and reverting to savagery.

Here Pellam plays a crucial role, not only because his refusal to pay
tribute to Arthur (ll. 3–5) and to police his realm draws Balan's gentle
governance away from his unruly brother, but also because Pellam's superstitious icons—savage totems covered in the trappings of a later
phase of civilization—illuminate Balin's practice. Balin, like the former
heathen Pellam, merely seeks a new totem rather than more highly developed religious practice. He seizes on worship of the queen, and the
image of her crown, as the key to civilized behavior: "'Some goodly cognizance of Guinevere, / In lieu of this rough beast upon my shield, /
Langed gules, and toothed with grinning savagery'" (ll. 191–93). His
substitution of her crown for the beast's "langed gules" mirrors Pellam's
substitution of Catholic relics for pagan images. Significantly, Balin does
not, as in Malory, pierce Pellam with the holy spear found in the King's
shrine room; rather, Balin stabs the more highly developed Balan with
the spear, itself a piece of fraudulent superstition ("Point-painted red" [l.
406]) that could fool only the most credulous.

There is, however, another threat to Arthur's kingdom, and to Balin, abroad in the realm; and though superficially opposed to Pellam's celibacy it is aligned with it as another vestige of pagan practice surviving into a later stage of civilization. In "Balin and Balan" Tennyson introduces Vivien, whose unbridled pagan sensuality is as opposed to Christian marriage as is Pellam's celibacy. According to Victorian anthropologists, savages were characterized not only by animistic religion but also by promiscuity among both men and women. As J.F. McLennan observed, women "'among rude tribes' were 'usually depraved' . . ." (Stocking, p. 202). Vivien enters, notably, praising the animistic practice of sun-worship and the delights of sexual "depravity":

> "Old priest, who mumble worship in your quire—
> Old monk and nun, ye scorn the world's desire,
> Yet in your frosty cells ye feel the fire!
> The fire of Heaven is not the flame of Hell.
>
> . . . .
> "The fire of Heaven is lord of all things good,
> And starve not thou this fire within thy blood. . . ."
>   (ll. 438–41, 446–47)

When Vivien lies to Balin on hearing the names of Guinevere and Lancelot, claiming to have witnessed an adulterous dalliance between the two (ll. 495–516), Balin's veneer of civilization breaks up at a touch. He reverts to savagery in an instant—"his evil spirit upon him leapt, / He ground his teeth together, sprang with a yell" (ll. 529–30)—and his death soon follows.

Yet Balin's vulnerability to the savage reversions exemplified by Pellam and Vivien is also occasioned by Lancelot and the Christian wife Guinevere, whose polished phrasings echo the superstitions of the former. In a disturbing encounter between the lovers witnessed by Balin, Lancelot retreats from sexual involvement with the queen because of the power of a dream the night before of saints and virginity:

> "Last night methought I saw
> That maiden Saint who stands with lily in hand
> In yonder shrine.
>
> . . . .
> Lo! these her emblems drew mine eyes—away."
>   (ll. 255–57, 260)

Guinevere, in answer, celebrates the riotous fecundity of nature and embodies the female sensuality celebrated by Vivien: "'Sweeter to me' she said 'this garden rose / Deep-hued and many-folded! sweeter still / The wild-wood hyacinth and the bloom of May'" (ll. 264–66). Savagery does not merely come from without, in the form of a Pellam, Vivien, or Balin, but resides within, as vestigial survivals even among the greatest of the land (always excepting Arthur). Hence the very queen can harbor traces of instincts more openly evinced by the profligate Vivien. If "Balin and Balan" continues to inscribe Protestant marriage as a norm that renders Catholic celibacy scandalous, its swerve to the discourses of anthropology to make this claim also introduces the disturbing possibility that institutions in advanced civilizations might not differ entirely from primitive precursors. In theological terms this suggests a possible link between Anglican and more "primitive" Roman Catholic practices, a possibility that illuminates the poem's anxiety to identify primitive remnants that constantly threaten developments to which an advanced culture aspires.

CONCLUSION

Tennyson's final Grail poem, "Balin and Balan," is as extreme a reaction against ritualism and celibacy as his first, "Sir Galahad," was a celebration of ritual and virginity. As I have suggested throughout this essay, one reason for the mutating treatments of the Grail quest within Tennyson's work was the particular configuration of religious and gender ideology implicitly linked to the Grail through the rise and development of Anglo-Catholicism and, to a lesser degree, through Victorian anthropology. Tennyson's Grail poems encode, if they also complicate, the dominant ideologies of his day. Examining the Grail poems in the context of the Oxford Movement illuminates responses to scandals of faith and gender embedded in these works. Above all, resituating the Grail poems in their historical context suggests that Tennyson was less a complacent, self-satisfied bowdlerizer of Malory than a complex poet coping with intricate skeins of cultural and gender norms that have yet to be fully unraveled today.

NOTES

1. For a recent overview of the Oxford Movement, see Robin Gilmour, *The Victorian Period: The Intellectual and Cultural Context of English Literature 1830–1890* (London: Longman, 1993), pp. 76–81.

2. John Henry Newman, *Newman's* Apologia Pro Vita Sua, *The Two Versions of 1864 & 1865, Preceded by Newman's and Kingsley's Pamphlets*, intro. Wilfrid Ward (Oxford: Oxford University Press; London: Humphrey Milford, 1913), p. 226. Subsequent references will be given as in-text citations. Kingsley's pamphlet will also be cited as "Newman," followed by the relevant page number.

3. R.D. Middleton, *Newman at Oxford: His Religious Development* (London: Oxford University Press, 1950), pp. 187–88.

4. Hallam Tennyson, *Alfred Lord Tennyson: A Memoir*, 2 vol. (London: Macmillan, 1897), II, 65.

5. Eve Kosofsky Sedgwick, *Between Men: English Literature and Male Homosocial Desire* (New York: Columbia University Press, 1985), p. 3. Subsequent references to Sedgwick will be given as in-text citations.

6. David Hilliard, "Unenglish and Unmanly: Anglo-Catholicism and Homosexuality," *Victorian Studies*, 25 (1982), 191. It is significant that the *Norfolk News* article appeared less than four months after Newman concluded the last installment of *Apologia Pro Vita Sua*. The newspaper indicates the heightened awareness of scandalous religious and gender issues in the wake of the Kingsley-Newman exchange. Subsequent references to Hilliard are given as in-text citations.

7. A number of scholars have traced Kingsley's agitation over Newman's doctrinal practices to Kingsley's extreme asceticism during his undergraduate days and later "rescue" of his wife from a nunnery. See, for example, Owen Chadwick, *The Spirit of the Oxford Movement* (Cambridge: Cambridge University Press, 1990), p. 126; and Oliver S. Buckton, "'An Unnatural State': Gender, 'Perversion,' and Newman's *Apologia Pro Vita Sua*," *Victorian Studies*, 35 (1992), 360 ff. Though Buckton and I cite different sections of the Kingsley-Newman debate, and though the role of women in the controversy plays a larger role in my examination than in Buckton's, our arguments about the interrelatedness of gender and religion in this episode of Victorian history parallel each other closely. Subsequent references to Chadwick are given as in-text citations.

8. "What I have said is, that monks and nuns are patterns of Christian perfection; and that Scripture itself supplies us with this pattern. Who can deny this? . . . Again, what is meant but this by St. Paul's saying, 'It is good for a man not to touch a woman?' and, when speaking of the father or guardian of a young girl, 'He that giveth her in marriage doeth well; but he that giveth her not in marriage doeth better?' And what does St. John mean but to praise virginity, when he says of the hundred forty and four thousand on Mount Sion, 'These are they which were not defiled with women, for they are virgins?' And what else did our Lord mean, when He said, 'There be eunuchs who have made themselves eunuchs for the kingdom of heaven's sake. He that is able to receive it, let him receive it?'" (Newman, p. 376).

9. Two passages distance Newman from the issue of celibacy. In the first he answers Kingsley's charge directly:

> He says that I teach that the celibacy of the clergy enters into the *defini-tion* of the Church. I do no such thing; that is the blunt truth. Define the Church by the celibacy of the clergy! why, let him read 1 Tim. iii.; there he will find that bishops and deacons are spoken of as married. How, then, could I be the dolt to say or imply that the celibacy of the clergy was a part of the definition of the Church?
>
> (Newman, p. 379)

He returns to the issue a few pages later:

> (At the same time I cannot conceive why the mention of Sacramental Confession, or of Clerical Celibacy, had I made it, was inconsistent with the position of an Anglican Clergyman. For Sacramental Confession and Absolution actually form a portion of the Anglican Visitation of the Sick; and though the 32nd Article says that "Bishops, priests, and deacons, are not *commanded* by God's law either to vow the state of single life or to abstain from marriage," and "therefore it is *lawful* for them to marry," this proposition I did not dream of denying, nor is it inconsistent with St. Paul's doctrine, which I held, that it is "*good* to abide even as he," i.e. in celibacy).
>
> (Newman, p. 382)

10. Martin Harrison and Bill Waters, *Burne-Jones* (London: Barrie & Jenkins, 1973), p. 11.

11. Debra Mancoff, *The Arthurian Revival in Victorian Art* (New York: Garland, 1990), pp. 105, 135. Subsequent references to Mancoff will be given as in-text citations.

12. Mark Girouard, *The Return to Camelot: Chivalry and the English Gentleman* (New Haven: Yale University Press, 1981), p. 178. Subsequent references to Girouard will be given as in-text citations.

13. "John Keble," *Blackwood's Edinburgh Magazine*, 105 (April 1869), 411. Subsequent references to this article will be cited in the text as "Keble," followed by the page number.

14. All citations of Tennyson's poems are from *The Poems of Tennyson*, ed. Christopher Ricks (1969; New York: W.W. Norton, 1972).

15. Confirmation of the account in *Blackwood's* is suggested by the Oxford Diaries of Arthur Hugh Clough, later a religious skeptic, who matriculated to Balliol College in 1836. In 1838 he recorded these events for Friday, May 18:

8 1/2 to 9	D<evotio>ns—
10-10 1/2	D<evotio>ns—
10 1/2-11	Loitered sadly
12-4	Essay 3 hours—Calls
4-7 1/2	Wine Party —Goulburn
8 1/2-9 1/2	I have been loitering & taking my ease again

See *The Oxford Diaries of Arthur Hugh Clough*, ed. Anthony Kenny (Oxford: Clarendon, 1990), p. 60. Though the references to homework and drinking parties suggest undergraduates not unlike those of the late twentieth century, it is notable that the young Clough spent two half-hour periods in religious devotions. Other entries in the diary link the devotions to the Tractarian emphasis on sanctity. In *Hellenism and Homosexuality in Victorian Oxford* (Ithaca and London: Cornell University Press, 1994), Linda Dowling also comments on the connection between "Galahad" and the tone of the early Oxford movement (p. 42).

16. As Robert Browning wrote after "The Holy Grail" was published in 1869, "The old 'Galahad' [of 1842] is to me incomparably better than a dozen centuries of the 'Grail,' 'Coming of Arthur,' and so on. I ought to be somewhat surprised to hear myself thinking so, since it seems also the opinion of everybody. . . ." Quoted by J. Phillip Eggers, *King Arthur's Laureate: A Study of Tennyson's Idylls of the King* (New York: New York University Press, 1971), p. 94. Subsequent references to Eggers will be given as in-text citations.

Like James Eli Adams (*Dandies and Desert Saints: Styles of Victorian Masculinity* [Ithaca and London: Cornell University Press, 1995], pp. 75–106), I argue that anxiety over same-sex desire as a potential implication of the celibacy celebrated by Tractarians did not emerge until the 1860s. Because normative heterosexuality is so marked a feature of "The Holy Grail," however, the work of Sedgwick is more central to my argument than Adams's, which focuses on reserve and theatricality, social combinations and individuality, as issues related to emergent norms of masculinity.

17. W.S.F. Pickering, *Anglo-Catholicism: A Study in Religious Ambiguity* (London: Routledge, 1989), p. 202. James Bentley also notes the vogue of ritualism, which he assigns to the period 1864–67, when there was a marked change in vestments worn by younger priests. See *Ritualism and Politics in Victorian Britain: The Attempt to Legislate for Belief* (Oxford: Oxford University Press, 1978), pp. 20–21.

18. S.L. Ollard, *A Short History of the Oxford Movement* (1915; rpt. London: Faith Press Reprints, 1963), pp. 101–02.

19. Linda K. Hughes, *The Manyfacéd Glass: Tennyson's Dramatic Monologues* (Athens: Ohio University Press, 1987), pp. 185–88.

20. The term is drawn from Eve Kosofsky Sedgwick, "The Beast in the Closet: James and the Writing of Homosexual Panic," in *Sex, Politics, and Science in the Nineteenth-Century Novel*, ed. Ruth Bernard Yeazell (Baltimore:

Johns Hopkins University Press, 1986), p. 182. Subsequent references to Sedgwick's essay will be given as in-text citations.

Richard Dellamora also observes the inscription of homophobia in "The
Holy Grail" yet notes that the loving relationship of Ambrosius and Percivale becomes a "touchstone of human affection," which, in contrast to the "evidently
neurotic character of the nun's practice," suggests the value of warm desire between men. See *Masculine Desire: The Sexual Politics of Victorian Aestheticism*
(Chapel Hill: University of North Carolina Press, 1990), p. 155. See also Herbert
Sussman, who argues that Robert Browning's "Fra Lippo Lippi" sexualizes a
monk much as Tennyson sexualizes the Grail quest; Sussman views Browning's
poem as "the sign in mid-century artistic discourse of . . . unnatural male
celibacy" ("Robert Browning's 'Fra Lippo Lippi' and the Problematic of a Male
Poetic," *Victorian Studies*, 35 [1992], 189).

21. According to David Hilliard (above, note 6), if intimate friendships between men were common in the Victorian era, celibacy was not, nor were religious brotherhoods, which could provide an alternative to marriage for gay men
(185).

22. Raymond Chapman notes a contemporary indication of this anxiety in a
novel by Charlotte Yonge, in which a character remarks, "Look here my dear, the
last generation was that of mediaevalism, ecclesiology, chivalry, symbolism,
whatever you may call it. Married women have worked out of it. It is the middle-
aged maids that monopolise it. Ours is that of common sense." See Chapman,
"Last Enchantments: Medievalism and the Early Anglo-Catholic Movement," in
Medievalism in England, ed. Leslie J. Workman (Cambridge, Eng.: Brewer,
1992), p. 184. See also the chapter on sisterhoods in Martha Vicinus, *Independent Women: Work and Community for Single Women 1850–1920* (Chicago: University of Chicago Press, 1985), pp. 46–84; and John Shelton Reed, "'A Female
Movement': The Feminization of Nineteenth-Century Anglo-Catholicism," *Anglican and Episcopal History*, 57 (1988), 199–238.

23. The point is also made by Sedgwick, *Between*, p. 119, and by Linda M.
Shires, "Rereading Tennyson's Gender Politics," in *Victorian Sages and Cultural
Discourse: Renegotiating Gender and Power*, ed. Thais E. Morgan (New
Brunswick, NJ: Rutgers University Press, 1991), pp. 49 ff.

24. See also Clyde de L. Ryals, *From the Great Deep: Essays on "Idylls of
the King"* (Athens: Ohio University Press, 1967), p. 165.

25. I borrow the term from Mary Poovey, *Uneven Developments: The Ideological Work of Gender in Mid-Victorian England* (Chicago: University of
Chicago Press, 1988), p. 3 and passim.

26. Sir Thomas Malory, *Malory: Works*, ed. Eugene Vinaver, 2nd ed. (Oxford: Oxford University Press, 1971), p. 52.

Since "Balin and Balan" figures less frequently in discussions of Tennyson's treatment of the Grail legend, a summary may be in order. The idyll opens as Arthur sends emissaries to learn why King Pellam, the former ally of Lot, no longer pays tribute. Meantime Arthur hears that two stranger knights in the forest challenge all passers-by. Arthur himself sallies out and overthrows Balin and Balan, then welcomes the brothers—here twins—to his court. Balin, earlier exiled from court for striking a servant, functions as a type of the prodigal son until a report of Pellam arrives. Formerly pagan, Pellam has converted to Christianity, become an ascetic, and now refuses to pay tribute because he is done with worldly things. Garlon, his heir and regent, is suspected by some of being the wood demon who rides invisible through Pellam's realm and strikes unwary knights from behind. Balan departs in search of the wood demon and Balin, deprived of his brother's controlling influence, falls prey to his savage moods once more. Seeking an external prop, he turns to Lancelot and Lancelot's worship of the queen as a model. When, however, he witnesses a troubling téte-à-téte between Guinevere and Lancelot in the garden, he flees court, eventually coming upon Pellam's castle with its room full of relics (in Tennyson's Protestant poem these are clearly fakes). When Garlon suggests openly that the queen whose crown adorns Balin's shield is engaged in adulterous intrigue with Lancelot, Balin kills Garlon, escapes the castle by pole-vaulting out a window by means of the spear reputed to have pierced Christ's side, and flees into the surrounding woods. Here he encounters Vivien, chief villainess—and seductress—of the *Idylls*. When Vivien seems to confirm Balin's worst fears about what he witnessed in the garden between Guinevere and Lancelot—though in fact Vivien is lying—Balin's psychic defenses crumble in an instant. Shrieking, he tramples the queen's crown affixed to his shield. Balan, in quest of the wood demon, mistakes the shriek for the demon's own, enters, and attacks. The brothers are both mortally wounded and die locked in one another's arms, though not before they discover each other's identity and express hope for the afterlife.

    27. Quoted by Raymond Chapman (above, note 22), p. 170. Paul Turner argues that Pellam reflects the Oxford Movement, Newman's conversion, and the "Papal Aggression" of the Catholic hierarchy founded in England in 1850 by Cardinal Wiseman, as well as the "anti-liberal pronouncements" of Pope Pius IX. See Turner's *Tennyson* (London: Routledge and Kegan Paul, 1976), p. 153. I concur with Turner but locate the idyll's perspective on Catholicism in discourses more specific to the early 1870s.

    28. George W. Stocking Jr., *Victorian Anthropology* (New York: Free Press, 1987), pp. 161–63. Subsequent references to Stocking are given as in-text citations. Tennyson's personal library included volumes by Victorian anthropologists John Lubbock and E.B. Tylor. See Nancie Campbell, comp., *Tennyson in Lincoln: A Catalogue of the Collections in the Research Centre*, 2 vols. (Lincoln, Eng.: Tennyson Society, 1971–73), I, 69, 102.

CHAPTER 14

"Pure Hearts and Clean Hands"
The Victorian and the Grail

DEBRA N. MANCOFF

In 1859, an expectant British audience welcomed a new collection of poems by Alfred Tennyson (1809–1892). The high anticipation was not surprising. Since his literary debut in 1842 Tennyson enjoyed widespread popularity and critical acclaim, and his appointment as the poet laureate in 1850 gave him commanding authority as well as official sanction. Any new publication of Tennyson's work was justly regarded as an important literary event. But, in this case, it was the subject as much as the poet that heightened public excitement. The *Idylls of the King* contained four long poems based on the tales of King Arthur and the Knights of the Round Table. The venerable and grand tale, celebrating romance, adventure, and national identity, was now revitalized and told anew for the modern world. But the strong reception was tempered with an element of disappointment. The critic for *Blackwood's Edinburgh Magazine* expressed a common opinion when he urged the laureate to continue his Arthuriad and return to the saga of the Grail quest and the good knight Sir Galahad, that "noble type of true Christian chivalry—of that work of heaven on earth which only pure hearts can love, clean hands can do."[1]

With his first, brief poem on the Grail knight, "Sir Galahad" of 1842, Tennyson captivated his public by portraying a perfect youth, charged with purpose and idealism. His strength, innocence, and earnest determination defined both his quest and its objective. But in the years that followed, Tennyson and other modern interpreters of the legend found that recasting the saga of Galahad and his search for spiritual knowledge and fulfillment would prove as elusive as the search for the Grail itself. Yet, the centrality of the Grail and the Grail knight to the time-honored legend drew poets and painters to the subject again and again. The challenge of portraying that "pure heart" and those "clean hands" ran counter to the pragmatic and self-defining view of the Arthurian Revival. To tell the tale of Galahad was to create a standard of ethics and resolve that few modern men or women could accept, so it was with longing and reluctance that the Victorians reached for the Grail.

For over a century, the prospect of reviving the saga of King Arthur and the Knights of the Round Table inspired the national imagination. The legend, neglected since the Middle Ages, was recovered in the course of the Gothic Revival's quest to reconstruct and romanticize British cultural patrimony. In the eighteenth and early nineteenth centuries, fragments of the legend appeared in literary anthologies, creating a new audience and context for the forgotten epic.[2] Renowned poets, including Walter Scott and Robert Southey, announced plans to republish Sir Thomas Malory's *Morte Darthur*, out of print since 1634.[3] By 1817, three versions had appeared, including a de luxe edition edited by Southey in his official capacity as poet laureate.[4]

Fueling this interest was a new identification of the British gentleman with the chivalric knight, inspired by the romantic novels of Scott, with diverse results that included the collecting of armor, scholarly and philosophical treatises, mock tournaments, and even the formation of Young England, a political party dedicated to a belief in *noblesse oblige*.[5] The accession of Queen Victoria in 1837 strengthened the association of knight and gentleman, as the men of Britain swore allegiance to protect their land and their lady. Early in the Queen's reign, Gothic Revival interest focused upon Arthurian subjects as the finest and most authentic examples of the chivalric tradition in Britain.

Like many poets of the era, Alfred Tennyson dreamed of recasting the saga for his own generation. In the 1830s, he drew up and abandoned a series of Arthurian projects, searching in vain for an appropriate form to revitalize the legend.[6] The publication of *Poems*, a two-volume collection of 1842, made his reputation and gave the public his first serious and polished attempts to address Arthurian subjects. Three lyric works, "The Lady of Shalott," "Sir Launcelot and Queen Guinevere," and "Sir Galahad," evoked a spirit of romance and adventure, while the epic "Morte d'Arthur" revived the nobility and heroism of the ancient tradition. More important, Tennyson's account of the tragic end of the legend stood as a gesture of intention to undertake the complete cycle, and in the years that followed, his audience waited patiently and eagerly for him to fulfill his own promise of Arthur's return.[7]

Tennyson's contemporary critics, as well as modern literary scholars, attribute the success of the first installation of the *Idylls* to his transformation of the legendary characters into vital men and women, portrayed with complexity and humanity. The writer in the *Saturday Review* described Tennyson's characters as "fabulous knights and ladies," but also as "true men and women."[8] Sympathy for them sprang from empathy with them, and, in the words of the critic of the *Athenaeum*, readers responded to their experiences and emotions, "weeping with the weeper, warming under the influences of the great of soul, and smiling, perhaps sometimes fearing, as scenes and incidents pass before us."[9] Tennyson's success in translating the epic of the past for the audience of the present was ensured by his ability to let the readers identify with his characters. In the *Idylls of the King* Tennyson struck a chord of familiarity—in feeling, in words, in sentiment—that encouraged his readers to see the modern soul in the medieval knight or lady, a habit of interpretation that had endured from the earliest days of the Gothic Revival in literature.

It was precisely this bond of association that had made Tennyson's poem "Sir Galahad" of 1842 such a resounding success. Written in Galahad's own voice, the poem proclaims the young knight's creed of chivalry and purity with confidence and conviction. "My good blade carves the casques of men, / My tough lance thrusteth sure, / My strength is as the strength of ten, / Because my heart is pure" (ll. 1–4).[10] True to his oath of honor, he respects womanhood and swears an oath of protection, but he abstains from accepting their physical favors in gratitude, preferring a higher reward: "More bounteous aspects on me beam,/ Me mightier transports move and thrill; / So keep I fair thro' faith and prayer / A virgin heart in work and will" (ll. 21–4). His way through life is solitary, facing dangerous adventures and supernatural phenomena, but he holds fast to his quest, never questioning, always determined, his fate guided by angelic voices that urge him forward: "'O just and faithful knight of God! / Ride on! the prize is near'; All-arm'd I ride whate'er betide, / Until I find the Holy Grail" (ll. 79–80; 83–84).

While the path Tennyson chose for his Galahad was traditional, the spirit of his Grail knight was thoroughly modern. His exuberance, his earnestness, and his unrestrained joy in his youth, strength, and destiny reflect Victorian boyhood rather than medieval spirituality. In "Sir Galahad" little attention was paid to the reason for the quest; the knight, with his code of conduct, restless energy, and sterling character, was the focus of popular attention. The ringing tones of "Sir Galahad" flashed before the Victorian public like sunlight on shining armor. No Arthurian poem enjoyed greater popularity. It quickly became a favorite work, praised for its realization of an ideal youth, a model for young men of modern society, motivated by honor and dedicated to a life of clean living and social service. In the Victorian mind, the Grail represented Galahad's code rather than spiritual fulfillment, and this submerging of the symbol in the character and his purpose would endure throughout the Arthurian Revival.

Even before the 1859 *Idylls* appeared, Tennyson's critics, fans, and even his family urged him to expand upon "Sir Galahad." Friends wrote him letters, but, in 1859, when the Duke of Argyll suggested that "The 'Grail' ought to be written forthwith," Tennyson replied that he had given up the subject long ago, questioning its viability. "I doubt whether such a subject could be handled in these days without incurring a charge of irreverence. It would be too much like playing with sacred things. The old writers *believed* in the Grail."[11] It was not the character of Galahad that made him hesitate; it was the actual progress of the quest. Tennyson found it difficult to translate it into modern terms. Spiritual mysteries and holy vessels conflicted with Tennyson's practical Protestantism, and he feared that a contemporary version of the saga would compromise both his own beliefs and the legend's original significance. He did try to approach the difficult topic from another angle, framing the quest from Lancelot's experience, but he gave that up as well.

Artists faced similar difficulties in interpreting the subject. William Dyce (1806–1864) hoped to feature the subject as the central image in an ensemble of frescoes he designed for the Queen's Robing Room in the new Palace at Westminster. Early in the planning stages of his project he praised the Grail Quest as "a sort of 'Pilgrims Progress' of the middle ages, expressive with the force of a religious allegory."[12] But, after he researched the subject in a well-regarded, scholarly text, Algernon Herbert's *Britannia After the Romans* (1836), Dyce changed his mind. Herbert called the quest part of a literature that was "tedious and odious," a "blasphemous imposture," calculated "to pass off the mysteries of Bardism for direct inspirations of the Holy Ghost."[13] Within a few months, Dyce reassessed the subject, labeling tales of it as corrupt, "little else than a tolerably intelligible religious allegory, strongly tinctured with the monastic ideas of the 13th century, and seemingly, to some extent, intended to throw discredit on Chivalric greatness." He did maintain that the subject deserved a prominent place in his Arthurian cycle, but he strove to avoid what he feared were "matters of religious and antiquarian controversy, which had better be avoided" (Dyce to Eastlake, 23 November 1848, in J.S. Dyce, "Life, Correspondence," III, 58).

Trying to preserve the significance of the subject but evade the difficulties of its content, he chose to illustrate the moment the knights left Camelot. The design *Piety: The Knights of the Round Table Departing on the Quest for the Holy Grail* (1849; National Gallery of Scotland; Figure 14.1) was inspired by a passage in Malory's *Morte Darthur*.[14] The setting is the courtyard outside Camelot, where the knights, already mounted, still their restive horses to bid farewell to their sovereign and their ladies. Although the scene is vital and filled with vivid detail, nothing indicates the reason for the knights' quest. There is no vision of the Grail, no Grail Maiden, no angels or heavenly beings to inspire or guide their travels. Priests are present but relegated to a minor position, half hidden by Arthur, who openly displays his grief. Dyce depicts him as a noble patriarch, still proud and strong, but burdened with the concerns of leadership. His grand gesture echoes his words of lament to Gawaine, "Ye have nigh slain me with the avow and promise that ye have made; for through you ye have bereft me the fairest fellowship and the truest of knighthood that ever were seen together in any realm of the world; for when they depart from hence I am sure they all shall never meet more in this world."[15] In this interpretation Dyce presented the quest in a non-religious context, free from ancient heresy or any endorsement of Catholicism, Britain's minority religion. But his clients rejected the design, finding it too tragic for the monarchical chamber. By trying to mask the subject's spiritual meaning, Dyce had revealed one of the narrative functions of the quest. By drawing the knights

Fig. 14.1. William Dyce, *Piety: The Knights of the Round Table Departing on the Quest for the Holy Grail* (1849). Watercolor, 9 1/8"x 17 3/8". The National Gallery of Scotland. (See insert for greater detail.)

Fig. 14.2. William Dyce, *Religion: The Vision of Sir Galahad and His Company* (1851). Fresco, 11' 2 1/2"x 14' 6". Queen's Robing Room, Palace of Westminster, London. Reproduced by kind permission of the Palace of Westminster.

away from the court, it stood as a first step to the eventual destruction of the Round Table.

Dyce abandoned the design but not the subject of the Grail Quest. His final solution was the fresco *Religion: The Vision of Sir Galahad and His Company* (Queen's Robing Room, Palace of Westminster; Figure 14.2), which was completed in 1851. With *Le Morte Darthur* again as his source, Dyce selected the incident where the paths of the three young knights—Bors, Percival, and Galahad—crossed. In the company of Percival's sister, they followed four lions on the trail of a white hart. Coming to a rustic shack, they were surprised to hear the sounds of a mass in progress within. When they entered the shack, the lions turned into the four gospel writers and the hart into Christ (Malory, *Le Morte Darthur*, II, 249–50). The vision lasted only a moment, but the hermit priest who lived there explained it was a sign that one in their company would find the Grail. Dyce painted the momentary vision with Christ enthroned, born upon clouds and flanked by the evangelists and their symbolic beasts. To the right, Bors, Percival, and Percival's sister look on in reverence, while at the left, Galahad springs forward to embrace the vision. Once again the priest stands on the margins. He holds a simple mass cup, a symbol for the Grail, but, in this context, not its true substitute. Galahad's attention is riveted on Christ and the Gospel writers, suggesting a practical means to come to an understanding of Christian mysteries. Dyce also avoided the conclusion of the Quest, which would take Galahad out of the worldly sphere into heaven. His vision of the Grail knight is as enthusiastic and assertive as that of Tennyson; this Galahad is active rather than mystical. He seems to take his destiny in his own hands, and the course toward that destiny—undertaken with courage, resolve, and energy—seems more important than its goal.

In contrast, Dante Gabriel Rossetti (1828–1882) found the challenge of spiritual mystery enticing, and he continually returned to the subject of the Grail throughout his career. While Dyce hesitated to present Galahad as a solitary mystic, in an illustration for Tennyson's "Sir Galahad," published in 1857, Rossetti placed him at an isolated shrine, listening to the chants of his angelic guides, his ecstatic face glowing in the eerie illumination of a single burning candle. Rossetti was also one of the few artists who dared to portray the attainment of the Grail.

In 1857, Rossetti organized a small group of painters to design and execute murals in the upper story of the Debating Hall in the new Oxford Union.[16] Using Malory's *Morte Darthur* as his primary source, Rossetti chose to illustrate scenes from the quest for the Grail. Although he never completed his depiction of Galahad's attainment, he returned to the design in 1864 in the watercolor *How Sir Galahad, Sir Bors, and Sir Percival Were Fed with the Grael; but Sir Percival's Sister Died by the Way* (Tate Gallery, Figure 14.3). Here Galahad is the central figure of a solemn procession. He bows his head as he advances to the Grail Maiden; his companions remain a respectful distance behind him. As in Rossetti's *Damsel of the Sanc Grael* of 1857, the Grail Maiden is sumptuously dressed and surrounded by symbols of purity and salvation. Radiant lilies bloom at her feet, and behind her, above an altar cloaked with embroidered shields, a white dove flutters, swinging a smoking censer. But, in this close and confusing composition, Rossetti evokes more mystery that he can explain.

Although Rossetti portrayed Galahad several times, he believed that Lancelot and his failed quest better conveyed the message of the Grail. In this, Rossetti unwittingly conformed to the interpretative habit of self-identification that characterized the Arthurian Revival. Lancelot, with his good intentions but worldly ways, became a personal symbol for Rossetti. In *Launcelot's Vision of the Sangrael*, a design for another mural in the

Fig. 14.3. Dante Gabriel Rossetti, *How Sir Galahad, Sir Bors, and Sir Percival Were Fed with the Grael, but Sir Percival's Sister Died by the Way* (1864). Watercolor, 11 1/2"x 16 1/2". The Tate Gallery, London / Art Resource, NY. (See insert for greater detail.)

Oxford Union Debating Hall, Rossetti places the knight outside the chapel of the Grail, lost in a dream-like trance. The image is a free invention on a passage from Malory's *Morte Darthur* in which a hermit assures Lancelot that his life of carnal transgression has resulted in a singular good: the birth of Galahad. But, in Rossetti's interpretation, Lancelot's love for Guenevere bars the way to his salvation. Her form dominates the composition. Placed in the center, between two windows, she drapes her arms in the branches of an apple tree and sways with erotic languor. The apple tree and the coiling snake above the knight's head bind the image of Guenevere to Eve and original sin as the simple truth of the human condition. At the far left, beyond the failed knight's reach, an angel kneels, holding the Grail. Lancelot cannot cross the chasm between his sin and his salvation without confronting his love for Guenevere. But Rossetti does not condemn the knight. Instead, he suggests that Lancelot, and his choice for earthly rather than spiritual fulfillment, provides a more telling standard than Galahad to measure humanity.

Rossetti also planned to rewrite the legend from Lancelot's point of view. The idea came to him as early as 1858, inspired perhaps by the poetry of his friend William Morris or by his own designs for the Debating

Hall murals. Once again using Malory as his source, Rossetti took extensive notes on the events crucial to Lancelot's experience. He drew up a list of rhyming words, but he composed only a brief passage and abandoned the poem after 1871.[17] The evidence, although scant, reveals his intentions. He chose the title "God's Graal" and described its subject as "the loss of the Sangrael by Lancelot, a theme chosen to emphasize the superiority of Guenevere over God" (Rossetti to Algernon Charles Swinburne, 9 March 1870, in Baum, *Rossetti*, p. 42). While Rossetti's remark suggests irreverence, it should not be taken to disparage the story of salvation. Instead, Rossetti sought the most human—meaning to his mind the most passionate—dimension of the legend, and he found it in Lancelot's experience. His notes reveal that at the conclusion of the tale the sinners would sacrifice their love for their redemption. The single surviving fragment returns to the theme of the mural design, with Lancelot exhausted from his failed quest, dreaming of Guenevere and apple trees, but remembering in his sorrow that "God's Graal is good" (Baum, *Rossetti*, p. 239).

In 1869, Tennyson finally returned to the saga of the Grail search. "The Holy Grail," first published independently then added to the *Idylls* in 1870, surprised and even shocked his public. Rather than give them a triumphant tale of spiritual commitment and achievement, Tennyson offered his readers a tragedy, a saga of failure, exhaustion, ambivalence, and denial. The new poem focuses on Percivale, who, after his failure to find the Grail, has retreated to life in a monastery. As he recalls the quest to a fellow monk, he tells how it decimated the court and damaged his life and the lives of those he loved. His own sister, the first to behold the vision, starved herself in devotion. Lancelot descended into madness. Galahad, who rides through the poem like a phantom, severs all ties with his world, crying, "If I lose myself, I save myself" (l. 178).[18] From the beginning Arthur doubted the worth of the quest for most of the knights, asking them "What are ye? Galahads?" (l. 306), and when his broken men return he castigates them for leaving their common duties in search of a goal beyond them. In "The Holy Grail," Tennyson equates Galahad's goodness and spirituality with the elusive Grail itself, beyond the reach of most men, dangerous and hubristic to emulate or pursue. The courageous young lad who caught public favor in 1842 was transformed into a specter of Astrea, fleeing the world with the passage of the Age of Gold.

Few artists chose to illustrate Tennyson's vision of the quest. They preferred to recall the shining example of the earlier poem. Throughout the Victorian era and well into the twentieth century, artists portrayed Galahad as young, eager, androgynous, and active.[19] Always striving toward his goal, Galahad served as an icon of commitment rather than a symbol of spirituality. The Grail was always just beyond his reach. On occasion, the Grail would appear in another context. James Archer (1823–1904), for example, included it as a healing cup in *La Mort D'Arthur* of 1862 (Manchester City Galleries). As Arthur rests on the Isle of Avalon, an ethereal angel brings him the Grail, now a symbol of his promised return. But for most Victorians, while Galahad maintained his appeal, the Grail was regarded with ambivalence, drawing men from their duty to a quest in futility. This fear influenced depictions of the Grail Angel. As portrayed by Frederic Shields (1833–1911) in 1875, she seduced as well as inspired, entrancing the knights to follow her, like a siren, against their better judgment (William Morris Gallery; Figure 14.4).

Fig. 14.4. Frederic Shields, *Angel of the Holy Grail* (c. 1875). Red chalk, 25"x 22". William Morris Gallery, London.

The simple innocence of Galahad caught the attention of painter Edward Burne-Jones (1833–1898) in his youth, but a deep faith in idealism drew him back to the Grail in his late career. He first read Tennyson's poem as a twenty-year-old undergraduate at Cambridge University. He wrote of his enthusiasm for the work to a boyhood friend. "I have my heart set on our founding a Brotherhood. Learn Sir Galahad by heart. He is to be the patron of our Order."[20] This eager, childlike response, as well as his signature as the "General of the Order of Sir Galahad," reveals the typical Victorian view of the knight at mid-century. As a symbol of clean-living, resolute youth, Galahad offered a pattern that could—and should—be emulated.

Several years later, in 1858, while staying at the London home of his friend Valentine Prinsep, Burne-Jones met Alfred Tennyson. Although he had long since abandoned his notion of "The Order of Sir Galahad," he kept his interest in the poet's vision of the Arthurian hero. In partial tribute to Tennyson, Burne-Jones produced a small, exquisitely rendered drawing, based on the first two and the final stanzas of the 1842 poem (Fogg Art Museum; Figure 14-5). He portrayed Galahad as a dreamy,

Fig. 14.5. Edward Burne-Jones, *Sir Galahad Riding Through a Mysterious Wood* (1858). Pen and ink, 6"x 7 1/2". Courtesy of the Fogg Art Museum, Harvard University Art Museums, Bequest of Grenville L. Winthrop. (See insert for greater detail.)

self-contained youth, barely out of adolescence. He armed the knight according to Tennyson's description, with a "good blade" and a "tough
lance." The knight's sweet expression—beautiful, boyish, and pensive—
testifies to his strength-giving purity. He rides, undistracted, past men
and women who are enjoying each other's company. This distance between Galahad and the realm of earthly endeavor had never been so
clearly defined. Here, Galahad's serenity, rather than his energy and conviction, is emphasized. This Galahad is silent. He does not call attention
to his power or his weapons, nor does he beckon others to follow his
lead. For the artist, who now identified with the idealism rather than its
agent, the image had deep personal significance. He confessed, "I can't
look at Galahad yet to finish it, every stroke in it reminds one of some
dear little word or incident that happened as the pen was marking"
(Burne-Jones, *Memorials*, I, 181–82). With this small drawing Burne-
Jones opened a door on a private vision, a magical world of glittering
beauty where goodness reigned unchallenged.

In the years that followed, Burne-Jones put aside the icons of Galahad and his Grail. Other knights—St. George, Sir Degrevant—provided
chivalric subjects, and his interests in the Arthurian legend focused upon
the seduction of Merlin by Nimüe.[21] But the story of Galahad and the
Quest remained his favorite saga. At the end of his life he proclaimed,
"Lord! how that San Graal story is ever in my mind and thoughts continually. Was there ever anything in the world as beautiful as that is beautiful?" (Burne-Jones, *Memorials*, III, 333). The story of holding to an ideal
and seeking its often uncertain end embodied the ideal of beauty for
Burne-Jones, and it became a metaphor for his art.

The Grail resurfaced in Burne-Jones's iconography in a very private
endeavor. In 1882, he began to compile sketch ideas in a large book fas-
tened with leather thongs.[22] He called it his "Secret Book of Designs,"
and according to his wife Georgiana it revealed "sides of his nature that
none of his other work does" (Burne-Jones, *Memorials*, II, 118). Page
after page depicts chivalric imagery, but the overall theme is the questing
knight. Burne-Jones also recorded notations on heraldry in the "Secret
Book," and his interest continued long after the book was filled. In 1890
William Morris gave him a text on the arms of the Round Table Knights,
which he described in detail to his friend Lady Leighton-Warren. Expressing surprise that many of the renowned knights had "rather commonplace arms," he confessed a desire to "violate heraldry" and invent a
new device for Galahad. He envisioned a "gold cup on a silver ground"
or a black ground emblazoned with a silver chapel. Either design would

replace Galahad's traditional red cross on a white ground, which Burne-Jones believed was "so dull for him" (Burne-Jones, *Memorials*, II, 211).

The imagery in the "Secret Book" began to appear in his decorative arts designs. In 1886, he produced four highly finished cartoons for stained-glass panels depicting the Quest for the Grail for his home in Rottingdean (William Morris Gallery; Figure 14-6).[23] Using a simple organization, a limited ensemble of figures, and Gothic script captions, Burne-Jones told the story with an elegant economy. The four panels are joined by a river of light that gains in size and power as the attainment approaches. The slow rotation of the Grail Angel, marking the worthiness of each petitioner, speaks of the character of the knights and the qualities they personify. She turns her back on Gawain, who slumbers, dreaming of the "Deeds of Kings." She bypasses the well-armed Sir Lancelot, whose way is barred by a beautiful queen who represents "Such Love as Dwelleth in Kings Houses." Galahad is worthy of her glance, and he is the one she faces when, in the last panel, she arrives in Sarras to lead the young knight into the chapel of the Grail. Of the three knights, only Galahad is unreservedly beautiful; his graceful limbs and perfect profile bear a stronger resemblance to those of the Angel than to those of his fellow mortals. This emphasis on beauty was allied to the artist's aesthetic principles. To Burne-Jones the attainment of beauty was the objective of his art.

In 1891, Burne-Jones produced a set of designs for tapestry panels, telling the Quest in full. Commissioned by Australian mining magnate W.K. D'Arcy, the six arras tapestries with additional dado hangings were woven at William Morris's Merton Abbey Tapestry Works.[24] The scenes move swiftly through the narrative. In "The Summons to the Quest," the Grail Maiden appears in the court. "The Arming and Departure of the

Fig. 14.6. Edward Burne-Jones, Cartoon for *The Story of the Quest for the Holy Grail* (1886). Ink, sepia, and gouache, 17 7/8"x 132 7/8". William Morris Gallery, London. (See insert for greater detail.)

Knights" offers a telling contrast to Dyce's version of the subject, for there is no evidence of the impending tragedy, and King Arthur is conspicuously absent. Three scenes, "The Ship," "The Failure of Sir Gawain and Sir Ewain," and "The Failure of Sir Lancelot," move the story toward its conclusion. And in "The Attainment," Burne-Jones presents a metaphor for what he had been seeking throughout his career (Figure 14.7). The long, horizontal composition prompts the viewer to read the sequence left to right. At the far extent of the image, Bors and Percival look toward the holy chapel in the distance. Three tall angels bar their way, and, in a gesture borrowed from Quattrocento painting, the one nearest the chapel directs the gaze onward. At the chapel door where lilies bloom, Galahad kneels in wonder. Inside, three more angels attend the altar where the Grail is kept. Brightly lit and gleaming, the interior of the chapel is rarified, serene, and silent. The open door suggests Galahad's right to enter; soon he will be crowned the Prince of Sarras. Despite the title "The Attainment," what Burne-Jones portrays is the moment before, when Galahad recognizes the Grail. He is a petitioner at the chapel of beauty, and his reward is the vision rather than the possession.

One of the painter's final Grail images had deep personal significance. In 1896, he produced a oil version of the tapestry design for "Sir Lancelot at the Ruined Chapel." The figure of Lancelot was a souvenir of the painter's own lost youth. In 1857, when Rossetti was painting the mural of the same subject at the Debating Hall at Oxford, Burne-Jones posed for the figure of the failed knight. Alone, collapsed against the well, Lancelot is watched by a sympathetic angel. She has emerged from the chapel, which, despite its ruin, is brightly lit within. Her sorrowful glance and her graceful hands express pity for the fallen knight but no condemnation. Unlike Ros-

Fig. 14.7. Edward Burne-Jones, "The Attainment of the Grail," from *The Quest of the Holy Grail* (1891–94). Wool and silk on cotton warp, 96"x 273 1/2". Birmingham Museum and Art Gallery. (See insert for greater detail.)

setti's interpretation, however, Burne-Jones's makes no reference to Guenevere. Lancelot's failure appears to be one of recognition rather than action. He will not see the Grail and witness the revelation of its beauty. The failing health and imminent death of his friend William Morris had brought Burne-Jones to thoughts of his own mortality, and he feared, like Lancelot, that he would fail to complete his own quest.

In her *Memorials* of her husband, Georgiana Burne-Jones observed that the painter had little interest in historical or religious interpretations of the saga of the Grail Quest. "The question was impossible to discuss with [him], to whom it was a living power" (Burne-Jones, *Memorials*, II, 270–71). Burne-Jones had no need of scholarly explanations, for he had found a true and personal equivalent in his art for the Grail. Near the end of his life, he confessed to his friend and studio assistant Thomas Rooke that he felt out of step with his times, reflecting, "A pity it is I was not born in the middle ages. . . . People then would have known how to use me— now they don't know what on earth to do with me . . . .Well, what does that matter . . . . I've learned to know Beauty when I see it, and that's the best thing."[25] The Arthurian Revival taught Burne-Jones not just to enjoy or admire the legend but to find a way to identify with it. His pursuit was not for Galahad's Grail, but for his own—the beauty of his artistic vision—allowing him to approximate Tennyson's description of the "old writers." Like them, Burne-Jones "*believed* in the Sangreal" (H. Tennyson, *Memoir*, 1, 456–57) and that allowed him to see the end as greater than the means. While others of his generation were moved by a desire to be like Galahad, Burne-Jones sought only to define for himself a Grail, and through that he found a true faith in "the work of heaven on earth which only pure hearts can love, clean hands can do."

NOTES

Reprinted and revised with permission from *Der Gral: Artusromantik in der Kunst des 19. Jahrhunderts* (Dumont/Bayerisches National Museum, 1995), pp. 108–20.

1. Blackwood's *Edinburgh Magazine,* 86 (November 1859), 610.

2. Literary anthologies such as Thomas Percy's *Reliques of Ancient English Poetry* (1765) and George Ellis's *Specimens of Early English Romances* (1805) presented examples of medieval ballads and romance in drastically edited or summarized form with commentary on source, style, and meaning. These made "lost" literature accessible to general, and even young, audiences. See Debra N. Mancoff, *The Arthurian Revival in Victorian Art* (New York: Garland, 1990) pp. 37–41, and James Douglas Merriman, *The Flower of Kings: A Study of the Arthurian Legend*

in England Between 1485 and 1835 (Lawrence: The University Press of Kansas, 1973), pp. 93–99; 127–28.

3. For a full account of publications of *Le Morte Darthur*, see Barry Gaines, "The Editions of Malory in the Early Nineteenth Century," in *Papers of the Bibliographic Society of America* 68 (1974), 1–17. See also Merriman, pp. 127–28.

4. These were *The History of the Renowned Prince Arthur, King of Britain,* 2 vols. (London: Walker and Edwards, 1816); *La Mort d'Arthur: The Most Ancient and Famous History of the Renowned Prince Arthur and the Knights of the Round Table,* 3 vols. (London: R. Wilks, 1816); and *The Byrth, Lyf, and Actes of King Arthur,* 2 vols., ed. R. Southey (London: Longman, Hurst, Rees, Orme, and Brown, 1817). Both the Walker and Edwards and the Wilks edition were based on the 1634 text, which Merriman describes as "corrupt" (p. 129). They were also cheaply produced and inexpensive.

5. For the source and influences of the chivalric revival, see Alice Chandler, *A Dream of Order. The Medieval Ideal in Nineteenth-Century English Literature* (Lincoln: University of Nebraska Press, 1970); Mark Girouard, *The Return to Camelot, Chivalry and the English Gentleman* (New Haven: Yale University Press, 1981), and Mancoff, *Arthurian Revival*, pp. 27–64.

6. Tennyson began to work on Arthurian subjects in the early 1830s. He wrote a prose draft for a twelve-book epic in 1833 and outlined a musical masque in five acts sometime after. Although he did not publish his first Arthurian works until 1842, completed drafts of "Sir Galahad," "The Lady of Shalott," "Sir Launcelot and Queen Guinevere," and "Morte d'Arthur" date from this decade and were, for the most part, published with minor alterations.

7. Tennyson published the poems of his Arthuriad over a period of thirty years. The first installation of the *Idylls of the King* included "Enid," "Vivien," "Elaine," and "Guinevere." In 1862, he added the "Dedication" to Prince Albert. In 1869 he published *"The Holy Grail" and Other Poems*, including "The Coming of Arthur," "The Holy Grail," "Pelleas and Ettare," and "The Passing of Arthur." The 1872 publication of *"Gareth and Lynette" and Other Poems* contained "Gareth and Lynette" and "The Last Tournament." The epilogue "To the Queen" was written in 1873. In the same year Tennyson divided "Enid" into two poems, later retitling them "The Marriage of Geraint" and "Geraint and Enid." "Balin and Balan" was published in 1885 in *Tiresias and Other Poems*. By 1891 Tennyson placed the poems in the present order and made the last change to his text. For details of publication, see J. Phillip Eggers, *King Arthur's Laureate: A Study of Tennyson's "Idylls of the King"* (New York: New York University Press, 1971), and Kathleen Tillotson, "Tennyson's Serial Poem," in Geoffrey Tillotson and Kathleen Tillotson, *Mid-Victorian Studies* (London: University of London; The Atholone Press, 1965), pp. 80–109.

8. *Saturday Review,* 16 (July 1859), 76.

9. *Athenaeum* (July 1859), 74. For an overview of the reception of the 1859 *Idylls of the King,* see Linda K. Hughes, "Tennyson's Urban Arthurians: Victorian Audiences and the 'City Built to Music,'" in Valerie M. Lagorio and Mildred Leake Day, eds., *King Arthur Through the Ages,* 2 vols. (New York: Garland, 1990), II, 39–61, especially 42–49.

10. Alfred Tennyson, "Sir Galahad," in *The Poetical Works of Tennyson,* ed. G.R. Stange, (Boston: Houghton Mifflin Company, 1974), p. 101.

11. Tennyson to the Duke of Argyll, 3 October, 1859, in, Hallam Tennyson, *Alfred Lord Tennyson: A Memoir by His Son,* 2 vols. (New York: Macmillan, 1897), I, 456–57.

12. Dyce to Charles L. Eastlake, 20 July 1848, in James Stirling Dyce, "Life, Correspondence, and Writings of William Dyce, R.A. Painter, Musician, and Scholar, by His Son," 4 vols. (Unpublished Manuscript, Aberdeen City Art Gallery, Department of Manuscripts), III, 49.

13. Algernon Herbert, *Britannia After the Romans; Being an Attempt to Illustrate the Religious and Political Revolutions of that Province in the Fifth and Succeeding Centuries* (London: 1836), p. vi.

14. Dyce's design was submitted in a watercolor rendering to the Fine Arts Commission, the governing board for the decoration of the new Palace, in 1848, and exhibited at the Royal Academy in 1849. The Fine Arts Commission rejected the work but their reasons were never clearly stated. See Mancoff, *Arthurian Revival,* p. 125.

15. Sir Thomas Malory, *Le Morte Darthur,* 2 vols. (London: J.M. Dent, 1919), II, 172.

16. In 1857 Rossetti arranged the commission with architect Benjamin Woodward. The artists included Edward Burne-Jones, William Morris, Arthur Hughes, J. Hungerford Pollen, Valentine Prinsep, and J. Rodham Spencer Stanhope. Of these artists, including Rossetti, only Pollen had experience painting murals. The interior also posed extremely difficult technical and compositional challenges, including damp brick walls and large windows that made viewing difficult. The project, on a whole, was a failure, and many of the artists left before completing their works. Deterioration occurred almost immediately, and over the years the murals have undergone repeated restoration and conservation treatments, the most recent of which, completed in 1989, was the most successful. See Mancoff, *Arthurian Revival,* pp. 156–60 and John Christian, *The Oxford Murals* (Chicago: University of Chicago Press, 1981).

17. A notebook in the Duke University Library records Rossetti's plans for "God's Graal," including twenty-six pages of notes and extracts from Malory's *Morte Darthur,* revealing how he would edit the story from Lancelot's point of

view. See Paull Franklin Baum, *Dante Gabriel Rossetti: An Analytical List Of Manuscripts in the Duke University Library* (Durham, North Carolina: Duke University Press, 1931), pp. 41–43; 78–79.

18. Alfred Tennyson, "The Holy Grail," in *Poetical Works*, pp. 400–13.

19. George Frederick Watts and Joseph Noel Paton each painted several notable and popular images of Galahad of this type. For information on their images of the Grail knight, see Marilyn Lincoln Board, "Art's Moral Mission: Reading G.F. Watts's *Sir Galahad*," and Richard Schindler, "Sir Noel Paton and the Grail Quest: The Arthurian Mythos as Christian Art," in Debra N. Mancoff, ed., *The Arthurian Revival: Essays on Form, Tradition, and Transformation* (New York: Garland, 1992), pp. 132–54 and 115–31 respectively. For the appeal of Galahad as a model for boys, see Debra N. Mancoff, *The Return of King Arthur: The Legend Through Victorian Eyes* (New York: Harry N. Abrams, 1995), pp. 101–28.

20. Burne-Jones to Cormell Price, 1 May 1853, in Georgiana Burne-Jones, *Memorials of Edward Burne-Jones,* 2 vols. (London: Macmillan Company, 1906), I, 77.

21. Burne-Jones first interpreted the subject of Merlin's enchantment in 1857, working on the Debating Hall Murals at Oxford. He refined the subject in a gouache and watercolor of 1861, now in the collection of the Victoria and Albert Museum in London. His best-known version, *The Beguiling of Merlin*, was painted during the years 1874–76 and caused a critical sensation when it was shown at the Grosvenor Gallery in 1877. The painting is now in the Lady Lever Art Gallery in Port Sunlight. See Mancoff, *Arthurian Revival*, pp. 218–21.

22. Burne-Jones left the sketchbook to the British Museum in London.

23. The windows were removed from their original location and conserved by the Victoria and Albert Museum in 1980. See Debra N. Mancoff, *Burne-Jones* (Rehnart Park, CA: Pomegranate, 1998), p. 95.

24. The tapestries were designed for D'Arcy's home, Stanmore Hall in Uxbridge. For photographs *in situ*, see "The Arras Tapestries of the San Graal at Stanmore Hall," *Studio* 15 (1899), 98–104. The Merton Abbey Tapestry Works produced two other sets from Burne-Jones's designs: a set of three panels for Laurence Hodson in 1895–1896, and a full set for D'Arcy's partner George Mc-Colloch in 1898–1899.

25. 29 May 1897, in Mary Lago, ed., *Burne-Jones Talking: His Conversations 1895–1898 Preserved by His Studio Assistant Thomas Rooke* (London: John Murray, 1981), pp. 146–47.

CHAPTER 15

From Logres to Carbonek
The Arthuriad of Charles Williams

KARL HEINZ GÖLLER

Among the modern poets of today, Charles Williams (1896–1945) has yet to receive the acknowledgement which he deserves, although he is one of the major shapers and remakers of the Arthurian legend, as C. S. Lewis and others have pointed out.[1] Of course, Lewis' *Arthurian Torso* will always remain an indispensable guide through the labyrinthine passages of the poet's work; and yet many paths remain to be explored.

In his incomplete prose work *The Figure of Arthur* Charles Williams delineates the intention of his poetic works *Taliessin Through Logres* and *The Region of the Summer Stars*.[2] They are meant to portray the development of the legends of Arthur and the Grail, their gradual coalescence and fusion and the fate of the Grail world. Two subjects are of primary importance for Williams: the realm of King Arthur and that of the Grail. When these two focal points of Williams' *Arthuriad* are compared with medieval treatments—as for instance that of Malory, whose *Morte Darthur* can be regarded as one of Williams' main sources—the modern poet's originality becomes clear. The love story of Lancelot and Guinevere, which is perhaps the most appealing to modern audiences, is only allotted marginal treatment. The centre of the entire myth, and therewith the *raison d'être* of Williams' work, is clearly the Grail. The poet sees the union of the world of Arthur with that of the Grail less as a legendary or historical phenomenon, and far more as a complex symbol of the union of Empire and Christendom, that is to say as a symbol of the Ultimate Epiphany, the Second Advent of Christ.

Logres is the name Charles Williams gives to Arthur's realm in conformity with the Old French prose version.[3] It is a part or a province of the Byzantine Empire, which for Williams represented the incarnation of Divine Order. From the point of view of medieval Arthurian romance, the Roman Empire would have been a more appropriate choice. But for Williams, Byzantium was connected to the idea of a strictly hierarchical power with an organic structure. Divine order was for him a matter of geometrical precision, with complete harmony of all the component parts. Rivalry of the member states of the Empire, or manifestations of national thought, did not fit into his conception.

Others besides Charles Williams used Byzantium as a symbolic vehicle, for example W. B. Yeats. Both were connected with the Golden Dawn Group of Chelsea occultists. The originality of Charles Williams lies in the utter Christianisation of the image; one might even say he baptized *goetia*.

One of the mystery writers of the Golden Dawn period, Arthur Machen, may have inspired Williams to the idea of a modern *parousia* symbolised by the grail. His story "The Great Return" (1915) is an account of the Grail and its effect on a modern Welsh parish church. The idea of *perichoresis* or interpenetration may also have been suggested by one of Machen's stories.[4]

Thus Williams gives the story of King Arthur an entirely new slant. Its meaning can only be understood through a closer look at the development of earlier treatments of the Arthurian story. The idea of order already plays a prominent role in the *Historia Regum Britanniae* of Geoffrey of Monmouth.[5] The learned bishop of St Asaph is less interested in the heroic deeds of the historical King Arthur than in the idea of kingship, of which Arthur is a symbol. Geoffrey constructs a glorious past, in which Britain was a major power by reason of its unity and singleness of purpose, which enabled it to rival the Roman Empire. The historian's aim is the foundation of a political ideology, the creation and dissemination of the idea of an Anglo–Norman Empire. To this end he emphasises the *primordia urbis* and makes Arthur a figure larger than life, greater than Hector and Aeneas, Alexander and Charlemagne, a visible symbol of a realm which far surpassed that of the Romans in brilliance and in power. The foundation of the Empire sketched by Geoffrey was meant to lie beyond the reaches of the medieval *imperium;* his Arthur is meant as a negation of the uniqueness of the imperial office.[6]

In literary works after Geoffrey nationalist tendencies become more apparent,[7] and more emphasis is given to the conflict with Rome. The most complex Middle English treatment of the fate of King Arthur, the *Alliterative Morte Arthure*,[8] places the conflict with Rome at the focal point of the action. Even in the chronicles we can recognise a gradual shifting of interest in this direction.[9] In Geoffrey's history Arthur is about to climb the Alpine passes when the news of Mordred's treason reaches him, forcing a quick retreat. According to Peter of Langtoft[10] Arthur has already crossed the Alps and the trumpets in Pavia are announcing a feast, when the bearer of bad tidings from Britain reaches Arthur. John Hardyng[11] places the final battle between Romans and Britains in the Toscana in central Italy. In the *Annals of Worcester*[12] which follow the *Liber de Compositione Castri Ambaziae*[13] in this respect, Arthur is forced to turn back shortly before reaching the city gates of Rome, where he hears about Mordred's betrayal. And finally Jean de Preis has Arthur marching into Rome in his *Mer des Histoires,*[14] and we see him crowned as Emperor. In a similar manner in the French prose version, as reflected in Sir Thomas Malory's *Morte Darthur,*[15] Arthur is crowned as emperor in Rome after a great victory over the Empire.

Charles Williams provides us with a completely different concept of the Arthurian myth. The major innovation consists in the exclusion of an antithetical opposition of *Logres* and Rome. Even in Tennyson's version, Rome was only the "slowly fading mistress of the world"; the poet devotes one meagre sentence to the battle against Rome.[16] Williams saw the fight against the Roman emperor as a very unfortunate element of the Arthurian myth, and preferred to omit it. "No national myth was ever the better for being set against a more universal authority," the poet tells us.[17] The result of dropping the rivalry between *Logres* and Rome is a denationalisation of the Arthurian myth. Arthur's realm is now an integral part of the Byzantine Empire.

The concept of organism is meant literally by Charles Williams. His point of departure is Wordsworth's idea that the human body is an index of a greater universal order—the old medieval topos of microcosm and macrocosm.[18] The words which appear in an index also appear in the corresponding text, and in a similar manner the qualities and the structural features of the human body are found in counterpart in the universe. The Empire of *Logres is* conceived as an analogy to the human body. The head is *Logres,* for the historical source of the myth lies in Britain; it gains consciousness here and is given verbal form.[19] The breasts are the country of France, which fed Christendom with the milk of knowledge and of faith ("the breasts of *intelligo* and *credo*").[20] Rome is represented through the hands of the Pope, which convey the blessing of the Church to the faithful. The navel stands for Byzantium, the organic centre and seat of the Empire; the loins are Jerusalem, where Christ was crucified and the new

Adam born.[21] Thus the Empire is seen as an organism, and the human body, in turn, as a mirror of the Empire, the Kingdom of God.[22]

Beyond this Empire to the South is *P'o-l'u,* the land of the Antipodes, where order dissolves into anarchy. Octopi with giant tentacles creep over the slimy sea and stare with lidless eyes at the coast of the Empire. Images from Coleridge's *Ancient Mariner* and Wells' *War of the Worlds* blend with the medieval concept of the Antipodes, which interestingly enough were seen as a negative counterpart of the Arthurian world in the *Draco Normannicus* of Etienne de Rouen.[23]

P'o-l'u is a kind of Hell, the sphere of power of the Headless Emperor. To the West of *Logres* lies *Broceliande,* [24] the mysterious world of making and shaping, of the *Apeiron.* The mistress of this forest is Nimue. She appears in mortal guise, but as the "Mother of Making" she combines earthly existence with the transcendent. Nimue's children are Merlin and Brisen, perceptible and active embodiments of time and space. In the forest of *Broceliande,* beyond the borders of the Empire, stands the castle of *Carbonek* where the Grail and the Bleeding Lance are kept. Merlin and Brisen are preparing the union of Byzantium and *Carbonek,* the welding of the worldly and religious ideals, the perfection of Christendom on earth—namely the *parousia.*

Logres, which medieval authors did not localize geographically, has become a spiritual landscape in the writings of Charles Williams, one whose main characteristic is geometrical order. But order is not seen as a value in itself, rather, it stands as a sign for the sacred, directing us to God, the operation of whose Providence is revealed in the harmony of mathematical and geometrical symbols. According to Williams, religion is to be expressed in terms of mathematical clarity, whose contours are clearly visible. Sin is seen accordingly as the destruction of an ordered pattern or structure, the derangement of God's plans through man.[25]

Logres with its hierarchical order and rationality thus refers to an ordered universe, for which it can stand as an index in the same way as the human body stands for the Empire. But *Logres* is only a passing realization of an ideal society, the creation of a happy moment in time, and thus vulnerable and instable. It is dependent upon human cooperation with the overall plan. When selfless love is lacking and man makes himself the centre of this world, chaos breaks in: "Things fall apart, the centre cannot hold."[26]

Compared with Malory's account of the dissolution of the Round Table and of the Arthurian world, that is to say the destruction of secular power, the dimensions have been expanded by Williams. They remind us of Milton and of his representation of the fall of mankind.[27] Heaven and earth are joined in a new mythic kingdom which is by no means unreal because it lacks historical existence, nor is it merely an archetypical description of an utopian *Phantastikón*. It is far more a representation of man's situation in this world, and therefore of universal validity even for modern man. Besides its historical applicability, the myth shaped by Williams has a life of its own, and this is what gives it meaning and depth.

In much the same way as he transforms the world of King Arthur, Williams also presents the world of the Grail in a form not previously found in English literature. Perhaps we could say that the legend of the Grail had never been given adequate poetic treatment in English literature before Charles Williams. Besides the insignificant work of Henry Lovelich,[28] there are five further English treatments of the early history of the Grail which must already have been known in England by 1250, as an interpolation in *De Antiquitate Glastoniensis Ecclesiae*[29] shows. The oldest of the versions which have been preserved is a fragment contained in the alliterative poem *Joseph of Arimathia*.[30] The *Queste del Saint Graal*,[31] however, is only found in English in Thomas Malory's *Morte Darthur*,[32] which Charles Williams evidently used as a major source.

Malory had little sympathy for the secret of the Grail and its mystic function.[33] Spiritual knighthood was far less important to him than worldly glory and honour. And yet it is not necessarily a contradiction that his entire account of the Quest follows his sources more closely than the remaining parts of his work. He adopts only the matter *(matière),* while at the same time changing the *sens* entirely. The transcendental goal of the Quest was meant to direct the knight away from his entanglement in the earthly code of honour towards the true purpose of life. Malory, however, makes the Grail an integral part of his world of knighthood,[34] a fact which Williams seems to have overlooked. The hierarchical world of values of the French prose version culminates in Galahad, a saintly Christ-like figure, from whom even adventures retreat to allow him free passage. Although he belongs to the court of Arthur and to the Round Table, his true home and destiny is the mythic Sarras, and in place of jousting and tournaments his mission is the Grail. And yet the French author never doubts the fact that Galahad is the best knight in the world, far better than all the others. Malory, however, in sharp contrast to his sources, insists on the fact that Lancelot was a better knight than his son Galahad. In this way Malory has basically secularized his source. Through the figure of Lancelot he places spiritual knighthood on an equal footing with secular knighthood. The Quest becomes one knightly adventure among many others.[35]

Malory's attitude towards the Quest of the Grail is by no means to be seen as the failing of an individual author who is far too earth-bound. On the contrary, such a reaction to the Quest of the Grail seems to be wide-spread, even today, in England and everywhere else in the world. The Grail seems to have become a stumbling stone for modern man, who is no longer capable of appreciating the ascetic ideal of life. John W. Donald-son, one of the more recent editors of Malory, has thus omitted the Quest entirely. He justifies this step by pointing out that this part of the story ev-idently stems from monastic interpolation and cannot be reconciled with the spirit of knighthood. In his eyes, the ideals of chastity and atonement are completely foreign elements, alien to the tenor of the narrative. Don-aldson's conclusion is that this leads to completely false conceptions of Arthur and his knights.[36] In a similar manner, Tennyson had portrayed the Quest of the Grail as the adventure of the three mystics Galahad, Perceval and Bors, one which was instigated by the ecstatic visions of holy virgins. The Round Table, and with it common man, had no part in the Grail.[37]

Charles Williams is acquainted with such ideas. He has Mordred, the traitor and cynic, say: "My father often thought about the value of the Grail for his salvation; but I can do without such fairy mechanisms. Should something like the Grail really exist, which is hardly likely, I shall send a dozen of my knights in order to destroy it."[38]

For Williams, the Grail is no theatrical prop, but rather a tangible spiritual power. A large portion of his later poetry is aimed at restoring the Grail to its proper position, an undertaking which was certainly coura-geous, if not very promising.

Williams goes about his task as a scholar and a poet. His prose work *The Figure of Arthur* shows an astounding knowledge of the nearly over-whelming store of Arthurian secondary literature. His hypothesis on the origin of the Grail is unequivocal and, it must be admitted, reveals a cer-tain amount of prejudice. Whether the Grail be a chalice or a bowl or some other kind of vessel, its first appearance in European literature is bound up with the Sacred Host. Chretién's Grail has no connection with the Celtic fairy-tale vessel or Cauldron of Plenty. It provides food not for the body, but for the soul. Thus Williams regards the Grail as a ciborium containing the Holy Bread of the Eucharist.[39] In contrast to the versions of Malory and Tennyson, it does not serve a small elite, but is destined for all mankind.

Williams sees the wound of the Fisher-King as a physical and spiri-tual hurt suffered by the entire human race. Naturally he does not ignore the sexual connotations of the wound; but he places them in proper perspective by viewing them in terms of their symbolic and allegorical value. The reader acquainted with his poems is led immediately to think of Jerusalem and its significance in the myth of the organic body, an analogy which provides a deeper understanding of what happens in the Castle of the Grail.[40]

Perceval's failure is attributed by Williams to an inner feeling of guilt which forbids him to approach the sanctuary. The reason first given by Chrétien—respect for the advice of Gournemant—is disregarded by Williams as being too minor. Perceval's guilt is far more to be seen in his cruel impatience towards his mother, in a natural, unreflected and unholy impulse, in short: in natural sin.

Williams goes on to treat the various continuations of Chrétien's unfinished narrative, whose main contribution to the legend of the Grail lies in the combination and sublimation of images already present. The combination of the Grail and the Bleeding Lance with Christian tradition is clearly evident in these authors, as well as the great benefit which Perceval's question might have meant for the country. A new element is to be seen in the introduction of the Waste Land motif to the myth, a concept originally pagan, according to which natural fertility is dependent upon the sexual potency of the ruler. The wound of the Fisher-King is explained by the Dolorous Blow of the sword, which gains supreme importance in Williams' new version of the myth as a symbol of original sin. Williams attributes similar importance to the visit of the entire Round Table to the Grail Castle on the occasion of Perceval's coronation. Here we see an Arthurian world given a dynamic orientation towards a new spiritual centre.

The last version of the Grail story discussed by Williams is *Perlesvaus*. It is easy to see why Williams took such an interest in this particular work. Its exposition conveys the impression that Arthur and the Grail are to be combined in a single story. In order to restore his lost reputation, Arthur rides through the land in search of adventure. In the chapel of a hermitage he experiences the mystery of the Eucharist. He has a vision of a beautiful woman on the altar with a child upon her knee. While the Hermit celebrates Mass, the child is transformed into the Man of Sorrows with a crown of thorns upon his head. Arthur sees himself in this figure, and pity draws tears to his eyes. Immediately Christ is retransformed into the child, and with the *ite missa est* the vision and the light which framed it are extinguished. Full of new resolutions, Arthur returns to Cardoil and promises Guinevere that he will do the will of God from that time onward.

At this point, according to Williams, Arthur has come as close to the mystery as he ever will. In no other version is the king accorded such measure of grace, with the exception perhaps of Galahad's appearance at the royal court in Malory. A fusion of the two worlds, however, does not take place. The world of the Grail and the Arthurian world hardly come in contact in *Perlesvaus.* Williams, however, saw the combination of these two subjects as his major task.

II

The poem on the calling of Taliessin to his vocation is contained in the volume of poetry entitled *The Region of the Summer Stars,* which for the most part was composed later than the poems in the previous volume *Taliessin Through Logres.* Both taken together compose the Arthuriad of Williams: ". . .in general the argument of the series is the expectation of the return of Our Lord by means of the Grail and the establishment of the kingdom of Logres (or Britain) to this end by the powers of the Empire and Broceliande."[41]

According to the chronology of the Arthurian kingdom, *The Calling of Taliessin* forms the beginning of the cycle. Here the poet and seer Taliessin[42] learns in a dream vision of the establishment of the Kingdom of Logres in which he is to play a part. It is true that he cannot understand the full connotations of his task because he is still too much involved in the druidism and magic lore of his native land; and yet he is faintly aware of the greatness of his mission, the enormous appeal of the ideas of Byzantium and of the Grail. On the other hand, he also sees the possibility of the fall of Logres, even if it is only a vague premonition. Thus at the very beginning of Taliessin's way to Byzantium, the fate of Arthur's realm is foreshadowed.

The poem *The Calling of Taliessin* begins in the style of the *Mabinogion* with the description of the origin of Taliessin. No one knows from whom the poet and seer is descended. The beginnings of poetry and prophecy are veiled in clouded darkness. But already the discovery of the infant Taliessin in a weir of the River Wye is a kind of sign for everything that is to follow. Subtle associations and the use of anticipation and innuendo recall biblical parallels, many of them barely noticeable for the reader at first and only fully understandable after the whole has been read. Taliessin is carried down the river in a willow basket covered with leather, and is brought to land by King Elphin. He is thus comparable to the Hebrew *Mosheh,* for this name means: one drawn out of the water.

What Moses was for the people of the Jews, Taliessin is to become for Logres and for Britain.

King Elphin is rooted in paganism and the bloody handiwork of war; his connection with poetry is limited to a hearty song after the feast. And nevertheless he accepts the gift of the river, and the child has already begun to sing: on the druidic lore of reincarnation, on the preordained law of transformation whose circle begins with fish and ends again with fish, namely: ". . . from shapes that eat / to shapes that are eaten, and then to the fish split / to be at once on the dish and again in the sea."[43]

This law of Karma rules Taliessin, and with him the entire pagan world; for God has not yet led them into the land of the Trinity and set them free. And yet as much as this senseless movement back to the point of departure might seem a closed circle, it is rather a sign of something new and final, the perfection of the cycle of destiny and therewith the liberation and emancipation of the individual. Bread and fish recall the mystery of the Eucharist of which Williams says: ". . . they were eaten, yet they themselves received the eater into themselves; they were separate, yet they were one."[44] This is almost certainly the antitype of the "shapes that eat / to shapes that are eaten." The metamorphosis which takes place under the law of Karma as a historical or mythical reality serves at the same time as a prototype, which is later fulfilled in the Christian Empire of Byzantium. The mystic sense of the pagan world is to be seen in such prototypes, which foreshadow the Empire to come, even if it is only in the unconscious song of a poet who has not yet attained maturity as a prophet.

The account of Taliessin's childhood and youth is likewise full of allusion, anticipation and connotation. It is Williams' myth of the rise of poetic genius.[45] Again we have an interlacing of various threads, motifs and types of the poetic message; the individual tones of the son echo in a chord of exotic harmony. The point of departure is the Celtic image of the Cauldron of Ceridwen, from which the art of poetry spills forth. Superimposed upon this, however, is a kind of cosmic story of the Muse whose origins are unknown. Taliessin was already at the Throne of God when the world was created. His spirit moved over the waters during the flood, and it ascended into the third heaven, his true home, where the summer stars shine—symbols of the eternal ideas. Here we hear an echo of William Blake's *Songs of Experience:* "Hear the voice of the bard, who Present, Past and Future sees," and yet there is a clearly Christian accent. Although he has not yet found the formula of the Empire, the pillar of Christianity, Taliessin has a premonition of the coming liberation from the cycle of destiny, although, for the time being, merely in the form of vague correspondences and similarities.

Taliessin lives not only on a physical plane, but also in the poetic breath of the spirit, and life and knowledge coalesce in the trinity of verse, again a typological image which creates anticipation in the poem and sets a new pole, a new focal centre for the action and for the thoughts of the reader: "I was thrall to Ceridwen and free in the manger of an ass"[46]— mysterious connotations of Bethlehem and the salvation and rebirth of mankind. Thus the personality of the poet comes into focus as the individual vessel of the Muse who transforms man, makes him a tool and thereby raises him above his kind. At the same time, however, she makes the poet a chimera, neither fish nor fowl, so terribly divided from other men that no woman can love him, a man still heard by scholars but no longer heeded, a man closer to the dead than to the living.

The Empire (and here this means Christendom) is at first unknown to Taliessin, save in the form of mysterious and vague allusions. Minor external objects are explained to him, the pantry of the monks, the bread and beans of the hermits, the outer shells of symbols whose significance Taliessin senses because he knows the laws of correspondence. But one day he learns of the Kingdom of God and of its history on earth, of the original sin of Adam and the salvation of mankind through Christ, whose unbelievable, all-comprehending love transformed the tree of Adam into the cross of crucifixion. According to an early Christian legend, Paradise and Mount Calvary were both located in the same place, called *medium terrae*.[47] This is where creation began, and here Adam was born and reborn. And the wood of the cross, according to the same legend, was that of the tree of Adam. The message which reaches Taliessin is only fragmentary and vague, but nevertheless it suffices to make everything he has heard so far appear black and white magic (*goety,* black magic and *theurgy,* white magic). Even the poetry of the pagan world appears shabby in comparison with the shadowy dream of the Empire, whose component parts materialize from the imagination of the poet, take on the semblance of a human body, a microcosm which mirrors in itself all aspects of the Empire. The seed has been sown in Taliessin's heart. His thirst has been awakened for the metaphysics of salvation. He wants to learn more about it than he can gather on the River Wye. For this reason he departs for Byzantium, the image of the City of God.

Taliessin's way leads him along the western coast of England towards the Channel. On his left lies the waste land that is one day to become Logres, and on his right the wood and the sea of Broceliande, the mysterious realm of making, the *Apeiron,* home of Nimue who shapes all earthly things according to their celestial ideas. Beyond Broceliande lies the castle of the Grail, and beyond that the holy land of Sarras. Broceliande is borderland, the realm between the here and the beyond, and thus known only to the elect. No one returns unchanged from this land— some come again as saints, others as empty-headed prattlers who unashamedly preach their metaphysics as if it were gospel. Taliessin only passes through the outer fringes of the wood, and yet his soul is seized by fear and doubt. In the face of the monumental task which lies before him he very nearly despairs: "dividing word from thing and uniting thing to word," that is the separation of the word or concept from the archetypes of celestial truths, and the fusion of these words with their natural objects on Earth in poetic images and symbols.

While he waits, trying to gather himself, he is approached by a shining form which divides into two parts, and becomes a man and a woman—Merlin and Brisen, "time and space, duration and extension." They come from Broceliande and intend to establish a kingdom in Logres in which Byzantium and Broceliande will be united. We hear about the kingdom for the first time in this passage, and we know no more than Taliessin what it is all about. But like the poet we sense that in Logres the divine mystery will take form, that the creation of the perfect man is to take place. Taliessin is not granted more knowledge than that. He must be happy if his spirit can comprehend the space which divides him from Carbonek. He is not allowed to enquire after Sarras, for he has not yet been to Byzantium and is thus still in the stage of the Druid poet who can sense parallels and analogies but is earth-bound by nature and cannot yet participate in the *Feeling Intellect.*

With a cosmic image of sublime beauty, Williams introduces the mysterious magic of Merlin and Brisen. The day draws to a close, the sun sinks to the Antipodes, and the Earth casts its conic shadow into space.[48]

This image is taken from the *Divine Comedy, Paradiso* IX. 118.[49] According to Dante's view (indeed according to medieval astronomy in general), the universe is entirely lighted by the sun. Night is caused by the cone-shaped shadow cast by the Earth. Because the Earth stands at the centre of the universe and the sun revolves around it, we must imagine Earth's shadow moving like the rotating hand of a clock.[50] It reaches no further than the sphere of Venus, thus darkening only the inner planetary heavens, whose spheres according to Dante symbolize the lower levels of imperfect holiness still tinged with earthliness. Williams likewise allows the point of the cone to reach the sphere of Venus, but at this point the image loses its concrete form and dissolves into an abstract concept. The third heaven, as Williams emphasises, is nonspatial: this must definitely be seen as a conscious device of the poet, who always takes the material world as his point of departure, only to pass over to the abstract ideal. In the case in question, the reader is additionally struck by the suspicion that the medieval model of the universe composed of spheres with the Earth at its centre must, for obvious reasons, be disguised. For naturally Williams knew that Earth's shadow could not fall in the sphere of Venus, which is nearer to the sun than the Earth.

The transformation of the image into an abstract one distracts from the geocentrical orientation of the model which forms the basis for Williams' thought and poetry. This becomes particularly clear in *The Coming of Galahad*. In *The Calling of Taliessin,* Williams was less concerned with the idea of an ordered universe, than with the opposition between idea and reality. For him the third heaven is the non-spatial home of likewise non-spatial ideas, according to whose archetypes Nimue creates objects and living beings on Earth. The sphere of Venus is transformed into a Platonic realm of celestial love and beauty, and the light of the ideas which have their home here is seen when the sun sinks, and all earthly things, the images of the ideas, are cast into invisibility. This is when Merlin and Brisen are able to hear the activity of the *Feeling Intellect* as a faint humming at the point of the conic shadow, a sign of the coming establishment of Logres and the advent of Sarras.

Taliessin does not understand the magic formula itself, and he experiences it only half-consciously as within a dream. Fate is determined by space and time (Brisen and Merlin), and the seer can only perceive it and portray it. Merlin marks the magic pentagram on the floor, the Druidic sign which was regarded as a symbol of perfection by the Platonists, Pythagoreans and Gnostics. Under Merlin's hands the flames of potential intellect rise up, and much in the same way as the shadow of Earth falls into space, reaching the third heaven, and darkness renders the ideas visible, so the shadow of Brisen falls upon Logres, which is still waste land waiting for the advent of Sarras. The images of celestial ideas are not yet evident.

Only the accidentals of the magic act sink into Taliessin's heart. He does not yet understand the substance of the magic. And yet its connotations suffice to give him an idea of the sequence of coming events and of his own mission. At first he only sees Brisen's back: she stares into the fire as if in a hypnotic trance. The flames throw red signs on her back, which for Taliessin is slowly transformed into snow-covered mountains—as can only happen in a dream. At first he sees the mountains in the ruby light of the fire, then the dreamer sees green meadows and steep mountain passes, and he sees himself as a wanderer in this landscape. He crosses the Apennine Mountains, and sails across the Caspian Sea in a storm. Brisen's back thus becomes a landscape in the dream of the poet, a world which as a macrocosm contains all the counterparts of the qualities and features of the human body, which can serve as an index for it. Each part of the land must be sought out by Taliessin in his search for wisdom.

Suddenly and unexpectedly a city is seen on the coast, bright and lovely beyond words, illuminated by rays of a mystic sun. Both city and light lie beyond the reach of Taliessin's dream. Poetry cannot reach that far, not even in a dream. Shortly before the final goal, the shining ray of glory is hidden from the poet by a cloud and becomes again the back of Brisen, which Williams calls "recapitulatory." Again the focus shifts from Brisen's back to the shadows that fall on Logres, and now Taliessin sees the stones in the waste land burst into light and shine like the summer stars—hope and anticipation of the fruitful union of Carbonek and Caerleon.

Taliessin, entangled in the pagan codex of the purely factual, can only take part in Merlin's magic through the medium of a dream vision. And yet from accidental details the seer and the reader are able to gain a glimpse of the Empire. The metamorphosis of the images takes place with dreamlike ease, and transitions, as in dreams, are often motivated by a single feature, such as the ruby colour of the fire as a *tertium comparationis* to completely unrelated and unvisualised objects, which develop according to a law of their own from images already present. Brisen's back becomes a snow-covered mountain, the Apennines, the Caspian Sea at the foot of the Caucasus, and once again the body of Brisen. The light of the magic flame in the pentagram is transformed to firelight on the snow-covered mountains, to the light of Sarras which originates from suns beyond the sun, then becomes the shining glory of deepest truth, and once again is transformed back to the gentle flickering fire of Merlin.

And yet we never have the impression that metaphors are manipulated at will; indeed there is never the slightest suspicion of intentional vagueness and mysteriousness on the side of the poet. The key image, that of the "recapitulatory body," acts as an aid towards easy comprehension of the poetic message, which does not attempt more clarity for the simple reason that it is not based on facts or logical concepts, but rather on visionary premonitions.

Although the summer stars disappear the next morning with the dawning of light, the world (Logres) has changed. Dawn is seen in the rosy hue of porphyry, like the imperial stairway, the womb of woman, or the *largesse* of the emperor. And yet, for a short while, there is a new focal point in Logres, the eye of the storm which has devoured all the summer stars, as tiny as can be, but lit from within like the egg of a glow-worm. It is the light of the three-fold Trinity, the symbol of the task now given to Taliessin by Merlin: go to Byzantium! Taliessin hears and un-derstands Merlin. His eyes fall on Brisen, and again her shadow is trans-formed, this time to an immense monumental stairway which leads from the brain (Logres) down to the base (Broceliande). The way from the Forest of Making and Shaping to Camelot is free. Above all, however, Carbonek can now be brought to Logres, and thus the king awaits the ad-vent of the Trinity on the topmost peak of the stairway.

The idea that the salvation and perfection of mankind should take place in Britain is not a private mythology of Williams, but has a long his-tory of development.[51] In the words of William Blake, who is spiritually very much akin to Charles Williams, we read in *Jerusalem* (pl. 27): "All things Begin and End in Albions Ancient Druid Rocky Shore . . . You have a tradition, that Man anciently contain in his mighty limbs all things in Heaven and Earth: this you received *(sic)* from the Druids. But now the Starry Heavens are fled from the mighty limbs of Albion."[52] According to Blake, Jerusalem is the emanation of the giant Albion, and Britain the first home of patriarchal religion, and therefore the original Holy Land.

Taliessin sees himself as a poet and singer at the foot of the throne of the Dragon. The entire court stares out upon the sea and sees a ship, ap-parently from Sarras, carrying the Grail which rests in the hands of Helayne, the daughter of the Grail king. In order not to divulge the se-cret, Williams uses the device of a dream within a dream: Taliessin finds himself suddenly aboard ship; and there, in a state of ecstasy, he senses the nature of the object concealed under the saffron yellow cloth. Shortly after this, however, his limbs lose their stiffness, and still caught up in the dream he sees himself in the magic pentagram. The stairway gradually disappears from sight, and those that stood at its top fly into empty space together with the throne of the Dragon—a psychologically subtle, even superb account of gradual awakening from a deep dream.

Taliessin appears to be unable to detach himself from the vision. He is still caught up in it, but his intellect cannot encompass its imaginative world. He dozes in half-consciousness, and again he receives Merlin's command: son of the bard, go to Byzantium! He and Brisen have already taken the possible failure of the Empire into account, and have conse-quently kept their rite ambivalent. Already there is a gentle undertone of approaching catastrophe, the first signs of disaster, namely the downfall of Logres, which cannot come up to the demanding task. And yet Merlin has taken precautions against even this eventuality. Taliessin will lead his followers in Logres along the same spiritual paths marked by Galahad, the chosen one of the Grail. This concludes the poem, and each one goes his way: Brisen to Carbonek, Merlin to Camelot and Taliessin to Byzantium.

The spiritual tension of the poem is marked by the poles of light and darkness. But they do not form a simple symbolic equation: light for truth and wisdom, and darkness for falsehood and ignorance. On the contrary, the light of the idea can only shine when it has become dark on Earth, when the hard and sober light of the sun, which Williams (like Wordsworth) associates with the negative connotations of human *ratio,* has been extinguished, when a shadow is cast on the object of perception, thus enabling it to shine of its own accord. Paradoxically, it is Earth itself which casts its shadow upon things and into space, thus enabling the summer stars of the ideas to shine. The concrete image of Earth and its spatial extension is Brisen. Her shadow falls upon Logres, and the land which is at first dark begins to shine in a reflection of the stars mirrored again in the waste land—an earthly equivalent of the cosmic darkening of space through the conic shadow of Earth, and of the shining of the summer stars which is thereby made possible.

Alongside this polarity, and at the same time interpenetration of light and darkness, we find the image of the waste land, a key symbol for both Charles Williams and T. S. Eliot. Logres has not yet achieved the state of perfect order. It is not lack of water which makes the land a waste land, nor sterility and infertility, but rather the anarchy of civil war, the lack of law and order. Logres is still wilderness, it has not yet taken on the form of *res publica,* for its members are still in a state of strife. Automatically the reader thinks of: "Omne regnum in se ipsum divisum desolabitur."[53] Waste land for Williams means egotism, isolation and autonomy expressed through the image of barter or communication made impossible. The opposite pole is represented by the harmonious integration of the individual in the greater organic whole. Such an integration is only possible by means of *largesse* and exchange, concretely symbolised by the wagon and the ship at the Golden Horn, by human interaction and exchange. The individual states and kingdoms are not autonomous; they belong together in the same way that the limbs and organs of the body do, and what connects them with one another is *largesse* and exchange. But this is not presented to us as a general principle; it is demonstrated in an exemplary way by Taliessin, who, before he can learn to think in Merlin's style, must first travel many miles through the Empire. Only "ranging the themes," that is to say, travelling through the provinces of the Empire, will lead him to comprehend the organic unity of the world, and enable him to fulfil his role in it.

The image of the waste land is connected with the idea of Advent. Logres and the world await salvation on the border of Broceliande and Sarras, whence the Trinity is to come. The Grail carried by Helayne is a symbol of Divine Love, which is to bring about the birth of perfect man on earth. It is the symbol of *parousia,* the Second Advent of Christ, and therewith of God's Kingdom on earth.

Taliessin appears to us as a visible embodiment of the metaphysical drive of man, which Williams has portrayed in a way far more subtle, complex and many-sided than other modern poets. Taliessin's function as a servant of both the Empire and the advent of Sarras causes his own development and significance to recede into the background. He may be a pagan, but at the same time he is *anima naturaliter christiana,* a man in quest of truth, relentless and uncompromising to the point of total self-annihilation. In addition, however, Taliessin is a poet who knows the images and the facts behind them, and who with the help of the law of correspondences senses the spiritual connections. His true home is the realm of ideas, the third heaven of the summer stars where "unriven truths" dwell. As poet and *vates* he has known the world from the beginning and has a right to be heard, not because of his greater knowledge, but because he has literally experienced the doctrine of *largesse* and because he knows the theory of exchange, according to which each of us can and must bear the burden of others.[54]

Taliessin's followers are enslaved of their own free will: they enter the obligation on the basis of a decision of conscience and a vow, and thus their position is higher than that of the poet of the king, who has received his faith through grace.

Taliessin can preserve the image of Divine Love in his heart, even if Logres should fall. He will continue to have his following in the land, which will then be called Britain, and all those who live in love will belong to his following. And thus the poem of the *Calling of Taliessin* concludes on an almost hesitant note of resignation. Mankind "shall follow in Logres and Britain the spiritual roads". What binds these men together, however, and what remains after the fall of Logres, is only love, that is to say *largesse* or *caritas.*

III

The manner in which a call to the royal court or to the service of the Queen is issued is shown in *The Queen's Servant,* a difficult poem, but one of poignant beauty. Its appeal and charm lie in its conceptual terseness, its delight in magic ritual and metamorphosis. The poem sparkles with hidden energy and dynamism, and yet at the same time it relays an impression of static, almost liturgical ceremoniousness. Its beauty and charm appear to be closely akin to the baroque pomp of a high feast—they are like the scent of incense and the sound of organ music for the senses of those readers who cannot grasp the rational meaning of such intricate complexity, but who are nevertheless moved by sensual impressions, and have much the same effect as that of murmured Latin psalms, only half-understood, in a Church service.

The poem's point of departure is a letter of the seneschal Kay to Taliessin with the request to send an intelligent girl to court to serve the Queen. She must be equal to high demands: to be able to read and translate Greek, as well as to plant a rose garden, to know court ceremonial, and to understand the great art of imaginative poetry as well. The reader may be troubled in so far as he is accustomed to associating Guinevere and her sinful love with the Queen—an association which does not correspond to the intention of the poet. [55] There is still a hope of *parousia* in which the Arthurian Empire and the royal court are to play a role. This is the task for which the servant of the Queen is called from Taliessin's household to court. She is to provide a connection to the emperor in Byzantium, that is to the *civitas,* to serve Order on the spiritual plane. She is to care for it and cultivate it in the analogy of the rose garden. This double task demands a "grand art" from her in the same manner as that possessed by the poet Taliessin. Above all it is a task which could not be entrusted to a slave. Whoever is to fulfill such an important function at court must possess the complete freedom of the Children of God. In *The Queen's Servant* we learn of the emancipation of the individual from the chains of natural concupiscence, and of the vocation and preparation for a spiritual task.

Taliessin has one of his trusted servants who is still a slave come to him, and he sets her free with a laconic word: '"Now be free". The slave's reaction is all but enthusiastic. Rather sarcastically she answers: "So! Freedom, I see, is the final task of servitude." Which is as much to say, unasked for, undesired freedom is just as repressive, perhaps even more of a burden, than the service of a bondsman. One freed in this manner has to pay the ransom of her own liberation, though it is with a golden coin she has received from Taliessin. The slave knows that her liberation is not a matter of social status, but that Taliessin has signed the warrant which frees her from the entanglement of the senses and the body, thus discarding the old Adam. From this it follows that Taliessin acts as a type of Christ in these poems. The slave is commissioned to put on the new Adam, and thereby to leave behind her the barbaric status of servitude in favour of human perfection in a Christian sense and service in freedom.

Taliessin himself bought the slave in a district of Caucasia. In the anatomic myth of Williams, Caucasia means chastity and fertility of the human body, youthful freshness and the virginal unapproachability of the young girl, physical animality which forms the basis of human life; it is at the same time the location of Prometheus' martyrdom. Caucasia is therefore less a specific part of the body than the entire human body in all its naturalness: joy, energy, beauty, health, in short: the old Adam, though for the present only nature, and thus still egocentric and not yet capable of taking on the transcendental. In the organic harmony of the human limbs and their spotless beauty, Caucasia mirrors the ideal order of Byzantium as well as all that is natural. To the natives of Caucasia, however, this transcendental beauty is hidden; they do not perceive the symbolism of their country's miracles, the lambs in the rose gardens, the shining snow flakes on the golden fleece of the landscape.

A prerequisite for this is an overview of the provinces of the Empire, but above all the knowledge of Byzantium and of the Imperial Palace whose throne room symbolises the omnipresence of God. All creation and therewith all themes of the realm are ultimately an expression and reflection of this central unity. The direct vision of the idea, however, is reserved for the visitor to Byzantium. Outside of the throne room there are images and symbols whose significance is only clear to those who know the idea. Only through the transcendental can the natural be understood; only intellect knows that it knows.

The slave has never been in Byzantium and will probably never reach it. But she is capable of grasping the referential character of her body intellectually—through the study of metaphysical books or through Merlin's maps, or even through the mysterious little book from the library of the emperor. But there is an easier and quicker approach: man becomes capable of receiving the transcendental when he puts off the old Adam. "Unclothe" is the command which Taliessin gives to the slave, and therewith she stands before him in the immaculate beauty of her shining nakedness. Taliessin gazes at the organic unity of beauteous soul in beauteous body, and in it he sees a premonition of the prayer of the nun Dindrane and the benediction of Galahad.

As in *The Calling of Taliessin,* the body of the woman is transformed under the meditative stare of Taliessin into the world. A few hints lead us to conclude that Taliessin's eyes rest on the back of the maiden, and that this in turn becomes identical with the shadow of Caucasia, in which the tiny but clearly visible shadow of Byzantium blossoms, and even the meadows of Sarras beyond the sea. This second metamorphosis of the human back excludes the possibility of a coincidental play on images, and this applies to *The Calling of Taliessin* as well. In my opinion, this is Williams' central metaphor. The human body is in itself a microcosm, which is simultaneously a reflection of the greater world and a world in itself. The term alone implies the existence of a macrocosm with similar features and qualities. Williams expresses the universe in terms of the image of the human body, which not only serves as a major symbol of the poet's concept of life and the world, but also as the focus of his poetic vision.

The origin of the image is possibly to be seen in Exodus XXXIII. 23 which states that Moses may only see the back of God: ". . . and [I] will cover thee with my hand until I have passed by: and I will take away mine hand, and thou shalt see my back: but my face shall not be seen." The back of God is usually interpreted as the material world. Thus Moses experiences in his vision the entirety of the world in an image similar to that seen by his successor Taliessin who reveals parallels to his great predecessor in more than this point. But even the Bible is not alone in this image. We find similar forms in many myths of creation, for instance in the Nordic Song of Ymir, according to which the sea was made from the blood of the arch-giant Ymir, the mountains from his bones, the land from his flesh, the stones from his teeth and the trees from his hair.

The most striking parallel to Williams is to be found in Blake whose giant Albion contained everything in himself before his fall: sun, moon, stars, and sea.[56] Only the imagination is capable of uniting the interior with the exterior in a manner which may even approach the mystical, so that in human society we catch a glimpse of the true presence of the divine body of Christ.[57]

Williams is also concerned with the relation of nature and the transcendental, but they do not represent separate units for him; they are intermingled. Caucasia has cast its shadow on Sarras, and thus rendered it visible like an image or a metaphor which contains its object of reference in a figurative sense in itself. Only when the body of the slave is naked and humbled, is it prepared for the glorious robe of an all-encompassing reality which is given to man with his freedom. In place of her old garb, the girl is given a robe of roses and wool. Only the old girdle is to be retained as a reminder of her former servitude, and as a warning to remain true to her new obligation.[58]

The central image of the poem is the exchange of clothes. It derives from Paul's *Epistle to the Corinthians,* V.4 ff.: "For verily in this we groan, longing to be clothed upon with our habitation which is from heaven: if so be that being clothed we shall not be found naked. For indeed we that are in this tabernacle do groan, being burdened; not for that we would be unclothed, but that we would be clothed upon, that what is mortal may be swallowed up of life . . . Wherefore if any man is in Christ, he is a new creature: the old things are passed away; behold, they are become new." The apostle compares man's earthly body with a temporary tent, the heavenly body with a permanent house. But he wishes to put on the heavenly body in this life, without having to first cross the threshold of death.

The exchange of clothes in Charles Williams can only be understood in the context of the *Epistle to the Corinthians.* It stands for a spiritual metamorphosis, the transition from the status of natural corporality to a new life in the spirit. The poetic metaphor which symbolises this is the cloak of golden lambs' wool and red roses; nor are these just any roses, but rather Caucasian centifoliae. The characteristic of this species is their scarlet colour and the heart-shaped centre of their petals. This is a good example of the way Charles Williams uses metaphors: they glow from within with rich sensuality and yet at the same time they are transformed into an abstract concept which can only be derived from the original image through abstraction and thoughtful reflection. It is much the same as the manner in which the poet Taliessin plucks the string of his harp and immediately grasps it with two fingers to prevent it from resonating further. The scarlet colour of the rose and the shape of the heart, the wool of the symbolic animal, the lamb, all signal the meaning of the clothes and at the same time the metamorphosis of the slave.

The way to sanctification leads through nature, that is through the works of Nimue, who continually shapes the things of this world according to their archetypes in the third heaven. The transformation requires the "rhythms of ceremony," the "grand art," but also grace. By grand art Williams apparently means a sacramental, liturgical art, and by grace the divine power from which art stems. Both are necessary for the sanctification of flesh and blood.

The liberation of the slave ends with an act of exchange, *largesse.* Taliessin imbues her with his entire power and energy, and there is a genuine exchange of qualities and features. Williams believed quite literally in the possibility of such a substitution. He not only rediscovered the doctrine of the Atonement and reinterpreted it back into art and experience; he was also convinced that each of us could take upon himself the burden of another, and, in turn, share his energy and power with his neighbour.[59] "Substitutionary love transcends the 'fallacy of rational virtue' which says we are judged by our own works—*only*."[60] The power of Taliessin pours into the slave in a blast of union. This blast means both a union of nature and spirit, as well as the descent of the Spirit, the experience of the Divine. Through this the slave has become an equal of Taliessin, she henceforth belongs to Taliessin's Society. "Be as Ourself in Logres." This command is valid to death, even beyond death, for afterwards there can be no fear of death but only yearning for the beyond, as we read in St. Paul.

The ceremonial conclusion of the act of liberation is thus to be seen as a kind of confirmation *(confirmatio)* which finds expression in the blow to the cheek. This detail originates from the Roman ceremony of the freeing of prisoners, but here it carries the additional sense of making one strong for the battle of life, but last not least also the kind of salvation "after the kind of Christ and the order of Logres." The central idea of the poem is God:

"Depart, with God," She said: "Remain, in God."

IV

The girl from Caucasia is called to the royal court. Although she is liberated and belongs to Taliessin's following, she is still a child in a spiritual sense and thus in constant danger of a relapse. With *The Coming of Galahad,* however, the new Adam comes to Arthur's court. Mysterious things happen which cause everyone to recognise that the prophecies of the arrival of the Chosen One are about to be fulfilled: Galahad takes his seat at the Round Table, the famous *Siège Périlleux,* without being swallowed up by the earth, as his unworthy predecessors had been. The knights receive from the Grail everything they wish in the way of food and drink, and the water Galahad washes his hands with glitters and sparkles like a thousand stars. At the close of the evening the knight of the Grail is led to Arthur's bed in a ceremonial procession. He, takes possession of it after a mysterious rite: the New Adam takes the place of the Old.[61]

We view all this with Taliessin as outsiders from the perspective of servants and kitchen-boys. The king's poet has not joined the procession. He passes through offices and kitchens to the exterior courtyard, from where he views the torch-lit procession to the king's bed seen through the windows of towers and halls: "He stood looking up among the jakes and latrines," and even the nursery rhyme which he sings to his own

accompaniment on the harp contains the descending motion which we
have just passed through with the poet:

> Down the porphyry stair the queen's child ran,
> There he played with his father's crown . . .

We have already reached the lowest point of descent, for we stand in
the outer courtyard before the latrines and therewith at the outer point of
Williams' organic and physiological symbolism. This is where the discussion between Taliessin, Gareth and a slave takes place, and its topic is
"preference," the hierarchy of Logres and the significance of Galahad,
the keeper of the Grail: "Lord, tell me of the new knight!" "What man is
this for whom the emperor lifts the Great Ban?" For Williams the answer
to this question was particularly important, since it was decisive for the
values and meanings of his own philosophy of life. Religion, philosophy,
poetry, love: each of these represented a closed, autonomous world for
him, one which resisted integration into an overall structure.

Taliessin sings the Song of Songs for Galahad. He has no doubt that
this knight stands at the top of the world hierarchy and that he is justified
in taking his place in Arthur's bed. But Taliessin sings among the jakes
and latrines, he stands at the other end of the scale, among human excre-
ment which reminds him and others of the fact that the flight to the mysterious heights of the Grail must start from the basis of human nature,
and that all paths to the realm must lead through the door of man's animality. I would see the jakes as a first hint of man's feet of clay—his
weakness and proneness to error, and thus a premonition of the eventual
failure of a union of Camelot and Carbonek.

The poem of *The Coming of Galahad* is dominated by the symbolism of stone and shell which Williams has taken from Wordsworth's *Prelude*. The fifth book of this work begins with a dream of the poet. In the
midst of a desert, a mounted Bedouin appears bearing a stone in one
hand, in the other a shell of exquisite beauty. The stone stands for the
doctrine of Euclid, geometry, and the shell for poetical song, poetry. The
stone and shell become the poles of Williams' thought, and symbolise for
him order and life, Byzantium and Broceliande, Nimue and the third
heaven. Stone and shell are fused, and become one in the person of Galahad. He is the image of the new Adam and an example of the necessary
union of the realms of Arthur and the Grail in Logres.

Taliessin believes that he has seen the union in five different houses:
in poetry; in the life of the senses and of the body; in the intellect; in reli-

gion; and in the imaginative vision (Byzantium), and even in double form in each house. Intellectual Gaul requires the shell in order to reach perfection; corporeal Caucasia requires the stone. All the houses are intimately connected with each other, each is autonomous, but requires the other to give and receive validity and permanence. It seems to me that Taliessin speaks a clear and understandable language at this point. He sees the five houses transformed into the triangle of the pentagram which before had played such a great role in Merlin's magic as a symbol of perfection.

The direct source of Williams and thus the key to a better understanding of his imagery may well be seen in the Middle English romance *Sir Gawain and the Green Knight,* in which Gawain carries the pentagram as a heraldic symbol on his shield. The allegorical meaning of this symbol rests in the idea of the "endless knot," so named because the star is composed of an unbroken connection of five lines which, when traced, lead right back to the point of departure. Taliessin traces the lines of the pentagram with his finger, and the individual significance of the houses is lost from sight. One dissolves into another. Taliessin's skill fails him, for it is only adequate for the single categories. In the pentagram, however, they are submerged in a single identity.

The recognition of identity is made possible by the fusion of shell and stone, the creation of a new quality. Logres likewise can only gain its identity from a similar synthesis. At first, the dual character of truly fulfilled existence is to be observed in each individual house. Lewis describes the first and foremost task of life as: "to 'fit' the stone and the shell in whatever House you occupy, to retain poetic vision in the midst of hard thinking, to study 'precision' in your highest poetry, to offer even to the *body* of the beloved a 'Euclidean love.' "[62]

But the balance achieved in this way is only valid in the individual house, and this is not the end of the task. The category province remains an organic part of the Empire, that is to say of the higher order. True identity can only be achieved by a fusion of the categories with one another: "The clerks of the Emperor's house study the redaction of categories into identity: so we."[63] In the person of Galahad, a shoot of the third heaven has taken root in Logres; the symbol of the pentagram is tailored to fit him. It stands for the fusion of categories to a single identity and therewith transcends Taliessin's comprehension: "What then . . . when the cut hazel has nothing to measure?"[64] The poet is forced to retreat, modest and humble. A new measure must be applied in the future:

> . . . The eyes of my lord are the measure of intensity
> and his arms of action; the hazel, Blanchefleur, he.[65]

The Coming of Galahad concludes with Taliessin's vision of the ascent of the soul to the innermost heaven. Similar to Dante who had seen the planetary spheres in analogy to the different grades of holiness, Williams draws an analogy between the planets and their zones and the spiritual and mental development of man. Four zones divide the Empire from the throne of God and are to be passed through in the development of man and therewith of the City. In the face of a geocentric structure of the universe in *The Calling of Taliessin,* this centripetal movement appears contradictory and illogical.[66] But we must recall that according to Dante and to other medieval authorities spatial order mirrors the spiritual one. According to this view, the earth is located at the outermost fringe of the universe, that is to say before the walls of the City. Man was once the centre of the universe and now stands on its fringes.

The last part of the poem is difficult because the basic concept of the interior part of the courtyard of the palace is meant to stand as a kind of base for the planetarium. Williams says that four zones separate the Empire from the throne of God, and these zones are "slanted to each cleft in each wall, with planets planted." In this we hear an echo of the beginning of the poem: "till he came by a door cleft in a smooth wall." Thus Taliessin stands in the interior courtyard and views the spheres of the planets slanted towards the sightholes in the wall, on the one side Mercury and Venus, on the other Jupiter and Saturn. He himself stands upon the Earth, "seen and strewn by the four." To the careful reader, this passage reveals a correction of the medieval planetarium: Mercury and Venus circulate beneath the Earth around the sun, Jupiter and Saturn are planets with larger orbits. It is possible that Williams superimposed this modern view of the planetary system intentionally upon the original model, not to mystify the reader, but in order to demonstrate that the poetic mode is not tied to the "Discarded Image," but is an appropriate and valid vehicle of the twentieth century and its view of the world. The basis of the poem at any rate is a geocentrical view of the universe. Earth is symbolised by the courtyard, on which the spheres of the individual planets are slanted like the props of a baldachin which rise up to the firmament and direct the meditative gaze of the *Vates* towards the throne of God.

The first step of the ascent is marked by the planet Mercury; it corresponds to the God of Conflict and Change, the as yet undecided state of rivalry among the houses. Venus represents the sphere of the focussing of human thought on a certain goal ("Venus preference"), an interior turning towards a loved one. Jupiter with its moons indicates irony and irony vanquished, which no longer bruises itself on the unavoidable, but accepts the wonderful absurdity of it all and laughs about it. And finally Saturn is the star of loneliness and meditation,[67] of the promise and image of Golden Age.[68] Logres, as Taliessin sees, has only reached the sphere of Jupiter. Here Galahad and Lancelot still live with one another, unrest of the heart and earthliness. Future developments are already anticipated: the huge powers of Broceliande have created Galahad but have exhausted themselves in the act. Logres bows down to Britannia; Carbonek and Camelot are by no means one, but are farther apart than ever before.

V

The poem *The Meditation of Mordred is* far clearer and simpler than the preceding ones. We hear no more of mystic Sarras and of the perfection of man on earth. The subject is now Logres, which is to develop into historical Britain. The aureole of the transcendental gradually recedes, giving way to the naked reality of things which are only reflections and which have lost their tie with the third heaven. Mordred himself is a totally down-to-earth type, one no longer ambivalent but completely autonomous, evil, perverted, and cynical. He is the incestuous son of Arthur, and thus the symbol of destructive egotism which Williams calls Gomorrha.

The reader is not led to judge Mordred on the basis of his deeds, but rather on his state of inner consciousness. The entire poem consists of an interior monologue which makes a brutally open description of the happenings in Logres possible. Mordred is not subject to any restrictions or inhibitions. His thoughts are disjointed and only connected by association. The single law of his psychology is a perverted yearning for recognition, aimed at a paradise in the style of the cruel dictators of the Antipodes.

The names and events are taken from Malory's *Morte Darthur,* which is to be seen as a background for the entire cycle. The date of the events can be fixed through the name of Pope Deodatus, who succeeded Boniface IV and was head of the church from 615 to 618. The introduction of this historical personage into the world of cryptic mythology can be seen as a confirmation of the tendency towards reality. The clouds of phantasy begin to recede, the transcendentally beautiful figures of a long-awaited, imaginatively anticipated *parousia* disappear like swirls of mist before the noon-day sun. The world shows her true face.

The first lines of the poem contain a play on the various meanings of *wood* and *elm.* Usually, the elm is connected with pleasurable associations in poetry. It represents the human qualities of beauty, charm, graciousness and stateliness.[69] But Arthur has all the elms of his country torn down to make poles and oars, to carry his knights across the Channel: "The king has poled his horsemen across the Channel." And once they are on the other side of the Channel, the poles of elm become human-like beings which stand motionless about Lancelot's castle.

In Mordred's eyes, the reason for this campaign is miserable, unworthy and banal. In Malory's *Morte Darthur,* the underlying law of war was determined by the tragic inevitability of a world approaching its downfall, one which sucked Arthur into its vortex. According to Williams' Mordred, the only reason for the siege is: "lest . . . the king should be cheated with another by his wife the queen." Disinterested and completely detached, the traitor sees, in his imagination, the besieging troops from the roof of the palace. In his vivid fantasy the knights of King Arthur are transformed into spears of elmwood. But these elms break into bud, "the elms bud in steel points," and these are directed against the walls of Benwick, behind which Lancelot rests secure and safe from danger.

From Arthur and Lancelot, the traitor's thoughts turn to Guinevere who has evidently hidden herself in the Convent of Almesbury out of fear and disdain for Mordred. According to a number of other versions, Guinevere plots with Mordred, thereby sinking to his moral level. Williams sees her in the image of "stone fitting itself to its echo,"[70] entangled in her own circle of life like sound and echo, infertile and pale, basically unworthy of her great lover Lancelot. In Mordred's eyes, Guinevere is a whore, and Arthur correspondingly an old cuckold. In this respect his cynicism is unparalleled: "It is laidly alike to be a wittol and a whore."[71]

Mordred's opinion of the inhabitants of London is no higher. In his eyes they are capable of stoning Guinevere in a sudden attack of fanatic righteousness, should he decide to drag the Queen out of the Convent by force and lead her through the streets of London. This is evidently a thought with which Mordred has played for a long time—a result of his disappointment in Guinevere. All Londoners are self-righteous and have thus forfeited the grace of coinherence. Catholic morals and catholic mockery are counterpoised. Catholic, in the first word-pair, is capitalized and means Catholic in the ecclesiastical sense. In contrast, the "catholic" paired with mockery is not capitalized and carries the meaning "universal," widespread. But this play on the meaning of words is more than a simple pun, for the term catholic mockery designates at the same time the degeneration of catholic morality to a self-righteous, loveless condemnation of the sins of one's neighbour: exchange and *largesse* are dead in the land, London has regressed from the City to the wood: "London is become a forest. . . bare grinning leaves, a whole wood of moral wantons, whose spines are tree-stretched up towards me, their hope." For Williams the forest represents the primeval and the wild, as yet unformed chaos, lacking definition and horizon.[72] The principle of order has been lost. Camelot is no longer the head of the realm which is to see the birth of the new Adam. It has made itself independent, in the rebellion against its Byzantine centre.

The unity symbolized by an organic body has been destroyed. The old tribute is abolished. The gold coins with the sign of the dragon will remain in the country: London has declared its autonomy. But the symbol of the dragon is not only found on the coins; it is also Mordred's coat of arms, so that he is entitled to say: "Kin to kin presently, children; I too am a dragon." Like many other symbols in the poem, the dragon which was once the heraldic cognizance of Uther and Arthur has taken on an ominous connotation and appearance, and thus carries a different meaning to that in previous treatments of the Arthurian material.[73] With right, Taliessin says in a previous conversation with Kay:

> Sir, if you made verse you would doubt symbols.
> I am afraid of the little loosed dragons.
> When the means are autonomous, they are deadly; . . . [74]

The loosed dragons which are directed against their own country remind the reader of the *Alliterative Morte Arthure*[75] in which Arthur dreams of a dragon which will one day destroy his land. The philosophers and interpreters of the dream assure the king that he himself is symbolized by the dragon. His own *hubris* will cause the downfall of his realm. But also his son Mordred (Welsh *mordraig* = sea dragon) plays an important part in this. In Charles Williams, this same Mordred is practically the incarnation of the sinful egotism of his father. Thus we should not reproach the son when he says; "Like son, like father."

Mordred regards the holy vessel of the Grail in a very similar way. Even here, we see an all-pervading degeneration of values. In *The Calling of Taliessin* Ceridwen's cauldron was a typological anticipation of the Grail. But Mordred does not believe in such a Grail. He recalls that his father often pondered the importance of this holy vessel for his salvation. But he will and can do without such a fairy mechanism. If there were something like the Grail, he says, he would have it carried off by a dozen knights. His cooks would be pleased to possess such a magic cauldron.

The Grail seen as a cooking pot in Mordred's kitchen—this represents the absolute depth of degradation of the mystical and the sacred. All associations with the Eucharist and the creation of a new Adam have been abandoned. For Mordred the Grail is no more than a magic device to be handled with care, because a fairy might be summoned to the room at a rubbing as with Aladdin's lamp.

The idea of Aladdin's lamp leads Mordred's thoughts to exotic climes. All the themes and provinces of the Byzantine Empire have been destroyed, for they have lost their coherence. And now Mordred dreams of a kingdom of his own, a kind of Anti-Empire, "beyond miles of bamboo" (12.1), one which has a number of similarities to P'o-lu , which lies even beyond this terrible country: "beyond P'o-l'u / he told of another Empire. . . where a small Emperor sits" (13.2–4). This emperor becomes a model for Mordred, who is evidently impressed most by his relationship to his small, slant-eyed wives; once or twice every seven years he has one brought into his bed or thrown into a swamp in a bamboo cage. This is the type of tyrant Mordred wants to be. He intends to establish an Empire in London, as soon as his father is fallen in the wood of elms. His paradise is to be like that of the tyrant of the Antipodes, and he wants to live there by himself and to be admired by all other men.

Mordred is not Satan; he is probably not even the incarnation of evil. Williams sees him as a man of flesh and blood, the product of criminal incest and the expression of Arthur's egotistic love of self: "her arm was stretched to embrace his own stretched arm; she had his own face."[76] Thus Mordred is exclusively self-directed in all his thoughts and intentions. He rejects the attempt at integration into a larger society and draws his standard of value for his action solely from his own impulses. ". . . Mordred is entire egotism, Arthur's self-attention carried to the final degree. This is why it is he who wrecks the Table."[77]

The difference between father and son rests in the fact that Arthur desires the good but is too weak to achieve it, in spite of others and himself. Mordred, however, embodies the diabolic aspect of the dragon. Of course, he is also an exemplary embodiment of original sin and man's need for salvation. But in addition he is an individual, and as such he has freedom of choice and can decide for himself. There were a number of other possibilities open to him—Charles Williams has shown them clearly enough. But Mordred's decision is a selfish one—against *largesse,* exchange and coherence. And thus it appears to me that we have more than just the archetype of evil in a mythological poem and more than a fascinating, clearly visualized figure in a lyric cycle. Here we have the prototype of modern man, who is incapable of loving his neighbour unless he needs him for his own purposes, who takes the salvation of the soul into his own hands and prunes morality as the situation demands, who holds the spiritual world for no more than fairy magic and superstition.

We recognise him: he is the autonomous man cut off from all attachments; he is the succubus in love with his own image, the narcissist who transforms coinherence into incoherence and will nevertheless be respected, admired and honoured. Not until the concluding poem, *The Prayers of the Pope*, does it become clear where these developments lead.

VI

The Prayers of the Pope represents a turbulent, eventful crescendo of historical events and developments which lead to the final catastrophe—the downfall of the realm and the dissolution of Taliessin's fellowship. The event is not described in an epic way by the poet, but rather as the reflection of the young Pope Deodatus, as he prepares himself for the Eucharistic service of Christmas by a meditation in the Lateran Church: "slender, white-haired, incandescent, seeming in his trance of prayer a third twin of Merlin and Brisen . . ."[78] The white hair of the young man is a sign of premature aging under the burden of an office of great responsibility. We know that the historical Deodatus II once invested his entire strength in the attempt to bring Rome and Byzantium together. But for Williams the symbol of white hair means a great deal more: "And do you think the Pope, who is young, with white hair, brilliant, the image of Merlin (only M[erlin] has black hair), might be Merlin + [sic] loss? If you get me. The Pope (let us say) is time losing its beauties (by deprivation or will, not by mere passing change) but affirmatively. O I write it badly . . ."[79]

As welcome and interesting this foot-note of Williams may be, it does not seem to me as necessary for the understanding of the poem as Anne Ridler maintains: "I could not see how any reader would be able to guess the significance of the Pope's white hair or understand why he is said to be *rich* in loss without such a hint."[80] My own impression is that the poet is meditating upon his own poem, and that the results of his reflection are just as unique and unusual as his use of metaphor and symbolism in the poem. The only prerequisite actually necessary for an understanding of the poem is the basic structure of the Byzantine Empire, and even that could be interpolated from a close reading of the poems themselves.

The individual images, concepts and thoughts behind the poem gain a general imaginative relevance through a continual transposition of levels and perspectives. They are not restricted to a single case or historical fact, as for instance the invasion of the Huns, the break between Papacy and Patriarchy (1054), the World War; rather they represent a kind of law of history in a metaphorical manner. Every Logres has become Britannia in the course of its historical development. Grail, Christ and the Eucharist are manifested on earth, but men do not live on earth untouched by history. The call goes unheeded, the image recedes and is lost for ever. There is no consolation in the fact that after all it is only an image that has been lost, that is to say something transitory and unstable. Williams objects:

> But each loss of each image
> is single and full, a thing unrequited,
> plighted in presence to no recompense, . . .[81]

To live in and with images belongs to the nature of man, who is met halfway by God in that he relinquished his own essence and became man.[82] Therewith God reaffirms the justification of the images through and in himself. Thus the Pope prays: ". . . confirm / nor thee in thine images only but thine images in thee."[83]

With particular clarity and audibility, connotations of the last World War are felt. Williams, with his poet's sensibility, experienced and suffered its ordeal to a degree hardly rivalled by another Englishman. In London and Paris, the poet says, the peace talks were silenced, the cities of Logres "felt the sliding planes of the raiders' sails." Very gradually this vision of the Second World War is replaced by images of the invasion of the Huns, who cross the Weichsel, Danube and Rhine and flood Europe: "the land shook / as band after band stamped into darkness cities / whose burning had lamped their path." Finally these cruel images of war are matched by implications of the Japanese invasion of India, a case of uncanny foresight, since this part of the poem was first written before the war.[84] At the same time, however, it is also strongly reminiscent of the octopus-like menace described in Wells' *War of the Worlds*. But perhaps one should not interpret the image of the octopi who creep from coast to coast with their giant tentacles, "feeling along Burma, nearing India" too concretely. The basic conception is the extension of the headless Emperor's power and that of his realm (P'o-l'u) through the destruction of the Empire.

Hardly a word is wasted at this point on the realm of Arthur and the knights of the Round Table. We learn of the complex events which lead to downfall, not through the poet's direct account, but through rumours which reach the ears of the Pope via various indirect channels. At first we hear only of Arthur's war against Lancelot, of Gawain's irreconcilability and his preference for private vengeance, but most of all of Mordred, the incarnation of treachery and discord. The letters of the Pope have achieved nothing at all, the disease of chaos has spread in the whole country, and mobs storm through the streets of London—a symbol for interior rebellion, the dissolution of the City. Mordred takes possession of the Round Table and fills it with pagan chieftains. With the demon of his own desire, he fashions a world of false images without any mutual relationship or coherence: "Logres was void of Grail and Crown."

From Taliessin's mouth we hear the account of the end of Arthur's realm. In terse words the poet and seer informs his followers that Arthur and all the lords of the Round Table are dead: "the Table may end tomorrow." This example makes it particularly evident that Williams' intention differs from that of Malory. The core of the matter is no longer the ascent and the downfall of the realm of Arthur, but the destruction of the Empire, that is of order and unity, of organic coherence and *largesse* among men, of the ceasing of exchange, and the loss of coinherence.

And thus it is the downfall of the kingdom that forms the subject of the poem. The inhabitants live in a constant state of fear of others; they become isolated and strive for complete autonomy and self-justification. They exist solely in the aura of their own glory, and as a necessary consequence, view their fellow man as a natural enemy. This is true of groups, as well as of individuals. Those who reject the society of the city and would place the nation, race, or people in its stead require a counterbalance against which they can clarify and consolidate their own goals. Nationalism, racism and class-conflict all entail enmity against someone—foreigners, Jews or capitalists:[85] "forsaking the Emperor, they chose among themselves, / here one and there one, foes / among themselves, puppets of reputation, / void of communicated generation of glory."[86]

Even the form in which the message of the poem is couched is indicative of the collapse of order and coherence. Interjected parenthetical remarks break sentence periods into small groups, independent both in rhythm and content and loosely joined by apposition. The resultant impression is one of incoherence and dissolution. The identity of the kingdom as an organic whole dissolves, the categories become autonomous, and there is no longer a Merlin to unite them in the pentagram. At the same time, the disintegration of the provinces also means the dissolution of the organic body— that is to say, death: "all gave their choice to the primal curse and the grave, . . ."[87] Each is prepared to consign his neighbour to eternal damnation; each becomes a Mordred, or a Khan of the Huns, or the Calif of Asia in his heart. The city gives way to autonomous sects, and the poets are replaced by men who either cannot speak at all, or are only capable of spouting empty rhetoric. Magicians conjure up the ghosts of the past, which rise from Hell and from their graves to form a macabre procession—an army of mindless bodies in mechanical motion at the fore of the pagan hordes. This part of the poem, with its terrible visions, reveals the depth of Williams' "knowledge of darkness,"[88] his painful, nightmarelike certainty of the true existence of evil as the result of original sin.

But for Williams there are no clear-cut lines between Good and Evil. He refuses to join in the biased, one-sided condemnation of the enemy and the self-justification of "Our Side" and its motivation. "Where is the difference between us?" asks the Pope. "Causes and catapults they have and we have." He refuses to sit in judgment, "alive are they in us and we in them. / We know how we have sinned; we know not how they."[89] The only difference lies in the fact that the Pope's side acknowledges *coinherence*, whereas the other side denies it. Herein lies the true task of the Church in Williams' eyes: to realize its Catholicity and its universality. In all things Williams preferred the whole to the parts; he rejected the Roman Catholic Church for denying true Catholicism when it proclaimed itself the sole guardian of Christian truth, thereby creating a schism with the universal church. But this did not mean that he rejected Rome or the Papacy. For Williams, Byzantium, Canterbury, Jerusalem and Rome represented provinces of a single Christian church.[90]

Williams has Pope Deodatus sense the schism in his own heart, the collapse of order and the return of chaos. All the prayers of the Pope close with the same repeated lines, which echo like a refrain: "Send not, send not the rich empty away!" Pope Deodatus feels the disintegration and spiritual death in his soul—the downward progress of the Kingdom has reached its lowest point. Charles Williams leaves us in a world similar to that of T. S. Eliot's *Waste Land,* where the Fisher King's question is answered by a nursery rhyme: "London Bridge is falling down, falling down, falling down . . ." There is no reprieve from the curse of sterility.

But Williams also leaves us a small gleam of hope: Taliessin's household will survive. Although the poet relinquishes his task to God and formally dissolves the existing bonds, the ideal society will live on, and all will belong who are united by love. Secretly, unbeknownst to each other, and completely on their own, men will continue to love their neighbour and to serve their fellow man. They will continue to do good, for good in this world can no more be stamped out than can evil.

And Taliessin gives the reader a further hope: Broceliande will live forever. Even though the tentacles of P'o-l'u approach the coast of India, they encounter resistance: they are held fast and prevented from further progress by something similar to them and yet completely alien—the roots of the magic forest of Broceliande. They twine themselves firmly about the powerful arms of P'o-l'u; the powers of death and the Under-world are held in check by the Mother of Making.

Thus hope for mankind lies in the fact that evil can never gain total ascendancy. Broceliande and P'o-l'u merge, and there is continual en-counter between the outgrowth of Evil and the seedling-like growth of Good, which may at times be forced to retreat, but can never be fully overcome. This is the hope which lives on in mankind and inspires the lords and consuls whose hearts preserve the dream of the Empire and who continue to hope for the advent of Sarras in spite of all darkness and despair.

NOTES

Reprinted with permission from *Arthurian Literature* I (1981), 121–73. Section VII has been omitted with the author's permission.

1. For engaging insights into the personal side of the poet, see James T. Como, ed., *C. S. Lewis at the Breakfast Table and other Reminiscences* (New York, 1979); particularly the lively accounts of Derek S. Brewer, Erik Routley, Nathan C. Starr. No less vivid is the portrait sketched by Alice Mary Hadfield in her "The Relationship of Charles Williams' Working Life to his Fiction," in *Shadows of the Imagination: The Fantasies of C. S. Lewis, J. R. R Tolkien, and Charles Williams,* ed. M. R. Hillegas (Carbondale, 1969; new ed. 1979). The Charles Williams Society of London, which was founded in 1975, issues a Newsletter with essential criticism and interpretation. Additional contributions are found in *Mythlore* (Los Angeles) which is devoted to Williams, Tolkien and Lewis. I particularly wish to express my appreciation to Martin Moynihan, Esq., who encouraged me to delve deeper into the mystic world of Charles Williams and who kindly brought me into contact with Mary Hadfield, one of the founder members of the Charles Williams Society.

2. Charles Williams, *Taliessin Through Logres* and *The Region of the Sum-mer Stars* (London, 3rd ed. 1954). *Taliessin through Logres, the Region of the*

Summer Stars by Charles Williams and Arthurian Torso by Charles Williams and C. S. Lewis, introd. by Mary McDermott Shideler (Grand Rapids, Michigan, 1974). Frequent use was made of Williams' most important work in prose on Arthurian mythology, *The Arthurian Torso,* as it was entitled by its editor, C. S. Lewis (London, 2nd ed. 1952). See also, his *The Image of the City and Other Essays,* ed. Anne Ridler (London, 1958). A bibliography of secondary literature on Williams is to be found in John Heath-Stubbs, *Charles Williams,* Writers and their Work, No. 63 (London, 1955), 40–4. Additional mention must be made of Mary McDermott Shideler, *The Theology of Romantic Love. A Study in the Writings of Charles Williams* (New York, 1968), which includes a comprehensive bibliography of Williams' writing together with the reviews it received. Rev. by William V. Spanos in *JEGP,* 67 (1968), 719–22.

3. Logres as a name for the image of an ideal place and the destination of life's journey is analogous to St. Augustine's New Jerusalem and Tolkien's True West. Cf. Jonnie Patricia Mobley, *Towards Logres: The Operation of Efficacious Grace in Novels by C S. Lewis, Charles Williams, Muriel Spark, and Gabriel Fielding* (Diss., University of Southern Califorrna, 1973).

4. This I owe to a friendly communication of Martin Moynihan, Esq. Cf. *The Caerleon Edition of the Works of Arthur Machen,* 9 vols. (London, 1923), "The Great Return," Vol. 7, 191 ff.

5. Editions: *The Historia Regum Britanniae of Geoffrey of Monmouth,* ed. A. Griscom (London and New York, 1929); *Historia Regum Britanniae, A Variant Version,* ed. J. Hammer (Cambridge, Mass., 1951).

6. On Geoffrey's intention, cf. W.F. Schirmer, *Die Frühen Darstellungen des Arthurstoffes* (Köln and Opladen, 1958), 19 ff; further: Heinrich Pähler, *Strukturuntersuchungen zur Historia Regum Britanniae des Geoffrey of Monmouth* (Diss., Bonn, 1958), chapters 6 and 7.

7. The fact that Arthur was a mortal enemy of the Anglo-Saxons was gradually forgotten by Geoffrey's successors. Both Henry II and Edward I fought to suppress the troublesome legend of Arthur's return by having his body exhumed. A number of English kings liked to envision themselves in the role of *Arthurus redivivus.* The son of Henry VII was even baptized under the name of Arthur. On the legends of the Return, cf. R. S. Loomis, "The Legend of Arthur's Survival," in *Arthurian Literature in the Middle Ages,* ed. R. S. Loomis (Oxford, 1959), 64–71.

8. Valerie Krishna, ed., *The Alliterative Morte Arthure. A Critical Edition* (New York, 1976). For a re-evaluation of this unique work see *The Alliterative Morte Arthure: A Reassessment of the Poem,* ed. Karl Heinz Göller (Woodbridge, 1981).

9. On the development of the figure of Arthur in historiography, cf. Herta Brandenburg, *Galfried von Monmouth und die frühmittelenglischen Chronisten* (Diss., Berlin, 1918).

10. *Chronicle of Peter of Langtoft,* 2 vols., ed. T. Wright (London, 1866–68).

11. John Hardyng, *The Chronicle, Together with the Continuations by R. Grafton,* ed. H. Ellis (London, 1812).

12. *Annales de Wigornia,* in *Annales Monastici IV,* ed. H.R. Luard, Rolls Series (London, 1869).

13. *Liber de Compositione Castri Ambaziae,* in *Chroniques des Comtes d'Anjou,* ed. P. Marchegay and A. Salmon (Paris, 1871).

14. *Mer des Histoires,* in *Chroniques Belges,* 6 vols., ed. A. Borgnet, S. Bormans, Belgian Royal Academy (Brussels, 1864–80).

15. *The Works of Sir Thomas Malory,* ed. Eugene Vinaver (London, 2nd ed., 1967).

16. "The Coming of Arthur," in A. Tennyson, *Poetical Works* (London, 1954), 295.

17. *Arthurian Torso,* 83.

18. Cf. "The Index of the Body," *The Image of the City,* 80–7.

19. Cf. J. Heath-Stubbs, *Charles Williams,* 36.

20. *Taliessin Through Logres,* 8.

21. In regard to Jerusalem as the site of Christ's crucifixion and the birth-place of the New Adam, one can ask whether Williams was familiar with the ancient Omphalos concept; cf. Arno Esch, "Paradise and Calvary," *Anglia,* 78 (1960), 74–7.

22. *Arthurian Torso,* 107–8. As source for Williams' geographical myth, Dante, among others, must be mentioned, who saw Jerusalem as the centre of civilized earth. But even more significant is the poetic geography found in Blake, and the symbolic meaning he saw in the four directions—North, South, East and West. The verious *states* correspond to parts of Williams' anatomical myth. Cf. Maung BaHan, *William Blake: His Mysticism* (Bordeaux, 1924), 78: "They (the four 'states') are sometimes spoken of as 'the four worlds of humanity in every man' . . . and sometimes personified as the 'four mighty ones . . . in every man.' They are designated the four 'Zoas' or 'Lifes' in Eternity, and their names are Urthona (or Los), Urizen, Luvah and Tharmas. The Directions of their seats 'in eternal times' were respectively North, South, East and West."

23. *The Draco Normannicus of Etienne de Rouen,* ed. R. Howlett, Rolls Series (London, 1885).

24. On Broceliande, cf. McDermott Shideler, *The Theology of Romantic Love,* 102 ff.

25. Cf. *The Image of the City,* 145; as well as, Charles Moorman, *Arthurian Triptych, Mythic Materials in Charles Williams, C. S. Lewis and T. S. Eliot* (New York, 1960), 67.

26. William Butler Yeats, "The Second Coming," in *The Collected Poems* (London,1958), 211.

27. Cf. Nathan Comfort Starr, *King Arthur Today: The Arthurian Legend in English and American Literature 1901–1953* (Gainesville, 1954), 178.

28. *The History of the Holy Grail,* by Henry Lovelich, skynner, ed. F. J. Furnivall, EETS ES 20/24, 28/30 (London, 1874–78); Dorothy Kempe, *The Legend of the Holy Grail, its Sources, Character and Development* ("Introduction" to, and Part V of Henry Lovelich's Verse "History of the Holy Grail") (London, 1905). This work, which dates back to 1430, is a translation of the French *Estoire del Saint Graal* without any additions or alterations whatsoever. In fact, the language is so stiff and halting, and the treatment so little suited to the elevated nature of the topic, that we sympathize with the wry remark of the editor that Lovelich must have felt unfulfilled by his trade as a furrier.

29. *William of Malmesbury, Liber de Antiquitate Glastoniensis Ecclesiae,* in J. P. Migne, *Patrologia Latina,* Vol. 179, cols. 1682–1734.

30. *Joseph of Arimathia,* ed. W. W. Skeat, EETS OS 44 (London, 1871).

31. On the background of the Quest of the Grail, see Loomis, *Arthurian Literature,* esp. R. S. Loomis, "The Origin of the Grail Legends," 274–294; Jean Frappier, "The Vulgate Cycle," 295–318; Fanni Bogdanow, "The *Suite du Merlin* and the Post-Vulgate *Roman du Graal,*" 325–335.

32. In his account of the Quest of the Grail, Malory follows the Old French prose version, which seems to have been of monastic origin, at least for this part. The hermit who interprets the hierarchy of virtues places Chastity and Virginity at the height of the scale, a surprising turn-about-face after Courtly Love has just been explained as the main inspiration and code of behaviour of knighthood and Chivalry. Virginity is followed in descending order by Humility, Patience, Righteousness, and Love. During the Vigil before Whitsunday, the tables in Arthur's hall are placed in the same position prescribed for this feast in the Rule of Citeaux. In addition, the central problem of the nature of Grace and the repeated discussions of Trans-substantiation give rise to the idea that the author must have been a Cistercian monk. Cf. Loomis, *Arthurian Literature,* 306.

33. Cf. E. Vinaver, *The Works of Sir Thomas Malory,* 1, 70 ff.

34. This is particularly easy to demonstrate in the case of Lancelot, Malory's explicit favourite and, as in the French version, still "le meilleur chevalier du monde." Naturally as such he had to be excluded from the Quest. Malory had already portrayed his adulterous love for Guinevere, thus stamping Lancelot as sinful and unworthy of the vision of the Grail.

35. The somewhat neglected tale of the healing of Knight Urry is revealing on this point. Lancelot cures him merely by the laying on of hands and by prayer, an incident inserted by Malory without an apparent source. As in his account of

the Quest, Malory has elevated the role of earthly knighthood here. Cf. P. E. Tucker, "A Source for 'The Healing of Sir Urry' in the 'Morte Darthur,'" *MLR*, 50 (1955), 490–2.

36. *Arthur Pendragon of Britain* (New York, 1943).

37. "The Holy Grail," in A. Tennyson, *Poetical Works*, 401.

38. "The Meditation of Mordred," in *The Region of the Summer Stars*, 47–9, here 48.

39. According to Chrétien, however, the Grail is a vessel for food in which common salmon and lampreys are served, and thus its transformation from a profane object to a sacred one in the form of a chalice or ciborium is a phenomenon that remains to be explained.

40. In regard to the Grail and Bleeding Lance, Williams points out that they appear for the first time in this form in Chrétien. There were Celtic lances which blazed lightning and fire, but not one that bled. One cannot blame Williams for not finding the reason for the new image. Of course, Chrétien has a different lance in mind in the procession than the one that wounded the king. Thus the bleeding of the spear, and the healing of the wound with the blood of the spear must be explained. Williams has evidently thought of the lance of Longinus which pierced the side of Christ in this connection, in the context of his discussion of the *Conte du Groal*.

41. *The Region of the Summer Stars*, "Preface," vii.

42. The historical Taliessin lived in the sixth century, and the poetry attributed to him has been preserved in the *Book of Taliessin* (c. 1275). Twelve historical poems from this collection date back to the sixth century and are regarded by Celtic scholars as "the genuine work of Taliessin." Cf. A. L. Owen, *The Famous Druids* (Oxford, 1962), 201 ff. Lady Charlotte Guest translated the story of Taliessin in her *Mabinogion*. The following passage quoted from the translation ("Taliessin," in *The Mabinogion*, transl. by Lady Charlotte Guest (London, 1877), 471–94) casts helpful light on our poem:

And my original country is the region of the summer stars; . . .
I was with my Lord in the highest sphere,
On the fall of Lucifer into the depth of hell:
I have borne a banner before Alexander; . . .
I have been loquacious prior to being gifted with speech; . . .
I am able to instruct the whole universe.
I shall be until the day of doom on the face of the earth;
And it is not known whether my body is flesh or fish. (pp. 482–3)

43. *The Region of the Summer Stars*, 6; cf. on Celtic concepts of reincarnation: Jan de Vries, *Keltische Religion* (Stuttgart, 1961), 252.

44. *Arthurian Torso*, 22; on the earlier tradition of Taliessin, cf. Owen, *Famous Druids*, 213.

45. In what follows, Williams, in my opinion, failed to distinguish clearly enough between bards, *vates,* and Druids. The Celtic priesthood fulfilled several functions which can no longer be clearly separated today. Cf. Jan de Vries, *Keltische Religion,* 216–7.

46. *The Region of the Summer Stars,* 7.

47. *The Book of the Cave of Treasures,* transl. from the Syriac Text of the British Museum MS. Add. 25875 by Sir E. A. Wallis Budge (London, 1927), 63; cf. also n. 21, Esch.

48. On the imagery of the shadow, cf. Carl Dee Dockery, *The Myth of the Shadow in the Fantasies of Williams, Lewis and Tolkien* (Diss., Auburn University, 1975).

49. Cf. the useful commentary on Dante's concept of the universe in *The Divine Comedy of Dante Alighieri,* introd. by C. H. Grandgent, trans., by J. A. Carlyle and P. H. Wicksteed (New York, 1944).

50. Cf. C. S. Lewis, *The Discarded Image* (Cambridge, 1964), 111–2.

51. Cf. C. C. Dobson, *Did Our Lord Visit Britain?* (Glastonbury, 7th ed., 1958).

52. G. E. Bentley, ed., *William Blake's Writings,* 2 vols. (Oxford, 1978), I, 470.

53. Luke 11.17.

54. On the nature and function of the poet, see William Matthew Roulet, *The Figure of the Poet in the Arthurian Poems of Charles Williams* (Diss., St John's University, 1965). The figure of the artist has a similar function in Charles Williams' novels, see Robert C. Holder, "Art and Artist in the Fiction of Charles Williams," *Renascence,* 27 (1975), 81–7.

55. Cf. Veronica L. Skinner, "Guinevere's role in the Arthurian poetry of Charles Williams," *Mythlore,* 4 (1977), 9–11.

56. According to Blake, the main characteristic of John Locke's philosophy is the externalisation of the existence of material objects.

57. Cf. Northrop Frye, *Fearful Symmetry. A Study of William Blake* (Boston, 3rd ed., 1967), 349 ff. A comparison of the stars in heaven with the body of Christ is to be found in Richard Rolle. It is an interesting fact that he writes: "Also, swet Jhesu, þe sterres ben cause of euche þynge þat is grene, or groweth, or bereth fruyt . . . Also sterris ben cause of mynys, metaill, and of precious stonys . . . ." *English Writings of Richard Rolle,* ed. H. E. Allen (Oxford, 1963), 35. The Metaphysical poets often compare the human body to the universe (e.g. George Herbert, in "Man"), as does mystical poetry in general. Cf. John Charles Earle, "Bodily Extension": ". . . Thus every man / Wears as his robe the garment of the sky—/ So close his union with the cosmic plan, / So perfectly he pierces

low and high—/ Reaching as far in space as creature can, / And coextending with immensity." *Oxford Book of English Mystical Verse* (Oxford, 1962), 510.

58. Gawain's reason for wearing the green girdle was a similar one. In general, this item of clothing appears to have borne a corresponding function in courtly poetry.

59. On the problem of "exchange" and Williams' doctrine of substitution and its psychological and existential foundation, see J. J. Boies, "Existential Exchange in the Novels of Charles Williams," *Renascence,* 26 (1974), 219–229.

60. Martin J. Moynihan, in a private communication to the author.

61. Cf. Charles Moorman, *Arthurian Triptych,* 72.

62. *Arthurian Torso,* 168.

63. "The Coming of Galahad," in *Taliessin Through Logres,* 69–77, here 73.

64. "The Coming of Galahad," 72.

65. "The Coming of Galahad," 73.

66. Cf. C. S. Lewis, *The Discarded Image,* 58.

67. *The Divine Comedy of Dante Alighieri,* Paradiso, Canto XXI, 532–537.

68. Cf. Ferdinand Piper, *Mythologie der christlichen Kunst von der ältesten Zeit bis in's* [sic] *sechzehnte Jahrhundert* (Weimar, 1851), 215.

69. Gertraud Jobes, ed., *Dictionary of Mythology, Folklore and Symbols* (New York, 1961).

70. "The Coming of Galahad," 74.

71. "The Meditation of Mordred," in *The Region of the Summer Stars,* 47–9, here 47. The word "laidly" presents difficulties in the interpretation. In my opinion, it is to be seen both as a pun on "ladylike" and on the verb "to lay," to which it could be considered an adverb; the passage clearly contains a sexual innuendo, and the Scottish "laidly" in the sense of "repulsive," "hideous," "offensive," appears a less likely probability. "Wittol" is an old word for cuckold.

72. *The Image of the City,* "Introduction," lii.

73. Cf. the author's treatment in "Die Wappen König Arthurs in der Hs. Lansdowne 822," *Anglia,* 79 (1961), 253–266, here 253.

74. "Bors to Elayne: On the King's Coins," in *Taliessin Through Logres,* 42–5, here 44.

75. Ed. Krishna (New York, 1976).

76. "Lamorack and the Queen Morgause of Orkney," in *Taliessin Through Logres,* 38–41, here 40.

77. *The Image of the City,* 176.

78. "Prayers of the Pope," in *The Region of the Summer Stars,* 50–61, here 50.

79. *The Image of the City,* "Introduction," lxv.

80. *The Image of the City,* "Introduction," lxv.

81. "Prayers of the Pope," 50.

82. On the Neoplatonic character of Williams' imagery, and his theological basis in Thomas Aquinas' *analogia entis,* see Sape Anne Zylstra, *Charles Williams: An Analysis and Appraisal of his Major Work* (Diss., Emory University, 1969).

83. "Prayers of the Pope," 55.

84. *Arthurian Torso,* 185.

85. Cf. *Arthurian Torso,* 182.

86. "The Prayers of the Pope," 51.

87. "The Prayers of the Pope," 51.

88. Cf. the chapter of the same name in A. M. Hadfield, *An Introduction to Charles Williams* (London, 1959).

89. "The Prayers of the Pope," 53.

90. Cf. Hadfield, *Introduction,* 131.

CHAPTER 16

T. S. Eliot

CHARLES MOORMAN

So much has been written about T. S. Eliot's literary and philosophical development that it would seem unnecessary to comment further on these matters. But although critics have made much of Eliot's swing from restless poetic innovation and fierce social and religious criticism to metrical formality and acceptance of a tradition-bound society and church, little has been said concerning the basic attitude, present in Eliot's work from the beginning, which underlies and in a sense motivates these seemingly irresponsible changes. Since this attitude has a great deal to do with Eliot's use of myth, it will be necessary to attempt a definition of this prevailing point of view.

I have already attempted to define the sort of mentality involved in the creation of literary myth. Basically, the mythmaker is a primitive; he sees no division between himself and the nature that exists outside himself. To quote again from Henri Frankfort:

> The world appears to primitive man neither inanimate nor empty, but redundant with life; and life has individuality, in man and beast and plant, and in every phenomenon which confronts man—the thunderclap, the sudden shadow, the eerie and unknown clearing in the wood, the stone which suddenly hurts him when he stumbles on a hunting trip. Any phenomenon may at any time face him, not as "It," but as "Thou." In this confrontation, "Thou" reveals its individuality, its qualities, its will. "Thou" is not contemplated with intellectual detachment; it is experienced as life confronting life, involving every faculty of man in a reciprocal relationship.[1]

A modern version of this same attitude, it seems to me, is contained in Eliot's famous description of the unified sensibility:

> When a poet's mind is perfectly equipped for its work, it is constantly amalgamating disparate experience; the ordinary man's experience is chaotic, irregular, fragmentary. The latter falls in love, or reads Spinoza, and these two experiences have nothing to do with each other, or with the noise of the typewriter or the smell of cooking; in the mind of the poet these experiences are always forming new wholes.[2]

In both instances, primitive man and modern poet, we have a point of view suggested which regards the universe as a reconcilable and unified, if not thoroughly systematic, whole. The principles of identity and reconciliation are present in both statements and represent a quality that is common to and necessary for both the mythmaker and, in Eliot's view, the poet.

This identification of mythmaker and poet seems to me to throw a good deal of light on Eliot's basic attitude toward poetry and toward the world. This point of view, which I call "sacramental," seems to me to underlie all of Eliot's work. Basically, the sacramentalist, like primitive man, can see no difference between himself and the world of natural things which surrounds him; he has, in Eliot's phrase, a "unified sensibility" that enables him to see all experience, however disparate it may first appear, as a whole and unified complex of meaning, unified because it is interpreted in terms of its relation to the whole milieu of experience by a mind that is not only cognizant of those relations, but ready and able to interpret them as they relate to one another and to his own personality. In short, the "odour of a rose," in Eliot's view, becomes a total part of Donne's experience and personality;[3] Donne unites that odor with the total complex of his experience, seen under the aspects of both time and space, of which it is a part. *Sub specie aeternitatis*, therefore, Donne is of no more importance in the total experience than is the rose that originally started the chain of reaction; they exist as equal parts of a total experience.

In addition to seeing no difference between the "I" of self and the "It" of nature, the sacramentalist also constantly identifies symbol and object. To use again the most obvious nonliterary example, there is no essential difference to a communicant who accepts the doctrine of the Real Presence in the "reality" of the actual Body and Blood of Christ and the wafer of unleavened bread and cup of wine which symbolize that Body and that Blood. No matter how the particular relationship of symbol and object is defined, whether as transubstantiation or consubstantiation, the main point, grasped and adhered to certainly by an act of faith, is that that symbol and object do exist in some sort of unity, which though certainly undefinable is nevertheless "real." Because of this, reason and thus definition cannot be used to explain the phenomenon; it is only properly felt and believed by a mentality unaccustomed, whether unconsciously or consciously, to analysis and unused to the separation of man and nature, self and nonself. This is, of course, precisely the same habit of thinking that primitive man employs when he blames the stone that he kicked for hurting him. Thus it is that the poetry of Charles Williams admits no difference in kind between the modern world and the Arthurian myth that he uses as its symbol. Thus it is that Donne is able to compare his ailing body to a map[4] and Marvell the progress of his love to a set of geometrical equations[5] with no sense of insecurity, or of unreality, or of ineptness. These poets and primitives see man and nature, seen and unseen, object and symbol as parts of a total experience, unified in spite of itself by their sacramental points of view. To them the word is made flesh at all times and on an infinite number of levels.

These two aspects of the sacramental point of view—the fusion of man and nature and of symbol and object—seem to me to underlie all of Eliot's career from "The Love Song of J. Alfred Prufrock" through "Little Gidding"; they are demonstrable in his poetry long before his conversion to Anglo-Catholicism. That he has continued them in his later religious poetry is obvious, since Eliot's current belief in the Incarnation as the unifier of all experience ("Here the impossible union / Of spheres of existence is actual")[6] has led him further from the analytical abstracting of the scientific mind than did his early theory of the dissociation of sensibility, which is primarily a matter of literary history. But even before *For Launcelot Andrewes*, the sacramental viewpoint was there, exhibiting itself in a form totally unlike that of any poet (with the possible exceptions of Coleridge and Hopkins) since the metaphysicals. This is nowhere so graphically illustrated as in the mythopoetic method of *The Waste Land*.

It is a commonplace that the secret to any interpretation of *The Waste Land* lies in an analysis of Eliot's use of myth in that poem. But more often than not this fact is singled out for scorn rather than for praise. At first glance, the poem appears chaotic, disunified; the profusion of references to myth and literature and the lack of transitional statements between the swift changes in scene give the poem a cluttered appearance. Because of this, some critics have claimed that the poem lacks any sort of unity, except perhaps for a purely artificial and mechanical unity of method and for an over-all unity of effect based on the shaky principle of imitative form.[7] This so-called "fallacy of imitative form" we can, I think, safely ignore since it is concerned only with partial effect and is not therefore really connected with any principle of total unity. The question of artificial unity of method, on the other hand, comes closer to the truth of the matter.

The mechanical unity of the poem is said to lie in Eliot's trick of setting a scene from myth or literature and a contemporary scene in close proximity and then settling back to watch the immediate effect of that comparison.[8] A good example of this method appears in the use of Tiresias in the seduction scene of "The Fire Sermon."[9] Eliot in his notes to the poem quotes a section of the *Metamorphoses* which explains two essential facts about the Greek seer—(1) he has been both man and woman, and (2) he is able to know the future. Both of these miraculous qualities, moreover, are caused by his having been involved in situations involving sexual relations. He was condemned to live for seven years as a woman because he interfered with the mating of two snakes; he was privileged to see the future as compensation for the blindness imposed on him by Juno when he judged against her on a question of sexual pleasure. Thus, Tiresias "though blind, throbbing between two lives, / Old man with wrinkled female breasts, can see" and judge the sordid affair between the callous "typist home at teatime" and the vain carbuncular clerk. Passages involving Tiresias occur three times during the scene—(1) in the short introductory passage I have quoted, (2) just before the entrance of the clerk when it is said that Tiresias "perceived the scene, and foretold the rest," and (3) at the moment of intercourse when he says that he has "foresuffered all / Enacted on this same divan or bed," he who has "sat by Thebes below the wall / And walked among the lowest of the dead." Here then is a mythological figure, both man and woman, seer and prophet, set beside a cheap, effortless and mechanical seduction, the most striking quality of which is its obvious triviality. The effect of the comparison is, to me at least, immediate and overwhelming. Here is Tiresias, representing the world of myth, who knows the sexual act both as a man knows it and as a woman knows it, who has been condemned and honored for interference in sexual situations, who has been involved in the great tragedy of Oedipus, who has held communion with the tragic living and "walked among the lowest of the dead"—here is Tiresias, in whose life the sexual act has been of tremendous meaning and importance, forced to watch with disgust a sexual act that is wholly mechanical and totally void of meaning.

Sexual intercourse, which in past time has driven men to war, murder, and poetry and for which men once lost the world and thought the world well lost, has become, in the contemporary waste land, a matter of routine, as mechanical as combing one's hair or placing a record on the phonograph. In short, the waste land itself is by implication devoid of meaning.

The conclusion of the scene between the typist and the clerk affords another instance of Eliot's general method. As an example of a past world in which love had meaning, Eliot here uses a scrap of a song in Goldsmith's *The Vicar of Wakefield*.[10] After the clerk has gone, the typist remarks that she is "glad it's over," and at this point appear the lines:

> When lovely lady stoops to folly and
> Paces about her room again, alone,
> She smooths her hair with automatic hand,
> And puts a record on the gramophone.
>   (11. 253–256)

The lines from *The Vicar of Wakefield* which Eliot is parodying begin:

> When lovely woman stoops to folly,
> And finds too late that men betray,
> What charm can soothe her melancholy?
> What art can wash her guilt away?

and conclude with the observation that the only "art her guilt to cover" is "to die." Again the contrast is immediate and overwhelming. Eliot's ironic use of this eighteenth-century lyric, and especially of the sexual connotations of "to die," expresses directly and forcefully a contrast between modern sexual ennui and an older concept of romantic honor by suggesting, in the twisting of Goldsmith's lyric, the difference between two civilizations.

I bring forward these interpretations in demonstration of a kind of unity which underlies the poem and which can be clearly demonstrated by an analysis of Eliot's method at any point in the poem. Yet it is manifestly a mechanical unity, imposed from without by an intellect extremely conscious of the trick it is using. An organic unity must, by definition, come from within the poem's elementary structure, guiding and shaping the tenor and structure of the whole poem rather than of the parts. Two comments on organic structure, in specific application to Eliot and *The Waste Land*, come immediately to mind. The first is: This organic unity must proceed out of what I have previously called a sacramental point of view that, as I have defined it, either will not or cannot see that the compared and contrasted items, no matter from where in time or space they may be drawn, are of any essential difference in kind. In short, just as Donne's comparison of the body and map or of the lovers and compass is perfectly natural to a mind used to this sort of mythopoetic thought, so must the presence of Tiresias in the room of the typist proceed not from a conscious trick of methodology but from a mind, like Donne's, which sees neither strangeness nor trickery in the comparison.

The existence of such an attitude is manifestly undemonstrable except perhaps by the method I have previously suggested, i.e., that the poet is able to work with equal ease with either set of terms involved in the comparison. Unfortunately, the comparisons introduced in *The Waste Land* are too limited in duration to allow this method. But the presence of the sacramental point of view may also be indicated by the nature of the images used by Eliot in the poem; with this matter I wish to deal in the second of these two general comments on organic unity in *The Waste Land*. The objections of those critics who give to *The Waste Land* mechanical but not organic unity may be reduced, it seems to me, to a single statement—*The Waste Land* consists of too great a variety of comparisons to have any one organically unifying principle. These critics have a point; *The Waste Land* is on first glance a hodgepodge. Yet the varying images and seemingly disconnected comparisons of *The Waste Land* may be shown to be variations of one image and one comparison, a fact that would seem to point to the presence of the sacramental point of view. That basic metaphor involves the waste land of the Arthurian myth.

Eliot's introductory note to the poem states that "not only the title, but the plan and a good deal of the incidental symbolism of the poem were suggested by Miss Jessie L. Weston's book on the Grail legend: *From Ritual to Romance*." It is almost certain, judging from Eliot's note, that he came to know the myth from Miss Weston's book. He thus saw the myth primarily from her ritualist and Celticist point of view and accepted her interpretation of the major symbols. The Fisher King-wasteland myth, according to Miss Weston's interpretation, is primarily sexual in conception and function. The Fisher King is interpreted as a symbolic representative of the life principle whose maimed condition indicates a failure in his virility; his traditional wound in the thigh becomes a symbolic castration. This wounding of the Fisher King's virility, moreover, is reflected in the blight visited upon his land. Having quoted a passage from the *Sone de Nansai* which lists among the blights that strike the waste land the facts that

> Ne enfes d'omme n'e nasqui
> Ne puchielle n'i ot mari
> Ne arbres fueille n'i porta
> Ne nus pres n'i reverdia,
> Ne nus oysiaus n'i ot naon
> Ne se n'i ot beste faon. . . .[11]

Miss Weston says concerning this passage:

> Now there can be no possible doubt here, the condition of the King is sympathetically reflected on the land, the loss of virility in the one brings about a suspension of the reproductive processes of Nature on the other.[12]

According to Miss Weston, this legend, which has its roots in fertility rituals, becomes associated in the Middle Ages with the growing body of the Arthurian materials, and the cup and lance of the older legend (both of which are patently sexual in origin in Miss Weston's view) become the Grail and Bleeding Lance of the Christian story.

I have already quoted in connection with Charles Williams, Eliot's remarks on a poet's method of operation. The gist of those remarks is that the poet is, by nature, a man of "unified sensibility," who sees all experience, however disparate, as potential material for art. The theory of the "objective correlative," moreover, assumes that emotional states are transmitted not by abstractions, but by these disparate poetic concretions that serve in turn to evoke like states of mind in the reader. It seems to me that Eliot finds in Miss Weston's discussion of the Fisher King-wasteland legend a perfect objective correlative to his own generalized emotion toward contemporary society. To Eliot, the modern world *is* a waste land, devastated by moral and spiritual wounds that have affected its reproductive organs and creative functions. The modern world cannot create, cannot reproduce; it is, in essence, a dead land. In the myth, as it exists in Miss Weston's reading, this death is intimately connected with sterility, and it is my contention that this central image of sexual sterility forms the underlying foundation of all the supposedly varied and disunified metaphorical allusions in the poem. My case for organic unity, and hence for the sacramental point of view in *The Waste Land,* therefore, lies in Eliot's use of the sterility image of the Fisher King-waste-land myth as it comes to him from Jessie Weston's *From Ritual to Romance.*

One need only glance at the wealth of exegetical studies of *The Waste Land* to realize that every detail of the poem has already been interpreted in the light of its possible connections with myth generally and with the Grail myth in particular. Grover Smith states in prefacing a complete examination of the text that *"The Waste Land* summarizes the Grail legend, not precisely in the usual order, but retaining the principal incidents and adapting them to a modern setting."[13] There is thus no need for my explicating the poem in detail. The Grail myth can be seen to underlie the poem at every point, either in images that refer directly to the myth (the protagonist's "fishing in the dull canal," the journey to the Chapel Perilous) or indirectly to the sexual sterility that, in Miss Weston's interpretation, is a vital part of the myth (the frustrated women of "A Game of Chess," the homosexual Mr. Eugenides).

The use of the Grail myth as a unifying image thus allows for the presence of the sacramental point of view in that the myth provides a kind of matrix out of which and about which all of Eliot's images, drawn from wherever or whenever, may evolve and cluster. The Arthurian myth establishes for Eliot by means of its own inclusiveness and unity the artistic equivalent of Charles Williams' "co-inherence of souls." Just as the concept of the co-inherence allows Williams to mix magical and commonplace, living and dead, so Eliot's over-all waste-land myth allows him to fuse Marvell's "Coy Mistress," Day's goddess Diana, and the exfighter Apeneck Sweeney into a single image that contains within itself the opposites of attraction and repulsion, past and present, mythical and modern and *is* itself a sacramental fusing of image and idea.

A few examples from the poem should demonstrate how the Grail myth serves to permit Eliot's sacramentalism to operate in *The Waste Land.*

The poem begins with a section "identifying the class and character of the protagonist."[14] Yet the first seven lines of the poem serve also to introduce the general theme of sexual sterility which underlies the poem, and thus prepare us for the introduction of the myth. April is generally associated with the regeneration of the earth and thus with love and birth. But in Eliot's poem, April is "cruel": "the dull roots" are stirred by the rain; the lilacs are simply "bred" out of a "dead soil" (ll. 1–7). Birth is an uncomfortable process; winter with its "forgetful snow" and "dried tubers" was sterile, yet safer than this birth-giving April. It is in this context that we first see the waste land itself:

> A heap of broken images, where the sun beats,
> And the dead tree gives no shelter, the cricket no relief,
> And the dry stone no sound of water.
>   (ll. 22–24)

But even in the midst of this desert lies a hope:

> There is shadow under this red rock,
> (Come in under the shadow of this red rock).
>   (11. 25–26)

Under this "rock," then, exists some kind of regeneration; there is "shadow" here. The symbol of the rock is here ambivalent, referring as it does to Christ ("the shadow of a great rock in a weary land"), to the Grail itself (in Wolfram's *Parzifal*, "the Grail is said to be a stone, and those who are called to its quiet are said to be called as children and to grow up under its shadow")[15] and to Chrétien's castle of ladies, "la roche de Sanguin."[16] Thus, in the midst of images of sterility, the Grail itself is present to remind us of a kind of religious fertility and order which may revitalize the waste land.

There follow immediately in the poem two other sets of symbols referring again to this pattern of sexual sterility and demonstrating the presence of the sacramental point of view (ll. 31–42). The hopeful cry of the sailor accompanying Isolde to Cornwall and its answer, the dismal report of the shepherd who watches the empty sea for Isolde's return, are used to frame the protagonist's encounter with the hyacinth girl. The hyacinth girl, "arms full and hair wet," obviously a symbol of sexual fertility, is greeted by her lover (to Grover Smith, the Grail quester himself), who, neither "living nor dead," cannot in any way partake of her sexuality and is stunned by her vibrant life; he "knew nothing, / Looking into the heart of light, the silence." Thus, in this opening description of the waste land, Eliot presents in rapid succession an image (the red rock) which refers directly to the Grail legend and, in the Isolde and hyacinth girl sections, images that refer indirectly to the sterility-fertility dichotomy that underlies the Grail myth. This opening passage, moreover, indicates quite clearly the type of methodology and the kind of poetic mentality which pervade the poem; an image of great potential fertility drawn from whatever source (the seaman's song, the hyacinth girl) is presented and then immediately fused with a contrary image or with a denial of the original image in its own terms (the shepherd's song, the protagonist's refusal to accept the girl). The sacramental point of view, stemming from the unified sensibility, thus allows Eliot to "amalgamate disparate experience" in images that unite oppositions in time, place, and attitude.

Other images show the same process at work. In Eliot's presentation of Madame Sosostris, the fortuneteller (11. 43–59), the Tarot deck of cards, which once played a part in ancient fertility rituals, is here seen as a mere fortunetelling device used, significantly, by a society fortuneteller who has a "cold," which is generally in Eliot a sterility symbol.[17] The characters as they appear on the cards also become symbols connected with the basic fertility-sterility image pattern that dominates the poem. The "drowned Phoenician sailor" is later connected with the Phoenician merchant who suffers "death by water" and so becomes, as Brooks suggests, a "type of the fertility god whose image was thrown into the sea annually. . . ."[18] "Belladonna [symbolically a modern poisoning of the image of the Blessed Virgin], the Lady of the Rocks" is a denial of Divine Motherhood, hence motherhood itself, in terms of the waste land. She has become simply the "lady of situations," a phrase that would seem to carry connotations of illicit sexual relationships. The "man with three staves" is associated by Eliot himself with the maimed Fisher King; the one-eyed merchant later becomes associated with the homosexual Mr. Eugenides, who represents another kind of sexual sterility; the Hanged Man of the Tarot deck is associated by Eliot with Frazer's Hanged God and so directly with Christ and indirectly with the Grail. Thus again, the emphasis of the scene is directed to the principal themes and symbols of the Fisher King myth—sexual sterility and the saving power of the Grail.

One could go on demonstrating the same point in almost every line. The fusion of the passionate fertility of myth (Cleopatra, Dido, Eve) with the frustration and sterility of modern society in "A Game of Chess," the intermingling of the various river scenes in "The Fire Sermon," the journey to the Chapel Perilous and the final images of fragmentation in "What the Thunder Said"—all of these images indicate clearly the use of the Grail myth as objective correlative and as matrix.

It should be clear also that this fusing of images within the organic unity of the poem differs from the simple mechanical unity obtained by setting past and present side by side. This latter device corresponds to the "illustrative" use of metaphor; it is a comparative device, and from this point of view the image of Tiresias in "The Fire Sermon" is simply compared with the image of clerk and typist. However, by means of the sacramental point of view the images are not compared, but identified, and in the seduction scene it will be noted that Tiresias is physically present and that he both sees the scene before him and feels (by means of his "foresuf-fering") the emotions of both (because of his dual sexuality) typist and clerk. Tiresias, in the poem, is not compared with the modern lovers; he is identified with them in terms of the sterility-fertility myth of which they are both a part. Eliot himself reinforces in the notes to the poem this no-tion of the kind of unity exhibited in the poem by stating that "just as the one-eyed merchant, seller of currants, melts into the Phoenician Sailor, and the latter is not wholly distinct from Ferdinand Prince of Naples, so all the women are one woman, and the two sexes meet in Tiresias."[19]

So in Eliot's poem, all literature and all myth become aspects of one literature and one myth. The poem's much discussed contrasts between Elizabethan England and modern England, Eastern religion and Western secular thought, fertility and sterility all exist within the context of the poem as parts and aspects of a legend and symbol that Eliot uses to con-trol the material that goes into the making of his vision of his own time.

This use of the sacramental point of view to suggest by means of allu-sion whole structures and attitudes, moreover, is seen throughout Eliot's work. In four well known lines from "Sweeney among the Nightingales," Eliot alludes in passing to four myths:

> The nightingales are singing near
> The Convent of the Sacred Heart,
> And sang within the bloody wood
> When Agamemnon cried aloud.

The reader, perhaps unfairly, is expected to enlarge upon each of these al-lusions, bringing to bear on the poem the whole weight of the full situa-tion that each allusion suggests. He must know that the legends concerning the rape of Philomel, the Crucifixion of Christ, the murder of the priest in the sacred wood at Nemi, and the murder of Agamemnon by Aegisthus and Clytemnestra are all basically concerned with high crimes involving murder, sex, violence, and treachery. The reader must also apply this information to the text of the whole of Eliot's poem in order to understand the contrast that Eliot is enforcing, a contrast between these ancient crimes, all of which involve violence and meaning and purpose, and the proposed murder of Sweeney, which is confused and most obvi-ously meaningless and purposeless. But, to repeat, the whole force and impact of the poem depend upon the reader's ability to supply the full meaning of the mythical situations to which Eliot merely alludes. This method is typical of Eliot's general handling of myth. A name, a place, an allusion is enough to suggest the whole situation from which the key word comes. Thus it is that in *The Waste Land* the twisted lines from Marvell and Day suggest the whole poems from which they are taken as well as the total milieu and cultural situation which produced those poems.

This reliance on myth and on the sacramental point of view may well be, as I have suggested earlier, the unifying thread that binds all of Eliot's work together. Grover Smith points out, quite conclusively it seems to me, that the mythical pattern of death and rebirth underlies almost all of Eliot's creative work,[20] and I would maintain that the sacramental method is the means whereby this pattern is presented in terms and symbols which, though they shift from work to work, are nevertheless consistent in that they constantly reflect that pattern, and that it is also the means whereby Eliot's works acquire organic unity.

Certainly, from one point of view, the earlier poems can be seen as quests, if not for the specifically Christian Grail of the Arthurian myth, then at least for the fertility and purpose and vision which the Grail symbolizes. Though it is perhaps an error to see specific allusions to the Grail myth in poems such as "The Love Song of J. Alfred Prufrock," "Mr. Apollinax," and "Gerontion," there is nevertheless demonstrated in these poems the same sacramental use of myth which determines the form and meaning of *The Waste Land.*

"Prufrock" fuses into a series of images two worlds, the world Prufrock envisions (the redeemed and fertile waste land) and the world as it is (the waste land itself). Thus the famous image of "the evening . . . spread out against the sky / Like a patient etherised upon a table" fuses Prufrock's romantic expectation (he expects the evening to be "spread out" in a magnificent fashion) with his actual perception (the etherized patient). And the same sacramental fusion is present in the images drawn from myth and literature. The socialite, culture-conscious "women" of Prufrock's own society and Michelangelo (here representing the most vigorously masculine and fertile creativity) are fused into a single image. Prufrock is ironically compared, again by means of this same kind of image, with Hamlet, with Lazarus, with John the Baptist, with Marvell's lover, and through the epigraph to the poem, with Guido de Montefeltro, all of whom represent the fertile, active, decisive life for which Prufrock is searching.

This same technique is perceptible in other early poems of Eliot. In "Mr. Apollinax," the hero, a "charming man," is sharply ridiculed by images in which he is linked, and so ironically compared, with Priapus, the old man of the sea, and the centaur. "Gerontion" defines the sterility and ineffectualness of the modern waste land by fusing images of modern sterility (the old man's house, his blindness, the sneezing woman, the hazy international set of lines 23–29, the distorted images of history, the final fragments) with images of fertility (Thermopylae, the pirates, the goat, Christ the tiger, May, passion). In "Sweeney Erect," Apeneck Sweeney, here awakening in a brothel, is identified with Polyphemus and the "epileptic on the bed" with Nausicää. In each of these poems, the sacramental method controls both meaning and structure by yoking items of "disparate experience," all of which ultimately stem from the central image of the failure of the quest for fertile life in the midst of a sterile world.

The sacramental fusion of images is even more readily apparent in the poems, and incidentally the plays, following *The Waste Land*, though here specifically Christian images, drawn principally from Dante, St. John of the Cross, and the liturgy, take the place of the older pagan symbols. In these poems, the "still point," the point of fusion of time and timelessness, matter and spirit, man and God comes more and more to fill Eliot's mind and to dominate and so give organic unity to his poems. The image of the still point, or in specifically Christian terms the Incarnation, which appears in *Four Quartets* and in *The Family Reunion* and *Murder in the Cathedral* is itself the supreme image of the sacramental consciousness:

> Here the impossible union
> Of spheres of existence is actual,
> Here the past and future
> Are conquered and reconciled. . . .
>
> ("The Dry Salvages")

It is toward this "impossible union" that Eliot continually strives in his later work. Hence one finds in these poems an even greater clustering and fusing of images drawn from myth and literature, images that again are determined by the constant pervading and unifying influence of the death-rebirth pattern. In "Journey of the Magi," ordinary temporality is ignored as the wise men encounter images of the crucifixion ("three trees on the low sky," "six hands at an open door dicing for pieces of silver") as they approach Bethlehem. Once there, they find the "birth" to be "hard and bitter agony for [them], like Death." In "Ash Wednesday," images taken from *The Divine Comedy*, St. John of the Cross, Shakespeare's sonnets, the bestiaries, the Scriptures, the liturgy, Grimm's fairy tales, and Guido Cavalcanti flow together with perfect ease to form a single unified image of penitence. Grover Smith finds in sixty lines of the "second movement" of "Little Gidding" possible allusions to Kipling, Tourneur, Shakespeare, Mallarmé, Milton, Swift, Ford, Yeats, Johnson, and Dante fused into an image "showing past time as simultaneously alive";[21] and almost any given section of *Four Quartets* would, I expect, yield similar fruit.

One might be disposed to treat such a use of allusion as mere virtuosity, a delight in erudition and obscurity for their own sakes. But it can also be seen as Eliot's attempt to make his poetry itself an image of the "impossible union / Of spheres of existence," to create within his poetry a single concentrated image of life, seen *sub specie aeternitatis*, an image distilled out of time and space by means of the sacramental point of view.

But specifically how and why does Eliot use the Arthurian myth in *The Waste Land?* It is obvious, first of all, that I cannot say as I did concerning C. S. Lewis that Eliot selects and uses parts of the myth to suggest the whole meaning of the myth. Neither can I say as I did of Charles Williams that what we have in *The Waste Land* is a complete recreation of the whole legend. On the other hand, it is perfectly clear that the symbols of the Fisher King and the waste land dominate and control the movement of the poem. One solution I would suggest is this: Eliot finds in these two symbols almost perfect objective correlatives by which he can express the emotion he feels toward the modern world. Here in the legend are symbols that express Eliot's own disillusion (this is in spite of Eliot's statements that he was never disillusioned) and disgust—the maimed ruler and the sterile land. The advantage of this particular myth lies then in the fact that it at once focuses and interprets Eliot's general feeling toward his own age. Thus, the myth Eliot adopts in *The Waste Land* becomes the sort of image to which he can transfer his emotion and by which he can express it in art.

Eliot's own remark on myth is probably the best single statement of the point of view I am attempting to define in this study. This statement may be used, furthermore, to help define Eliot's own use of the Arthurian myth in *The Waste Land*. Myth, in Eliot's terms, becomes a "way of controlling, of ordering, of giving a shape and a significance to the immense panorama of futility and anarchy which is modern history."[22] That *The Waste Land* involves as its major theme "the futility and anarchy of modern history" no one will doubt. And I have tried to show that the Fisher King-waste-land myth "is a way of controlling, of ordering, of giving a shape and a significance" to Eliot's vision. Certainly, at any rate, if this single myth and image along with the images of sterility which it naturally implies can be traced throughout the poem, then this part of the myth does in a very real sense order and control *The Waste Land*. If, however, it is objected that it is foolish to cry "order and control" in the face of such a manifestly chaotic poem as *The Waste Land*, let me retort that Eliot's own statement on myth is made apropos of what seems superficially to be one of the most obviously chaotic novels of our time— Joyce's *Ulysses*. The point is, I think, that superficial eccentricities and difficulties do not necessarily point to a central disunity. There is no "fallacy of imitative form" actually present in *The Waste Land*; there are merely superficial difficulties engendered by the difficulty of writing a poem based on many facets of a single myth and by Eliot's notion that since "our civilization comprehends great variety and complexity," the poet must seek a central order in a surface disorder, thus producing a poetry that, in Eliot's opinion, "must be difficult."[23] But in *The Waste Land*, as in *Ulysses*, the surface variants of the basic myth (the Fisher King-waste-land theme in Eliot, the Ulysses search theme in Joyce) always point inward to the central unity. All the images, like all the characters, of *The Waste Land* are in essence one image, and this single myth, embracing as it does all the variant myths of the poem, does give order, shape, and significance to Eliot's picture of modern society.

But why, again, does Eliot pick this particular myth? One answer I have already suggested; the Fisher King-waste-land myth involves not simply fertility and sterility, but more particularly religious fertility and secular sterility, a concept implicit, though undeveloped, in Chrétien, the Vulgate Cycle, and Malory. The Fisher King, at least in the later versions that connect the whole Arthurian myth with the Grail material, is the keeper of the Grail. His only cure in these legends lies in a resanctification of his person and his mission. He awaits the coming of the pure hero who can win the Grail and use it to cure him. Thus, the waste land itself becomes an image of secularism and the Fisher King an image of the failure of religion. Significantly, and this fact must have been obvious to Eliot at the time, the only cure possible for the modern world, as well as for the waste land, is religious in nature. In spite of Miss Weston's protestations, this section of the Arthurian myth is principally a homily on the destructiveness of complete secularism. Eliot himself, of course, has since said the same thing; from 1934 onward, it has become his principal text:

> If you do away with this struggle, and maintain that by tolerance, benevolence, inoffensiveness, and a redistribution or increase of purchasing

power, combined with a devotion, on the part of an elite, to Art, the world
will be as good as anyone could require, then you must expect human beings to become more and more vaporous.[24]

    . . . the struggle of our time [is] to concentrate, not to dissipate; to
renew our association with traditional wisdom; to re-establish a vital
connexion between the individual and the race; the struggle [is], in a
word, against Liberalism. . . .[25]

Thus although we find Eliot preaching no direct sermons in *The Waste
Land*, it is sure that the very image, the myth that guides and controls the
poem, preaches the required sermon by implication. To the general reader,
as to the student of Miss Weston, the Grail myth has to do first of all with
religion. Talk of mystery rites is apt and pertinent (and we have no evidence that Eliot did not accept Miss Weston's theory), but the myth at heart
is religious, and by virtue of this fact *The Waste Land* is a religious poem.

It will be helpful, I think, to approach this problem of myth and
unity from another vantage point. The difficulties of the poem occur not,
as some critics maintain, from Eliot's failure to unite the various cultures
he draws upon, but from a misunderstanding of Eliot's attitude toward
the whole problem of unification. Eliot's purpose is certainly not to foster a belief in the various myths he uses. Although the great variety of
myths involved hinders a superficial reading of the poem, it does not
negate the possibility that the poem has unity or that it represents more
than a chaos of unassimilated knowledge and impression. Myth is in itself a way of ordering knowledge, of stating precisely what the poet feels
to be the state of modern society, and it is altogether possible that this
"way of ordering knowledge" becomes not only the principal device of
the poem, but one of its major themes as well. As in "Sweeney among the
Nightingales," Eliot is involved in contrasting both the modern world in
which nothing has meaning with a world where all actions have meaning
and, at the same time, the secular viewpoint that sees no meaning in action with his own sacramental point of view that sees meaning in all
things. Thus, the myths in *The Waste Land* may very well have a double
function; they may serve not only to contrast the fertile religious order of
the past with the sterile secular chaos of the present, but also to contrast
the modern dissociation of matter and form with the poet's own viewpoint that asserts the inseparability of matter and form. *The Waste Land*
not only opposes spiritual life-in-death with secular death-in-life, but
also a sacramental habit of thought with a dissociated sensibility that forbids any assimilation of experience. Seen in this light, Eliot's own atti-

tude toward the poem becomes clear. The myths themselves may be of less importance in the poem than the attitude toward myth which unites them; Eliot everywhere suggests through his use of myth a consistent world viewpoint capable of uniting these mythical elements of the poem in contrast to a modern world view that sees all experience as disjunctive. There are thus two sets of contrasts in *The Waste Land*: a contrast of order and chaos and a contrast of the sacramental and whole world view with the secularized and partial world view.

The sacramental point of view that can equate evening and etherized patient in "The Love Song of J. Alfred Prufrock" can be seen identifying the fire and the rose in "Little Gidding"; Eliot's sacramental viewpoint orders and controls his poetry throughout his career. *The Waste Land*, moreover, would seem to be a *locus classicus* of this particular sort of method and mentality. Here, Eliot, beginning with a single myth and a single image, is able to expand that myth and that image in all directions, seeing applications of the basic principle in many times and literatures, yet never losing the single thread of imagery which controls and unifies all the subsidiary imagery of the poem. The Fisher King-waste-land section of the Arthurian myth, involving as it does religious fertility and secular sterility, thus becomes the center of Eliot's poem. In a sense, then, the Arthurian myth assumes in Eliot, just as it does in Williams and Lewis, a position of central importance.

NOTES

Reprinted with permission from *Arthurian Triptych: Mythic Materials in Charles Williams, C.S. Lewis, and T.S. Eliot* (Berkeley and Los Angeles: University of California Press, 1960). Chapter 5, "T.S. Eliot," pp. 127–48 and Notes, pp. 162–63.

1. *The Intellectual Adventure of Ancient Man* (Chicago: University of Chicago Press, 1946), p. 6.

2. "The Metaphysical Poets," *Selected Essays: 1917–1932* (New York: Harcourt, Brace, 1932), p. 247.

3. *Ibid.*

4. In *A Hymn to God, My God, in My Sickness.*

5. In *The Definition of Love.*

6. "The Dry Salvages," *Four Quartets* (New York: Harcourt, Brace, 1943), p. 27.

7. See especially Yvor Winters' condemnation of this theory in connection with Eliot that "modern art must be chaotic in order to express chaos." According

to Winters, who denies any unity to *The Waste Land*, imitative form in the poem results only in confusion (*The Anatomy of Nonsense* [Norfolk: New Directions, 1943], pp. 163–165).

8. This opinion is upheld most effectively by Edmund Wilson, who finds in Eliot's apparent fragmentariness a certain proportion and order (*Axel's Castle* [New York: Scribner, 1931], p. 112). Although Cleanth Brooks in his excellent analysis (*Modern Poetry and the Tradition* [Chapel Hill: University of North Carolina Press, 1939], pp. 136–172) treats the problem of unity only by implication, he would seem to find some unity in the poet's use of irony and "the obverse of irony" as reflected in Eliot's method of contrasting myth and contemporary reality. Other critics (see note 7 above on Yvor Winters) find that Eliot's poetic method has not even mechanical unity. Stephen Spender complains that Eliot's greatest weakness is his "fragmentariness" (*The Destructive Element* [Boston: Houghton Miffllin, 1936], p. 154). F. R. Leavis finds that the "comprehensiveness" of *The Waste Land* has been achieved at the "cost of structure" (*New Bearings in English Poetry* [London: Chatto and Windus, 1932], p. 112). This same criticism lies at the base of Richard Chase's comment that Eliot's prose statement that myth is an ordering device "is constantly belied by his use of myth in his own poems" (*Quest for Myth* [Baton Rouge: Louisiana State University Press, 1949], pp. v–vi).

9. All the quotations from Eliot's poetry other than *Four Quartets* are taken from the American edition of the *Collected Poems, 1909–1935* (New York: Harcourt, Brace, 1936). As far as I know, none of the materials that I have used in explication are original with me, nor can I always be sure from what commentaries they are taken. The fullest explications of *The Waste Land* are those of F. O. Matthiessen in *The Achievement of T. S. Eliot* (New York: Oxford University Press, 1947), Cleanth Brooks in *Modern Poetry and the Tradition*, and Grover Smith, Jr. in *T. S. Eliot's Poetry and Plays* (Chicago: University of Chicago Press, 1956). Smith's notes contain a full bibliography of the important commentaries on the poem.

10. Although in *The Waste Land*, Eliot's point of reference to past glories includes both literary and mythological allusions, it is clear that they fulfill exactly the same function in that both are used to suggest total situations or milieus that can be compared to the modern waste land.

11.   Nor was any child of man born there,
      Nor was any maiden married there,
      Nor did the trees there bear leaves,
      Nor any meadow blossom,
      Nor did any birds bear young,
      Nor any beast faun.

12. *From Ritual to Romance* (Cambridge: Cambridge University Press, 1920), p. 21.

13. *Op. cit.*, p. 70.

14. Brooks, *op. cit.*, p. 139.

15. Maynard Mack et al., *Modern Poetry*, "English Masterpieces" Series (New York: Prentice-Hall, 1950), p. 124.

16. Smith, *op. cit.,* p. 73.

17. See "Gerontion": "The goat coughs at night in the field overhead." The goat is normally a fertility symbol.

18. *Op. cit.*, p. 142.

19. *Collected Poems*, p. 94.

20. *Op. cit., passim.*

21. *Op. cit.*, p. 284.

22. " 'Ulysses,' Order, and Myth," *Dial*, LXXV, 5 (Nov., 1923), 483.

23. "The Metaphysical Poets," p. 248.

24. *After Strange Gods* (New York: Harcourt, Brace, 1934), p. 46.

25. *Ibid.*, p. 53.

CHAPTER 17

Walker Percy's Grail

J. DONALD CROWLEY AND
SUE MITCHELL CROWLEY

In the concept of the Second Coming the motif of Withdrawal-and-Return attains its deepest spiritual meaning. . . . In the myth of the Second Coming of Arthur, . . . the vanquished Britons consoled themselves for the failure of the historic Arthur to avert the ultimate victory of the English barbarian invaders.

—Arnold Toynbee

I think
that we
Shall never more, at any future time,
Delight our souls with talk of knightly deeds,
Walking about the gardens and the halls
Of Camelot, as in the days that were.
I perish by this people which I made,—
Tho' Merlin swore that I should come again . . .

—Tennyson, "Morte D'Arthur"

Since Walker Percy has characterized himself as a Catholic existentialist,[1] it is not surprising that his fictional heroes are questers, that each is *homo viator*,[2] a sovereign wayfarer. Nor is it surprising that both the way and the goal of these spiritual travelers inheres in sacrament. Insofar as Percy's "knights" inhabit a postmodern world, they suffer and confront both the internal monsters of Kierkegaardian dread and despair and the Heideggerrian malaise of everydayness, endemic with its external monsters of a desacralized culture. This double trajectory—a fiction that projects philosophical and theological understandings and values and, at the same time, criticizes the civilization that has lost those values—has marked Percy's work since his first novel, *The Moviegoer.*[3] How, he seems always to have asked, does one speak to a secular culture? How does one begin, particularly in America (and, to be sure, as a Catholic), to begin again, to make a "new earth" or, more properly, renew the old, old one. Possessed of a prophetic-apocalyptic quality in plot and tone, conceived in the complexly linear time structure of the Judaeo-Christian tradition, Percy's works as fictional critique ponder the past and present and thrust forward into an increasingly uncertain future. Binx Bolling of *The Moviegoer* (1961) and Will Barrett of *The Last Gentleman* (1966) are on horizontal searches for faith; Dr. Tom More, a fallen version of his namesake (Percy's own knight of faith—that eminently practical saint who stood against the adultery of his king and tried to save the old church in England, Sir Thomas More), is in *Love in the Ruins: The Adventures of a Bad Catholic at a Time Near the End of the World* (1971) and *The Thanatos Syndrome* (1987) struggling against a wasteland of secularism in which science and sex, both exclusively genital now, reign supreme.

As Percy's theologically based critical commentary has evolved, his readers have become growingly aware that it is born out of a broad sweeping mythical-historical vision. Percy is in his historical understanding greatly indebted to Arnold Toynbee's *Study of History,*[4] particularly to Toynbee's views on the endurance of the Jews in history, and the Incarnation, the god-man, as the ultimate and only lasting conception of withdrawal and return. Though their own religious convictions are quite disparate, Percy is, no less than Toynbee, fascinated with the manner in which the thought of the Mediterranean world was a crucible of Christianity. He is concerned, too, with the negative as well as positive influence of Greek and Roman philosophy on later Christian thought. This long view is personalized in all Percy's fiction because of his overriding need, in the light of his own conversion to Roman Catholicism, to work through what he calls the southern Stoicism of his own ancestors, especially of William Alexander Percy, the man of letters who raised him.

In a 1956 *Commonweal* essay, "Stoicism in the South," Percy makes the connections that will frequently inform his later fiction: preeminent among those ideas are Roman Stoicism, the southern tradition, and the Arthurian legends:

> The greatness of the South, like the greatness of the English squirearchy, had always a stronger Greek flavor than it ever had a

Christian. Its nobility and graciousness was the nobility and graciousness of the old Stoa. . . . If the Stoic way was remarkably suited to the Empire of the first century, it was quite as remarkably suited to the agrarian South of the last century. . . . It was a far nobler relationship than what usually passes under the name of paternalism. The nobility of Sartoris . . . was the nobility of the natural perfection of the Stoics, the stern inner summons to man's full estate, to duty, to honor, to generosity toward his fellowmen and above all to his inferiors—not because they were made in the image of God and were therefore lovable in themselves, but because to do them an injustice would be to defile the inner fortress which was oneself. . . . For the Southern Stoic the day has been lost and lost for good. . . . Southern society was above all a society of manners, an incredible triumph of manners, and a twilight of manners seems a twilight of the world. For the Stoic there is no real hope. His finest hour is to sit tight-lipped and ironic while the world comes crashing down around him.

It must be otherwise with the Christian. The urban plebs is not the mass which is to be abandoned to its own barbaric devices, but the lump to be leavened. The Christian is optimistic precisely where the Stoic is pessimistic. . . . We in the South can no longer afford the luxury of maintaining the Stoa beside the Christian edifice. In the past we managed the remarkable feat of keeping both, one for living in, the other for dying in. But the Church is no longer content to perform rites of passage; she has entered the arena of the living and must be reckoned with.[5]

Arthurian motifs occur often in the densely allusive texture of Percy's fiction: they serve regularly as paradigms for the southern code of Stoicism in the face of defeat. Where Percy employs the Arthurian legends he does so with two very complexly interrelated intentions. On the one hand, he parodies the chivalric code which he associates with the Stoicism of the ante- and post-bellum South; on the other hand, he discovers an antidote for that Stoa, that Roman inheritance of aristocratic paternalism, absolute reliance on reason, and heroic resignation before the dictates of fate, in a conception of the human being as incarnate creature, participating both in the fall and its many consequences—most pointedly in a quest, both individual and communal, for the Grail, not as provocative literary and legendary symbol but in its ultimate incarnational meaning as sacrament.

Percy's earliest fictional embodiment of southern Stoicism is Binx Bolling's Aunt Emily Cutrer (a portrait, in fact of his "Uncle" Will Percy) in *The Moviegoer.* If Binx is the Kierkegaardian aesthete, Emily is the ethical dowager who values manners and doing "the right thing." Certain of Binx's ancestors, like Percy's own, have been well-known military men. Emily's brother Alex, the one with "the Rupert Brooke-Galahad sort of face" (24), died in the Argonne a hero's death held "as fitting since the original Alex Bolling was killed with Roberdaux Wheat in the Hood breakthrough at Gaines Mills in 1862" (24–25). And so, when Binx's little brother dies his aunt explains that he must "act like a soldier" (4). Emily, the darling of her brothers, sees herself as "the female sport of a fierce old warrior gens" (26). After a career in volunteer public service which culminated in Red Cross service in the Spanish Civil War, she has married a well-to-do Creole and settled in the Garden District to become "as handsome and formidable as her brothers, soldierly in both look and outlook, . . . at sixty-five still the young prince" (27). Her husband Jules, participating, if more passively, in her chivalric code, can describe a Tulane goal-line stand against LSU as "King Arthur standing fast in the bloodred sunset against Sir Modred and the traitors" (30). So goes one of Percy's anticly postmodern transmogrifications of Arthurian materials.

Emily regards herself as "an Episcopalian by emotion, a Greek by nature and a Buddhist by choice" (23). A patron of good causes and the arts and possessed of a Socratic manner, she is strongly individualistic, philosophical, serene, and self-righteous. Like the Roman Stoics and Arthur in his defeat, she fears that "the fabric is dissolving" (54) but, adds Percy, "for her even the dissolving makes sense. She understands the chaos to come." She sees the "barbarians at the inner gate" (133) with no one to defend the West, and the future as her own "Dover Beach" of "the going under of the evening land" (54). The world itself is "an insignificant cinder spinning away in a dark corner of the universe," and the reason for human existence "a secret which the high gods have not confided" to her (54). She is the embodiment of William Alexander Percy's devotion to the resignation of Marcus Aurelius. She is less than resigned, however, when she suspects that Binx has betrayed her code by sexually compromising her stepdaughter Kate; Emily, "as erect and handsome as the Black Prince" (221), accuses him of breaking his trust. In fact, Binx and Kate's failed sexual encounter on the train to Chicago is the outward sign of that inner grace which permits their mutual discovery of a deeper intimacy as creatures in despair on a common journey, as co-questers in the religious mode.

Percy symbolises Emily's moral rectitude and lack of a supernatural religious understanding with a distinctly Arthurian metaphor. As she confronts Binx on his return from Chicago, they both gaze at a letter opener, a small Excalibur, the "soft iron sword she has withdrawn from the grasp of the helmeted figure on the inkstand" (221). Emily realizes that the tip of the blade is bent, and Binx, ever the existential questioner, is acutely conscious now that, years before, he himself had bent it in trying to open a drawer. Emily, relentless Stoic, now accuses him of breaking "sacred trust" that involves the common assumptions of "gentlefolk" who share "a native instinct for behavior, a natural piety or grace," a certain kind of "class," over against the "common" people, who have "enshrined mediocrity" as a national ideal. Emily "raises the sword to Prytania Street" (222–24) and explains that she has tried to "save" him: "More than anything I wanted to pass on to you the one heritage of the men of our family, a certain quality of spirit, a gaiety, a sense of duty, a nobility worn lightly, a sweetness, a gentleness with women—the only good things the South ever had and the only things that really matter in this life" (224). However, Binx will find his Grail, not in an idealized past but rather in the present of the communal feast of fish with his mother and her family, in the Mass they attend together, in his handicapped and holy brother Lonnie's devotion to sacramental Penance and his request for the last rites, and, finally, in his love for and marriage to Kate.

If Percy has given us Binx as his Kierkegaardian "knight of faith," in the "knight" of his fourth novel, *Lancelot*,[6] the reader is confronted with a complete antihero in search of an Unholy Grail. This "grail" Lancelot Andrewes Lamar will define as sin and, then more precisely, as sexual sin. He relives his quest as he makes a deeply perverse anticonfession to an old friend and failed priest-psychiatrist, whom long years ago in his youth he had begun to call "Percival." His unconscious self-revelation continues for 257 pages and forms the basis of the very complex structure of the novel. Lance tells the priest:

> I don't know why I want to talk to you or what I need to tell you or need to hear from you. . . . I have to tell you in order to know what I already know. . . . Perhaps I talk to you because of your silence. (85)

The confessor with his "hooded look" speaks only in the last two pages of the novel and then, like the knight of the Wasteland, to infer a question and to imply, cryptically, that there is an answer. At the same time, however, Percy controls Lancelot's narrative in such a way that Percival—who, as much as his Arthurian prototype, has had a life of relentless difficulty and uncertainty in defining his true vocation—becomes extraordinarily present as a character, and the reader begins to understand that, for him as well, "there is something wrong." For Percival will come to know the nature of his own quest only when he hears the story of Lance's antithetical one. As the medieval friends Lancelot and Percival sought each other during their Grail quests, so these two twentieth-century souls are deeply interdependent and, in Percy's word, potentially "intersubjective." They share a story fraught with Arthurian names, symbols and situations, and give that story two possible endings, not totally unlike the divergent destinies of their paradigms. Percy's parodic art leaves little doubt that there are also in *Lancelot* echoes and correspondences to the homecoming of Odysseus, but these are by no means as dominant as the parallels to Arthurian materials in his scheme here of employing myth to illustrate history.

The legendary Launcelot understood his singleminded passion for Guinevere as a guilty love. For a time he wandered in the forest, driven mad by public scorn and personal shame. Though he struggled to tear his two loves asunder in his heart, his one poisonous sin was inextricably bound to his quest, and he was doomed to follow wandering fires to the end of his days. On the other hand, Percival was characterised as "The Pure," that is, possessed, not only of chastity but of purity of intention, purity of heart. All his other endeavors turned to dust because he was destined for a single quest. Readers of Malory will recall that after Launcelot has been sent from "the holy place" where the knight was healed, he curses the day of his birth and comprehends that it is his adultery with the queen and his betrayal of his king that have prevented him from an actual vision of the Sangreal. Then, coming upon a hermitage and a hermit, Launcelot "prayed him for charity for to hear his life" (Xl, 190).[7] The hermit, a man of great good will, marvels that the knight looks so "abashed," and he senses somehow that God must love him. The hermit warns Launcelot that, though he is the greatest knight in the world, he has been deeply presumptuous in seeking to be "where His flesh and His blood was" while still unshriven of his "lechery." Though Launcelot makes his confession and is enjoined to do penance, he is nonetheless never free of his love of Guinevere and forgets "the promise and the perfection that he made in the quest."[8]

Percy's Lance has as his hermitage a New Orleans "Center for Aberrant Behavior" following the explosion of his ancestral home, Belle Isle, in which the bodies of his wife and three others are found, and it is only late in the course of the novel that the reader knows that Lance has been incarcerated for having wreaked his vengeance by multiple murder violent and obscene. From the cell Lance and, later, Percival as well look down on both "Lafayette Cemetery," suggestive of both revolutionary chivalry and death, and "Annunciation Street," evocative of new, redemptive life in the Incarnation. This dual view points directly to the opposing choices open to Lance and his old friend at the end of the novel.

Lance sees Percival, in his J. C. (a singular but typical Percy word-play) Penney pantsuit, standing in the graveyard with a woman who is scrubbing the white New Orleans tombs and who apparently asks the priest to pray for the dead. It is All Souls' Day, a feast that (like Christmas) would permit Father John to say three masses, but he apparently refuses the request. Percy seems to be indicating that the priest considers himself unworthy because he himself knows that he suffers from the "sickness unto death." Lance, too, suffers from despair and has a shock of recognition; at the sight of Percival he feels he is "overtaken by the past" and is seeing himself. Lance, however, suffers from what Kierkegaard calls the despair of defiance, truly demonic despair, so what he encounters in Percival is a former self or the self he might have been. Lance invites Percival to "Come into my cell" (3). These two deconstructed—or reconstructed—Arthurian knights then reenact in a radically postmodern and desacralized setting essential elements of the relationship between their literary/legendary ancestors.

In earlier days when he lived at Northumberland near Belle Isle, Percival, though he was not pugnacious but brilliant, obscure and withdrawn, bore the misnomer Harry Hotspur. He was built "like Pius XII" but called Prince Hal because he seemed happy only in whorehouses. "Also," Percy writes in an emphatic fragment—"as Percival and Parsifal, who found the Grail and brought life to a dead land" (10). Now he is Father John, either because he is a loner like the Baptist, or because he loved much like the Evangelist. Like Percival, Lance was part of the gone-to-pot Anglo-Saxon aristocracy which inhabited the River Road, called "the English Coast" since it was an enclave of British gentry united by a crazy-quilt dislike both of Catholics and the Longs. Unlike the Creoles who have mastered the secret of living ordinary lives well, making money and "making" Mardi Gras, their "honorable" families "lived from one great event to another, tragic events, triumphant events, with years of melancholy in between. They lost at Vicksburg and Shiloh, fought duels, defied Huey Long, and were bored to death between times" (23–24). In contrast to the River Road, Percy characterizes New Orleans proper as a Catholic city, not really part of the South, a city which has had no heroes in three hundred years and has its cathedral set in the Vieux Carré in a concentration of sin.

The Anglo-Saxon backgrounds shared by Lancelot and Percival have, however, resulted in strikingly different careers. Percival, perhaps because the men in his family are prone to depression and early suicide, has found Louisiana "not good enough for him" and chosen to work in Biafra. Lance, whose life peaked in college when he became a Rhodes scholar, had become a nonpracticing lawyer and a liberal gone sour, devoted on the one hand to rather paternalistic civil rights endeavors and, on the other, to publishing nostalgic essays on Civil War skirmishes in the *Louisiana Historical Journal.* In all this he had rather forlornly repeated the same dilettante efforts of his own father without knowing it. And he had done so because, being one of Percy's seemingly incurable romantics who puts his most cherished ideals just out of his reach, he is drawn, like his father (and, to be sure, Nick Carraway besides), inexorably into the past. That father, Maury, had been poet-laureate of Feliciana Parish, busying himself with publishing vignettes of historical events and non-Roman churches. His library was filled with romantic English poetry, the Waverley novels, Episcopal Church history, southern history and biographies of Robert E. Lee. He loved Lee "the way Catholics love St. Francis" (116): the Confederate hero had become for him "as legendary and mythical as King Arthur and the Round Table." The books indicate the reasons for the name given him by his father:

> Do you think I was named Lancelot for nothing? The Andrewes was tacked on by him to give it Episcopal sanction, but what he really had in mind . . . was that old nonexistent Catholic brawler and adulterer, Lancelot du Lac, King Ban of Benwick's son, knight of the Round Table and—here was the part he could never get over [or, it seems, get right]—one of only two knights to see the Grail (you, Percival, the other); and above all the extraordinariness of those chaste and incorrupt little Anglican chapels set down in this violent and corrupt land besieged on all sides by savage Indians, superstitious Romans, mealy-mouthed Baptists, howling Holy Rollers. (116)

"What's in a name?" all Percy's work would seem to ask. In this novel and in Lance's name there are, clearly, genes and destiny, the maddened living and killing, and the need both to tell and hear of it, the re-living of the whole after the fact.

Whether Lance's father and mother saw themselves in this romantic light, or Lance chooses to recall them in this way is unclear. But the romance dissolved in each case as the young Lance made his first discoveries of evil. The first took the form of an ill-gotten $10,000 found under the argyle socks in Maury's drawer. Lance recalls his sense of delight as his eyes devoured the money, "the sweet shameful heart of something, the secret."

The reader has an early clue to his later quest: "There is no secret in honor. If one could but discover the secret at the heart of dishonor" (213). While his father had been tending to such business, Lance's mother Lily had been having a kind of courtly love relationship with "Uncle" Harry Wills, a Mardi Gras krewe knight in a Duke's costume, who gives Lance gifts of a glass pistol with candy inside and a Swiss army knife. Thus, Maury, a cuckold, a sorrily trivialized Arthur, became a sort of role model for his son, precursor of Lance's own cuckolding. And Lily, a clear parody of the maid of Astolat, was "like a lovebird. She lived for love. Literally. Unless she was loved, she withered and died" (212). In this mix love seems to join money as twin bitch goddesses in Percy's postmodern American culture.

It is Lance's mysterious Cousin Callie who, appearing from out of the hurricane at the end of the novel, wearing an out-of-season camellia, like Dumas' Camille, pinned to her shoulder, provides us with Lance's reminiscence of Lily. In fact, Lance begins to confuse the two, perceiving them both as fallen women. He remembers Lily in a picture of a VMI military wedding, prankishly "proffering an unsheathed sword" to the photographer (225): "The sword is upright, the blade held in her hands, the hand guard making a cross." There he sees her as a Joan of Arc, but his ultimate mental picture of Lily has her with Uncle Harry "in the linoleum-cold gas-heat-hot tourist cabin" (216). Are these two his mother and father? The reader, with Lance, wonders. With all his rich heritage of names, Lance literally—and spiritually—does not know, cannot know whence he sprang. He must question his own paternity as he will later that of his daughter.

Continually within the point of view of his gnostic—even Manichean—hero's memory and current consciousness, Percy complicates these pictures of human evil with one of surd evil. Lancelot recalls that he was "in love" with Lucy Cobb. As a Louisiana football hero, from a state in which people valued fistfights and cockfights, Lance met the Georgian Lucy in Highlands, North Carolina, where the easy decorous manners of the eastern South prevailed. They were married, moved to Belle Isle and had two children. "Then," Lance says, "she died." Of Elaine, the Lily Maid of Astolat, who simply ceases breathing and dies of her love for Lancelot, Tennyson writes:

> She grew so cheerful that they deem'd her death
> Was rather in the fantasy than the blood.[9]

In Lucy the cause is leukemia and the fantasy in the mind and character of her husband, as Percy creates another, radically different version of the romantic Lily Maid.

Lance himself is unromantically discharged from the army, "not bloody and victorious and battered by Sir Turquine but with persistent diarrhea" (28). In the second generation Lance has witnessed not only the end of heroism but the decay of courtly love. The antithesis of the pure knight of the Grail, his son is no Galahad—consummate finder of the real grail—but bisexual and living in an old streetcar. And this Galahad has a sister seduced by a lesbian.

If Lucy was Lance's romantic past, Margot, his second wife, despite her infatuation with the crafts, the artifacts of the past, becomes his present. Belle Isle, fallen on hard times, opens its doors to tourists on the Azalea Trail, and Margot, from Texas with ten million, has become a "belle." Though it is impossible for new money to participate in the Comus ball, the Azalea Festival is a uniting of the oil rich and old, broke River Road gentry, the very same "rare royal betrothal" Margot and Lance will make. Less coy than Scarlett, Margot, Percy tells us, met the master of Belle Isle and promptly doffed her ante-bellum costume in order to become its mistress: "Damned if the hoop skirt didn't work like chaps" (75). Margot has a Morgan le Faye-like gift for transformations.

Now, in his cell, Lance feels that he himself was transformed by Margot. He ponders what love is and speaks to Percival: "For by your dear sweet Jesus I did love her there for her droll mercinariness and between her sweet legs and in her mouth . . ." (81). The "there," where he first made love to Margot, is the pigeonnier of Belle Isle. Along with the hospital cell, the pigeonnier is a critically important place of discovery in the novel, at once the Oriel of Launcelot and Guinevere and the Chapel Perilous of a question to be answered. It is there that Lance and Percival had first read *Ulysses* and discovered sex and the anger of an Odyssean hero whose wife has other suitors.[10] Margot can (or could), however, be like Morgan, both helpful and malicious in her crafts. Lance describes how this "Texas magician" transformed Belle Isle with its Carrara mantelpiece, English antiques and slave chairs, back to its original state. In addition, she turned the pigeonnier into a kind of "hunting lodge"-office for Lance. But, Lance explains, when she was finished with Belle Isle, she was finished with him.

Margot's new project involves a film crew at work on the new enchantment, twentieth-century cinematic magic, which will employ Belle Isle as well as a miniature steamboat on False River as settings. Margot has only a bit part and acts as girl Friday to Merlin, the Hemingwayesque director; Lance, in the background off-stage, is adviser on matters of southern history. Margot, having transformed the ancestral home to a celluloid stage-set, has her future sights set on playing Nora in "A Doll's House" for Janos Jacoby, co-director and alter-Merlin, who seems actually to be in charge.

It is during the filming that Lance makes his great "discovery." He is in the pigeonnier where he first made love to Margot and will later have his vision of the Lady of the Camellias. What Lance discovered, in glancing at his daughter Siobhan's camp application, and now remembers so vividly, is the letter "O" (significantly grailshaped) in her blood type, which indicates that she cannot be both his and Margot's daughter. Old bills and a bit of figuring confirm that she was in Texas with Merlin during the time Siobhan would have been conceived. He has discovered his wife's infidelity. And it is at this point that the nature of the quest he is reliving with Percival becomes explicit. If "the greatest good," Lance says, "is to be found in love, so is the greatest evil" (139). Armed with this new knowledge, the gnostic Lancelot seems restored to health. No longer a victim of the malaise, he quits drinking and with a virtually insidious lucidity develops his plan to seek the ultimate sin. Margot had been his "absolute," his "infinite," his "feast," his grail: "That was my communion, Father—no offense intended, that sweet dark sanctuary guarded by the heavy gold columns of her thighs, the ark of her covenant" (171). Now he would seek sin in the same place. As he tells it, "So Sir Lancelot set out, looking for something rarer than the Grail. A sin" (140).

His decision has caused Lance to take a hard look at himself in the mirror. What he saw was a man gone to seed: "Do you remember the picture of Lancelot disgraced, discovered in adultery with the queen, banished, living in the woods, stretched out on a rock, chin cupped in both hands, bloodshot eyes staring straight ahead, yellow hair growing down over his brows? But it's a bad comparison. My bloodshot eyes were staring too but it was not so much the case of my screwing the queen as the queen getting screwed by somebody else" (64). He engages Elgin, a black MIT engineering senior and liveried tour guide at Belle Isle, to "watch" and to film the sexual encounters of the film crew at the motel. When Lance views Elgin's flawed films he sees tiny reddish figures in a Dantesque hell, with tiny Pentecostal flames flickering over each head. Percy readers will recognize in the delta shape of the Margot-Merlin-Jacoby *menage à trois* and the "rough swastikaed triangle" (192) of Raine Robinette and Troy Dana, the film's stars, and Lucy, Lance's daughter by his first wife, a ghastly parody in which perverted sex becomes the horrible inversion of Percy's own intersubjective theory of symbol which he describes in his essay, "The Delta Factor."[11] With his suspicions empirically validated, he devises his own plot—a marplot whose events, in initiating life's evils, totally outstrip them in their killing cruelty—by which the crew will move into Belle Isle and be blown up by leaking methane gas from the well upon which the old mansion sits. He sends away both his daughters as well as Merlin, with whom he shares a sense of perverse fellowship as cuckold. Ironically, it is the Christmas season, the tree is lighted in the living room, and the traditional bonfires are burning on the levee to celebrate the Incarnation. At the same time Lance is planning his elaborately staged destruction, a great hurricane is threatening the coast. Percy, a lover of puns and word games and jokes, names the hurricane "Marie." Raine, whose name may signify "rein" or "reign" or "raines," the fabric of Guinevere's shroud, insists that they take "champagne" up to the belvedere atop Belle Isle and "have a party named 'Goodbye movie, hello Marie'" (204).

As he relives the events with Percival, he recalls for the first time how he performed their old Bowie knife test, sticking the blade, supposed to have belonged to Jim Bowie himself, into the cypress wall and trying to withdraw it. The Excalibur of their youth would become Lancelot's instrument of an act by which he discovers, beyond envy and revenge, no secret but only the nothingness at the heart of evil.

Knowing understood as a gnostic grasp of esoteric fact and "knowing" in the biblical sense become one in his dark ritual; both are essential to Lance's plan as he visits the bedrooms of Belle Isle, where Elgin's concealed cameras convert living into mere acting, home into cinematic stage-set, and sex into sheer obscenity. In Raine's room, Troy Dana—the "faggot" as Lance calls him—lies stoned on the far side of the bed. Lance, seeing his daughter Lucy's sorority ring on Raine's hand, sodomizes the willing actress in order to discover her "secret." Then he finds Margot and Janos Jacoby in the great Calhoun bed whose design, complete with its buttresses, gargoyles and altar screen, resembles a Gothic cathedral. Lance the new knight sees the two as the new beast and squeezes them more tightly together: "Mashed together, the two were never more apart, never more themselves" (240). Then all three seem to float in the methane-filled air. They, in fact, replicate Dante's Paola and Francesca, destined to be inseparable and driven forever by the winds of the Inferno. Their sin?—their adultery, of course, which resulted from their having read the story of Lancelot and Guinevere.

Lancelot consummates his nihilistic quest in wreaking vengeful judgment on the new barbarians. He slits Jacoby's throat with his Bowie knife, given him years before by that ambiguously fallen woman, the

Lady of the Camellias, his Lady of the Lake. After the explosion in which Lance is blown free, he returns to the ruins, not to find the four bodies but to retrieve the knife. Later judged incompetent to stand trial, he will be freed when he is declared sane. Although guilt is not seen to be an issue for either the law or Lance, Percy's reader, like Percival, knows that this unholy knight's unholy grail is in himself.

And so a year later he carries on his curiously compulsive monologue with Father John, who makes him feel that he is overtaken by his past, by his self. Lance, having confessed to Percival, the hooded knight, senses that Percival still has a question: "Do you love?" Lance has an answer ready, though it is hardly the one Percival has in mind. Because he cannot stand the world as he finds it, Lance has been developing a Utopian vision of a new order and a theory of sexual love by which to defend himself against the barbarism and start the world over. Behavior will be based, he insists manically, not on Catholicism or any other ism but on a stern new code for "gentlemen," who will hold a "gentleness toward women and an intolerance of swinishness, a counsel kept, and above all a readiness to act, and act alone if necessary" (157). This third revolution will take place in Virginia and follow the other two—that of 1776, won because the British were stupid, and the second, in 1861, which failed because, as Lance says, "we got stuck with the Negro thing and it was our fault" (157). His new knight will look like the Virginian, with his gun across his shoulders standing on the Blue Ridge, a perfect reembodiment of the broad sword tradition.

Lance explains that such new men would "have felt at home at Mont-Saint-Michel, the Mount of the Archangel with the flowing sword, or with Richard Coeur-de-Lion at Acre. They believed in a God who said he came not to bring peace but the sword" (157). As opposed to Christian *caritas,* Lance's code involves a "stern rectitude," a "tight-lipped courtesy toward men," and "chivalry toward women," who "must be saved from the whoredom they have chosen" (158). Women, for their part, will be either virgins or whores.

Lance's abstracted history of sex relates directly, if unbeknownst to him, to his own biographical revelations. First, there was the romantic period in which he "fell in love" with Lucy, the figure of light in the Paradiso, whom he insists was a virgin. The current period, represented by Margot and the film company, is like a "baboon colony" or a "soap opera." The third stage he insistently predicts will be a clarification by way of catastrophe, a living death, when everything will become desert. This phase and the "new earth" that it will for him ensure is symbolized by the third

woman in Lance's life, Anna, a young woman made autistic as a result of
gang-rape with whom he communicates by tapping in Morse Code on the
cell wall. From Lance's skewed perception, she is both whore, as a victim
of rape, and virgin in that she is now like a ten-year-old. He will take her to
Virginia and build a log cabin and they will be the New Adam and Eve of
the third revolution—still another attempt, stupidly and self-righteously
Utopian, to redefine a gnostically solipsistic Grail.

The film story within the novel depicts Lancelot's second phase, or
the current state of sex in America. In addition, the film and its stars, in
turn, constitute Percy's comic indictment of a particular scholarly work
on the Grail legend. Perhaps the most fascinating parody related to
Arthurian materials in *Lancelot* is the one Percy works on Jessie Weston's *From Ritual to Romance*.[12] Merlin believes, and rightly so, that he
has "created" Troy Dana, whose name evokes both paganism and the
heroic code of the Homeric epics. In himself Troy is "nothing, a perfect
cipher," but with his helmet of golden hair he is perceived in the film as a
"creature of light" (147), with a temperature "around 101. He actually
glows." Everyone else in the film is "hung up" and, therefore, dead. Not
only is Troy free in this universe of cinematic glare, he offers resurrection; he frees others, if only pathetically, for that false world. "Perhaps he
is a god. At least he is a kind of Christ-type" (148). He frees Sarah, the li-
brarian-initiate, played by Margot, in the stacks. "It is not just screwing,"
Merlin explains, "but a kind of sacrament and celebration of life. He
could be a high priest of Mithras [in Weston, responsible for the initiation of women]."[13] Merlin expounds in postmodern doublespeak that the
film will not treat love but be content with "the erotic which in any form
at all, is always life-enhancing." The sharecropper of the vegetation-rit-
ual film finds his celluloid Beatrice in the aristocratic girl. Jacoby explains: "'It is the aristocrat in this case who has the life-embracing
principle and not the sharecropper, as is usually the case, since he is usually shown as coming from the dirt.' 'Soil,' said Margot" (114).

If indeed the Grail legends, as Weston believes, have their kernel,
their sole origin, in the Vegetation Ritual, the Life-Cult, what, Percy
seems to ask, has become of the fertility ritual in the twentieth century?
While Percy is, on the one hand, pronouncing judgment on the gnosticism, which Weston associates with the cults of Mithra and Attis, and the
violence of his hero, much of Lance's critique of the American scene is
the author's own—gone crazy, as the author knows. Percy would believe
that the sort of Grail conception which is Weston's—divorced as it is
from the source of the Grail, Christ—results in the very infertility that

announces the true Wasteland of our time. Albeit through his unreliable narrator, he has provided a novel full of examples of desacralized sex so that the fiction may itself be read as a statement on Weston's theory: the discovery of the adulterous female symbol as sign of fertility in the letter "O"; the ultimate impotence of both Merlin and Lancelot; the unerotically perverted sex of the film crew; the unspeakable rape of Anna; and, finally, the parodic rape in the film which takes place in the pigeonnier-Oriel of Belle Isle. *Lancelot* is Percy's fullest fictional dramatization of those conditions describing the character of postmodern American sexuality as seen by the noted American psychiatrist quoted by Percy: "In Harry Stack Sullivan's words, the mark of success in the culture is how much one can do to another's genitals without risking one's self-esteem unduly."[14] Joyous Gard or Camelot, clearly, Percy says, lies in a world elsewhere. Merlin's film satirizes Weston's pre-Christian ideas directly, as does Lance's own post-Christian story. In both love is divorced from spiritual as well as physical fertility and, therefore, from the source of love and life alike. Clearly, Lance has no genuine conception of authentic love, of caritas. His chauvinistic new chivalry is very old and very false, and it will not recreate a lost civilization. The role of Percival in the novel is to hold and transmit the secret that will.

For Percy, the existentialist, the question which still hangs in the air of this Chapel Perilous should not find its answer in an abstracted definition of love but in an act. What is the Grail? Whom shall it serve? The seeming ambiguity of the structure and, in particular, of the openendedness of the novel almost hides Percy's answers. In the first sentence of the novel Lancelot has said to Percival: "Come into my cell. Make yourself at home."[15] As the priest's visits go on, Percy, in the manner of Flannery O'Connor, has Lance address him by what might almost be termed "taking the name of the Lord in vain," in a coincidence of opposites. "Jesus, come in and sit down" (84). Lance has referred to Father John as one "obsessed with God" (216), as one who chose "the time-place god" (31). Twice the priest looks like Isaiah's "man of sorrows" (53:3) and, thus Percy implies, he must himself be "acquainted with infirmity." Lance sees Percival's sadness as nothing more than a "tolerant Catholic world-weariness" (131) which loses all distinctions and loves everything. But his cynical statement is precisely Percy's ironic affirmation of Percival as incarnate creature and of the need for participation in both the fall and the healing Incarnation. Percy has conceived of Percival, as Malory did, as one of the very few people who "believed in our Lord Jesus Christ . . . who believed in God perfectly."[16]

In his final visit, Percival wears what Lance calls his "priest uni-form" (163). Lance asks if he is "girding for battle or dressed up like Lee for surrender" (163). In Lance's scheme the priest might join the third revolution or retain the old Stoicism, but Percival has his own ideas of spiritual battle and surrender, closer perhaps to the dark night of the soul and that surrender to the love of God described by the mystics. The time is still November, the month of All Souls, when the last meeting occurs, and Father John has now begun to pray for the dead, for himself and Lance, those knights whose wounds are secret. Lance will soon be leav-ing and he will stroll down Annunciation Street. Will there be a fullness of message for him, an annunciation of incarnation, in what has been the only partially seen billboard sign from the "little view" from his cell?

The question for this knight of the Unholy Grail may well have been formulated at the very beginning of the novel when Lance points out the fragmented "message":

> Free &
>   Ma
>   B

The gnostic Lance has missed the significance of the phonetic hiero-glyph that would tell him what Percival "knows," that each of them—and Percy's reader as well—is free and may *be;* to "be," for Walker Percy, is both to become and to believe. But Lance, feeling very cold, complains: "Why did I discover nothing at the heart of evil? There was no 'secret' after all. . . . There is no question. There is no unholy grail as there was no Holy Grail" (253). Percival gazes at him with his same steady sad-ness, and Lancelot once again formulates the priest's perennial question: "Do I think I can ever love anyone?" (254). Each knight must make a de-cision and a new beginning, because there is a secret.

Lance refuses to live in the world he sees as Sodom and seems perched to create his own world with Anna in Virginia, even if it takes an apocalyptic sword to protect his Utopia. Yet Percy's endings always leave his characters open to possibility, and in this novel Lancelot seems willing to "wait" and give Percival's God "time," as he says. Curiously, it is Lance who jocularly describes Percival's grail: "So you plan to take a little church in Alabama, Father, preach the gospel, turn bread into flesh, forgive the sins of Buick dealers, administer communion to suburban housewives?" (256). Then, as if he is only now realising what he must do, Percival looks straight at Lancelot. Under that gaze of the hooded knight, Lance says, "You know something you think I don't know, and you want to tell me but you hesitate" (256). Then Percival, speaking for the first time in the novel, says simply, "Yes." And his continued affirmations, his "yeses" (he says "yes" twelve times in this final scene, "no" just once), project into the future, they stand over against the "no's," the deep negations of Lancelot that have been the structure of the past, of his unholy quest. The Grail question still remains in the final lines. Lancelot: "Is there anything you wish to tell me before I leave?" Percival utters the novel's final word: "Yes." Unlike his paradigmatic predecessor, Lancelot has not done penance and he does not love, but he is free and he "may," because in Percy's grace-filled, redeemed world, anything may "happen." Percival, who will find the Grail, knows that secret.

It is in Tennyson's and then again Toynbee's understanding of the failure of the Arthurian myth before the onslaught of the barbarians that Percy finds sanctions for his attack on Stoicism and the chivalric codes of courtly love and the broad sword as they have developed in the 1900's in America. As the concept of a second coming of Arthur was completely inadequate to the Britons before the onslaught of the barbarians, so are those Arthurian values inadequate to the barbarism of sexual abuse and modern violence which define the postmodern world of Lancelot Andrewes Lamar.

Arthur's Christian realm was destroyed by the barbarians within— the adultery and resultant blood feuds—as much as by Modred and the barbarians without. When his knights departed on their separate quests, Arthur sorrowed that he would not see many of them again and realized that the Round Table and its code were at an end. Percy, like Malory and Tennyson, is deeply concerned with "decline and fall"[17] and the available alternatives to that decline and fall. One is what Will Percy called "the unassailable wintry kingdom of Marcus Aurelius"; still another is Lance's apocalyptic third revolution of individualistic conservatism; the third is implicit in all Percy's work: "Compared to the fatalism of his aristocratic Uncle Will and the messianism of Lancelot, Percy says he has much more hope. 'I'm a Catholic, and I believe that with all the difficulty it is having, the Judaeo-Christian tradition is the last best hope of sustaining democracies.'"[18] In that tradition Percy sees the world as full of signs: words (even on billboards), events, people, sacraments. Each work ends with sacrament, Walker Percy's Grail. In *The Moviegoer* Binx follows the Mardi Gras of his life with the penitential understanding of Ash Wednesday. Like Chrétien's Percival on Good Friday, he then has the potential to see the Grail. He can reject the "knowing" Stoicism of his Aunt Emily and begin to "do" the works of faith, to love and marry Kate, to care for his brothers and sisters, whom he has hitherto thought of only as his "half-brothers and -sisters." *The Last Gentleman* ends with a baptism in Santa Fe, *Love in the Ruins* with a Christmas Mass. *The Second Coming,* the novel which follows *Lancelot,* is as much about life as *Lancelot* is about death. It offers an answer to both the malaise and the old and new adulteration of love in the truly life-enhancing coming together and marriage of Will Barret and Allie, herself a sacrament for Will. "The Space Odyssey," the last chapter of *Lost in the Cosmos,* concludes with the ancient Abbot Liebowitz offering Mass for an extraordinarily ecumenical group of survivors as the world begins over again after the nuclear holocaust of the obscene year 2069. *The Thanatos Syndrome,* Percy's most recent fiction, concludes with a Mass of the Epiphany, the feast which celebrates Christ's being shown forth to the world. Walker Percy's grail is, quite simply, what it has always been in the Christian tradition, the cup of the last supper and the blood of the crucified Christ. Percy, both piously and parodically a new Joseph of Arimathea, would save it for the wasteland of the postmodern world.

NOTES

Reprinted with permission from *King Arthur Through the Ages,* ed. Valerie M. Lagorio and Mildred Leake Day (New York: Garland, 1990), II, 255-77.

1. Zoltán Abádi-Nagy, "A Talk with Walker Percy," (1973), *Conversations with Walker Percy,* eds. Lewis A. Lawson and Victor A. Kramer (Jackson, 1985), 73.

2. Percy adopts this Thomistic term from Gabriel Marcel's title. Marcel's work, like that of Søren Kierkegaard and Martin Heidegger, has been a definitive influence in Percy's thought.

3. Walker Percy, *The Moviegoer* (New York, 1967) (cited by page numbers hereafter within the text). The novel was first published by Alfred A. Knopf in 1961 and won the 1962 National Book Award.

4. The epigraph to this essay is from D. C. Somervell's abridgement of Toynbee's multivolume work (New York, 1947) 1, 223.

5. Walker Percy, "Stoicism in the South," *Commonweal* 64, 14 (July 6, 1956), 343-44.

6. Walker Percy, *Lancelot* (New York, 1977) (cited by page numbers hereafter within the text).

7. Sir Thomas Malory, *Le Morte D'Arthur* (London, 1906) 2, 190-91. Percy is clearly familiar with Malory and Tennyson, but any critic who knows his thoroughgoing habit of research may well imagine he has read older texts as well.

8. Malory, 2, 271.

9. *Idylls of the King,* in *The Works of Tennyson,* ed. Hallam Lord Tennyson (New York, 1931), 406.

10. "Personified by the driven-to-murder Lancelot is 'what my Uncle Will used to call the broad-sword tradition, that goes back to Ulysses taking revenge on all the suitors who were hanging around his house when he got back from his long voyage to Troy. He doesn't just throw them out. He kills them all, you know. If somebody offends you, you kill them.'" (Percy in a 1977 interview with William Delaney in "A Southern Novelist Whose CB Crackles with Kierkegaard," *Conversations with Walker Percy,* eds. Lewis A. Lawson and Victor A. Kramer [Jackson, 1985], 154).

11. Walker Percy, *The Message in the Bottle* (New York, 1954).

12. Jessie L. Weston, *From Ritual to Romance* (New York: Peter Smith, 1941). See also John Edward Hardy, *The Fiction of Walker Percy* (Urbana: University of Illinois Press, 1987), 146–49.

13. Weston, quoting Cumont, describes Mithra as "le génie de la lumière céleste," 156.

14. *The Message in the Bottle,* 100.

15. The verb "come" resonates in Percy's fiction in the title of the novel that follows *Lancelot, The Second Coming;* in the final words of *Lost in the Cosmos,* "Come back." In his essay on faith, "The Message in the Bottle," Percy explains that the apostle who delivers the good news may, when "everyone is saying, 'Come!,' when radio and television say nothing else but 'Come!,'" find that "the best way to say 'Come!' is to remain silent." *The Message in the Bottle,* 148.

16. Malory, 2, 198.

17. Delaney interview, 152.

18. Delaney interview, 157.

CHAPTER 18

The Grail in Modern Fiction
Sacred Symbol in a Secular Age

RAYMOND H. THOMPSON

As in medieval accounts, modern treatments of the Grail legend offer two distinct ranges of possibility: it may be more or less Christian, and it may be more or less linked to Arthur's realm. At its first appearance in the *Perceval* of Chrétien de Troyes, the Grail is undoubtedly mysterious, but not particularly holy. It was left to Robert de Boron to identify it as the vessel of the Last Supper used by Joseph of Arimathea to catch Christ's blood after the Crucifixion. To the voluminous medieval romances on the Grail, later scholars have added learned commentary upon its nature and origins. Modern authors, thus, may perceive it as either pagan or Christian, endowed in either case with a rich history that precedes its manifestation to the Round Table. Moreover, despite the claim in the Vulgate *Queste del Saint Graal* and Sir Thomas Malory's *Morte Darthur* that the Grail was removed from this sinful world forever, it has returned in the pages of modern fiction more often than even King Arthur himself.[1] Indeed, interest in the Grail has quickened in the 1990s with the publication of several anthologies of short stories.[2]

At times, this interest may amount to no more than the borrowing of isolated elements of the legend in works with other interests. The Grail is transferred to a new guardian in Marion Zimmer Bradley's "Chalice of Tears, or I Didn't Want That Damned Grail Anyway" (1992). The Siege Perilous transports the hero of Andre Norton's *Witch World* (1963) to a magical otherworld. Parsifal tests the valor of the protagonist in *Bring Me the Head of Prince Charming* (1991) by Roger Zelazny and Robert Sheckley; and as Peredur he is one of the mythic figures who haunt a magical forest in Robert Holdstock's *Mythago Wood* (1984). The motif of the maimed Fisher King and the resultant wasteland appear in Darrell Schweitzer's "The Faces of Midnight" (1981, revised and published the same year as "Midnight, Moonlight, and the Secrets of the Sea"), Gael Baudino's Dragonsword series (1991–92), *The Grail and the Ring* (1994) by Teresa Edgerton, and *Merlin's Bones* (1995) by Fred Saberhagen. These characters and elements are undeveloped, however: they remain convenient plot devices in those works where they appear.

These are all fantasies, but elements of the Grail story turn up in "realistic" fiction also.[3] Among those in a contemporary setting are a handful of mystery and suspense novels.[4] In *The Grail Tree* (1979) by Jonathan Gash, for example, murder is committed to gain possession not of the battered pewter cup reputed to be the Grail, but of the ornate silver casket in which it is placed. While there is no suggestion of spiritual values in the novel, that the thieves should be punished for their materialism is not inappropriate to the Grail theme.

More frequently, however, elements of the legend are introduced into a realistic contemporary setting by the process of transposition. Suggestive parallels are created rather than features actually borrowed. The figure of the Fisher King is evoked in Richard Chizmar's short story "The Sinner King" (1994); in Tony Cosier's as yet unpublished novel *Perceval*, of which six excerpts have appeared in various magazines since 1983; in Nicole St. John's *Guinever's Gift* (1977), which recreates the Arthur-Guenevere-Lancelot love triangle; in *The Paper Grail* (1991) by James P. Blaylock, where the Grail is a nineteenth-century Japanese sketch that was once folded into the shape of a cup and used to gather blood; in *The Fisher King* (1991), a novel by Leonore Fleischer based on the motion picture; in Tim Powers's *Last Call* (1992), in which the renewal of the reign of the goddess-queen and her consort, the young king who replaces his predecessor, is reenacted among a group of gamblers in Las Vegas; and in *The Green Knight* (1993) by Iris Murdoch, which loosely transposes not only the account of Gawain's encounter with the Green Knight, but also the motifs of the Castle of Marvels and the Holy Fool, as well as the Fisher King, from Grail legend.

The figure of Perceval, the Holy Fool, who appears with the Fisher King in several of the above-mentioned works, is an equally popular borrowing among novels that transpose parts of the Grail legend. His Grail Quest is used by J.H. Shorthouse to condemn women committed to socialism in *Sir Perceval* (1886); by John Cowper Powys to assert the power of mysticism in a material world in *A Glastonbury Romance* (1933); by Bernard Malamud to recount the career of a gifted baseball player in *The Natural* (1952); by Raja Rao in the structure of *The Serpent and the Rope* (1960); by David Lodge to mock the idiosyncrasies of the academic conference circuit in *Small World* (1984); by John Crowley to reveal the scholarly fascination with research in *Ægypt* (1987); and by Katherine Patterson to explore the anguish of a young boy's search for information about his father who died in Vietnam in *Park's Quest* (1988).

By contrast, Galahad is transposed in only one very short story, "The Christmas of Sir Galahad" (1871) by Elizabeth Stuart Phelps, where he remains faithful to a very trying wife, although he does turn up as a reincarnation in both Theodore Sturgeon's "Excalibur and the Atom" (1951) and *The Forever King* (1992) by Molly Cochran and Warren Murphy. Lancelot's Quest is hardly more popular, but his pursuit of the "Unholy Grail"—to expose the corruption that lies behind the glittering facade of modern America in general and Hollywood in particular—in Walker Percy's *Lancelot* (1978) marks one of the most impressive achievements in modern Grail fiction. The Grail sought in *The Grail: A Novel* (1963) by Babs H. Deal is an unbeaten football season which the team's quarterback, Lance, only just fails to pull off. It also turns up as the mischievously named Platter of Plenty in *The Lyre of Orpheus* (1988), Robertson Davies's novel about staging an Arthurian opera.

These works offer only tantalizing fragments and echoes of Grail tradition. A far larger number actually send their characters on a Quest for the Grail itself; or sometimes have them stumble across it unawares, as did Perceval on his first visit to the Grail Castle. The experience may take place in a future portrayed by science fiction: in David Bischoff's *Star Spring* (1982), the search takes place in a computer-generated fantasy world; in Andre Norton's "That Which Overfloweth" (1992), it happens in a distant future of a waning earth; in John Gregory Betancourt's "Dogs Questing" (1992), it is conducted by dogs seeking to restore their ancient bond with mankind; in Patricia Kennealy-Morrison's Keltiad series (1984–), it is for one of the Thirteen Treasures of a Celtic race that has taken its customs into space. Or it may take place in an alternate universe imagined in fantasy: one in which Hitler won the war, as in Brad Linaweaver's "Under an Appalling Sky" (1992); or one even more crassly commercial than our own, as in Adam-Troy Castro's "Jesus Used a Paper Cup" (1994).

More commonly, however, the Quest for the Grail takes place in a contemporary setting. In one group of short stories, all published in 1992, this involves time travel: in Neil Gaiman's "Chivalry," Galaad comes forward in time to bargain with an old-age pensioner who bought the Holy Grail in an Oxfam shop; in "The Steel American" by S.P. Somtow and "That Way Lies Camelot" by Jenny Wurts, it is Perceval's turn to make the trip; in "Greggie's Cup" by Rick Wilber, the fabric of time is torn aside when a modern boy meets Lancelot. Conversely, people in the modern world attempt to retrieve the Grail from the past in "A Knyght There Was" (1963) by Robert F. Young, and *The Fetch* (1991) by Robert Holdstock. The Grail is also found by a Canadian teenager who is transported first to the world of Nwm, then to her own world's Arthurian past, in *The Third Magic* (1988) by Welwyn Wilton Katz. There she discovers that she herself is none other than Morgan le Fay.

In many of the modern Grail Quests, the heroes find themselves in competition with evil-doers who scheme to wield the power of the Grail for their own destructive ends. In *The Sleepers* (1968) by Jane Curry (where the Grail is one of the Thirteen Treasures of Britain), Sanders Anne Laubenthal's *Excalibur* (1973), and *The Return of Merlin* (1995) by Deepak Chopra, these foes are traditional Arthurian figures like Morgan Le Fay, Morgause of Orkney, and Mordred. They are religious cults in Sherard Vines's *Return, Belphegor!* (1932); evil magicians in both *A Wheel of Stars* (1989) by Laura Gilmour Bennett and *The Forever King* (1992) by Cochran and Murphy; Nazis in *Indiana Jones and the Last Crusade* (1989), a novel adapted by Rob MacGregor from the film screenplay; neo-Nazis in Jerry and Sharon Ahern's "Siege Perilous" (1992); and criminals in Jack C. Haldeman II's "Ashes to Ashes" (1992). In Charles Williams's *War in Heaven* (1930) and Susan Cooper's Dark Is Rising series (1968–77), the heroes must struggle against the supernatural force of evil itself.

Traditional figures or their modern equivalents appear not only as foes, however. Spiritual successors to the Fisher King appear in C.S. Lewis's *That Hideous Strength* (1945) as Ransom, the Pendragon and leader of the struggle of good against evil; and in *The Column of Dust* (1909) by Evelyn Underhill, where he turns over guardianship of the Holy Grail to a woman. Edwin Casson-Perceval, the naive narrator and friend of Hitler in *The Ring Master* (1987) by David Gurr, desperately excavates various sites in a misguided search for the Grail amidst the wasteland of wartorn Europe. Like Perceval, modern protagonists fail to ask the vital question in two short stories, "A Deal with God" by Pat Cadigan and "Storyville, Tennessee" by Richard Gilliam, both published in 1992. Arthur Machen develops the contrast between the spiritual and material worlds in *The Great Return* (1915) and in *The Secret Glory* (1922) where the hero's high-minded impracticality compares favorably with the cruelty and hypocrisy of the world in which he lives. As in the latter novel, modern characters are inspired by the Grail to lead better lives in *The Sparrow Child* (1958) by Meriol Trevor, *The Flowering Thorn* (1961) by Elizabeth Yunge-Bateman,[5] Nancy Holder's "To Leave If You Can," and Lawrence Watt-Evans's "Visions" (both 1992).

The Grail is sought and/or found not only in the modern period, but in earlier ones also: the nineteenth century in Lee Hoffman's "Water" (1992), in which a cowboy's discovery of it breaks a drought in the American West, and in Karl Edward Wagner's "One Paris Night" (1992), in which two adventurers melt it down for silver bullets to shoot a werewolf; the High Middle Ages in *The Hidden Treasure of Glaston* (1946) by Eleanore M. Jewett and *Kingdom of the Grail* (1992) by A.A. Attanasio (in both of which it performs miracles), "Castle of Maidens" (1992) by Richard Lee Byers and *Merlin's Destiny* (1993) by Sigmund Brouwer (in both of which it turns up in unlikely places); and the years shortly after the battle of Camlann in Christopher Webb's *Eusebius the Phoenician* (1969).

Most Grail Quests (or encounters) in modern fiction do, however, take place in King Arthur's day. Many of the historical novels are set in post-Roman Britain during the Dark Ages, but in keeping with the attempts to create a sense of authenticity, they demystify the Grail. In Victor Canning's Crimson Chalice Trilogy (1976–80), the traditions linked with the chalice are recounted, but it comes into the possession of Arturo's mother who passes it on to her son as a cherished talisman, rather than the object of a Quest. It is one of the ancient Treasures of Britain sought in both Thomas Clare's *King Arthur and the Riders of Rheged* (1992) and Mary Stewart's Arthurian novels (1970–). In *The Prince and the Pilgrim* (1995), however, Stewart's most recent addition to the series, she introduces another, more Christian Grail, brought over to Britain by a royal Merovingian refugee. In some novels, the Grail exercises a negative influence upon characters and events: in *The Emperor Arthur* (1967) by Godfrey Turton, Galahad's credulity is exploited by an ambitious Church; in George Finkel's *Twilight Province* (1967, published in the United States as *Watch Fires to the North*, 1968), Glahad [*sic*] becomes a religious fanatic; in *The Pendragon* (1978) by Catherine Christian, the Grail seems to be no more than a delusion resulting from the madness of Peredur. Others, however, present it in more positive terms: in *Excalibur!* (1980) by Gil Kane and John Jakes, it is the land of Britain itself; in Parke Godwin's *Firelord* (1980), it is a battered cup of uncertain authenticity that challenges people's faith; in *Guinevere: The Legend in Autumn* (1991), the conclusion to Persia Woolley's Guinevere trilogy (1987–91), it means many things to many people. Alone among these historical novels in a Dark Age setting, Jim Hunter's *Percival and the Presence of God* (1978) focuses upon the Grail Quest rather than includes it as but one episode in the course of Arthur's career.

Also set in the Dark Ages are six fantasies: in *The Mists of Avalon* (1982) by Marion Zimmer Bradley, the cup, dish, and spear are relics sacred to the worship of the Mother Goddess; in Sharan Newman's *Guinevere Evermore* (1985), the Quest follows that in Malory except that Palomides replaces Bors; in *Arthur* (1989) and again in *Pendragon* (1994), both by Stephen R. Lawhead, the mortally wounded Arthur goes for healing by the Grail to the Fisher King's palace in Avallon, though only in the latter novel does he return; in "The Cup and the Cauldron" (1992) by Mercedes Lackey, a follower of the Goddess and a Christian nun must overcome their religious prejudices before they can become Grail Maidens; in Judith Tarr's "Silver, Stone, and Steel" (1995), Merlin dreams of the coming of the Grail to Britain and into the custody of three queen-goddesses. Like these, *The City of Sarras* (1887) by U. Ashworth Taylor and Michael L. Nelson's "Perceval and the Holy Grail" (1979), two works set in the High Middle Ages, invoke the mystical aspects of the Grail, but whereas the first six stress the oneness of all worship, the latter pair emphasize its Christian identity.

More commonly, however, fiction set in the High Middle Ages explores character rather than mystical experience. Although he is sometimes overshadowed by others, Galahad is important to Mary Southworth's *Galahad, Knight Errant* (1907), John Erskine's *Galahad: Enough of His Life to Explain His Reputation* (1926), and Gwendolyn Bowers's *Brother to Galahad* (1963). Gawin's [*sic*] confusion and Perceval single-mindedness are examined in Dorothy James Roberts's *Kinsmen of the Grail* (1963); Aglovale's struggle with a strict conscience in *The Life of Sir Aglovale de Galis* (1905) by Clemence Housman; the sins and final repentance of Kundry and Amfortas in *The Grail of Hearts* (1992) by Susan Shwartz; the religious fanaticism of Mador in "Sir Mador Seeks the Grail" (1987) and the perplexity of Lancelot in "Prelude to the Quest" (1989), two stories by David Gareth from a projected collection dealing with the Quest for the Grail. T.H. White offers penetrating insights into Gawaine, Lionel, Aglovale, and Lancelot, each of whom relates the adventures he encountered on his Quest in *The Ill-Made Knight* (1940, later incorporated into *The Once and Future King*, 1958). Two novels depart from tradition to celebrate the steadfastness of women who achieve the Grail: in *A Lady of King Arthur's Court* (1909) by Sara Hawks Sterling, it is one of Guenever's damsels, disguised as a monk; in *The King's Damosel* (1976) by Vera Chapman, it is ever-adventurous Lynett.

The last group consists of ironic fiction. This too is set in the High Middle Ages, but it measures the gap between expectations and results, rather than heroic achievements. Some of these make use of the Grail legend to condemn human failings: Robert Nye's *Merlin* (1978), Richard Monaco's Grail series (1977–85), and Erin Caine's erotic novel *Knights of Pleasure* (1992; reissued in 1994 as *Avalon Nights* by Sophie Danson, another pseudonym) describe, in graphic detail, the depravity of humanity; Monaco's *Broken Stone* (1985) and "The Unholy" (1994) by Doug Murray unfold plans to wield an evil counterpart of the Holy Grail; Tanith Lee's "Exalted Hearts" (1994) reveals that more is lost than gained by the Quest.

Others, by contrast, react to our follies with affectionate laughter: the uncertain nature of the Grail generates humor in *A Connecticut Yankee in King Arthur's Court* (1889) by Mark Twain, *To the Chapel Perilous* (1955) by Naomi Mitchison, and Thomas Berger's *Arthur Rex* (1978); in "Maureen Birnbaum and the Saint Graal" (1993) by George Alec Effinger and in Tom Holt's *Grailblazers* (1994), where the object of the Quest is a berry bowl and a washing-up bowl respectively; and in "The Awful Truth in Arthur's Barrow" (1992) by Lionel Fenn, where it turns out to be a "hideously gorgeous woman" named Holy Gail. The Grail questers themselves are the source of comedy in Matt Cohen's *Too Bad Galahad* (1972) and in "The Power in Penance" (1994) by Edward E. Kramer, where the Holy Grail consumes in flames all who try to drink from it save only the bishop's cat named Percy.

This rapid survey of modern fiction reveals significant developments in Grail tradition. Some authors have been influenced by scholars who argue that the Grail evolved from the Cauldron of Plenty in Celtic legend: Katz takes her description of the Grail from that of the cauldron in the ancient Welsh poem *The Spoils of Annwfn*; Clare, Curry, and Kennealy-Morrison include it among the Thirteen Treasures of Britain; Stewart and Bradley link it with sword, spear, and dish as ancient relics of power. Bradley and Mitchison, among others, make it sacred to the worship of the Mother Goddess.

Most authors who make this identification are women, and they, along with others, not only pay closer attention to female characters like Elaine of Corbenic, Kundry, and successive Grail maidens, but also expand the role of women in the Grail story. Both Katz and Bradley make Morgan le Fay the Grail bearer; Underhill, Norton, and Bradley (in her short story) have guardianship of the Grail transferred to women; Chapman, Kennealy-Morrison, Mitchison, and Sterling send women to quest for the Grail; and girls are among the group of young people who seek it in the juvenile novels of Cooper, Trevor, and Yunge-Batemen.

Among the figures from Grail legend, Perceval and the Fisher King have exercised the strongest fascination for modern authors. The Waste Land has also manifested itself in an intriguing variety of ways, from drought in the otherworld of fantasy, to the desolation of modern, post-industrial cities. Evil is sometimes identified with contemporary manifestations like religious cults and the Nazis. The attempts of such evildoers to use the power of the Grail for selfish ends are a departure from medieval tradition that insists upon its purity. Perhaps aware of this, some authors have invented an Unholy Grail.

Another departure from tradition is the use of irony. While the composers of medieval romances were ready to parody the conventions of the genre, they were much more respectful in their treatment of Grail legend, whether out of Christian belief or fear of Church censure. Irony does appear in Chrétien's *Perceval* and the fourteenth-century English verse *Sir Perceval of Galles,* but the former predates identification of the Grail with the cup used at the Last Supper, while the latter omits the Grail altogether. By contrast, modern authors are ready not only to laugh at the impracticalities of the Grail Quest, but even to condemn an often intolerant Church for exploiting it. It is one measure of how the Church's authority has waned in the twentieth century.

I wish now to examine more closely four of these novels, chosen partly for their representative nature, but mainly for their success in dealing with the Grail legend.[6] The first is Parke Godwin's *Firelord*, which shows how it has been integrated into an account of Arthur's full career in a Dark Age setting.[7] Since the novels set in the Dark Ages are concerned with verisimilitude, many choose either to omit all reference to the Grail, dismissing it as a legend that attached itself to Arthur as tales of his achievements spread, or else to rationalize it. *Firelord* falls into the latter category.

Here the Grail found by Peredur in the well at the foot of Wyrral Tor turns out to be "An ordinary shallow bowl of pitted bronze" (359). To those who see it for the first time, it is a disappointment, "not what we thought" (357), but as Peredur points out, "It's the reaching, the hope and the faith that really count. How can any reality shine like the dream of it?" (360). In this respect, the Grail mirrors a central theme of the novel, the inspiration provided by the vision of "bright tomorrows you carved out of wishes and painted with dreams" (7).

The integration of the Grail legend into the structure of the novel is demonstrated by a scrutiny of the conclusion. As Arthur lies dying, he has a dream in which he is visited in succession by various figures who have been important in his life. First comes Merlin, here a projection of Arthur himself, with his dream of a brighter world, like that offered by the Grail itself. Then comes Ambrosius, who insists "I've got to save *some* of you for the historians" (392). His commitment to Roman logic is matched by that of Peredur in his search for the Grail, as Arthur recognizes: "His faith might have sent him down into the well, but a keen, critical mind led him there" (361). Peredur even retains an element of skepticism about his find: "if there was a Grail, it would look like nothing so much as this" (360).

The next visitors to the dying Arthur are Trystan and Geraint, who sweep him off into legend "that will endure as long as men dream" (392–93). Because the Grail is equally inspiring, the faithful pray at the bier of Peredur who "touched an enduring need in their hearts" (361). Trystan and Geraint are followed by Guenevere, her mind full of political concerns. These too are an important dimension in Godwin's Grail story. From the outset Arthur must learn to cope with the religious intolerance of the Grail's most fervent believers. The skill with which he masters the lesson is demonstrated when he uses the Grail to help reconcile the rebels led by Guenevere and Lancelot.

If this performance reveals Arthur's political astuteness, his final visitor, Morgana, releases "the last and best" part of him (395). She it was who taught him to love, and this is the quality that makes him such a beloved leader. It also brings him the Grail, for out of love for his old friend he allows Peredur to seek the holy vessel when policy might argue more secure restraint for so valuable a captive. "Someone who heeded fallen sparrows," he prays, "might take a moment for Peredur" (352). The Quest for the Grail is thus freely adapted by Godwin to fit into his vision of a leader worthy of the legend that has reverberated down through the ages.

Like *Firelord*, Jim Hunter's *Percival and the Presence of God* is a first-person narrative set in the Dark Ages (though there is a timeless quality about this world).[8] Whereas the Grail Quest is but a minor episode in the former, however, it dominates the latter which is told from Percival's point of view. Despite temptations to abandon his heroic quest, first for Arthur's court, then for the castle of the fisher-lord, Percival stubbornly persists. To it, he dedicates his life.

Yet his search for Arthur's course leads him only to a gutted castle and a ruined chapel within which he is trapped by a fallen beam. As he lies, "dying in an absurdity" (133), the only pattern he can discern in events is "either of an immense and grand cruelty, or of a vast indifference. Percival was simply not of interest to God" (125). The castle, he later learns, belonged not to Arthur but to a king named Poel, though the stories told about him were similar. Nor is his search for the castle of the fisher-lord, where he failed to ask the vital question during his first visit, any more successful. Hope of a quick return gradually fades.

What Percival undergoes is a "slow and baffled" (141) learning journey:

> I think I do now accept that either things are truly arbitrary, an utter haphazardness of God, or their direction is likely to be too difficult for us to understand, so that they appear arbitrary though they are not so.
> To some this is cynicism, and to others it is faith. (138)

Nor does his persistence bring consolation: "To address God is to address a remoteness. God doesn't blaze and touch me now, as in my adolescence, and possibly will never do so again" (139). He does not, however, yield to despair, rather to "a gentler counterpart: disappointment, and acquiescence" (137). As the novel ends, Percival confesses, "I no longer believe in Arthur, it being all I can manage to believe in God. . . . Remote one, stay within reach of my mind" (140–41).

While medieval questers may reject worldly for spiritual values, they never wonder whether Arthur's court and its ideals actually exist; and while they may doubt their worthiness to find the Grail, they never question God's purpose and concern with mankind. Hunter has transformed the legend from a medieval journey toward faith into a modern exploration of Christian existentialism: "self-sacrifice is not harder but easier, when there is no certainty of meaning. In a blank windless world, without confident directions of our own, we are most free to respond to needs outside ourselves" (138–39). His is a Grail Quest for a less spiritually confident age.

Thomas Berger's *Arthur Rex* is set, not in the Dark Ages, but in the High Middle Ages.[9] Like *Firelord*, however, it deals with the entire career of Arthur, and so the Quest for the Grail occupies but a small part of the novel, made even smaller because most adventures are not reported in detail. Berger integrates the stories of both Percival and Galahad, but it is the former who achieves a vision of the Holy Grail and who heals the maimed King Pelles. Thereafter, he and Galahad die with the rest of Arthur's knights in the last battle against Mordred.

These changes are necessary to Berger's ironic purpose. Since so spiritual an undertaking offers limited opportunities for humor, the Quest is moved largely into the background, so that attention may focus on those elements with most comic potential: Galahad's conception, Perceval's naïveté, and the obscure nature of the Grail so assiduously sought. The first two, however, are largely detached from the Grail Quest, for Galahad does not actually go on the Quest, and most of the comic scenes involving Percival occur before he starts his.

Most of the humor is thus directed at the dubiousness of the undertaking: "Methinks it is strange that an hundred knights are questing for that which they do not even know the look of," observes Arthur when Leodegrance explains the absence of his knights, to which that monarch replies, "The very mystery of it is a lure" (73). This, however, is only part of its fascination. When Percival later marvels that the Grail should be found so close to Camelot after he and others have searched far and wide, Galahad points out, "But if you had known where it was immediately, would you have had so many interesting adventures?" (450). This question brings Percival to an important realization: "I think I was happy in not finding it straightway. For all I ever wanted was to be a knight and to have adventures" (450).

Since the Grail "can not be seen except by him who is perfectly pure and without sin altogether" (73), it really is unattainable. Even Percival, who is "almost perfect" (424), is granted but a brief glimpse of the Grail. What is important, for Percival and all the other knights, is to pursue the vision, for only by striving may we improve ourselves, whatever our shortcomings. This is in keeping with a central theme of the novel for, as the ghost of Gawaine reminds his uncle, "though man be eternally contemptible, he should not be contemptuous of that which he can achieve" (483). This explains why Percival's completion of the Grail Quest is so anticlimactic. It is the Quest itself that is important, not the fleeting glory of an incomplete achievement. Just as the Grail maiden tells Percival, "Do not despair, for wert thou not as good a man as thou art, thou shouldst not see it at all" (424), so Arthur comforts Bedivere, "Do not weep. . . . Rather thank God in joy that for a little while we were able to make an interregnum in the human cycle of barbarism and decadence" (495).

In Naomi Mitchison's *To the Chapel Perilous,* the Grail Quest is central once again.[10] Although set in the High Middle Ages, it anachronistically introduces a press with modern standards, struggling to deal with conflicting stories on the one hand and political manipulation on the other. The result is a fascinating combination of delightful irony and thoughtful insight.

The problem for Lienors and Dalyn, the reporters waiting outside the Perilous Chapel, is that more than one Grail is found: Gawain finds a cauldron of plenty, Lancelot a cup and a lance that drips blood, Peredur/ Perceval a stone that spills forth gold coins, Bors the dish of the Last Supper, Galahad a cup full of blood that "threw a curious illumination through his fingers" (19). Other knights find other things. When Dalyn wonders, "we always supposed—there was only one Grail," the hermit responds, "Yes, indeed . . . and each knight won it" (15).

Yet they cannot simply report this fact. There are too many interests to take into consideration: sub-editors trying to angle the stories, publishers anxious to placate advertisers, readers with expectations they want fulfilled, influential figures like Elayne and Guinevere, and powerful institutions like the Court and an increasingly intolerant Church. Since none of these wants a multiplicity of Grails, it becomes necessary to choose one. It is the Church that finally wins the day, endorsing Galahad's as the true Grail and condemning any pagan associations in reports of the other finds: "they had very clear ideas of what it ought to be like, so it was quite easy for them to do it out of their heads or else to consult those who had recently had visions" (89).

Mitchison's approach offers valuable insights into both Grail tradition and the modern news media. Since she is not forced to adhere to one particular version of the legend, she is able to include as much material as she chooses. Thus she recalls the devils that take on the guise of beautiful women to tempt questers when Bors mistakes Lienors for just such a "temptation" (70); and she explores the more primitive aspects of the Perceval story by having him revert to his pagan roots in the Foret Sauvage where he is known as Peredur. Kundrie, the loathly damsel who reproaches Perceval for not asking the appropriate question of the Fisher King, is linked with the Flower Bride of Celtic tradition by a reporter from the Cymric People. The modern skepticism of the reporters provides rich opportunity for irony.

Yet the modern world has its own failings, as is revealed by how news stories are shaped. Where the Cymric People gives extensive coverage to Peredur/Perceval, the Northern Pict shows more interest in Gawain, each appealing to national and regional preoccupations. Lancelot's encounter with Elayne of Corbyn "had been a marvellous story, but they'd had to kill it. You couldn't risk a row with the Round Table attaches over a Court release" (19). Reports of more than one Grail displease Lord Horny, the newspaper publisher: "people . . . might all start off questing and who'd be left to read the advertisements?" (21). He worries, "it might set people thinking. We couldn't have that" (55). To gain the release of Lienors, the Camelot Chronicle publishes the unconfirmed and highly suspect story of Galahad's experiences in Sarras provided by the Church.

The trouble is that many patterns can be discerned in life, and each is represented by a different Grail.

> "And each pattern uncovers a different aspect of the heart: a different means of wisdom. . . . And each pattern is dangerous to the other patterns and must seem hateful to their followers. . . . Most people are much too frightened to be tolerant. And at any one time and place there's always one pattern on top." (159)

Since "truth" may be distorted, we must look for the underlying pattern: "the wound is healed, the secret told, the riddle becomes plain, the reconciliation is made between man and what surrounds him" (170). To achieve this, we, like Lienors and Dalyn, must abandon our detachment from life and each seek our own Grail: "It would be sad beyond all telling if the finding of the Grail were to happen once for all. Because then it could not happen again for anyone" (171). Only thus can we find our own pattern, discover what is important to us, not just to those who exercise power for their own advantage.

What all four novels offer is insight into the human heart and, through it, a glimpse of the eternal. The yearning for a better world than that in which we live drives the knights to seek the Grail, however formidable the obstacles, great the sacrifice, and uncertain (perhaps doomed) the outcome. Thus the Grail may be seen as a more refined and spiritual image of the whole Arthurian world, the dream of which continues to lure us down through the ages.

Significantly, though, this spiritual Quest is one that, by and large, takes place without the mediation of the Church. Whereas priests and hermits offer valuable guidance in most medieval Grail romances, the Church is more of a hindrance than a help in these four novels: because of the abbot's advice, Hunter's Percival keeps silent in the castle of the fisher-lord; despite the Christian principles of Arthur and his knights in Berger's novel, the bishops of the Church are characterized as corrupt "caitiffs" (34); the Church and its most fervent supporters are power hungry and intolerant in the novels of Godwin and Mitchison. Mitchison's hermit alone is estimable, but he seems to have few links with the Church and his answers to questions are enigmatic. He prefers to leave people to make their own decisions.

The predominantly negative portrayal of organized religion in all four novels reflects a widespread attitude throughout modern Arthurian fiction. The Church's intolerance and craving for power are frequently criticized. Even more important, however, is its frequent exclusion from the deepest mysteries of the Grail. The Grail Quest is a spiritual journey that must, in the final analysis, be taken alone, for we are each responsible for our own salvation. The authors and readers of modern fiction are clearly warier of external authorities than were our medieval ancestors. We have, after all, been witness to the cruelty and oppression perpetrated on others in the name of organized religion, not only down the centuries, but still today.

Amidst the sterile wasteland of a materialistic world driven by greed, self-interest, and the lust for power over others, our thirst for spiritual sustenance is fiercer than ever. It may only be slaked, however, by undertaking the Quest for our own Grail. It will not be easy, for we must struggle against our own obstinately recalcitrant nature, against the temptation to neglect our wider responsibilities, and against the efforts of others to exploit our good intentions for base purposes. Yet the rewards are beyond all reckoning. And if modern fiction is a guide to what we may expect to find, then the Grail that awaits us is love, compassion, forgiveness—love of God, compassion for others, forgiveness of ourselves. Whether we shall ever find it, or recognize it if we do, is uncertain. But the Quest itself is a more glorious endeavor than any other we might choose, and that in itself may prove enough in this broken world.

NOTES

1. For bibliographical information on the fiction discussed in this article, see individual author entries in *The New Arthurian Encyclopedia*, ed. Norris J. Lacy et al., Updated Paperback Edition (New York: Garland, 1996); for a summary of the evolution of the Grail in both medieval literature and modern scholarship, see particularly the entries by Richard O'Gorman (pp. 212–13) and Marylyn Parins (pp. 406–09); for a discussion of the motif of Arthur's return, see Geoffrey Ashe's entry (pp. 381–82) and *King Arthur's Modern Return*, ed. Debra N. Mancoff (New York: Garland, 1998).

2. First published in two limited editions as *Grails: Quests, Visitations, and Other Occurrences*, ed. Richard Gilliam, Martin H. Greenberg, and Edward E. Kramer (Atlanta: Unnameable, 1992), this anthology was augmented with additional stories and reissued as two separate volumes: *Grails: Quests of the Dawn* and *Grails: Visitations of the Night*, both published in New York by Roc / Penguin, 1994.

3. These works are realistic in their approach to the Grail material rather than to such elements as plot and character. For a fuller discussion of the rationale for the categories of fiction that I adopt, as well as many of the novels mentioned, see Raymond H. Thompson, *The Return from Avalon: A Study of the Arthurian Legend in Modern Fiction* (Westport, CT: Greenwood, 1985). Several works mentioned in this article might be placed in more than the one category I have chosen for ease of discussion.

Many of the novels are also discussed by Beverly Taylor and Elisabeth Brewer, *The Return of King Arthur: British and American Literature since 1800* (Woodbridge, Eng.: Boydell and Brewer; Totowa, NJ: Barnes and Noble, 1983); and by Maureen Fries, "Trends in the Modern Arthurian Novel," in *King Arthur Through the Ages*, ed. Valerie M. Lagorio and Mildred Leake Day, 2 vols. (New York: Garland, 1990), II, 207–22.

4. For a discussion of Mystery and Suspense Fiction, see Daniel Nastali's entry in *The New Arthurian Encyclopedia*, pp. 339–40.

5. For a fuller discussion of the Grail quest in these two novels, as well as those by Jewett and Webb below, see Raymond H. Thompson, "From Inspiration to Warning: the Changing Role of Arthurian Legend in Fiction for Younger Readers," *Bulletin of the John Rylands University Library of Manchester*, 76, No. 3 (Autumn 1994), 238.

6. Among the novels that might have been explored further are those by White and Percy. For a discussion of the Grail quest in the former, see John Crane, *T.H. White* (New York: Twayne, 1974); Martin Kellman, *T.H. White and the Matter of Britain* (Lewiston, NY: Mellen, 1988); and Elisabeth Brewer, *T.H. White's The Once and Future King* (Woodbridge, Eng.: Brewer, 1993). For a discussion of the Grail quest in Percy, see J. Donald Crowley and Sue Mitchell Crowley, "Walker Percy's Grail," Chapter 17 in this anthology; and John Bugge, "Arthurian Myth Devalued in Walker Percy's *Lancelot*," in *The Arthurian Tradition: Essays in Convergence*, ed. Mary Flowers Braswell and John Bugge (Tuscaloosa: University of Alabama, 1988), pp. 175–87.

7. Although the author describes the novel as a fantasy in the Acknowledgements, he does try to preserve what he calls "the bone of historical fact," based upon studies like *The Age of Arthur* (1973) by John Morris. All quotations are from the first edition (Garden City, NY: Doubleday, 1980), and are cited parenthetically in the text.

8. (London: Faber and Faber, 1978). Quotations are cited parenthetically in the text.

9. *Arthur Rex: A Legendary Novel* (New York: Delacorte, 1978). Quotations are cited parenthetically in the text. For a discussion of the role of Galahad, see

Jay Ruud, "Thomas Berger's *Arthur Rex*: Galahad and Earthly Power," *Critique*, 25 (1984), 92–100.

10. (London: Allen and Unwin, 1955). Quotations are cited parenthetically in the text. See also Marilyn K. Nellis, "Anachronistic Humor in Two Arthurian Romances of Education: *To the Chapel Perilous* and *The Sword in the Stone*," *Studies in Medievalism*, 2, No. 4 (1983), 57–77.

CHAPTER 19

Hollywood's New Weston
The Grail Myth in Francis Ford Coppola's *Apocalypse Now* and John Boorman's *Excalibur*

MARTIN B. SHICHTMAN

Ever since J. D. Bruce's well-reasoned attack on Jessie Weston's works, scholars of Arthurian romance have generally dismissed her writings.[1] Still, members of the artistic community, perhaps inspired by T. S. Eliot's fondness for *From Ritual to Romance*, continue to emphasize Weston's importance.[2] In two recent films, *Apocalypse Now* and *Excalibur*, directors Francis Ford Coppola and John Boorman demonstrate a heavy reliance on Weston's perception of the Grail quest as a romanticized version of ancient fertility rituals.[3]

Despite differing world views, Coppola and Boorman both strive to return to those early rituals on which the medieval Grail stories were founded; they attempt to arrive at the essence of the Grail myth, thereby to capture its universality. Thus, the directors turn to Jessie Weston, for her writings indicate that it is possible to determine the activities which gave birth to the Grail stories. According to Weston, "in the Grail King we have a romantic literary version of that strange mysterious figure whose presence hovers in the shadowy background of our Aryan race; the figure of a divine or semi-divine ruler, at once god and king, upon whose life and unimpaired vitality, the existence of his land and people directly depends."[4] It is because this king has either been maimed or fallen sick that his land has gone to waste, and only the Grail knight, Weston's "Medicine Man," can bring relief. Weston suggests that "the Doctor, or Medicine Man, did, from the very earliest ages, play an important part in Dramatic Fertility Ritual . . . that of restoring to life and health the dead, or wounded, representative of the Spirit of Vegetation."[5] She goes on to insist:

the Grail story was originally a loan from a ritual actually performed, and familiar to those who first told the tale. This ritual, in its earlier stages comparatively simple and objective in form, under the process of an insistence upon the inner and spiritual significance, took upon itself a more complex and esoteric character, the rite became a Mystery, and with this change the role of the principal actors became of heightened significance. That of the Healer could no longer be adequately fulfilled by the administration of a medicinal remedy; the relation of Body and Soul became of cardinal importance for the Drama, the Medicine Man gave place to the Redeemer.[6]

Coppola and Boorman rely on Weston to uncover for them the basis of the Grail myth, for if this can be discerned, then its import can be communicated to twentieth-century movie-goers. Like Weston, who looks to anthropological archetypes for her answers, they too seek the truth of paradigms.

Much has been made of Francis Ford Coppola's indebtedness to Joseph Conrad's *Heart of Darkness* in his writing of *Apocalypse Now*.[7] Several articles have also pointed to Coppola's use of Sir James Frazer's *The Golden Bough*.[8] But virtually no mention at all has been made concerning the director's reliance on Weston's book. Still, Coppola expresses his appreciation for *From Ritual to Romance* with a brief cinematic footnote, and he incorporates Weston's theories to demonstrate some of the ironies of the Vietnam war.[9] For Francis Ford Coppola, at least in *Apocalypse Now*, Vietnam is the Wasteland.

From the film's beginning, the viewer is inundated with images of death and destruction. Forsaking opening credits, Coppola turns his camera on a jungle suffering the effects of napalm bombing. In the background, Jim Morrison and The Doors sing "The End," a terrifying piece about a desperate land "desperately in need of a stranger's hand," a place where "all the children are insane, waiting for the summer's rain."[10] The viewer is then introduced to Coppola's Grail knight, his "Medicine Man," Captain Willard. To some degree, Willard is an insane child of the Wasteland. Staggering about in a drunken stupor, he recalls how his fondness for the Vietnam war caused the failure of his marriage. He then proceeds to trash his already squalid hotel room, finally destroying even an image of himself as he throws a punch through a mirror. But Coppola gives his viewer some hope for Willard. The captain recognizes the waste around him and laments that he has been in Saigon "a week now, waiting for a mission, getting softer." When soldiers arrive from I-Corp to take him away, Willard insists: "I wanted a mission, and for my sins they gave me one." This unlikely redeemer needs to be given a cleansing shower, a comic baptism, to sober him up and prepare him for the quest.

The most often used word in Willard's lexicon is "shit," and it appropriately describes his surroundings. But, as Willard maintains, he was "going to the worst place in the world and didn't even know it yet." In the Wasteland of Vietnam, even the decadent captain is a relative innocent, and he is played by Martin Sheen with wide-eyed naiveté. During his brief stay with that all-knowing power, Military Intelligence, the self-appointed god of the Vietnam war, Willard learns the tale of Colonel Kurtz. Much like the Fisher King of Arthurian romance, Kurtz suffers from wounds which will not heal; in a transmission intercepted by I-Corp, he compares himself to "a snail crawling on the edge of a straight-razor . . . and surviving." Willard is told that Kurtz was an outstanding officer, humanitarian, man of wit; he was "a good man." Now, however, Kurtz's ideas and methods have become "unsound." Furthermore, Kurtz has established an empire in Cambodia which has begun to reflect its leader's madness and corruption. Willard is dispatched to relieve both the lord and his land from affliction. Nevertheless, unlike Weston's Grail knight, who benignly restores fertility to lord and land, Coppola's hero is ordered to terminate Colonel Kurtz's command "with extreme prejudice." For the Grail knight of the twentieth century, for the Grail knight of the Vietnam war, healing involves putting the sick out of their misery and letting the land revive itself.

As Willard journeys up the river towards his meeting with Kurtz, he becomes more familiar with the Wasteland. Sterility, or the fear of it, is pervasive. The captain is accompanied by a group of young sailors, "rock and rollers" as he calls them, for whom Mick Jagger's "I can't get no satisfaction"[11] has become something of an anthem. He flies with air cavalry members who sit on their helmets so that they won't get their "balls blown off." At a USO show, he watches as three Playboy Playmates perform a masturbatory dance and then run from the hordes of sex-starved soldiers who desire them. These soldiers, promised "entertainment we know you are going to like," are only teased, left frustrated. There is no sexual consummation in Coppola's Vietnam. All acts of sexual intent, even attempted rape (if this can be called an act of sexual intent), are interrupted. Soldiers fighting the war can only hope to sustain their sexual potentiality, but this seems doubtful. As Willard's testimony at the beginning of the film suggests, all human relations, even those between husband and wife, are undermined by the war.

Willard likewise finds death and destruction all around him. Colonel Kilgore, an insane air cavalry officer assigned to assist Willard on the journey, flips "death cards" on the bodies of dead Viet Cong soldiers, plays "Ride of the Valkyries" as his choppers descend to carry off the souls of the enemy, has "death from above" printed on his command helicopter, claims to "love the smell of napalm in the morning," and orders his men to surf during a battle. Nor does Kilgore's insanity appear to be an isolated case. As Willard continues on his quest, he sees a jungle littered with the wreckage of war machines and the bodies of men. He even finds himself killing an innocent woman to expedite his mission. The violence is, for the most part, arbitrary and mindless, and Willard is forced to wonder just why his superiors really want Kurtz assassinated; he realizes; "It wasn't just [for] insanity and murder, there was enough of that here for anyone." And the madness of the Do Lung bridge seems to make Willard's case for him. Described as "the asshole of the world" by one soldier, the Do Lung bridge stands between Vietnam and Cambodia. It is a last outpost, and it is in chaos. Soldiers fire weapons at non-existent enemies; there is nobody in charge, no commanding officer. The only sound is the music of men screaming.

But compared to what lies ahead, the Do Lung bridge is actually an outpost of rationality. The bridge separates this world from the otherworld. Once beyond this point, Willard is in the land of Kurtz's Grail castle, a depraved parody of the Arthurian romance building which houses the cup of the Last Supper and the spear of Longinus. Coppola claims: "From the bridge on, I started moving back in time, because I wanted to imply that the issues and themes were timeless. . . . As you went further up the river, you went deeper into the origins of human nature . . . what we were really like."[12] Nothing that Willard has seen prepares him for Kurtz's compound, for this is truly a Wasteland. Willard notes that "the place was full of bodies . . . It smelled like slow death." For Kurtz and his followers, murder has become a ritual; it has become a sustaining part of their lives. They have forfeited even that little bit of humanity maintained by maniacs like Kilgore. They know nothing but death.

Willard is told by one of Kurtz's apologists (a crazed photo-journalist): "The man likes you . . . He's got something in mind for you . . . The man is clear in mind, but his soul is mad. He's dying, I think. He hates this . . . He likes you because you're still alive." The captain's vitality is seemingly reflected in the rain which begins falling from the moment of his arrival in Kurtz's compound. This traditional symbol of renewal is likewise associated with the Grail knight, who frees the waters of the Wasteland.[13]

But the rain which accompanies Willard is muddy, dirty. There is, in fact, no place in Vietnam for the pure, righteous redeemer of Arthurian romance; he belongs to a world divided into simple binary oppositions, a world in which the forces of goodness must inevitably emerge victorious from their psychomachian battles with evil. The situation in Vietnam is much more ambiguous, and it demands a more ambiguous Grail knight. Willard, a professional murderer, an accomplished assassin, is only slightly more alive than the depraved Colonel Kurtz. The hope he conveys is a tenuous one at best. In this botch of a world, the Grail knight can only be another agent of death.

Prior to meeting Kurtz, Willard is virtually ready to pardon him, to let him live. After a series of encounters, he changes his mind: "Everybody wanted me to do it. Him most of all. I felt like he was up there waiting for me to take the pain away. Even the jungle wanted him dead, and that's who he took his orders from anyway." Willard realizes that, in the perverted world of Vietnam, killing brings relief. As he commits the murder, Kurtz's people are sacrificing a bull. Coppola cuts back and forth from one scene to the other, fusing them as separate but similar rituals. Coppola claims: "The notion is that Willard is moved to do it, to go once more into that primitive state, to go and kill. He goes into the temple, and he goes through a quasiritual experience, and he kills the king. The native people there were acting out what was happening. They understood, and were acting out, with their icons, a ritual of life and death. Willard goes in and he kills Kurtz, and as he comes out he flirts with the notion of being king, but something does not lure him."[14] This episode may be a bit more complex than even Coppola admits; it hearkens back to Mithraic cult rituals which, according to Weston, were, from the beginning, associated with the achievement of the grail:

> Mithraism taught the resurrection of the body—Mithra will descend upon earth, and will revive all men. All will issue from their graves, resume their former appearance and recognize each other. All will be united in one great assembly, and the good will be separated from the evil. Then in one supreme sacrifice Mithra will immolate the divine bull, and mixing its fat with the consecrated wine will offer the righteous the cup of Eternal Life.[15]

Weston suggests that, like Mithra, the Grail knight was viewed as a messianic conveyer of the feast of resurrection; it was often the task of this knight to heal the wounded Fisher King and then replace him, presiding over the now revitalized populace of the Wasteland.[16] After he kills Kurtz, Willard calls in an air strike on the colonel's followers. The film ends as it began, with the flash of napalm. Willard both serves and undermines his mythic purpose; he brings about an ironic restoration of order by completely annihilating everything around him. There is no revivification of the Spirit of Vegetation from Willard's chemically induced immolation.[17]

John Boorman claims, in the closing credits for *Excalibur*, that his film is based on Sir Thomas Malory's *Le Morte d'Arthur*. In fact, Boorman's Grail quest is pure Jessie Weston. The director's respect for Malory is somewhat suspect, as he believes that "Malory was really the first hack writer . . . When Caxton built his printing press, he asked poor old Malory to write something, and he obliged by putting together all the stories he knew: all the stories that had been handed down through the oral tradition."[18] This remark indicates that Boorman doesn't know all that much about Sir Thomas Malory.[19] But then, it may never have been the director's intent really to retell Malory's story. According to Harlan Kennedy, "Boorman first got interested in the [Arthurian] legend by reading T. S. Eliot's *The Waste Land* and went on to read Jessie L. Weston's book about the Grail Quest, *From Ritual to Romance*."[20] Nor does ignorance of Malory necessarily invalidate Boorman's vision of the Grail story. The director incorporates Weston's theories to make the story more accessible to modern audiences, to transform a complex myth, filled, in Arthurian romance, with religious and cultural ambiguities, into a simple tale of loyalty and patriotism.

Boorman insists:

> The Arthurian legend is about the passing of the old gods and the coming of the Age of Man, of rationality, of laws—of man controlling his affairs. The price he pays for this is the loss of harmony with nature, which includes magic. As we tried to state in the film, that magic passes into our dreams and is lost—and consequently we feel nostalgic about what was lost in the human past. The only way to regain it is by some form of transcendence, which the quest for the grail represents— to transcend the material world and find a spiritual solution.[21]

Thus John Boorman is drawn to a fertility ritual which emphasizes the delicate balance between man and nature, between the leader and his land. No sooner does Arthur pull Excalibur from the stone than he is told by Merlin, "You will be the land and the land will be you. If you fail, the land will perish. When you thrive, the land will prosper." In accepting his assigned role, Arthur answers the prayers of priests who call on heaven to "give us a true king . . . The land weeps. The people suffer." For a time, at least, Arthur acts as this true king, establishing for himself and his followers a glorious, glittering empire.

In prosperity, however, Arthur becomes cut off from his people, his land. Satisfied with his achievements, the king fails to recognize the discontent growing around him. Boorman uses Lancelot's affair with Queen Guinevere to illustrate Arthur's increasing indifference to disruptive events. While all Camelot gossips about Guinevere's infidelity, Arthur refuses to acknowledge it. Despite early warnings from Merlin, the king cannot admit betrayal by his wife and the best of his knights. It is only when the issue is forced on him that Arthur finally attempts to take action, and by this time it is too late. The king proves ineffectual in bringing the lovers to justice. No longer able to wield Excalibur—the symbol of his sovereignty as well as his potency—against traitors, Arthur discards it. In essence, the king relinquishes his reign and with it his ties to the land. Lancelot, appreciating the horror of the situation, runs into the forest screaming "the king without a sword, the land without a king." According to Boorman, this is the beginning of the Arthurian empire's disintegration and downfall. With the king's failure to assert authority, the land begins to waste away.

Nevertheless, in Boorman's film, the affair between Lancelot and Guinevere marks only the onset of the king's emasculation; the process is completed by Arthur's sister, the witch Morgana. Disguised as Guinevere, Morgana enters Arthur's chamber and seduces him. This, however, is no ordinary seduction; it is more like a rape. Morgana dominates Arthur in bed; she cajoles, threatens, and laughs at him. Like the mythical succubus, from whom Boorman seemingly drew her character, Morgana robs the king of his sexual vitality. In return, she bears him a demon child, Mordred. The child embodies the sterility which will overcome both Arthur and his land, for he is sick, twisted, a perversion; he is decadence and death.

Boorman's *Excalibur* is the only Arthurian romance in which Arthur himself becomes the helpless lord of the Wasteland.[22] Weston claims: "taking the extant and recognized forms of the ritual into consideration, we might expect to find that in the earliest, and least contaminated, version of the Grail story the central figure would be dead, and the task of the Quester that of restoring him to life."[23] By making significant changes in the legend, Boorman in some ways attempts to return to this paradigm. In *Excalibur*, Mordred's birth brings about the figurative, if not the literal, death of Arthur. Invoking the spirit of such classic horror films as the original *Frankenstein*, Boorman provides a bestormed, old gothic castle as the scene for Mordred's nativity. Once having established these monstrous associations for Mordred, the director then cuts to Arthur's court where all are assembled to pray: "God save us from Morgana and her unholy child." Instead of receiving grace, however, Arthur is struck down by a thunderbolt. From this time onwards, the king exists in a netherworld between life and death; he is later to explain: "I didn't know how empty was my soul." As the land goes completely to ruin, Arthur collects his knights and pleads: "We must find what was lost . . . Only the Grail can restore leaf and flower."

Boorman's Grail quest is, therefore, a very specialized account of Weston's fertility rituals; the Grail knight of *Excalibur* must undergo an ordeal of loyalty and patriotism in order to redeem Arthur and the land. Still, Boorman's Grail quest and knight owe far more to Weston than to Malory. Galahad is the foremost quester in Malory's work; his mission is a deeply religious one, influenced profoundly by the Cistercian spirituality of Malory's source for the story, the French *Queste del Saint Graal*.[24] Boorman completely rejects Galahad as his hero, perhaps because Weston reckoned this knight too far removed from the original protagonist of the Grail ritual: "Galahad I hold to be a literary, not a traditional hero; he is the product of deliberate literary invention and has no existence outside the frame of later cyclic redactions."[25] The director instead chooses Perceval, a knight whom Weston associated with early Celtic accounts of the Grail legend. Whereas Malory's Galahad journeys towards personal salvation, performing marvelous, redemptive deeds along the way, Boorman's Perceval—and Weston's paradigmatic hero—pursues his quest for the sole purpose of saving an afflicted king.

At first glance, Boorman seems to have taken his Grail knight from any of the many medieval romances dealing with Perceval. Like the Perceval of early romance, Boorman's hero is depicted as a boorish young man who, impressed by Arthur's knights, devotes himself to a life of chivalry.[26] But Boorman's knight is decidedly different. In no Arthurian source is Perceval so overcome by his devotion to Arthur.[27] To aid his king, Boorman's Perceval travels through rain, snow, and desert. He finds the hideously decayed bodies of dead comrades who failed on the quest, and yet he pushes on. Barely able to move in his rusted armor, he comes upon a laughing child. This child, Mordred, and his mother, Morgana, attempt to corrupt Perceval, offering comfort to the knight who, through his long, hard journey has "found nothing but death and sorrow." When Perceval refuses to be tempted, they order him hanged, a punishment to which the knight submits rather than betraying Arthur.

As he suffers in the noose, Perceval has his first vision of the Grail castle. A drawbridge lowers, and the knight is temporarily blinded by a light which emanates from inside the building. He then sees a cup, filled with an unidentified red substance, and hears a deep, masculine voice ask the questions: "What is the secret of the Grail? Who does it serve?" Frightened, Perceval runs from the castle. It is of some significance that in this sequence Boorman greatly alters the standard medieval renditions of the Grail ceremony. There is no semi-religious Grail procession in *Excalibur*. The eucharistic associations of the Grail cup have all but been forgotten in the film.[28] In essence, the director attempts to strip the ceremony of its Christian veneer and restore it to a pre-Christian fertility ritual, much like the one about which Weston speculates. Boorman's efforts are only partially successful. Without Christian underpinnings, the Grail ceremony becomes somewhat confusing and obscure; meaning is lost. Nor does the film offer any real explanation as to the significance of the whole affair. The viewer is simply left to marvel at the dedication which brings Perceval to the Grail castle and to wonder at the timidity which drives him from it. Boorman's Perceval is not frightened by being witness to a religious Mystery, a miracle—as is usually the case in Arthurian romance; rather, he is scared by a bright light and a loud voice.

The director redeems both himself and his protagonist with Perceval's second visit to the Grail castle. After escaping death at the hands of Mordred and Morgana, Perceval resumes his quest, though with little hope. He endures more pain and suffering and then comes upon a group of religious fanatics who accost him screaming: "Look at the great knight. Peace and plenty they promised. But what did they give us, famine and pestilence. Because of their pride, they made themselves God, and Christ has abandoned us." Perceval is thrown into a deep stream where he quickly submerges, losing his armor during the descent. Suddenly, the knight has his second vision of the Grail castle. Naked, except for a loincloth, he approaches the Grail and is again asked the pertinent questions; his answers are most unusual, at least by traditional Arthurian standards:

What is the secret of the Grail? Who does it serve?
You, my lord.
Who am I?
You are my lord and king. You are Arthur.
Have you found the secret I have lost?
Yes. You and the land are one.

With this realization, the Grail is achieved. Perceval brings the Grail cup to Arthur and bids him drink from it, again insisting "you and the land are one."

The questions appearing in medieval versions of the Grail quest have long puzzled scholars.[29] These questions, which resemble the ones raised in Boorman's film, are supposed to be asked by the Grail knight, not of him. Furthermore, they are never answered. Some scholars have assumed that these questions, having little to do with the Christianized Grail ceremony, must be the legacy of an earlier, pre-Christian ritual, perhaps even a fertility ritual like the one described by Weston. By following Weston's suggestions, Boorman can, then, simplify and condense the Grail story while, at the same time, believing that he is more closely approximating the original rites. He can also make the story more accessible to modern viewers who are unfamiliar with the complexities of the Christianized Grail. Most important, by incorporating Weston's theories, Boorman can bring home a simple message of loyalty and patriotism to an audience which may appreciate these virtues only as remnants of a nostalgic, happier time.

In the end, Boorman, like Coppola, uses the Grail legend in an ironic fashion. His film is, after all, about the death of a world and a world view, about the ways man has lost contact with magic and nature. The Grail only restores the Arthurian society for a short period, just long enough to strengthen the king for his final, cataclysmic battle against Mordred. Still, Boorman's vision remains less ironic than Coppola's, for it suggests that there was once a time when mankind possessed magic and harmony with nature, and that through the achievement of the Grail this time could be briefly regained. The bloodbath with which *Excalibur* concludes does not offer modern audiences much hope, but there is a glimmer. So long as there is nostalgia for the glittering world of Camelot, Arthur's dream endures.

Both John Boorman and Francis Ford Coppola depict the Grail as being attainable. But while Boorman is somewhat relieved with its attainment, Coppola is made more uncomfortable. Boorman recognizes that mankind is so fallen that there can never again be a permanent vindication of magic and reintegration with nature. He also looks fondly at that time when loyalty and patriotism were great enough to achieve the Grail, great enough to bring back, if just for a short while, the glory of Camelot. The horror of Coppola's film is that it offers no hope, no dream. There is nothing redeeming in the Wasteland of Vietnam, where only total destruction can alleviate the agony.

NOTES

Reprinted with permission from *Post-Script: Essays in Film and the Humanities*, 4, no. 1 (Fall 1984), 35–48. Minor corrections have been made by the author.

1. See James Douglas Bruce "Miss Weston's Gawain Complex," in *The Evolution of Arthurian Romance from the Beginnings down to the Year 1300* (Baltimore: The Johns Hopkins University Press, 1923), II, 91–103. Also see Jessie L. Weston, *From Ritual to Romance* (1920; rpt. New York: Doubleday Anchor Books, 1957).

2. In his notes to "The Waste Land," T. S. Eliot claims:

Not only the title but the plan and a good deal of the incidental symbolism of the poem were suggested by Miss Jessie L. Weston's book on the Grail legend: *From Ritual to Romance* (Cambridge). Indeed so deeply am I indebted, Miss Weston's book will elucidate the difficulties of the poem much better than my notes can do; and I recommend it (apart from the great interest of the book itself) to any who think such elucidation of the poem worth the trouble.

See *T. S. Eliot: Collected Poems 1909–1962* (New York: Harcourt, Brace and World, Inc., 1963), p. 70.

3. Francis Ford Coppola, dir., *Apocalypse Now*, United Artists, 1979; and John Boorman, dir., *Excalibur*, Orion, 1981.

4. Weston, p. 62.

5. Weston, p. 109.

6. Weston, pp. 109–110.

7. In "The Literary Roots of *Apocalypse Now*," *New York Times* 21 Oct. 1979, Sec 2, p. 21, John Tessitore discusses the reductiveness of using this approach alone. He explains that Coppola's conclusion is radically different from Conrad's: "the film does rely on Conrad's novella for its characters and plot structure, but it still does not explain Mr. Coppola's ending."

8. Tessitore, p. 21, for instance, claims that "*Heart of Darkness* has taken Mr. Coppola just so far; to follow the film to its conclusion we must turn to *The Golden Bough*."

9. Towards the end of *Apocalypse Now*, Coppola focuses on a table containing several books. He zooms in and allows his camera to linger for several seconds. *From Ritual to Romance* is one of the books sitting on that table (as is Frazer's *The Golden Bough*). Certainly this scene is no accident; it is means for the director to acknowledge influences.

10. The Doors, "The End," Nipper Music, 1967.

11. Mick Jagger and Keith Richard, "Satisfaction," Immediate Music, Inc., 1965.

12. Greil Marcus, "Journey up the River: An Interview with Francis Coppola," *Rolling Stone*, 1 Nov. 1979.

13. Concerning the Grail knight's task of "The Freeing of the Waters" of the Wasteland, see Weston, pp. 25–33.

14. Marcus, p. 55.

15. Weston, p. 166.

16. See Weston, p. 60.

17. Compare, for instance, Coppola's use of the baptism ritual at the conclusion of *Godfather I*, where the audience understands that the ritual is being incorporated ironically and against its original intention as Michael is baptized into murder and blood, not cleansed of sin by water and witnessing.

18. Harlan Kennedy, "The World of King Arthur According to John Boorman," *American Film*, 6 (1981), 33.

19. For a more scholarly approach to the life of Sir Thomas Malory, see William Matthews, *The Ill-Framed Knight: A Skeptical Inquiry Into the Identity of Sir Thomas Malory* (Berkeley: The University of California Press, 1966).

20. Kennedy, p. 35.

21. Dan Yakir, "The Sorcerer: John Boorman Interviewed by Dan Yakir," *Film Comment,* 17 (1981), 50.

22. According to Malory, Arthur opposes the Grail quest in part because his kingdom is already prosperous, and the mission can only serve to deprive the court of valuable knights:

> "Alas!" seyde kynge Arthure unto sir Gawayne, "ye have nygh slayne me for the avow that ye have made, for thorow you ye have berauffte me the fayryst and the trewyst of knyghthode that ever was sene togydir in ony realme of the worlde. Fro whan they departe from hense I am sure they all shall never mete togydir in thys worlde, for they shall dye many in the queste. And so hit forthynkith nat me a litill, for I have loved them as well as my lyff. Wherefore hit shall greve me ryght sore for the departicion of thys felyship, for I have had an olde custom to have hem in my felyship."

The Works of Sir Thomas Malory, ed. Eugène Vinaver (Oxford: Oxford University Press, 1977), p. 522.

23. Weston, p. 120.

24. On the sources for Malory's Grail quest, see Charles Moorman, " 'The Tale of the Sankgreal': Human Frailty," in *Malory's Originality*, ed. R. M. Lumiansky (Baltimore: The Johns Hopkins University Press, 1964), pp. 184–204.

25. Weston, p. 189.

26. This is the way Perceval appears in the first of the Grail stories, Chrétien de Troyes' *Le Conte du Graal*, ed. Felix Lecoy (Paris: Librairie Honore Champion, 1972); his characterization changes little throughout medieval romance.

27. Perceval usually becomes involved in the Grail quest to absolve himself of a transgression caused by his clumsiness. He selects the quest of his own volition rather than being ordered on it. In fact, Arthur rarely has anything to do with the Grail quest. He is significant to the quest only insofar as it is his knights that take up the mission.

28. On the Christianized Grail, see Bruce, I, 219–68.

29. See Jean Frappier, "Chrétien de Troyes," in *Arthurian Literature of the Middle Ages*, ed. Roger Sherman Loomis (Oxford: The Clarendon Press, 1959), p. 190.

CHAPTER 20

Eric Rohmer and the Holy Grail

LINDA WILLIAMS

Compared to the younger, more prolific, and often more radical directors of the French New Wave—Godard, Rivette, Resnais, Varda, Truffaut, Marker—Eric Rohmer, the senior member of this illustrious group, has often seemed a throwback to many of the values the New Wave once opposed. A moralist in the heyday of leftist political cinema, a literary sensibility in an age when the French film was finally freeing itself from the literary standards of the "well-made film," a Catholic in both his cinematic themes and his film criticism, Rohmer has always seemed an unmistakably original, but decidedly conservative, talent.[1]

His major work of the sixties and seventies, *Six Contes Moraux,* a loosely related cycle of six films dealing with the romantic and intellectual obsessions of mostly male, middle class heroes, is a visually static, television style work in which characters endlessly debate the ethical and intellectual dimensions of erotic temptation: to spend a night at Maud's, to touch or not to touch Claire's knee. In these chaste, aggressively uncinematic films of temptation, James Monaco has gone so far as to observe the "faintly glowing embers" of the literary traditions of courtly love.[2]

Given these predilections, it was not surprising that Rohmer turned his attention to the filming of Chrétien de Troyes' courtly medieval romance, *Perceval le Gallois.* Here, finally, was a film in which Rohmer's Catholic and moral sensibilities, refined literary taste, even his interest in the archaic tradition of courtly love could happily converge. But what one was not prepared for in this adaptation was the uncommon beauty and originality of a film whose visual and narrative conception are like no other ever made.

With *Perceval,* Eric Rohmer has outdone himself. The film's dazzlingly innovative narrative style and total re-thinking of filmic space are as radical for 1979 as *The Cabinet of Dr. Caligari* was in 1919. Yet these innovations derive from an adaptation of a twelfth-century literary source to which Rohmer, who himself wrote the modern French translation, is remarkably faithful. In the following analysis I hope to clarify the ways in which Rohmer's film adapts both the narrative form of Chrétien's text and the spatial organization of medieval art to its own, peculiarly modernist cinematic ends.

CHRÉTIEN'S TEXT

Modern readers of medieval literature encounter works of such profound religiosity as to seem almost inscrutable to our own more doubting sensibilities. Yet in these works we also encounter fragmented, digressive narratives, one dimensional characters and a total disregard of reality that seems very similar to the scrambled narratives and anti-realism of our own recent literature. Nowhere is this more true than in the Arthurian romances of the twelfth-century French poet Chrétien de Troyes. In the gracefully rhymed, Old French couplets of Chrétien's courtly romances, we encounter an emblematic world of obscure signs. In these secular texts, based on the orginally pagan legends of King Arthur, the earthly love of the knight-in-shining-armor for the fair maiden-in-distress frequently stands as an imperfect metaphor for the divine love of Christ. The reader is intended, as in all medieval art, both to enjoy the superficial charm and beauty of this world and to see through it to the spirit of the next.

In *Perceval,* the last and most thematically religious of Chrétien's romances, the movement from earthly to divine love seems to constitute the very meaning of the tale. From the very beginning, Chrétien's text poses the problem of the reading/interpretation of obscure signs—a reading which is further complicated by the incompletion of the text itself. Perceval is an ignorant Welsh lad who, one day spying the shining armor of a knight, mistakes him first for a devil and then for an angel. Although the knight sets him straight as to the nature and function of this armor, the tale continues to revolve around Perceval's naive "understanding" of the true meaning of the knightly quest—his persistent inability to question and interpret its signs. Leaving his mother for Arthur's court where he soon becomes a knight himself, Perceval's subsequent adventures comprise a slow process of knightly education in which he too often learns to obey the letter, but not the spirit, of the chivalric code.

Perceval's initial failure is dramatized in the palace of the maimed Fisher King where he repeatedly fails to inquire about the meaning of the mysterious grail and bleeding lance paraded before him. Confronted with these mysterious signs, Perceval remains silent out of mere *politesse:* in a previous encounter with an older knight, the normally inquisitive and incessantly talkative Perceval had been instructed to curb his tongue. His new-found silence is a superficial form, not yet informed by genuine faith and charity. Moreover, this dutiful *corteisie* causes Perceval to miss the chance to restore the health of the Fisher King and his wasteland. Thus, although the romance shows Perceval's eventual progress from a country bumpkin to an accomplished knight in command of the rules of combat, polite discourse and loyal service to king and lady, Chrétien emphasizes his knight's often comic misunderstanding of the meaning of this proper behavior.

Since the tale is incomplete,[3] it is hard to say whether Chrétien intended to bring Perceval back to the grail castle for a second chance. Some continuators of the tale do, as does Wolfram von Eschenbach in his thirteenth-century, more christianized and allegorical *Parzival.* What is clear, however, is that, as far as it goes, the poem appears to establish an opposition between the outward form of *corteisie* and a true *corteisie* informed by faith. For even though Chrétien's text does not appear to be a religious allegory (courtly romance operates within a secular code that is quite separate from that of the church), in an age where religious faith is so much a part of all life, a proper understanding of the chivalric code must, in some sense, include the gloss of divine love.

The parameters of this gloss are indicated early in the text. Perceval not only mistakes his first view of a knight for a devil and then an angel; he also mistakes the tent of a maiden for a church. In both cases a naive religious interpretation is corrected by a more sophisticated courtly one: the armor encloses a knight whom Perceval besieges with questions, paying no attention to the knight's own requests for information; the tent houses a woman—from whom Perceval rudely extorts several kisses, again following the letter, but not the spirit, of his first instruction in chivalry. The ultimate goal of these early comic episodes is to suggest that Perceval's true education will entail the knowledge of the ideals for which both knight and maiden stand. Perceval's original over-valuation of their religious meanings thus seems intended to be corrected by a later, truly religious interpretation of the courtly ideal.

All this is suggested, but not fully demonstrated by the "end" of the Perceval section of Chrétien's romance. After his failure at the grail castle and in spite of his recent successes at setting right the repercussions of his early misdeeds as a knight, Chrétien informs us that Perceval had forgotten God. In a few abrupt verses the text then relates how he wandered for five years in this godless state, until one Good Friday, he came upon the chapel of a Hermit. The Hermit informs Perceval that it was his early sin of leaving his mother that caused his silence in the grail castle. He also informs Perceval, who has by now acquired his name but not his full identity, that he and the Fisher King are Perceval's uncles, brothers to his mother. He then absolves Perceval of his sin, enjoining him to go to mass each day to ask forgiveness. The section ends with the summary statement, "Thus Perceval learned how God was crucified and died on a Friday, and on Easter Day he received the communion. Of him the tale tells no more at this point."[4]

Although the romance continues with the adventures of Gawain, whose perfect adherence to the chivalric code is in strong contrast to Perceval's bumbling enthusiasm, these adventures break off, incomplete. Thus the real climax—if not the actual end—of the tale as it stands is Perceval's acceptance of Christ in the chapel. It is not surprising then, that Rohmer's adaptation ends the tale here in the chapel and not, where Chrétien's tale actually breaks off, in the middle of the second Gawain episode. Yet the film does preserve a significant sense of the original text's fragmentation by breaking off an earlier Gawain episode in the midst of a particularly suspenseful situation to which it never returns. Thus, as we shall see, Rohmer chooses to be faithful to the text fragment as it stands rather than to a hypothetical projection of the completed text.

FILMING THE MIDDLE AGES

The unfathomable error of most film versions of medieval texts has been to sacrifice the peculiar charm and style of the narration for the concrete particularity of its historically known world. Such films opt for authentic castles, real forests and bone-crunching battles in place of the spiritual ideals for which they stand. The sheer size, weight of detail and splendor of such films defeat the very spirit of the age by imposing a novelistic fullness and depth, an epic historicism, upon the delicate economy, enigmatic charm and style of the romance form. (Monty Python's 1975 excursion into Arthurian romance in *Monty Python and the Holy Grail* parodies these jarring contradictions in its absurd mixture of the excessively bloody physical reality of combat with the extreme stylization of a standing joke which has Arthur and his knights prance about on imaginary horses followed by servants with coconut shells providing the appropriate sound-effects).

Rohmer's film offers a radical departure from nearly all previous strategies for the adaptation of medieval works (whether Walt Disney or Robert Bresson) by 1) incorporating the narrative voice and tone of the original text into his own dramatization and 2) avoiding the temptation to recreate the historical Middle Ages, adapting instead the visual style of medieval painting and illumination to film. Not since Rohmer's own earlier self-conscious quotation of Ingres in his adaptation of Kleist's *The Marquise of O* has a film so closely imitated the painting of a previous age. Yet here Rohmer does more than borrow a visual style. Taking his cue from the flat perspectives, disproportionate scale, surface richness and graceful lines of medieval painting, Rohmer also adapts these qualities to the three dimensionality of the cinema soundstage, the physical presence and movements of live actors and even to camera movement itself. In a similar manner, Rohmer also adapts his narrative, discovering the surprising affinity of medieval romance to the fragmented, self-conscious and anti-realist narratives of much post-modern literature. The result is a film which captures the naive style and religious spirit of the original text *and* its similarities with the self-conscious anti-realism and ironic tone of much post-modern art and literature.

SHOWING AND TELLING

One of the most important contributions of the French New Wave has been the restoration of a sense of narrative telling—not just dramatic showing—to film. Godard, Truffaut, Rohmer, Marker, Resnais—all at one time or another have re-inscribed a modern novelistic voice in their films. In place of the straight-forward enactment of events, these works complicated their unfolding with a combination of narrative telling and cinematic showing. In many of their films a narrative voice either duplicates, diverges from, or ironically comments upon the dramatic action. In *Jules et Jim* Truffaut's fast-talking impersonal voice-over narrator tends to defuse the melodrama, often working in counterpoint to the dramatic events of the tale; in *Deux ou trois choses que je sais d'elle,* Godard's confiding authorial whisper offers an intimate, philosophical commentary on the existential meaning of simple objects; in *Providence* Resnais' dying novelist spinning stories in the night manipulates "real" events and characters into outrageous fictions, self-consciously controlling and "rewriting" his text. Rohmer, too, has often preferred to have his heroes tell their own tales. In the preface to the published version of his *Contes Moraux,* Rohmer explains that his intention has never been to film "raw events, but the *narrative* that someone makes of them."[5]

Chrétien is similarly aware of his role as narrator and animator of what for him was already a traditional collection of narrated events. His narrator self-consciously selects and judges the actions of his hero, informing us of his decision to tell, or even more strikingly, not to tell a particular detail, as in the following account of Perceval's battle with the knight Anguingueron in defense of his beloved Blanchefleur.

> Anguingueron fell from his saddle, painfully wounded in the arm and side. The youth [Perceval is unnamed as yet], not knowing how to deal with him on horseback, sprang to the ground, drew his sword, and laid on again. I cannot describe all the strokes. but they were heavy and the fight lasted long, until Anguingueron fell. [6]

In a later combat in defense of the same lady, Chrétien's narrator omits even more detail:

> They struck each other so that the shields and the lances were broken, and they were both thrown to the earth. But they quickly sprang up and renewed the combat on foot with their swords, and long the issue hung in the balance. If I wished I could describe it fully, but I will not, since one word is as good as twenty.[7]

These self-conscious condensations continually announce the narrator's manipulation of the tale's events. At the beginning of his tale, along with the usual flattery to his patron, Chrétien stresses the fact that although the traditional source of his tale is good (after all his patron "gave him the book"), what really counts is how Chrétien "acquits himself" of his task of putting it into rhyme.[8] Rohmer, too, inscribes the act of re-telling a traditional tale into his film. But where Chrétien makes us aware of his role as narrator-animator of an already existing source, to which he is nevertheless faithful, Rohmer doubles this awareness by making us aware both of Chrétien's self-conscious animation and his own animation of Chrétien.

The film begins in a leisurely fashion as five women musician-singers in medieval dress sing directly to the audience the opening verses of Chrétien's tale—a description of the "season when trees bloom, bushes put forth their leaves," etc. As they sing of the birds who "sing at dawn" the camera tracks laterally to reveal not birds but an adjacent group of four male musicians who make bird sounds with their instruments. This male "chorus" then joins the sung narration to tell how, in this season, the "son of the widow lady" went out from his mother's castle into the "great forest."

In long shot we next see Perceval on his horse riding forth from his mother's tiny castle, onto an astroturf meadow and through the three or four silver-colored trees of the "forest." As Perceval rides, the sung narration of the chorus ceases and Perceval himself takes over in a spoken, though still rhymed, verse. Then, in a radical breach of conventional narrative form, he speaks of himself in the third person, describing how "the youth" dismounts to cast his spears, "now before, now behind, now high, now low." Perceval dismounts, but instead of actually throwing his spears, he simply mimes the gesture, holding back his arm with the spear, in an elaborately stylized fashion.

In this opening sequence the narrative is dispersed and redistributed in a number of different ways. It begins with a sung narration by a group of onscreen narrators who sing directly to the film audience, then moves to a redundant telling and showing in which a similar group narrates off-screen what we see on. Then the character within this narration begins simultaneously to narrate and enact his own adventure. Finally, this character narrates and only symbolically acts it out through stylized gesture.

Even more diverse redistributions of the narrative function follow: at times a single male or a single female voice acts as a simple offscreen narrator, usually in moments of ellipsis as when Perceval journeys from one castle to the next. At other times, portions of the same male or female chorus take on minor roles as attendants to the various lords and ladies Perceval encounters in the course of his adventures, shifting easily from characters within the tale to observers outside. In the course of the film these chorus members become familiar presences, silently bringing on the feast in some scenes, simultaneously spying on and narrating the action in others. When, for example, Perceval's mother explains to her son why she has tried to keep him ignorant of knighthood, her serving women—a portion of the female chorus—freely share the task of this explanation with her, speaking as if they too were Perceval's mother.

At still other times this chorus interrupts the speech of a character, narratively abbreviating a story we already know. When Perceval begins to tell Gornemant de Gohort how he was knighted, for example, a bell rings to interrupt his tale, "to tell it again would be a bore." During this narrative abbreviation, Perceval and Gornemant continue to face each other in semi-frozen postures, ready to resume the drama when the chorus has finished its momentary interruption. Here the chorus merely does as a group what Chrétien's narrative does: it interrupts the dramatic showing of a dialogue to save us the repetition of information we already know, the characters are not visibly present on the "stage" of his drama; thus they are not visibly interrupted. But when Rohmer's chorus-narrators perform the same abbreviating function we are made acutely aware of the interruption of one form of discourse by another. Showing and telling rub against one another, revealing the intrinsic differences of their discursive means.

The case is the same when a character begins simultaneously to narrate and enact an event. The redundancy and occasional inconsistency— as with the throwing of the spears—exaggerate what readers of Chrétien's text experience as a certain naiveté, even as they also lend it a paradoxically modern complexity. It is as if Rohmer realized that, since we can never grasp the "final" meaning of a work so remote from our own age, the only honest recourse of the modern film adaptor is to make us aware that what we see is, in a very literal sense, a dramatic reading of a traditional narration. Without actually having his actors read their lines, and without any of the usual trappings used to create a rehearsal atmosphere, Rohmer nevertheless suggests that what we are witnessing is an incomplete transformation from narrative to drama in which the tensions between the two forms of discourse generate an interest all their own.

These tensions make explicit an impression of naiveté inherent in any modern reading of medieval literature: as, for example, the modern readers' initial sense that such narratives are charming but inept, unable to handle such complexities as psychological consistency of its characters, or coherent, unitary narrative. In much the same way, we tend to view similar contradictions of scale and perspective in medieval art as naive, as if the painter would have liked to render perspective and scale "correctly" but lacked the technical means. The truth is, of course, that to the medieval artist, the faithful representation of the complete physical world was of little interest, even though these artists were often capable of a meticulous rendering of its surface detail.

Rohmer's adaptation of Chrétien's romance intentionally exaggerates these false impressions of naiveté in order to emphasize what, after all, is simply a result of the reader's own imprisonment within an already outmoded realist aesthetic which judges all breaches of psychological consistency, unitary narrative and historical, geographical reality as simple incapacity, however charming. By refusing to adapt his film to this aesthetic, Rohmer both preserves the modern reader's original impression of the tale's naiveté and, at the same time, calls the legitimacy of this impression into question, suggesting the possibility of an aesthetic system that can, like the inconsistent perspectives of medieval art, accomodate contradiction. Nowhere is this accommodation of contradiction more pronounced than in the radical shift from Perceval's story to the enactment of Christ's passion at the end of the film.

Where Chrétien's tale merely informs us that Perceval finally learned "how God was crucified," Rohmer, in the only instance of significant divergence from his source, chooses to demonstrate this understanding in a coda which re-enacts the passion. Once again the film combines showing and telling. Only here, the narration is the Latin text of the gospel sung in an austere manner by the male chorus, then enacted in a highly stylized pantomime in the small round space of the Hermit's chapel. In this pantomime of the seizure, condemnation and crucifixion of Christ, Perceval plays Christ, Blanchefleur is Mary Magdalen and Perceval's mother is Mary. As Christ, Fabrice Luchini acquires a beard and an aura of spirituality that eluded him as Perceval. With each new stage of the drama he is led roughly, in tight little circles, around the small round space of the chapel.

Both the transformation of this tiny bare space of the Hermit's chapel to symbolize the last days of Christ's life and the transformation of the same actor who played Perceval to symbolize Christ are deeply affecting in a way that a more sentimentalized, realistic crucifixion could never be. What Rohmer miraculously manages to convey in this scene is the overwhelming power of a faith that can transcend the boundaries of individual identity: we see Perceval both as himself and as Christ, and we see the chapel—the space for the performance of the mass—both as chapel and scene of the passion.

Shifts of character and decor have already become common in this film. The obvious re-use of the same few trees to represent different forests, the easy way chorus members take on different roles, or the way a character shifts from first to third person often combining direct address ("where do you come from?") and narration ("she said gently") in the same sentence, all suggest very fluid notions of both human identity and the space of its activity. The pantomime of the passion offers an even greater fluidity. In the Middle Ages Christ's passion was conceived both as an historical moment in the life of an individual, and as a timeless sacrifice shared with all humanity—a moment that could be endlessly re-enacted in the mass's own ritualized mixture of telling and showing.

Rohmer thus shows that in this pantomime Perceval does not only come to understand the historical fact of Christ's sacrifice; he actually becomes Christ. Perceval's assumption of Christ's role becomes a gloss on the meaning of Chrétien's incomplete text. Without radically tampering with the tale itself—Rohmer "ends" with Perceval resuming his role and riding on through the forest—the film nevertheless suggests what seems to be the emotional intent of Chrétien's narrative: the setting straight of a confused, secular ideal of the court with the Christian ideal of divine love. Although Perceval never returns to the grail castle to fulfill his spiritual mission, Rohmer's expansion of Chrétien's very brief reference to the crucifixion suggests that it is precisely through the merging of his own mysterious identity with that of Christ that the young knight will finally be able to comprehend his relation to the maimed Fisher King. Perceval cannot know who he is until he learns to interpret the transcendent meaning of the signs of this world. To do this he must internalize the meaning of Christ's sacrifice. With this inspired shifting of roles, Rohmer inscribes what for Chrétien was a theme of identity into the very form of his film.

Where most directors have adapted the medieval text to a more realistic aesthetic, Rohmer has exaggerated the very qualities in the text that contradict this aesthetic. By increasing the original narrative's self-consciousness, by multiplying its discursive means, by preserving the digressive and fragmented nature of the tale and by making textual naiveté an issue in itself, Rohmer manages to be faithful to his source and, at the same time, to suggest its affinities with a post-modern aesthetic which, for very different reasons, values these same qualities.

THE SPACE OF COURTLY ROMANCE

In the tightly condensed space of an obvious soundstage, against a patently artificial backdrop sky, Rohmer creates the spatial analogue of Chrétien's text. The same few, organically stylized metallic trees stand for the forest; green astroturf carpets stand for the perennially green fields of all romance. Even the castles, decked out from scene to scene in different banners, are recognizable as the same sets recycled in new narrative contexts. This economy and stylization of form is typical of the medieval paintings and miniatures which have clearly inspired the film. Flat lighting, primary colors with a dominant use of gold decoration also enhance the surface splendor of the film in a perfect imitation of the flat decorative space of medieval painting.

Even the position of the human figure within this space imitates, as much as possible, the stylized gesture and disproportionate scale of medieval art. Not only do these human figures dwarf their architectural surroundings—a damsel leaning out of a tower appears nearly as tall as the tower itself—but they are also just as often insubstantially perched, in stylized poses on the very edge of their benches, as if not fully integrated into their spatial surroundings. Perceval himself is rather thin and insubstantial, given his character of an exuberant and very physical country bumpkin who overpowers all opponents in hand-to-hand combat. Although not quite the bloodless icon of medieval painting, Perceval does take on some of the ethereal, sinuous qualities of such figures. Gestures too are stylized, especially when the actors freeze in momentary tableaux during periods of narration.

Yet at the same time, the cinematic requirement of filming the movement of real people in real space requires an accommodation of static gesture to the greater naturalism of the motion picture. Rohmer explains how he discovered the key to the translation of stylized gesture into movement in a recent interview.[9] Noticing that in the Middle Ages expressive movement is always governed by the elbow remaining tight against the body, Rohmer devised an entire system of gesticulation based on the relation of the elbow to the body. He then taught his actors, in the full year of rehearsal preceding filming, to pivot their forearms with outstretched palms around the elbow as a basis for all movement. The more mannered, courtly characters, especially the women, move almost exclusively in this fashion, offering a stylized but not stilted translation into movement of the sinuous shapes of the medieval figure; while Perceval himself, because he does not initially belong to this courtly milieu, is given a freer, more spontaneous range of movement.[10]

This translation of stylized static gesture to cinematic movement is paralleled, in a similar translation of the flat perspective of medieval painting, to three dimensional space. For although the scale of relations between human figure, castle and trees may be disproportionate, each has a solid existence in real space. Rohmer does not attempt the intentional disorientation of the mixture of human figure and trompe l'oeil backdrop of a film like *The Cabinet of Dr. Caligari*. In *Caligari*, confused perspectives, jarring angular lines and contradictory mixtures of painted and solid decor were intended to express the subjective confusion of the mind of the film's narrator-protagonist. The very different anti-realism of Perceval's space suggests no such subjective confusion, no malaise between individual and environment. Here disproportionate space suggests an idealized, hierarchical world of symbolic meaning, in which a forest can be represented by a few trees, a castle by a few towers and holiness by a halo. But at the same time this space can contain the physical reality of real persons who fight very real combats.[11]

Perhaps the most inspired translation of medieval, painted space into a three dimensional, cinematic space occurs in Rohmer's depiction of movement in his knight's repeated trajectories from castle to forest to castle. In this movement Rohmer finds an intriguing analogue to the symbolic space of both medieval painting and Chrétien tales. In courtly romance, when a knight sets forth in search of adventure, he sets out in the morning on what is most often a difficult and tortuous path, and he arrives in the evening at a castle where he inevitably encounters a new adventure. The narrative contains no extraneous detail; when the knight sets forth again, he will ride through the same formulaic "wild forest," arriving at yet another "well-placed" or "noble" castle.

We have already seen how Rohmer visually emphasizes the formulaic, repetitive nature of this by recycling the same castle and forest in each new narrative context. But even more striking is the condensed, convoluted and continuous nature of this space. Typically, we see Perceval on horseback emerging from a tiny castle on screen right and proceeding in a continuous shot towards the left, riding through the trees and the forest. The action of riding through this forest is usually represented by repeated circular windings in and around these trees, until emerging from the forest and still moving towards the left, Perceval arrives at the next castle, having completed what is supposed to be a day's ride in a single shot. When he embarks on his next adventure he will emerge from this same castle, now on screen right, and proceed once again to the left. Thus Rohmer needs only two castles at each end of his sound stage connected by a small "forest" of trees, in order to symbolize the space of his tale.

The condensed, continuous representation of this journey into one shot is reminiscent of a form of narrative condensation peculiar to medieval art called continuous narration. Continuous narration allowed the medieval artist to defy the temporal limitations of painting to approach what to us must seem a nearly cinematic progression in time. The form commonly appears in manuscript illuminations accompanying written narratives. In a very limited space the artist represents various stages in a narrative sequence continuously within a single frame. In an early example, cited by Janson in his *History of Art*, we see various episodes from the story of Jacob strung out on a single "C" shaped path: Jacob wrestling the angel, Jacob receiving benediction from the angel, etc.[12]

Such illustrations are conceived as linear progressions to be read, like the lines of the text they accompany, continuously in time rather than, as most visual art, simultaneously in space. Janson describes this particular example of the path of Jacob's life as a "frieze turned back upon itself."[13]

In a much later example, "The Meeting of Saint Anthony and Saint Paul,"[14] this convoluted trajectory takes on the form of an even more sinuous "S" shape. This work shows Anthony setting out alone at the top of an "S" shaped path and then later, towards the bottom, embracing St. Paul. In the limited space of the illuminated manuscript, contiguous points along the same path come to represent separate movements in time; contiguity in space becomes the signifier of temporal progression.[15] Since Rohmer is already working in a linear, temporal medium, he has no need to temporalize space in this way. But there is a sense in which the sinuous trajectory of his knight's movements from castle to forest to castle approximates this circular turning upon itself of continuous narration. For if we look closely at the camera movements which follow the trajectory of Chrétien's knight, we find an anomaly: the distance between any two (outdoor) points is never traversed in a straight line. This is not only the case in the obvious circular wandering through the trees but in what at first appears to be a direct movement from point A to point B. In my own case I recall, on first viewing, wondering whether the various shots following Perceval's journey were pans or travelings. Since the camera was keeping up with the lateral movement of the knight and horse, it seemed likely that the movement was a traveling, but if so, there was something disorienting about the relation of foreground to background which suggested the stationary revolution on its own axis of a pan.

The solution is simple but was not clear to me until Rohmer explained in the same interview quoted above, his peculiar method of building his set.[16] In an effort to compensate for the rigid lack of variation of the cinema's rectilinear frame, which is so unlike the curves of the illuminated manuscript (whose frames are often the irregularly curved shape of an initial letter), Rohmer built his entire set in the form of a semi-circle; when a character appears to walk straight ahead, his movement, in fact, describes a curve. This is the cause of the confusion between pan and traveling mentioned above; what appeared to be a lateral traveling was in fact a semi-circular pan. Thus the linear trajectory of a given character becomes like the "frieze turned back upon itself" of continuous narration. Any trajectory through outdoor space in Rohmer's film will, if continued long enough, turn back upon itself in a circular arc, like the "S" and "C" shaped paths of continuous narration. Although this never happens entirely (Rohmer only built a *semi*-circular set), the effect nevertheless offers a striking translation of the symbolic space of medieval iconography into the three-dimensional space of film.

This curved movement through a three-dimensional space continually re-used in different time continuum, becomes a cinematic analogue of the miniature artist's curving paths. The condensed, emblematic space traversed by these paths—a space often created in the interstices of an ornate letter—is never intended to represent real space, but to stand as a metaphor of the soul's journey through life. It is fascinating to note that for Rohmer the cinematic equivalent of these paths begins as a suggestion of curved movement turning back upon itself, but ends up as even more stylized and geometrically exact circles in the ritual enactment of the passion at the end of the film. Here the time continuum of the last days of Christ's life is radically condensed into a few minutes as Perceval-as-Christ moves from scene to scene in tight circles in the small round space of the chapel. In this final sequence, Rohmer completely transforms and condenses the linear time of the narrative into a truly circular movement through symbolic space, creating the cinematic equivalent of a miniature.

Rohmer's subversion of rational and realist space has several implications. In an intriguing article on "Postmodern Hermeneutics of Performance," Richard Palmer has written that "modernity" in Western consciousness emerges with the rise of perspective in Renaissance drawing.[17] Borrowing notions from Jean Gebser and William M. Ivins Jr., Palmer points out that perspective is a "rationalization of sight" which leads to a sense of the world as a measurable entity.[18] This rational, measuring spirit made possible both a materialism which divides the world into clear categories of subject and object and a linear notion of time as "progress," leaving behind Neo-Platonic, "pre-modern," notions of a matter governed by spirit, a language bearing the mark of that which it speaks, history moving in great cosmic cycles. These "modernist" attitudes have limited the "speaking power" of the "pre-modern" literary and sacred texts, forcing us to read them as simple expressions of human subjectivity, vicarious experiences of another person's suffering.

Palmer proposes instead a "postmodern" hermeneutics that can reclaim "the sense of spiritual depth and mystery in life that was available to pre-modern consciousness."[19] Such a hermeneutics would include a conception of time as round and whole rather than abstract and linear, a time capable of holding both past and future; a multi-perspectival consciousness of space; a view of the subject as a perpetual mask, or persona, through which god-like forces play; and finally, a conception of truth as generated by the mediation of language.

Of course Palmer has not invented these aspirations; they are recognizably part of a continuous avant-garde, anti-realist impulse at work in all the most innovative works of modernist or "postmodern" culture in which both writing and performance have ceased to be processes of representation. The value of Palmer's formulation here is that it so neatly summarizes what appears to have been Rohmer's strategy with *Perceval*. For Rohmer's film invents a cinematic antidote to the "rationalization of sight" by refusing to allow the viewer to "measure" visually the space of his sets or the geometric trajectories of his characters. Rohmer similarly breaks down the clear categories of subject and object in his merging of the subjective and dramatic *I* with the objective and narrative *he*. This process culminates in the final merging of the Perceval persona with that of Christ—a merging which additionally presupposes a non-linear conception of time capable of fixing two disparate moments in an eternal present.

All of the above are "postmodern" features regularly found both in the literary productions of the French New Novelists and the cinematic productions of the French New Wave. Rohmer's special insight with *Perceval* has been to demonstrate the extent to which the purging of the usual "modern" interpretation of a medieval, "pre-modern" text can produce a "post-modern" work of dazzling originality. Only by eliminating all possible sentimental, tragic or psychological recuperation of the "pre-modern" text, does Rohmer's film move beyond linear and dramatic enactment to a deeper level of ritual performance. This deeper level does not merely represent the religious spirit of the age; it actually becomes that spirit incarnate. This, I think, is the reason for the strangely affecting quality of so unsentimental and untragic a film. For once we are moved by a truly godlike Christ whose love is never meant to be understood in human terms.

NOTES

Reprinted with permission from *Literature/Film Quarterly* 11 (1983), 71–82.

1. Rohmer and Claude Chabrol have co-authored *Hitchcock* (Paris: Editions universitaires, 1957), a highly respected and extremely Catholic study of the films of Alfred Hitchcock.

2. James Monaco, *The New Wave* (New York: Oxford University Press, 1976), p. 294.

3. Chrétien completed 9234 lines out of what we might estimate, on the basis of his other romances, to have been a 12000 to 15000-line project.

4. "Perceval or the Story of the Grail," in *Medieval Romances,* ed. Roger Sherman Loomis (New York: The Modern Library, 1957), p. 87.

5. Quoted in Monaco, *The New Wave,* p. 299.

6. Roger Sherman Loomis, p. 43.

7. Loomis, p. 51.

8. Loomis, p. 9.

9. "Rohmer's Perceval," Gilbert Adair, *Sight and Sound,* 47 (Autumn 1978), pp. 230–234.

10. Rohmer adds that his actors practiced this movement every day, "like scales." "It was a means of access to a new kind of expression which enabled us to rediscover—in particular, with the women—a certain behavioural grace, close to that of the dance and now quite obsolete." Adair interview, *Sight and Sound,* pp. 233–234.

11. The one exception to this is the grail castle itself which is defined in the text as a semi-imaginary, magical realm not on the same level as the space in the rest of the film. In Chrétien's text this becomes apparent after the fact: other characters doubt the very existence of the castle Perceval has just visited. Rohmer makes this doubt even more explicit by showing the magical appearance and disappearance of the castle, transforming what could have simply been Perceval's faulty vision into an overt declaration of another order of space.

12. W. H. Janson, *History of Art* (New Jersey: Prentice Hall, 1962), p. 166.

13. Janson, p. 166.

14. By Sassetto (active 1423–1445) in the National Gallery, Washington, D.C.

15. I am indebted to Bruce Kawin for the above example and for clarifying to me the scroll-like quality of continuous narration.

16. Interview with Adair, *Sight and Sound,* p. 234.

17. Palmer, "Postmodern Hermeneutics of Performance," *Performance in Postmodern Culture,* Michel Benamou, Charles Caramello eds., (Madison: Coda Press, 1977), pp.19–31.

18. Palmer, p. 22.

19. Palmer, p. 27.

AEB-9453

Gramley Library
Salem Academy and College
Winston-Salem, N.C. 27108